►► Barney Rosset, editor

Evergreen Review Reader 1957-1961

►► Grove Press, Inc. / New York

First Evergreen Edition 1979
First Printing 1979
ISBN: 0-394-17095-4
Grove Press ISBN: 0-8021-4267-2
Library of Congress Catalog Card Number: 79-52055

LIBRARY OF CONGRESS CATALOGING IN PUBLICATION DATA
Main entry under title:
Evergreen review reader.
   CONTENTS: pt. 1. 1957-1961.—pt. 2 1962-1967.
   I. Rosset, Barney. II. Evergreen review.
AC5.E76 1979   808.8'004'5   79-52055
ISBN 0-394-17095-4 (v. 1)
ISBN 0-394-17490-9 (v. 2)

Manufactured in the United States of America

Distributed by Random House, Inc., New York

GROVE PRESS, INC., 196 West Houston Street, New York, N.Y. 10014

Picture essays are indicated by ▶

►► Contents

1957-1961

EVERGREEN REVIEW

VOL. 1
NO. 1

SARTRE   BECKETT   SCHORER   MICHAUX
DODDS   HAMBURGER   PURDY   FEINSTEIN

$1.00

No. 3
$1.00

↓ EVERGREEN REVIEW

CAMUS
BECKETT
ARNAUD
SOUTHGATE
ROBBE-GRILLET
IONESCO
O'HARA
AND OTHERS

No. 4
$1.00

↓ EVERGREEN REVIEW

OLSON
GINSBERG
TROCCHI
DODDS
IONESCO
KEROUAC
ADAMOV
FERLINGHETTI
AND OTHERS

2210

No. 2
$1.00

↓ EVERGREEN

SAN FRANCISCO SCENE

MILLER   REXROTH   GINSBERG   KEROUAC
DUNCAN   FERLINGHETTI   MILES   RUMAKER

1957

▶▶ Samuel Beckett

Dante and the Lobster

It was morning and Belacqua was stuck in the first of the canti in the moon. He was so bogged that he could move neither backward nor forward. Blissful Beatrice was there, Dante also, and she explained the spots on the moon to him. She shewed him in the first place where he was at fault, then she put up her own explanation. She had it from God, therefore he could rely on its being accurate in every particular. All he had to do was to follow her step by step. Part one, the refutation, was plain sailing. She made her point clearly, she said what she had to say without fuss or loss of time. But part two, the demonstration, was so dense that Belacqua could not make head or tail of it. The disproof, the reproof, that was patent. But then came the proof, a rapid shorthand of the real facts, and Belacqua was bogged indeed. Bored also, impatient to get on to Piccarda. Still he pored over the enigma, he would not concede himself conquered, he would understand at least the meanings of the words, the order in which they were spoken and the nature of the satisfaction that they conferred on the misinformed poet, so that when they were ended he was refreshed and could raise his heavy head, intending to return thanks and make formal retraction of his old opinion.

He was still running his brain against this impenetrable passage when he heard midday strike. At once he switched his mind off its task. He scooped his fingers under the book and shovelled it back till it lay wholly on his palms. The Divine Comedy face upward on the lectern of his palms. Thus disposed he raised it under his nose and there he slammed it shut. He held it aloft for a time, squinting at it angrily, pressing the boards inwards with the heels of his hands. Then he laid it aside.

He leaned back in his chair to feel his mind subside and the itch of this mean quodlibet die down. Nothing could be done until his mind got better and was still, which gradually it did. Then he ventured to consider what he had to do next. There was always something that one had to do next. Three large obligations presented themselves. First lunch, then the lobster, then the Italian lesson. That would do to be going on with. After the Italian lesson he had no very clear idea. No doubt some niggling curriculum had been drawn up by someone for the late afternoon and evening, but he did not know what. In any case it did not matter. What did matter was: one, lunch; two, the lobster; three, the Italian lesson. That was more than enough to be going on with.

Lunch, to come off at all, was a very nice affair. If his lunch was to be enjoyable, and it could be very enjoyable indeed, he must be left in absolute tranquility to prepare it. But if he were disturbed now, if some brisk tattler were to come bouncing in now big with a big idea or a petition, he might just as well not eat at all, for the food would turn to bitterness on his palate, or, worse again, taste of nothing. He must be left strictly alone, he must have complete quiet and privacy to prepare the food for his lunch.

The first thing to do was to lock the door. Now nobody could come at him. He deployed an old *Herald* and smoothed it out on the table. The rather handsome face of McCabe the assassin stared up at him. Then he lit the gas-ring and unhooked the square flat toaster, asbestos grill, from its nail and set it precisely on the flame. He found he had to lower the flame. Toast must not on any account be done too rapidly. For bread to be toasted as it ought, through and through, it must be done on a mild steady flame. Otherwise you only charred the outsides and left the pith as sodden as before. If there was one thing he abominated more than another it was to feel his teeth meet in a bathos of pith and dough. And it was so easy to do the thing properly. So, he thought, having regulated the flow and adjusted the grill, by the time I have the bread cut that will be just right. Now the long barrel-loaf came out of its biscuit-tin and had its end evened off on the face of McCabe. Two inexorable drives with the bread-saw and a pair of neat rounds of raw bread, the main elements of his meal, lay before him, awaiting his pleasure. The stump of the loaf went back into prison, the crumbs, as though there were no such thing as a sparrow in the wide world, were swept in a fever away, and the slices snatched up and carried to the grill. All these preliminaries were very hasty and impersonal.

It was now that real skill began to be required, it was at this point that the average person began to make a hash of the entire proceedings. He laid his cheek against the soft of the bread, it was spongy and warm, alive. But he would very soon take that plush feel off it, by God but he would very quickly take that fat white look off its face. He lowered the gas a suspicion and plaqued one flabby slab down on the glowing fabric, but very pat and precise, so that the whole resembled the Japanese flag. Then on top, there not being room for the two to do evenly side by side, and if you did not do them evenly you might just as well save yourself the trouble of doing them at

all, the other round was set to warm. When the first candidate was done, which was only when it was black through and through, it changed places with its comrade, so that now it in its turn lay on top, done to a dead end, black and smoking, waiting till as much could be said of the other.

For the tiller of the field the thing was simple, he had it from his mother. The spots were Cain with his truss of thorns, dispossessed, cursed from the earth, fugitive and vagabond. The moon was that countenance fallen and branded, seared with the first stigma of God's pity, that an outcast might not die quickly. It was a mix-up in the mind of the tiller, but that did not matter. It had been good enough for his mother, it was good enough for him.

Belacqua on his knees before the flame, poring over the grill, controlled every phase of the broiling. It took time, but if a thing was worth doing at all it was worth doing well, that was a true saying. Long before the end the room was full of smoke and the reek of burning. He switched off the gas, when all that human care and skill could do had been done, and restored the toaster to its nail. This was an act of dilapidation, for it seared a great weal in the paper. This was hooliganism pure and simple. What the hell did he care? Was it his wall? The same hopeless paper had been there fifty years. It was livid with age. It could not be disimproved.

Next a thick paste of Savora, salt and Cayenne on each round, well worked in while the pores were still open with the heat. No butter, God forbid, just a good foment of mustard and salt and pepper on each round. Butter was a blunder, it made the toast soggy. Buttered toast was all right for Senior Fellows and Salvationists, for such as had nothing but false teeth in their heads. It was no good at all to a fairly strong young rose like Belacqua. This meal that he was at such pains to make ready, he would devour it with a sense of rapture and victory, it would be like smiting the sledded Polacks on the ice. He would snap at it with closed eyes, he would gnash it into a pulp, he would vanquish it utterly with his fangs. Then the anguish of pungency, the pang of the spices, as each mouthful died, scorching his palate, bringing tears.

But he was not yet all set, there was yet much to be done. He had burnt his offering, he had not fully dressed it. Yes, he had put the horse behind the tumbrel.

He clapped the toasted rounds together, he brought them smartly together like cymbals, they clave the one to the other on the viscid salve of Savora. Then he wrapped them up for the time being in any old sheet of paper. Then he made himself ready for the road.

Now the great thing was to avoid being accosted. To be stopped at this stage and have conversational nuisance committed all over him would be a disaster. His whole being was straining forward towards the joy in store. If he were accosted now he might just as well fling his lunch into the gutter and walk straight back home. Sometimes his hunger, more of mind, I need scarcely say, than of body, for this meal amounted to such a frenzy that he would not have hesitated to strike any man rash enough to button-hole and baulk him, he would have shouldered him out of his path without ceremony. Woe betide the meddler who crosed him when his mind was really set on this meal.

He threaded his way rapidly, his head bowed, through a familiar labyrinth of lanes and suddenly dived into a little family grocery. In the shop they were not surprised. Most days, about this hour, he shot in off the street in this way.

The slab of cheese was prepared. Separated since morning from the piece, it was only waiting for Belacqua to call and take it. Gorgonzola cheese. He knew a man who came from Gorgonzola, his name was Angelo. He had been born in Nice but all his youth had been spent in Gorgonzola. He knew where to look for it. Every day it was there, in the same corner, waiting to be called for. They were very decent obliging people.

He looked sceptically at the cut of cheese. He turned it over on its back to see was the other side any better. The other side was worse. They had laid it better side up, they had practised that little deception. Who shall blame them? He rubbed it. It was sweating. That was something. He stooped and smelt it. A faint fragrance of corruption. What good was that? He didn't want fragrance, he wasn't a bloody gourmet, he wanted a good stench. What he wanted was a good green stenching rotten lump of Gorgonzola cheese, alive, and by God he would have it.

He looked fiercely at the grocer.

"What's that?" he demanded.

The grocer writhed.

"Well?" demanded Belacqua, he was without fear when roused, "is that the best you can do?"

"In the length and breadth of Dublin," said the grocer, "you won't find a rottener bit this minute."

Belacqua was furious. The impudent dogsbody, for two pins he would assault him.

"It won't do" he cried, "do you hear me, it won't do at all. I won't have it." He ground his teeth.

The grocer, instead of simply washing his hands like Pilate, flung out his arms in a wild crucified gesture of supplication. Sullenly Belacqua undid his packet and slipped the cadaverous tablet of cheese between the hard cold black boards of the toast. He stumped to the door where he whirled round however.

"You heard me?" he cried.

"Sir" said the grocer. This was not a question, nor yet an expression of acquiescence. The tone in which it was let fall made it quite imposible to know what was in the man's mind. It was a most ingenious riposte.

"I tell you" said Belacqua with great heat "this won't do at all. If you can't do better than this" he raised the hand that held the packet "I shall be obliged to go for my cheese elsewhere. Do you mark me?"

"Sir" said the grocer.

He came to the threshold of his store and watched the indignant customer hobble away. Belacqua had a spavined gait, his feet were in ruins, he suffered with them almost continuously. Even in the night they took no rest, or next to none. For then the cramps took over from the corns and hammer-toes, and carried on. So that he would press the fringes of his feet desperately against the end-rail of the bed or, better again, reach down with his hand and drag them up and back towards the instep. Skill and patience could disperse the pain, but there it was, complicating his night's rest.

The grocer, without closing his eyes or taking them off the receding figure, blew his nose in the skirt of his apron. Being a warm-hearted human man he felt sympathy and pity for this queer customer who always looked ill and dejected. But at the same time he was a small tradesman, don't forget that, with a small tradesman's sense of personal dignity and what was what. Thruppence, he cast it up, thruppence worth of cheese per day, one and a tanner per week. No, he would fawn on no man for that, no, not on the best in the land. He had his pride.

Stumbling along by devious ways towards the lowly public where he was expected, in the sense that the entry of his grotesque person would provoke no comment or laughter, Belacqua gradually got the upper hand of his choler. Now that lunch was as good as a *fait accompli,* because the incontinent bosthoons of his own class, itching to pass on a big idea or inflict an appointment, were seldom at large in this shabby quarter of the city, he was free to consider items two and three, the lobster and the lesson, in closer detail.

At a quarter to three he was due at the School. Say five to three. The public closed, the fish-monger re-opened, at halfpast two. Assuming then that his lousy old bitch of an aunt had given her order in good time that morning, with strict injunctions that it should be ready and waiting so that her blackguard boy should on no account be delayed when he called for it first thing in the afternoon, it would be time enough if he left the public as it closed, he could remain on till the last moment. Benissimo. He had half-a-crown. That was two pints of draught anyway and perhaps a bottle to wind up with. Their bottled stout was particularly excellent and well up. And he would still be left with enough coppers to buy a *Herald* and take a tram if he felt tired or was pinched for time. Always assuming, of course, that the lobster was all ready to be handed over. God damn these tradesmen, he thought, you can never rely on them. He had not done an exercise but that did not matter. His Professoressa was so charming and remarkable. Signorina Adriana Ottolenghi! He did not believe it possible for a woman to be more intelligent or better informed than the little Ottolenghi. So he had set her on a pedestal in his mind, apart from other women. She had said last day that they would read *II Cinque Maggio* together. But she would not mind if he told her, as he proposed to, in Italian, he would frame a shining phrase on his way from the public, that he would prefer to postpone the *Cinque Maggio* to another occasion. Manzoni was an old woman, Napoleon was another. *Napoleon di mezza calzetta, fa l'amore a Giacominetta.* Why did he think of Manzoni as an old woman? Why did he do him that injustice? Pellico was another. They were all old maids, suffragettes. He must ask his Signorina where he could have received that impression, that the 19th century in Italy was full of old hens trying to cluck like Pindar. Carducci was another. Also about the spots on the moon. If she could not tell him there and then she would make it up, only too gladly, against the time. Everything was all set now and in order. Bating, of course, the lobster, which had to remain an incalculable factor. He must just hope for the best. And expect the worst, he thought gaily, diving into the public, as usual.

Belacqua drew near to the school, quite happy, for all had gone swimmingly. The lunch had been a notable success, it would abide as a standard in his mind. Indeed he could not imagine its ever being superseded. And such a pale soapy piece of cheese to prove so strong! He must only conclude that he had been abusing himself all these years in relating the strength of cheese directly to its greenness. We live and learn, that was a true saying. Also his teeth and jaws had been in heaven, splinters of vanquished toast spraying forth at each gnash. It was like eating glass. His mouth burned and ached with the exploit. Then the food had been further spiced by the intelligence, transmitted in a low tragic voice across the counter by Oliver the improver, that the Malahide murderer's petition for mercy, signed by half the land, having been rejected, the man must swing at dawn in Mountjoy and nothing could save him. Ellis the hangman was even now on his way. Belacqua, tearing at the sandwich and swilling the precious stout, pondered on McCabe in his cell.

The lobster was ready after all, the man handed it over instanter, and with such a pleasant smile. Really a little bit of courtesy and goodwill went a long way in this world. A smile and a cheerful word from a common working-man and the face of the world was brightened. And it was so easy, a mere question of muscular control.

"Lepping" he said cheerfully, handing it over.

"Lepping?" said Belacqua. What on earth was that?

"Lepping fresh, sir" said the man, "fresh in this morning."

Now Belacqua, on the analogy of mackerel and other fish that he had heard described as lepping fresh when they had been taken but an hour or two previously, supposed the man to mean that the lobster had very recently been killed.

Signorina Adriana Ottolenghi was waiting in the little front room off the hall, which Belacqua was

naturally inclined to think of rather as the vestibule. That was her room, the Italian room. On the same side, but at the back, was the French room. God knows where the German room was. Who cared about the German room anyway?

He hung up his coat and hat, laid the long knobby brownpaper parcel on the hall-table, and went prestly in to the Ottolenghi.

After about half-an-hour of this and that obiter, she complimented him on his grasp of the language.

"You make rapid progress" she said in her ruined voice.

There subsisted as much of the Ottolenghi as might be expected to of the person of a lady of a certain age who had found being young and beautiful and pure more of a bore than anything else.

Belacqua, dissembling his great pleasure, laid open the moon enigma.

"Yes" she said "I know the passage. It is a famous teaser. Off-hand I cannot tell you, but I will look it up when I get home."

The sweet creature! She would look it up in her big Dante when she got home. What a woman!

"It occurred to me" she said "apropos of I don't know what, that you might do worse than make up Dante's rare movements of compassion in Hell. That used to be" her past tenses were always sorrowful "a favourite question."

He assumed an expression of profundity.

"In that connexion" he said "I recall one superb pun anyway: 'qui vive la pieta quando è ben morta . . .'"

She said nothing.

"Is it not a great phrase?" he gushed.

She said nothing.

"Now" he said like a fool "I wonder how you could translate that?"

Still she said nothing. Then:

"Do you think" she murmured "it is absolutely necessary to translate it?"

Sounds as of conflict were borne in from the hall. Then silence. A knuckle tambourined on the door, it flew open and lo it was Mlle Glain, the French instructress, clutching her cat, her eyes out on stalks, in a state of the greatest agitation.

"Oh" she gasped "forgive me. I intrude, but what was in the bag?"

"The bag?" said the Ottolenghi.

Mlle Glain took a French step forward.

"The parcel" she buried her face in the cat "the parcel in the hall."

Belacqua spoke up composedly.

"Mine" he said, "a fish."

He did not know the French for lobster. Fish would do very well. Fish had been good enough for Jesus Christ, Son of God, Saviour. It was good enough for Mlle Glain.

"Oh" said Mlle Glain, inexpressibly relieved, "I caught him in the nick of time." She administered a tap to the cat. "He would have tore it to flitters."

Belacqua began to feel a little anxious.

"Did he actually get at it?" he said.

"No no" said Mlle Glain "I caught him just in time. But I did not know" with a blue-stocking snigger "what it might be, so I thought I had better come and ask."

Base prying bitch.

The Ottolenghi was faintly amused.

"Puisqu'il n'y a pas de mal . . ." she said with great fatigue and elegance.

"Heureusement" it was clear at once that Mlle Glain was devout "heureusement."

Chastening the cat with little skelps she took herself off. The grey hairs of her maidenhead screamed at Belacqua. A virginal bluestocking, honing after a penny's worth of scandal.

"Where were we?" said Belacqua.

But Neopolitan patience has its limits.

"Where are we ever?" cried the Ottolenghi, "where we were, as we were."

Belacqua drew near to the house of his aunt. Let us call it winter, that dusk may fall now and a moon rise. At the corner of the street a horse was down and a man sat on his head. I know, thought Belacqua, that that is considered the right thing to do. But why? A lamplighter flew by on his bike, tilting with his pole at the standards, jousting a little yellow light into the evening. A poorly dressed couple stood in the bay of a pretentious gateway, she sagging against the railings, her head lowered, he standing facing her. He stood up close to her, his hands dangled by his sides. Where we were, thought Belacqua, as we were. He walked on, gripping his parcel. Why not piety and pity both, even down below? Why not mercy and Godliness together? A little mercy in the stress of sacrifice, a little mercy to rejoice against judgment. He thought of Jonah and the gourd and the pity of a jealous God on Nineveh. And poor McCabe, he would get it in the neck at dawn. What was he doing now, how was he feeling? He would relish one more meal, one more night.

His aunt was in the garden, tending whatever flowers die at that time of year. She embraced him and together they went down into the bowels of the earth, into the kitchen in the basement. She took the parcel and undid it and abruptly the lobster was on the table, on the oilcloth, discovered.

"They assured me it was fresh" said Belacqua.

Suddenly he saw the creature move, this neuter creature. Definitely it changed its position. His hand flew to his mouth.

"Christ!" he said "it's alive."

His aunt looked at the lobster. It moved again. It made a faint nervous act of life on the oilcloth. They stood above it, looking down on it, exposed cruciform on the oilcloth. It shuddered again. Belacqua felt he would be sick.

"My God" he whined "it's alive, what'll we do?"

The aunt simply had to laugh. She bustled off to the pantry to fetch her smart apron, leaving him goggling down at the lobster, and came back with it on and her sleeves rolled up, all business.

"Well" she said "it is to be hoped so, indeed."

"All this time" muttered Belacqua. Then, suddenly aware of her hideous equipment: "What are you going to do?" he cried.

"Boil the beast" she said, "what else?"

"But it's not dead" protested Belacqua "you can't boil it like that."

She looked at him in astonishment. Had he taken leave of his senses?

"Have sense" she said sharply, "lobsters are always boiled alive. They must be." She caught up the lobster and laid it on its back. It trembled. "They feel nothing" she said.

In the depths of the sea it had crept into the cruel pot. For hours, in the midst of its enemies, it had breathed secretly. It had survived the Frenchwoman's cat and his witless clutch. Now it was going alive into scalding water. It had to. Take into the air my quiet breath.

Belacqua looked at the old parchment of her face, grey in the dim kitchen.

"You make a fuss" she said angrily "and upset me and then lash into it for your dinner."

She lifted the lobster clear of the table. It had about thirty seconds to live.

Well, thought Belacqua, it's quick death, God help us all.

It is not.

▶▶ **James Purdy**

Cutting Edge

Mrs. Zeller opposed her son's beard. She was in her house in Florida when she saw him wearing it for the first time. It was as though her mind had come to a full stop. This large full-bearded man entered the room and she remembered always later how ugly he had looked and how frightened she felt seeing him in the house; then the realization it was someone she knew, and finally the terror of recognition.

He had kissed her, which he didn't often do, and she recognized in this his attempt to make her discomfort the more painful. He held the beard to her face for a long time, then he released her as though she had suddenly disgusted him.

"Why did you do it?" she asked. She was, he saw, almost broken by the recognition.

"I didn't dare tell you and come."

"That's of course true," Mrs. Zeller said. "It would

have been worse. You'll have to shave it off, of course. Nobody must see you. Your father of course didn't have the courage to warn me, but I knew something was wrong the minute he entered the house ahead of you. I suppose he's upstairs laughing now. But it's not a laughing matter."

Mrs. Zeller's anger turned against her absent husband as though all error began and ended with him. "I suppose he likes it." Her dislike of Mr. Zeller struck her son as staggeringly great at that moment.

He looked at his mother and was surprised to see how young she was. She did not look much older than he did. Perhaps she looked younger now that he had his beard.

"I had no idea a son of mine would do such a thing," she said. "But why a beard, for heaven's sake," she cried, as though he had chosen something permanent and irreparable which would destroy all that they were.

"Is it because you are an artist? No, don't answer me," she commanded. "I can't stand to hear any explanation from you. . . ."

"I have always wanted to wear a beard," her son said. "I remember wanting one as a child."

"I don't remember that at all," Mrs. Zeller said.

"I remember it quite well. I was in the summer house near that old broken-down wall and I told Ellen Whitelaw I wanted to have a beard when I grew up."

"Ellen Whitelaw, that big fat stupid thing. I haven't thought of her in years."

Mrs. Zeller was almost as much agitated by the memory of Ellen Whitelaw as by her son's beard.

"You don't like Ellen Whitelaw," her son told her, trying to remember how they had acted when they were together.

"She was a common and inefficient servant," Mrs. Zeller said, more quietly now, masking her feelings from her son.

"I suppose *he* liked her," the son pretended surprise, the cool cynical tone coming into his voice.

"Oh, your father," Mrs. Zeller said.

"Did he then?" the son asked.

"Didn't he like all of them?" she asked. The beard had changed this much already between them, she talked to him now about his father's character, while the old man stayed up in the bedroom fearing a scene.

"Didn't he always," she repeated, as though appealing to this new hirsute man.

"So," the son said, accepting what he already knew.

"Ellen Whitelaw, for God's sake," Mrs. Zeller said. The name of the servant girl brought back many other faces and rooms which she did not know were in her memory. These faces and rooms served to make the bearded man who stared at her less and less the boy she remembered in the days of Ellen Whitelaw.

"You must shave it off," Mrs. Zeller said.

"What makes you think I would do that?" the boy wondered.

"You heard me. Do you want to drive me out of my mind?"

"But I'm not going to. Or rather it's not going to."

"I will appeal to him, though a lot of good it will do," Mrs. Zeller said. "He ought to do something once in twenty years at least."

"You mean," the son said laughing, "he hasn't done anything in that long."

"Nothing I can really remember," Mrs. Zeller told him.

"It will be interesting to hear you appeal to him," the boy said. "I haven't heard you do that in such a long time."

"I don't think you ever heard me."

"I did, though," he told her. "It was in the days of Ellen Whitelaw again, in fact."

"In *those* days," Mrs. Zeller wondered. "I don't see how that could be."

"Well, it was. I can remember that much."

"You couldn't have been more than four years old. How could you remember then?"

"I heard you say to him, *You have to ask her to go.*"

Mrs. Zeller did not say anything. She really could not remember the words, but she supposed that the scene was true and that he actually remembered.

"Please shave off that terrible beard. If you only knew how awful it looks on you. You can't see anything else but it."

"Everyone in New York thought it was particularly fine."

"Particularly fine," she paused over his phrase as though its meaning eluded her.

"It's nauseating," she was firm again in her judgment.

"I'm not going to do away with it," he said, just as firm.

She did not recognize his firmness, but she saw everything changing a little, including perhaps the old man upstairs.

"Are you going to 'appeal' to him?" The son laughed again when he saw she could say no more.

"Don't mock me," the mother said. "I will speak to your father." She pretended decorum. "You can't go anywhere with us, you know."

He looked unmoved.

"I don't want any of my friends to see you. You'll have to stay in the house or go to your own places. You can't go out with us to our places and see our friends. I hope none of the neighbors see you. If they ask who you are, I won't tell them."

"I'll tell them then."

They were not angry, they talked it out like that, while the old man was upstairs.

"Do you suppose he is drinking or asleep?" she said finally.

"I thought he looked good in it, Fern," Mr. Zeller said.

"What about it makes him look good?" she said.

"It fills out his face," Mr. Zeller said, looking at the wallpaper and surprised he had never noticed what a pattern it had before; it showed the sacrifice of some sort of animal by a youth.

He almost asked his wife how she had come to pick

out this pattern, but her growing fury checked him.

He saw her mouth and throat moving with unspoken words.

"Where is he now?" Mr. Zeller wondered.

"What does that matter where he is?" she said. "He has to be somewhere while he's home, but he can't go out with us."

"How idiotic," Mr. Zeller said, and he looked at his wife straight in the face for a second.

"Why did you say that?" She tried to quiet herself down.

"The way you go on about nothing, Fern." For a moment a kind of revolt announced itself in his manner, but then his eyes went back to the wallpaper, and she resumed her tone of victor.

"I've told him he must either cut it off or go back to New York."

"Why is it a beard upsets you so?" he wondered, almost to himself.

"It's not the beard so much. It's the way he is now too. And it disfigures him so. I don't recognize him at all now when he wears it."

"So, he's never done anything of his own before," Mr. Zeller protested suddenly.

"Never done anything!" He could feel her anger covering him and glancing off like hot sun onto the wallpaper.

"That's right," he repeated. "He's never done anything. I say let him keep the beard and I'm not going to talk to him about it." His gaze lifted toward her but rested finally only on her hands and skirt.

"This is still my house," she said, "and I have to live in this town."

"When they had the centennial in Collins, everybody wore beards."

"I have to live in this town," she repeated.

"I won't talk to him about it," Mr. Zeller said.

It was as though the voice of Ellen Whitelaw reached her saying, *So that was how you appealed to him.*

She sat on the deck chair on the porch and smoked five cigarettes. The two men were somewhere in the house and she had the feeling now that she only roomed here. She wished more than that the beard was gone that her son had never mentioned Ellen Whitelaw. She found herself thinking only about her. Then she thought that now twenty years later she could not have afforded a servant, not even her.

She supposed the girl was dead. She did not know why, but she was sure she was.

She thought also that she should have mentioned her name to Mr. Zeller. It might have broken him down about the beard, but she supposed not. He had been just as adamant and unfeeling with her about the girl as he was now about her son.

Her son came through the house in front of her without speaking, dressed only in his shorts and, when he had got safely beyond her in the garden, he took off those so that he was completely naked with his back to her, and lay down in the sun.

She held the cigarette in her hand until it began to burn her finger. She felt she should not move from the place where she was and yet she did not know where to go inside the house and she did not know what pretext to use for going inside.

In the brilliant sun his body, already tanned, matched his shining black beard.

She wanted to appeal to her husband again and she knew then she could never again. She wanted to call a friend and tell her but she had no friend to whom she could tell this.

The events of the day, like a curtain of extreme bulk, cut her off from her son and husband. She had always ruled the house and them even during the awful Ellen Whitelaw days and now as though they did not even recognize her, they had taken over. She was not even here. Her son could walk naked with a beard in front of her as though she did not exist. She had nothing to fight them with, nothing to make them see with. They ignored her as Mr. Zeller had when he looked at the wallpaper and refused to discuss their son.

"You can grow it back when you're in New York," Mr. Zeller told his son.

He did not say anything about his son lying naked before him in the garden but he felt insulted almost as much as his mother had, yet he needed his son's permission and consent now and perhaps that was why he did not mention the insult of his nakedness.

"I don't know why I have to act like a little boy all the time with you both."

"If you were here alone with me you could do anything you wanted. You know I never asked anything of you. . . ."

When his son did not answer, Mr. Zeller said, "Did I?"

"That was the trouble," the son said.

"What?" the father wondered.

"You never wanted anything from me and you never wanted to give me anything. I didn't matter to you."

"Well, I'm sorry," the father said doggedly.

"Those were the days of Ellen Whitelaw," the son said in tones like the mother.

"For God's sake," the father said and he put a piece of grass between his teeth.

He was a man who kept everything down inside of him, everything had been tied and fastened so long there was no part of him any more that could struggle against the stricture of his life.

There were no words between them for some time; then Mr. Zeller could hear himself bringing the question out: "Did she mention that girl?"

"Who?" The son pretended blankness.

"Our servant."

The son wanted to pretend again blankness but it was too much work. He answered: "No, I mentioned it. To her surprise."

"Don't you see how it is?" the father went on to the present. "She doesn't speak to either of us now and if you're still wearing the beard when you leave it's me she will be punishing six months from now."

"And you want me to save you from your wife."

"Bobby," the father said, using the childhood tone and inflection. "I wish you would put some clothes on too when you're in the garden. With me it doesn't matter, you could do anything. I never asked you anything. But with her . . ."

"God damn her," the boy said.

The father could not protest. He pleaded with his eyes at his son.

The son looked at the father and he could see suddenly also the youth hidden in his father's face. He was young like his mother. They were both young people who had learned nothing from life, were stopped and drifting where they were twenty years before with Ellen Whitelaw. Only she, the son thought, must have learned from life, must have gone on to some development in her character, while they had been tied to the shore where she had left them.

"Imagine living with someone for six months and not speaking," the father said as if to himself. "That happened once before, you know, when you were a little boy."

"I don't remember that," the son said, some concession in his voice.

"You were only four," the father told him.

"I believe this is the only thing I ever asked of you," the father said. "Isn't that odd, I can't remember ever asking you anything else. Can you?"

The son looked coldly away at the sky and then answered, contempt and pity struggling together, "No, I can't."

"Thank you, Bobby," the father said.

"Only don't plead any more, for Christ's sake." The son turned from him.

"You've only two more days with us, and if you shaved it off and put on just a few clothes, it would help me through the year with her."

He spoke as though it would be his last year.

"Why don't you beat some sense into her?" The son turned to him again.

The father's gaze fell for the first time complete on his son's nakedness.

Bobby had said he would be painting in the storeroom and she could send up a sandwich from time to time, and Mr. and Mrs. Zeller were left downstairs together. She refused to allow her husband to answer the phone.

In the evening Bobby came down dressed carefully and his beard combed immaculately and looking, they both thought, curled.

They talked about things like horse racing, in which they were all somehow passionately interested, but which they now discussed irritably as though it too were a menace to their lives. They talked about the uselessness of art and why people went into it with a detachment that would have made an outsider think that Bobby was as unconnected with it as a jockey or oil magnate. They condemned nearly everything and then the son went upstairs and they saw one another again briefly at bedtime.

The night before he was to leave they heard him up all hours, the water running, and the dropping of things made of metal.

Both parents were afraid to get up and ask him if he was all right. He was like a wealthy relative who had commanded them never to question him or interfere with his movements even if he was dying.

He was waiting for them at breakfast, dressed only in his shorts but he looked more naked than he ever had in the garden because his beard was gone. Over his chin lay savage and profound scratches as though he had removed the hair with a hunting knife and pincers.

Mrs. Zeller held her breast and turned to the coffee and Mr. Zeller said only his son's name and sat down with last night's newspaper.

"What time does your plane go?" Mrs. Zeller said in a dead, muffled voice.

The son began putting a white paste on the scratches of his face and did not answer.

"I believe your mother asked you a question," Mr. Zeller said, pale and shaking.

"Ten-forty," the son replied.

The son and the mother exchanged glances and he could see at once that his sacrifice had been in vain: she would also see the beard there again under the scratches and the gashes he had inflicted on himself, and he would never really be her son again. Even for his father it must be much the same. He had come home as a stranger who despised them and he had shown his nakedness to both of them. All three longed for separation and release.

But Bobby could not control the anger coming up in him, and his rage took an old form. He poured the coffee into his saucer because Mr. Zeller's mother had always done this and it had infuriated Mrs. Zeller because of its low-class implications.

He drank viciously from the saucer, blowing loudly.

Both parents watched him helplessly like insects suddenly swept against the screen.

"It's not too long till Christmas," Mr. Zeller brought out. "We hope you'll come back for the whole vacation."

"We do," Mrs. Zeller said in a voice completely unlike her own.

"So," Bobby began, but the torrent of anger would not let him say the thousand fierce things he had ready.

Instead, he blew savagely from the saucer and spilled some onto the chaste white summer rug below him. Mrs. Zeller did not move.

"I would invite you to New York," Bobby said quietly now, "but of course I will have the beard there and it wouldn't work for you."

"Yes," Mr. Zeller said, incoherent.

"I do hope you don't think I've been . . ." Mrs. Zeller cried suddenly, and they both waited to hear whether she was going to weep or not, but she stopped herself perhaps by the realization that she had no tears and that the feelings which had come over her about Bobby were likewise spent.

"I can't think of any more I can do for you," Bobby said suddenly.

They both stared at each other as though he had actually left and they were alone at last.

"Is there anything more you want me to do?" he said, coldly vicious.

They did not answer.

"I hate and despise what both of you have done to yourselves, but the thought that you would be sitting here in your middle-class crap not speaking to one another is too much even for me. That's why I did it, I guess, and not out of any love. I didn't want you to think that."

He sloshed in the saucer.

"Bobby," Mr. Zeller said.

The son brought out his *What?* with such finished beauty of coolness that he paused to admire his own control and mastery.

"Please, Bobby," Mr. Zeller said.

They could all three of them hear a thousand speeches. The agony of awkwardness was made unendurable by the iciness of the son, and all three paused over this glacial control which had come to him out of art and New York, as though it was the fruit of their lives and the culmination of their twenty years.

►► **Larry Gara**

Baby Dodds' Story

[Larry Gara writes: "I met Baby Dodds at George Lewis' first Chicago appearance in March of 1953. That evening he sat in on several numbers and later, during conversation, I got the idea of recording his life story. Baby was a superb narrator and I still recall with joy the many Sundays I spent in his 51st Street, Chicago, apartment while he recounted the details of his long and varied career. Baby Dodds played in many great jazz bands, including some led by Papa Celestin, Fate Marable, King Oliver, Bunk Johnson, Jimmie Noone, and Baby's brother, the clarinetist, Johnny Dodds. He made records with Jelly Roll Morton, Louis Armstrong, Mutt Carey, Natty Dominique, and many other famous jazz musicians.

"Baby Dodds developed a style of his own which is sharp and clear but never obtrusive. He has a special type of press roll and often used to shimmy as he drummed. He considers drumming an art and, like other New Orleans jazzmen, he prefers to work as a part of a group rather than to dominate a band. His drumming is relaxed yet full of drive. The rhythm is always steady and without the rumble that so many drummers produce. Baby is as versatile as he is original; he has played drums for New Orleans street parades, for small Chicago outfits, for fourteen-piece orchestras, for recorded drum solos and for the dancer Merce Cunningham.

"Although he has had three strokes Baby Dodds is far from disabled. He can still play wonderful music and continues to think of ways to further perfect his style. Recently he has made some fine recordings with Natty Dominique's band which will be issued by William Russell on his American Music label. They will help give a much deserved recognition of Baby's contribution to American jazz music. For, as his old friend and fellow-musician, Natty Dominique, said: 'Baby Dodds has a rhythm of his own. It will be Baby Dodds' as long as he lives, and for all the days that's coming. Baby Dodds is the world's greatest drummer.'"]

1. New Orleans Beginnings

When I was just a youngster my mother taught me a poem which I always remembered. It was an ideal which I tried to follow throughout my musical career and it went like this:

All you do, do with your might
Because things done by halves
Are never done right.

Be the labor great or small,
Do it well or not at all.

I always worked to improve my drumming and I never drummed just for money. I loved it and I felt that drums have as much music in them as any other instrument. And I think the idea of the guy who invented drums was to have a person beat drums to get something out of them. Quite natural the guy who made them first knew what was supposed to be gotten out of them. But I doubt if anyone knows it today. In my estimation drums should play according to the melody and still keep time. Those to me are the drummer's two specific jobs. Although a drummer can't make a bad note, he provides a very important foundation for the rest of the musicians. You can't get into a locked house without a key and the drum is the key to the band.

Although I never forgot my mother's lesson, I don't remember too much about her because she died when I was only nine years old. I know that she was a very good-looking, brown-skinned woman. She had high cheek bones and a very long Roman nose with a hump in it. I don't recall that she played any musical instrument but she used to sing religious songs with the rest of our family. In school I was always first or second in my class and my mother wanted to send me to Tuskegee to become a doctor. But of course, after she passed away, things turned out differently.

But when I was little I was inspired by music all around. Besides my brother John, who played his clarinet, my father and his brother used to play violin. One of my sisters played a melodeon, and my father and sister also used to play harmonicas. My sister used to play some blues and I tried to pick it up. The rest of the family didn't know it because I would get off by myself and try to play different things my sister played. But I didn't think I was so good with it and I gave it up. My dad also played quills. He took green bamboo reeds and removed the soft spongy material in them. That would leave a clear hole in the reed and then my father would cut them down to about three to six inches, each one a little longer than the other. Then he would put a plug in the top and cut it down, like any other whistle, and he would blow these quills and make very nice music. There was one quill for each note of the scale and he could play almost anything on them. It sounded just like a flute but there was no fingering. I made myself a little set of quills and my father helped me but I didn't make out so well on them. My father was very religious and he only played and sang hymns and sacred music. In fact, everybody in the family used to sing. It was the most beautiful quartet you ever heard, to hear that outfit sing. I could sing soprano or tenor and my brother John used to sing real high tenor. And do you know what took it away from him? Clarinet! And do you know what took mine away? Whisky!

My father worked on a farm part of the time and he was also a handyman for a while. And for a time he worked in a warehouse. He never went to school but he was very good at figures. He was better at arithmetic than I was and he didn't need a pencil and paper to do it. He taught himself to read and write while working in the warehouse. He was also a first deacon in the Baptist Church. His job was to open the church when the pastor wasn't there and he had to take care of the library. We kids all went to Sunday school, which started at nine-thirty or ten, and we had to stay for the eleven o'clock service which lasted until noon. Since our dad was there we didn't dare leave. And during the service you could hear a pin drop. We didn't dare chew gum or even look up. If we weren't gentlemen on the street, we were gentlemen in church. And church was different from what it is now; there was no hollering or whooping. And they didn't have music in the church; there was only singing.

In those early days I also used to hear classical music. Negroes were not allowed in the places where it was played so I heard it by standing on the outside. Many times I heard symphonies that way. Sometimes we used to stand in the hallway of the Tulane Theatre in New Orleans. One side was an opera house and the other was this theater and we'd stand in between to hear the music. That is where I learned to like symphony music and I especially loved to hear the flutes. I even wanted to study to be a flute player. I don't see how in the world I ever wanted to play the flute, because there was no field for colored people in classical music. That's why I never took it up. I always liked symphonies and still do. But, being a jazz man, when I hear a symphony I pick out different things which I feel I can use in jazz. And I learned quite a bit from such listening. I used to carry any melody on the snare drums that a band played. I got that idea from listening to symphonic music and also from playing in street parades. They still do that in New Orleans parades, but not as distinctly as they used to.

I began to be interested in becoming a musician when I saw what my brother John was doing. We used to go around to different houses and ask for old bottles which we could sell to the guy that picked up rags and things. Instead of money he'd pay us with candy and whistles. That's where John got a little tin flute. It had only six holes but he was blowing it around, and he would play little things on it. One day my dad asked him what he really would like to play and John said the clarinet. And then my dad got him a clarinet. And the minute my brother began to play it he had a perfect tone. That was around 1909, when John was about seventeen and I was only fifteen years old. Of course this interested me. I wanted to get something too and the instrument I wanted was a flute. Since it was out of the question for me to play in a pit orchestra I never got a flute but I still wanted something.

John played his clarinet in the neighborhood and on Sundays he would go and play in parties and he would get all the ice cream and cake. Now I didn't like that. I was the baby in the family and felt I should get the treats. I was especially jealous when John went to different parties and I wasn't even in-

vited. So I finally got an idea. I took a lard can and put holes in the bottom and turned it over and took nails and put holes around the top of it. Then I took some rounds out of my mother's chairs and made drumsticks out of them. Sometimes we used to go in the back yard, to our back place. There was a baseboard and I used to kick my heels against the baseboard and make it sound like a bass drum, using the can as a snare drum. With a clarinet it sounded so good that all the kids in the neighborhood came around to get in on the fun.

By that time I had already got my name "Baby." I was born in New Orleans on Christmas Eve, 1894. Except for my baby sister, Hattie, who was born a few years later, I was the youngest of six children. My name was the same as my father's, Warren. My mother would call "Warren," and I would answer. She'd say, "I'm calling your father." Then she'd say "Warren," and my father would answer, and she'd say "I'm calling the baby." That's where the "Baby" came in. My sisters and brothers picked it up and Johnny carried it to school. Of course that did it. I used to get angry about it and I've jumped on many kids and fought them for calling me Baby. When I got out of grammar school the larger girls would call me Baby, and I liked that. I didn't resent the girls using the name but I did the boys. And, of course, anything a person resents is going to happen. After I got into the music business, people found out my name was Baby and it fit perfectly. Baby Dodds is much shorter than Warren and for some reason an alias, or a nickname, will go much farther in life than a real name. And so it was with me, even before I got my first drums.

But I wanted a real drum set. I told my father and he said, "You don't get any drum. How on earth could we stand all that noise! It's bad enough around here now. You'd chase everybody out of the neighborhood." I thought that was very bad. It hurt me and I couldn't understand why he would buy my brother a clarinet and not buy me drums. I knew drums would not cost as much. Of course, in those days, any child who turned out to be a musician was considered no good. As a musician one had to play in places where there was liquor and the chances were he would drink a lot. And I had begun drinking before I started playing music. It wasn't that I had anything on my mind, or drank to drown my troubles, but I used to love the taste of liquor and always have. Then again we had to play in the tenderloin district. We were looked upon as nobody. Musicians were also very raggedy, and many of them didn't care about their appearance.

But I was determined to get drums and finally my

father consented to let me have them if I bought them myself. Well, I didn't mind working because I had helped my father work around the little farm where he worked as handyman. We kids used to help him tend the cows, chickens, ducks, hogs and goats. I used to plant and tend the different vegetables, but I hated to churn the butter which my father made to sell. He wouldn't let me fool around with the cows, but I used to feed, curry and clean the horses for him. We were living at Waveland, Mississippi, then, so I went to New Orleans and found a job. I was about sixteen years old and got work with a wealthy Jewish family named Levi. My brother's wife worked there as a cook and that's how I got the job. When I went there they asked me if I knew how to wait on tables. I didn't know how and had never waited on a table, but I told them "yes." I worked as a butler and fixed salads, cleaned the rug and took care of the dining room. On Thursdays and Fridays I did the yard work. I worked there about a year and a half and kept that job going until I was able to save up money and buy some secondhand drums. I got only four dollars and six bits a week but managed to save around ten or twelve dollars to buy my first drum. It was a single-head snare drum. I also got some sticks and different little things but it took so long to save up enough to get more drums that I got a job at Mentes bag factory.

At the bag factory I got a dollar and a quarter a day. I did a little bit of everything there. I worked in the drier. We had to hang the sacks on a hook, and after a certain period of time they would go through and come out dry. When they came out I had to count them and put so many in a bundle. There were fifty sacks in a bundle and it was very heavy work. They made sacks of different quality burlap. They used the first-class stuff for sugar sacks. Out of others they made coarser grade sugar sacks, coffee sacks, rice sacks and oyster sacks. There were about two hundred and fifty people working at Mentes but quite naturally the colored fellows couldn't get any of the better jobs. They did the heavy work like trucking the bales of burlap in and out, picking up the work off the sewing machines and packing up the bags to go to the press. I worked there for three or four years and did a little bit of everything except the cutting and sewing.

While working there I bought the rest of my drum set, one piece at a time. I bought a bass drum, which was a big high thing with ropes like the drums they used in school bands. I had to pull them to tighten and after they were pulled a while the ropes got slick. Then I would let my fingers slide on the rope. It cost me about ten dollars. It was a big, narrow thing and I

had no cymbal, foot pedal or anything else. Finally I got a foot pedal, put the set together, and by jimmy, I come to make a noise! I amused the kids in the neighborhood and was real satisfied with myself. Then I added little traps that I needed, like a cymbal, wood block, and a ratchet and whistles and things of that sort. I got them all second hand at a pawnshop but they were as good as new to me. I loved them as much as if they had just come from a factory. It was the hard way and the best way since I knew that I had to take care of them. And I've always tried to take care of my drums. I believe that professional musicians should always try to keep up their instruments. Many drummers don't care how bad their drum sets look. If they can make a dollar on them, they don't worry. I never was that way. I've had some bad-looking drums in my day, but it wasn't that the heads had holes in them, or patches, nothing like that. I think that's lazy. If a person makes a living on something and doesn't keep it in top working shape, well, he's just not much good. You can be lazy, but be lazy in some other way, not on the instrument you make your bread on.

The man who was my inspiration when I first started drumming was a fellow named Mack Murray. I first heard him when I was about fifteen, before I had a chance to get hold of any drums. He was a very tall skinny guy and what a drummer! He played in street parades and in the Robichaux Band. When playing for dancing Mack Murray used a very small snare drum which looked like a banjo, and my inspiration came from his drumming. He used ebony sticks and you would never know that they were so heavy. He played beautiful drums. When he made a roll it sounded like he was tearing paper. It was a marvelous thing. Another wonderful drummer was a Creole fellow named Louis Cottrell. He was very good at examining drums. He could take a snare drum and pick it up and turn it over and examine it to tell if it was any good or not. And he never bought his drums. When the music stores in New Orleans got a new set of drums they would send for Cottrell, who would try them out and tell if they were good. He had a very light technique and played both parades and dance-band music. He was with the Excelsior Orchestra.

Of course, when I began drumming I soon wanted a teacher because I wanted to know what I was doing and how to do it. I got a teacher by the name of Dave Perkins. He was very light, like a white fellow, and was a straight man in music. He had an awful big class and taught all kinds of drumming to all colors although he was in a colored neighborhood. But he taught me individually and I paid him by the lesson rather than go in the class. Dave Perkins gave me the rudiments of drumming. And I did all right with him. He gave me a drum pad to use but he didn't want me to use a bass drum. Well, he didn't know I owned one so I practiced there with the pad, and I'd go home at night and execute what I knew on both bass drum and snare. I got along so well Dave wanted to know if I played anywhere or if I had a bass drum. I told him I didn't have any, and he said, "No, I don't want you to touch it." I stayed with him at least a year, and after I got so far advanced, and did so well on my bass drum, I went to another teacher.

Meanwhile I had done a lot of street parade work with Bunk Johnson's band. I used to tell them how good I was but still I wanted to go to a teacher some more. I went to a fellow named Walter Brundy. He used to play with Robichaux and was a very good drummer. He was a reading drummer and that's what I wanted to learn—to read music. I didn't get that from Perkins. Brundy taught me the fundamentals of reading music and I found out that everything I had been doing was wrong. He taught me that the right hand was "mammy" and the left "daddy," and I soon learned how to get my two hands working differently. This was, of course, after I mastered having both hands do the same thing. After I got that pretty well, Brundy gave me the two drums to work on. Brundy and Perkins were the only two teachers whom I paid, but I got ideas and pointers from lots of others who were playing in New Orleans at that time. I went to Cottrell and learned some more of the rudiments of technique from him. I also got some pointers from a very good drummer whose name was Paps, but we didn't call him Paps, we called him Rabbit. He was with tent shows and I heard that he used to drum for Ma Rainey. I never took lessons from him but learned just by sitting around and looking at him work. For a while he was my favorite drummer. He also played with Armand Piron's five- or six-piece band and I sat in several times with that outfit. It was a jazz band, but on a higher level. In those days I wasn't reading music so when the time came to read music I had to get up. But they liked my work very much. I got my press roll from Henry Zeno, Henry Martin and Tubby Hall. The guy who used it most effectively was Henry Martin. He played with Kid Ory and it was very effective. It was a pretty hard thing to learn but I worked at it until I got it. Of course I did it in my own way and according to my ability, and it never was exactly like someone else's. I used to study the rolls of different drummers at dances and in parades and worked out a long press roll which I preferred to the shorter ones. Tubby Hall's brother, Minor Hall, uses a shorter type press roll today. Where I used three beats, Minor Hall used only one, and of course that makes a different sound.

I also used to listen to some New Orleans drummers who didn't inspire my work. There was Black Benny who was a kind of rowdy fellow. He wasn't a taught drummer but just picked it up. He played so well at it and enjoyed drumming so much that all the fellows liked him from that point and hired him to play. He only played in street bands and there was nothing special about his drumming except that he would always do something to fill in and make some novelty out of it. I heard him when I was very young but his style of drumming was nothing that inspired me.

Of course, a great deal about drumming I had to work out for myself. When you work at something daily that's yours. I taught myself how to tune my drums and how to put the heads on and tuck them in. The skin was wet when I got them and I learned how to trim the edges and then tuck the heads on. Today they have regular tuckers but when I started we used to tuck them on with a spoon handle. We had to tuck it very tight. And today they don't sell drum heads that you have to wet. They are on the hoop when you buy them. Then we had to put them on the hoop. All those things I had to learn by myself. But when you want to be a drummer, nothing's too hard.

And when I was learning I picked up the different drum terms like the mammy and daddy stuff which Brundy taught me. I learned that a biff shot was one abrupt fast lick, a flam is sixteen notes, a flimflam is thirty-two, and a lick is when you just hit the drum. With a lick you just hit it, and with a biff you try to make it sound on something, either the rim or anything else solid. The pickup was the first beat and the rudiments are the things we did with a number to be played. It was just different things we did to make the number go and to make the other fellows play. In other words, in a calm, ordinary way you push the number and the other musicians too.

When I began playing I soon got a job with Willie Hightower's band, the American Stars. I got it through Robert Smith, the guitar player. I had been working as an ordinary laborer for his father who was a contractor. I started working with gravel and the wheelbarrow and that was pretty tough work. Then I began using the trowel and got paid a much better salary. After Bob found out that I could drum he asked me to come to rehearsal and I got the job with Hightower. With that outfit we played little ice-cream party dates and at first all I got was ice cream. I didn't even look for any money and didn't think that I was good enough to get money. I was only about sixteen when I started working with Hightower. It was a very nice little seven-man outfit. Hightower played a trumpet, Roy Palmer played trombone, Wade Whaley played clarinet, and we also had a violin in the group. Hightower was a very nice, even-tempered fellow and I never did see him drink. He played both jazz and straight horn and he'd play one chorus nice and then he would chop it up and play it jazzy.

We began playing at dances at lawn parties and fish fries, all outdoors. Through my playing the dates with the Hightower outfit my name began ringing around with different fellows. Roy Palmer, our trombone player, got a job in the tenderloin district, at the Fewclothes Café, and he insisted on getting me for a drummer. In the front of the place there was a bar and in the back was a dance floor, cabaret style. There were five of us, including a bass player. But Roy let the bass player go and that left only four. Sidney Desvigne played trumpet. He was a very light fellow with light hair and we used to call him "Sheep." Roy Palmer played trombone, Walter Decou, piano, and I played drums. We made some pretty nice music, too. The district was a big field for jazz men. We only made a dollar a night but we would also pass the hat around. Sometimes we took in ten to twenty-five dollars an evening. And that wasn't bad money between the four of us. If somebody asked for a number they would always give you money. Whatever we got we'd bring up and put in the kitty and later divide it among the whole group.

The girls who worked in the district really liked the music and they often sent up for different requests and sent money along. Sometimes they would work along with the band and have the fellows they were with ask for certain numbers. Sometimes they asked the men to give bigger tips for the musicians, too.

In those days we used to play all kinds of numbers. New Orleans is a seaport town and boats would come in from all parts of Europe. Many of the fellows had been on boats for three to five months when they came in and they were glad to find a dance hall and fast women in the district. Then we'd play *Over the Waves* for the sailors and different nationality songs. The men would pay for them because they hadn't heard their native songs in the United States before. We'd also jazz up songs like *In the Shade of the Old Apple Tree*. We used to take waltz tunes and change them into four-four time. And *High Society* we always played as a straight march. Now they play it as a jazz number. And the whole point of that number is the clarinet solo. It

was Picou's number and he did wonderfully on it. We played what was later called ragtime but was then called syncopation. It was picked up off Scott Joplin. It was called syncopation before I even started playing. Syncopation is tied with two groups of notes, or four groups, and in swing music it is four and six groups. It makes the time different. In jazz we call that a bundle of notes together. And we always stressed the melody. That's the secret of jazz music, to carry the melody at all times. The melody is supposed to be heard distinctly, carried by one specific instrument, the trumpet, trombone, clarinet, or violin.

On New Orleans dance dates we also had to play mazurkas, quadrilles, polkas, and schottisches. There were certain halls in New Orleans where you had to play all those things. Some of the Creole people went only for that music. If you couldn't play them you just didn't get the job.

Of course we also played the blues. Some of the guys would come in and drink with women and they would be blue about something, and they would ask us to play the blues. The blues that were popular were the *Memphis Blues*, the *St. Louis Blues*, and *Careless Love*. *Bucket Got a Hole in It* was also a blues type of number and *Ace in the Hole* was another. The blues were played in New Orleans in the early days very, very slow, and not like today, but in a Spanish rhythm.

After I left the Fewclothes outfit I worked for a piano player named Manuel Manetta, who also played in the district. The place was called the Casino. It was a little uppity place that had about five or six men in the band. It had been known as the Villa Café but some killing had gone on there and the owner changed the name to the Casino. Before long I left the district and went back to Hightower. I was glad to get away from the district, anyway. I didn't like that sort of life. Furthermore, I had a girl in the district who wanted to cut my throat.

In the meantime Hightower got a regular job playing at St. Catherine's Hall, which was a Catholic school. Ory's band had been playing there but he gave the job up, and when Hightower found out about it he spoke to the priest in charge. The school used to give dances every Friday and Sunday. We didn't get both days but we got the Sunday dates. When I first went there I didn't even think about whether I was going to get paid or not. I wasn't particular and I was especially excited about the work because my brother John had played in the same place with Ory. All I wanted to to do was to get a chance to play where my brother used to play. And we made very good and kept those Sunday dances for a long time. I played with the American Stars off and on for several years.

It was when I was working with Willie Hightower's outfit that I first realized how important drums were to a band. Sometimes when I had to go out and happened to hear the group start to play, I could feel that something was missing. And the greatest satisfaction of my entire musical career was knowing that I belonged there. Without the drum there was something lacking. No instrument can take the drum's place. With all the outfits I played, I felt that I was just as essential in the outfit as any other instrument in it. I knew I had to do my part. I had to beat drums because nothing else answers. Without my filling in my part it would mean a difference. Of course, I never worked any place where I felt I was the whole thing. I felt that all the other instruments were needed too. No one can do anything by himself. If there are more than two it's a group, and I feel that all members are essential. In playing music I always felt that I was part of the group and not an individual performer.

When I first started playing in New Orleans I heard a lot of good jazz musicians. There were Buddy Petit, Joe Johnson, George Larroque and Andrew Kimball, trumpet players, and Frankie Dusen, trombone player. There was also a tall dark fellow by the name of Eddie Jackson who used to play very good tuba. He could play both sweet and hot. But in those days they only used tubas in street parades, never in dances. Sometimes I used to go out to Lincoln Park where both Buddy Bolden and John Robichaux were playing. Robichaux had a sweet band and they would sometimes play the classics in swing. Those days they didn't call it jazz, but they called it swing. Robichaux played in a closed-in place like a pavilion and the better-class people came to hear his band. Bolden had a band which played in an open place with only a roof over it. The sporting class of people would go to hear Bolden, but both bands played for dancing and the people went to dance, not just to listen. We used to call it a "honky-tonk" where Bolden played and his men were the "bums." I heard Bolden play but can't remember anything about him or the music. He was one of the big guys of the day. Those days they had four or five trumpet men that were very good but Bolden was supposed to be king of them all. I also heard Picou play clarinet when I was little and he was really great. George Baquet was another guy playing clarinet who was just about as great as Picou. And of course, besides hearing jazz music played for dancing, I heard jazz in all the New Orleans parades. I also knew Jelly Roll Morton from the time I was a kid, and the great

pianist Tony Jackson. I used to work in the place where he worked but that group of men were older and I never got close to them. To even get in a conversation with them I had to buy them a lot of drinks or just pass by and take what I could get and go in. In those days a beginner wasn't allowed to be with a bunch of men that played such a high class of music. They wouldn't have anything to do with us.

I played with Big Eye Louis Nelson in different bands and at different times. He used to play clarinet with the Dusen band, not as a regular player, but just now and then. He was a very determined fellow, especially on the young musicians just starting up. He'd show a youngster all he knew but he had a very glum disposition. He knew he had to be stern with those of us who were learning. He didn't kid around much and we never got to be close friends. He lived downtown, and I lived uptown. He was on the north side of town and I lived on the east side. In other words, he was a Creole and lived in the French part of town. Canal Street was the dividing line and the people from the different sections didn't mix. The musicians mixed only if you were good enough. But at one time the Creole fellows thought the uptown musicians weren't good enough to play with them, because most of the uptown musicians didn't read music. Everybody in the French part of town read music. Then too, the Creole people in New Orleans were very high strung. Most of them had a little better education and it seems as though they had a little more money. When they went into music they were given money to get a teacher and they would learn music from the start. My brother and I were really exceptions in that we both got teachers and became reading musicians.

Of course in those days the instrumentation was different. When I first started out they had no piano. They mostly used bass viol, guitar, clarinet, trumpet, trombone and drums. The guitar carried only rhythm in the bands. Actually you have a much sweeter jazz band when you have a guitar and no piano. In that way the drums couldn't outplay the other guys, because the drummer had to keep in touch with the guitar. The guitar is not a harsh instrument but a very melodious one. When the piano came in it was harsher and louder than the guitar, although in my time we had some guitar players that were awful loud. There were Johnny St. Cyr, Brock Mumford and Lorenzo Stalls. Later they switched to banjo. I think the first band to switch was Frankie Dusen. They made the change because the banjo was a novelty. And they used two types of banjo. The regulation and the tenor.

In many places they had nothing but just piano

and drums. In fact, on one occasion, I had to play a whole evening with nothing but drums and trombone. That was with Jack Carey. We had a date to play uptown in what they called the Irish Channel. The Irish people liked the colored music and they hired Jack Carey's outfit. He had no regular drummer but would hire individuals for different dates, and that time he wanted me to play with the group. It had rained in the afternoon and a lot of fellows failed to appear at the dance. Only Jack Carey and I showed up with our drums and trombone. Well, those Irishmen were very tough on colored fellows and we wanted to avoid a misunderstanding. We knew if we played the best we could they'd be satisfied. After waiting a half-hour we noticed that a lot of the Irish fellows were getting drunker and we knew what would happen if the music didn't start soon. So we began to play that way and played the whole dance through. I think it sounded all right, too. Carey played a rough, tailgate style trombone and they liked it very much. He carried the melody and quite natural I was there with the time, so there was nothing to worry about. We both had to work very hard though, because on the drums I had to do everything to fill in, to make it sound like something. We knew we couldn't sound like a full band, but they danced to it and there was no trouble.

Jack Carey was a wild and quick-tempered fellow. He was older than his brother Mutt, who played trumpet. Sometimes he was quite loud and boisterous. Mutt was very quiet. Jack wanted to have things perfect but when he tried to explain something carefully he couldn't do it, and then he would get all upset. Mutt had more of an ability to explain things than Jack. They were different in all ways. Mutt was a very light fellow and Jack had a dark skin. Mutt was always kidding and joking and I never saw him really angry. And they used to call *Tiger Rag* "Play, Jack Carey." The part where they say "hold that tiger," Jack Carey would make on the trombone, and they used to say "Jack Carey, Jack Carey!" Everybody played it that way saying "Jack Carey" instead of "hold that tiger."

While I was playing around with different outfits my brother was established and playing with Kid Ory's band. He had studied clarinet under different fellows. One was Papa Tio, the old man Lorenzo, and Charlie McCurdy was another one. They were both straight musicians, not jazz men. And when John came along, he came along against Sidney Bechet. That meant he really had to fight. John got the job with Ory through Pops Foster. Foster was with the Ory band and they were using Wade Whaley on clarinet. Pops Foster happened to come

by the house and hear John's clarinet. He stopped on the sidewalk and knocked on the door and asked my brother if he wanted to join a band. My brother said "yes," and Pops Foster told Ory and everybody he had a pretty clarinet player he would like them to hear. They had a rehearsal of some sort and John joined Ory, and he played with him a number of years.

Sometimes I would go around to dances in New Orleans where my brother was playing with Ory. I used to go to the drummer, Henry Martin, and get him to let me drum. He would get up and I would sit down in the band. And then the band fellows would look around and see it wasn't the same style of drumming. My brother and Ory and the others didn't think that I was capable or good enough to play in that band, and they'd walk off the stand one by one, until all the fellows were off but the bass player and me. The bass player was Eddie Garland, and the next thing he would be laying the bass down, and I'd know there was nothing for me to do but get down. And when I'd get down the band would all come back again. It was very embarrassing. They pulled that quite a few times, made me feel awfully bad. I was determined, though. I felt as though a baby must crawl before it can walk, and I felt that I wasn't quite ready to walk yet and just took it for granted. And for an encouragement I would go around and do the same thing all over again. That gave me ambition to learn. I was trying to play with someone who was capable of playing. And many times later I returned the compliment. But I never did get over the feeling I had towards Ory. Later I played with him on the West Coast but I never got close enough to Ory to know him. It's a respect that I gave him that I perhaps wouldn't give anyone else.

The musicians of those days were remarkable men. When the leader of an orchestra would hire a man, there was no jealousy in the gang. Everybody took him in as a brother, and he was treated accordingly. If a fellow came to work with anything, even a sandwich or an orange, the new man would be offered a piece of it. That's the way they were. They believed in harmony. That's how they played music, in harmony. And that's the way the fellows were, those oldtimers. And I was young and I had to give them a lot of respect. If those men would happen to like you enough to pick you up, they would either make a musician out of you, or you wouldn't be any musician. In their way, they were rough, but in a way they weren't rough. Everything they told you they would make you do for your own benefit. But I used to try to drum and I'd drum my best and they knew I was doing my best and they all said the same thing. They said, "Someday he's going to be a good drummer because he pays attention. He wants to learn." And I did.

But while I was learning I kept playing and I left the American Stars to join Frankie Dusen's Eagle Band. Dusen was a very high-strung good-looking fellow. He was part Indian and had a brown skin but reddish complexion. He had a high nose with a lump in the middle—real Indian nose—and very long curly hair. He played tailgate trombone, something like Ory, but a little smoother and with a bit more polish. Bunk Johnson played trumpet in that outfit. The little fellow that was the drummer, Henry Zeno, got sick and died, practically overnight. He ate raw oysters and drank whisky, and it killed him. I had built such a reputation around New Orleans that they said, "Let's get Babe." Then that made me play the street parades, too. It was the first time I played them. Different social clubs in the city would hire our band. They would have bands to turn out with a parade or for some other function. Sometimes it was anniversaries or social occasions and sometimes the funeral of a member. With the brass band I only had one drum, the snare drum. Someone else played the bass drum. We also played for dancing with the Dusen Band but it was a bigger outfit when we played parades.

There was a traditional line-up for the New Orleans parades. The trombone was always first. They always used two or three trumpets and they came next. Behind the trumpets would be the heavy instruments, like bass, tubas, and baritones. Then behind them were the altos, two or three alto horns, and behind them were the clarinets. It was very good if there were two. Usually it was only one, an E flat. Then behind the clarinet would come the drums, only two, a bass drum and a snare drum. That was for balance. For funeral marches the snare drum is muffled by pulling the snares off. When the snares are off it's the same as a tom-tom. But you don't muffle drums with parades, or going back from the cemetery. At the most there were eleven or twelve men in the whole brass band. I never noticed what the people who followed the bands did because my attention was all on my music. Maybe I'd cast my eye and perhaps see something funny, but it was only a minute, and then right back to my music. In the parades they had horses and men with sashes and the like, but the music was all I was interested in.

Sometimes the groups would have several bands in a parade. Then the main band had to start first and finish last and all the other bands had to go through this leading band at the end of the parade. Of course the head band would always be the best. And it was one of the most exciting things I ever did to play music and go through another band that was playing. The main band was lined up on both sides and we had to go between them and keep playing. I remember the first time it happened. I don't remember who was drumming in the main band but I think it was Ernest Trepagnier who was beating bass drum. The snare I don't remember. But my snare was a four-inch drum, and this fellow had a six-inch snare drum. When we got going through I couldn't hear my drumming anymore so I didn't know what I was doing. And I picked up with the other drummer, who was playing six-eight in contrast to the two-four time we had been playing. I should have displaced the other fellow's drumming with concentrating on what I was doing, but that time I heard the other guy's part and not my own, and of course we were playing altogether different numbers. But it's those experiences which make you know what music is, and it's the hard way of learning.

I played many a funeral with brass bands in New Orleans. The first time I ever heard the number *Didn't He Ramble* was in a street parade after the burial of a corpse. He had been a member of a secret society and so they hired a band to play for his funeral. He was the type of fellow who would go out and have a good time, and cheat on his wife. In other words he was the type of person who would throw a brick and hide his head. But when he came home he was a saint. And so they made this number. They claim that Buddy Bolden made it but I don't know. If the musicians found out that this was the kind of man who was being buried they would play this song. It meant a lot of things that weren't just out and spoken.

Of course we played other numbers coming back from funerals. We'd play the same popular numbers that we used to play with dance bands. And the purpose was this: As the family and people went to the graveyard to bury one of their loved ones, we'd play a funeral march. It was pretty sad, and it put a feeling of weeping in their hearts and minds and when they left there we didn't want them to hear that going home. It became a tradition to play jazzy numbers going back to make the relatives and friends cast off their sadness. And the people along the streets used to dance to the music. I used to follow those parades myself, long before I ever thought of becoming a drummer. The jazz played after New Orleans funerals didn't show any lack of respect for the person being buried. It rather showed their people that we wanted them to be happy.

On other occasions we played jazz on the streets to advertise dances and lawn parties. Private individuals used to sponsor these parties and they were held in outdoor pavilions rather than dance halls. They'd have just a tarpaulin or tent over the top to keep the night air off, and sometimes they would have a tarpaulin stretched out on the ground for the people to dance on. Sometimes they'd dance on the natural ground. They'd smooth it off nice. And the only advertising they had would be to get the band on a wagon and put a couple of posters on the side. We would sit there and go from block to block or corner to corner, and play. Of course when the people came out to hear the band they would see the posters. I used to play on such wagons when I first started with the American Stars and later with Frankie Dusen's Eagle Band, and still later with Celestin. For a fact, all the bands used to advertise that way. We would start out about two o'clock in the afternoon and wouldn't get back till around five.

When some other outfit was also advertising and we met each other along the street in those wagons it used to make it very interesting. The guys would put the wheels together and tie them so the band that got outplayed could not run away. That made us stay right there and fight it out. And we used to draw quite a crowd of people in the street that way. We didn't call them cutting contests, but if we said that a band cut you on the street, that meant they outplayed you. And that was passed along through jokes. We talked about who got chased, or which band "fixed them guys," and that sort of talk.

I'll never forget one time when we were stopped on the streets. I was playing with Jack Carey on that occasion. I didn't belong to the band but they used to get me to play. Jack Carey played trombone, his brother Mutt, cornet, and Carey's nephew named Zeb, clarinet, and we ran across Ory's band. Quite natural the Ory band had the best of it all. Besides Ory, my brother was in that band, and Joe Oliver. Of course we didn't have a chance, but we had to stay there. When we played a number there wouldn't be much applause, but when Ory played we would hear a lot of people whistling and applauding. When we heard that, quite natural our courage went down and we wanted to get away. But the wheels were tied together. It lasted an hour and a half or two hours and it was very discouraging. I wasn't so good. I was just starting and Ory's drummer, Henry Martin, was a finished musician, but those things are what made us want to become good musicians because it made us know what we had to do better.

But I improved as time went on and I left the Dusen Band to join Sonny Celestin's outfit. Sonny had heard that I was young but wanted to learn and he hired me. We played at a place called Jack Sheehan's Roadhouse. It was a cabaret style place. They'd sell setups and glasses, and people could either bring their own whisky or buy it there. It was prohibition but they sold whisky anyway because it was on the outskirts of New Orleans. They also had roulette wheels for gambling and some card games. We

R. Rewal

played only for dancing and there were six of us in the outfit: Celestin on trumpet; Baby Ridgeley, trombone; Zutty Singleton's uncle, Willie Bontemps, played bass and guitar; and Lorenzo Tio, clarinet. It was mostly a reading band. Only two didn't read music. And we had a girl piano player. She was a very good-looking, light-colored girl named Emma Barrett. She had big eyes; we used to call her "Eyes." She was a very thin girl but, oh my God, she could play nice piano. She played like any man.

They were all good musicians. Celestin played very sweet horn. He never was much of a jazz man on horn. He played mostly straight. Still, with everybody else jazzing and him playing straight, it sounded awfully good. Baby Ridgeley was also a very nice guy who played nice trombone. His playing wasn't rough but sweet, more like Honoré Dutrey's. Willie Bontemps was a very big fellow who weighed two hundred pounds or more. He suffered from asthma and had to use an atomizer. Lorenzo Tio was more of a Mexican type fellow. He was Creole, very tall with very straight black hair. He was a very easygoing fellow and he used to love to play. He had a cute little joke which he liked to play on Sonny. Celestin was very sleepy; we used to say he was lazy, but he was just a sleepyhead. After playing he'd put his horn down in his lap and go to sleep. Then for a trick Tio would take some newspaper, tie it to the back of Sonny's chair, and set fire to it. One night Celestin jumped up and almost ran out of the place. He was very angry with Lorenzo and Tio had to hide from him for about half an hour until he got his temper down. It's the only time I've ever seen Celestin really mad. He was pretty sore but later he took it as a joke, too.

When I was with Celestin we played more pop numbers than when I was in the Dusen Band. We didn't call them pop numbers though, we called them classical numbers. That is, not the rowdy type, such as blues, nothing like that. The customers at Jack Sheehan's were all white and the blues would not have been appreciated. It wouldn't be any use to play them. One of the main numbers which we played was *Liza Jane*. I used to sing that and Sonny would put his horn in his lap and start clapping in time. But before he got the time he'd be going asleep. I'd have to say "Come on, Sonny!" and then he'd wake up and join in the number again. Later, after I left the band, Sonny sang the number himself and then all the fellows joined in. Before that I don't think Celestin knew he could sing.

It was at Jack Sheehan's that I worked out my shimmy beat. It was wartime, around 1918. One night a French soldier came in. When he heard the music he couldn't dance to it, but he just started to shake all over. That's the way it affected me. I saw him do it and I did it, too. The people got such a kick out of seeing me shaking like him that they all came around and watched. Then when I saw that it caused such a big sensation and brought credit to myself and my drumming, I continued it. I used to shimmy at the same time I used my press roll and a full beat. It was perfect. I slapped my left foot, the right foot was busy, and it worked very nicely. I used it ever since that time and it became a specialty with me.

Although I didn't realize it at the time, my days of playing in New Orleans were coming to an end. Before long I joined the Fate Marable Band and played on the riverboats, and from there I went to the West Coast and Chicago with King Oliver. But it was in New Orleans that I got my start.

2. *Jazz on the River*

It was around the latter part of 1918 when Pops Foster got me the job playing on the riverboat. I had been playing with Sonny Celestin's Band and left that outfit to work on the boat. Pops also wanted to get Louis Armstrong. He figured that I could do more with Louis than he could and he asked me to get him for the band. Louis was playing with the Ory Band. So was my brother John. So I was fighting to get Louis on the boat, and my brother was fighting to make him stay with Ory. Finally, I won out. It was a big job but I made it and we had Louis with us on the boat. Louis and I stayed on the boats from the fall of 1918 until September of 1921.

The boats belonged to the Streckfus line. They had jazz bands for dancing on all their boats. At first I played on the steamer *Sidney*, working out of St. Louis in the summer, and out of New Orleans for seven winter months. After my first year on the boat they brought the steamer *St. Paul* out of dry dock. It was a much larger boat. The *Sidney* held only about eight hundred but the *St. Paul* had a capacity of thirty-five hundred. After that they used the *Sidney* in New Orleans only. I played on four boats in all: the *Sidney*, the *St. Paul*, the *J.S.* and the *Capitol*. Later they added the *President*. I was on that boat when it came out of dry dock but I didn't work on it. We would leave New Orleans around the fifteenth of May and head up the river for St. Louis. We played in St. Louis from about the fifteenth of June until the fifteenth of September, but we also took trips out of some towns farther up the river. We went all the way up to St. Paul and stopped in Davenport, Dubuque and Keokuk, Iowa; LaCrosse, Wisconsin; and Red Wing, Minnesota, on the way.

In St. Louis they used to give colored excursions every Monday night. It was one of the most wonderful things you've ever seen carried on. The boat was packed and we got such a kick out of it because it gave us a free kind of sensation for working. We worked all the week for white people and this one night we could work for colored. It gave us an altogether different sensation because we were free to talk to people and the people could talk to us, and that's a great deal in playing music. We were less tense because it was our own people. I especially loved it because I made a big sensation with my shimmy beat. I used to shimmy and drum at the same time, shake all over. The colored people had never seen anything like that. I used to have a bunch around me backed up five or six deep; and Louis Armstrong would have a bunch five or six deep backed up around him. It was a wonderful thing, and we were the two sensational men on the boat, Louis and I.

We certain enjoyed working on the boats and we were paid well, too. We were getting fifty dollars a week and five dollars a week bonus. That was to force us to stay on the whole season; we wouldn't receive the bonus until the season was over. We also got our room and board on the boat. The bunks were very comfortable but we stayed down in the hold. However, it was very clean and nice. The band and the roustabouts were the only colored people on board. The fourteen of us in the Marable Band all ate at a separate table. Some of the fellows thought the food was good but I didn't think so. We had mostly stews, salads, wieners and things like that. That's nothing to feed anybody. When we got to St. Louis we preferred to board ourselves rather than stay on the boat and eat that food.

And they were pretty strict about what we did, too. After we left New Orleans to go up the river, we had nothing to do but be on the boat. We ate and slept right on the boat. Every time we got off work we went right back down in the hold and went to sleep, or did what we wanted to do at night: play cards, or shoot craps, or something. There was nobody to win money from except one another. When we went out at night there was a curfew. And if we weren't there at a certain time we didn't get on the boat. We got off work at eleven and we could leave the boat until curfew, which was about one-thirty.

The bosses demanded discipline. I remember once when I was in Keokuk, Iowa, I got into a humbug. We all piled off the boat one day and I got so drunk I couldn't see. They were using this homemade beer, they used to call it "bust-head" in Keokuk, and I came back to the boat so drunk with the stuff that I just couldn't walk up the gangplank. They tied me to a post and one of the bosses said I should have been horsewhipped. I said "Yeah? I'll bet it would be the worst horsewhipping you ever saw if you'd let me alive when you got through." They were kind of shy of me. I didn't care about anything in those days so maybe I would have done something, I don't know.

But my heart was in my music, and that was some of the sweetest music I ever played. It was a wonderful outfit. Besides the standard jazz and popular numbers, we played classical numbers and also played for ordinary singing. The Marable Band was the first big band that I worked with. We had about fourteen men. It was a pleasure to work with that bunch of men. We didn't have to work hard. Of course, we worked hard but we didn't have to. We played strictly by music. And music is not so hard if you get with a bunch that's playing together. But it's an awful strain to play jazz with one fellow going this way and another fellow going another. That makes for hard work. It's like anything else. If you run an automobile and the gears are meshing easy you can run it pretty fast. But if the gears are meshing badly, they're going to hit each other. It's the same thing with music. Regardless of what the number is, if everybody's together, and if everybody knows his business, when the notes are joined they'll come out even. The music would sound so pretty, especially on the water. And the melophone set the band off and gave it a different tone from any other band I worked with. It was something great to hear. Everybody was so congenial, too. We had so much harmony in that band.

The leader, Fate Marable, was a very light-colored man with red hair. He was a pretty stern fellow who kept strict order. Marable had worked for Streckfus so long, and he looked so white, that people used to say he was Streckfus's son. He was the best calliope player I ever heard. I've heard them played in the circus but no one could play like that guy. He had a calliope on top of the boat which he used to play alone. Three decks down, where the band played, he had a little electric chimes, which worked just like a calliope. He played mostly piano with the band but he would use the chimes just to make the band sound a little different at times.

There were some other wonderful musicians in the riverboat band besides Fate Marable. There was Joe Howard, who was a very even-tempered, nice-going fellow. He would try to tell you everything right if he possibly could and would show us anything that he could to improve the group. But he would get angry with himself sometimes and we could see the different expressions on his face. He would never bother anybody though. He helped Louis a great deal with the mastering of musical ability.

Davey Jones, who played melophone, was another easy-tempered fellow who didn't drink at all. His musical ability was also very high and he would show anyone all he knew. And his melophone gave the band a sound you don't often hear. He played it with the bell of the horn in his lap. Other players turned it up. The sound from the bell would come in his lap. It muffled the tone and made it sound so beautiful.

Sam Dutrey was a fine fellow but he was very high strung. However, he and I used to get along beautifully. We were close friends, just as his brother, Honoré, was my best friend in the Oliver outfit later. He also tried to get me to save some of my money.

Of course, Louis was also with us. I remember, when he first came on the boat, he didn't have a horn. And in Davenport, Iowa, Bix Beiderbecke and some of the other white musicians came on the boat to listen and talk to the different musicians. Louis told Bix he didn't have a horn, so Bix said, "Well, meet me when I go out and I'll see if I can get you a horn." And Bix took him out afterwards and helped him pick out a horn.

There's a story about Louis and some of the others buying bootleg liquor on the boat. It was during prohibition time and we were glad to get even a drink of liquor, especially good liquor. One day a fellow came on the boat with a suitcase out of which he pulled a bottle. We all had a taste of it and we asked him how much he wanted. He said "Twenty-five dollars a quart." We knew whisky was tough to get so we all said "yes." He said he would have to come back and bring it to the dock at a certain time, and we planned a time to have it on our intermission so we could meet him. When he came during intermission we were waiting. I don't know what happened but I ducked out of it and decided I didn't want any. Then Fate borrowed the twenty-five I had put in. He and Louis had earlier paid for one quart each, so that meant the fellow got seventy-five dollars. But when we got back on the boat we found out there was nothing in the suitcase but three bricks. Naturally, we lost all of the money and never saw the fellow again. But we had a big laugh and kidded Louis and Fate a long while about it. It was a real laugh for me, because even though my money went, I had backed out of it after I had been one of the instigators. And of course everybody knew I loved whisky.

But with all our joking we never got away from the music and we always tried to work out new ideas. Louis was especially versatile. Once Streckfus bought some trick instruments for the different people in the band. He bought Louis a slide trumpet and me a slide whistle and different little trinkets that were to go with my drums. That's what they call traps. A snare drum isn't a trap drum. Rather traps are such things as blocks, triangles, slide whistles, horns, tambourines, cocoa blocks and things like that. In those days nobody handled these traps but the drummers. And if you couldn't handle the traps you didn't get a job. Well, Streckfus bought this slide whistle for me but I didn't even look at it. Louis did. He played it and years later he used it sometimes with the Oliver Band. Joe wanted him to make a recording with it so he took the whistle along to a recording session and played it on the Oliver record of *Sobbin' Blues.*

Louis also had a lot to do with the popularizing of jazz words. He used certain expressions on the riverboats, like "Come on, you cats," and "Look out there, Pops," and the like. These were his own ideas. I had never heard such words as "jive" and "cat" and "scat" used in New Orleans. There was one exception, however, which you don't hear now. We used to call white musicians "alligators." That was the way we'd describe them when they'd come around and we were playing something that we didn't want them to catch on to. We'd say "Watch out, there's an alligator!" But these other terms Louis had a lot to do with.

I think it was on the riverboat where Louis developed his gravel voice. He had a cold all the time and we used to kid him around, laughing and joking. Once he took a whole course of Scott's Emulsion. It cleaned him out perfectly and then he got plenty of rest on the boat since there was no special place to go. He got rid of the cold but the voice had developed like that and he's been like that ever since.

Louis learned a lot about music from Joe Howard on the boats, and I also learned a great deal about music during that time. I knew how to spell when reading music but I didn't know how to read well and fast. We had loads of fun and had an hour and a half or two hour rehearsal almost every day, all new music. That's why we learned to be such good readers. New music every day, and the same music we rehearsed in the day we played at night. And we had to be perfect with it. There were three Streckfus brothers, and they were all musicians. I think two of them played piano and one, violin. And they made Fate demand frequent rehearsals of the band. It was wonderful for me and everyone else concerned. It made us tidy up our music, it made our eyes fast, and it made us fast on our instruments. That was the first place I learned what "time" was. They would hold a metronome on me, and a stop clock, and I wouldn't know anything about it. I had to be a very strict time keeper in those days. I used to listen to everybody in the group and try to give each one what he wanted. Nobody tried to outplay the other fellow. We all played together, and Louis was the only one who took solos in the Marable Band.

It was on the riverboat that I began using the rims instead of the wood blocks. I don't remember the number but on one that called for wood blocks I used the rims of the bass drum instead. And it sounded so pretty. The wood block gave a loud sound, and I substituted the shells of the drums, and it sounded so soothing and soft. Sometimes I used faster beats on the rims. Then again, when it was a slow number, I'd do it in triplets. It was pretty and soft, and still it would make the number lively. I worked out these things by myself on the boat because I knew I had to make good. That's also where I learned to be so tough on drumming. At that time I could sit down and drum a pretty long time.

On the boat I also worked out the technique of hitting the cymbal with the sticks. I worked that out around 1919. Now everybody's using it, but it came from me on the riverboat. There was a side cymbal that used to be on the drum. I took that off and then it was a straight boom, boom, boom. Of course, I still used the two cymbals on top of the bass drum. There was a regular cymbal and a Chinese cymbal. The Chinese cymbal had a different tone. We all used it in those days but Ray Bauduc's about the only one I know who uses it now.

It was about the same time that I helped cause the sock cymbals to be made. I was in St. Louis working on the steamboat and William Ludwig, the drum manufacturer, came on the boat for a ride. He was very interested in my drumming. I used to stomp my left foot, long before other drummers did, and Ludwig asked me if I could stomp my toe instead of my heel. I told him "I think so." For a fact I thought nothing of it. So he measured my foot on a piece of paper and the space where I would have it and where it would sit and he made a sock cymbal. Two cymbals were set up and a foot pedal with them. One day he brought one along for me to try. It wasn't any good, so he brought another raised up about nine inches higher. Well, I had just taken the cymbal off the bass drum because I didn't want to hear that tinny sound any more and I didn't like the sock cymbal either. I didn't like any part of them and I still don't. Now it's a big novelty for drummers. Some drummers can't drum without them. I can't drum with them.

But I made good, too, with my drumming and there's a story about my teacher Brundy which shows the progress I made. We were working on the steamer *St. Paul* and there was another excursion boat, the *J.S.*, which was a sister to the *St. Paul*. The only difference between the two boats was that the *St. Paul* was a flat-bottomed boat and the *J.S.* was a keel-bottomed boat. After we had made such a hit in St. Louis, Streckfus wanted to get another colored band for the *J.S.* They got an outfit from New Orleans and Brundy was in it. After he had played a while, Streckfus told him, "You come over on the steamer *St. Paul* and listen to that drummer." When Brundy came on and I saw who it was, I told Streckfus, "My God, I can't do no drumming. This fellow's my teacher. He taught me how to drum." He said, "It doesn't matter if he did, you can drum better than he can." And Streckfus told him so. Brundy replied, "If my scholar can drum better than I and I've got to learn under him now, I'll quit." And he did. He quit drumming entirely and started playing clarinet from that time on. I never heard him play clarinet but I understand he played it until he was killed when hit by a car sometime later.

Of course Streckfus liked my drumming or he wouldn't have hired me. He liked the whole band. He used to use a white band out of Davenport, Iowa, every year. They were jazz bands, too, or supposed to be. They called them jazz bands. But I guess he was losing money with the white bands. Red Nichols played on the boat one time, and also Miff Mole. Some of the white musicians didn't like the idea of playing with Fate, even though he was as light as any of them. I think that's why Mr. Streckfus wanted all Negroes.

The first year we went up the river we didn't do good at all. It was pitiful. We played up the Mississippi River and I think people used to come on the boat more for curiosity than anything else. And they sat down and looked at us. They'd advertise before we got there that we were colored. So people wouldn't be disappointed. Fate Marable and his Jaz-E-Saz Band, with Louis Armstrong, Baby Dodds, and so forth down the line. It was embarrassing to have the people stare at us but I didn't care about that. I looked at it this way: "Well, I'm doing something big or else there wouldn't be such astonishment." Often when we went to a town nobody would dance. Then when we'd go back for a second trip that same day, the boat would be packed.

Hannibal, Missouri, was a hard place. We played one trip out of there, and had an excursion for the women and children in the daytime. We had a nice load, not full capacity but a nice load. At night we had only a few, and what was there just sat down and looked at us. And do you think they started dancing? No. They just sat and stared. That was from nine o'clock until eleven o'clock. Nobody danced. We'd take an intermission, go off, come back, and they'd still look at us. And then later on the mayor or somebody ordered another trip back there. He ordered a special chartered trip. My God, you couldn't get them off the boat; the boat was packed to capacity. I think the first time it was a surprise for the people. They had never before seen Negroes on the boat. They saw Negro roustabouts but had never seen a Negro with a tie and collar on, and a white shirt, playing music. They just didn't know what to make of it. But they really liked it. They were the most dancingest people I ever found on the boat.

Sometimes the people would stand on the wharf and listen to the music. The boat was tied to the wharf and we'd play there for about a half-hour before we'd ship out. That was partly to attract people. We also had dancing on the boat while it was docked. Lots of people would feel more secure when it was standing than when it was running. And the people on the boat were not the rowdy kind. We were lucky to have just nice people. If they weren't nice before they got on the boat, they were gentlemen and ladies while on it. They had some pretty tough guys around like bouncers to keep order. No liquor was served and there was no gambling, excepting raffles for candy.

The band played strictly for dancing. We played all the standards of the day and we used to make the classics into dance tunes. There was a sign up "Requests filled," and the people could ask for special numbers. We played eleven or twelve numbers, and every one of them had an encore to it. Then we had only a fifteen-minute intermission, and started all over again. We worked pretty hard with that band.

But we didn't play many blues on the boat. The white people didn't go for blues like they do now. They try them now but they don't know the blues. They think any slow number is a blue type. That's wrong. Blues is blues. In New Orleans we used to play the blues and the very lowest type of dancers used to love such things. They were played very slow and fellows and their girl friends would stand almost still and just make movements. It was rowdy music, and yet it wasn't rowdy in a way, either. They often expressed some tragedy, just like *Frankie and Johnny*. *Frankie and Johnny* was one of this style of blues they used to sing a long time ago. It was about some woman and her man. Another one was *Ace in the Hole*. Those are really sporting numbers, which were played in the sporting houses, or when sporting people would get together.

The blues are something like a man drinking. If he drinks to extreme it's because there's something on his mind. And it's so deeply on his mind that the only cure he thinks he can find is a bottle. The blues is something of that sort. It may come from trouble in one's home, with his people, his wife or something, domestic troubles perhaps. That's what blues are. Something like this song *Laugh, Clown, Laugh*. Regardless of how heavy your heart may be you can't give in to that and make the people know you're sorry. You've got to make them laugh. That's the same with the blues.

In New Orleans we played the blues in very slow tempo. Blues today aren't played as slow as in the old days. It used to be so draggy. I've heard white people say at a dance, "We don't want any of that dead march music. That sounds like a funeral march." Well, they didn't know any different. The colored people understood. The only way the colored people could express themselves was through the blues, that perhaps nobody understood but themselves. That's the way they expressed themselves to themselves. It's very unnatural for some people, especially white people. In a way a white man has always had his chance to do anything he wanted to. A Negro's chances are always limited.

The Negro had something to be blue for. He could go only so far and then he was cut out, regardless of how good he was. Quite naturally, when he thinks about it, that he's in a limited place in life, why he gets blue about it. Then he sits down, and he'll either whistle to himself, or pat his foot, or do something. And maybe he sings some song that's very slow, and he takes his time to express himself in his way. When another guy comes along, he hears the tune and says, "What is this guy doing?" and asks, "What's the name of that tune?" The fellow answers, "Oh, just blues." And the second guy might ask, "Why blue?" and he answers, "Well, I got the blues, that's all it is." It's getting rid of your feelings within yourself. And it is expressed with a song. And it must have the feeling with it. If an individual doesn't have the feeling with the blues it doesn't mean anything.

I've heard some wonderful blues singers. I've listened to Ma Rainey sing the blues time and time again. And she would sing blues with words that coped with the situation. Like Mamie Smith. She had a voice and sang words that made you feel very sad. Bessie Smith was the same way. I think Bessie had one of the silver tones of blues singers. That's my opinion. Mamie Smith's voice was between contralto and alto, and Bessie Smith had a real clear alto voice. Ma Rainey had a baritone voice. Between the three singers, for my part, I would rather hear Bessie.

I didn't hear blues singers in St. Louis but I heard

practically all the bands that were around there at the time we were on the riverboats. I used to like St. Louis very much. Dewey Jackson had a band there and so did Charlie Creath. And there was a place called Jazzland where they had a band. It was a rendezvous for most of the colored traveling acts that came from other places like Chicago. Sometimes, but very seldom, we would sit in with the St. Louis bands. Everybody that was working on the boat was known there, and Louis and I used to travel together most of the time. And when we'd sit in there, we'd break it up. Naturally, I knew how to work with Louis and Louis knew how to work with me, so it turned out very nice. I met this drummer Red Muse, who was supposed to be very sensational, in St. Louis. It was a place called the Chauffeur's Club, a night club joined to a hotel. I was with Fate Marable and everybody was hollering when we came in the place. His drumming was very sensational, very good. He'd throw up sticks and things like that. I was actually afraid to sit down there. But one night Fate played piano, and Louis played trumpet and I played drums, and we broke up the place. So I had no more bother with Muse after that. Before that I was scared to death. But I shimmied when I drummed and that took the eyes of the people. It was something different and made a very good impression.

My drumming improved a great deal on the boats but eventually Louis and I left because of a misunderstanding which we had with the bosses. Streckfus wanted us to play differently and he told Marable so. Well Fate Marable had been with Streckfus so long that anything Streckfus asked for he'd tell us to do,

even if it meant breaking our necks. The Streckfuses were musicians and they knew what they wanted and they wanted us to beat a different time than we had been using. Some of the older people on the boat couldn't dance to our music and Streckfus wanted to introduce what he called "toddle time." It was really two-four time but he wanted four beats to the measure. It's what they are doing today. To me, four beats was all wrong. It has a tendency to speed up the music. But for the older people it was easier since instead of dancing to a step, they would just bounce around. Louis was also to play differently from what he had been used to. And I just couldn't do this toddle time on my drums. I felt that it would change me so much from my way of drumming and from what I had learned and had been doing all those many years. Louis couldn't do what they wanted him to do either. Well, we were the stars on the boat and we felt that if we were the stars, why monkey with us. We had already made a reputation with our music and the people were satisfied. So finally Louis and I left the boat together after handing in written resignations. That was about the first of September, 1921.

I often think what a shame it was that the riverboat band never recorded. If they had, people would really have heard something pretty. It was just like a clock. Even if we got off one or two beats, somebody knew it and told us about it. It made me very sad to leave the Marable outfit. I had been attached to the band for three years and that was a long time to be with a special bunch of people. But I soon joined another group in which I was just as happy—the King Oliver Band.

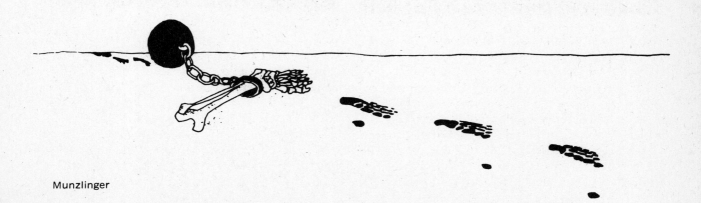

Munzlinger

Berkeley in Time of Plague

Plague took us and the land from under us,
Rose like a boil, enclosing us within.
We waited and the blue skies writhed a while
Becoming black with death.

Plague took us and the chairs from under us,
Stepped cautiously while entering the room

(We were discussing Yeats); it paused a while
Then smiled and made us die.

Plague took us, laughed and reproportioned us,
Swelled us to dizzy, unaccustomed size.
We died prodigiously; it hurt a while
But left a certain quiet in our eyes.

Psychoanalysis: An Elegy

What are you thinking about?

I am thinking of an early summer.
I am thinking of wet hills in the rain
Pouring water. Shedding it
Down empty acres of oak and manzanita
Down to the old green brush tangled in the sun,
Greasewood, sage, and spring mustard.
Or the hot wind coming down from Santa Ana
Driving the hills crazy,
A fast wind with a bit of dust in it
Bruising everything and making the seed sweet.
Or down in the city where the peach trees
Are awkward as young horses,
And there are kites caught on the wires
Up above the street lamps,
And the storm drains are all choked with dead
    branches.

What are you thinking?

I think that I would like to write a poem that is slow
    as a summer
As slow getting started
As 4th of July somewhere around the middle of the
    second stanza
After a lot of unusual rain
California seems long in the summer.
I would like to write a poem as long as California
And as slow as a summer.
Do you get me, Doctor? It would have to be as slow
As the very tip of summer.
As slow as the summer seems
On a hot day drinking beer outside Riverside
Or standing in the middle of a white-hot road
Between Bakersfield and Hell
Waiting for Santa Claus.

What are you thinking now?

I'm thinking that she is very much like California.
When she is still her dress is like a roadmap. High-
    ways
Traveling up and down her skin
Long empty highways
With the moon chasing jackrabbits across them
On hot summer nights.
I am thinking that her body could be California
And I a rich Eastern tourist
Lost somewhere between Hell and Texas
Looking at a map of a long, wet, dancing California
That I have never seen.
Send me some penny picture-postcards, lady,
Send them.
One of each breast photographed looking
Like curious national monuments,
One of your body sweeping like a three-lane highway
Twenty-seven miles from a night's lodging
In the world's oldest hotel.

What are you thinking?

I am thinking of how many times this poem
Will be repeated. How many summers
Will torture California
Until the damned maps burn
Until the mad cartographer
Falls to the ground and possesses
The sweet thick earth from which he has been
    hiding.

What are you thinking now?

I am thinking that a poem could go on forever.

After Budapest

[Jean-Paul Sartre's leading position among French intellectuals lends a special significance to his reactions to Russian intervention in Hungary and to his analysis of the situation in left-wing politics in France at that time. The following interview with Sartre was first published in the Paris Express, November 9, 1956.]

How did you learn of the events in Hungary and what were your first reactions?

My first reaction, anguish; there was this unbelievable error: the request for intervention by Russian troops, and no one knew as yet whether it was the last Rakosi-ist or the new Hungarian government which was responsible. After a few days, anguish gave way to hope and even joy; although the Russian command—which we had just learned was called in by Gero—had committed the criminal clumsiness of answering this call, it had then withdrawn its troops from Budapest.

We saw Soviet regiments withdrawing before the insurgents rather than fire on them; Russian soldiers deserting. The Kremlin seemed hesitant: it seemed as if the insurgents were going to win. Perhaps, in spite of this first terrible bloodshed, the Soviet Union wanted to resort to negotiations like those in Poland.

The anguish returned immediately after, more intense each day: it did not leave me with the emergence from prison on to the world scene of Cardinal Mindszenty. I thought: the USSR will be put on the spot: their Cardinal was returned to them; what about Horthy and integration with the Western powers? The Russians will have to abandon Hungary or resume the massacres. The neutrality asked for by Nagy was obviously only a minimum demand made under pressure of the insurgents and which would not satisfy them.

The return to the old parties, the hunt for members of the secret police and, undoubtedly, also of the Communist party workers, the return of the émigrés, the appearance of "suppressed local émigrés," the possible existence of a reactionary conspiracy in the army, all this showed that the Hungarian revolt was aiming at a complete liquidation of what is called the socialist foundations of the regime.

It was this tragic situation which one of the last members of the Nagy government described on Radio Budapest: "We are caught between the menace of a return of the reactionaries and that of a foreign occupation. This is what caused the Russian intervention. This is the explanation." But an explanation is not an excuse: from any angle, the intervention was a crime. And it is an abject lie to claim that the workers are fighting at the side of the Soviet troops.

Listen rather to the appeals of Kadar, last night: "Workers, help us! . . . Workers and peasants, fight with us! The Communist party is going through the most tragic phase of its history. We are breaking with the past; moreover, we have changed the name of the party." Would these appeals be necessary if everyone was supporting the insurgents? If the workers and the peasants, after having "manifested their legitimate discontent," to quote *Pravda*, had joined with the Nagy government to push back the émigrés, there probably would have been a civil war; however, not one dispatch, not one radio report, even in the popular democracies, made mention of a civil war. All is confusion and instability among the insurgent groups popping up everywhere.

Among these groups, united in their fight against the Soviets and in their demand for withdrawal, appeared reactionary elements and some which were foreign inspired. But the fact is there: workers, peasants, the entire populace fought at their side. The advanced Communist element, moved by the wish to democratize the regime, coexisted with the reactionaries in the same groups which contained, at the same time, many other tendencies and which seesawed from one side to the other in reaction to events, to changes in membership of the groups and, finally, to the Russian intervention.

In a word, it was on the entire population and not on a handful of armed émigrés that the Red Army was going to fire. It is the people, the workers and the peasants—the former victims of Horthy—who are still being massacred today.

The crime, for me, is not only the attack on Budapest by the tanks, it is that it was made possible and perhaps necessary (from the Soviet point of view naturally) by twelve years of terror and stupidity. If the right was predominant among most of the insurgents it is because they all shared one passion, completely negative: hatred of the Soviets and of Rakosism.

Those hunts in the sewers were horrible: as though it was necessary for the regime to make itself hated! Aside from a conscious minority—the intellectuals, the union of writers—quickly ignored by the masses, the workers and the peasants, after having recited their lessons learned by rote, found themselves in complete confusion, with no political or social education.

Generally, popular revolutions are leftist. For the first time—though everything is new in these tragic events—we have seen a political revolution evolving to the right. Why? Because nothing had been given to the people, neither material satisfaction nor a socialist faith, not even a clear viewpoint of the situation. The people were certainly mistaken, but even in their errors they have the right to liberty and respect: workers free themselves by means of errors, of experiments; errors are not corrected by cannon fire. Stalinism is *entirely* responsible for these very errors.

The right claims that the Hungarian agony constitutes a definite defeat for socialism. What do you think?

What the Hungarian people are teaching us with their blood is the complete failure of socialism as a Soviet-imported product. We know what socialism has cost the Soviet Union: the sweat, the blood, the crimes, also the courage, and the perseverance. But the country was also able to raise itself to the top rank of industrial powers. That is because historical conditions allowed it; the Communists of 1917 were taking over from a bourgeoisie which was not yet fully developed, but which had laid the foundations of a strong industrial complex.

It was absolutely absurd to impose a servile imitation of the Stalin type of organization on each satellite country in order to make it a USSR plaything, a small-scale model, without taking into account the difference in situations. Hungary, in particular, was as far removed as possible from a socialist revolution by reason of its overpopulation, mostly peasants, and governed before the war by a class of feudal landowners and a cowardly and resigned bourgeoisie which preferred a sort of semicolonization to its own development.

In 1939, the cities were unhappy under Horthy's dictatorship, but the peasants got along in spite of their misery; a practically nonexistent proletariat, a peasant class crushed under centuries-old prejudices:

that is what the Soviets were confronted with in 1945. The first elections brought a democratic front to power in which the Communists, all-powerful behind the scenes, officially occupied but a limited place: 57% of the votes had gone to the party of small landowners.

The formidable task of the new government was to forge ahead, parcel out the large landholdings, distribute the land to the peasants, but then to form a new concentration both bourgeois and socialist (cooperative farms, factories, population centers, by attracting the surplus of the peasant population to the cities). That is, to make these great changes *in place of* a bourgeoisie which had never known how to accept its responsibilities and *in favor of* socialism. Everything in this program went against the centuries-old habits of the peasants; as for the workers, they came from the country and they have remained more faithful to their villages than to the factories.

Nothing could be done without acceptance of a definite unpopularity and without exercising a certain restraint; it was necessary to feed these enlarged cities, this population of workers growing daily, and the peasants, less numerous and still badly equipped with tools, could only subsist by accepting taxes and a kind of collectivism.

This restraint has always existed in capitalist countries: only, the concentration and the various forms of expropriation which result from it seem to the individual to be the consequences of an anonymous destiny. In a socialist country this destiny often takes the form and name of the head of the government.

It was thus of *primary* importance that this restraint be as little irritating as possible, that the plans should be modest, and that progress toward socialism should proceed in stages over a long period; it was necessary to envisage an immediate rise in living standards so that everyone in the regime should have something to defend. Remember that it was the sale of the national wealth which was the strong point of our revolution. And besides, especially at this stage of evolution, the important thing was to convince. The Chinese say: "It is always necessary to explain." "Explain" does not mean propaganda. It is to inform, to educate, and also—for one does not convince with words only—to give something. Of those who are already persuaded that socialism is what their country needs, sacrifices can be asked. But of those who, like the majority of Hungarian peasants, are both against the foreign occupation and socialism, nothing can be asked: it is first necessary to conquer them, and to convince them. To demand from them the same thing as from those who already believe in socialism, is to create an ever increasing breach in the masses, to facilitate the growth of terrorism, to manufacture for oneself all the conditions necessary for a counter-revolution.

Nothing was explained: a series of events changed everything. First, the Marshall Plan; its avowed aim was to prevent the growth of socialism in the satellites: America's responsibility is undeniable in the present happenings. There followed, at the time, a sudden tightening of the ties between socialist countries: the "Iron Curtain" is a result of the Marshall Plan. Then came the first revolt of national communism: Titoism.

Everything moved toward stalinization: after the Marshall Plan the social-democratic party and the small landowners' party disappeared; after Titoism, the Communist party became bolshevized; that is, the nationalist elements which, as though by chance, were the only popular ones, were eliminated and replaced by Moscow-trained Communists. One can imagine the effect in Hungary of the Rajk trial (Rajk had fought alongside the peasants during the resistance) and the triumph of Rakosi (who had spent many years in the USSR).

Naturally, this transformation had two important economic consequences: the USSR, in turn, assumed the semicolonization of Hungary, and overindustrialization pushed collectivity to an extreme. Hungary, more than any other Central European country, resisted this regime by force. All observers—even the French Communists—are agreed on this point. Terrorism was necessary to maintain it. The White Terror which, with certain people, seemed to justify the recent Russian intervention, is but the consequence of the *Red Terror.*

The error is evident: the USSR had succeeded with the "socialization of one country"—its own; it was a matter of succeeding with the "socialization of several countries." It had preferred to reissue several "socialisms in one country." This façade allowed it to remain the only means of communication between one satellite and another, thus rejecting the self-imposed solution—a socialist commonwealth with interlocking economies—because of distrust and because it wanted interlocking economies only with its own country. The result: the total liquidation of a regime which was never accepted by anyone in Hungary.

There are some who say: "the foundations of socialism" should have been saved in Hungary. If the foundations of socialism had existed in Hungary, socialism would have saved itself. The Red Army intervened in Hungary to save the foundations of social-ism in the USSR—that is, the military positions (as Courtade admits) and the uranium mines.

You spoke of "democratization." Will you define exactly what it means to you in a socialist regime?

For me, democratization is something which cannot exist without a complete revision of the relations between the Soviet Union and its satellites.

This democratization can only be realized in an organization of satellite countries conceived in the light of their own interests more than those of the USSR. Consequently, it requires a veritable general planning at the level of all the countries combined. It would then be evident that it is not necessary for Poland to manufacture cars which cannot run, that Budapest does not need a flooded subway system, that Polish coal could be distributed more efficiently among the various Central European countries. This union of all socialist countries would be directed by the USSR; but this directorship would only be truly administered under a common foreign policy. Then, a rise in the living standards would become possible, and with it, democratization could take on concrete forms.

When the living standards are raised, you can tell the truth with no fear of trouble and even allow its expression by people not of your opinion. One lies to men who are dying of hunger and fatigue because, to them, governmental errors are a question of life and death. Democratization, for me, does not mean a return to a plurality of parties: the reappearance in Hungary of conservative parties almost made necessary the Russian presence (but not the brutal intervention). But one can return to a centralized democratization within the party; individual liberty can be restored, the right of habeas corpus; censorship can be abolished, and workers' councils can be set up. In a word, it is up to each government to decide, taking into account the situation and the demand of the masses. But most important, for me, democratization will begin when those abstract parties named Communist party of Hungary, Rumania, Bulgaria, etc., will have truly resumed—if it is not too late—contact with the masses.

Do you think that Stalinism is primarily concerned with foreign policy?

I am not sure. It seems to me that in the beginning the USSR, moreover legitimately, did not distinguish between foreign policy and the organization of socialism. From 1945 to 1948, she would have liked to attract the popular republics by a slow rise in living standards, by a progressive construction of socialist foundations, which, at the same time, gave her security and defended her against encirclement.

It was the Marshall Plan, once again, which provoked the fear of a rupture in the socialist front. In any case, I fear that it was not a question of military security which provoked Russian intervention in Hungary. Anyway, that is the opinion of Pierre Courtade who makes these "revelations" in *Humanité*:

Was there any need for hoping for the re-establishment, in the name of "liberty," of a feudal regime in Hungary?

Could the Soviet Union, whose forces were stationed in Hungary by treaty agreement, run the risk of a "break in alliances" which would have made of Hungary a stronghold of the Western powers in the middle of the popular democracies?

What attitude can men like yourself, who were its friends, now have toward the USSR?

I will say first that a crime does not involve an entire people. I do not think that the Russian people ever had much sympathy toward the Hungarians, any more than the Hungarians for the Russians. Moreover, there are very few Russians who know much about current events. For this it would be necessary to read the Hungarian and Polish press, if they are still distributed in Moscow. What happened in Hungary is thus, in my opinion, of little import to the Russian people, nor does it touch their lives very deeply. Especially because they are consciously being lied to. *Pravda* was writing last Sunday, a few hours after the Soviet aggression against Budapest: "The Hungarian people, its working class, all the true patriots of Hungary will find in themselves the necessary force with which to destroy reaction." There, certainly, is what the readers of the Soviet press believe. You know of course that the troops intervening in Hungary are of various non-Russian races: there is no chance that workers from Moscow will come back to say to their friends: we have fired on workers.

No, the Russian people is innocent, as are all peoples, except those who are involved through their silence in a system of concentration camps established in their own countries. In the USSR, the stupor of the population since the return of the prisoners proves that it was not aware. My personal sympathy for this great working and courageous people is not altered by the crimes of its government.

I was reading in *Combat* this morning: "Always full of discretion, Raymond Aron did not want to take the satisfaction which comes when one sees what he has written confirmed by recent events." Well! if Raymond Aron is satisfied to see his predictions confirmed by events, he must have a strong constitution!

Undoubtedly he thinks, and certain others with him, that de-stalinization was a mask, nothing but words. For my part, I think that that is an absolute error. De-stalinization was believed in by certain members of the Soviet government and its bureaucracy and it led them to taking a risk. Possibly some of them are already paying for this audacity? It was nevertheless to be desired, it was necessary, and I should like to express my personal gratitude and respect to those who first attempted it.

But it was necessary to know where they were heading and not to allow events to bypass them; they shouldn't have played this stupid game which the sinister Hermann calls in *Libération* "la douche écossaise" (the cold-water shock); they shouldn't have, in Hungary for example, called Nagy to power in 1953, promising higher investments in basic industries, then retracted, bringing back Rakosi after having criticized him, returning to the policy of the unconditional primacy of heavy industry, rehabilitating Rajk while allowing his accuser to remain in power, then suddenly firing Rakosi, the accuser, and replacing him with a greater mediocrity, Gero, and ending by calling in Nagy too late, when the blood was flowing, and taking away all his chances to regain the confidence of the people.

Yes, it was necessary to know what they wanted and where they were going; to make reforms without boasting about them first, but to make them progressively. From this point of view, the gravest fault was probably Khrushchev's report, for in my opinion the solemn public denunciation, with a detailed list of crimes of an enshrined personality who represented the regime for so long, is madness when such frankness is not accompanied by a considerable rise in the living standards of the population.

Malenkov had been much more skillful. He had started to inaugurate reforms without saying anything about Stalin. For example, it was he who had already replaced Rakosi with Nagy.

I do not consider Stalin to have been a cultured or extremely intelligent person. But from that to the story that he directed all of the operations of the war by following the movements of the armies on a school map, there is a considerable distance. Even Hitler was able to read a headquarters map. Thus, the Khrushchev report, instead of being a frank and complete explanation, was nothing but a web of tales. This report was a terrible blow. It confirmed the dictatorship of the party instead of reducing it.

I know very well that it was not written with full deliberation, that it was an improvisation, that it was probably the maneuvering of the group which wanted to push democratization ahead in order to preserve or to regain the reins of power. But the result was to reveal the truth to the masses which were not prepared to receive it. When we see to what extent, here in France, the report shook the intellectuals and the Communist workers, we can understand how the Hungarians, for example, were little prepared to understand this awful list of crimes and errors, given without explanation, without historical analysis, without discretion.

While Khrushchev was holding the reins, he said: "We will accept the consequences of de-stalinization as much as we can." After the spectacular reconciliation with Tito, and the Polish riots, you know what happened: this mixture of unbelievable and backward brutality which recalled the old Russian ways.

De-stalinization was also accompanied by honest attempts at democratization within Russia which benefited Russian society. I believe one should respect this attempt, even if it failed. Thus I believe in it, as long as it is not suddenly stopped today. But I fear this sudden stop: it is impossible to believe one word of the program brandished by Janos Kadar, impossible to think that he could ask for the withdrawal of Russian troops in Hungary, for then Russian intervention would not have made any sense. The Hungarian people are furious; there are still, we are told, small groups of resisters. How can one imagine that the Russian troops will leave? Once more, words will have signified the opposite of what they mean: Guy Mollet used the word "pacifying" to indicate "military operations"; Kadar says "democratization" to indicate "terror and foreign occupation."

Thus, in my opinion, democratization has ceased in Hungary, if it ever started. It has probably also been stopped elsewhere: one cannot imagine a country maintaining a dictatorship over others without maintaining one over itself. Consequently, I believe in democratization, but I also believe that it has stopped for a while, and that this cessation is evident even in important changes within the Soviet government.

In the light of this, how would you describe your position toward the USSR?

I condemn absolutely and unconditionally the Soviet aggression. Without rendering the Russian people responsible, I repeat that its present government has committed a crime and that a dispute between factions in its midst has resulted in giving the power to a group (of "hardboiled" military men; former stalinists?) which today is outdoing stalinism after having denounced it.

In history all crimes are forgotten; we have forgotten ours and other nations will forget them little by little. A time may come when we shall forget those of the USSR if its government changes and if the newcomers attempt to truly apply the principle of equality in relations with socialist and nonsocialist nations. For the moment, there is nothing to do but to condemn. I break off with regret, but completely, my relations with my friends the Soviet writers who do not (or cannot) denounce the massacre in Hungary. One can no longer feel friendly toward the governing faction of the Soviet bureaucracy: it is horror that is reigning.

If Hungary had been left independent, Marshal Bulganin's proposal to Eisenhower for common intervention in the Egyptian affair could have been taken seriously. But this idea of an urgent action by the two great powers, launched in the wake of the crushing of Hungary, becomes a mockery, a political maneuver. It finishes by discrediting any possible UN action. Consider the idea that now we would find ourselves before a situation such as this: on the one hand, the U.S., with England and France, eventually intervening in Hungary against the USSR; on the other hand, the U.S., with the USSR, eventually putting themselves between Egypt and Israel, against England and France, in the Suez.

I don't know if the UN ever was worth anything, but this absurd confusion proves that it is no longer of any use. Moreover, if there should be a Big Five conference in Switzerland, then peace would have been found once more outside the UN.

What consequences will the events in Hungary have for the French left?

The sad reality today, for me, is that the French left risks extinction by these events unless there is a change in its parties, and unless the minorities take things in hand.

I was reading in this morning's papers that the Socialist party is making a new appeal to the active Communist party members to abandon the party and join the S.F.I.O. [French Socialist party]. This is singularly audacious. It means: quit that impossible Communist party which approves of the crushing of Budapest and come join us in acclaiming those who are torturing Algeria. Before such a contradiction, what remains of the left?

As for the Radical party, I will tell you frankly

what I think: I don't think it ever was really leftist. Moreover, it has been representing the right for a number of years. The changes which were imposed on it by M. Mendès-France, a man who is perfectly respectable in his thoughts and actions, provoked the first schism. In spite of this schism, the other day M. Mendès-France represented only one-fifth of the two thirds of the Radical party in a decisive vote.

In the [Paris] *Express*, you once said of me: "Jean-Paul Sartre has been put out of action." I can say now: "Mendès-France wanted to be part of the action, and he has in turn been put out of action."

Thus I cannot believe anything which comes, from now on, out of what used to be called, at election time, the "Republican Front."

The Socialist party is in a shocking state. It has betrayed its voters. And it has betrayed its socialist mission. It is now occupying—the most unbelievable thing possible—a position at the side of the English Conservatives against the Laborites. The bad conscience of its leaders has become a repugnant cynicism. Did you hear M. Pineau on the radio Sunday? In a whimpering tone, one of unbearable condolences, he had but a few words for the courageous insurgents in Budapest. Then, all of a sudden, his voice became bitter, caustic, and glorious: The UN, he said, had preferred to busy itself with an "Egyptian dictator."

The French Communist party has about 180,000 members, I believe, of which 170,000 are devoted and 10,000 are permanent party workers at 40,000 francs a month, which completes the organization. As long as it was a question of local French politics, up to recent years, the Communist party, in spite of its errors, kept a straight line: it was in contact with the masses; it could not cut itself off from them. For it is sometimes possible to cut oneself off from the masses in an authoritarian regime when one is in power, but not when one is in the opposition.

With some delay it tacked about in favor of the war in Indo-China, and finally steered a straight course. It had at first discouraged quite a few people, disconcerted by its attitude on Algerian politics; but finally, there also, it recovered in time. Some days after the events in Budapest, it was still gaining votes in the local elections.

But the Communist party is an international party. It is thus a party which must make foreign policy decisions. And these decisions are today being entirely dictated by an organization completely subservient to the most uncompromising viewpoint of the Soviet government.

The results are the most repugnant lies; like those we could read in this morning's *Humanité*: "As they

were fleeing, the rioters set fire to numerous buildings. Sunday evening Budapest was a sea of flames. One of the few radio stations left in the hands of the counterrevolutionaries Sunday evening was boasting that the glow from the fires was visible for several kilometers around."

I can hardly imagine the insurgents running from house to house in the Russian-encircled city, being bombarded with phosphorous bombs, setting fire to their own homes. It's the usual technique: one takes the reports of events, distorts and misrepresents them. This is the horrible habit the Communist leaders have got into of slandering people before killing them.

What hope is there, in your analysis, for the gravely affected French left?

It is obvious that as far as we are concerned—many intellectuals think as I do—we are maintaining our complete sympathy toward those thousands of militant Communists who are today in the throes of anguish and who, I understand quite well, at the moment when their party is being criticized on all sides —through its own fault of course—have no desire to abandon it. With those people one can sympathize, for they are not responsible for the massacres in Budapest. They are honest people, earnest and disturbed, and there are some among the ten thousand party workers of the organization. But the leaders are totally and irremediably responsible.

As much as it might be possible after years of anxiety, rancor, and bitterness, to resume relations with the Soviet Union—a definite change in its political tendencies would suffice—it is not, and never will be, possible to resume relations with the present leaders of the French Communist party. Their every word, their every gesture, is the result of thirty years of lies and mental sclerosis. Their reactions have been those of irresponsible people.

In my opinion, the crime just committed is not the responsibility of those Communists who cannot speak, of those who do not leave the party because it is in danger, for it alone in France today represents the socialist movement; for if it has been slandered, it is not only because of its crimes but because it is the only one going toward socialism. Those men are against the dictatorial policy within the party.

Besides, I am certain that all the leftists would regroup themselves if, on the demand of individuals like Tixier-Vignancour, the Communist party was in danger of extinction.

In the Socialist party also, there is an honest and sincere minority at the head, over a mass of uneasy militants. Of course, this minority has not protested very much, or at least its protests have not as yet been very loud, against the policy of Mollet's government.

But if these Communists who are opposed to dictatorship could have the power and the strength to impose a change in policy, and if this socialist minority could come out with renewed principles, we would then find a sort of popular front which could be the "new left." The Christian left, which really exists and is really leftist, the dynamic elements of radicalism even, the disorganized: all could join this great movement. But if this does not happen, it must be said frankly: the left is lost.

With such a prospect, what do you think will be the relations between Socialists and Communists?

The Communists are dishonored, the Socialists are plunging themselves into the mire. They are accepting the rightist policies: this is what has regularly ruined leftist regimes that have let themselves be influenced. Remember the example of the German Weimar government. Yes, thanks to Guy Mollet, today the right is enjoying a sort of purity. It is not torturing Algeria; it is the Socialists who landed in Suez. If they disorient the French as much as that, how far will they go when the French protest, first about the taxes, then about gasoline, and finally about their sons—for, unfortunately, it will be in that order. They will then be tempted to go to the extreme right. Poujade well understood this; he who forbade his men in the Chamber to vote "for the Queen of England." Fortunately Poujade is an imbecile.

The outlook for the left is very difficult, almost impracticable perhaps, but it is the only hope. The "new left" is full of very intelligent people; it includes workers and small businessmen as well as intellectuals. But it actually represents today only some two hundred thousand people in the entire country. It is a very useful turntable for the making of alliances. But the real problem is elsewhere.

The real problem is in the relations between Socialists and Communists. Can the Communists overturn their own dictators, and can the minority Socialists leave the party? Up to now the militants and party workers of the S.F.I.O. have fought within the party. They have obtained no results. On the other hand, a certain number of Communists have left the party, one by one, where they felt stifled. These departures have had no results either.

One of the very terms of the socialist fight today is precisely the existence of these strong party structures: thus the Communist party headquarters constantly addresses itself "to the Socialists," without ever making the slightest distinction between members and leaders, thus contributing to the consolidation of these leaders. Considerable courage and strength would be necessary from all these opponents of both parties to succeed in changing things.

The other prospect is that popular unity would be achieved with the appearance of a dictatorship, that of Marshal Juin or of someone else. It would be the only way for the left to have its errors forgotten. The Socialist party could shed its own blood to pay for that which it caused to be shed. The Communist party, after having earned the admirable title of the Party of Martyrs, could today receive that of the Party of Murderers: its future martyrs will bring it honor and we of the left will pay for everything we were not able to prevent. I still have hope that this purge will be spared us.

How does this problem of the struggle within the party affect a Communist party member?

If, as everything seems to indicate, the honest and sincere Communists are agitated, let them look for support among the working classes, for example within the C.G.T.

As for the right, it has no right to make claims. Those who did not protest against the tortures in Algeria and against Suez have no right to protest against the events in Hungary.

What will be the reaction of the French Communist party to your stand?

Much as it displeases me to break with the Communist party, I can do it because I protested in time against the Algerian war: I am not opposed to all the sincere and honest leftists, even those who remain in the ranks of the Communist party. I remain with them, even if they should reject me tomorrow.

The leaders will say that they had long been right in calling me "hyena" and "jackal" when Fadeev—who committed suicide—spoke like today's *Humanité*: but I am completely indifferent to what they will say about me, given what they are saying of the events in Hungary.

►► Henri Michaux

Miserable Miracle

[Henri Michaux says that his new book, Miserable Miracle (from which we print here the second chapter) "is an exploration. By means of words, signs, drawings. Mescalin the subject explored." Miserable Miracle is Michaux's report on his experiments with mescalin pursued over many months. Louise Varèse, Michaux's translator, says that here Michaux "is both clinician and patient. His 'eye glued to the microscope,' he notes the demonic behavior of mescalin in himself while at the same time observing the grotesque, glittering, hyperbolic spectacles staged by the drug.

"In religious rites for countless centuries, Indians in Mexico have worshiped the god of peyotl, which is the mescal cactus bud from which mescalin, its active principle, is derived. In recent years the hallucinatory properties of mescalin have attracted the intensified interest of scientists in their search for the baffling secret of mental disease. In less scientific circles the drug is regarded as the open sesame to a new 'artificial paradise.' But it was not for the phantasmagoria of colors in the mescalin world, or a desire to escape from this one, that induced Michaux to join the scientists in their exploration. It was the curiosity which is known as scientific and which is shared by creators in all fields. Michaux's report on his experiments is a scientific document as well as a work of art.

"A painter as well as a poet, Michaux after his third experiment began recording his impressions in revealing drawings, two of which are reproduced here. He also kept a journal while under the influence of the drug which, though too illegible to serve as text, provided him with milestones to guide his memory back over the monstrous road he and mescalin had traveled together.

"Michaux differs from other writers on the subject in that he not only describes the often beautiful, always exorbitant, repetitious, robot-like, rushing, trembling, terrifying world of mescalin, not only details his hair-raising experiences: he comes close to giving us the experience itself."]

In a dimly lighted room, after taking ¾ of a 0.1 gr. ampule of mescalin

In a state of great uneasiness, of anxiety, of inner solemnity.—The world retreating in the distance, an ever-increasing distance.—Each word becoming more and more dense, too dense to be uttered from now on, word complete in itself, word in a nest, while the noise of the wood fire in the fireplace becomes the only presence, becomes important—strange and absorbing its movements . . . . In a state of expectancy, an expectancy that becomes with each minute more pregnant, more restive, more ineffable, more painful to endure . . . and to what point can it be endured?

shivers shivers gnawings

Far away, like a soft whistling of the wind in the shrouds, harbinger of storms, a shiver, a shiver lacking flesh and skin, an abstract shiver, a shiver in the workshop of the brain, in a zone where shivering with shivers is impossible. Shivering with what then?

That something can happen that a world of things can happen. Phenomenal swarmings of possible things that want to be, are hurrying, are imminent.

As if there were an opening, an opening which would be an assembling, which would be a world, which would be that something can happen, that many things can happen, that there is a crowd, that there is a swarming of what is possible, that everything is crawling with possibilities, that the person I vaguely hear walking outside might ring the bell, might enter, might set the place on fire, might climb up to the roof, might throw himself howling onto the pavement of the courtyard. Might everything, anything, without choosing, without any one of these actions having precedence over another. I am not particularly disturbed by it either. "Might" is what counts, this prodigious

might
might
might

Beginnings
of inner visions.
Knives long as
trajectories.
Dazzling knives
plow swiftly
through
empty space.
The torture
of enormous
stretchings.
Painful stretchings
as if the cells of
my body were being
forced (unless their
own convulsions are
themselves the
cause) to accompany
these terrible
accelerations to the
very limit of their
own elasticity.

from the tip
terribly high
to the base
terribly low
divergents
divergents
iMMense
terremoto
Mense.
Remarkable words
with letters
bigger than
aqueducts
ringed with
quicksilver,
flamboyant and
shocking, like
advertising.
In the midst of
this unceasing
earthquake,
I keep
thinking
of making
inordinately
rising
declarations.

A whiteness appears,
a whiteness
to blind you,
dazzling,
like molten metal

urgency of possibilities which have become enormous and continue to multiply.

(The sounds of the radio or of records, words or music, have no effect. Only reality sows and is productive.)

Suddenly, but first preceded by a vanguard-word, a courier-word, a word launched by my language central which receives the warning before I do, like those monkeys who feel earthquakes before men do, suddenly, preceded by the word "blinding," a knife, suddenly a thousand knives, suddenly a thousand dazzling scythes of light, scythes set with lightning, enormous, made to cut down whole forests, start furiously splitting space open from top to bottom with gigantic strokes, miraculously swift strokes which I am forced to accompany internally, painfully, and at the same unendurable speed, up to those same impossible heights and immediately afterward down into the same abysmal depths, with the stretchings ever more and more monstrous, dislocating, insane . . . and when is it going to end . . . if it is ever going to end?

Finished. It's finished.

Himalayas all at once spring up higher than the highest mountain, sharply pointed, false peaks though, diagrams of mountains, but not less high for all that, inordinate triangles with angles ever more acute, to the very edge of space, idiotic but immense.

While I am still occupied looking at these extraordinary mountains, the intense urgency that has me in its grip, having settled on the letters "m" of the word "immense," which I was mentally pronouncing, the double down strokes of these miserable "m's" begin stretching out into the fingers of gloves, into the nooses of lassos and these in turn, preposterously large, shoot up toward the heights—arches for unthinkable, baroque cathedrals, arches ridiculously elongated resting on their unchanged little bases. It is utterly grotesque.

Enough. I've understood. I mustn't think of anything! I mustn't think at all. Vacuity, and lie low! I mustn't give a single idea, not a single spare part to the mad mechanism. But already the machine has resumed its movement at a hundred images a minute. The Himalaya-producing machine, which had stopped, now starts again. Great plowshares plow up a stretch of space which doesn't seem to care. Enormous plowshares plow without any reason for plowing. Plowshares and again great scythes mowing empty space from top to bottom with enormous strokes that will be repeated fifty, a hundred, a hundred and fifty times. (Until the accumulators have run down.)

Why bother, since nothing can be done about it? The stretchings are less painful. Am I getting used to them?

And "White" appears. Absolute white. White whiter than all whiteness. White of the advent of white. White without compromise, by exclusion, by the total eradication of non-white. White mad, exasperated, shrieking with whiteness. Fanatical, furious, riddling the eyeball. White atrociously electric,

*pouring out of
a Bessemer
converter.
If a detonation
could be whiteness.
So white really
exists.
To have to live
always in
constant
scintillation.*

*An ocean that has no
salt, no iodine,
no breeze, does not
refresh, an ocean
for an optician.
Slashed to pieces
by reflections.
Through me the
sea undulates.
Torture of
undulation.
Breaking against
nothing.
Torture of
what is unstable,
of what is
impermanent,
torture
of being tickled
by iridescence.*

*I am being
hollowed out. . .
There is the fact
of its being
torrential,
there is the fact
of its plunging
headlong,
there is the fact
of its bursting.
the unforgettable
furrow
A lost phantom
was lying at
full length, probably
myself. A furrow
runs through this
motionless giant
while storms, smoke,
cuts, gashes were
torturing this
"no man's land."
The electric
rivulet
unspeakable
currents*

implacable, murderous. White in blasts of white. God of "white." No, not a god, a howler monkey. (If only my cells don't burst.)

Cessation of white. I feel that for me white will have something immoderate about it for a long time to come.

On the edge of a tropical ocean, in a thousand reflections of the silver light of an invisible moon, among the undulations of restless waters, ceaselessly changing. . . .

Among silent lappings, among the tremors of the shining expanse, in the swift ebb and flow, martyrizing patches of light, in the slashings of luminous loops, arcs, and lines, in the occulations, the reappearances, in the dancing flashes being decomposed, recomposed, contracted, spread out, only to be rearranged once more before me, with me, within me, I, drowned, and in the midst of an intolerable buffeting, my calm violated a thousand times by the oscillating tongues of infinity, sinusoidally overrun by the multitude of liquid lines, enormous with a thousand folds, *I was and I was not*, I was caught, I was lost, I was in a state of complete ubiquity. The thousands upon thousands of murmurings were the thousand slashings in myself.

Sensation of a fissure. I hide my head in a scarf in order to know, to recognize my surroundings.

I see a furrow. A furrow with little, hurried, transversal sweepings. In it a fluid, its brightness mercurial, its behavior torrential, its speed electric. Seemingly elastic too. Swish, swish, swish, it whisks along showing innumerable little tremors. I also see stripes.

Where is this furrow exactly? It is just as though it were crossing my skull from the forehead to the occiput. Yet I can see it. A furrow without beginning or end, and whose average breadth is appreciably the same above and below, a furrow which I'd say comes from the farthest ends of the earth.

My body's envelope (if I think or try to think about it) floats freely around the furrow (how can it?), enormous balloon containing this little river, for this great furrow, when I try to see my body at the same time, is only a rivulet, but still lively, untamed—champagne and spitting cat. An immense space between my body and the furrow, with the furrow running through the middle. Sometimes there is nothing in this space. (Strange, I thought I was full.) Sometimes there are little dots all over it.

So then, I contain the furrow, except at its extremities which disappear in the distance, and yet it is myself, it is my instants, one after the other, flowing in its crystalline flux. In this flux my life advances. Fractured into a thousand fractures, through this rivulet I have continual prolongation in time. It might stop. Perhaps. Yet no one seeing it would believe that it could ever stop flowing, leave me there.

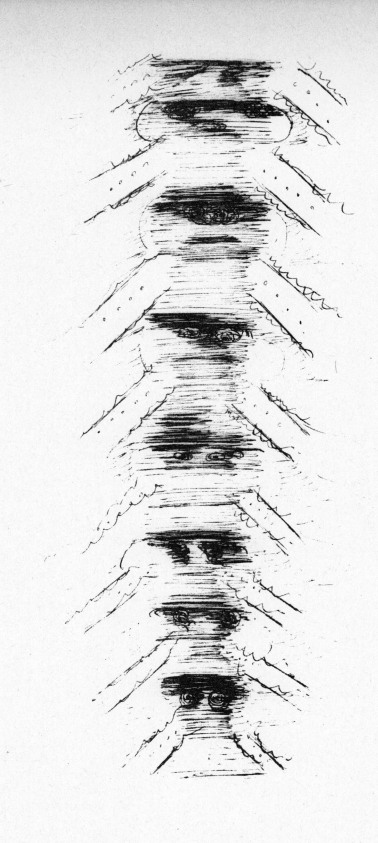

counter-acting
counting-flowing
cross-hatching
too, too shaken
this rock
corresponds to
I don't know what
in me which
breaks, and breaks
again, endlessly
re-forms and
breaks again.
cleavage
breaches
breaches
breaches everywhere
at the same time
angular rents in a bag,
intolerably
angular.

Now I am in front of a rock. It splits. No, it is no longer split. It is as before. Again it is split, entirely. No it is not split at all. It splits once more. Once more it ceases to be split, and this goes on indefinitely. Rock intact, then cleavage, then rock intact, then cleavage, then rock intact, then cleavage, then rock intact, then cleavage. . . .

Cardboard now, cardboard sheets, cardboard boxes, manufactures of cardboard, factories of cardboard, truckloads of cardboard . . . and finally an avalanche of cardboard. (Documentary film or sonata?)

Enormous sheets of cardboard, bigger than screens, of a gray that is unpleasant to look at and a texture that must be unpleasant to touch, are being handled very briskly by hands I do not see.

The devil take all this cardboard. I'm not interested!

Why all this cardboard? I have just noticed a certain numbness of my lip and upper jaw, the beginning of the well-known sensation (before the extraction of a tooth) of the "cardboard mouth."

Cessation.

First stage
toward visions
of colors.

"What, past noon already! Is it possible? And I haven't seen any colors yet, real, brilliant colors. Perhaps I am not going to see any." Annoyed, I wrap up in my scarf again. Then, apparently the result of my reflection,[1] released by the thought or by the switch-button word, I am submerged by thousands of little dots of colors, a tidal wave, a deluge, but with each tiny globule perfectly distinct, isolated, detached.

Cessation of the deluge.

Apparition
of colors.

Return of the deluge. . . . What is happening? An enemy of these colors? No longer any colors at all. Yet they are not quite absent either. Or are they vanishing too quickly now to be really perceptible? (Like an electric current not sufficiently strong or prolonged.) At moments it seems to me they are there. Certainly not much of a spectacle, or I might say that it is to a real spectacle what "noisily" is to "noise." Odd obliquity.

fusillade of
colors.

At last equivocation ends. This time color abounds. A hundred Empire State buildings at night, all windows lighted with all kinds of lights, would not fill with as many splashes of distinct unbelievable colors[2] the screen of my vision.

On one of my frontiers (I had at first called it my "Spitzberg") I am saturated with an impossibly immense area of colored bulbs.

Cessation.

---

[1] Or the reverse: the thought was launched by an imperceptible sensation, a pre-sensation.

[2] I know now, and will know even better soon, that the teeming drawings—"*burrées*," as Dr. Ferdière calls them—of some of the insane, are not exaggerated but give a *moderate* view of their extraordinary universe.

Not a single color. As if "it" no longer had the strength to be color.

It has come back, it begins again. The mechanism is once more running: Green!

Green?
Not green?

Green. Did I see it? Too fugitively seen. I know that there is green, that there is going to be green, that there is an expectation of green, that there is green frantically straining toward existence, a green that couldn't be greener. It is not, and there is any amount of it (!)

I emit "green."
Extinction
of green

Here it comes! It has come out. Fully.
I am honeycombed with alveolae of green. Greens like bright dots on the back of a beetle. The zone that emits green is in me. I am wrapped in green, immured. I end in green. (A kind of emerald green.)

A large plaque, fairly circular and as though elastic. A spasm causes it successively and almost imperceptibly to contract, then to expand again.

In the
pink sewer.

It is also as though elastically pink. Pink, then not pink, then pink, then not pink, or barely pink, then very pink. Pink spreads. Innumerable pink bulbs appear. Pink spreads more and more. I generate it, I sparkle with it. I am sprouting pink. I suffocate with pinkness, with pinkening. The pecking of this pink disturbs me, is odious.
Cessation.
Thank heaven!

Disjunction

I hear my cleaning woman's step in the hall. She has come back. Why! Does she want something? Is she going to knock on the door? I hope not.
At this moment I see (with inner sight) my fist suddenly strike out with violence in her direction, fifteen, twenty times in succession, at the end of my extended arm, but long, long, long, an arm three meters long, a meager arm and, like my childish fist, unrecognizable. Stupefying sight. Anger? But I feel none. *It* has burned up feeling. *It* has caught, not even the dynamic, but the kinetic side of anger, with all the emotional sensation conjured away. That is the strange part of this mechanism. To express an emotion it excludes all consciousness of emotion. That is why, like a stranger, I watch this unsuccessful mechanical gesture, wondering if it isn't really idiotic of me to want to interpret this ridiculous spectacle as a consequence of an anger which I don't know if I feel, and which at the very most corresponds to "If only no one opens the door!"
There is haste, there is urgency in me.[3]

Phenomenon
of breakings
and reversings
of the current.
a madman
with his hand
on the switch
The current
always being
switched on
switched off.

I should like. I should like to be rid of all this. I should like to start from zero. I should like to get out of here. Not to go out through an exit. I should like a multiple exit, like a fan. An exit that never ends, an ideal exit, an exit such that having gone out I should immediately start to go out again.
I should like to get up. No, I'd like to lie down, no, I'd like to get up immediately, no, I'd like to lie down at once, I want to get up, I am going to telephone, no, I'm not going to telephone. But I really must. No, I'm going to lie down. And thus, ten, twenty, fifty times in a few minutes, I shall decide, then decide the contrary, I shall come back to my first decision, go back to my second decision, return once more to the first, as wholeheartedly, fanatically eager as for a crusade one moment, and the next totally indifferent, uninterested, perfectly relaxed.

[3] What would happen if this accelerator were administered to slow-motion animals, to the chameleon, to the lazy three-toed sloth, or to the marmot just coming out of hibernation?

No question of saying, as in the case of the visual images, that I'm not fooled, that I understand the mechanism (which is the same). Twenty times I am on the point of getting up to telephone, as many times, indifferent, I give up. I'm on the shuttle line. Current off, current on, current off, current on. I shall be like that as many times as "it" wishes, completely mobile and then completely at rest and tranquil and serene on the platform of a single second. (Or perhaps of a double or triple second.)

On the tables and on those at the tables many crystals. The eye, when it enjoys, enjoys crystallinely

Once more there is haste. Great haste. Intolerable haste. Haste is about to present a spectacle, short and repeated over and over. Mesc. can only supply gags: I see an enormous restaurant..Numerous stories, and people are eating on all the balconies (yes, there are balconies *and* with pillarets!), thousands of tables, thousands of people eating, thousands of waiters in blue jackets. Funny idea! Dishes are served. Dishes are removed. Are served again. Are re-removed. No sooner is the dish served than the plate is taken away. No sooner is the plate set down than the dish is taken away. The speed is not even that of a gag, but of a metronome. It is not that of an alternating current either. Try to picture the details: these diners are like manikins, the waiters too. No expression one can remember. No individuality in the movements either.

Flashes of hunger Mesc. provokes desires which appear and disappear in an instant.

What possible explanation? Yet this utterly idiotic spectacle is the translation of a prodigious mechanism. One must realize that mescalin provokes the most violent sensations of hunger, present one minute, gone the next: *sparks of hunger*. For mescalin instantaneously "images" and realizes sensations or ideas without the least participation of the will, and without any consciousness of desire. The silly gag is the result of this perfect, automatic functioning.

The rest of the spectacle—what I detest the most: exhibitionism. That of clothes, that of the "pleasures of the table." The festive atmosphere and balconies where colors are displayed to give an air of gaiety, have not been forgotten either.

Pause.

Several pauses. A few colored plains.

Another pause.

This time it must surely be the end.

It was only the end of something, the end of the tremors.

The cellular brushings have ceased. Tickling is about to begin. And what will the cells do, not knowing how to respond to tickling with tickling.

I was going to find out. Something I should never have expected.

After a long blank period and in a kind of lull after battle (or was it my capitulation that was in preparation), the rapid motions were still there, much less violent, not lacerating at all, yet still master . . . as I was to have occasion to discover.

The retinal circus. In the paradise of everything flashy sickly forms perforated, hollow Monuments of

Then, for no particular reason, except—and it was reason enough—that I had been surprised not to hear any music (inner music), though the outside noises and even the distant strains of a band penetrated intact, I see, after many different blues, at least fifty trumpet players with raised trumpets looking perfectly ridiculous, dressed in blue and pink[4] costumes, of a sort I don't recognize and don't care to, but very operetta looking, and who begin to play or at least to go through the motions at an incredible speed, with half a city such as Orléans listening to them, also grotesquely dressed, and as conspicuous

---

[4] We think it wonderful to see colors appear when we think of music. Naturally, if one had that in addition! But the first thing one notices, and with much annoyance, is that one can no longer mentally evoke sounds. The circuit is closed. Why? Does one center inhibit another? Excessive attention fixed on one side (optic) preventing attention on the other (acoustic)?

It is a law I have remarked in normal life and it is flagrant under the influence of mescalin: a closing of one opening to create another. A new opening automatically starts the closing of another side. . . . Sensibility on one side calls for insensibility on the other. It is what graphologists find it so hard to understand.

What an absurdity, a total man, all parts of him equally present, important, accentuated.

*another
civilization.
the catching
word.*

*disorderly raid on
words, and so rapid
that there is no time
to charge them with
meaning. It is
only later that
one can consider
them from the
point of view of
meaning.
Horrible this
compulsory almost
muscular coopera-
tion with the dis-
graceful procession
of words.*

as a necktie. Besides I'd swear there must have been forty rows of balconies one above the other (and, so that nothing should be lacking, pillarets ridiculously elongated). And all of this, of course, in the colors of ribbons for young ladies and candy for children. Perfectly nauseating.

Ludicrous, all that! Intolerable! Why suddenly did this thought occur to me, why did I think of the word "solicit"? Who would ever suppose it to be so "soliciting"? Normally it means nothing to me and departs without leaving a ripple, without creating a ripple.

But now, hardly arrived, irresistibly it drags after it its brothers and cousins (in the most superficial way), its distant cousins that are barely related (I here choose the least farfetched), the irremediable, the inexhaustible, the inexorable, the indestructible, the indefinable, the ineradicable, the indefatigable, the incredible, the innumerable, the irrevocable, the incurable, the insuperable, the incontestable, to say nothing of the incompressible, the inacceptable, the indomitable, and a whole string of others which I really must interrupt, now that I can. For at the time, not only was I unable to interrupt the stupid enumeration but I had to pronounce all the words, repeating them in my mind rapidly and emphatically and very disagreeably. (A strange elastic bridge in fact connected me with each one of them.)

Impossible to stop them. The adverbs, the long adjectives in *able*, and the prefixes and the "ins"—"in" for mescalin, irresistible, of course.

(After all, mescalin was expressing itself in its own way. Expressing me. In these words, launched haphazardly, spasmodically, one recognized "obliquely" the unhappy situation.)

Cessation! At last!

Pause. Long pause.
A final volley.

Another pause . . .
Could it be finished?[5]

*caricature
of composition
and of creation.
Against a given
background, at a new
speed, certain
ideas alone can
circulate
Others are not
attached to any-
thing, do not
correspond to the
spasmodic jerkings
and consequently
will not show any
images on the film,
though they may well
count more than
others which in-
stantly open up
optical fairs.*

And now, at this idea of finished, the bad composer I have become, because of my weakened condition (?), because of the speed of the brain waves I have to conform to, because of the unwonted pace I am forced to keep up, here he is—here I am—beginning to employ the tritest topics of amplification and, in the silliest, most systematic way to draw up the easiest antitheses, even easier enumerations, everything that is finish, final, exit (and not only the images but, as supreme idiocy, even the words "saying themselves" headlong in me): signs with the directions "exit," ship moored "at the end of the quay," panorama, viewpoint at the end of the path! all this—stupid schoolboy stuff—begins filing past me to my utter bewilderment.

Ridiculous, outrageous, and unavoidable, and which I for the life of me could never have imagined.

---

[5] At about this moment, in the semi-darkness I start to get up—"Don't leave," says one of my companions who had wanted, I thought, a glass of water . . . "Don't leave." "Leave where?" I return laughingly in order, among other things, to dispel the idea that I am attempting more than they are and exposing myself to certain mishaps. They laugh. But the word coming back to me begins to function, combining with *finish* in an endless series. *Finish* and *leave* becoming inexhaustible.

*Impetus in jerks
impetus indefinitely
renewed.*

*Everything becoming
arrows shooting
desperately
toward the
final point.
discontinuous
progressions
Speed in
measured rhythm*

Yet what counts, what is prodigious in this grotesque phenomenon, is this mad, indefatigable urgency, this ever-recurring urgency which is such that at the final point and on the way out, one is still in a hurry, in a hurry to go on to the finish, a finish which is never final enough.[6] At the top of the acute angle of a mad triangle, the final point will become the starting point for the base of another triangle whose final point will beget still another triangle which in turn . . . and so on indefinitely. The urgency is in no way abated by a third final point, or by a fourth, or by a tenth, or by a branch, simultaneously developing collateral images, or by the image of an ocean liner leaving the dock, or by an airplane taking off, or by a sudden rocket, or by an intercontinental rocket passing through the stratosphere, or by an interplanetary rocket passing beyond the bounds of terrestrial gravitation. No matter how far away it is, it has to launch another rocket, which in turn, pausing, launches another rocket, which in turn, pausing, launches another rocket, perpetual forward spurts to give free scope to the craving for departure, craving for going beyond, false rockets, in fact, all of them, abstract, diagrammatic, but no less eager to reach, by successive stages, an ever-receding infinity.

*the experiment
of introducing images
into mescalin
visions.*

Into my inner visions I try to introduce an image from outside. With this intention, I turn over the pages of an abundantly illustrated zoology book open beside me and look at the pictures of different animals. Nothing happens. When I close my eyes they are not there. They are frankly excluded. No sign of any after-image. As soon as they are out of my sight they seem to have been cut by a knife. For all that, I try again, looking at the giraffes and the ostriches, elongated animals which ought to tempt mescalin's elongating propensity. But even while I am looking at them I know very well that I am not "detaining" them. When I close my eyes, not the slightest image. I pick up the book again, but tired of pictures (more than tired, I have no contact with them at all), in the flickering light of the wood fire I begin to glance at the text, with difficulty making out a few words: "the giraffe . . . a ruminant, between the antelope and the . . . by its shape. . . ." Wait! At these words something seems to stir. I close my eyes and, already responding to the mention of their name, two dozen giraffes are galloping in the distance, rhythmically raising their slender legs and their interminable necks. True, they have nothing in common with the muscular, beautifully colored animals of the photographs which I had just been looking at, and which had been unable to create any "inner" giraffe. These were diagrams in motion of the idea "giraffe," drawings formed by reflection, not reproduction.

*To enter into the
visions of mescalin
the giraffes must
grow even taller.*

But tall they certainly were. High as houses of seven stories but with bases not proportionately larger. In order to enter into the mescalin world they had been forced to become these slender giants, these ridiculous, vertiginous manikins that a mild mistral could have toppled over, their legs broken.

Cessation.

*ruins
ruins
perpetually
in ruin
(without ever
falling)
consolidations
dislocations
consolidations*

By means of zigzag strokes, by means of transversal flights, by means of flashing furrows, by means of I don't know what all, always beginning again, asserting itself, recovering itself, steadying itself, by means of punctuations, of repetitions, of hesitant jerks, by slow cantings, by fissurations, by indiscernible slidings, I see, being formed, unformed, reformed, a jerking building, a building in abeyance, in perpetual metamorphosis and transubstantiation, sometimes appearing to be the rough draft of an immense and almost orogenic tapir, or the still quivering *pagne* of a Negro dancer who has collapsed and is about to

[6] Gasoline, ether, carbon tetrachloride used by René Daumal —who from them derived an . . . astonishing faith—all products which violently eliminate fat and sugar from the brain, induced this same phenomenon.

dislocations

*"Mescalin
avoids form,"
Havelock Ellis.*

*Once more
besieged by pink
licked by pink.
A sort of perversion
applied to a color*

*Last signs of
speed.
the immense
endless belt
of faces*

fall asleep. But out of the sleep, and even before it occurs, the building magically rises.

And here it is again just as it was before, with more stories[7] than you can count, with a thousand rows of spasmodic bricks, a trembling, oscillating ruin, crammed, stuttering *Bourouboudour*.

Like the sensitive tip of the tongue at the height of its enjoyment, if this tip of the tongue became instantaneously a big, fat, pink hippopotamus replete with that enjoyment, and not only one, but a hundred big-bellied hippos, and ten thousand sows, suckling already biggish little pigs snuggling against their swollen flanks, and all this huddled together one against the other, and if the height of the enjoyment, thus spread out and multiplied, were solely the fact of being pink, pink, pink, stupidly, deliriously, paradisiacally pink, pink enough to make you howl, unless, that is, you had the soul of a whore and took a flabby pleasure in yielding to it, that was the way I was seeing pink, I was up to my eyes in pink, pink besieged me, licked me, wanted to confound me with itself. But I refused to fall for it. I'd have been ashamed.

From island to island, greater and greater slackening. Softening too. For the first time a face appears, if it is a face. Two or three hundred alternate rows of eyes and lips, blubber lips that is, blubber lips, blubber lips, blubber lips, and eyes slightly mongoloid, eyes, eyes, eyes, eyes, composed the face which kept gliding ceaselessly downward, each lower row disappearing, replaced by other rows appearing, of slanting eyes, of slanting eyes, of slanting eyes, or of great blubber lips, blubber lips with fleshy ridges like a rooster's comb, but not nearly so red. And they were indecipherable, the eyes, very narrow under immense heavy lids, slightly tremulous. And all this enormously rectangular, in fact like a moving carpet with the thickness and volume totally imperceptible, or rather seeming to be of the same thickness all over, the thickness of a comfortable carpet in which the eyes and lips were not so much in relief as excrescences, wasps, bellies, innumerable bellies, pinned there and still quivering. And the endless belt kept on rolling with its enigmatic eyes, and you couldn't decide which one to watch more than another. There was a slight incline, and the width of the face that kept sliding by was that of a moderately wide street, its height in proportion. A curious thing about it was that you had no more difficulty seeing the top than the bottom or the middle. And this great intent face, so exaggerated and devoid of any other part, visibly incapable of detaching itself from others, I was able to watch without fear and even without repugnance. I felt hardly any curiosity either. Like the other spectacles, it did not seem to be there for me. Mescalin, soon to be spent, had now become more subdued. If the faces, when I try to describe them, seem monstrous, they really were not, being without any apparent expression. The colors showed hundreds of different tints and the subtle tones of autumn woods and forests. Instead of a carpet it might also have been a landscape or a mountain of faces. It was simply that they were juxtaposed and their parallelism more mechanical than deliberate. Obviously mescalin did not know how to compose. I believe that the superabundance of colors which covered the entire space and refused to be suppressed disturbed both of us, mescalin and me. What was lacking in this huge spectacle was a gravity in proportion to its apparent extent. Immense without grandeur. Everything was growing indistinct. The storm of white lights was over and would not return.

The anopodokotolotopadnodrome was about to close.

---

[7] Endless, but never vertiginous. That would require a sense of distance and depth I don't have, which I am totally lacking.

J. P. in five words expressed what each of us was thinking. "One isn't proud of oneself." Not one of the three of us who were there had regarded it with reverence, but rather as a sort of prestidigitator's act. And we rose with the joyous sensation of having come from the ruin of a glassworks for which no one would hold us responsible.[8]

However, it was not all over as I had thought. Late in the evening, my head once more wrapped in a scarf, protected from the light of the lamp, I began seeing images again, certainly more colorful than any I was capable of myself. More blurred than they had been earlier, fainter yet characteristic—mescalin's, not mine.

Delicacy of the degradations. Miraculous attenuations.

All evening I followed with delight the delicacy of this progressive decline. In slow imperceptible degradations, the images now passing so slowly as to become pictures, but still enormous (notably a rug, and a beautiful one, as large as the Place de la Concorde), underwent an attenuation of coloring, in the end becoming lovely and "human," an attenuation of such delicacy I felt I should like to share it with someone. . . . This attenuated tone, a marvel of extreme tenuousness, at the very limit of perceptibility, seen half an hour later had undergone a new infinitesimal softening, final caress of the stranger who was leaving, and thus, through diminishing and subtly moving stages, the visions became memory images. There was a point at which they were no longer ordinary apparitions, at which everything was memory. You couldn't tell. You were always making mistakes, or you saw that previously you had been mistaken, so exact the superimposition always became. Images and memory images always eventually coinciding, something which never happens except at this stage. Time passed in the contemplation of these minute details. Now and then magnificent greens returned. I was never altogether asleep.

Thus the night wore on, shot through from time to time by wonderful images.

THIRD EXPERIMENT The very "little deaths" of mescalin from which one is constantly being resuscitated. to the mad motions of the disappearing images the body periodically responds with a slow, solemn rhythm, the four-minute rhythm. (Approximate time not sufficiently verified.)

If a person should become addicted to mescalin—but it is more apt to frighten anyone ("Grant that we do not go mad," was the prayer of Mexicans who, after fasting and continence, sought the god of the Peyotl)—it would certainly be for the periodic and ineffable shipwrecks one experiences. The exhaustion that follows the act of love is sometimes called the "little death." Compared to it, the extremely little death of mescalin is like the little death compared to the Great Death, so discreet it is, and gentle, but one suffers hundreds of them in the course of the day.

You go from little death to little death for hours on end, from shipwreck to rescue, succumbing every three or four minutes without the least apprehension, only to be gently, marvelously resuscitated once more. A deep sigh, which speaks volumes to those who know, is the only intimation of new rescues, but the voyage continues, a new death is preparing from which you will emerge in the same way. It is as though you had another heart whose systole and diastole occurred fifteen or twenty times an hour. Meanwhile, real or not, the indefatigable organ renews its strength and its drama and, though already weary, you are forced to take part until, at the fourth minute of the cycle, you give a sigh of relief which marks the end of the abstract coition.

And so it was with me the last time I delivered up my body and the tool that is called my head. It was also the time of the fracture, the gaping fracture, gaping for a long time perhaps, just as, in the case of a woman you have

---

[8] Several colors had been entirely absent for hours, as for example red, although red is a color I use frequently. On the other hand, green which I never use was, with white, violently present and in superabundance. Theory of Ewald Herling (*Theorie der Vorgänge*, 1890) according to which, if I am not mistaken, in drunkenness one sees only colors fitting the mood to the exclusion of all others. On the contrary, I was against most of mescalin's colors. They made me ashamed or furious.

possessed while remaining detached, it happens that without thinking, or through a feeling of tenderness, graver by far than love, one day you surrender yourself, and she enters you with the swiftness of a torrent and never to leave again.

And so that day was the day of the great opening. Forgetting the tawdry images which as a matter of fact all disappeared, I gave up struggling and let myself be traversed by the fluid which, entering me through the furrow, seemed to be coming from the ends of the earth. I myself was torrent, I was drowned man, I was navigation. My hall of the constitution, my hall of the ambassadors, my hall of gifts and of the interchange of gifts, to which the stranger is brought to me for a first inspection; I had lost them all, my halls and my retainers. I was alone, tumultuously shaken like a dirty thread in an energetic wash. I shone, I was shattered, I shouted to the ends of the earth. I shivered, my shivering was a barking. I pressed forward, I rushed down, I plunged into transparency, I lived crystallinely.

at the right the celestial stairway.

Sometimes a glass stairway, a stairway like a Jacob's ladder, a stairway with more steps than I could climb in three entire lifetimes, a stairway with ten million steps, a stairway without landings, a stairway up to the sky, the maddest, most monstrous ventures since the Tower of Babel, rose into the absolute. Suddenly, I didn't see it any longer. The stairway had vanished like the bubbles of champagne, and I continued my navigation, struggling not to roll, struggling against suctions and pullings, against infinitely small jumping things, against waiting webs and arching claws.

a gigantic starfish

At times thousands of little ambulacral tentacles of a gigantic starfish fastened to me so compactly that I could not tell if I was becoming the starfish or if the starfish had become me. I shrank into myself, I made myself watertight and contracted, but everything here that contracts must promptly relax again, even the enemy dissolves like salt in water, and once more I was navigation, navigation first of all, shining with a pure white flame, responding to a thousand cascades, to foaming trenches and to gyratory gougings. What flows cannot inhabit.

Streamings streamings.

The streamings that on this extraordinary day were something so immense, so unforgettable, unique, that I thought, that I never stopped thinking: "A mountain, in spite of its lack of intelligence, a mountain with its cascades, its ravines, its streaming slopes would be in the same state I am in now and better able to understand me than a man. . . ."

What you see when you keep your eyes open.

Many *peyotleros*, probably but little accustomed to dreaming, have no visions, or at least not visions strong enough to be interesting, and prefer to keep their eyes open and to observe the altogether novel, the iridescent and, as it were, vibrant beauty of familiar objects, especially the dullest ones, for they are improved the most, becoming really quite marvelous (in tone).

the colors of the very weak inner vision combine with those of perception to produce exquisite tones.
Distances uncertain.

As for me, in the very dim light, curtains drawn, blinds half closed, I noticed very little difference in the things around me, except that I could not fix their positions exactly. The distance from me to the walls, especially to the opposite wall, was no longer always the same. It wavered from being three meters away to three meters, fifty centimeters. It could not seem to make up its mind. But to this I had paid little attention, either because I found it hardly different from what I had experienced during a severe bout of fever, or because, as the sensation was rather disagreeable, I kept my eyes closed, interested only in the visions.

Meanwhile I had to get up to put a log on the fire. The noise seemed so formidable that I apologized to my companions for the earthquake I had provoked. They laughed in such a spontaneous and wholehearted manner that I realized their ears, made supersensitive like mine by mescalin, had heard the

same unprecedented din. I went on into the next room where the light hurt my eyes. Then I opened the door into the bathroom and turned on the switch. I stood aghast at what I saw in the washbasin: a fetus! I was utterly dumbfounded. It is true that a woman had been there a short time before, a woman I hardly knew, but who seemed so proper. It was unbelievable! I couldn't get over it! She had stayed there for a considerable length of time—I remembered it now—but still, a woman as modest as she seemed!

An accident evidently. The effect of the emotional shock, the traumatism of the drug. Fascinated, I stood stock-still staring at it. I am not very active by nature. But I really had to find out if the fetus was whole, otherwise, poor woman, her suffering was not over. She would come back. That is why she had been suddenly so perturbed. Something had to be done. With a feeling of disgust I touched the soft bluish head of the sticky bloodstained little thing. What a mess! Whole or not whole? Finally, with a stick I found in one corner, I begin energetically shoving the little body back and forth . . . it opens and falls apart. "Ah!" and I stand there overwhelmed as by another anomaly. The fetus no longer existed, yet it was still there, livid, bluish, bloodstained, such really delicate tones, almost iridescent, but which I failed to appreciate. . . . On the contrary, I was appalled. And what of the proof furnished by tearing it apart? No doubt, but the existence of the fetus, perfectly distinct and indubitable a few seconds ago, refused to be suppressed by the appearance, providential though it was, of this sort of rag or wet paper. I was still aghast. True, the case of the fetus seemed settled, but I had a vague feeling that if I were to discover another fetus, or worse, in a basin, in a sink, or in an empty flowerpot, it might not be explained away so happily and unexpectedly as at present. My behavior was not as childish as it appears. Feeling that I was in no state to resist the hallucination and preferring not to remain exposed to it, I quickly returned to the dim living room, where queer colored visions did indeed come, and would come again, in my inner vision, but no fetus, nothing resembling a fetus, nothing really dangerous. I was not worried on that score. Why? It would be hard to say. Perhaps because in the real world, as far as women, domestic animals, even turtles are concerned, I am always afraid of the consequences. Not very practical, I am afraid of anything that might become "material" and demanded quick, rational decisions, of being caught unprepared. All this was evident, if not materialized, in this incident which as a matter of fact was not a true hallucination since it did not occur without some support. But it has taught me more than dozens of pages on the subject, for it has made me realize how one could remain riveted to a hallucination, unable to tear oneself away. As for a supporting agent, one can always be found. What surface is so smooth as not to show enough variations for the imagination to seize upon? What atmosphere so free from particles of dust that there is not one to catch and hold a chimerical object?

fleeing from the hallucination.

I used to have a kind of respect for people who saw apparitions. No longer! I have no doubt they really see them, but in what state of mind! Certainly not when they are calm, for then they would indeed be extraordinary.

Everything moves, everything is vibrant and teeming with reality to the eye and the mind of anyone who is in the second state . . . or who has been.

One evening about three weeks after my last dose of mescalin, I decided to read Quercy on hallucination after going to bed. Later, trying to toss the book onto the couch and aiming badly, it fell to the floor and, opening, revealed a wonderful colored photograph inserted in the volume. I hastened to recover the book. I wanted to see those marvelous colors again and to find out the name of the painter of the original of the reproduction which I had barely glimpsed, but which I should recognize among all others. I turn over the pages: nothing. I shake the volume trying to make the loose page fall out. Impossible. I go over the book once more page by page, and again the next morning, even getting a friend to examine it too: nothing.

At the word "hallucination" I had had one.

Seeing the word on the cover I had functioned. Quick as thought it was realized. But not understanding, I had kept searching in vain for the admirable colored reproduction, more real than a real one, among the colorless pages of the book which had provoked it.   —*Translated by Louise Varèse*

►► Jack Kerouac

October in the Railroad Earth

There was a little alley in San Francisco back of the Southern Pacific station at Third and Townsend in redbrick of drowsy lazy afternoons with everybody at work in offices in the air you feel the impending rush of their commuter frenzy as soon they'll be charging en masse from Market and Sansome buildings on foot and in buses and all well-dressed thru working-man Frisco of Walkup ?? truck drivers and even the poor grime-bemarked Third Street of lost bums even Negroes so hopeless and long left East and meanings of responsibility and *try* that now all they do is stand there spitting in the broken glass sometimes fifty in one afternoon against one wall at Third and Howard and here's all these Millbrae and San Carlos neat-necktied producers and commuters of America and Steel civilization rushing by with San Francisco *Chronicles* and green *Call-Bulletins* not even enough time to be disdainful, they've got to catch 130, 132, 134, 136 all the way up to 146 till the time of evening supper in homes of the railroad earth when high in the sky the magic stars ride above the following hot-shot freight trains—it's all in California, it's all a sea, I swim out of it in afternoons of sun hot meditation in my jeans with head on handkerchief on brakeman's lantern or (if not working) on book, I look up at blue sky of perfect lostpurity and feel the warp of wood of old America beneath me and have insane conversations with Negroes in several-story windows above and everything is pouring in, the switching moves of boxcars in that little alley which is so much like the alleys of Lowell and I hear far off in the sense of coming night that engine calling our mountains.

But it was that beautiful cut of clouds I could always see above the little S.P. alley, puffs floating by from Oakland or the Gate of Marin to the north or San Jose south, the clarity of Cal to break your heart. It was the fantastic drowse and drum hum of lum mum afternoon nathin' to do, ole Frisco with end of land sadness—the people—the alley full of trucks and cars of businesses nearabouts and nobody knew or far from cared who I was all my life three thousand five hundred miles from birth-O opened up and at last belonged to me in Great America.

Now it's night in Third Street the keen little neons and also yellow bulblights of impossible-to-believe flops with dark ruined shadows moving back of torn yellow shades like a degenerate China with no money—the cats in Annie's Alley, the flop comes on, moans, rolls, the street is loaded with darkness. Blue sky above with stars hanging high over old hotel roofs and blowers of hotels moaning out dusts of interior, the grime inside the word in mouths falling out tooth by tooth, the reading rooms tick tock bigclock with creak chair and slantboards and old faces looking up over rimless spectacles bought in some West Virginia or Florida or Liverpool England pawnshop long before I was born and across rains they've come to the end of the land sadness end of the world gladness all you San Franciscos will have to fall eventually and burn again. But I'm walking and one night a bum fell into the hole of the construction job where they're tearing a sewer by day the husky Pacific & Electric youths in torn jeans who work there often I think of going up to some of 'em like say blond ones with wild hair and torn shirts and say "You oughta apply for the railroad it's much easier work you don't stand around the street all day and you get much more pay" but this bum fell in the hole you saw his foot stick out, a British MG also driven by some eccentric once backed into the hole and as I came home from a long Saturday afternoon local to Hollister out of San Jose miles away across verdurous fields of prune and juice joy here's this British MG backed and legs up wheels up into a pit and bums and cops standing around right outside the coffee shop—it was the way they fenced it but he never had the nerve to do it due to the fact that he had no money and nowhere to go and O his father was dead and O his mother was dead and O his sister was dead and O his whereabout was dead was dead—but and then at that time also I lay in my room on long Saturday afternoons listening to Jumpin' George with my fifth of tokay no tea and just under the sheets laughed to hear the crazy music "Mama, he treats your daughter mean," Mama, Papa, and don't you come in here I'll kill you etc. getting high by myself in room glooms and all wondrous knowing about the Negro the essential American out there always finding his solace his meaning in the fellaheen street and not in abstract morality and even when he has a church you see the pastor out front bowing to the ladies on the make you hear his great vibrant voice on the sunny Sunday afternoon sidewalk full of sexual vibratos saying "Why yes Mam but de gospel do say that man was born of woman's womb—" and no and so by that time I come crawling out of my warmsack and hit the street when I see the railroad ain't gonna call me till 5 A.M. Sunday morn probably for a local out of Bay Shore in fact always for a local out of Bay Shore and I go to the wailbar of all the wildbars in the world the one and only Third-and-Howard and there I go in and drink with the madmen and if I get drunk I git.

The whore who come up to me in there the night I was there with Al Buckle and said to me "You wanta play with me tonight Jim, and?" and I didn't think I had enough money and later told this to Charley Low and he laughed and said "How do you know she wanted money always take the chance that she might be out just for love or just out for love you know what I mean man don't be a sucker." She was a goodlooking doll and said "How would you like to oolyakoo with me mon?" and I stood there like a jerk and in fact bought drink got drink drunk that night and in the 299 Club I was hit by the proprietor the band breaking up the fight before I had a chance to decide to hit him back which I didn't do and out on the street I tried to rush back in but they had locked the door and were looking at me thru the forbidden glass in the door with faces like undersea—I should have played with her shurrouruuruuruuruuruuruuruurk-diei.

Despite the fact I was a brakeman making 600 a month I kept going to the Public restaurant on Howard Street which was three eggs for 26 cents 2 eggs for 21 this with toast (hardly no butter) coffee (hardly no coffee and sugar rationed) oatmeal with dash of milk and sugar the smell of soured old shirts lingering above the cookpot steams as if they were making skidrow lumberjack stews out of San Francisco ancient Chinese mildewed laundries with poker games in the back among the barrels and the rats of the earthquake days, but actually the food somewhat on the level of an oldtime 1890 or 1910 section-gang cook of lumber camps far in the North with an old-time pigtail Chinaman cooking it and cussing out those who didn't like it. The prices were incredible but one time I had the beefstew and it was absolutely the worst beefstew I ever et, it was incredible I tell you—and as they often did that to me it was with the most intensest regret that I tried to convey to the geek back of counter what I wanted but he was a tough sonofabitch, ech, ti-ti, I thought the counterman was kind of queer especially he handled gruffly the hopeless drooldrunks, "What now you do-

ing you think you can come in here and cut like that for God's sake act like a man won't you and eat or get out-t-t-t-"—I always did wonder what a guy like that was doing working in a place like that because, but why some sympathy in his horny heart for the busted wrecks, all up and down the street were restaurants like the Public catering exclusively to bums of the black, winos with no money, who found 21 cents left over from wine panhandlings and so stumbled in for their third or fourth touch of food in a week, as sometimes they didn't eat at all and so you'd see them in the corner puking white liquid which was a couple quarts of rancid sauterne rotgut or sweet white sherry and they had nothing on their stomachs, most of them had one leg or were on crutches and had bandages around their feet, from nicotine and alcohol poisoning together, and one time finally on my way up Third near Market across the street from Breens, when in early 1952 I lived on Russian Hill and didn't quite dig the complete horror and humor of railroad's Third Street, a bum a thin sickly littlebum like Anton Abraham lay face down on the pavement with crutch aside and some old remnant newspaper sticking out and it seemed to me he was dead. I looked closely to see if he was breathing and he was not, another man with me was looking down and we agreed he was dead, and soon a cop came over and look and agreed and called the wagon, the little wretch weighed about 50 pounds in his bleeding count and was stone mackerel snotnose cold dead as a bleeding doornail—ah I tell you—and who could notice but other half dead deadbums bums bums bums dead dead times X times X times all dead bums forever dead with nothing and all finished and out—there—and this was the clientele in the Public Hair restaurant where I ate many's the morn a 3-egg breakfast with almost dry toast and oatmeal a little saucer of, and thin sickly dishwater coffee, all to save 14 cents so in my little book proudly I could make a notation and of the day and prove that I could live comfortably in America while working seven days a week and earning 600 a month I could live on less than 17 a week which with my rent of 4.20 was okay as I had also to spend money to eat and sleep sometimes on the other end of my Watsonville chaingang run but preferred most times to sleep free of charge and uncomfortable in cabooses of the crummy rack—my 26-cent breakfast, my pride—and that incredible semiqueer counterman who dished out the food, threw it at you, slammed it, had a languid frank expression straight in your eyes like a 1930's lunchcart heroine in Steinbeck and at the steamtable itself labored coolly a junkey-looking Chinese with an actual stocking in his hair as if they'd just Shanghai'd him off the foot of Commercial Street before the Ferry Building was up but forgot it was 1952, dreamed it was 1860 goldrush Frisco—and on rainy days you felt they had ships in the back room.

I'd take walks up Harrison and the boomcrash of truck traffic towards the glorious girders of the Oakland Bay Bridge that you could see after climbing Harrison Hill a little like radar machine of eternity in the sky, huge, in the blue, by pure clouds crossed, gulls, idiot cars streaking to destinations on its undinal boom across shmoshwaters flocked up by winds and news of San Rafael storms and flash boats—there O I always came and walked and negotiated whole Friscos in one afternoon from the overlooking hills of the high Fillmore where Orient-bound vessels you can see on drowsy Sunday mornings of poolhall goof like after a whole night playing drums in a jam session and a morn in the hall of cuesticks I went by the rich homes of old ladies supported by daughters or female secretaries with immense ugly gargoyle Frisco millions fronts of other days and way below is the blue passage of the Gate, the Alcatraz mad rock, the mouths of Tamalpais, San Pablo Bay, Sausalito sleepy hemming the rock and bush over yonder, and the sweet white ships cleanly cutting a path to Sasebo.—Over Harrison and down to the Embarcadero and around Telegraph Hill and up the back of Russian Hill and down to the play streets of Chinatown and down Kearney back across Market to Third and my wild-night neon twinkle fate there, ah, and then finally at dawn of a Sunday and they did call me, the immense girders of Oakland Bay still haunting me and all that eternity too much to swallow and not knowing who I am at all but like a big plump long-haired baby worwalking up in the dark trying to wonder who I am the door knocks and it's the desk keeper of the flop hotel with silver rims and white hair and clean clothes and sickly potbelly said he was from Rocky Mount and looked like yes, he had been desk clerk of the Nash Buncome Association hotel down there in 50 successive heatwave summers without the sun and only palmos of the lobby with cigar crutches in the albums of the South and him with his dear mother waiting in a buried log cabin of graves with all that mashed past historied underground afoot with the stain of the bear the blood of the tree and cornfields long plowed under and Negroes whose voices long faded from the middle of the wood and the dog barked his last, this man had voyageured to the West Coast too like all the other loose American elements and was pale and sixty and

complaining of sickness, might at one time been a handsome squire to women with money but now a forgotten clerk and maybe spent a little time in jail for a few forgeries or harmless cons and might also have been a railroad clerk and might have wept and might have never made it, and that day I'd say he saw the bridgegirders up over the hill of traffic of Harrison like me and woke up mornings with same lost, is now beckoning on my door and breaking in the world on me and he is standing on the frayed carpet of the hall all worn down by black steps of sunken old men for last 40 years since earthquake and the toilet stained, beyond the last toilet bowl and the last stink and stain I guess yes is the end of the world the bloody end of the world, so now knocks on my door and I wake up, saying "How what howp howelk howel of the knavery they've meaking, ek and won't let me slepit? Whey they dool? Whand out wisis thing that comes flarminging around my dooring in the mouth of the night and there everything knows that I have no mother, and no sister, and no father and no bot sosstle, but not crib" I get up and sit up and says "Howowow?" and he says "Telephone?" and I have to put on my jeans heavy with knife, wallet, I look closely at my railroad watch hanging on little door flicker of closet door face to me ticking silent the time, it says 4:30 A.M. of a Sunday morn, I go down the carpet of the skidrow hall in jeans and with no shirt and yes with shirt tails hanging gray workshirt and pick up phone and ticky sleepy night desk with cage and spittoons and keys hanging and old towels piled clean ones but frayed at edges and bearing names of every hotel of the moving prime, on the phone is the Crew Clerk, "Kerroway?" "Yeah." "Kerroway it's gonna be the Sherman Local at 7 A.M. this morning." "Sherman Local right." "Out of Bay Shore, you know the way?" "Yeah." "You had that same job last Sunday—Okay Kerroway-y-y-y-y." And we mutually hang up and I say to myself okay it's the Bay Shore bloody old dirty hagglous old coveted old madman Sherman who hates me so much especially when we were at Redwood Junction kicking boxcars and he always insists I work the rear end tho as one-year man it would be easier for me to follow pot but I work rear and he wants me to be right there with a block of wood when a car or cut of cars kicked stops, so they won't roll down that incline and start catastrophes, O well anyway I'll be learning eventually to like the railroad and Sherman will like me some day, and anyway another day another dollar.

And there's my room, small, gray in the Sunday morning, now all the franticness of the street and night before is done with, bums sleep, maybe one or two sprawled on sidewalk with empty poorboy on a sill—my mind whirls with life.

So there I am in dawn in my dim cell—2½ hours to go till the time I have to stick my railroad watch in my jean watchpocket and cut out allowing myself exactly 8 minutes to the station and the 7:15 train No. 112 I have to catch for the ride five miles to Bay Shore through four tunnels, emerging from the sad Rath scene of Frisco gloom gleak in the rainymouth fogmorning to a sudden valley with grim hills rising to the sea, bay on left, the fog rolling in like demented in the draws that have little white cottages disposed real-estatically for come-Christmas blue sad lights— my whole soul and concomitant eyes looking out on this reality of living and working in San Francisco with that pleased semi-loin-located shudder, energy for sex changing to pain at the portals of work and culture and natural foggy fear.—There I am in my little room wondering how I'll really manage to fool myself into feeling that these next 2½ hours will be well filled, fed, with work and pleasure thoughts.— It's so thrilling to feel the coldness of the morning wrap around my thickquilt blankets as I lay there, watch facing and ticking me, legs spread in comfy skidrow soft sheets with soft tears or sew lines in 'em, huddled in my own skin and rich and not spending a cent on—I look at my little-book—and I stare at the words of the Bible.—On the floor I find last red afternoon Saturday's *Chronicle* sports page with news of football games in Great America the end of which I bleakly see in the gray light entering—the fact that Frisco is built of wood satisfies me in my peace, I know nobody'll disturb me for 2½ hours and all bums are asleep in their own bed of eternity awake or not, bottle or not—it's the joy I feel that counts for me.—On the floor's my shoes, big lumber-boot flopjack workshoes to colomp over rockbed with and not turn the ankle—solidity shoes that when you put them on, yokewise, you know you're working now and so for same reason shoes not be worn for any reason like joys of restaurant and shows.—Night-before shoes are on the floor beside the Clunkershoes a pair of blue canvas shoes à la 1952 style, in them I'd trod soft as ghost the indented hill sidewalks of Ah Me Frisco all in the glitter night, from the top of Russian Hill I'd looked down at one point on all roofs of North Beach and the Mexican nightclub neons, I'd descended to them on the old steps of Broadway under which they were newly laboring a mountain tunnel—shoes fit for watersides, embarca-deros, hill and plot lawns of park and tiptop vista.—

Workshoes covered with dust and some oil of en-gines—the crumpled jeans nearby, belt, blue railroad hank, knife, comb, keys, switch keys and caboose coach key, the knees white from Pajaro Riverbottom finedusts, the ass black from slick sandboxes in yard-goat after yardgoat—the gray workshorts, the dirty undershirt, sad shorts, tortured socks of my life.— And the Bible on my desk next to the peanut butter, the lettuce, the raisin bread, the crack in the plaster, the stiff-with-old-dust lace drape now no longer lace-able but hard as—after all those years of hard dust eternity in that Cameo skid inn with red eyes of rheumy oldmen dying there staring without hope out on the dead wall you can hardly see thru window-dusts and all you heard lately in the shaft of the roof-top middle way was the cries of a Chinese child whose father and mother were always telling him to shush and then screaming at him, he was a pest and his tears from China were most persistent and world-wide and represented all our feelings in brokendown Cameo tho this was not admitted by bum one except for an occasional harsh clearing of throat in the halls or moan of nightmarer—by things like this and neg-lect of a hard-eyed alcoholic oldtime chorusgirl maid the curtains had now absorbed all the iron they could take and hung stiff and even the dust in them was iron, if you shook them they'd crack and fall in tat-ters to the floor and spatter like wings of iron on the bong and the dust would fly into your nose like fil-ings of steel and choke you to death, so I never touched them. My little room at 6 in the comfy dawn (at 4:30) and before me all that time, that fresh-eyed time for a little coffee to boil water on my hot plate, throw some coffee in, stir it, French style, slowly carefully pour it in my white tin cup, throw sugar in (not California beet sugar like I should have been using but New Orleans cane sugar, because beet racks I carried from Oakland out to Watsonville many's the time, a 80-car freight train with nothing but gondolas loaded with sad beets looking like the heads of decapitated women)—ah me how but it was a hell and now I had the whole thing to myself, and make my raisin toast by sitting it on a little wire I'd especially bent to place over the hotplate, the toast crackled up, there, I spread the margarine on the still red hot toast and it too would crackle and sink in golden, among burnt raisins and this was my toast—then two eggs gently slowly fried in soft mar-garine in my little skidrow frying pan about half as thick as a dime in fact less a little piece of tiny tin you could bring on a camp trip—the eggs slowly fluffed in there and swelled from butter steams and I threw garlic salt on them, and when they were ready the yellow of them had been slightly filmed with a cooked white at the top from the tin cover I'd put over the frying pan, so now they were ready, and out they came, I spread them out on top of my already prepared potatoes which had been boiled in small pieces and then mixed with the bacon I'd already fried in small pieces, kind of raggely mashed bacon potatoes, with eggs on top steaming, and on the side lettuce, with peanut butter dab nearby on side.—I had heard that peanut butter and lettuce contained all the vitamins you should want, this after I had originally started to eat this combination because of the deliciousness and nostalgia of the taste—my breakfast ready at about 6:45 and as I eat already I'm dressing to go piece by piece and by the time the last dish is washed in the little sink at the boiling hot-water tap and I'm taking my lastquick slug of coffee and quickly rinsing the cup in the hot water spout and rushing to dry it and plop it in its place by the hot plate and the brown carton in which all the groceries sit tightly wrapped in brown paper, I'm already picking up my brakeman's lantern from where it's been hanging on the door handle and my tattered time-table's long been in my backpocket folded and ready to go, everything tight, keys, timetable, lantern, knife, handkerchief, wallet, comb, railroad keys, change and myself. I put the light out on the sad dab mad grub little diving room and hustle out into the fog of the flow, descending the creak hall steps where the old men are not yet sitting with Sunday morn papers because still asleep or some of them I can now as I leave hear beginning to disfawdle to wake in their rooms with their moans and yorks and scrapings and horror sounds, I'm going down the steps to work, glance to check time of watch with clerk cage clock—a hardy two or three oldtimers sitting already in the dark brown lobby under the tockboom clock, toothless, or grim, or elegantly mustached—what thought in the world swirling in them as they see the young eager brakeman bum hurrying to his thirty dollars of the Sunday—what memories of old home-steads, built without sympathy, hornyhanded fate dealt them the loss of wives, childs, moons—libraries collapsed in their time—oldtimers of the telegraph wired wood Frisco in the fog gray top time sitting in their brown sunk sea and will be there when this afternoon my face flushed from the sun, which at eight'll flame out and make sunbaths for us at Red-wood, they'll still be here the color of paste in the green underworld and still reading the same editorial over again and won't understand where I've been or what for or what—I have to get out of there or suffo-cate, out of Third Street or become a worm, it's al-right to live and bed-wine in and play the radio and

cook little breakfasts and rest in but O my I've got to tog now to work, I hurry down Third to Townsend for my 7:15 train—it's 3 minutes to go, I start in a panic to jog, goddam it I didn't give myself enough time this morning, I hurry down under the Harrison ramp to the Oakland-Bay Bridge, down past Schwei-backer-Frey the great dim red neon printshop always spectrally my father the dead executive I see there, I run and hurry past the beat Negro grocery stores where I buy all my peanut butter and raisin bread, past the redbrick railroad alley now mist and wet, across Townsend, the train is leaving!

Fatuous railroad men, the conductor old John J. Coppertwang 35 years pure service on ye olde S.P. is there in the gray Sunday morning with his gold watch out peering at it, he's standing by the engine yelling up pleasantries at old hoghead Jones and young fireman Smith with the baseball cap is at the fireman's seat munching sandwich—"We'll how'd ye like old Johnny O yestiddy, I guess he didn't score so many touchdowns like we thought." "Smith bet six dollars on the pool down in Watsonville and said he's rakin' in thirty four." "I've been in that Wat-sonville pool—." They've been in the pool of life fleartiming with one another, all the long poker-playing nights in brownwood railroad places, you can smell the mashed cigar in the wood, the spittoon's been there for more than 750,099 yars and the dog's been in and out and these old boys by old shaded brown light have bent and muttered and young boys too with their new brakeman passenger uniform the tie undone the coat thrown back the flashing youth smile of happy fatuous well-fed goodjobbed careered futured pensioned hospitalized taken-care-of railroad men—35, 40 years of it and then they get to be con-ductors and in the middle of the night they've been for years called by the Crew Clerk yelling "Cassady? It's the Maximush localized week do you for the right lead" but now as old men all they have is a regular job, a regular train, conductor of the 112 with gold-watch is helling up his pleasantries at all fire dog crazy Satan hoghead Willis why the wildest man this side of France and Frankincense, he was known once to take his engine up that steep grade—7:15, time to pull, as I'm running thru the station hearing the bell jangling and the steam chuff they're pulling out, O I come flying out on the platform and forget momen-tarily or that is never did know what track it was and whirl in confusion a while wondering what track and can't see no train and this is the time I lose there, 5, 6, 7 seconds when the train tho underway is only slowly upchugging to go and a man a fat executive could easily run up and grab it but when I yell to

Tomi Ungerer

brakeman and an old deadheading conductor ole Charley W. Jones, why he had seven wives and six kids and one time out at Lick no I guess it was Coyote he couldn't seen on account of the steam and out he come and found his lantern in the igloo regular anglecock of my herald and they gave him fifteen benefits so now there he is in the Sunday har har owlala morning and he and young rear man watch incredulously this student brakeman running like a crazy trackman after their departing train. I feel like yelling ":Make your airtest now make your airtest now!" knowing that when a passenger pulls out just about at the first crossing east of the station they pull the air a little bit to test the brakes, on signal from the engine, and this momentarily slows up the train and I could manage it, and could catch it, but they're not making no airtest the bastards, and I hek knowing I'm going to have to run like a sonofabitch. But suddenly I get embarrassed thinking what are all the people of the world gonna say to see a man running so devilishly fast with all his might sprinting thru life like Jesse Owens just to catch a goddam train and all of them with their hysteria wondering if I'll get killed when I catch the back platform and blam, I fall down and go boom and lay supine across the crossing, so the old flagman when the train has flowed by will see that everything lies on the earth in the same stew, all of us angels will die and we don't ever know how or our own diamond, O heaven will enlighten us and open your youeeeeeoueee—open our eyes, open our eyes—I know I won't get hurt, I trust my shoes, hand grip, feet, solidity of yipe and cripe of gripe and grip and strength and need no mystic strength to measure the musculature in my rib rack—but damn it all it's a social embarrassment to be caught sprinting like a maniac after a train especially with two men gaping at me from rear of train and shaking their heads and yelling I can't make it even as I halfheartedly sprint after them with open eyes trying to communicate that I can and not for them to get hysterical or laugh, but I realize it's all too much for me, not the run, not the speed of the train which anyway two seconds after I gave up the complicated chase did indeed slow down at the crossing in the airtest before chugging up again for good and Bay Shore. So I was late for work, and old Sherman hated me and was about to hate me more.

The ground I would have eaten in solitude, cronch —the railroad earth, the flat stretches of long Bay Shore that I have to negotiate to get to Sherman's bloody caboose on track 17 ready to go with pot pointed to Redwood and the morning's 3-hour work —I get off the bus at Bay Shore Highway and rush

Assistant Stationmaster "Where's 112?" and he tells me the last track which is the track I never dreamed I run to it fast as I can go and dodge people à la Columbia halfback and cut into track fast as off-tackle where you carry the ball with you to the left and feint with neck and head and push of ball as tho you're gonna throw yourself all out to fly around that left end and everybody psychologically chuffs with you that way and suddenly you contract and you like whiff of smoke are buried in the hole in tackle, cutback play, you're flying into the hole almost before you yourself know it, flying into the track I am and there's the train about 30 yards away even as I look picking up tremendously momentum the kind of momentum I would have been able to catch if I'd a looked a second earlier—but I run, I know I can catch it. Standing on the back platform are the rear down the little street and turn in—boys riding the pot of a switcheroo in the yardgoat day come yelling by at me from the headboards and footboards "Come on down ride with us" otherwise I would have been about 3 minutes even later to my work but now I hop on the little engine that momentarily slows up to pick me up and it's alone not pulling anything but tender, the guys have been up to the other end of the yard to get back on some track of necessity—that boy will have to learn to flag himself without nobody helping him as many's the time I've seen some of these young goats think they have everything but the plan is late, the word will have to wait, the massive arboreal thief with the crime of the kind, and air and all kinds of ghouls—ZONKed! made tremendous by the flare of the whole prime and encrudalatures of all kinds—San Franciscos and shroudband Bay Shores the last and the last furbelow of the eek plot pall prime tit top work oil twicks and wouldn't you?—the railroad earth I would have eaten alone, cronch, on foot head bent to get to Sherman who ticking watch observes with finicky eyes the time to go to give the hiball sign get on going it's Sunday no time to waste the only day of his long seven-day-a-week worklife he gets a chance to rest a little bit at home when "Eee Christ" when "Tell that sonofabitch student this is no party picnic damn this shit and throb tit you tell them something and how do you what the hell expect to underdries out tit all you bright tremendous trouble anyway, we's LATE" and this is the way I come rushing up late. Old Sherman is sitting in the crummy over his switch lists, when he sees me with cold blue eyes he says "You know you're supposed to be here 7:30 don't you so what the hell you doing gettin' in here at 7:50 you're twenty goddam minutes late, what the fuck you think this your birthday?" and he gets up and leans off the rear bleak platform and gives the high sign to the enginemen up front we have a cut of about 12 cars and they say it easy and off we go slowly at first, picking up momentum to the work, "Light that goddam fire" says Sherman he's wearing brandnew workshoes just about bought yestiddy and I notice his clean coveralls that his wife washed and set on his chair just that morning probably and I rush up and throw coal in the potbelly flop and take a fusee and two fusees and light them crack em Ah fourth of the July when the angels would smile on the horizon and all the racks where the mad are lost are returned to us forever from Lowell of my soul prime and single meditatee longsong hope to heaven of prayers and angels and of course the sleep and interested eye of images and but now we detect the missing buffoon there's the poor goodman rear man ain't even on the train yet and

Sherman looks out sulkily the back door and sees his rear man waving from fifteen yards aways to stop and wait for him and being an old railroad man he certainly isn't going to run or even walk fast, it's well understood, conductor Sherman's got to get up off his switch-list desk chair and pull the air and stop the goddam train for rear man Arkansaw Charley, who sees this done and just come up lopin' in his flop overalls without no care, so he was late too, or at least had gone gossiping in the yard office while waiting for the stupid head brakeman, the tagman's up in front on the presumably pot. "First thing we do is pick up a car in front at Redwood so all's you do get off at the crossing and stand back to flag, not too far." "Don't I work the head end?" "You work the hind end we got not much to do and I wanta get it done fast," snarls the conductor. "Just take it easy and do what we say and watch and flag." So it's peaceful Sunday morning in California and off we go, tack-a-tick, lao-tichi-couch, out of the Bay Shore yards, pause momentarily at the main line for the green, ole 71 or ole whatever been by and now we get out and go swamming up the tree valleys and town vale hollows and main street crossing parking-lot last-night attendant plots and Stanford lots of the world —to our destination in the Poo which I can see, and, so to while the time I'm up in the cupolo and with my newspaper dig the latest news on the front page and also consider and make notations of the money I spent already for this day Sunday absolutely not jot spent a nothing—California rushes by and with sad eyes we watch it reel the whole bay and the discourse falling off to gradual gils that ease and graduate to Santa Clara Valley then and the fig and behind is the fog immemoriates while the mist closes and we come running out to the bright sun of the Sabbath Californiay—

At Redwood I get off and standing on sad oily ties of the brakie railroad earth with red flag and torpedoes attached and fusees in backpocket with timetable crushed against and I leave my hot jacket in crummy standing there then with sleeves rolled up and there's the porch of a Negro home, the brothers are sitting in shirtsleeves talking with cigarettes and laughing and little daughter standing amongst the weeds of the garden with her playpail and pigtails and we the railroad men with soft signs and no sound pick up our flower, according to same goodman train order that for the last entire lifetime of attentions ole conductor industrial worker harlotized Sherman has been reading carefully son so's not to make a mistake:

"Sunday morning October 15 pick up flower car at Redwood, Dispatcher M.M.S."

►► **Alain Robbe-Grillet**

A Fresh Start for Fiction

The novel passes for a minor art only because of its obstinate attachment to exhausted techniques.

Nathalie Sarraute

It is scarcely reasonable, at first glance, to think that a *new* literature may one day—now, for example—be possible. The many attempts which have been made for more than fifty years to pull the art of narrative out of its rut have resulted, at best, in merely a few isolated works. None of these, whatever its interest, has attracted a public comparable to that enjoyed by the bourgeois novel. The only conception of the novel in effect today remains, in fact, that of Balzac.

Or one might go further and say, that of Madame de la Fayette. Already sacrosanct in her age, psychological analysis constituted the basis of all prose: presided at the conception of the book, at the description of its characters, at the development of its plot. A *good* novel, ever since, has remained the study of a passion—or a conflict of passions, or the absence of passion—in a given milieu. Most contemporary novelists of the traditional sort—those, that is, who actually win the approval of their readers—could insert long passages from *La Princesse de Clèves* or from *Père Goriot* into their own books without awakening the least suspicion in the vast public which devours whatever they turn out. They would scarcely need to change more than a phrase here and there, modify certain constructions, give a glimpse of their own "manner" by means of a word, a "daring" image, the rhythm of a sentence. . . . But all of them admit, without seeing anything peculiar about it, that their preoccupations as writers date back several centuries.

What is there to be surprised at in this? The raw material—the French language—has undergone only very slight modifications for three hundred years; and, while society has transformed itself little by little, while industrial techniques have made considerable progress, our intellectual civilization has remained precisely the same. We live according to essentially the same habits and prohibitions—moral, alimentary, religious, sexual, hygienic, familial, etc. And of course there is always the human "heart," which, as everyone knows, is eternal. There's nothing new under the sun, it's all been said before, we've come on the stage too late, etc.

The risk of encountering such objections is merely increased if one dares claim that this new literature is not only possible in the future, but is already being written, and that it is going to represent—in its fulfillment—a revolution more total than those from which such movements as romanticism and naturalism were born.

Such promises as "Now things are going to change!" will invariably meet with ridicule. How will they go about changing? In what direction? And—especially—why now?

The art of the novel, however, has achieved such a degree of stagnation—a lassitude noted and remarked on by almost the whole of criticism—that it is scarcely imaginable that it can survive for long without radical changes. To the minds of many, the solution is simple indeed: no change is possible, the art of the novel is in the process of dying. We have no such guarantees. History will reveal, in a few decades, whether the various fits and starts which have been noted are signs of a death agony or a rebirth.

In any case, one must not deceive oneself as to the difficulties such a revolution will encounter. They are considerable. The whole caste system of our literary life (from publisher to the most modest reader, including bookseller and critic) has no choice but to fight against the unknown form which is attempting to establish itself. The minds best disposed toward the idea of a necessary transformation, those most willing to countenance and even recognize the values of experiment, remain, in spite of everything, the heirs of a tradition. A new form always seems to be more or less an absence of any form at all, since it is unconsciously judged by reference to consecrated forms. In one of our most celebrated encyclopedic dictionaries, we can read, in an article on Schoenberg: " . . . author of audacious works, written without regard for any rules whatever"! This brief judgment is found under the heading *Music*, evidently written by a specialist.

The stammering, newborn work will always be regarded as a monster, even by those who find the experiment fascinating. There will be some curiosity, of course, some gestures of interest, always some provision for the future. And some praise; though what is sincere will always be addressed to the vestiges of what is already familiar, to all those bonds from which the new work has not yet broken and which desperately seek to imprison it in the past.

For if the norms of the past serve to measure the present, they also can be used to construct it. The writer himself, despite his will to be independent, is situated in an intellectual civilization and a literature —that is, what *has been* written, a literature of the past. It is impossible for him to escape altogether from this tradition of which he is the product. Sometimes even the elements he has tried the hardest to uproot seem, on the contrary, to bloom more vigorously than ever in the very work by which he had hoped to destroy them; and he will be congratulated, of course, with relief, for having cultivated them so reverently.

Thus it will undoubtedly be those who specialize in the novel (novelists, critics, fanatic readers) who will have the most difficulty pulling themselves out of its rut.

Even the least "conditioned" observer is unable to look at the world which surrounds him with entirely unprejudiced eyes. There is no question of reviving that naive concern for objectivity at which the analyst of the soul (subjective) finds it so easy to smile. Objectivity in the general sense of the term—total impersonality of observation—is all too evidently an illusion. But *freedom* of observation *should* be possible, and yet, unfortunately, it is not. At every instant, a continuous fringe of culture (psychology, ethics, metaphysics, etc.) is being added to things, disguising their real strangeness, making them more comprehensible, more reassuring. Sometimes the camouflage is complete: a gesture slips from our mind, supplanted by the emotions which supposedly produced it, and we remember a landscape as *austere* or *calm* without being able to evoke a single outline, a single determining element. Even if we immediately think, "that's literary," we don't try to react against it. We accept the fact that what is *literary* (the word has become pejorative) functions as a screen set with bits of variously colored glass that fracture our field of vision into tiny assimilable facets.

And if something resists this systematic appropriation of the visual, if an element of the world breaks in on us without finding any place in the interpretive screen, we can always make use of our convenient category of the "absurd" to absorb this awkward residue.

But the world is neither significant nor absurd. It *is*, quite simply. That, in any case, is the most remarkable thing about it. And suddenly this evidence strikes us with irresistible force. All at once the whole beautiful construction collapses: opening our eyes to the unexpected, we have experienced once too often the shock of this stubborn reality we were pretending to have mastered. Around us, defying the mob of our animistic or protective adjectives, the things *are there*. Their surfaces are clear and smooth, *intact*, neither dubiously glittering, nor transparent. All our literature has not yet succeeded in penetrating their smallest corner, in softening their slightest curve.

The innumerable filmed novels encumbering our screens provide us an occasion for reliving this curious experience as often as we like. The cinema, another heir of the psychological and naturalist tradition, more often than not has as its sole purpose the transposition of a story into images: it aims exclusively at imposing on the spectator, through the intermediary of some well-chosen scenes, the same meaning that the sentences had for the reader. But at any given moment the filmed story can draw us out of our interior comfort toward this proffered world with a violence that one would seek in vain in the corresponding text, whether novel or scenario.

One can readily perceive the nature of the transformation. In the original novel, the objects and gestures forming the very tissue of the plot disappeared completely, leaving behind only their *significations*: the empty chair became only absence or expectation, the hand placed on a shoulder became a sign of friendliness, the bars on the window became only the impossibility of leaving. . . . But in the cinema, one sees the chair *too*, the movement of the hand, the shape of the bars. What they signify remains obvious, but, instead of monopolizing our attention, it becomes something added, even something in excess, because what touches us, what persists in our memory, what appears as essential and irreducible to vague intellectual concepts, are the gestures themselves, the objects, the movements, and the contours, to which the image has suddenly (and unintentionally) restored their *reality*.

It may seem arbitrary that such fragments of crude reality in the film narrative, which the camera cannot help presenting, strike us so vividly, whereas identical scenes in real life do not suffice to free us of our blindness. Actually, it is as if the very conventions of the photographic medium (the two dimensions, the black-and-white images, the frame of the screen, the difference of scale between scenes) help to free us from our own conventions. The slightly "unaccustomed" aspect of this reproduced world reveals at the same time the unaccustomed character of the world that surrounds us: unaccustomed, too, to the degree that it refuses to conform to our habits of apprehension and to our demands.

Instead of this universe of "signification" (psychological, social, functional) we must try to construct a world both more solid and more immediate. Let it be first of all by their *presence* that objects and gestures impose themselves, and let this presence continue to make itself felt beyond all explanatory theory that might try to enclose it in some system of reference, whether sentimental, sociological, Freudian, or metaphysical.

In this future universe of the novel, gestures and objects will be "there" before being "something"; and they will still be there afterward, hard, unalterable, eternally present, mocking their own meaning, which tries in vain to reduce them to the role of precarious tools between a formless past and an indeterminate future.

Thus objects will little by little lose their inconsistency and their secrets; will renounce their false mystery, that suspect interiority which Roland Barthes has called the "romantic 'heart' of things." No longer will objects be merely the vague reflection of the hero's vague soul, the image of his torments, the mainstay of his desires. Or rather, if objects must still accept this tyranny, it will be only in appearance, only to show all the more clearly to what extent they remain independent and alien.

As for the novel's characters, they may in themselves be rich with multiple interpretations; they may, according to the preoccupations of each author, give rise to all kinds of commentaries—psychological, psychiatric, religious, or political, yet their indifference to these supposed riches will quickly be apparent. Whereas the traditional hero is constantly incited, cornered, and destroyed by these "interpretations" proposed by the author, and endlessly rejected into an immaterial and unstable *elsewhere*, always more remote and blurred, the future hero of the novel will remain, on the contrary, "there." It is the commentaries which will seek "elsewhere"; in the face of his irrefutable presence, they will appear useless, superfluous, even dishonest.

All this might seem very theoretical, very illusory, if something were not actually changing—changing totally, definitively—in our relationships with the universe. Which is why we glimpse an answer to the old ironic question, "Why now?" There is today, in fact, a new element that separates us—this time radically—from Balzac, as from Gide or Madame de la Fayette: it is the dismissal of the old myth of "depth."

We know that the whole literature of the novel was based on this myth, and on it alone. The traditional role of the writer consisted in excavating Nature, in burrowing deeper and deeper to reach some ever more intimate strata, in finally bringing to light some fragment of a disconcerting secret. Having descended into the abyss of human passions, he would send to the seemingly tranquil world (the one on the surface) triumphant messages describing the mysteries he had actually touched with his own hands. And the sacred dizziness that then seized the reader, far from causing him anguish or nausea, reassured him as to his power of domination over the world. There were chasms, certainly, but thanks to such valiant speliologists, their depths could be sounded.

It is not surprising, given these conditions, that the literary phenomenon par excellence has resided in this one word, so all-inclusive and unique, which attempts to summon up all the inner qualities, the hidden *soul* of things. *Profundity* has functioned like a trap in which the writer captured the universe in order to hand it over to society.

The revolution which has taken place is in proportion to the power of the old order. Not only do we no longer consider the world as our very own, our private property, designed according to our needs and readily domesticated, but we no longer believe in its "depth."

While essentialist conceptions of man were facing their destruction, the notion of "condition" replaced that of "nature," the *surface* of things ceased being the mask that concealed their "heart" (a door opening on the worst "beyonds" of metaphysics).

It is therefore the whole literary language that has to change, that is changing already. We witness from day to day the growing repugnance that people of greater awareness feel for words of a visceral, analogical, incantatory character. On the other hand, the visual or descriptive adjective—the word that contents itself with measuring, locating, limiting, defining—indicates a difficult but most likely direction for the novel of the future.

Translated by Richard Howard

Lawrence Ferlinghetti

►► Lawrence Ferlinghetti

from A CONEY ISLAND OF THE MIND

3

The poet's eye obscenely seeing
sees the surface of the round world
             with its drunk rooftops
             and wooden oiseaux on clotheslines
             and its clay males and females
             with hot legs and rosebud breasts
             in rollaway beds
and its trees full of mysteries
and its sunday parks and speechless statues
and its America
             with its ghost towns and empty Ellis Islands
and its surrealistic landscape of
                          mindless prairies
                          supermarket suburbs
                          steamheated cemeteries
                          cinerama holy days
                          and protesting cathedrals
a kissproof world of plastic toiletseats tampax and taxis
        drugged store cowboys and las vegas virgins
        disowned indians and cinemad matrons
        unroman senators and conscientious non-objectors
and all the other fatal shorn-up fragments
of the immigrant's dream come too true
        and mislaid
             among the sunbathers

6

They were putting up the statue
        of Saint Francis
    in front of the church
        of Saint Francis
             in the city of San Francisco
in a little side street
             just off the Avenue
                          where no birds sang
        and the sun was coming up on time
                                 in its usual fashion
                 and just beginning to shine
                          on the statue of Saint Francis
             where no birds sang
And a lot of old Italians
                    were standing all around
             in the little side street

just off the Avenue
watching the wily workers
who were hoisting up the statue
with a chain and a crane
and other implements
And a lot of young reporters
in button-down clothes
were taking down the words
of one young priest
who was propping up the statue
with all his arguments
And all the while
while no birds sang
any Saint Francis Passion
and while the lookers kept looking
up at Saint Francis
with his arms outstretched
to the birds which weren't there
a very tall and very purely naked
young virgin
with very long and very straight
straw hair
and wearing only a very small bird's nest
in a very existential place
kept passing thru the crowd
all the while
and up and down the steps
in front of Saint Francis
her eyes downcast all the while
and singing to herself

7

What could she say to the fantastic foolybear
and what could she say to brother
and what could she say
to the cat with future feet
and what could she say to mother
after that time that she lay lush
among the lolly flowers
on that hot riverbank
where ferns fell away in the broken air
of the breath of her lover
and birds went mad
and threw themselves from trees
to taste still hot upon the ground
the spilled sperm seed

Dog

The dog trots freely in the street
and sees reality
and the things he sees
are bigger than himself
and the things he sees
are his reality
Drunks in doorways
Moons on trees
The dog trots freely thru the street
and the things he sees
are smaller than himself
Fish on newsprint
Ants in holes
Chickens in Chinatown windows
their heads a block away
The dog trots freely in the street
and the things he smells
smell something like himself
The dog trots freely in the street
past puddles and babies
cats and cigars
poolrooms and policemen
He doesn't hate cops
He merely has no use for them
and he goes past them
and past the dead cows hung up whole
in front of the San Francisco Meat Market
He would rather eat a tender cow
than a tough policeman
though either might do
And he goes past the Romeo Ravioli Factory
and past Coit's Tower
and past Congressman Doyle
He's afraid of Coit's Tower
but he's not afraid of Congressman Doyle
although what he hears is very discouraging
very depressing
very absurd
to a sad young dog like himself
to a serious dog like himself
But he has his own free world to live in
His own fleas to eat

He will not be muzzled
Congressman Doyle is just another
fire hydrant
to him
The dog trots freely in the street
and has his own dog's life to live
and to think about
and to reflect upon
touching and tasting and testing every thing
investigating everything
without benefit of perjury
a real realist
with a real tale to tell
and a real tail to tell it with
a real live
                barking
                        democratic dog
engaged in real
                free enterprise
with something to say
                        about ontology
something to say
                about reality
                        and how to see it
                                and how to hear it
with his head cocked sideways
                at streetcorners
as if he is just about to have
                his picture taken
                        for Victor Records
                listening for
                        His Master's Voice
        and looking
                like a living questionmark
                        into the
                        great gramophone
                        of puzzling existence
with its wondrous hollow horn
        which always seems
        just about to spout forth
                some Victorious answer
                to everything

►► Kenneth Rexroth

Noretorp-Noretsyh

Rainy, smoky Fall, clouds tower
In the brilliant Pacific sky.
In Golden Gate Park, the peacocks
Scream, wandering through falling leaves.
In clotting night, in smoking dark,
The Kronstadt sailors are marching
Through the streets of Budapest. The stones
Of the barricades rise up and shiver
Into form. They take the shapes
Of the peasant armies of Makhno.
The streets are lit with torches.
The gasoline drenched bodies
Of the Solovetsky anarchists
Burn at every street corner.
Kropotkin's starved corpse is borne
In state past the offices
Of the cowering bureaucrats.
In all the Politisolators
Of Siberia the partisan dead are enlisting.
Berneri, Andreas Nin,
Are coming from Spain with a legion.
Carlo Tresca is crossing
The Atlantic with the Berkman Brigade.
Bukharin has joined the Emergency
Economic Council. Twenty million
Dead Ukrainian peasants are sending wheat.
Julia Poyntz is organizing American nurses.
Gorky has written a minifesto
"To the Intellectuals of the World!"
Mayakofsky and Essenin
Have collaborated on an ode,
"Let *Them* Commit Suicide."
In the Hungarian night
All the dead are speaking with one voice,
As we bicycle through the green
And sunspotted Californian
November. I can hear that voice
Clearer than the cry of the peacocks,
In the falling afternoon.
Like painted wings, the color
Of all the leaves of Autumn,
The circular tie-dyed skirt
I made for you flares out in the wind,
Over your incomparable thighs.
Oh splendid butterfly of my imagination,
Flying into reality more real
Than all imagination, the evil
Of the world covets your living flesh.

►► Robert Duncan

This Place, Rumord to Have Been Sodom . . .

This place, rumord to have been Sodom, might have
    been.
Certainly these ashes might have been pleasures.
Pilgrims on their way toward the Holy Places remark
this place. Plain as the nose on your face
these mounds are palaces. This was once a city
among men, a gathering together of spirit.
It was measured by the Lord and found wanting.

It was measured by the Lord and found wanting,
destroyd by the angels that inhabit longing.
Surely this is Great Sodom where such cries
as if men were birds flying up from the swamp

ring in our ears, where such fears that were once
desires walk, almost spectacular,
stalking the desolate circles, red-eyed.

This place rumord to have been a City surely was,
separated from us by the hand of the Lord.
The devout have laid out gardens in the desert,
drawn water from springs where the light was
    blighted.
How tenderly they must attend these friendships
or all is lost. All *is* lost.
Only the faithful hold this place green.

Only the faithful hold this place green,
where the crown of fiery thorns descends.
Men that once lusted grow listless. A spirit

wrappd in a cloud, ashes more than ashes,
fire more than fire, ascends.
Only these new friends gather joyous here,
where the world like Great Sodom lies under fear.

The world like Great Sodom lies under love
and knows not the hand of the Lord that moves.
This the friends teach where such cries
as if men were birds fly up from the crowds
gatherd and howling in the heat of the sun.
In the Lord Whom the friends have named at last
    Love
the Images and Love of the friends never dies.

This place rumord to have been Sodom is blessd in
    the Lord's eyes.

▶▶ **Brother Antoninus, O. P.**

Annul in Me My Manhood

"The Lord gives these favors far more to women than to men;
I have heard the saintly Fray Peter of Alcantara say that, and
I have observed it myself. He would say that women made
much more progress on this road than men, and gave excellent
reasons for this, which there is no point in my repeating here,
all in favor of women."   St. Teresa of Avila

Annul in me my manhood, Lord, and make
Me woman-sexed and weak
If by that total transformation
I might know Thee more.
What is the worth of my own sex
That the bold possessive instinct
Should but shoulder Thee aside?
What uselessness is housled in my loins,
To drive, drive, the rampant pride of life,
When what is needful is a hushed quiescence?
"The soul is feminine to God,"
And hangs on impregnation,
Fertile influxing Grace. But how achieve
The elemental lapse of that repose,
That watchful, all-abiding silence of the soul,

In which the Lover enters to His own,
Yielding Himself to her, and her alone?
How may a man assume that hiddenness of heart
Being male, all masculine and male,
Blunt with male hunger? Make me then
Girl-hearted, virgin-souled, woman-docile, maiden-
    meek;
Cancel in me the rude compulsive tide
That like an angry river surges through,
Flouts off Thy soft lip-touches, froth-blinds
The soul-gaze from its very great delight,
Out-bawls the rare celestial melody.
Restless I churn. The use of sex is union,
Union alone. Here it but cleaves,
Makes man the futile ape of God, all ape
And no bride, usurps the energizing role, inverts;
And in that wrenched inversion caught
Draws off the needer from his never-ending need, di-
    verts
The seeker from the Sought.

Clement Greenberg

Jackson Pollock

Jackson Pollock was born on January 28, 1912, in Cody, Wyoming, the youngest of five sons of Le Roy and Stella (née McClure) Pollock. His father, who was first a farmer and then a surveyor, had been born Le Roy McCoy, but took the name of Pollock from the family by which he was adopted as a child. (He died in 1933.) In 1915 the Pollocks moved to Arizona, and from there, in 1918, to Northern California, then back to Arizona in 1923, and finally to Southern California in 1925.

Pollock became interested in art during adolescence, following the example of his oldest brother, Charles, a painter who now teaches at Michigan State College. He studied art at Manual Arts High School in Los Angeles (where one of his classmates was Philip Guston) with the intention of becoming a sculptor but soon changed to painting. (Sculpture haunted him to his last days, though he made but few and desultory attempts at it in his maturity.) Leaving high school without graduating, Pollock came to New York in 1929 to study under Thomas Benton at the Art Students League, where he continued until 1931. He made several trips back to the West before 1935, but from then on lived more or

Jackson Pollock
Photo by Hans Namuth

less permanently in New York. From 1938 to 1942 he was employed on the Federal Art Project as an easel painter.

Pollock's work was first seen by the New York public in 1940, in a group show of French and American paintings organized by John Graham and held at the McMillan Gallery. Among the other Americans included were Willem de Kooning and Leonore (Lee) Krasner, a former student of Hans Hofmann's. She first met Pollock on this occasion, and they were married in 1944, but even before their marriage her eye and judgment had become important to his art, and continued to remain so.

In 1943 Pollock's work caught the attention of Peggy Guggenheim and her associate, the late Howard Putzel, and in November of the same year his first one-man show was held at their Art of This Century Gallery on West 57th Street. Miss Guggenheim's and Putzel's confidence in him showed itself in the form of a contract for his production that was renewed annually until the end of 1947, in which year Miss Guggenheim closed her gallery and returned to Europe. In 1946 the Pollocks were able to move out to Springs, near East Hampton on Long Island, and buy a house there.

He had a one-man show every year between 1943 and 1953: at Art of This Century until 1947; at the Betty Parsons Gallery from 1948 to 1951; and at the Janis Gallery in 1952 and 1953. His first retrospective was put on at Bennington and Williams colleges in 1952, his second at the Janis Gallery in 1954, and his third in 1957, after his death, at the Museum of Modern Art. A fourth retrospective, organized by the Museum of Modern Art, was presented at the 1957 Bienal in São Paulo, Brazil, and is now traveling in Europe. His first one-man show in Europe was held in Paris in 1952 at the Galerie Michel Tapié, Studio Paul Facchetti, and the same works were shown in the following year at the Kunsthaus in Zurich. Although the Museum of Modern Art and the San Francisco Museum of Art acquired Pollock's work early on, his first sales in appreciable quantity came only in 1949 and 1950. Another lean period followed during which purchases by Alfonso Ossorio, a fellow-painter, helped ease an otherwise trying situation, and it is only since 1952 or 1953 that Pollocks have been in steady demand.

Pollock produced relatively little during the last three years of his life. On the night of August 11, 1956, he was killed in an automobile accident. He was buried in Springs cemetery in accordance with a wish he had expressed some time before.

Jackson Pollock's studio
Photo by Hans Namuth

►► Patsy Southgate

A Very Important Lady

There was nothing in the house that Lilly could call her own. Ever since they had come East it had been that way. She had been unable to make so much as a fingerprint anywhere, and all the traces of her existence—a faint ring in the bathtub, powder spilled along the floor—were wiped away by the servants as soon as she left the room. Even her own clothes, leaning against each other in her closet, did not hold the shape of her, in no way seemed to stand for her. They were, like everything else now, his. She had become a little anxious lately, looking about her for a sign to tell that she still lived there.

"I should be home about six," Edward was saying, snapping shut his brief case, "but I shall have to be at my desk until dinner time. So will you see to it that a decent bottle of wine is chilled. Nothing too unusual, I should think." He was putting on his hat, the leather band sticking to his forehead in the heat, now his coat, his arms plunging into their sleeves. Lilly tried to listen, alarmed at how much like a fox he always looked in his hat. "I've asked the Julian Brills for eight o'clock, I think Julian could be helpful in Washington. So don't forget to tell Marie. And Lilly," he was smiling at her under his mustache, "do try and get at your checkbook today." The sun glinted on his teeth as he turned, and her "All right, Edward" was demolished in the crash of the wrought-iron door. After his steps rapping out under the archway had ended, the house was quiet.

Lilly stood like a little girl left alone. She was a woman of fifty lost in flesh which hung as heavily on her, when she moved, as an enormous snowsuit. She knew how unhealthy it was. Statistics about strained hearts and brief life spans always made her tremble with the urgency of cutting down, and starting way back somewhere with primordial bone and muscle. And she saw how ugly it was, hating her fat with a fury that often made her want to take a knife to it. She was aware, for example, that she looked each morning, standing in the marble hall, like a scrubwoman rigged out in the negligee of the lady of the house, monstrous in her peach chiffon. But she couldn't stop eating to save her soul.

It always surprised her to find her old self again, as she did now, in the early sunlight which glowed through the leaves and petals in the flower room. She was so much better already. This time, after Edward had left, it had taken only a few moments, and a short walk down the hall away from the front door. Here, among the curly vines and birds in their lacy cages, she almost felt at home. She almost lost a hundred pounds and had her hair redone. And although she knew it was silly, she could find her voice again when talking to the birds.

"You won't believe this," she told a small green parrot, "but I used to be beautiful when I was young. Even Edward thought so. And I was a dancer, too. When I was living in Wichita I studied all the ballets. *Sleeping Beauty*, and *Scheherazade*, I can remember them all so well. The music would take me up in its arms and I would move with it, as though I were going through a great palace where I could go in all the rooms. I could be everything it told me. It was the most marvelous thing!" She gave the parrot a little smile, he turning his head way low and around to peer at her. In the flower room all the life was so real: the standing stems, the gesturing flowers and the small thud of birds hopping in their private way from perch to perch. It is a nice room, Lilly thought, to find yourself in, with all your friends around you. "You sweetheart, you're such a plucky little red flower," she whispered to the first one of summer on a rose-geranium plant. "And you have very warm feet," she said to the elderly canary who could still get out of his cage and sit on her finger. "And you, you are greedy and disgusting," she told a huge rubber plant in the corner which had the habit of leaning way out across the window and hogging all the sunlight. "I will have to chop you down, someday."

But now I must go and tell John about the wine, she remembered. And do all the other things which I can't seem to think of now, but I will think of them in time.

Telling John things Edward had told her to tell him frightened Lilly, so she always did it first. John had been the butler for twelve years, and during that time all the towers of plates and rows of goblets in the pantry had become his. He dealt them out for dinner parties, selecting carefully for each occasion, and flanked them with silver from the dark chests, laying them on a lace or linen cloth. When everyone had left the table he gathered them back, washed and dried them knowingly, and returned them to their proper places. In the beginning Lilly used to say, Let's have the flowered plates with gold edges, or, I love the ones with midnight blue around them, John. But John would draw himself up into such a monument of horror, looking down at her with bulging eyes, that Lilly would apologize, and retreat from his domain.

She gathered her peach collar up around her throat, and moved uncertainly through the black and white hallway, through the Louis Quinze living room, across the Turkish rug in the dining room, coming to a halt behind the screen in front of the pantry door.

"You know," she told a lady in blue who was sitting on a bench on the screen, "When I was a little girl the circus only came to town once a year. We would all go down to the railroad tracks to watch them unload the animals. I always liked the camel best." Then she pushed open the door.

John was drying the breakfast dishes, his hands pink from the hot water, his dignity calm in rolled-up sleeves and an apron. Lilly noticed a chocolate mole on his forearm, hairy and big as a quarter, which she had never seen before, but he didn't try to cover it up. She couldn't imagine him ever being embarrassed, or laughing, or spilling coffee on his shirt and getting angry at himself. She raised her head to look at him squarely, which was the way to give orders to servants, and her heart sank at his patient expression.

"Mr. Hillman asked me to tell you," she began, while his ripe-olive eyes opened wider and wider, "that he would like a bottle of wine chilled for dinner." She wished she could stop her own eyes from widening in response to his, but it always happened. "Nothing too unusual, he thinks." They seemed to balloon out of her head, and her mouth felt dry. "Please," she added, lost now in his diluent stare. His towel began to circle around his plate as he said, with great resonance, "Yes indeed, madame." He blinked, and turned again to his dishwater.

"Thank you, John." Lilly backed out of the heavy door. When she let it go, it sucked itself back into its eternal alignment with the pantry walls.

"Dear me," she said to herself, "he ought to have that mole removed. Moles can get out of hand, and be dangerous. And I still say, he does have the worst habit with his eyes, even though Edward doesn't see it. Sort of queer, I think. I wonder if he used to be a hypnotist. I wonder if he does it to everybody, or if it's just me. Probably just me, since almost everyone seems to scare me these days, even Edward. I just can't seem to talk to anyone, any more, without wanting to run for my life. It's because I am so fat,

like a giant mushroom, and I repel everybody. I can feel them being repelled, and I don't blame them a bit. Not a bit. I will tell Marie to give me only celery for lunch, just two stalks, and a cup of consommé, and perhaps one of her almond cookies for dessert." Her short, peach form trudged back through the dining room, traveling across a Turkish wilderness woven, a hundred years ago, by dark untrustworthy hands in a place where she had never been.

Her breath came faster as she started up the stairs, and tiny beads of sweat formed across her upper lip. She was thinking now of the moment when, back in her own room, she would press the ivory button at her bedside and in some labyrinthian miraculous way her signal would ring near Marie, in the kitchen.

"Marie will hear me," she said, settling back onto her bed and crossing her ankles prettily. She still had pretty ankles. "She'll come up to me, and we'll have one of our long discussions." Lilly smiled at her door around which Marie would appear earnestly, unfailingly, to talk about food. Her steps were coming now.

"O Marie, here you are at last!"

"Ah yes, madame. It is not so easy for me to climb the stairs on a day like this. I am no longer so young, and in such a hot weather, I assure you, it is only for madame I make the effort."

"I know, Marie, I know," said Lilly, filled with sympathy and with the breath of delight that always came with it. Once she had said to Edward, "Marie and I understand each other perfectly. It's really quite remarkable, the understanding we have." And Edward had replied, "Why, not at all. It's very simple. Marie knows an easy job when she sees one, that's what she understands about you. And you, you find you have a deep feeling for a cook. It's not at all surprising, really." Lilly had been hurt, and had even cried a little as she used to in the old days when he teased her like that. But somehow her bond with Marie had survived, secretly, since she never mentioned it to Edward again, until it had become the happiest factor in her life. Out of the blur of unapproachable faces, Marie's would appear by her bedside, a round reassuring expanse with nothing in it to fear. The mouth could never say polite things which were untrue, and the eyebrows were silky and serene. It was the kind of face, Lilly felt, that she would like to have at her deathbed. Often she had wanted to ask, "Marie, what do you really think of me? Am I really hopeless?" certain that Marie's answer would be the most valuable of all.

"Madame must be careful not to catch cold on such a hot day," she was saying now in her brassy voice. "My kitchen, I tell you right now, it is no place for cooking. It is a big steam in there, like the breath of a mad dog, I give you my word." Her blue eyes were fierce at the outrage of it.

"I know, Marie," Lilly smiled, "it's perfectly dreadful. I will ask Mr. Hillman again about getting you an air conditioner, but I've asked him twice already, and he hasn't remembered." She stopped, caught by a dire and self-pitying dread which had crossed her mind before. "Why does he always forget the few things I think would be nice?" she asked, not daring to look up. "Sometimes, Marie, I hate to say this, but sometimes I think he does it on purpose, just to hurt me. Then I feel that he really hates me, and wishes that I would go out of his life, somehow."

"Ah, no, it is not so serious as this. Surely monsieur would not do this terrible thing, no. He is not a cruel man, madame, and you must not think these sinful thoughts. Besides, monsieur is a person of importance, who is in the business of making many big decisions. We must not worry too much with air conditioning such a man as this."

"But Marie, he won't remember. I just know he won't, and how will you breathe, this summer?"

"Then, madame, you have only to tell him a third time. Men always remember the third time, they are famous for this."

Lilly could have wept. It was so much more to her now than just a question of telling him a third time. She had had, she knew, a momentous last hope that Marie would say, "Ah madame, monsieur is indeed very thoughtless, not only of me and whether I cannot breathe in my kitchen, but also of you, my poor friend, and whether you cannot breathe any more." But Marie had only told her what a criminal she had been to expect so much. She had made a kindly rummage through the evidence of Edward's days: four telephones, big decisions, the sense of unimpeachable importance—and a judgment in his favor. Of course she was right. Edward was not really cruel. And why should he remember her now anyway, when there was no longer anything about her worth remembering?

Marie took her pencil from the historical black structure of hair on top of her head and her notebook from her apron pocket. Turning the pages carefully today, she prepared to record what they would eat.

"Just now," she declared, "I have fallen in love with a fish. Please don't laugh at me, madame (Lilly had almost laughed, or almost cried, not knowing which). It has never happened to me before. I see him in the fishman's window on my way home from mass, and right away I say: God has put you here for Marie. He is a salmon, gorgeous animal. I will prepare him cold, *sauce verte, garni de concombres.* Following, a little *salade cresson, fromages.* And to finish, my *Bavaroise au café.* No? It will be unforgettable!"

Since her mind had wandered off, unaccountably, after the fish, Lilly said nothing. Was it cucumbers they were having? She could still see the cucumber vines meandering all over the compost heap out back in the far Middle Western childhood which kept popping into her mind. How funny cucumber leaves had been, waving and flopping like summer hats on top of all that cow manure. She uncrossed her ankles for her thighs were getting sweaty. Then all at once she saw herself again, as she used to be, running all over in her floppy summer hats, only a little plump and so eager to be happy. Once Jimmy Thorne had said that her smile made him weak in the knees. And all her friends agreed that she was the prettiest. She thought she would probably have to cry, after Marie had left.

"Then, madame, we have decided everything. It only remains to telephone my fish. But my poor madame, why do you look so unhappy? Tell Marie, I beg you, please do not look like this!"

Lilly didn't know why. She and Edward had met beside a Kansas swimming pool, long ago. Their feet had touched underwater. They had danced together. Right away he had been her god, and every time he smiled at her, she had felt blessed. Everyone said then how lucky she was, that Edward had a brilliant mind and would get to the top before long. They had married in October, she all in white and biting her lip to hold back her tears of joy. Now they were like two enemies standing over a friend's coffin in a huge house. Once the burial was over, they would never meet again. Lilly saw herself in the coffin. No one had dared put the lid on, yet, but it would have to be done soon. O God, please help me, Lilly thought, not having thought of Him for ages.

Marie was still waiting. Dear Marie, who had climbed all the way up the stairs in the heat.

"Marie," she finally asked, "what do you think I should wear tonight? I want to look my best, my very best, in honor of your fish."

"If you please," Marie said quickly, "the lavender dress of lace that shows a little of the décolleté. This is the one to wear tonight. In this dress madame looks like a very important lady. Very very distinguished."

"Do you really think so?"

"Madame, there is no question." Lilly couldn't quite trust, to this extent, the grave face above her.

But she knew she loved it, and it had the power to make her feel oddly reckless, at times.

"And madame, to stay in this house all the time is very bad. Today you must go out a little, this afternoon."

"Well, I might, at that." Lilly nodded.

"Of course. One must have courage. Even in this terrible weather one must maintain oneself. So madame, you will do this, no? And I must go now, and see what all those crazy idiots have been doing to my kitchen. The minute I turn my back, they are all sitting down smoking cigarettes and making me sick. Good-bye for now, my dear madame."

"Good-bye."

Marie left the room, her whispering espadrilles going away through the carpeted hallways in the front of the house to the closed dividing doorway. Now, Lilly thought, she will go down the back hall that smells of linoleum, down the back stairs that are narrow, down into the kitchen. She will burst in and shout commands, her voice like a trumpet calling her maids and grocery boys and cats and pots and pieces of meat. There the fan sucks out the stale air, and the chairs have been sat in for years. Even the colors have meaning: new peas' green, radiant white of onions, blood of strawberries. The shaping and peeling and cutting and throwing away is an old habit.

I would like to live in the kitchen, Lilly thought. I would shell the peas for her, and rattle them into the pot like little bursts of machine-gun fire!

She grunted, getting off the bed, and started for the bathroom. She would run the water a long time, as she did every day, wondering about joining the Red Cross, or perhaps going to an art gallery. Nobody notices you in the Red Cross, she would tell herself. And paintings don't care what you look like. "If only I were thin," she would sigh. "I must ask Marie to read *Losing Weight and Loving It*, I'm sure she would help me with the rules."

When Lilly at last got at her checkbook it was almost five o'clock, the time of day when she wished most that she had children. First she would take them into the flower room to see the birds, then they would sit on the sofa in the library and she would read to them. She would probably read *The Little Red Hen*, making all the noises for the animals so that they would laugh. Who will help me plant the wheat? asked the Little Red Hen. Not I, said the fox. Not I, said the duck. Not I, said the pig. Then I'll do it myself, said the Little Red Hen, and she did. Lilly stared on at her checkbook, trying to find some sort of sense in the leaning towers of numbers. But she couldn't seem to concentrate today. Edward would

be home any minute now. He might come up to question her about it. Of course she would have to confess, since she had never told a lie to him in her life.

An hour later, when the checkbook had been put away and the cool air was unfurling in the evening trees outside, Lilly remembered, rather dizzily, what Marie had said. "In the lavender dress of lace, that shows a little of the décolleté, madame looks like a very important lady." Not knowing any reason, except that it was time for one last desperate attempt, Lilly decided to believe her. She decided to be, that night, a very important lady. It was the only way left of entering the living room, and besides, Marie had never told her anything that could be doubted. So tonight she would sit up straight on the needle-point sofa, smiling and talking to Julian and Helena, and asking John to pass around the peanuts once again, please. To Edward she would say how much checkbooks bored her, and would he be kind enough to have his secretary tend to hers in the future. And to them all, at the dinner table, she would relate the story of Marie's love affair with a fish, and in such a witty way that they all would laugh, even Edward, while she shrugged, murmuring lightly about what amusing things cooks came up with these days.

The improbability and daring of Lilly's decision alarmed her more than she realized. It had only made her lightheaded at first, but when she began to dress her hands were shaking, and the little beads of perspiration had appeared again along her lip. Dressing was a process that made her furious, an endless battle between her will and her resisting flesh. Bending over to pull on her stockings, she could scarcely control the desire to unhook her corset forever and just give up. But the decision had been made, and it was essential not to turn back now. She stepped into her pointed shoes.

When she had finished she went to stand before the mirror. There she observed her yellow-gray hair in its frizzy halo, and the low scoop of lace revealing the roots of her pent-up bosom with the crease between, like buttocks. She saw the enormity of her waistline and hips, and the flesh which hung from her arms like extra breasts. She saw herself with a final clarity, knowing that she was as deeply absurd as ever in her lavender best. But she had her decision firmly in hand, like a sword, and the heedless fluttering butterfly hope from Marie.

It was eight o'clock. Edward would have finished bathing, and would be waiting for her. The cocktail tray would have been brought in. The row of bottles would be standing behind the silver bowls of lemon

peel and olives. She would go down now, and pause in the doorway to smile her good evening. With slow tread, like a precarious queen, she started off.

When she got to the living room, Edward was talking on the telephone in the library, so she waited, standing up, near the piano. Then he came in carrying the evening paper. "They're fifteen minutes late," he said, not looking at her. "Julian ought to know better. I could do a lot for him, if he showed the proper spirit." He sat in his chair by the fire. She could only see the top of his head which was bald except for a few well-trained hairs combed straight across it. He would be frowning, she knew, while he read, his mouth slightly puckered as though he were whistling a perpetually inaudible little tune.

"Edward," she called to him across the intervening furniture. "I would like to talk to you a minute."

"Yes?"

"It's about my checkbook."

He turned a page of the paper and rattled it into place.

"I wish you would have your secretary do it for me in the future, please."

"My secretary? Why on earth should she do it? Can't you figure it out for yourself?"

"Well, I suppose I could. But it's begun to bore me so."

"Bore you, Lilly? How strange. What did you expect it to do?"

"Nothing. I don't know." Lilly pulled at the loose skin on her elbow.

"Checkbooks have bored people for years, Lilly, ever since they were invented. And any time you have something better to do, you come and tell me, and I'll give it to my secretary. But it doesn't seem to me that your life is busy enough, at this point, to warrant taking such a step."

Then the doorbell rang. Edward said, "Ah!" and strode into the front hall to greet the Brills. While he was gone, Lilly edged over to the sideboard. She popped four of Marie's hot cheese canapés into her mouth. Then she rearranged the parsley on the doily so that nothing showed.

Julian and Helena had never been as charming as they were that night. Helena sat before an open French door where her flickering face and white dress were perfect against the troubled leaves and darkness outside. It was always a shock to hear her voice, for she looked as though she might have come out of a convent for just one evening, and would have only gentle opinions, or at worst, might make a starlit vow of adoration to a handsome man far off in a corner of the garden. But Helena was apt to throw back her head and make a surprisingly noisy attack upon the position of the government in Egypt. Lilly thought the men must wish she would just sit quietly so they could look at her, but they seemed delighted to listen and even accorded her the respect they usually reserved for each other.

Everyone was talking now, Helena's laughter ringing in, Julian mostly clearing his throat, Edward making his points, licking his lips between, pronouncing obscurely the names of obscure Moslem chieftains. Lilly sat straight still in her corner of the sofa, smiling from one to the other. She said nothing because she never read the front part of the paper any more, only the column where a lady answered people's problems, and articles about dogs finding lost babies. Edward would never talk about her parts of the paper, unless there were an exceptionally brutal murder which he would retell, with great relish, as a joke. And everyone would laugh.

Lilly had hardly finished her third drink when John appeared again and took her glass. She couldn't hear the others very clearly any more, so she thought about John's mole bristling darkly under his white coat, and wondered whether his wife had minded it, if he had had a wife. When he brought her drink back, she noticed with some resentment that he had forgotten the cherry. Her shoes had begun to hurt, by now.

"I do think all this talk about foreign affairs gets to be an awful bore, don't you, Lilly?" Julian was leaning toward her, his jaw thrust out in a rather menacing way. "If they want to blow up the pyramids, we'll just get Edward here to build us some more, won't we?" Lilly nodded, and drank another large swallow to give her time to think of something to say. But her mind was blank as a piece of glass, and her only sensation a cold one, ice bumping against her upper lip. She could see Edward dimly, just beyond Julian's ear. He gestured in her direction and said something to Helena which she could not hear. Then he and Helena laughed.

Julian cleared his throat. "Tell me, Lilly," he went

on, "I haven't seen you in a long time. What have you been doing with yourself lately?"

"Well," Lilly looked down at her gigantic lavender lap. Through the small inward shattering in her head, she heard her voice saying, quite loudly, "Well, Julian, to tell you the truth, today I thought I would go to the Forty-ninth Street Gallery, so I did. I had a marvelous time, too. There were so many paintings there, so many new things." She had spilled some bourbon on her knee, and the stain was growing. She dabbed at it with a tiny paper napkin which said "Lillian and Edward" in green capital letters. Edward was looking at her now.

She stood up abruptly and raised her heavy arms until they were perpendicular to her body. The purple spots of underarm sweat were crescent moons as she turned her palms upwards and, looking at Edward, she said very quietly in the silence, "The most beautiful painting of all is of a Madonna and Child. The Child is looking straight ahead, and so is the Madonna. They are both looking at me, all the time, even now. Because I am a very important lady, in my way."

On her way out of the living room she knocked against an end table, almost turning it over. When she got to the flower room there was hardly any light, but she could still make out her friends. "You are very sleepy, I know," she whispered to them, "and trembling and wobbling a bit the way you always do at night. But I came to say good-bye to you, because I am going away. I am going out to walk in the street." She could see clearly now how they all were shivering in the dark, so she turned around slowly to comfort them. "Dear thing," she said to the little red flower, the first one on the rose-geranium plant, "I will take you with me, if you want to come."

She picked it and stuck its stem into the lace at her bosom, where it nodded its head as she moved with unsteady grandeur out across the hallway.

Edward and the Brills were talking in low voices in the living room. They probably think I'm drunk, Lilly said to herself. She tried to close the front door quietly, but it always gave a clang, no matter how careful you were. As she reached the archway she heard Edward calling behind her, "Lilly, come back this minute. This is insane. Lilly! Where do you think you're going?" She began to run, then, with the preposterous haste of a frightened cow, until she was out of sight beyond the street light at the corner.

Marie found her the next morning when she came down to start the coffee. Her mistress must have come in, after everyone had gone to bed, by the kitchen door, and gotten only halfway up the back stairs before she collapsed. Marie summoned John, and between them they managed to haul her the rest of the way up and lift her into her bed. But they were unable to rouse her, though Marie put cold washcloths on her forehead.

Edward had to fly to California that morning. He called the doctor, and looked in on Lilly before he left. As he closed her door, he thought once more how lucky it was that only the Brills had been there. He would telephone Julian from Los Angeles and propose the business in Washington he had in mind.

►► Allen Ginsberg

Howl

for Carl Solomon

I

I saw the best minds of my generation destroyed by madness, starving hysterical naked,
dragging themselves through the negro streets at dawn looking for an angry fix,
angelheaded hipsters burning for the ancient heavenly connection to the starry dynamo in the
        machinery of night,
who poverty and tatters and hollow-eyed and high sat up smoking in the supernatural darkness of
        cold-water flats floating across the tops of cities contemplating jazz,
who bared their brains to Heaven under the El and saw Mohammedan angels staggering on
        tenement roofs illuminated,
who passed through universities with radiant cool eyes hallucinating Arkansas and Blake-light
        tragedy among the scholars of war,
who were expelled from the academies for crazy & publishing obscene odes on the windows of
        the skull,
who cowered in unshaven rooms in underwear, burning their money in wastebaskets and listening
        to the Terror through the wall,
who got busted in their pubic beards returning through Laredo with a belt of marijuana for New
        York,
who ate fire in paint hotels or drank turpentine in Paradise Alley, death, or purgatoried their torsos
        night after night

with dreams, with drugs, with waking nightmares, alcohol and cock and endless balls,

incomparable blind streets of shuddering cloud and lightning in the mind leaping toward poles of Canada & Paterson, illuminating all the motionless world of Time between,

Peyote solidities of halls, backyard green tree cemetery dawns, wine drunkenness over the rooftops, storefront boroughs of teahead joyride neon blinking traffic light, sun and moon and tree vibrations in the roaring winter dusks of Brooklyn, ashcan rantings and kind king light of mind,

who chained themselves to subways for the endless ride from Battery to holy Bronx on benzedrine until the noise of wheels and children brought them down shuddering mouth-wracked and battered bleak of brain all drained of brilliance in the drear light of Zoo,

who sank all night in submarine light of Bickford's floated out and sat through the stale beer afternoon in desolate Fugazzi's, listening to the crack of doom on the hydrogen jukebox,

Who talked continuously seventy hours from park to pad to bar to Bellevue to museum to the Brooklyn Bridge,

a lost battalion of platonic conversationalists jumping down the stoops off fire escapes off windowsills off Empire State out of the moon,

yacketayakking screaming vomiting whispering facts and memories and anecdotes and eyeball kicks and shocks of hospitals and jails and wars,

whole intellects disgorged in total recall for seven days and nights with brilliant eyes, meat for the Synagogue cast on the pavement,

who vanished into nowhere Zen New Jersey leaving a trail of ambiguous picture postcards of Atlantic City Hall,

suffering Eastern sweats and Tangerian bone-grindings and migraines of China under junk-withdrawal in Newark's bleak furnished room,

who wandered around and around at midnight in the railroad yard wondering where to go, and went, leaving no broken hearts,

who lit cigarettes in boxcars boxcars boxcars racketing through the snow toward lonesome farms in grandfather night,

who studied Plotinus Poe St. John of the Cross telepathy and bop kabbala because the cosmos instinctively vibrated at their feet in Kansas,

who loned it through the streets of Idaho seeking visionary indian angels who were visionary indian angels,

who thought they were only mad when Baltimore gleamed in supernatural ecstasy,

who jumped in limousines with the Chinaman of Oklahoma on the impulse of winter midnight streetlight small-town rain,

who lounged hungry and lonesome through Houston seeking jazz or sex or soup, and followed the brilliant Spaniard to converse about America and Eternity, a hopeless task, and so took ship to Africa,

who disappeared into the volcanoes of Mexico leaving behind nothing but the shadow of dungarees and the lava and ash of poetry scattered in fireplace Chicago,

who reappeared on the West Coast investigating the F.B.I. in beards and shorts with big pacifist eyes sexy in their dark skin passing out incomprehensible leaflets,

who burned cigarette holes in their arms protesting the narcotic tobacco haze of Capitalism,

who distributed Supercommunist pamphlets in Union Square weeping and undressing while the sirens of Los Alamos wailed them down, and wailed down Wall, and the Staten Island ferry also wailed,

who broke down crying in white gymnasiums naked and trembling before the machinery of other skeletons,

who bit detectives in the neck and shrieked with delight in policecars for committing no crime but their own wild cooking pederasty and intoxication,

who howled on their knees in the subway and were dragged off the roof waving genitals and manuscripts,

who let themselves be fucked in the ass by saintly motorcyclists, and screamed with joy,

who blew and were blown by those human seraphim, the sailors, caresses of Atlantic and
Caribbean love,

who balled in the morning in the evenings in rosegardens and the grass of public parks and
cemeteries scattering their semen freely to whomever come who may,

who hiccupped endlessly trying to giggle but wound up with a sob behind a partition in a Turkish
Bath when the blond & naked angel came to pierce them with a sword,

who lost their loveboys to the three old shrews of fate the one-eyed shrew of the heterosexual dollar
the one-eyed shrew that winks out of the womb and the one-eyed shrew that does nothing
but sit on her ass and snip the intellectual golden threads of the craftsman's loom,

who copulated ecstatic and insatiate with a bottle of beer a sweetheart a package of cigarettes a
candle and fell off the bed, and continued along the floor and down the hall and ended
fainting on the wall with a vision of ultimate cunt and come eluding the last gyzym of
consciousness,

who sweetened the snatches of a million girls trembling in the sunset, and were red eyed in the
morning but prepared to sweeten the snatch of the sunrise, flashing buttocks under barns
and naked in the lake,

who went out whoring through Colorado in myriad stolen night-cars, N.C., secret hero of these
poems, cocksman and Adonis of Denver—joy to the memory of his innumerable lays of
girls in empty lots & diner backyards, moviehouses, rickety rows on mountaintops in caves
or with gaunt waitresses in familiar roadside lonely petticoat upliftings & especially
secret gas-station solipsisms of johns, & hometown alleys too,

who faded out in vast sordid movies, were shifted in dreams, woke on a sudden Manhattan, and
picked themselves up out of basements hungover with heartless Tokay and horrors of
Third Avenue iron dreams & stumbled to unemployment offices,

who walked all night with their shoes full of blood on the snowbank docks waiting for a door in
the East River to open to a room full of steamheat and opium,

who created great suicidal dramas on the apartment cliff-banks of the Hudson under the wartime
blue floodlight of the moon & their heads shall be crowned with laurel in oblivion,

who ate the lamb stew of the imagination or digested the crab at the muddy bottom of the rivers
of Bowery,

who wept at the romance of the streets with their pushcarts full of onions and bad music,

who sat in boxes breathing in the darkness under the bridge, and rose up to build harpsichords in
their lofts,

who coughed on the sixth floor of Harlem crowned with flame under the tubercular sky
surrounded by orange crates of theology,

who scribbled all night rocking and rolling over lofty incantations which in the yellow morning
were stanzas of gibberish,

who cooked rotten animals lung heart feet tail borsht & tortillas dreaming of the pure vegetable
kingdom,

who plunged themselves under meat trucks looking for an egg,

who threw their watches off the roof to cast their ballot for Eternity outside of Time, & alarm
clocks fell on their heads every day for the next decade,

who cut their wrists three times successively unsuccessfully, gave up and were forced to open
antique stores where they thought they were growing old and cried,

who were burned alive in their innocent flannel suits on Madison Avenue amid blasts of leaden
verse & the tanked up clatter of the iron regiments of fashion & the nitroglycerine shrieks
of the fairies of advertising & the mustard gas of sinister intelligent editors, or were run
down by the drunken taxicabs of Absolute Reality.

who jumped off the Brooklyn Bridge this actually happened and walked away unknown and
forgotten into the ghostly daze of Chinatown soup alleyways & firetrucks, not even one
free beer,

who sang out of their windows in despair, fell out of the subway window, jumped in the filthy
Passaic, leaped on Negroes, cried all over the street, danced on broken wineglasses barefoot

smashed phonograph records of nostalgic European 1930's German jazz finished the
whiskey and threw up groaning into the bloody toilet, moans in their ears and the blast
of colossal steamwhistles,

who barreled down the highways of the past journeying to each other's hotrod-Golgotha jail-
solitude watch or Birmingham jazz incarnation,

who drove crosscountry seventy-two hours to find out if I had a vision or you had a vision or he
had a vision to find out Eternity,

who journeyed to Denver, who died in Denver, who came back to Denver & waited in vain, who
watched over Denver & brooded & loned in Denver and finally went away to find out
the Time, & now Denver is lonesome for her heroes,

who fell on their knees in hopeless cathedrals praying for each other's salvation and light and
breasts, until the soul illuminated its hair for a second,

who crashed through their minds in jail waiting for impossible criminals with golden heads and the
charm of reality in their hearts who sang sweet blues to Alcatraz,

who retired to Mexico to cultivate a habit, or Rocky Mount to tender Buddha or Tangiers to boys
or Southern Pacific to the black locomotive or Harvard to Narcissus to Woodlawn to the
daisychain or grave,

who demanded sanity trials accusing the radio of hypnotism & were left with their insanity & their
hands & a hung jury,

who threw potato salad at CCNY lecturers on Dadaism and subsequently presented themselves on
the granite steps of the madhouse with shaven heads and harlequin speech of suicide,
demanding instantaneous lobotomy,

and who were given instead the concrete void of insulin metrasol electricity hydrotherapy
psychotherapy occupational therapy pingpong & amnesia,

who in humorless protest overturned only one symbolic pingpong table, resting briefly in catatonia,

returning years later truly bald except for a wig of blood, and tears and fingers, to the visible
madman doom of the wards of the madtowns of the East,

Pilgrim State's Rockland's and Greystone's foetid halls, bickering with the echoes of the soul,
rocking and rolling in the midnight solitude-bench dolmen-realms of love, dream of life
a nightmare, bodies turned to stone as heavy as the moon,

with mother finally fucked, and the last fantastic book flung out of the tenement window, and
the last door closed at 4 AM and the last telephone slammed at the wall in reply and the
last furnished room emptied down to the last piece of mental furniture, a yellow paper
rose twisted on a wire hanger in the closet, and even that imaginary, nothing but a hopeful
little bit of hallucination—

ah, Carl, while you are not safe I am not safe, and now you're really in the total animal soup of
time—

and who therefore ran through the icy streets obsessed with a sudden flash of the alchemy of the use
of the ellipse the catalog the meter & the vibrating plane,

who dreamt and made incarnate gaps in Time & Space through images juxtaposed, and trapped
the archangel of the soul between 2 visual images and joined the elemental verbs and set
the noun and dash of consciousness together jumping with sensation of Pater Omnipotens
Aeterna Deus

to recreate the syntax and measure of poor human prose and stand before you speechless and
intelligent and shaking with shame, rejected yet confessing out the soul to conform to
the rhythm of thought in his naked and endless head,

the madman bum and angel beat in Time, unknown, yet putting down here what might be left to
say in time come after death,

and rose reincarnate in the ghostly clothes of jazz in the goldhorn shadow of the band and blew the
suffering of America's naked mind for love into an eli eli lamma lamma sabacthani
saxophone cry that shivered the cities down to the last radio

with the absolute heart of the poem of life butchered out of their own bodies good to eat a
thousand years.

II

What sphinx of cement and aluminum bashed open their skulls and ate up their brains and
        imagination?

Moloch! Solitude! Filth! Ugliness! Ashcans and unobtainable dollars! Children screaming under
        the stairways! Boys sobbing in armies! Old men weeping in the parks!

Moloch! Moloch! Nightmare of Moloch! Moloch the loveless! Mental Moloch! Moloch the heavy
        judger of men!

Moloch the incomprehensible prison! Moloch the crossbone soulless jailhouse and Congress of
        sorrows! Moloch whose buildings are judgment! Moloch the vast stone of war! Moloch
        the stunned governments!

Moloch whose mind is pure machinery! Moloch whose blood is running money! Moloch whose
        fingers are ten armies! Moloch whose breast is a cannibal dynamo! Moloch whose ear is
        a smoking tomb!

Moloch whose eyes are a thousand blind windows! Moloch whose skyscrapers stand in the long
        streets like endless Jehovahs! Moloch whose factories dream and croak in the fog!
        Moloch whose smokestacks and antennae crown the cities!

Moloch whose love is endless oil and stone! Moloch whose soul is electricity and banks. Moloch
        whose poverty is the specter of genius! Moloch whose fate is a cloud of sexless hydrogen!
        Moloch whose name is the Mind!

Moloch in whom I sit lonely! Moloch in whom I dream Angels! Crazy in Moloch! Cocksucker
        in Moloch! Lacklove and manless in Moloch!

Moloch who entered my soul early! Moloch in whom I am a consciousness without a body!
        Moloch who frightened me out of my natural ecstasy! Moloch whom I abandon!
        Wake up in Moloch! Light streaming out of the sky!

Moloch! Moloch! Robot apartments! invisible suburbs! skeleton treasuries! blind capitals! demonic
        industries! spectral nations! invincible madhouses! granite cocks! monstrous bombs!

They broke their backs lifting Moloch to Heaven! Pavements, trees, radios, tons! Lifting the city to
        Heaven which exists and is everywhere about us!

Visions! omens! hallucinations! miracles! ecstasies! gone down the American river!

Dreams! adorations! illuminations! religions! the whole boatload of sensitive bullshit!

Breakthrough! over the river! flips and crucifixions! gone down the flood! Highs! Epiphanies!
        Despairs! Ten years' animal screams and suicides! Minds! New loves! Mad generation!
        down on the rocks of Time!

Real holy laughter in the river! They saw it all! The wild eyes! the holy yells! They bade farewell!
        They jumped off the roof! to solitude! waving! carrying flowers! Down to the river! into
        the street!

III

Carl Solomon! I'm with you in Rockland
        where you're madder than I am
I'm with you in Rockland
        where you must feel very strange
I'm with you in Rockland
        where you imitate the shade of my mother
I'm with you in Rockland
        where you've murdered your twelve secretaries
I'm with you in Rockland
        where you laugh at this invisible humor
I'm with you in Rockland
        where we are great writers on the same dreadful typewriter
I'm with you in Rockland

where your condition has become serious and is reported on the radio
I'm with you in Rockland
where the faculties of the skull no longer admit the worms of the senses
I'm with you in Rockland
where you drink the tea of the breasts of the spinsters of Utica
I'm with you in Rockland
where you pun on the bodies of your nurses the harpies of the Bronx
I'm with you in Rockland
where you scream in a straitjacket that you're losing the game of the actual pingpong of the abyss
I'm with you in Rockland
where you bang on the catatonic piano the soul is innocent and immortal it should never die ungodly in an armed madhouse
I'm with you in Rockland
where fifty more shocks will never return your soul to its body again from its pilgrimage to a cross in the void
I'm with you in Rockland
where you accuse your doctors of insanity and plot the Hebrew socialist revolution against the fascist national Golgotha
I'm with you in Rockland
where you will split the heavens of Long Island and resurrect your living human Jesus from the superhuman tomb
I'm with you in Rockland
where there are twenty-five thousand mad comrades all together singing the final stanzas of the Internationale
I'm with you in Rockland
where we hug and kiss the United States under our bedsheets the United States that coughs all night and won't let us sleep
I'm with you in Rockland
where we wake up electrified out of the coma by our own souls' airplanes roaring over the roof they've come to drop angelic bombs the hospital illuminates itself   imaginary walls collapse   O skinny legions run outside   O starry-spangled shocks of mercy the eternal war is here   O victory forget your underwear we're free
I'm with you in Rockland
in my dreams you walk dripping from a sea-journey on the highway across America in tears to the door of my cottage in the Western night

►► Eugène Ionesco

The Photograph of the Colonel

One afternoon the municipal architect and I went to see the wealthy residential district: a suburb of white houses surrounded by gardens full of flowers and wide streets lined with trees. Shiny new cars stood before the entrances, the paths, and the gardens.

Bright sunlight flooded down from a blue sky. I took off my topcoat and carried it over my arm.

"In this part of town," my companion said to me, "the weather is always fine. The land commands a high price, and the villas are constructed of the best materials; only well-to-do people, the cheerful, the healthy, the likable, live here."

"So I see. Here," I pointed out, "the trees are already in leaf and the light is filtered, but not so much as to shade the façades of the houses, while in all the rest of the city the sky is as gray as an old woman's hair, frozen snow still clings to the edges of the sidewalks, and the wind blows cold. This morning it was freezing when I got up. How curious it is to find ourselves in the midst of spring here, as though we had suddenly been transported a thousand miles to the south. When you take a plane, you often have the feeling that you are witnessing the transfiguration of the world. And yet you'd have to go to the airfield and fly for at least two hours in order to see the landscape metamorphose itself into the Riviera, for instance. But here, we've done no more than take a short streetcar ride, and the trip, if you can even call it a trip, took place in the same places, if you'll permit me this little play on words, which, moreover, is unintentional, I assure you," I said with a smile which was both witty and constrained. "How do you account for it? Is this district more sheltered? But I don't see any hills around to protect it from bad weather? In any case, as everyone knows, hills don't turn away the clouds, nor do they protect us from the rain. Are there bright, warm currents of air coming from below or above? But if that were the case, surely we'd have heard of it. There's no wind, although the air smells fresh. It's very curious."

"It's an island, quite simply," the municipal architect replied, "an oasis, just as sometimes in the desert you see astonishing cities rise up in the midst of arid sand, covered with fresh roses and surrounded with fountains and rivers."

"Ah, yes, that's right. You mean the kind of cities we call 'mirages'!" I said, to show that I was not completely ignorant.

At that time we were strolling alongside a park which I noticed had a pool in its center. We walked for almost a mile and a half through the villas, private residences, gardens and flowers. The calm weather was perfect; relaxing—too much so, perhaps. It began to be disturbing.

"Why don't we see anyone in the streets?" I asked. "We're the only strollers out. No doubt it's the hour for lunch and all the people are at home. But why don't we hear laughter and the clinking of glasses? There's not a sound. All the windows seem to be closed!"

We had stopped before two buildings that appeared to have been abandoned before they were finished. There they stood half erected, white in the midst of the greenery, waiting for the builders.

"It is so pleasant here!" I said. "If I were rich—alas, I earn but little—I'd buy one of these lots. In a few days the house would be built and I'd no longer have to live among the unhappy, in that dirty suburb, on those factory streets darkened by winter, dust, or mud. Here, the air smells so good," I said, inhaling the soft yet potent air which intoxicated my lungs.

My companion knit his brows: "The police have suspended all construction in this area. It was a pointless regulation, for no one is buying these lots today, anyway. The residents of the district even want to move out. But they have no other place to live. If it weren't for that, they'd have all packed their bags by now. Perhaps with them it's also a point of honor not to flee. They prefer to remain hidden in their beautiful homes. They don't go out except in case of extreme necessity, and then in groups of ten or fifteen. Even so, there is still danger."

"You're joking! Why are you putting on this serious air? You're darkening the day; do you want to discourage me?"

"I'm not joking, I assure you."

I felt a sudden pain in my heart. Everything clouded over for me. The resplendent landscape, in which I had taken root, which had, all at once, become part of me or of which I had become part, detached itself, became completely exterior to me, was no longer anything but a landscape in a frame, an inanimate object. I felt myself alone, outside of everything, lost in a dead clarity.

"Explain yourself!" I implored. I who had looked forward to a pleasant outing! "I was so happy a few moments ago!"

We were retracing our steps, as it happened, toward the pool.

"This is the place," the municipal architect said. "Right here is where they find two or three drowned, every day."

"Drowned?"

"Come and see for yourself that I'm not exaggerating."

I followed him. From the edge of the pool, I could see that there was, in fact, the swollen corpse of an officer in the engineering corps, floating in the water, as well as that of a little boy of five or six years, rolled up inside his hoop, and still holding his rod in his clenched hand.

"There are three today," my guide murmured. "There's another," he pointed with his finger.

A red head, that I had taken, for a moment, to be aquatic vegetation, emerged from the depths, but remained caught beneath the marble rim of the pool.

"How horrible! It's a woman, I believe."

"Apparently," he said, shrugging his shoulders. "The other is a man, and there's a child. That's all we know."

"Maybe she's the mother of the little one. . . . How sad! Who did this?"

"The murderer. It's always the same person. They can't catch him."

"But our life is in danger. Let's get out of here," I cried.

"As long as you're with me you're not in danger. I am the municipal architect, a city functionary; and he doesn't attack the administration. When I retire, it will be a different matter, of course, but, for the present . . ."

"Let's get away from here, anyway," I said.

We walked away at a fast clip. I was in a hurry to leave the wealthy residential district. The rich are not always happy, I thought, experiencing an indescribable distress. I suddenly felt dead tired, sick at heart, that existence was in vain. "What good is anything," I said to myself, "if this is what we end up with?"

"You surely expect that he'll be apprehended before your retirement begins?" I asked.

"That's not so easy! . . . You must know that we are doing everything we can . . ." he replied with a mournful air. Then he added: "Not that way, we'll lose our direction, we'll keep going around and around in circles . . ."

"Show me the way. . . . Ah! the day began so well. But now, I will always see those drowned people, that image will never leave my memory!"

"I should not have let you see them . . ."

"It can't be helped; it is better to know everything, better to know everything."

In a few moments we had reached a way out of the district, at the end of a drive on the edge of the outer boulevard and across from the streetcar stop. Some people were standing there, waiting. The sky was somber. I was cold, frozen. I put on my topcoat and wrapped my scarf around my neck. Thin rain was falling, water mixed with snow, and the pavement was wet.

"You don't have to go home right away, do you?" the commissioner asked me (that is how I learned that he was also a commissioner). "Surely you have time for a drink with me . . ."

The commissioner seemed to have regained his cheerfulness. Not I.

"There's a bar over there, near the streetcar stop, just a step from the cemetery; they sell wreaths there too."

"I don't feel very thirsty now, you know . . ."

"Don't worry about it. If one dwells on all the misfortunes of humanity, one cannot go on living. Every day children are massacred, old people starve, the widows, the orphans, the dying."

"Yes, Mr. Commissioner, but having seen this close up, seen it with my own eyes. . . . I cannot remain unconcerned."

"You are too impressionable," my companion replied, giving me a hearty slap on the shoulder.

We entered the bar.

"We're going to try to cheer you up! . . . Two beers!" he ordered.

We sat down near the window. The stout proprietor, wearing a vest and with his rolled-up shirt sleeves exposing his enormous hairy arms, came to serve us:

"For you, I have real beer!"

I started to pay him.

"No, no," said the commissioner, "it's on me!"

I was still heavy-hearted.

"If only you had his description!" I said.

"But we do have it. At least the one under which he operates. His portrait is posted all over the city."

"How did you get it?"

"From the drowned. Some of his victims, in their final agony, have regained consciousness for a moment and have been able to give us additional details. We also know how he goes about his game. As a matter of fact everybody in the district knows."

"But then why aren't they more prudent? All they have to do is to be on their guard."

"It's not so simple as all that. I tell you, every evening there are always two or three who fall into his trap. But he, he never lets himself get caught."

"I still can't understand."

I was astonished to perceive that this appeared to amuse the architect.

"Look," he said, "over there at the streetcar stop is where he makes his attack. When the passengers get off, on their way home, he goes up to them, disguised as a beggar. He whines, begs for money, tries to work on their pity. That's his usual dodge. He'll say that he's just been discharged from the hospital, has no job but is looking for one, has nowhere to spend the night. But that's only the opening. He singles out a kindly soul. He engages her in conversation, hooks onto her, doesn't let go for a moment. He offers to sell her various small objects that he takes out of his basket: artificial flowers, scissors, obscene pictures, all kinds of things. Generally, his offers are refused, the good soul is in a hurry, she hasn't got time. Spieling all the while, he moves along with her until they're near the pool that you saw. Then, all of a sudden, he pulls his master stroke; he offers to show her the photograph of the colonel. It's irresistible. Since there's no longer much light, the good soul bends over in order to see it better. At that moment she is lost. Seizing his chance while she is looking at the photograph, he pushes her and she falls into the pool. She drowns. The deed is done. All he has to do is to look for a new victim."

"What's so amazing is that they recognize him and yet they let him surprise them."

"It's a trap, that's what it is. He's crafty. He's never been caught in the act."

Mechanically, I looked through the window at the people descending from the streetcar, which had just arrived. I didn't see any beggar.

"You won't see him," the commissioner said, divining my thought. "He won't show himself, for he knows that we are here."

"Perhaps you ought to post a plain-clothes man on permanent duty at this place."

"That's not possible. Our inspectors are snowed under with work, they have other duties to perform. Moreover, they too would want to see the photograph of the colonel. Five of them have already been drowned in just that way. Ah! if we only had some evidence, we wouldn't have any trouble finding him!"

I parted company with my companion, not without having thanked him for being kind enough to take me to see the wealthy residential district, and also for so amiably permitting himself to be interviewed on the subject of all these unpardonable crimes. Alas, his instructive revelations will never appear in any newspaper: I am not a journalist, nor have I ever claimed to be one. The information of the architect-commissioner had been given to me entirely gratuitously. And it had filled me with anguish, gratuitously. Overcome with an indefinable malaise, I regained my house.

Edouard was waiting for me in the low-ceilinged, gloomy, autumnal sitting room (the electricity doesn't work during the day). There he was, seated on the chest near the window, dressed in black, very thin, his face pale and sad, his eyes burning. Presumably he still had a touch of fever. He noticed that I was distraught and asked me the reason. When I began to tell him of my experiences, he stopped me at the first words; he knew the whole story, he said, in a trembling, almost childish voice, and he was even surprised that I myself had not heard of it long before this. The whole city knew about it. That was why he had never spoken of it to me. It was something that everyone had talked about for a long time and now that it was old news it had been assimilated. But regrettable, certainly.

"Very regrettable!" I said.

In my turn, I did not conceal my surprise that he was not more disturbed. But perhaps I was unjust, perhaps his thoughts were on the disease that was consuming him, for he was tubercular. One can never hope to know the heart of another.

"Would you like to go for a little stroll?" he asked. "I've been waiting for you for a whole hour, and I'm freezing here in your house. Surely it must be warmer outside."

Although I was depressed and exhausted (I'd much rather have gone to bed), I agreed to go with him.

He got up and put on his felt hat with its black ribbon, and his dark-gray topcoat; then he lifted up his heavy, bulging brief case, but let it fall before he had taken a step. It fell open as it hit the floor. We both bent down, at the same time. From one of the pockets of the brief case some photographs had slipped out; they showed a colonel in full-dress uniform, mustachioed—an ordinary colonel with a good, even rather striking head. We placed the brief case on the table to look through it more easily; we took out several hundred more photographs, all of the same subject.

"What does this mean?" I demanded. "This is the photograph, the famous photograph of the colonel! You had it here and you never told me a word about it!"

"I don't keep looking in my brief case all the time," he replied.

"Still, it's your brief case, and you always carry it with you!"

"That's not a reason."

"Anyway, let's make use of the opportunity while we can, let's look further."

He plunged his white, sick man's hand, with its crooked fingers, into the other pockets of the enormous black brief case. Then he drew out (how was it able to contain so much?) incredible quantities of artificial flowers, of obscene pictures, of candies, of toy banks, of children's watches, of brooches, fountain pens, cardboard boxes, of I don't know what all —a hundred objects and some cigarettes. ("Those belong to me," he said.) The table was filled to overflowing.

"These are the things the monster uses!" I cried. "And you had them there!"

"I was unaware of it."

"Empty it all out," I encouraged him. "Go ahead!"

He went on taking out more things. There were calling cards with the name and the address of the criminal, his card of identity complete with photograph, and then, in a little case, some slips of paper on which were written the names of all the victims, and an intimate diary that we leafed through, with all its revealing details, his projects, his plan of action minutely described, his declaration of faith, his doctrine.

"You've got all the evidence right here. We can have him arrested."

"I didn't know," he mumbled, "I didn't know . . ."

"You could have saved so many human lives," I reproached him.

"I feel embarrassed. I didn't know. I never know what I have, I'm not in the habit of looking in my brief case."

"It's a condemnable negligence!" I said.

"I apologize. I'm very sorry."

"And really, Edouard, these things couldn't have got into your brief case all by themselves. Either you've found them or you've received them!"

I felt pity for him. He had flushed red, he was truly ashamed.

He made an attempt to remember.

"Ah, yes!" he cried after several seconds. "I recall it now. The criminal sent me his private diary, his notes, his lists, a long time ago, begging me to publish them in a literary review—that was long before he carried out the murders and I had completely forgotten all about it. At the time it never occurred to me that he would perpetrate them; it was only later that he must have decided to carry out his plans; as for me, I regarded all this as so much daydreaming, without any relation to reality, a sort of science fiction. Now, of course, I regret that I did not carefully consider the matter, that I did not associate his papers with subsequent events.

"In any case the relationship is between intention and realization, neither more nor less; it's as clear as the light of day."

From the brief case he also took out a large envelope that we opened; it contained a map, a very detailed map carefully marked to show all the places where the assassin had been encountered and it gave his exact schedule, minute by minute.

"It's simple," I said. "We'll notify the police, and all they have to do is nab him. Let's hurry, the office of the prefecture closes before nightfall. If we're late, there'll be no one there. And by tomorrow he may have changed his schedule. Let's go to the architect and show him the evidence."

"All right," said Edouard, rather indifferently.

We left on the run. In the hallway, we bumped into the concierge, who cried, "What do you mean by . . ." The rest of her sentence was lost in the wind.

By the time we had reached the main avenue we were winded and had to slow down. To the right, plowed fields extended as far as the eye could see. To the left were the first buildings of the city. And straight ahead of us, the setting sun was purpling the sky. Some bare trees straggled along both sides of the avenue. Only a few people were out.

We followed along the rails of the streetcar tracks (had it already stopped running?) which extended far into the distance.

Three or four large military trucks (I don't know where they came from) suddenly blocked our way. They were parked along the sidewalk, which, at this point, lay beneath the level of the roadway, which seemed, because of this difference of level, to be raised.

It was fortunate that Edouard and I had to pause to catch our breath, for I suddenly noticed that my friend did not have his brief case with him.

"What have you done with it? Here I assumed that you were carrying it with you," I said. The scatterbrain! In our hurry he had left it in the house. "There's no point in going to see the commissioner without our evidence! What were you thinking of? You're incomprehensible. Go back quickly and look for it. I'll run on so that I can at least warn the commissioner in time and get him to wait. Hurry back to the house and try to rejoin me as soon as possible. The prefecture is at the end of the street. I don't like being alone on an errand like this: it's unnerving, you understand."

Edouard disappeared. I began to experience a sensation of fear. Here the sidewalk descended even lower, so much so that some steps should have been built, four to be exact, so that pedestrians might have access to the roadway. By now I was very close to one of the big trucks in the center of the line (the others were ahead and behind). This was an open truck, with rows of benches on which were sitting, pressed tightly together, forty young soldiers in dark-colored uniforms. One of them held a big bouquet of red carnations in his hand. He was using it as a fan.

Several policemen came up to direct the traffic, loudly blowing their whistles. I was grateful for their help: the traffic jam was holding me up. These policemen were unusually tall. One of them, who was standing near a tree, looked taller than the tree itself when he raised his night stick.

Then I saw a small, modestly dressed gentleman with white hair, hat in hand, standing before the policeman whose great height made him appear even smaller; he was asking him very politely, perhaps too politely, but with real humility for some small item of information. Without interrupting his signaling, the policeman, in a rough voice, replied abruptly to the retiring gentleman (who might perfectly well have been his father, given the difference in age, but excluding the difference in stature, which did not favor the old man). The policeman sent him on his way with a rude word, turning back to continue his work and blowing his whistle.

The policeman's attitude shocked me. In any case it was his *duty* to be polite to the public—surely that was incorporated in the regulations. "When I see his chief, the architect, I will try to remember to speak to him about this!" I said to myself. As for us, we are all too polite, too timid with the police; we've encouraged them in their bad habits and it's basically our fault.

A second policeman, as huge as the first, came over and stood near me on the sidewalk. He was visibly annoyed by the traffic jam, about which, it must be admitted, he had every right to be annoyed. Having no need of steps to mount up from the sidewalk to the roadway, he approached very near the truck full of soldiers. Although his feet were on a level with mine, his head was somewhat higher than their heads. Accusing them of tying up the traffic, he harshly reprimanded the soldiers, who were scarcely to blame, least of all the young man with the bouquet of red carnations.

"You've nothing to do but amuse yourself with this?" he asked him.

"I'm not doing anything wrong, Mr. Policeman," replied the soldier very gently, in a timid voice. "This isn't holding up the truck."

"Insolence, it's jamming the motor!" cried the policeman, slapping the soldier, who didn't say a word. Then the policeman grabbed the flowers and threw them away; they disappeared.

I was personally outraged by this behavior. I firmly believe that there is no hope for a country where the police have the upper hand over the army.

"Why are you meddling in this? Is it any of your business?" he said, turning toward me.

In no wise had I expressed my thoughts aloud. They must have been easy to divine.

"In the first place, what are you doing here?"

I seized upon his questions as an excuse to explain my case, possibly to ask his advice, even his assistance.

"I have all the evidence," I said, "and now the murderer can be arrested. I must hurry on to the prefecture. It's not very far from here. Can you go there with me? I'm a friend of the commissioner, of the architect."

"That's not my branch. I'm in traffic control."

"Yes, but . . ."

"That's not part of my job, don't you understand! Your story doesn't interest me. Since you're connected with the chief, go on and see him and get the hell out of here. You know the way, get going, nothing's stopping you."

"All right, Mr. Policeman," I said, as politely as the soldier but in spite of myself: "Very well, Mr. Policeman!"

The policeman turned to his colleague who was standing beside the tree and said with harsh irony: "Let the gentleman pass!"

This man, whose face I could see through the branches, gave me the signal to advance. As I passed near him, he screamed at me in a rage, "I hate you!" Though surely it was I who had more of a right to say that than he.

I found myself alone in the center of the road, the trucks already far behind me. Onward I hurried, straight toward the prefecture. Night was fast approaching, the north wind was freezing, and I was worried. Would Edouard be able to rejoin me in time? And I was furious with the police: these people are good for nothing but to annoy us, to teach us good manners, but when we have a real need for them, when it is a question of defending us—then it's a case of "tell it to the Marines"—they let us down every time!

On my left there were no more houses. Only gray fields on both sides of the road. There seemed to be no end to this route, or this avenue, with its streetcar rails. I walked and walked: "If only he's not too late, if only he's not too late!" I thought to myself.

Abruptly, he surged up in front of me. There could be no doubt of it: it was the murderer; and all about us there was only the darkened plain. The wind was wrapping an old sheet of newspaper around the trunk of a gaunt tree. Behind the man, at a distance of several hundred yards, I could see in profile, against the setting sun, the prefecture office buildings, not far from the stop where the streetcar had just arrived; I could see some people descending —they seemed very small at that distance. No help was possible, they were much too far away, they would not be able to hear me.

I stopped short, frozen in my tracks. "These lousy cops," I thought, "they've left me alone with him on purpose. They want people to think that it was only a private quarrel!"

We were face to face, but two steps from each other. I looked at him in silence, on my guard. He stared at me and he was almost laughing.

He was a man of middle age, skinny, stunted, very short of stature, and ill-shaven; he appeared to be weaker than I. He was wearing a dirty, worn gabardine coat, torn at the pockets, and some of his toes were sticking out of the gaps in his broken-down shoes. He had a dilapidated, almost shapeless hat on his head; he kept one hand in his pocket, while with the other he clenched a knife with a large blade that reflected a livid gleam. He fixed me with his single cold eye, made of the same material and glittering with the same light which was reflected from his weapon.

Never had I seen an expression so cruel, of such hardness—and why?—of such ferocity. An implacable eye, that of a snake, perhaps, or of a tiger, a heedless murderer's. No word, friendly or authoritative, no reasoning would be able to persuade him; no promise of happiness, not all the love in the world would be able to touch him; nor could beauty cause him to give way, nor irony shame him, nor all the sages of the world succeed in making him comprehend the vanity of crime, which is as vain as charity.

The tears of the saints might fall on this lidless eye, on this steely look, without softening it in the least; battalions of Christs could have followed one another to their Calvaries for him in vain.

Slowly I drew from my pockets my two pistols, and in silence, for two seconds, held them aimed at him. He did not flinch. I lowered them, let my arms fall. I felt myself disarmed, desperate: what could bullets—any more than my feeble strength—do against the cold hate and obstinacy, against the infinite energy of this absolute cruelty, without reason and without mercy?

Translated by Stanley Read

►► Albert Camus

Reflections on the Guillotine

Shortly before World War I, a murderer whose crime was particularly shocking (he had killed a family of farmers, children and all) was condemned to death in Algiers. He was an agricultural worker who had slaughtered in a bloody delirium, and had rendered his offense still more serious by robbing his victims. The case was widely publicized, and it was generally agreed that decapitation was altogether too mild a punishment for such a monster. I have been told this was the opinion of my father, who was particularly outraged by the murder of the children. One of the few things I know about him is that this was the first time in his life he wanted to attend an execution. He got up while it was still dark, for the place where the guillotine was set up was at the other end of the city, and once there, found himself among a great crowd of spectators. He never told what he saw that morning. My mother could only report that he rushed wildly into the house, refused to speak, threw himself on the bed, and suddenly began to vomit. He had just discovered the reality concealed beneath the great formulas that ordinarily serve to mask it. Instead of thinking of the murdered children, he could recall only the trembling body he had seen thrown on a board to have its head chopped off.

This ritual act must indeed be horrible if it can subvert the indignation of a simple, upright man; if the punishment which he regarded as deserved a hundred times over had no other effect on him than to turn his stomach. When the supreme act of justice merely nauseates the honest citizen it is supposed to protect, it seems difficult to maintain that this act is intended—as its proper functioning *should* intend it—to confer a greater degree of peace and order upon the city. Justice of this kind is obviously no less shocking than the crime itself, and the new "official" murder, far from offering redress for the offense committed against society, adds instead a second defilement to the first. This is so apparent that no one dares speak openly of the ritual act itself. The officials and the journalists whose responsibility it is to speak of it, as if conscious of the simultaneously provocative and shameful aspects of such justice, have devised a kind of ceremonial language for dealing with it, a language reduced to the most stereo-typed formulas. Over breakfast we may read, on some back page of our newspaper, that the condemned man "paid his debt to society," that he "expiated his crime," or that "at five o'clock this morning justice was done." Officials deal with this man as "the accused," "the patient," or merely refer to him as the C.A.M. (*Condamné à mort*). Capital punishment, one might say, is written about only in whispers. In a highly organized society such as ours we acknowledge a disease is serious by the fact that we do not dare speak of it openly. In middle-class families, it was long the rule to say that the oldest daughter had a "weak chest," or that Papa suffered from a "growth": to have tuberculosis or cancer was regarded as something of a disgrace. This is even more certainly true in the case of capital punishment: everyone does his best to speak of it only in euphemisms. The death penalty is to the body politic what cancer is to the individual body, with perhaps the single difference that no one has ever spoken of the necessity of cancer. Yet we do not usually hesitate to describe the death penalty as a *regrettable necessity*, justifying the fact that we are killing someone because it is "necessary," and then not speaking of what we are doing because it is "regrettable."

My intention, on the contrary, is to speak of it crudely. Not out of a taste for scandal, and not, I think, because I am morbidly inclined. As a writer I have always abhorred a certain eagerness to please, and as a man I believe that the repulsive aspects of our condition, if they are inevitable, must be confronted in silence. But since silence, or the casuistry of speech, is now contributing to the support of an abuse that must be reformed, or of a misery that can be relieved, there is no other solution than to speak out, to expose the obscenity hiding beneath our cloak of words. France shares with Spain and England the splendid distinction of being among the last countries on this side of the iron curtain to retain the death penalty in its arsenal of repression. This primitive rite survives in our country only because an ignorant and unconcerned public opinion has no other way to express itself than by using the same ceremonial phrases with which it has been indoctrinated: when the imagination is not functioning, words lack the resonance of their meanings and a deaf public scarcely registers a man's condemnation to death. But expose the machinery, make people touch the wood and the iron, let them hear the thud of heads falling, and a suddenly aroused public imagination will repudiate both vocabulary and punishment alike.

When the Nazis staged public executions of hostages in Poland, they first gagged their prisoners with rags soaked in plaster so they could not cry out some final word of liberty or rebellion. It may seem an effrontery to compare the fate of these innocent victims with that of our condemned criminals, but apart from the fact that it is not only criminals who are guillotined in France, the method is the same: we gag our guilty with a stuffing of words, though we cannot justly affirm the legitimacy of their punishment unless we have first considered its reality. Instead of saying, as we always have, that the death penalty is first of all a necessity, and afterwards that it is advisable not to talk about it, we should first speak of what the death penalty really is, and only then decide if, *being what it is*, it is necessary.

Speaking for myself, I believe the death penalty is not only useless but profoundly harmful, and I must record this conviction here before proceeding to the subject itself. It would not be honest to allow it to appear as if I had arrived at this conclusion solely as a result of the weeks of inquiry and investigation I have just devoted to the question. But it would be equally dishonest to attribute my conviction to sentimentality alone. I stand as far as possible from that position of spineless pity in which our humanitarians take such pride, in which values and responsibilities change places, all crimes become equal, and innocence ultimately forfeits all rights. I do not believe, contrary to many of my illustrious contemporaries, that man is by nature a social animal; the opposite, I think, is probably nearer the truth. I believe only that man cannot now live outside a society whose laws are necessary to his physical survival, which is a very different thing. I believe that responsibility must be established according to a reasonable and effective scale of values by society itself. But the law finds its final justification in the benefit it provides, or does not provide, the society of a given place and time. For years I have not been able to regard the death penalty as anything but a punishment intolerable to the imagination: a public sin of sloth which my reason utterly condemns. I was nevertheless prepared to believe that my imagination influenced my judgment. But during these weeks of research, I have found nothing which has modified my reasoning, nothing which has not, in all honesty, reinforced my original conviction. On the contrary. I have found

new arguments to add to those I already possessed; today I share Arthur Koestler's conclusion without qualification: capital punishment is a disgrace to our society which its partisans cannot reasonably justify.

It is well known that the major argument of those who support capital punishment is its value as an example. We do not chop off heads merely to punish their former owners, but to intimidate, by a terrifying example, those who might be tempted to imitate their actions. Society does not take revenge—society merely protects itself. We brandish the newly severed head so that the next prospective murderer may therein read his future and renounce his intentions. All of which would indeed be an impressive argument if one were not obliged to remark: (1) That society itself does not believe in the value of this much advertised example. (2) That it has not been ascertained whether capital punishment ever made a single determined murderer renounce his intentions, while it is certain that its effect has been one of fascination upon thousands of criminals. (3) That the death penalty constitutes, from other points of view, a loathsome example of which the consequences are unforeseeable.

First of all, then, society does not believe its own words. If it did, we would be shown the heads. Executions would be given the same promotional campaign ordinarily reserved for government loans or a new brand of *apéritif*. Yet it is well known on the contrary, that in France executions no longer take place in public—they are perpetrated in prison yards before an audience limited to specialists. It is less well known why this should be so, and since when it has been so. The last public execution took place in 1939—the guillotining of Weidmann, a murderer several times over whose exploits had brought him much notoriety. On the morning of his execution, a huge crowd rushed to Versailles; many photographers attended the ceremony and were permitted to take photographs from the time Weidmann was exposed to the crowd until the moment he was decapitated. A few hours later *Paris-Soir* published a full page of pictures of this appetizing event, and the good people of Paris were able to discover that the lightweight precision instrument used by their executioner was as different from the scaffold of their history books as a Jaguar is from an old de Dion-Bouton. The officials connected with the event and the government itself, contrary to every hope, regarded this excellent publicity in a very dim light, declaring that the press had only appealed to the most sadistic impulses of its readers. It was therefore decided that the public would no longer be permitted to witness executions, an arrangement which, shortly afterward, made the work of the Occupation authorities considerably easier.

Logic, in this case, was not on the side of the lawmakers. Logically, in fact, they should have voted a medal to the editor of *Paris-Soir* and encouraged his staff to do still better next time. If punishment is to be exemplary, then the number of newspaper photographs must be multiplied, the instrument in question must be set up on a platform in the Place de la Concorde at two in the afternoon, the entire population of the city must be invited, and the ceremony must be televised for those unable to attend. Either do this, or stop talking about the value of an example. How can a furtive murder committed by night in a prison yard serve as an example? At best it can periodically admonish the citizenry that they will die if they commit murder; a fate which can also be assured them if they do not. For punishment to be truly exemplary, it must be terrifying. Tuaut de la Bouverie, representative of the people in 1791 and a partisan of public execution, spoke more logically when he declared to the National Assembly: "There must be terrible spectacles in order to control the people."

Today there is no spectacle at all—only a penalty known to everyone by hearsay and, at long intervals, the announcement of an execution couched in soothing formulas. How shall a future criminal, in the very act of committing his crime, keep in mind a threat which has been made increasingly abstract by every possible effort? And if it is really desirable that the incipient murderer preserve a vision of his ultimate fate that might counterbalance and ultimately reverse his criminal intent, then why do we not burn the reality of that fate into his sensibility by every means of language and image within our power?

Instead of vaguely evoking a debt that someone has paid to society this morning, would it not be more politic—if we are interested in setting an example—to profit by this excellent opportunity to remind each taxpayer in detail just what sort of punishment he can expect? Instead of saying, "If you kill someone you will pay for it on the scaffold," would it not be more politic—if we are interested in setting an example—to say instead: "If you kill someone, you will be thrown into prison for months or even years, torn between an impossible despair and a constantly renewed fear, until one morning we will sneak into your cell, having taken off our shoes in order to surprise you in your sleep, which has at last overcome you after the night's anguish. We will throw ourselves upon you, tie your wrists behind your back, and with a pair of scissors cut away your

shirt collar and your hair, if it should be in the way. Because we are perfectionists we will lash your arms together with a strap so that your body will be arched to offer unhampered access to the back of your neck. Then we will carry you, one man holding you up under each arm, your feet dragging behind you, down the long corridors, until, under the night sky, one of the executioners will at last take hold of the back of your trousers and throw you down on a board, another will make sure your head is in the lunette, and a third one will drop, from a height of two meters twenty centimeters, a blade weighing sixty kilograms that will slice through your neck like a razor."

For the example to be even better, for the terror it breeds to become in each of us a force blind enough and powerful enough to balance, at the right moment, our irresistible desire to kill, we must go still further. Instead of bragging, with our characteristic pretentious ignorance, that we have invented a swift and humane means of killing those condemned to death, we should publish in millions of copies, read out in every school and college, the eyewitness accounts and medical reports that describe the state of the body after execution. We should particularly recommend the printing and circulation of a recent communication made to the Academy of Medicine by Doctors Piedelièvre and Fournier. These courageous physicians, having examined, in the interests of science, the bodies of the condemned after execution, have considered it their duty to sum up their terrible observations thus: "If we may be permitted to present our opinion on this subject, such spectacles are horribly painful. The blood rushes from the vessels according to the rhythm of the severed carotids, then coagulates. The muscles contract and their fibrillation is stupefying. The intestine undulates and the heart produces a series of irregular, incomplete, and convulsive movements. The mouth tightens, at certain moments, into a dreadful grimace. It is true that the eyes of a decapitated head are immobile, the pupils dilated; fortunately, they cannot see, and if they exhibit no signs of disturbance, none of the characteristic opalescence of a cadaver, they at least have no capacity for movement: their transparency is that of life, but their fixity is mortal. All this may last minutes, even hours, in a healthy subject: death is not immediate. . . . Thus each vital element survives decapitation to some extent. There remains, for the physician, the impression of a hideous experiment, a murderous vivisection followed by a premature burial."

I doubt that many readers can read this dreadful report without blanching. We can, in fact, count on its power as an example, its capacity to intimidate. What is to prevent us from adding to it the reports of witnesses that further authenticate the observations of medical men. If the severed head of Charlotte Corday is supposed to have blushed under the executioner's hand, we shall hardly be surprised after examining the accounts of more recent observers. Here is how one assistant executioner, hardly likely to cultivate the sentimental or romantic aspects of his trade, describes what he has been obliged to see: "There was one wild man, suffering from a real fit of delirium tremens, whom we had to throw under the knife. The head died right away. But the body literally sprang into the basket, where it lay struggling against the cords that bound it. Twenty minutes later, in the cemetery, it was still shuddering." The present chaplain of La Santé, the reverend father Devoyod, who does not appear to be opposed to the death penalty, tells, nevertheless, the following remarkable story in his book *Les Délinquants* (which renews the famous episode of a man named Languille whose severed head answered to its name): "The morning of the execution, the condemned man was in a very bad humor, and refused to receive the succor of religion. Knowing the depths of his heart and his true regard for his wife, whose sentiments were genuinely Christian, we said to him, 'For the love of this woman, commune with yourself a moment before you die.' And the condemned man consented, communing at length before the crucifix, and afterwards scarcely seemed to notice our presence. When he was executed, we were not far from him; his head fell onto the trough in front of the guillotine, and the body was immediately put into the basket. But contrary to custom, the basket was closed before the head could be put in. The assistant carrying the head had to wait a moment until the basket was opened again. And during that brief space of time, we were able to see the two eyes of the condemned man fixed on us in a gaze of supplication, as if to ask our forgiveness. Instinctively we traced a sign of the cross in order to bless the head, and then the eyelids blinked, the look in the eyes became gentle again, and then the gaze, which had remained expressive, was gone. . . ." The reader will accept or reject the explanation proposed by the priest according to his faith. But at least those eyes that "remained expressive" need no interpretation.

I could cite many other eyewitness accounts as hallucinatory as these. But as for myself, I hardly need or know how to go further. After all, I make no claim that the death penalty is exemplary: indeed, this torture affects me only as what it is—a crude surgery practiced in conditions that deprive it of any edifying

character whatsoever. Society, on the other hand, and the State (which has seen other tortures) can easily bear such details; and since they favor preaching examples, they might as well make them universally known so that a perpetually terrorized populace can become Franciscan to a man. For who is it we think we are frightening by this example constantly screened from view; by the threat of a punishment described as painless, expedient, and on the whole less disagreeable than cancer; by a torture crowned with all the flowers of rhetoric? Certainly not those who pass for honest (and some are) because they are asleep at such an hour, to whom the *great example* has not been revealed, and who drink their morning coffee at the hour of the premature burial, informed of the operation of justice, if they happen to read the newspapers, by a mealy-mouthed bulletin that dissolves like sugar in their memory. Yet these same peaceful creatures furnish society with the largest percentage of its homicides. Many of these honest men are criminals without knowing it. According to one magistrate, the overwhelming majority of the murderers he had tried did not know, when they shaved themselves that morning, that they were going to kill someone that night. For the sake of example and security alike, we should brandish rather than disguise the agonized face of our visitor before the eyes of every man as he shaves himself in the morning.

This is not done. The State conceals the circumstances and even the existence of its executions, keeps silent about such reports and such accounts. It does not concern itself with the exemplary value of punishment save by tradition, nor does it trouble to consider the present meaning of its act. The criminal is killed because he has been killed for centuries, and furthermore he is killed according to a procedure established at the end of the eighteenth century. The same arguments that have served as legal tender for centuries are perpetuated as a matter of routine, contradicted only by those measures which the evolution of public sensibility renders inevitable. The law is applied without consideration of its significance, and our condemned criminals die by rote in the name of a theory in which their executioners no longer believe. If they believed in it, it would be known, and above all it would be seen. But such publicity, beyond the fact that it arouses sadistic instincts of which the repercussions are incalculable and which end, one day or another, by satisfying themselves with yet another murder, also risks provoking the disgust and revolt of public opinion itself. It would become more difficult to execute by assembly line, as we do in France at this very moment, if such executions were translated into the bold images of popular fantasy. The very man who enjoys his morning coffee while reading that justice has been done would certainly choke on it at the slightest of such details. And the texts I have quoted may go far toward supporting the position of certain professors of criminal law who, in their evident incapacity to justify the anachronism of capital punishment, console themselves by declaring with the sociologist Tarde that it is better to kill without causing suffering than it is to cause suffering without killing. Which is why we can only approve the position of Gambetta, who as an adversary of the death penalty nevertheless voted against a bill proposing the exclusion of the public from executions, asserting: "If you do away with the horror of the spectacle, if you perform executions in the prison yards, you will also do away with the public reaction of revolt which has shown itself in recent years, and thereby establish the death penalty all the more firmly."

We must either kill publicly, or admit we do not feel authorized to kill. If society justifies the death penalty as a necessary example, then it must justify itself by providing the publicity necessary to *make* an example. Society must display the executioner's hands on each occasion, and require the most squeamish citizens to look at them, as well as those who, directly or remotely, have supported the work of those hands from the first. Otherwise society confesses that it kills without consciousness of what it does or what it says; or that it kills yet knows, too, that far from intimidating belief, these disgusting ceremonies can only awaken a sense of criminality, and thoroughly undermine public morale. Who could be more explicit than a judge at the end of his career?—Counselor Falco's courageous confession deserves careful attention: "On only one occasion during my years on the bench I recommended a verdict in favor of execution of the accused and against the commutation of his punishment; I decided that despite my position I would attend the ceremony—with complete objectivity, of course. The man in question was not at all sympathetic, not even interesting: he had brutally murdered his little daughter and then thrown her body down a well. Nevertheless, after his execution, for weeks, and even for months, my nights were haunted by this memory. . . . I served in the war like everyone else, and I saw an innocent generation killed before my eyes; yet confronted with the memory of that dreadful spectacle, I still can say I never once experienced the same kind of bad conscience I felt as I watched the kind of administrative assassination known as capital punishment."

But after all, why should society believe in the value of such an example, since it does not affect the incidence of crime, and since its effects, if they exist at all, are invisible? For capital punishment cannot intimidate a man who does not know he is going to commit murder, who decides on it in an instant and prepares his action in the heat of passion or an *idée fixe*; cannot intimidate a man who starts off for an assignation carrying with him a weapon to frighten his faithless mistress or his rival and then, at the last minute, makes use of it, although without any such intention—or without thinking he had any such intention. In short, capital punishment cannot intimidate the man who throws himself upon crime as one throws oneself into misery. Which is to say that it is ineffective in the majority of cases. It is only fair to point out that in France, at least, capital punishment is rarely applied in cases of "crimes of passion." Yet even "rarely" is enough to make one shudder.

But does the death penalty act as a deterrent, at least, upon that "race" of criminals it claims to affect —those who live by crime? Nothing is less certain. Arthur Koestler reminds us that in the period when pickpockets were punished by hanging in England, other thieves exercised their talents in the crowds surrounding the scaffold where their fellow was being hanged. Statistics compiled during the past fifty years in England show that out of 250 men hanged, 170 had previously attended one or even two public executions. Even as late as 1886, out of 167 men condemned to death in the Bristol prison, 164 had attended at least one execution. Figures corresponding to these cannot be ascertained in France because of the secrecy which surrounds executions here. But those we have remind us that in that crowd my father stood among to watch a public execution, there must have been a considerable number of future criminals who did not run home and vomit. The power of intimidation operates only on those timid souls who are not dedicated to crime, and gives way before precisely those incorrigibles whom it is concerned to correct.

Yet it cannot be denied that men fear death. The deprivation of life is certainly the supreme punishment, and arouses in each of us his decisive fear. The fear of death, rising from the obscurest depths, ravages the self; the instinct for life, when threatened, panics and flounders among the most dreadful agonies. The legislator may with some justice assume that his law affects one of the most mysterious and powerful motives of human nature. But the law is always simpler than nature. When, in its attempt to establish its sovereignty, the law ventures into the blind realms of being, it runs a terrible risk of being impotent to control the very complexity it attempts to set in order.

Indeed if the fear of death is one kind of evidence, the fact that this same fear, no matter how great it may be, has never sufficed to discourage human passions, is still another. Bacon was right: no passion is so weak that it cannot confront and master the fear of death. Vengeance, love, honor, grief, even fear of something else—all are victorious over the fear of death in one circumstance or another. And shall cupidity, hatred, or jealousy not accomplish all that love or patriotism or the human passion for liberty are able to achieve? For centuries the death penalty, often accompanied by various barbarous refinements, has tried to restrain the incidence of crime; yet crime persists. Why? Because the instincts which confront and war against each other within man are not, as the law would have them, constant forces in a state of equilibrium. They are variable forces that die and triumph one after another, whose successive imbalances nourish the life of the mind in the same way that electrical oscillations, occurring with sufficient frequency, establish a current. Consider the series of oscillations passing from desire to satiation, from decision to renunciation, which all of us experience in a single day and then multiply these variations to infinity and we may form an idea of the extent of our psychological proliferation. These imbalances, these disequilibriums are generally too fugitive to permit any one force to gain control of the entire self. Yet it sometimes happens that a single element of the soul's resources can break free and occupy the entire field of consciousness; no instinct, even that of self-preservation, can then oppose the tyranny of this irresistible force. In order that the death penalty be really intimidating, human nature itself would have to be different from what it is, would have to be as stable and serene as the law itself. It would no longer be life, but still life.

But life is not still life, is not stable, not serene. Which is why, surprising as it may seem to those who have not observed or experienced in themselves the complexity of the human situation, the murderer for the most part considers himself innocent when he commits his crime. Before being judged, the criminal acquits *himself*. He feels he is—if not entirely within his rights—at least extenuated by circumstances. He does not reflect; he does not foresee; or if he does, it is only to foresee that he will be pardoned —altogether or in part. Why should he fear what he regards as highly unlikely? He will fear death after being judged, not before his crime. Therefore, in order to intimidate effectively, the law must permit the murderer *no escape*, must be implacable *in ad-vance*, must admit no possibility of an extenuating circumstance. Who among us would dare to demand this?

And even if we did, there is still another paradox of human nature to consider. The instinct of self-preservation, if it is a fundamental one, is no more so than that other instinct less often discussed by academic psychologists: the death instinct which at certain times demands the destruction of the self or of others. It is probable that the desire to kill frequently coincides with the desire to die or to kill oneself. The instinct of self-preservation thus finds itself confronted in variable proportions by the instinct for self-destruction. The latter is the only means by which we can altogether explain the numerous perversions which—from alcoholism to drug addiction —lead the self to a destruction of which it cannot long remain ignorant. Man desires to live, but it is vain to hope that this desire can control all his actions. He desires to be annihilated as well—he wills the irreparable, death for its own sake. It so happens that the criminal desires not only his crime, but the misery that accompanies it, especially if this misery is unbounded and inordinate. When this perverse desire grows until it gains control of the self, the prospect of being put to death is not only impotent to restrain the criminal, but probably deepens even further the abyss into which he plunges: there are situations in which one kills in order to die.

Such singularities suffice to explain how a punishment that seems calculated to intimidate the normal mind has in reality nothing whatever to do with ordinary psychological processes. All statistics show, without exception—in the countries which have abolished it, as well as in the others—that there is no connection between the death penalty and the incidence of crime. This incidence, in fact, neither rises nor falls. The guillotine exists; crime exists: between them there is no other apparent connection than that of the law. All we are entitled to conclude from the figures provided by statisticians is this: for centuries crimes other than murder were punished by death, and this supreme punishment, deliberately repeated, caused none of these crimes to disappear. For several centuries these crimes have no longer been punished by death, yet they have not increased in number, and the incidence of some has even diminished. Similarly, murder has been punished by capital punishment for centuries, yet the race of Cain has not disappeared from the earth. In the thirty-three nations that have abolished the death penalty or no longer impose it, the number of murders has not increased. How can we therefore conclude that the death penalty is really intimidating?

Its partisans can deny neither these facts nor these figures. Their only and ultimate reply is significant; it explains the paradoxical attitude of a society which so carefully conceals the executions it claims as exemplary: "It is true that nothing proves that the death penalty is exemplary; it is even certain that thousands of murderers have not been intimidated by it. But we cannot know who *has* been intimidated by such a penalty; consequently, nothing proves that it does not serve as an example." Thus the greatest of all punishments, the penalty that involves the ultimate forfeiture of the condemned man and concedes the supreme privilege to society, rests on nothing more than an unverifiable possibility. Death, however, does not admit of degrees of likelihood; it fixes all things—blame and body alike—in its definitive rigidity. Yet it is administered in our country in the name of a possibility, a calculation of likelihood. And even if this possibility should be reasonable, would it not have to be certitude itself to authorize certain and absolute extinction? Yet the man we condemn to die is cut in two not so much for the crime he has committed as for the sake of all the crimes that might have happened, but which *have not* happened —which could occur, but somehow *will not* occur. Hence, the greatest possible uncertainty appears to authorize the most implacable certitude of all.

I am not the only one to be astonished by this dangerous contradiction. The State itself disapproves, and its bad conscience explains in turn all the contradictions of the official attitude. This attitude suppresses the publicity of executions because it cannot affirm, faced with the facts, that they have ever served to intimidate criminals. It cannot escape the dilemma which Beccaria had already pointed to when he wrote: "If it is important to show the people frequent proof of power, then executions must be frequent; but in that case crimes must be frequent too, which will prove that the death penalty is far from making the desired impression; thus this penalty is at the same time useless and necessary." What can the State do about a punishment both useless and necessary, except conceal it without abolishing it? And so it will be preserved in obscurity, continued with perplexity and hesitation, in the blind hope that one man at least, one day at least, will be intimidated by consideration of the punishment that lies ahead, and will abandon his murderous intent, thereby justifying, though no one will ever know it, a law which has no support in reason or experience. To persist in its claim that the guillotine is exemplary, the State must raise the incidence of real murders in order to avoid an unknown murder of which it cannot be sure (will never be sure) that it would ever have been committed at all. Is it not a strange law, that recognizes the murder it commits, and remains forever ignorant of the crime it prevents?

But what will remain of this power of example, if it is proved that capital punishment has another power, this one quite real, which degrades men to the worst excesses of shame, madness, and murder?

The exemplary effects of these ceremonies can readily be traced in public opinion—the manifestations of sadism they reveal, the terrible notoriety they arouse in the case of certain criminals. Instead of an operatic nobility of attitude at the foot of the scaffold, we find nothing but disgust, contempt, or perverse pleasure. The effects are well known. Propriety too has had its share in effecting the removal of the scaffold from the square in front of the city hall to the city walls, and from the walls to the prison yard. We are less well informed about the sentiments of those whose business it is to attend this kind of spectacle. Let us listen to the words of the director of an English prison, who speaks of "an acute sense of personal shame," of a prison chaplain who speaks of "horror, shame, and humiliation"; and let us consider especially the feelings of the man who kills because it is his trade—I mean the executioner. What shall we think of these civil servants of ours, who refer to the guillotine as "the bike," the condemned man as "the client" or "luggage," except, in the words of the priest Bela Just, who served as prison chaplain for more than thirty executions, that "The idiom of the executors of justice yields nothing in point of cynicism or vulgarity to that of its violators." Here, furthermore, are the reflections of one of our assistant executioners on his official travels across the country: "When it came time for our trips to the provinces, the real fun began: taxis, good restaurants, everything we wanted!" The same man, boasting of the executioner's skill in releasing the knife, says: "One can *indulge oneself in the luxury* of pulling the client's hair." The depravity expressed here has other, more profound aspects. The clothing of the condemned man belongs, by custom, to the executioner. We learn that old father Deibler hung all the clothing he had collected in a shack and that he used *to go look at his collection from time to time.* There are more serious examples. Here is our assistant executioner again: "The new executioner has guillotine fever. Sometimes he stays at home for days at a time, sitting in a chair, ready to go, his hat on his head, his overcoat on, waiting for a summons from the public prosecutor."

And this is the man of whom Joseph de Maistre said that his very existence was accorded by a special decree of divine power and that without him, "order gives way to chaos, thrones collapse, and society disappears." This is the man by means of whom society gets rid of its culprit, and once the executioner signs the prison release, he is permitted to walk out, a free man. The honorable and solemn example, as conceived by our legislation, has had one certain effect, at least—it perverts or destroys the human quality and reason of all who participate in it directly. It will be objected that we are discussing only a few exceptional creatures who make a living out of such degradation. There might be fewer protests if it were known that there are hundreds of men who offer their services as executioner *without pay*. Men of my generation, who have survived the history of our times, will not be surprised to learn this. They know that behind the most familiar, the most peaceful face lies the instinct to torture and to kill. The punishment which claims to intimidate an unknown murderer unquestionably provides a number of known monsters with their vocation as killers. Since we are not above justifying our cruelest laws by considerations of probability, let us not hesitate to admit that out of these hundreds of men whose services are refused, one, at least, has satisfied in some other way the bloody impulses which the guillotine awakened within him.

If we are to maintain the death penalty, let us at least be spared the hypocrisy of justification by example. Let us call by its right name this penalty about which all publicity is suppressed, this intimidation which does not operate upon honest men to the degree that they are honest, which fascinates those who have ceased to be honest, and which degrades and disorders those who lend their hands to it. It is a punishment, certainly, a dreadful physical and moral torture, but one offering no certain example save that of demoralization. It forbids, but it prevents nothing —when it does not in fact arouse the will to murder itself. It is *as if it were not*, except for the man who suffers it—in his soul for months or years, and in his body during the desperate and violent moment when he is cut in two without being altogether deprived of life. Let us call it by a name which, lacking all patents of nobility, at least provides that of truth—let us recognize it for what it ultimately is: a revenge.

Punishment, penalizing rather than preventing, is a form of revenge: society's semiarithmetical answer to violation of its primordial law. This answer is as old as man himself, and usually goes by the name of *retaliation*. He who hurts me must be hurt; who blinds me in one eye must himself lose an eye; who takes a life must die. It is a feeling, and a particularly violent one, which is involved here, not a principle. Retaliation belongs to the order of nature, of instinct, not to the order of law. The law by definition cannot abide by the same rules as nature. If murder is part of man's nature, the law is not made to imitate or reproduce such nature. We have all known the impulse to retaliate, often to our shame, and we know its power: the power of the primeval forests. In this regard, we live—as Frenchmen who grow justifiably indignant at seeing the oil king of Saudi Arabia preach international democracy while entrusting his butcher with the task of cutting off a thief's hand— in a kind of middle ages ourselves, without even the consolations of faith. Yet if we still define our justice according to the calculations of a crude arithmetic, can we at least affirm that this arithmetic is correct, and that even such elementary justice, limited as it is to a form of legal revenge, is *safeguarded* by the death penalty? The answer must again be: No.

We scarcely need to point out how inapplicable the law of retaliation has become in our society: it is as excessive to punish the pyromaniac by setting his house on fire as it is insufficient to punish the thief by deducting from his bank account a sum equivalent to the amount he has stolen. Let us admit instead that it is just and even necessary to compensate the murder of the victim by the death of the murderer. But capital punishment is not merely death. It is as different, in its essence, from the suppression of life as a concentration camp from a prison. It is undeniably a murder which arithmetically cancels out the murder already committed; but it also adds a regularization of death, a public premeditation of which its future victims are informed, an *organization* which in itself is a source of moral suffering more terrible than death. There is thus no real compensation, no equivalence. Many systems of law regard a premeditated crime as more serious than a crime of pure violence. But what is capital punishment if not the most premeditated of murders, to which no criminal act, no matter how calculated, can be compared? If there were to be a real equivalence, the death penalty would have to be pronounced upon a criminal who had forewarned his victim of the very moment he would put him to a horrible death, and who, from that time on, had kept him confined at his own discretion for a period of months. It is not in private life that one meets such monsters.

Here again, when our official jurists speak of death without suffering, they do not know what they are talking about, and furthermore they betray a remarkable lack of imagination. The devastating, degrading fear imposed on the condemned man for months or even years is a punishment more terrible than death itself, and one that has not been imposed on his victim. A murdered man is generally rushed to his death, even at the height of his terror of the mortal violence being done to him, without knowing what is happening: the period of his horror is only that of his life itself, and his hope of escaping whatever madness has pounced upon him probably never deserts him. For the man condemned to death, on the other hand, the horror of his situation is served up to him at every moment for months on end. Torture by hope alternates only with the pangs of animal despair. His lawyer and his confessor, out of simple humanity, and his guards, to keep him docile, unanimously assure him that he will be reprieved. He believes them with all his heart, yet he cannot believe them at all. He hopes by day, despairs by night. And as the weeks pass his hope and despair increase proportionately, until they become equally insupportable. According to all accounts, the color of his skin changes: fear acts like an acid. "It's nothing to know you're going to die," one such man in the Fresnes prison said, "but not to know if you're going to live is the real torture." At the moment of his execution Cartouche remarked, "Bah! a nasty quarter of an hour and it's all over." But it takes months, not minutes. The condemned man knows long in advance that he is going to be killed and that all that can save him is a reprieve which operates, so far as he is concerned, like the will of heaven itself. In any case he cannot intervene, plead for himself: he is no longer a man, but a thing waiting to be manipulated by the executioners. He is kept in a state of absolute necessity, the condition of inert matter, yet within him is the consciousness that is his principal enemy.

When the officials whose trade is to kill such a man refer to him as "luggage," they know what they are saying: to be unable to react to the hand that moves you, holds you, or lets you drop—is that not the condition of some package, some *thing*, or better still, some trapped animal? Yet an animal in a trap can starve itself to death; the man condemned to death cannot. He is provided with a special diet (at Fresnes, diet No. 4 with *extras* of milk, wine, sugar, perserves, and butter); he is encouraged to eat well— if necessary he is forced to eat. The animal must be in good condition for the kill. The thing—the animal —has a right only to those corrupted privileges known as caprices. "You'd be surprised how sensitive they are!" declared one sergeant at Fresnes without a trace of irony. Sensitive? Unquestionably—how else recover the freedom and dignity of will that man cannot live without? Sensitive or not, from the moment the death sentence is pronounced, the condemned man becomes part of an imperturbable

mechanism. He spends several weeks within the cogs and gears of a machine that controls his every gesture, ultimately delivering him to the hands that will lay him out on the last device of all. The luggage is no longer subjected to the operations of chance, the hazards that dominate the existence of a living being, but to mechanical laws that permit him to foresee in the minutest perspective the day of his decapitation.

His condition as an object comes to an end on this day. During the three-quarters of an hour that separates him from his extinction, the certainty of his futile death overcomes everything: the fettered, utterly submissive creature experiences a hell that makes a mockery of the one with which he is threatened. For all their hemlock, the Greeks were humane: they provided their criminals a relative liberty at least, the possibility of postponing or advancing the hour of their own death; and of choosing between suicide and execution. For reasons of security, we carry out our justice by ourselves. Yet there could not be real justice in such cases unless the murderer, having made known his decision months in advance, had entered his victim's house, tied him up securely, informed him he would be put to death in the next hour, and then used this hour to set up the apparatus by which his victim would be dispatched. What criminal has ever reduced his victim to a condition so desperate, so hopeless, and so powerless?

This doubtless explains the strange quality of submission that is so often observed in the condemned man at the moment of his execution. After all, those who have nothing to lose by it might make a last desperate effort, preferring to die by a stray bullet or to be guillotined in a violent struggle that would numb every sense: it would be a kind of freedom in dying. And yet, with very few exceptions, the condemned man walks quite docilely to his death in dismal impassivity. Which must be what our journalists mean when they tell us the condemned man died courageously. What they *really* mean, of course, is that the condemned man made no trouble, no attempt to abandon his status as luggage, and that we are all grateful to him for his good behavior. In so disgraceful a business the accused has shown a commendable sense of propriety in allowing the disgrace to be disposed of as soon as possible. But the compliments and character references are just another part of the general mystification that surrounds the death penalty. For the condemned man often behaves "properly" only to the degree that he is afraid, and deserves the eulogies of our press only if his fear or his despair are sufficiently great to sterilize him altogether. Let me not be misunderstood: some men— political prisoners or not—die heroically, and we must speak of them with the admiration and respect they deserve. But the majority of those condemned to death know no other silence than that of fear, no other impassivity than that of horror, and it seems to me that the silence of fear and horror deserves still more respect than the other. When the priest Bela Just offered to write to the relatives of one young criminal only a few minutes before he was to be hung, and received these words in answer: "I don't have the courage, not even for that," one wonders how a priest, at such a confession of weakness, could keep from falling on his knees before what is most miserable and most sacred in man. As for those who do not talk, those who show us what they have gone through only by the puddle they leave in the place they are dragged from, who would dare say they died as cowards? And by what name shall we call those who have brought these men to their "cowardice"? After all, each murderer, at the moment of his crime, runs the risk of the most terrible death, while those who execute him risk nothing, except perhaps a promotion.

No—what the condemned man experiences at this moment is beyond all morality. Neither virtue, nor courage, nor intelligence, not even innocence has a share in his condition at that moment. Society is reduced at one blow to that condition of primitive terror in which nothing can be judged and all equity, all dignity, have vanished. "The sense of his own innocence does not immunize the executed man against the cruelty of his death. . . . I have seen terrible criminals die courageously, and innocent men walk to the knife trembling in every limb." When the same witness adds that, in his experience, such failures of nerve are more frequent among intellectuals, he does not mean that this category of men has less courage than any other, but that they have more imagination. Confronted with an inescapable death, a man, no matter what his convictions, is devastated throughout his entire system. The sense of powerlessness and solitude of the fettered prisoner, confronted by the public coalition which has *willed* his death, is in itself an unimaginable punishment. In this regard, too, it would be far better if the execution were held in public: the actor that is in every man could then come to the aid of the stricken animal, could help him keep up a front, even in his own eyes. But the darkness and the secrecy of the ceremony are without appeal: in such a disaster, courage, the soul's consistency, faith itself—all are merely matters of chance. As a general rule, the man is destroyed by waiting for his execution long before he is actually killed. Two deaths are imposed, and the first is worse than the second, though the culprit has

killed but once. Compared to this torture, the law of retaliation seems like a civilized principle. For that law, at least, has never claimed that a man must be blinded in both eyes to pay for having blinded his brother in one.

This fundamental injustice, moreover, has its repercussions among the relatives of the man who is executed. The victim has his relatives too, whose sufferings are generally infinite and who, for the most part, wish to be revenged. They are revenged, in the manner I have described, but the relatives of the executed man thereby experience a misery that punishes them beyond the bounds of all justice. A mother's or a father's expectation during the endless months, the prison parlor, the awkward conversations which fill the brief minutes they are allowed to spend with the condemned man, the images of the execution itself—all are tortures that have not been inflicted on the relatives of the victim. Whatever the feelings of the latter, they cannot require their revenge to exceed the crime to such an extent, and torment those who violently share their own grief. "I have been reprieved, Father," writes one man condemned to death, "and I still don't really believe in my good luck. The reprieve was signed April 30, and they told me Wednesday, on my way back from the parlor. I sent them to tell Papa and Mama, who had not yet left the prison. You can imagine their happiness." We can imagine their happiness only to the degree that we can imagine their unceasing misery until the moment of the reprieve, and the utter despair of those who receive another kind of news, the kind that unjustly punishes their innocence and their misery.

As for the law of retaliation, it must be admitted that even in its primitive form it is legitimate only between two individuals of whom one is absolutely innocent and the other absolutely guilty. Certainly the victim is innocent. But can society, which is supposed to represent the victim, claim a comparable innocence? Is it not responsible, at least in part, for the crime which it represses with such severity? This theme has been frequently developed elsewhere, and I need not continue a line of argument which the most varied minds have elaborated since the eighteenth century. Its principal features can be summed up, in any case, by observing that every society has the criminals it deserves. As far as France is concerned, however, it is impossible not to draw attention to circumstances which might make our legislators more modest. Answering a questionnaire on capital punishment in *Figaro* in 1952, a colonel declared that the establishment of perpetual forced labor as the supreme penalty amounted to the same thing as the establishment of schools of crime. This superior officer seems to be unaware—and I am happy for his sake—that we already have our schools of crime, which differ in one particular from our reformatories—that fact that one can leave them at any hour of the day or night: they are our bars and our slums, the glories of our republic. And on this point, at least, it is impossible to express oneself with moderation.

According to statistics, there are 64,000 overcrowded living accommodations (three to five persons to a room) in the city of Paris alone. Now of course the man who murders children is a particularly unspeakable creature, scarcely worth working up much pity over. It is probable, too (I say probable), that none of my readers, placed in the same promiscuous living conditions, would go so far as to murder children: there is no question of reducing the guilt of such monsters. But would such monsters, in decent living conditions, have an occasion to go so far? The least one can say is that they are not the only guilty parties: it is difficult to account for the fact that the right to punish these criminals is given to the very men who prefer to subsidize sugar beets rather than new construction.

But alcohol makes this scandal all the more striking. It is well known that the French nation has been systematically intoxicated by its parliamentary majority for generally disgraceful reasons. Yet even with such knowledge in our grasp, the determined responsibility of alcohol for crimes of blood is still astounding. One lawyer (Guillon) has estimated that it is a factor in 60 per cent of all such cases. Dr. Lagriffe sets the rate somewhere between 41.7 and 72 per cent. An investigation conducted in 1951 at the distribution center of the Fresnes prison, among inmates guilty of breaches of common law, revealed 29 per cent were chronic alcoholics and 24 per cent had alcoholic backgrounds. Finally, 95 per cent of all murderers of children have been alcoholics. These are all fine figures, but there is one we must consider which is still finer: that of the *apéritif* manufacturer who declared a profit of 410,000,000 francs in 1953. A comparison of these figures authorizes us to inform the stockholders of this company, and the assemblymen who voted for sugar beets rather than for buildings, that they have certainly killed more children than they suspect. As an adversary of capital punishment, I am far from demanding the death penalty for these individuals. But to begin with, it seems to me an indispensable and urgent duty to conduct them under military escort to the next execution of the murderer of a child, and at the conclusion of the

ceremony to present them with a table of statistics which will include the figures I have been discussing.

When the state sows alcohol, it cannot be surprised if it reaps crime. And it is *not* surprised, after all—it merely restricts itself to chopping off the same heads for which it poured out so much alcohol. It imperturbably executes its justice and sets itself up as a creditor: its good conscience is not affected. Hence we have one representative of the interests of alcohol indignantly answering the *Figaro* questionnaire: "I know what the most outspoken abolitionist of capital punishment would do if he were suddenly to discover assassins on the point of killing his mother, his father, his children, or his best friend . . . *Alors!*" This "*Alors!*" seems a little drunk already. Naturally the most outspoken abolitionist of capital punishment would fire, and with every justification, at the assassins, and without affecting in the slightest his reasons for outspokenly urging the abolition of capital punishment. But if his ideas led to consequences of any value, and if the same assassins smelled a little too much of alcohol, would he not subsequently turn his attentions to those who make it their business to intoxicate our future criminals? It is even a little surprising that the parents of victims of alcoholic crime have never had the notion of requesting a few elucidations from the floor of the Assembly itself. But the contrary is the rule, and the State, armed with the confidence of all, with the full support of public opinion, continues to punish murderers, even and especially when they are alcoholics, somewhat the way a pimp punishes the hard-working creatures who provide his livelihood. But the pimp doesn't preach about his business. The State does. Its jurisprudence, if it admits that drunkenness occasionally constitutes an extenuating circumstance, is unaware of chronic alcoholism. Drunkenness, however, accompanies only crimes of violence, which are not punishable by death, whereas the chronic alcoholic is also capable of premeditated crimes, which gain him the death penalty. The State thus maintains the right to punish in the very case in which its own responsibility is profoundly involved.

Does this come down to saying that every alcoholic must be declared nonresponsible by a State which will strike its breast in horror until the entire populace drinks nothing but fruit juice? Certainly not. No more than it comes down to saying that the facts of heredity eliminate responsibility and guilt. A criminal's real responsibility cannot be determined exactly. All calculation is powerless to take into account the total number of our ancestors, alcoholic or not. At the other end of time, such a number would be 10 times greater than the number of inhabitants of the earth at present. The total of diseased or morbid tendencies which could be transmitted is thus incalculable. We enter the world burdened with the weight of an infinite necessity, and according to logic must agree on a situation of a general nonresponsibility. Logically, neither punishment nor reward can be distributed accurately, and therefore all society becomes impossible. Yet the instinct of self-preservation, in societies and individuals alike, requires, on the contrary, the postulate of individual responsibility; a responsibility that must be accepted, without daydreaming of an absolute indulgence which would coincide with the death and disappearance of any society whatsoever. But the same line of reasoning that compels us to abandon a general nonresponsibility must also lead us to conclude that there is never, on the other hand, a situation of total responsibility, and consequently no such thing as absolute punishment or absolute reward. No one can be rewarded absolutely, not even by the Nobel prize. But no one must be punished absolutely if he is found guilty, and with all the more reason if there is a chance he might be innocent. The death penalty, which neither serves as an example nor satisfies the conditions of retaliative justice, usurps in addition an exorbitant privilege by claiming the right to punish a necessarily relative guilt by an absolute and irreparable penalty.

If, in fact, the death penalty serves as a questionable example of our gimcrack justice, one must agree with its supporters that it is eliminative: capital punishment definitively eliminates the condemned man. This fact alone, actually, ought to exclude, especially for its partisans, the discussion of all the other dangerous arguments which, as we have seen, can be ceaselessly contested. It would be more honest to say that capital punishment is definitive because it must be, to point out that certain men are socially irrecoverable, constituting a permanent danger to each citizen and to the social order as a whole, so that, before anything else, they must be suppressed. No one, at least, will question the existence of certain beasts in our society, creatures of incorrigible energy and brutality that nothing seems capable of subduing. And although the death penalty certainly does not solve the problem they present, let us at least agree that it goes a long way toward eliminating it.

I will return to these men. But first, is capital punishment confined only to them? Can we be absolutely certain that not one man of all those executed is recoverable? Can we even swear that one or another may not be *innocent?* In both cases, must we not admit that capital punishment is eliminative only to the degree that it is irreparable? Yesterday, March 15, 1957, Burton Abbott, condemned to death for the murder of a 14-year-old girl, was executed in California: it was certainly the kind of crime that I imagine would class him among the irrecoverables. Although Abbott had constantly protested his innocence, he was condemned. His execution was scheduled for March 15 at 10 in the morning. At 9:10 a reprieve was granted to allow the defense to present an appeal. At 11 o'clock the appeal was rejected. At 11:15 Abbott entered the gas chamber. At 11:18 he began to breathe the first fumes of gas. At 11:20 the secretary of the reprieve board telephoned the prison: the board had changed its decision. The governor had been called first, but he had gone sailing, and they had called the prison directly. Abbott was removed from the gas chamber: it was too late. If the weather had been bad the day before, the governor of California would not have gone sailing. He would have telephoned two minutes earlier: Abbott would be alive today and would perhaps see his innocence proved. Any other punishment, even the most severe, would have permitted this chance. Capital punishment, however, permitted him none.

It may be thought that this case is exceptional. Our lives are exceptional too, and yet, in the fugitive existence we have been granted, this exception occurred not ten hours by plane from where I am writing. Abbott's misfortune is not so much an exception as it is one news item among many others, an error which is not at all isolated, if we examine our newspapers (for example, the Deshay case, to instance only the most recent). The jurist Olivecroix, applying a calculus of probabilities to the chance of judiciary error, concluded in 1860 that approximately one innocent man was condemned out of every 257 cases. The proportion seems low, but only in relation to moderate punishment. In relation to capital punishment, the proportion is infinitely high. When Hugo wrote that he preferred to call the guillotine Lesurques, he did not mean that every man who was decapitated was a Lesurques, but that one Lesurques was enough to wipe out the value of capital punishment forever. It is understandable that Belgium definitely abjured pronouncing capital punishment after one such judiciary error, and that England brought up the question of its abolition after the Hayes case. We can readily sympathize with the conclusions of that attorney general who, consulted on the petition for reprieve of a criminal who was most probably guilty but whose victim's body had not been recovered, wrote as follows: "The survival of X assures the authorities the possibility of effectively examining at their leisure every new sign that may subsequently be discovered of the existence of his wife (the victim, whose body had not been recovered). . . . On the other hand, his execution, eliminating this hypothetical possibility of examination, would give, I fear, to the slightest evidence of her still being alive a theoretical value, a pressure of regret which I consider it inopportune to create." The man's feeling for both justice and truth are admirably expressed, and it would be advisable to cite as often as possible in our assize courts that "pressure of regret" which sums up so steadfastly the danger with which every juryman is confronted. Once the innocent man is dead, nothing more can be done for him except to re-establish his good name, if someone is still interested in asking for such a service. His innocence is restored—actually he had never lost it in the first place. But the persecution of which he has been the victim, his dreadful sufferings, and his hideous death have been acquired forever. There is nothing left to do but consider the innocent men of the future, in order to spare them such torments. It has been done in Belgium; but in France, apparently, there are no bad consciences.

Why should our consciences be bad if they are based on our conception of justice: has not this conception made great progress, does it not follow in the footsteps of science itself? When the learned expert gives his opinion in the assize courts, it is as if a priest had spoken, and the jury, raised in the religion of science—the jury nods. Nevertheless several recent cases—particularly the Besnard affair—have given us a good idea of the comedy such expertise can provide. Guilt is not better established because it can be demonstrated in a test tube. Another test tube can prove the contrary, and the personal equation will thereby maintain all its old significance in such perilous mathematics as these. The proportion of scientists who are really experts is the same as that of judges who are really psychologists—scarcely more than that of juries that are really serious and objective. Today, as yesterday, the chance of error remains. Tomorrow another expert's report will proclaim the innocence of another Abbott. But Abbott will be dead, scientifically enough, and science, which claims to prove innocence as well as guilt, has not yet succeeded in restoring the life it has taken.

And among the guilty themselves, can we also be sure of having killed only "irrecoverables"? Those who like myself have had to attend hearings in our assize courts know that a number of elements of sheer accident enter into a sentence, even a death sentence. The looks of the accused; his background (adultery is often regarded as an incriminating circumstance by some jurors: I have never been able to believe that all are completely faithful to their wives and husbands); his attitude (which is only regarded as being in his favor if it is as conventional as possible, which usually means as near play-acting as possible); even his elocution (one must neither stutter nor speak too well) and the incidents of the hearing sentimentally evaluated (the truth, unfortunately, is not always moving)—all these are so many accidents that influence the final decision of a jury. At the moment the verdict recommending the death penalty is pronounced, one can be sure that this most certain of punishments has only been arrived at by a great conjunction of uncertainties. When one realizes that the verdict of death depends on the jury's estimation of the extenuating circumstances, particularly since the reforms of 1832 gave our juries the power to admit undetermined extenuating circumstances, one can appreciate the margin left to the momentary humors of the jurors. It is no longer the law which establishes with any precision those cases in which the death penalty is recommended, but the jury which, after the event, estimates its suitability by guesswork, to say the least. As there are no two juries alike, the man who is executed might as well have been spared. Irrecoverable in the eyes of the honest citizens of Ile-et-Vilaine, he might well be granted the shadow of an excuse by the good people of Var. Unfortunately, the same knife falls in both departments. And it is not concerned with such details.

The accidents of the times combine with those of geography to reinforce the general absurdity. The communist French worker who was just guillotined in Algeria for having planted a bomb, discovered before it could explode, in the cloakroom of a factory was condemned as much by his act as by the times, for in the Algerian situation at present, Arab public opinion was to be shown that the guillotine was made for French necks too, and French public opinion, outraged by terrorist activities, was to be given satisfaction at the same time. Nevertheless, the minister in charge of the execution counted many communist votes in his constituency, and if the circumstances had been slightly different, the accused would have got off lightly and perhaps one day, as his party's deputy, might have found himself drinking at the same bar as the minister. Such thoughts are bitter and one might wish they remained fresh a little longer in the minds of our governors. These gentlemen should be aware that times and manners change; a day comes along when the criminal who was executed too quickly no longer seems quite so guilty. By then it is too late, and what can you do but repent or forget? Naturally, one forgets. But society is nonetheless affected: one unpunished crime, according to the Greeks, infects the whole city. Innocence condemned to death, or crime excessively punished, leaves a stain no less hideous in the long run. We know it, in France.

Such is the nature of human justice, it will be said, and despite its imperfections, after all, even human justice is better than the operation of despotism or chance. But this rueful preference is tolerable only in relation to moderate punishment. Confronted by death sentences, it is a scandal. A classic work on French law excuses the death penalty from being subject to degree in the following words: "Human justice has not the slightest ambition to insure proportion of this nature. Why? Because it knows itself to be imperfect." Must we therefore conclude that this imperfection authorizes us to pronounce an absolute judgment, and that society, uncertain of realizing justice in its pure state, must rush headlong with every likelihood of error, upon the supreme injustice? If human justice knows itself to be imperfect, might not that knowledge be more suitably and modestly demonstrated by leaving a sufficient margin around our condemnations for the eventual reparation of error? This very weakness in which human justice finds extenuating circumstances for itself in every case and on every occasion—is it not to be accorded to the criminal himself as well? Can the jury in all decency say, "If we condemn you to death by mistake, you will surely forgive us in consideration of the weaknesses of the human nature we all share. But we nevertheless condemn you to death without the slightest consideration of these weaknesses or of this common nature"? All men have a community in error and in aberration. Yet must this community operate in behalf of the tribunal and be denied to the accused? No, for if justice has any meaning in this world, it is none other than the recognition of this very community: it cannot, in its very essence, be separated from compassion. Let it be understood that by compassion I mean only the consciousness of a common suffering, not a frivolous indulgence that takes no account of the sufferings and rights of the victim. Compassion does not exclude punishment, but it withholds an ultimate condemnation. It is revolted by the definitive, irreparable measure that does injustice to man in general since it does not recognize his share in the misery of the common condition.

As a matter of fact, certain juries know this well enough, and often admit the extenuating circumstances of a crime which nothing can extenuate. This is because they regard the death penalty as too extreme and prefer to punish insufficiently rather than to excess. In such cases, the extreme severity of the punishment tends to sanction crime instead of penalizing it. There is scarcely one session of the assize courts of which one cannot read in our press that a verdict is incoherent, that in the face of the facts it appears either insufficient or excessive. The jurors are not unaware of this. They simply prefer, as we should do ourselves, when confronted with the enormity of capital punishment, to appear confused, rather than compromise their sleep for nights to come. Knowing themselves imperfect, at least they draw the appropriate consequences. And true justice is on their side, precisely to the degree that logic is not.

There are, however, great criminals that every jury will condemn, no matter where and when they are tried. Their crimes are certain, and the proofs elicited by the prosecution correspond with the admissions of the defense. What is abnormal and even monstrous in their crimes unquestionably determines their category as pathological, though in the majority of such cases psychiatrists affirm the criminal's responsibility. Recently, in Paris, a young man of rather weak character, but known for the sweetness and affection of his nature and his extreme devotion to his family, described himself as being annoyed by his father's remarks on the lateness of the hours he had been keeping. The father was reading at the dining room table. The young man took an ax and struck his father several mortal blows with it from behind. Then, in the same fashion, he struck down his mother, who was in the kitchen. He removed his bloody trousers and hid them in the closet, changed his clothes, and after paying a visit to the family of his fiancée without revealing the slightest discomposure, returned to his own house and informed the police his parents had been murdered. The police immediately discovered the bloody trousers, and easily obtained the parricide's unperturbed confession. The psychiatrists agreed on his responsibility for these "murders by irritation." The young man's strange indifference, of which he gave other indications in prison (rejoicing that his parents' funeral had been so well attended: "Everyone liked them," he said to his lawyers), can nevertheless scarcely be considered as normal. But his reason was apparently intact.

Many "monsters" offer a countenance just as impenetrable. They are therefore eliminated upon consideration of the facts alone. Because of the nature or the degree of their crimes it is inconceivable that they would repent or even wish to change their ways. In their case, a recurrence is what must be avoided, and there is no other solution than to eliminate them. On this—and only this—aspect of the question is the discussion of the death penalty legitimate. In all other cases the arguments of its partisans cannot withstand the criticism of its opponents. At this point, in fact, at our present level of ignorance, a kind of wager is established: no expertise, no exercise of reason can give the deciding vote between those who think a last chance must always be granted to even the last of men and those who consider this chance as entirely illusory. But it is perhaps possible, at this very point, to override the *eternal* opposition between the partisans and opponents of the death penalty, by determining the advisability of such a penalty *at this time, and in Europe.* With considerably less competence, I shall attempt to parallel the efforts of professor Jean Graven, a Swiss jurist who writes, in his remarkable study of the problems of capital punishment: ". . . Regarding the problem that once again confronts our conscience and our reason, it is our opinion that the solution must be based not upon the conceptions, the problems, and the arguments of the past, nor on the theoretical hopes and promises of the future, but on the ideas, the given circumstances, and the necessities of today." One could, in fact, argue forever about the advantages or devastations of the death penalty as it has been through the ages or as it might be contemplated in some eternity of ideas. But the death penalty plays its part here and now, and we must determine here and now where we stand in relation to a contemporary executioner. What does the death penalty mean for us, halfway through the twentieth century?

For the sake of simplification, let us say that our civilization has lost the only values that, to a certain degree, could justify the death penalty, and that it suffers, on the contrary, from every evil that necessitates its suppression. In other words, the abolition of the death penalty should be demanded by the conscious members of our society on grounds of both logic and fidelity to the facts.

Of logic, first of all. To decide that a man must be definitively punished is to deny him any further opportunity whatsoever to make reparation for his acts. It is at this juncture, we repeat, that the arguments for and against capital punishment confront one another blindly, eventuating in a fruitless checkmate. Yet it is exactly here that none of us can afford to be positive, for we are all judges, all party to the dispute. Hence our uncertainty about our right to kill and our impotence to convince others on either side. Unless there is absolute innocence, there can be no supreme judge. Now we have all committed some transgression in our lives, even if this transgression has not put us within the power of the law and has remained an unknown crime: there are no just men, only hearts more or less poor in justice. The mere fact of living permits us to know this, and to add to the sum of our actions a little of the good that might partially compensate for the evil we have brought into the world. This right to live that coincides with the opportunity for reparation is the natural right of every man, even the worst. The most abandoned criminal and the worthiest judge here find themselves side by side, equally miserable and jointly responsible. Without this right, the moral life is strictly impossible. None among us, in particular, is entitled to despair of a single man, unless it be after his death, which transforms his life into destiny and admits of a final judgment. But to pronounce this final judgment before death, to decree the closing of accounts when the creditor is still alive, is the privilege of no man. On these grounds, at least, he who judges absolutely condemns himself absolutely.

Barnard Fallot of the Masuy gang, who worked for the Gestapo, confessed to the entire list of terrible crimes of which he was accused, and later went to his death with great courage, declaring himself beyond hope of reprieve: "My hands are too red with blood," he said to one of his fellow prisoners. Public opinion and that of his judges certainly classified him among the irrecoverables, and I would have been tempted to put him in that category myself, had I

not read one astonishing piece of evidence: after having declared that he wanted to die bravely, Fallot told the same prisoner: "Do you know what I regret most of all? Not having known sooner about the Bible they gave me here. If I had, I wouldn't be where I am now." It is not a question of surrendering to the sentimentality of conventional imagery and conjuring up Victor Hugo's good convicts. The age of enlightenment, as it is called, wished to abolish the death penalty under the pretext that man was fundamentally good. We know, of course, that he is not (he is simply better or worse). After the last twenty years of our splendid history we know it very well. But it is because man is not fundamentally good that no one among us can set himself up as an absolute judge, for no one among us can pretend to absolute innocence. The verdict of capital punishment destroys the only indisputable human community there is, the community in the face of death, and such a judgment can only be legitimated by a truth or a principle that takes its place above all men, beyond the human condition.

Capital punishment, in fact, throughout history has always been a religious punishment. When imposed in the name of the king, representative of God on earth, or by priests, or in the name of a society considered as a sacred body, it is not the human community that is destroyed but the functioning of the guilty man as a member of the divine community which alone can give him his life. Such a man is certainly deprived of his earthly life, yet his opportunity for reparation is preserved. The real judgment is not pronounced in this world, but in the next. Religious values, especially the belief in an eternal life, are thus the only ones on which the death penalty can be based, since according to their own logic they prevent that penalty from being final and irreparable: it is justified only insofar as it is not supreme.

The Catholic Church, for example, has always admitted the necessity of the death penalty. It has imposed the penalty itself, without avarice, at other periods. Today, its doctrines still justify capital punishment, and concede the State the right to apply it. No matter how subtle this doctrine may be, there is at its core a profound feeling which was directly expressed by a Swiss councilor from Fribourg during a discussion of capital punishment by the national council in 1937; according to M. Grand, even the worst criminal examines his own conscience when faced with the actuality of execution. "He repents, and his preparation for death is made easier. The Church has saved one of its members, has accomplished its divine mission. This is why the Church has steadfastly countenanced capital punishment, not only as a means of legitimate protection, *but as a powerful means of salvation*. . . . [My italics.] Without becoming precisely a matter of doctrine, the death penalty, like war itself, can be justified by its quasi-divine efficacity."

By virtue of the same reasoning, no doubt, one can read on the executioner's sword in Fribourg the motto "Lord Jesus, thou art the Judge." The executioner is thereby invested with a divine function. He is the man who destroys the body in order to deliver the soul to its divine judgment, which no man on earth can foresee. It will perhaps be considered that such mottos imply rather outrageous confusions, and certainly those who confine themselves to the actual teachings of Jesus will see this handsome sword as yet another outrage to the body of Christ. In this light can be understood the terrible words of a Russian prisoner whom the executioners of the Tsar were about to hang in 1905, when he turned to the priest who was about to console him with the image of Christ and said: "Stand back, lest you commit a sacrilege." An unbeliever will not fail to remark that those who have placed in the very center of their faith the overwhelming victim of a judicial error should appear more reticent, to say the least, when confronted by cases of legal murder. One might also

remind the believer that the emperor Julian, before his conversion, refused to give official posts to Christians because they systematically refused to pronounce the death sentence or to aid in administering it. For five centuries Christians believed that the strict moral teaching of their master forbade them to kill. But the Catholic faith is derived not only from the teachings of Christ, it is nourished by the Old Testament, by Saint Paul, and by the Fathers as well. In particular the immortality of the soul and the universal resurrection of the body are articles of dogma. Hence, capital punishment, for the believer, can be regarded as a provisional punishment which does not in the least affect the definite sentence, but remains a disposition necessary to the terrestrial order, an administrative measure which, far from making an end of the guilty man, can promote, on the contrary, his redemption in heaven. I do not say that all believers follow this reasoning, and I can imagine without much difficulty that most Catholics stand closer to Christ than to Moses or Saint Paul. I say only that the belief in the immortality of the soul has permitted Catholicism to formulate the problem of capital punishment in very different terms, and to justify it.

But what does such a justification mean to the society we live in, a society which in its institutions and manners alike has become almost entirely secular? When an atheist—or skeptic—or agnostic judge imposes the death penalty on an unbelieving criminal, he is pronouncing a definitive punishment that cannot be revised. He sits upon God's throne, but without possessing God's powers and, moreover, without believing in them. He condemns to death, in fact, because his ancestors believed in eternal punishment. Yet the society which he claims to represent pronounces, in reality, a purely eliminative measure, destroys the human community united against death, and sets itself up as an absolute value because it pretends to absolute power. Of course society traditionally assigns a priest to the condemned man, and the priest may legitimately hope that fear of punishment will help effect the condemned man's conversion. Yet who will accept this casuistry as the justification of a punishment so often inflicted and so often received in an entirely different spirit? It is one thing to believe and "therefore know not fear," and another to find one's faith through fear. Conversion by fire or the knife will always be suspect, and one can well understand why the Church renounced a triumph by terror over infidel hearts. In any case, a secularized society has nothing to gain from a conversion concerning which it professes complete disinterest: it enacts a consecrated punishment, and at the same time deprives that punishment of its justification and its utility alike. Delirious in its own behalf, society plucks the wicked from its bosom as if it were virtue personified. In the same way, an honorable man might kill his son who had strayed from the path of duty, saying, "Really, I didn't know what else I could do!" Society thus usurps the right of selection, as if it were nature, and adds a terrible suffering to the eliminative process, as if it were a redeeming god.

To assert, in any case, that a man must be absolutely cut off from society because he is absolutely wicked is the same as saying that society is absolutely good, which no sensible person will believe today. It will not be believed—in fact, it is easier to believe the contrary. Our society has become as diseased and criminal as it is only because it has set itself up as its own final justification, and has had no concern but its own preservation and success in history. Certainly it is a secularized society, yet during the nineteenth century it began to fashion a kind of ersatz religion by proposing itself as an object of adoration. The doctrines of evolution, and the theories of selection that accompanied such doctrines, have proposed the future of society as its final end. The political utopias grafted onto these doctrines have proposed, at the end of time, a Golden Age that justifies in advance all intermediary enterprises. Society has grown accustomed to legalizing whatever can minister to its future, and consequently to usurping the supreme punishment in an absolute fashion: it has regarded as a crime and a sacrilege everything that contradicts its own intentions and temporal dogmas. In other words, the executioner, formerly a priest, has become a civil servant. The results surround us. Halfway through the century, our society, which has forfeited the logical right to pronounce the death penalty, must now abolish it for reasons of realism.

Confronted with crime, how does our civilization in fact define itself? The answer is easy: for thirty years crimes of state have vastly exceeded crimes of individuals. I shall not even mention wars—general or local—although blood is a kind of alcohol that eventually intoxicates like the strongest wine. I am referring here to the number of individuals killed directly by the State, a number that has grown to astronomic proportions and infinitely exceeds that of "private" murders. There are fewer and fewer men condemned by common law, and more and more men executed for political reasons. The proof of this fact is that each of us, no matter how honorable he is, can now envisage the *possibility* of someday being put to death, whereas such an eventuality at the beginning of the century would have appeared farcical at best. Alphonse Karr's famous remark, "Let my lords the assassins begin," no longer has any meaning: those who spill the most blood are also those who believe they have right, logic, and history on their side.

It is not so much against the individual killer that our society must protect itself then, as against the State. Perhaps this equation will be reversed in another thirty years. But for the present, a legitimate defense must be made against the State, before all else. Justice and the most realistic sense of our time require that the law protect the individual against a State given over to the follies of sectarianism and pride. "Let the State begin by abolishing the death penalty" must be our rallying cry today.

Bloody laws, it has been said, make bloody deeds. But it is also possible for a society to suffer that state of ignominy in which public behavior, no matter how disorderly, comes nowhere near being so bloody as the laws. Half of Europe knows this state. We have known it in France and we risk knowing it again. The executed of the Occupation produced the executed of the Liberation whose friends still dream of revenge. Elsewhere, governments charged with too many crimes are preparing to drown their guilt in still greater massacres. We kill for a nation or for a deified social class. We kill for a future society, likewise deified. He who believes in omniscience can conceive of omnipotence. Temporal idols that demand absolute faith tirelessly mete out absolute punishments. And religions without transcendence murder those they condemn en masse and without hope.

How can European society in the twentieth century survive if it does not defend the individual by every means within its power against the oppression of the State? To forbid putting a man to death is one means of publicly proclaiming that society and the State are not absolute values, one means of demonstrating that nothing authorizes them to legislate definitively, to bring to pass the irreparable. Without the death penalty, Gabriel Péri and Brasillach would perhaps be among us still; we could then judge them, according to our lights, and proudly speak out our judgment, instead of which they now judge us, and it is we who must remain silent. Without the death penalty, the corpse of Rajk would not still be poisoning Hungary, a less guilty Germany would be received with better grace by the nations of Europe, the Russian Revolution would not still be writhing in its shame, and the blood of Algeria would weigh less heavily upon us here in France. Without the death penalty, Europe itself would not be infected by the corpses accumulated in its exhausted earth for the last twenty years. Upon our continent all values have been overturned by fear and hatred among individuals as among nations. The war of ideas is waged by rope and knife. It is no longer the natural human society that exercises its rights of repression, but a ruling ideology that demands its human sacrifices. "The lesson the scaffold always provides," Francart wrote, "is that human life ceases to be sacred when it is considered useful to suppress it." Apparently it has been considered increasingly useful, the lesson has found apt pupils, and the contagion is spreading everywhere. And with it, the disorders of nihilism. A spectacular counterblow is required: it must be proclaimed, in institutions and as a matter of principle, that the human person is above and beyond the State. Every measure which will diminish the pressure of social forces on the individual will also aid in the decongestion of a Europe suffering from an afflux of blood, will permit us to think more clearly, and to make our way toward recovery. The disease of Europe is to believe in nothing and to claim to know everything. But Europe does not know everything, far from it, and to judge by the rebellion and the hope in which we find ourselves today, Europe does believe in something: Europe believes that the supreme misery of man, at its mysterious limit, borders on his supreme greatness. For the majority of Europeans faith is lost, and with it the justifications faith conferred upon the order of punishment. But the majority of Europeans are also sickened by that idolatry of the State which has claimed to replace their lost faith. From now on, with divided goals, certain and uncertain, determined never to submit and never to oppress, we must recognize both our hope and our ignorance, renounce all absolute law, all irreparable institutions. We know enough to be able to say that this or that great criminal deserves a sentence of perpetual forced labor. But we do not know enough to say that he can be deprived of his own future, which is to say, of our common opportunity for reparation. In tomorrow's united Europe, on whose behalf I write, the solemn abolition of the death penalty must be the first article of that European Code for which we all hope.

From the humanitarian idylls of the eighteenth century to its bloody scaffolds the road runs straight and is easily followed; we all know today's executioners are humanists. And therefore we cannot be too suspicious of humanitarian ideologies applied to a problem like that of capital punishment. I should like to repeat, by way of conclusion, that my opposition to the death penalty derives from no illusions as to the natural goodness of the human creature, and from no faith in a golden age to come. On the contrary, the abolition of capital punishment seems necessary to me for reasons of qualified pessimism, reasons I have attempted to explain in terms of logic and the most realistic considerations. Not that the heart has not made its contribution to what I have been saying: for anyone who has spent several weeks among these texts, these memories, and these men—all, intimately or remotely, connected with the scaffold—there can be no question of leaving their dreadful ranks unaffected by what one has seen and heard. Nevertheless, I do not believe there is no responsibility in this world for what I have found, or that one should submit to our modern propensity for absolving victim and killer in the same moral confusion. This purely sentimental confusion involves more cowardice than generosity, and ends up by justifying whatever is worst in this world: if everything is blessed, then slave camps are blessed, and organized murder, and the cynicism of the great political bosses—and ultimately, blessing everything alike, one betrays one's own brothers. We can see this happening all around us. But indeed, with the world in its present condition the man of the twentieth century asks for laws and institutions of *convalescence* that will check without crushing, lead without hampering. Hurled into the unregulated dynamism of history, man needs a new physics, new laws of equilibrium. He needs, most of all, a reasonable society, not the anarchy into which his own pride and the State's inordinate powers have plunged him.

It is my conviction that the abolition of the death penalty will help us advance toward that society. In taking this initiative, France could propose its extension on either side of the iron curtain; in any case she could set an example. Capital punishment would be replaced by a sentence of perpetual forced labor for criminals judged incorrigible, and by shorter terms for others. As for those who believe that such punishment is still more cruel than capital punishment itself, I wonder why, in that case, they do not reserve it for Landru and his like and relegate capital punishment to secondary offenders. One might also add that such forced labor leaves the condemned man the possibility of choosing his death, whereas the guillotine is a point of no return. On the other hand, I would answer those who believe that a sentence of perpetual forced labor is too mild a punishment by remarking first on their lack of imagination and then by pointing out that the privation of liberty could seem to them a mild punishment only to the degree that contemporary society has taught them to despise what liberty they have.

That Cain was not killed, but bore in the sight of all men a mark of reprobation is, in any case, the lesson we should draw from the Old Testament, not to mention the Gospels, rather than taking our inspiration from the cruel examples of the Mosaic law. There is no reason why at least a limited version of such an experiment should not be attempted in France (say for a ten-year period), if our government is still capable of redeeming its vote for alcohol by the great measure in behalf of civilization which total abolition would represent. And if public opinion and its representatives cannot renounce our slothful law which confines itself to eliminating what it cannot amend, at least, while waiting for a day of regeneration and of truth, let us not preserve as it is this "solemn shambles" (in Tarde's expression) which continues to disgrace our society. The death penalty, as it is imposed, even as rarely as it is imposed, is a disgusting butchery, an outrage inflicted on the spirit and body of man. This truncation, this living severed head, these long gouts of blood, belong to a barbarous epoch that believed it could subdue the people by offering them degrading spectacles. Today, when this ignoble death is secretly administered, what meaning can such torture have? The truth is that in an atomic age we kill as we did in the age of steelyards: where is the man of normal sensibility whose stomach is not turned at the mere idea of such clumsy surgery? If the French state is incapable of overcoming its worst impulses to this degree, and of furnishing Europe with one of the remedies it needs most, let it at least reform its means of administering capital punishment. Science, which has taught us so much about killing, could at least teach us to kill decently. An anesthetic which would permit the accused to pass from a state of sleep to death, which would remain within his reach for at least a day so that he could make free use of it, and which in cases of refusal or failure of nerve could then be administered to him, would assure the elimination of the criminal, if that is what we require, but would also provide a little decency where today there is nothing but a sordid and obscene exhibition.

I indicate these compromises only to the degree that one must sometimes despair of seeing wisdom and the principles of civilization impose themselves upon those responsible for our future. For certain men, more numerous than is supposed, knowing what the death penalty really is and being unable to prevent its application is physically insupportable. In their own way, they suffer this penalty too, and without any justification. If we at least lighten the weight of the hideous images that burden these men, society will lose nothing by our actions. But ultimately even such measures will be insufficient. Neither in the hearts of men nor in the manners of society will there be a lasting peace until we outlaw death.

Translated by Richard Howard

►► **Frank O'Hara**

A Step Away from Them

It's my lunch hour, so I go
for a walk among the hum-colored
cabs. First, down the sidewalk
where laborers feed their dirty
glistening torsos sandwiches
and Coca-Cola, with yellow helmets
on. They protect them from falling
bricks, I guess. Then onto the
avenue where skirts are flipping
above heels and blow up over
grates. The sun is hot, but the
cabs stir up the air. I look
at bargains in wristwatches. There
are cats playing in sawdust.
                     On
to Times Square, where the sign
blows smoke over my head, and higher
the waterfall pours lightly. A
Negro stands in a doorway with a
toothpick, languorously agitating.
A blonde chorus girl clicks: he
smiles and rubs his chin. Everything
suddenly honks: it is 12:40 of
a Thursday.

Neon in daylight is a
great pleasure, as Edwin Denby would
write, as are light bulbs in daylight.
I stop for a cheeseburger at JULIET'S
CORNER. Giulietta Massina, wife of
Federico Fellini, *è bell' attrice.*
And chocolate malted. A lady in
foxes on such a day puts her poodle
in a cab.
                There are several Puerto
Ricans on the avenue today, which
makes it beautiful and warm. First
Bunny died, then John Latouche,
then Jackson Pollock. But is the
earth as full as life was full, of them?
And one has eaten and one walks,
past the magazines with nudes
and the posters for BULLFIGHT and
the Manhattan Storage Warehouse,
which they'll soon tear down. I
used to think they had the Armory
Show there.
                A glass of papaya juice
and back to work. My heart is in my
pocket, it is Poems by Pierre Reverdy.

►► **Alexander Trocchi**

from CAIN'S BOOK

It is not far from Flushing to the Village. There is a
train direct to 42nd Street. But again I won't go in.
There is nothing for me to go there for now. It is as
though a quick and spasmodic plague wiped out our
shadow city. And the rest fled. Only the citadel remains, for each of us alone who is not behind bars.

Centre everywhere, circumference nowhere. Lethal
dose, variable.

It happened to some of us that we could no longer
go outside the citadel.

I remember nights without, cold streets, unfriendly saloons, great distances. Fear. Nine hours

until daylight (not that that made much difference, except that you could sit in the park amongst people who played), no reason for being anywhere rather than anywhere else, and without. This is the steel edge of hysteria, the point of a knife against an indrawn abdomen. It is difficult to breathe.

There is no one in this city before whom I can weep.

Noticing things, like traffic signals, and lights in porches and on empty lots. The failure to notice will bring back the reality of being without the citadel.

I noticed such things last night.

The city had never seemed so unfriendly, the faces so unlovable.

The bars blared and the automobiles were particularly like spaceships. A corner drugstore opened its crocodile jaws and exhaled yellow light. Four crooked figures set wide apart at the bar, four men, and a stand of bright paperbacks (the dispensary was in the rear).

Walk along Eighth Street after midnight and watch the men lean towards you.

No it is not that, and it is not that, and it is not that!

And there were the nights on pot, a long way from Midhou, *fumeur du hashish et raconteur*, when we played without fear, but those nights come seldom now, and the rest is grey and the same. Was everything always as it is? Does a man spend all his life waking up from a dream?

An old man called Molloy or Malone walked across country. When he was tired he lay down and when it rained he decided to turn over and receive it on his back. The rain washed the name right out of him.

It is a question of making an inventory.

This afternoon I stood in the yard of the Mac Asphalt and Construction Corporation and felt like making an inventory of the things and relations that are near me now. It wasn't the first time I'd felt like making such an inventory. I've tried more than once. Indeed, everything I write is a kind of inventorizing, and I don't expect ever to be able to do much more. And the inventories will always be unfinished. The most I can do is to die like Malone with a last dot of lead pinched between forefinger and thumb, writing perhaps: *mais tout de même on se justifie mal!*

And from time to time I think up epilogues for *Cain's Book.* God knows if I'll ever be able to put a stop to this habit. I'd need an eye in the back of my head and a hand that could propel me by the scruff of my own neck. Wanting them, and with the creeping behind, the sudden onsets of panic, that and the inventorizing are easily explained. To have some-

thing to be existing in relation to. A tradition for example, or a set of mental objects, or a turd, or a fag end. And to be able to fix the existence, with finality. Anyway, I became sure my literature had to begin with the inventory, and perhaps end with it. It's a question of what is left to us, what has not been bled by amputators and polishers of all blasphemy, and it's a narrow territory now. You must know that before you can begin. You must "fix" yourself as a mariner does before the storm strikes.

When I came to the city I came to a woman I had loved in Europe. That was Chloe, the one who was right or wrong about Jody, or who was concerned for me. Chloe was a smallish girl with soft, saffron-tinted flesh and black hair she sometimes wore like an American Indian. She had large, beautiful brown eyes, and a high-cheekboned, Madonna-like face. When she lay naked on the bed her body was like the *Rokeby Venus* by Velasquez.

When Chloe left me to return to America I suppose I wanted her to go. Since then, I have been with no other woman for long. I have been with many. In Europe, in Paris and in London, her image always came to me when I was with another woman. I never found one who was as beautiful as Chloe had been. But when I came to New York there was more than a year's experience we had lived apart, more than a year during which I had lived even more precariously than we had done together in Paris and during which she, returned to her own country, had not.

She was cool from the moment I arrived. (All America was cool from the moment I arrived.) And yet she loved me too. And so we grew away from one another gently, and terribly. And, except for a small Negro who, back in his own environment, was becoming more inconspicuous every day, she was all I had in New York out of the past.

There were many moments when I despaired of others, gave them up, let them stray out of the circle of light and definition, and they were free to come and go, bringing panic or chaos or joy, depending on my own mood, my state of readiness.

Readiness. There is the virtue of the citadel.

I thought that only in America could such hysteria be. Or in Russia. Only where the urge to conform has become a faceless President reading a meaningless speech to a huge, faceless people in a pink plastic eating barracks, only where machinery has impressed its forms deep into the fibres of the brain so as to make efficiency and the willingness to co-operate the only flags of value, where all extravagance, even of love, is condemned, and where a million faceless mind-doctors stand in long corridors in white coats, ready to observe, adjust, shockoperate . . . only here could such hysteria be. I thought that there were werewolves everywhere in the wake of the last great war, that in America they were referred to as "delinquents," a pasteurized symbol, obscuring terrible profundities of the human soul. And I thought: Now I know what it is to be a *European* and far from my native soil. And I saw a garbage truck, one of those great grey anonymous tanklike objects which roam the streets of New York, move beetle-like out of Tenth Street into Sixth Avenue, and on its side was a poster which read: "I am an American, in thought and deed." And there was the Statue of Liberty too.

Sometimes, at low moments, I felt that my thoughts were the ravings of a man mad out of his mind to have been placed in history at all, having to act, having to consider. A victim of the fixed insquint. Sometimes I thought: What a long distance History has taken me out of my way! And then I said: *Let it go, let it go, let them all go!* And inside I was intact and brittle as the shell of an egg. I pushed them all away from me again and I was alone like an obscene little Buddha, looking in.

At what point does liberty become license?

And a question for lawyers: *How many will hang that the distinction may crystallize?*

A quarter of an hour ago I gave myself a fix.

My scow is tied up in the canal at Flushing, N.Y., alongside the landing-stage of the Mac Asphalt and Construction Corporation. It is just after five in the afternoon. Today at this time it is still afternoon, and the sun, striking the cinderblocks of the main building of the works, has turned them pink. The motorcranes and the decks of the other scows tied up round about are deserted. Cain is at his orisons, Narcissus at his mirror.

I stood the needle and the eye-dropper in a glass of cold water and lay down on the bed. Inside the dropper the water was tinged pink.

It was a heavy dose. I felt giddy almost at once. I had to be careful. Two of the building-yard workmen in wide blue dungarees and wearing baseball caps were hanging about. From time to time they crossed my catwalk. They were inquisitive. They had heard the noise of my typewriter during the afternoon and that was sufficient to arouse their curiosity. It is not usual for a scow captain to carry a typewriter.

The canal water is smooth and dark green, its mirror-like surface bearing a scum of oil, dust, paper, and an occasional plank of wood. There are two yellow sand scows at a yard at the other side of the canal. The scow which is nearly light looms over the loaded scow like a pier over a low-lying jetty. On the scow which rides high out of the water there is a Portuguese Negro and his woman. The cabin of the other scow is locked up. For a while during the afternoon I sat outside on my catwalk and watched the Negro who stood watching his scow being unloaded. The unloading crane had a distinctive putter. Even across the short breadth of the canal it seemed to come from a great distance, like the sound of a tractor in a field far away, and that sound mingled with the sound of all the other cranes working on the canal, and they swung about, the grabs rising and falling, hawsers straining, and they were like big steel birds with no wings and no plumage, nodding and pecking all the afternoon. The Negro was smoking a pipe. His woman came out of the cabin from time to time with a bucket of slop or to hang out some wet clothes. I was too far away from her to see her features clearly. She is blond and wears a colourless smock. One time she looked across at me.

Lying on the bed I heard the buzz of a fly and I noticed it was worrying the dry corpse of another fly which was half-gouged into the plank of the wall. I wondered about that and then my attention wandered. A few minutes later I heard it buzz again and saw that it was still at its work, whatever it was, settled on the rigid jutting legs of the corpse. The legs grew out of the black spot like a little sprout of eyelashes. The live fly was busy. I wondered whether it was blood it wanted and whether flies like wolves or rats will eat off their own kind.

The mind under heroin is quite as evasive as it is ordinarily; one is aware only of contents. The form itself is not available to perception. But this whole way of posing the question, of dividing the mind from that of which it is aware, is fruitless. Nor is it so much that the objects of perception are altered as they are said to be under mescalin, nor that they are perceived more intensely or in a more enchanted or detailed and chaotic way as I have sometimes found them to be under marijuana; it is that perceiving turns inward, the eyelids droop, the blood is aware of itself, and the flesh; it is that the organism has a sense of being intact and unbrittle, and, above all, inviolable—for the attitude born of this sense of inviolability some Americans have invented the word "cool."

It is evening now. The cabin is cooler and the objects are growing dim. In a few moments I'll get up and light my lamps.

What the hell am I doing here?

I do not seriously pose this question here and now lying on my bunk, and under the influence of heroin, inviolable. That is one of the virtues of the drug, that it empties such questions of all anguish, transports them to another region, a painless, theoretical region, a play region, surprising, fertile, and unmoral. One is no longer grostesquely involved in the becoming. One simply is. I remember saying to Sebastian, before he returned to Europe with his new wife, that it was imperative to know what it was to be a vegetable. I should have added "as well."

. . . The illusory sense of adequacy induced in a man by the drug. Illusory? Can such sense-data be false? Inadequate? In relation to what? The facts? What facts? Marxian facts? Freudian facts? Mendelian facts? More and more I found it necessary to suspend such facts, to exist simply in abeyance, to give up, if you will, and I came naked to comprehension.

(Time on the scows . . .

Day and night soon became for me merely light and dark, daylight or oil-lamp, and often the oil-lamp became paler into the long dawn. It was the warmth of the sun that came on my cheek and on my hand through the window which made me get up and go outside and find the sun already far overhead and the skyscrapers of Manhattan suddenly and impressively and irrelevantly there in a haze of heat. And as for that irrelevance . . . I often wondered how *far out* a man could go without being obliterated. It is an oblique way to look at Manhattan, seeing it islanded there for days on end across the buffering water like a little mirage in which one is not involved, for at times I knew it objectively and with anxiety as a nexus of hard fact, as my very condition. Sometimes it was like trumpets, that architecture.

It is not possible to come quite naked to comprehension and it is difficult to sustain even an approximate attitude without shit, horse, heroin. Details, impressionistic, lyrical. I became fascinated by the minute to minute sensations, and when I reflected I did so repetitively and exhaustingly on the meaningless texture of the present moment, the cries of gulls, a floating spar, a shaft of sunlight, and it was not long before the sense of being alone overtook me, alone and lost and without hope of ever entering the city with its complicated relations, its plexus of outrageous purpose. And then I was at the brink of hysteria.)

What the hell am I doing here?

The question threw itself at me from all the drab walls of my cabin as one evening the tug *Buchanan* pulled my scow far out into the estuary of the Hudson River, tied her to a stakeboat in the middle of Upper Bay, and, for reasons known no doubt to some bookkeeper, abandoned me there in wind and rain for four nights and four days.

In the America I found nothing was ever in abeyance. Things moved or they were subversive. Perhaps it was thus, to leave America without going away, to retreat into abeyance, that I came to be on a riverscow. (Other places I might have come to: prison, madhouse, morgue.)

It had been so unexpected. I was not prepared. It was on a Friday evening around eight. The phone rang at Chloe's flat in the Village. There had been a change of plans. They were going to pull out my scow from Pier 72 in an hour. I was to get on board at once. I was short on stores, short on water, and short on cigarettes. I had expected to have the weekend free. All week I had been alone, moving slowly up and down rivers with my load of stone. To have chosen (almost hysterically) to be alone, to be a man continually choosing to be alone, and to have chosen not to be alone, and then to have been for one hour with Chloe, and then to be forced to be alone again, seeing on Chloe's face no answering panic, but its utter absence, and the sudden flicker of guilt as she became conscious of what I missed, and the quick look of tenderness which came then, gratuitously given, and for a terrible instant of awareness rejected by *me*—I was struck dumb.

Je pense donc je suis. Perhaps, considering the plundered Tree of Knowledge, Descartes spoke of suffering.

"Oh, darling!" Chloe said. And her voice was not false, but neither was it mine.

The Eighth Avenue bus took me to 34th Street, the Crosstown on 34th to Pier 72. The tug was already there and I boarded the *Edward J. Mulroy* under a flood of insults from the tugboat captain. The scowman is the leper of the New York waterfront, he is old and can't work or he is a zombie who won't. The four scows linked together single file lay with the down tide from a corner of Pier 73 for three hours. Shortly after midnight the tug returned and the short slow haul down the North River to the stakeboat in Upper Bay began. Mine was the last scow and I sat aft at my open cabin door and watched the dark west waterfront of Manhattan slide away to the right. I thought of a night two months before when I had a girlfriend aboard for a short trip and how at the same kind of midnight we went naked over the end of a long tow, each in the hempen eye of a dockline, screaming sure and mad off Wall Street as the dark waves struck.

We arrived at *Bronx Stakeboat Number 2* shortly after three in the morning and the tug, churning

foam on the black water, backed away, its bell clank-
ing instructions to the engine-room. She slewed
round then and moved quickly away into the darkness. I watched her for a few minutes until the glow
from her decklights dimmed and only the mast-lights
were visible. Then I entered the cabin.

A chair, a typewriter, a table, a single bed, a coal
stove, a dresser, a cupboard, a man in a little wooden
shack, a mile from the nearest land.

This night was going to be interminable.

I split a log and got the fire going. That helped.
For a few moments until I smoked a cigarette,
stubbed it in an overflowing ashtray, and wondered
what to do next.

Even then, and all this is some months ago now, I
was no sooner alone than I would begin urgently to
take stock.

I had come to New York from London and when
I realised that Chloe was no longer in love with me I
got a job on the scows. Time to think, to take stock.
The grey table in front of me strewn with papers,
inventories from the past, from Paris, from London,
notes neatly typed, notes deleted, affirmations, de-
nials, short bursts of coherence, sudden terrifying
contradictions, a mass of evidence that I had been in
abeyance, far out, unable to act, for a long time.

I wrote for example: "If I write: it is important to
keep writing, it is to keep me writing. It is as though
I find myself on a new planet, without a map, and
having everything to learn. I have unlearned. I have
become a stranger."

Everywhere throughout the notes the haunting
sense of dispossession. It was as though I were writing hesitantly, against the tide, with the growing suspicion that what I was writing was no more or less
than a confession that I was in some criminal sense
against History, that in the end it could lead me only
to the hangman. I thought that it wasn't surprising
that many writers, particularly of my class, underprivi-
leged in a dying culture, shied away from the painful
consciousness of their isolation and longed to be immersed in what was safe, without risk, in what was
objective. It was dangerous to be in this sense "free"
. . . in its lust after extinction the human soul has
learned promiscuous ways.

There was, for example, Tom's place, near the
Bowery.

Fay and I walked over together from a place on
Sheridan Square. We walked quickly, knowing that
Tom would arrive at the same time, or shortly after,
with the heroin.

"It's going to be good, baby," Fay said.

The room had a low sloping ceiling with two small
windows on one side and a fireplace on a raised brick
hearth in an opposite corner, at the far end of the
adjacent side. Sometimes the Negro burned a few
sticks in the grate and we sat with our knees at the
level of the fire which cast shadows on the dirty ceiling and walls and on the bricks of the fireplace, the
three of us on a small backless couch spread over
with a fawn blanket, looking into the fire, Fay in the
centre, still wearing her moth-eaten fur coat, her
arms folded, her head sunk on her chest, her slightly
bulbous, yellowish eyes closed. We sat there after we
had fixed and watched wood burn. The white box-
wood burned quickly. The Negro leaned forward and
added a few sticks to the blaze. He was a tall man in
his late twenties, lean, with a beautiful, pale, lean
face expressionless often as porcelain, the nose long,
the eyes half-closed and heavily lidded under the
drug.

I also am tall. I was wearing my heavy white seaman's jersey with a high polo neck, and I sensed that
the angularity of my face—big nose, high cheekbones, sunken eyes—was at present softened by the
shadows and smoothed—the effect of the drug—out
of its habitual nervousness. I had come from Europe
a few months before. My name is Joseph Necchi. My
eyes were closed. My elbows rested on my thighs and
my hands were clasped in front of me. The Negro,
who sometimes spoke of the West Indies, was called
Tom Tear.

At that moment I felt impelled to speak and I
said: "My father had false teeth."

I was aware that I flashed a quick, intimate glance
first at Tom, across Fay's line of vision, and then,
turning my head slightly, I caught the glint of appraisal in her protruding brown eyes.

"Yes," I said, and my face grew radiant, encourag-
ing them to listen, "he had yellow dentures."

Tom's teeth—they were long and yellowish and
gave his mouth a look of bone—were clenched in a
tight smile, the pale lips falling away, exposing them.
It was almost a mask of ecstasy, *part of the game*, I
should have said in some contexts, in some rooms.

Fay's face was more reserved. Swinish? More like a
pug than a pig. Her untidy dark hair tumbled into
her big fur collar. A yellow female pigdog, her face
in its warm nest beginning to stir with knowing.

"He was outside in the hall, spying on the lodg-
ers," I said. "My father was a born quisling, and he
had false teeth."

Tom Tear's face was patient and serene. The
flicker of the fire stirred in the sparse black stubble
on his lower face, making the hairs glint.

I went on for the friendly silence: "While he was
in the hall his false teeth were squatting like an octo-

pus in a glass of water on the kitchen dresser. The plates were a dark orange brick colour and the teeth were like discoloured piano-keys. They seemed to breathe at the bottom of the glass. The water was cloudy and tiny bubbles clung to the teeth. That was the kitchen where we lived, and they sat there like a breathing eye, watching us."

Fay's bluish lips had fallen apart in a smile. She made a grunt of understanding through her decayed teeth. Fay was forty-two. She had lived all her life in this city.

Tom Tear leaned forward and threw more wood on the fire. Wood was plentiful. We gathered it when we could be bothered on the streets.

"He went on tiptoe about the hall for nine years," I said, "in tennis shoes and without his teeth. The hall was no man's land."

Tom Tear nodded as he leaned back again away from the fire. His right cheek, which was all I saw from where I sat, was impassive, long and smooth.

"If someone came to the front door he came flying back into the kitchen for his teeth. He came in puffing and blowing with his hand on his paunch. He wore a collarless shirt with a stud in it and he went around in his shirt-sleeves and this old grey, sleeveless pullover." I paused. A white stick darkened and burst into flame. "When he grew older he became less frantic about the teeth," I said, smiling. "He slipped them into his mouth furtively in front of the visitor as though he suddenly remembered and didn't want to give offence. Perhaps he no longer needed defences."

"He'd given up by that time," Fay said. She looked straight into the fire.

We were all silent for a moment. I felt I had to go on. I said: "I'll tell you a story . . ."

The others smiled. Fay touched the back of my hand with her fingertips. I noticed she had prominent eyeteeth.

"It's not really a story," I said. "It's something I read somewhere, about a river bushman. This man wanted to track down some bushmen and he went to a place called Serongo in the swamps. One day he caught sight of a bushman paddling alone in a boat and he asked his head bearer if he would speak to him and get him to lead them to his tribe. The bearer told him he had known the bushman for thirty years, that he lived alone on a termite mound in the middle of the swamps, and he was deaf and dumb as well."

The others looked at me. I moved my clasped hands forward and stared at the thumbs. They were dirty at the knuckles and at the nails.

"We've all given up," I said then.

We were all silent.

"It's necessary to give up first," I began tentatively, "but it should be a beginning . . ." I sensed an ambiguity, something not quite authentic, and stopped speaking.

"Go on," Tom said after a moment.

But the mood had left me and I shook my head. I closed my eyes.

Again we were all silent. The smoke from the burning wood wound its way towards the chimney, some of it spilling outwards into the room where it clung to the low ceiling.

"Does anyone want to go out?" Fay said.

When neither of us answered she made the motion of snuggling inside her warm fur coat. "It's cold outside, too cold," she said.

I was sitting hunched forward with my eyes closed, my chin deep in the high woollen collar. The phrase "ex *nihil nihil fit*" had just come to me. It seemed to me that nothing would be beginning, ever. And I almost smiled.

Tom Tear, who a moment before had moved to a stool at the side of the fireplace was leaning backwards against the wall and his soft black eyelashes stirred like a clot of moving insects at his eyes. His face had the look of smoke and ashes, like a bombed city. It was at rest, outwardly.

There was a bed in the room, a low double bed on which three dirty grey army blankets had been stretched. On the wall between the two square windows—they were uncurtained and at night the four panes of glass in each were black and glossy—was a faded engraving, unframed. It curled away from the wall at one corner where the scotch tape had come away. There were two similar engravings on two other walls, both of them warped and one of them with a tear at the corner. On the fourth wall there was an unskilful pencil sketch of some trees and a water-colour of a woman's face, vague and pink, and painted on flimsy paper. This was the work of Tom Tear's girlfriend. A self-portrait. He talked of her now and again, always vaguely. She was kicking her habit in some clinic out of town. The last piece of furniture, apart from the backless couch and the stool on which Tom Tear sat, was a draughtsman's table which tilted on a ratchet to any required angle. This was the table on which Tom Tear would work if ever he became an architect. At that moment the table was horizontal and there was a clock on it, and an electric lamp which didn't work, and a burning candle, and a radio with a plastic cabinet in which another clock was inlaid. Both clocks said twenty-five past nine. That was all there was on the table, apart from the spike, and the glass of water, and the spoon.

We had fixed over an hour ago. We had used all the heroin.

Each of us was conscious of the well-being of the others. The blaze of wood in the fireplace made our cheeks glow. Our faces were smooth, and serene.

"I can't do with it and I can't do without it," Fay had said earlier as she prodded the back of her left hand—the flesh thin there and waxy—in search of a possible vein. At the third attempt she found a vein and the blood rose up through the needle into the eye-dropper and appeared as a dark red tongue in the colourless solution. "Hit," she said softly, with a slow smile. When she put the eye-dropper with the needle attached back into the glass of water and dabbed the back of her bluish hand with tissue paper there was no longer any fear in her eyes, only certainty, and in their yellowish depths ecstasy. I knew at that moment she was impregnable. I laughed softly at her and touched the slack flesh of her cheek lightly with my fingers. At that moment I was happy for her and I knew that she, when she watched me fix, in a moment now, would be happy for me. Gratuitously.

Each of us was conscious of the well-being of the others. The sense of well-being in each of us was reinforced by that consciousness.

I said suddenly that the wheel hadn't been invented yet. "The wheel hasn't been invented yet," I said.

We were sitting, three white faces towards the fire, a crude fire, and gloom beyond our shoulders. Fay's moth-eaten fur coat was gathered under her chin like an old animal-skin. "Outside," Fay said, her protruding yellow eyes glinting dully in the firelight, "there is the jungle." She laughed huskily and laid her friendly blue hand on my knee.

Tom's face tilted towards the ceiling, remained idyllic, inviolable.

"And it's raining outside," she said softly.

A moment later, she said: "You said your father was a spy, Joe. You mean he was inquisitive?"

I said: "The job he had before he became unemployable was a spy's job. He was a musician to begin with but he became a spy. His job was to snoop round clubs and concert halls to see that no one infringed copyrights. He was the fuzz, the executioner, the man. He was always closing curtains . . ." I leaned across and whispered loudly in Fay's ear . . . "Don't you know that people can see in?"

I said: "In the end he identified himself so completely with Authority that he became unemployable, he took too much upon himself, he felt himself free to make executive decisions, even if he was only the doorman. When he was summoned during the war for selling confectionery at black market rates without coupons . . . he sold it by the quarter pound to anyone who expressed conservative sentiments . . . he ranted against socialism and red tape. When he was arrested for soliciting on the street he pleaded with tears in his eyes that he was only trying to control a queue."

Fay was poking at the fire with a stick, smiling like a yellow idol.

"I'll go and break some more wood," I said. I got up and moved over to the door. As I opened it Tom's dog bounded in. "That damn dog again," I heard Fay say as I crossed the large, low studio, now brimming over with lumber and other materials, into which the door led. I selected a flimsy box and began to break it into pieces.

My mother was proud and my father was an unemployed musician with the name of an Italian. The blue-black hairs on my father's legs gave to his flesh the whiteness of beeswax. I associated him with the odours of pomade and *Sloan's Liniment*. The bathroom was his lair and his unguents were contained in a white cabinet affixed by four screws to a green wall. The pomade came in a squat jar with a red cap, the liniment in a flat bottle on whose label was an engraved likeness of Dr. Sloan. Because of his strange mustache I always thought of Dr. Sloan as an Italian. It was not until today that it occurred to me to suspect that he was not. The name of the maker of the pomade was Gilchrist, and yet it too was oily and glistened in my father's scalp.

In my father's obsequiousness there was an assurance but as he grew older he became reflective during the winter months. His step quickened but his distances were less ambitious. He spent more time in smokerooms over coffee and didn't move out again into the street until the waitresses had begun to sweep away the fag ends which had been trodden into the carpet and to polish the glass tops of the tables. At that point he glanced at the clock he had been aware of since he came in, pretended to have found himself once again in time confronted by an overlooked appointment, and walked purposively to the swing doors. In one of his ungloved hands he carried a small leather briefcase which contained the morning paper, the evening paper, and a pale blue box of deckled notepaper with envelopes to match. Sometimes he stopped abruptly on the pavement and fingered the lapel of his heavy coat. He looked guiltily at the feet of the people who passed him on either side. And then he walked more slowly. Every so often, just in that way, he remembered his angina. The word stuck in his throat. He was afraid to die on the public thoroughfare.

Sunday. My father would be awake before the milk and morning newspapers were delivered. He slept four or five hours at most. After the death of my mother he lived alone. At nine he shaved. Not before. The number of such necessary enterprises was very meagre. He had to spread them thinly over the day to prevent the collapse of his world. The fort wall was a frail one between my father and his freedom. He shored it up daily by complex ordinance. He was chosen for by an old selector system of tested rites. He gargled, watching his eyes in the mirror. He polished his shoes. He prepared his breakfast. He shaved. After that he staved off chaos until he had purchased the morning paper. Births, marriages, and deaths. He moved up and down the columns at the edge of himself. But with the years he achieved skill. Either way he was safe. If none of the names meant anything to him he could enjoy relief; if a friend had died he could after that first flicker of triumph be involved in solemnity. His hours were lived in that way, against what was gratuitous, but because he was all the time envious . . . at the brink. There is no suspicion so terrible as the vague and damning awareness that one was free to choose from the beginning.

Notes towards the making of a monster . . . That was one title I had considered. When at one of those bad moments, when the dykes crumble, there is a certain relief in inventing titles.

4 A.M. And it was as though I watched a robot living himself, watching, waiting, smiling, gesticulating . . . writing . . . for even as I prepare this document, saying I cannot sleep, I watch myself preparing it. I have stopped at this moment. Ten seconds? Five? The robot goes on writing, recording, unmasking himself, and there are two of us, the one who enters into the experience and the one who, watching, assures his defeat. To look into oneself endlessly is to be aware of what is discontinuous and null; it is to sever the *I* who is aware from the *I* of whom he is aware—and who is *he*? What is *I* doing in the third person? Identities, like the successive skins of onions are shed each as soon as it is contemplated; caught in the act of pretending to be conscious, they are *seen*. The confidence men.

Cain's Book, then.

Cain's Book is Cain's consciousness and its transcending. Look at him. He is lean as Cassius. Mark him well. He is shifty. He has travelled in many places. There is in him an ancient man, a doubter, and his hands are strong. Mark the mass above the eyes, the forehead sloping back, the long head, the small, close-set ears. It was not for nothing that Midhou was Cain's friend and Cain Midhou's. Cain is much alone. Thus when he is amongst men he can play, generously. Generosity sits on his mouth like a plume. And his jaw is strong.

What the hell am I doing here?

At certain moments I find myself looking on my whole life as leading up to the present moment, the present being all I have to affirm. It is somehow undignified to speak of the past or to think about the future.

From these sprawling notes:

The present is shored up by the past, and the not yet, a void haunted by naked will, is too slickly furnished by the world's orators, like a harem in a Hollywood film, with no short hairs.

When I was three I went to bed at night with a stuffed white bird. It's feathers were soft against my face. But it was a dead bird and sometimes I looked at it hard and for a long time. Sometimes I ran my thumbnail along the split in the rigid beak. Sometimes I sucked the blue beads that had been sewn in place of the eyes, tasting thought. And when the beak was prised open and wouldn't close again I disliked the bird and sought justifications. It was indeed a bad bird.

Another note:

There are times when the Citadel becomes a cell and the prisoner has the impulse to grasp the bars and shout out to the warden for a key, for a map; the desert is too thick, the sun scorching; but beneath the blue cap is the same familiar face; on the hip is the same familiar gun.

At such times Cain had to have his drugs. As they were inflicted upon himself they were condemned, as those were praised which Abel inflicted upon others. Abel was an honourable man; upright like a pillar, he had the good of others at his arse.

My father peeped out of doors. He watched the movements of others. When I was four I fell from a swing and broke my arm. When it was set in plaster I asked for a big box with a lid on it, like the one the cat slept in. I put it in a corner near the fire in the kitchen and climbed into it and closed the lid. I lay for hours in the dark, hearing sounds, of my mother's moving about, of the presence of others in the kitchen, and inside sensing the heat of my own presence. I was not driven from my box until after my arm was healed, and then at my father's insistence. It was a stupid game, he said. And the box was in the way. A boy needed fresh air. And when I looked at my father he could not look me in the eye.

When I write I have trouble with my tenses. Where I *was* tomorrow is where I *am* today, where I *would be* yesterday. I have a horror of committing fraud. It is all very difficult, the past even more than the future, for the latter is at least probable, calculable, while the former is beyond the range of experiment. The past is always a lie, clung to by the odour of ancestors. It is important from the beginning to treat such things lightly. As the ghosts rise upwards over the grave-wall, I recoffin them neatly and bury them.

And the present is wordless.

When I returned to the small room with my arms full of broken sticks, the terrier, a bone in its mouth now, growled savagely. That dog had a mad eye. I looked down at the shaggy brown head, at the shining wet fangs, and at the mad eyeball, and I said quietly: "What a fucking animal!"

"Get out!" Tom Tear yelled at the dog. "Get the hell out of here, you ill-mannered bitch!" He got up, grabbed the dog by the collar, and ran it into the next room.

I put the sticks down near the fireplace and added a few to the flames.

"He should get rid of it," Fay said before Tom returned.

"He's mad," I said. "You know last night in the street another dog tried to mount her. Tom went

stark raving mad. He's so damn proud she's a thoroughbred."

"I don't want her knocked up by any lousy mongrel!" Fay mimicked. "He's too much."

(Tom, the American Negro who claimed birth in the West Indies—many pale American Negroes claim similar descent, a mark of caste—and who claimed Scotch, Welsh, and Indian as well as Negro ancestry did not want his blue-blooded terrier interfered with by any mongrel cur. "*For Chrissake, Tom, think!*"

"That dog is me," Tom said once. And it was. It was vicious and untrustworthy and it bit his friends. "She was badly treated by her first owner!" Evidently she attacked even those who fed her. Like Tom, she never had a chance . . .)

"Jesus," Fay said, "all that sentimental crap makes me sick. I don't know why he doesn't get rid of it."

Tom Tear came back, closing the door behind him. The dog whimpered on the far side of it. Tom sat down on the stool at the side of the fireplace. For a few minutes none of us spoke.

"Seen Jody lately?" Fay asked me.

"No. Have you?"

Fay shook her head. "Tom saw her yesterday," she said.

I looked over at Tom.

"In Jim Moore's," he said. "She wanted to score but she didn't have the loot."

"How was she?" I said mechanically. The question came from a theoretical part of me, and yet I was involved in it, and I was more interested in a possible answer than either of the others knew. I supposed I loved Jody. Lately, anyway, I had been acting as if I did . . . I love Jody. But it was almost a sensation, intense, fragile, relative, a state of being, a hint of possibility. If Jody had been in the room at that moment, lying on the bed, and if she said: "Come and lie down beside me, Joe," I would have gone and lain down beside her.

"O.K.," Tom said. "She looked O.K."

But I had no impulse to go out and look for her. If I had known then she was sitting in Jim Moore's I would not have gone to Jim Moore's to pick her up.

"You mean she was sweating her ass off for a fix but was looking all the same fine, Tom?"

"Yeah!" Fay said.

"She doesn't sweat much," Tom said. "She's not hooked."

Listening to the tone of his voice I wondered why he didn't like Jody. I had asked him more than once but he was always evasive in his replies.

"She's no chippie, man!" Fay said to Tom, fixing

her bilious yellow eyes on him. They glinted like yellow ivory in the firelight.

Tear said he didn't say she was but she didn't use enough shit to have a real habit.

"A 'real' habit," Fay said ironically. "She takes all she can get, man."

"She could hustle, she could boost more," Tear said.

"Sure, she could make a profession of it," I said, with pain and irony.

"That's the trouble in this country," Fay said. "You take shit and it becomes your profession."

. . . Feed my habit, I was thinking. That's what Chloe had said to me: "Jody! She just uses you! She lies in her little nest and waits for you to come and feed her. She's like a bird, a fat, greedy little bird!" The thought only amused me. It was not that I hadn't thought about it myself. Jody would "burn" me mercilessly. I amused myself by telling Chloe that I loved Jody. "And she loves you, I suppose! You're a fool, Joe! She loves horse! My God, it makes me mad! And you come to me for money to buy shit for her! She doesn't even let you screw her!" "Yes, that's too much," I said quickly, "but it doesn't matter, Chloe, not in the way you think, and not as much as you think it does." I remembered Jody saying: "When we do make love, Joe, it'll be the end!" The "end love," she meant, the ultimate. . . . Like an overdose, Jody?

"When you're not on," Fay said, "you're looking for it or looking for money to get it with."

"It simplifies things," I said with a smile. "Are you ready to simplify things, and become a professional, Tom?"

Fay laughed huskily.

"I'm gonna kick tomorrow," Tom said woodenly. We both looked at him.

"I mean it, fuck it all!" he said. "I've been on this kick long enough. It's no fucking good. I spend most of my time in the subway. Backwards and forwards. To cop."

"Yeah," Fay said, poking the fire again. "It's a big drag."

Of course I knew I was playing with them as I always played. And they were playing with me and with each other. I wondered whether it wasn't always like that. In all living how could you expect other people to act except "as if"? At this point I was involved once again in the feeling of thinking something not quite authentic and I allowed the heroin to come back and take me entirely, and then only the room existed, like a cave, like "Castle Keep," and if other people existed it didn't matter, it didn't matter at all. The jungle could encroach no further than the tips of my fingers. No matter what went before, from the moment of the fix. And I thought again of Jody, and of how plump she was from eating too many cakes, of the soft wad of her belly, of our thighs with no urgency interlaced, of her ugly bitten hands, of the mark on the back of her left hand, high, between forefinger and thumb . . . it looked like a small purple cyst . . . into which she drove the needle each time she fixed. "That's your cunt, Jody," I said once, and I remember how she looked at me, softly and speculatively, drawing out the needle and watching the bead of blood form on the back of her hand, how she put that hand then to my mouth.

"Even without dollies," Tom Tear said, "I could kick it in three days."

"Sure, three days is plenty," Fay said elliptically. She clasped her hands at her knees and leaned forward towards the fire to lay her chin on them.

"I wouldn't need dollies," Tear said, leaning backwards again and closing his eyes.

"What would you do all day if you didn't have to look for a fix?" I said to him.

"You write," Fay said, glancing sideways and upwards at me. "*Cain* is great."

"For me," I said. "Not necessarily for anyone else. It's like a map, and sometimes I can read it. It's all I've got, except NOW . . . you know what I mean?"

Whether the others understood or not, I didn't know. I suspected that to some extent they did, Fay anyway. Tom probably not. Tom acted most of the time with a kind of eager anti-intelligence, like his own mad dog. But Fay was still a talented metal sculptor, though she didn't work much now. I didn't care. "Me" was something only I could know about. I didn't care then, for at that moment they were both with me, all three of us inviolable, under heroin.

"I want to read *Cain*," Tear said.

"Any time," I said. "I wrote it for us. It's a textbook for dope-fiends and other moles."

Fay laughed huskily into the fire.

"It's great," she said. "What's that thing you begin it with, Joe?"

I smiled with pleasure at being able to quote myself.

"If a gallows is clean," I said, "what more can a criminal expect?"

I showed Jody *Cain's Book*. Something prevented her having any response whatsoever. She said she couldn't understand it. She looked blank and shook her head.

"Nothing?" I said incredulously.

Fay had understood at once. Tom, the sentimentalist, would never understand. He rubbed his woolly head. His dog had the same woolly hair, only it was chestnut. Fay understood. "That's it," she said. "You gotta keep at it. You gotta do something. If you don't do anything it's a big drag. If only I could get a place to work!"

"Go to Mexico or back to Paris," I said. "You'd have to get out of this whole context. Here in New York you can only do as you're doing."

"You can say that again," Fay said. She added irrelevantly: "It's no good without a pad where I can work."

There was always something irrelevant. I had heard it all before from every junkie I had ever known. Yet I hesitated to deny all validity to this kind of talk. And when someone who had not used junk spoke easily of junkies I was full of contempt. It was not simple, any kind of judgment here, and the judgments of the uninitiated tended to be final, hysterical. The rigidity of fear. No, when one pressed the bulb of the eye-dropper and watched the pale, blood-streaked liquid disappear through the nozzle and into the needle and the vein it was not, not only, a question of feeling good. It was not a question of kicks. The ritual itself, the powder in the spoon, the little ball of cotton, the matches applied, the bubbling liquid drawn up through the cotton filter into the eye-dropper, the tie round the arm to make a vein stand out, the fix often slow because a man would stand there with the needle in the vein and allow the level in the eye-dropper to waver up and down, up and down, until there was more blood than heroin in the dropper—all this was not for nothing; it was born of a respect for the whole chemistry of alienation. When a man fixed he was "turned on" almost instantaneously . . . some spoke of a flash, a tinily murmured orgasm in the blood-stream. At once, and regardless of preconditions, a man entered "Castle Keep." In "Castle Keep," and even in the face of the enemy, a man could accept the fact of being alone. I could see Fay in her fur coat walking in the city at night close to walls. At every corner a threat: the Man and his finks were everywhere. She moved like a beast full of apprehension and for the Man and the values he sought to impose on her she had the beast's unbounded contempt.

A few hundred years ago Fay would have been burned as a witch and she would have hurled curses and insults at her destroyers from the stake, the unkempt black hair alive with shock, her gleaming yellow eyes mad, and her whole face contorted and hideous with hate to override her pain. Who knows how she may die today? Limits have been closing in; you can hang for dealings with a "minor," or rather, you can be electrocuted. Perhaps that is how Fay will die, strapped to a very old-fashioned-looking chair—it is a curious fact that the death-chair has such a quaint, old-fashioned look!—whinnying hate through purple nostrils, her outraged torso exuding blue smoke. But for the moment she is a forlorn figure slipping quickly through dark streets, desperate for a private place, for a burrow, for a "Castle Keep." There, in that low-ceilinged room, I had often said to Fay and to Tom that there was no way out but that the acceptance of this could itself be a beginning. I talked of plague, of earthquake, as being no longer contemporary, of the death of tragedy which made the diarist more than ever necessary. I exhorted them to accept, to endure, to record. As a last act of blasphemy I exhorted them to be ready to pee on the flames.

Lying on top of the bunk I must have fallen asleep about 5 A.M. I awoke less than two hours later and found myself lying with my eyes closed and a vague sense of panic at my bowels. A new day. I could hear the rain drumming at the small square window directly above my head and on the tin roof of the cabin. After a few moments I became aware that the rain had stopped.

The Edward J. Mulroy of New York, deck-scow, bobbed around on tide and currents, a low-slung coffin on the choppy grey water. The day was dull. The sky was low and grey-white. Tugs would come and go, hauling linked scows, like toy boats playing dominoes. They came here suddenly out of the mist which obscured Manhattan Island, hooting importantly. Leave two, take one. That went on all the time the scows lay there and there were now eleven of them strung out on wet ropes at the stakeboat. The stakeboat which provided temporary moorings for scows on their way to unloading stages in Brooklyn and Newark, N.J., was uninhabited. It was simply an engineless hulk painted green and red and set with bollards, a winch, cleats, and a few hawsers. A painted wooden board identified it as Bronx Stakeboat No. 2. The stakeboat swung about its anchors with the tide. The scows stranded out behind it in three rows, like beads on a string. Somewhere, not far off but invisible, a bell clanked dully and monotonously, a Banshee wailing her dead. It came from a marking buoy which flashed at night at regular intervals, a sudden explosion of white light which seemed to hesitate before it occluded. And at night, if the mist rose, the lights on the lower end of Manhattan struck upwards out of the dark like an electric castle.

It was still early when I went out on to the catwalk. The sun was struggling to break through a low mist and the surface of the water, glassy at this hour, was vaguely tinted with colour. I counted four scows behind me, a chain of three lying directly behind the stake, and, on the far side, three brick scows piled high with red bricks and two yellow sand scows. The front scow of the centre chain was grey and red. It was one of seventeen scows of a small sea transport corporation. I sat on an upturned bucket at my stern at the port side and gazed across towards the gradually appearing Brooklyn waterfront. I had drunk three cups of coffee and smoked a marijuana cigarette. The smooth water, grey-yellow, the tilting black cones of the distant buoys, and the passing freight which moved slowly across the estuary towards the North and East rivers all contributed to the profound sense which had come over me that I was living out of time. It was cool on deck. I was waiting to catch the junkboat which came out to the moorings from time to time to buy old ropes and to sell newspapers and cigarettes.

I had already decided to visit some of the other scows to see what I could borrow or buy. But it was a bit early for that, just after 7 A.M., and the decks of all the other scows as far as I could see them were deserted. I must have thought then about what the hell I was doing.

►► Paul Blackburn

Song for a Cool Departure

When the track rises
the wires sink to the fields
Trees absorb them in and blot them out:
black running
pencil lines against the fields' green
Shrubbery close to the track goes by
            so fast it hurts the eyes

Rain has quit
We have arrived
at Salut or Castelnaudary

            A woman laughs harshly in the corridor
            The soldiers on either side sleep beautifully
            peacefully, one
            with his mouth open
            The other has his closed
            The world is certainly diverse!
                    Wires begin again to
                    fall and rise
            Small fruit trees stand in quadrangles
            in a field otherwise planted
            The brook tries to escape notice
                    and where shall I put 2
            cypresses,
            3 elms?

Old woman in the corner
wrestles her rented pillows and cannot sleep
One finally arranges itself
under her right arm, the other
            entirely out of control, she clutches
on her lap, the comfortable weight,
her rented buffers against a hard world
and stares direct in front of her and cannot sleep

My wife holds her face up for a kiss
Brow puckered and tired, she also cannot quite sleep,
worrying about a pair of sunglasses we
left at someone's house yesterday
            in the round of farewells

Having left that town
we have left nothing behind

The world is surely diverse enough
and if the information is sound, one
could ride forever and never fall off
let others sleep—
I am so wide-awake I want to sing, while
the wheels turn, the windows clatter, the door
jogs, the wires
rise and change and fall
and the green grass grows all round, all round
and the green grass grows all round—

▶▶ **Charles Foster**

The Troubled Makers

Accusing. Two orange eyes set in dead white, staring up at him, accusing. And a rising curl of gray smoke past his eyes.

There was a tinkle of shells and a waft of air. Gray smoke eddied toward his face, rose up his nostrils. His nose twitched.

He sneezed. "Scope," he said.

His eyes blinked four times, rapidly.

He wiped his nose on the sleeve of his shirt and looked down at the counter that was tilting up toward him or away from him—which was it? And now he knew what the orange eyes were. Eggs. Sunnyside up. Hash-brown potatoes on the side. And coffee now, please, miss.

"Yes sir," she said, "right away, sir."

Had he said it out loud? And had he said it just now—or was he remembering having said it when he walked into this place, out of the awful rain? But she had already turned away, toward the terrace of six silexes in back of the counter.

She had short legs. Like goat legs? No. They were straight and rounded—not crooked or bony. But her trunk long in proportion. Erect she stood and walked. Rhythmic. Backstrap of her bra through the translucent nylon dimpled waitress dress going this way and that way as her shoulders went this way and that way.

Not slender, she wasn't. Young. Already too soft-rounded to be slender. And later on not slender at all. With love and children and food she'd spread. But with love. Black hair and skin in desert colors. Hints of ocher and sand and brown in the flesh. Desert Princess.

And brown eyes. Liquid brown. Not orange. Not accusing orange eyes idiot-set in frizzled mires of dead white with airholes.

He sneezed again.

He looked down. His right hand was resting on the edge of the counter, the counter that kept sloping this way and that way. Loving counter, nubile and waiting counter.

He saw the long thin cigar in his hand. That was the smoke. It had a soft gray ash three-quarters of an inch long and the smoke curled whitely toward his face. The firm brown wrapper of the slender cigar was faintly green in places.

"Seventy-five cents," he said.

"Did you say something to me, sir?" The girl turned back to him.

"Seventy-five cents, Desert Princess," he said. "Somewhere for this Havana Panatela . . . Havana Panatela . . . I paid seventy-five cents."

"Of course," Desert Princess said. "You got it here."

She was close to him, just above him across the yawing, shifting counter. Hips, waist, breasts, shoulders, liquid warm brown eyes and the clean smell of herself. How could anybody smell so much like herself?

"You bought it here, sir," she said with a smile hinting at the full flesh of her lips. "You said it might protect you from the rain. You bought it and then you lit it and you went out."

"I did? Nonchalant, into the red rain, smoking a seventy-five cent Havana Panatela. Devil a care . . . never a backward glance . . . leaving you flat? How could I do it, Desert Princess?"

"Oh, I didn't worry, sir. Your friend worried but I didn't worry, I knew you'd be back. At least, I was pretty sure you'd be back. And now you are back, aren't you?"

"Am I?" he said. "Yes, I suppose I am. And with a seventy-five cent Havana Panatela. But we'll soon fix that."

He grasped the panatela like a spear between the thumb and first two fingers of his right hand. So poised, he waited for the yaw and pitch of the counter to settle a little. And then he plunged it down, swiftly hard and true, down right into the center of the first of the two orange accusing eyes.

Liquid yolk spurted.

There was another musical tinkle of shells. He looked up and back along the deep, narrow lunchroom. The writhing counter ended four stools farther down—and there was an archway, ornate with plaster angels and lilies growing at its curving edges. Had he made it? He supposed so. And down from the arch hung a curtain made of shells. Shells that tinkled as, blown by air, they sounded one against another.

And now the shells had parted. And two brown hands were on the edges of the arch.

The Watusi Chief.

Six feet four inches tall he was. Maybe taller when he straightened up? But now he stooped under the arch.

"You shouldn't oughta done that, Boss," Watusi Chief said.

"Why not?" the man called Boss asked.

"Nobody oughta waste food, Boss. It ain't right, with people hungry."

"You call *this* food? And you call *them* out there people? I'll show you what's food and what's people!"

Boss lifted the dripping end of the Havana Panatela out of the egg yolk, leaving a mound of ash, gray slowly wetting to black. "I'll show you!"

And he plunged the end of the Havana Panatela deep into the center of the second orange eye. Again, liquid yolk spurted. It splashed on the heaving counter, the nylon of Desert Princess, the dirty, red-spattered khaki of the Boss's shirt.

"I'll show you what's food, you black bastard! I'll show you what's people! I'll show you what's what!"

Calmly, Watusi Chief took two big steps along the billowing counter. His long, evenly muscled right arm snaked down and under Boss's arms and around his belly. He lifted and hauled Boss up into the air, up over the counter. Desperately, Boss reached down to retrieve his Havana Panatela from the middle of the second orange eye. But his fingers only brushed it, knocking it off the edge of the plate onto the pulsing counter.

The counter surged and Havana Panatela flipped up on the crest of the surge and then off the counter and down, down between two stools.

Boss screamed in mid-air. "Something to suck. Gotta have something to suck. Something to mouth!" Boss screamed and screamed again.

"Maybe you better give him some mints," Desert Princess said.

"Could be," Watusi Chief said. "Gimme a box of 'em, please."

Desert Princess walked along the counter to the cash register, up at the front of the long narrow room.

Watusi Chief hoisted Boss up to his shoulder and let him hang there. "You try to calm down, Boss," he said. "You suck some mints and calm down, okay? Because we've got to find us a job before we run into the Town Marshal again—you remember, the bastard who stopped us out on the highway this morning?"

But Boss wasn't listening. Because down there in front of him was Desert Princess, one hand on the cash register, smiling up at him.

"Honey," he wailed to her, over the vast distances between them, the tremendous distances between everybody, "desert honey. Desert honey in the cool light and shadow of the oasis where the wild bees murmur. I must go now, I must leave thee, O desert princess of my honeycomb, dripping with desert ardor. I am borne on cruel wings of duty—but the memory of your sweet honey will stay ever on my tongue. Loved I not honor more, I'd curry and hurry the spice of your honey'd favor, and here I'd make my stand, to love or die for honey . . ."

"How much do we owe ya?" Watusi Chief asked.

"One eighty-seven," Desert Princess said. "Including the Havana Panatela and the sales tax."

Watusi Chief pulled two bills and a coin out of his pants pocket. "Here you are, miss. And you keep the change for your trouble."

"Oh, it wasn't hardly what you'd call trouble at all," Desert Princess said, smiling. "Why, gee, I kind of like him. The nice things he said, even if he did splash egg on my dress. I really do."

Boss began chanting, in a high falsetto. "Mints, mints, mints—mints pie in the mints sky when I mints mints mints die. Hot slices and slabs of mints sky girl princess of minks and princess of mints, succulent mints and singing minks. And when the mints sky was opened they all rained down—the shining furs of mints, the running laughter of the minks. And all the kings began to sing, O what a princess dish to set before the minsky pie of my mint-deminted eye . . ."

"Here's your mints, Boss. You can simmer down, now."

Boss saw the pink palm of Watusi Chief's brown left hand coming up toward his mouth. Two round white mints in the palm. Boss craned down, mouth open, tongue out. He lapped up and sucked up the two mints. And then he twisted his neck up and around till he could see the ceiling.

"Well, miss, I guess we'll be running along now," Watusi Chief said. "Could you tell me how we get to the state employment office from here?"

"Why, surely," Desert Princess said. "You just cross Main at the next crossing—the one with the light. That's Second. Walk two blocks down and turn left on Elm. Employment office's in the middle of the block. You can't miss it."

Desert Princess looked up at Boss, on Watusi Chief's shoulder. And then, beyond him, she saw what was happening on the ceiling. Or in the ceiling. She gasped.

There was a dwarf apple tree. Not exactly painted on—or in—the ceiling. It was in bas-relief, half in and half out, as if the ceiling were wet cement and a real apple tree had been picked up by a giant hand and pushed on its side halfway into the cement. Except instead of cement, or ceiling, there was a yellow sky behind—or above—the tree.

Desert Princess felt sure—if she could only reach up that high—she could pick one of the apples and bite into it and it would be a real apple. A tremendously real apple. Suddenly, she wanted one of the apples very much.

And she wanted the blossoms, the gigantic white-and-gold apple blossoms that nestled in sets of three around each of the big round red ripe apples. Whoever heard of apple blossoms and ripe apples growing together? And never on any tree, either apples or blossoms like these.

But instead of reaching up she just stared, mouth open. Because on the gnarled and crooked lowest limb of the dwarf apple tree a girl was suddenly sitting.

Bare feet and bare legs dangled down from the low limb, almost touching the ground. But the girl's body was wrapped in a short cape. Desert Princess had never in her life seen a cape anything like that cape but she was immediately sure that she had to have one just like it. For when she stared at it, all she could think of was a fan coral with delicate tracery veins of blood, taken from the turquoise deeps of a warm and liquid tropic sea, carried up and up to the surface of the world of air, and there transformed to texture sheer and smooth as incredible silk, silk passed by gentle hands through an adhering cloud of dust of butterfly wings.

"At it again," Watusi Chief groaned. "Jesus Christ, Boss, don't you *ever* relax?"

But Desert Princess hardly heard Watusi Chief. Because now she saw the face of the girl. And it was her face. Duplicated exactly in every detail, right down to the almost imperceptible forceps mark on her left cheek bone. But somehow, through the perfection of the likeness, there glowed a beauty, both ethereal and sexy, that Desert Princess had never herself discerned when she looked into her mirror.

"Gee," Desert Princess said, "am I *really* like that?"

"Boss says so, why then it's so," Watusi Chief said. "But he's sure takin' a long time saying it."

"Was I really like that—before? Or—did he, just now—did he just now *make* me that way?"

Watusi Chief sighed, resigned. "The Boss only brings out what's really there all the time, miss. He knows it's there because he can see it. And then he makes you see it too—with words, or colors, or sounds—or little scenes like this . . ."

"Goddamnit," Boss said, "I wanna nother mint. Gotta have something to *suck!*"

As Watusi Chief handed another mint up to Boss, Desert Princess saw a new figure appearing on the ceiling. Was it what they called a "centaur"? It had four legs—but they sure weren't horse legs. They looked more like the legs of a goat. And instead of hide—horsehide or goathide—the body was covered with the finest of white feathers. Pure white, except around the brisket. There they were tipped with scarlet. And above the brisket a man's body—covered with a swirling cape of feathers. A cape cut along the same lines as the cape of Desert-Princess-in-the-apple-tree.

The head above the cape was the head of Boss—except that the single twisted spear of a unicorn horn grew out of the middle of the forehead, just below the wind-tangled hair.

Two massively muscled arms held a shiny clarinet to the lips. And goat-legged, horned, feathered and caped, Boss galloped across the ceiling toward Desert Princess on the apple tree, his head thrown far back, blowing joy into the clarinet. The sound he made filled the lunchroom.

That sound—it seemed to well up from the floor, to travel up from the toes along the quivers of nets of nerves of legs and body, to be heard by all the body, bone and flesh and glands and nerves, before it even reached the drums of the ears. Because who could ever *hear* such sounds without feeling them first?

"Hey, that's something new you got on that clarinet, ain't it, Boss" Watusi Chief said. "What is it, chrome?"

"Purest silver," Boss said. "Silver pillaged by marauding barbarian hordes of the sun as they struck down in rapine the long-forgotten mountain fastness of an ancient race, an ancient people."

"Christmas sakes!" Desert Princess breathed, "a pure silver clarinet!"

"Nah," Boss said. "I was exaggerating. Kind of a pure silver alloy. I sort of threw in a little tungsten and platinum and antimony to, well, to give it body and feel and weight and touch and resonance and timbre. Stuff like that. Gimme another mint." Boss seemed calmer now, absorbed in his work.

Desert Princess herself handed up two more mints to Boss and his lips brushed across her fingers as he took them. She looked up and saw that now her cape was opening, opening wider as Boss the centaur approached closer and closer.

But it was not really a cape at all. It was a pair of wings! They fluttered up and down, opened wide and up and out over her shoulders and back, then down, closing in and around her bare shoulders. Up and down, with a movement like the flutter of a cape and the beat of wings at the same time—keeping the beat and the time of the sound from the silver and platinum and tungsten and antimony clarinet, swooping up and down.

Under her wings, Desert Princess' arms were folded over her naked breasts. In her hands she held a short bow and an arrow, both blood red. The feathers of the arrow with their scarlet tips might have been plucked from the centaur's chest.

With the centaur galloping closer across the ceiling, Desert Princess unfolded her arms. She fitted a blood-red arrow to the gold string of the blood-red bow. She pulled back till the bow bent and strained in a tense arc. Bowstring taut as a song, nipples of her bare breasts taut as the bowstring, taut as the red skin of the apples, taut apples bursting with ripeness.

She released the string and the arrow sang higher than the clarinet.

But in the midflight instant, they sang together—the arrow and the clarinet. Their songs blended into one new sound. And then both stopped. Stopped in shattering silence.

"Judas Priest! What have I done now!" Desert Princess screamed. She covered her eyes and leaned forward, bending over the cash register. "Oh, I can't bear it. I can't bear to look."

"Go ahead and look," Watusi Chief said. "You didn't do no harm. Boss is having too good a time right now to let anything tragic happen."

Desert Princess peered up, between her fingers. Watusi Chief was right. Now the silver and tungsten and antimony and platinum clarinet was clenched in Boss's right hand. And the blood-red arrow he had caught, caught in midflight and at the midpoint of its shaft, between his teeth.

Boss trotted forward, lifting his goat legs high, prancing triumphantly. The golden point of the blood-red arrow glinted at the sun while his eyes, under the single unicorn horn, glinted at Desert Princess . . .

"Sque-e-e-ak—BANG!" said the screen door.

"What the hell is going on here?" said the fat man who came in through the door.

"Why nothin' at all, Uncle," Desert Princess said.

"Fellers, this is my uncle, the Town Marshal."

"We've met," Watusi Chief said.

"What d'ya mean—nothin' at all? If it's nothin' at all, then what's that tree doin' growin' outa my ceiling?"

"Your ceiling?" Watusi Chief said. "Looks to me like it's mostly Boss's ceiling now."

"Fifty-one percent of the stock in this here lunch-room's mine," the Town Marshal said. "I guess that makes it my ceiling, don't it? Well, don't it?"

"But forty-nine percent is *mine*," Desert Princess said, "so I guess I got *some* say in what . . ." Desert Princess broke off, her voice choked with disappointment. She was staring at the ceiling.

The Town Marshal looked up. The ceiling, one hundred percent of it, was just as it had always been. The plaster wore the dead gray, powdery gray coat of dirt and calcimine it had always worn. The three big brown stains and the five small brown stains were back, where they had always been. Over the stove and grill, behind the counter, the same layer of smoke and slimy grease spread out in its half-circle, just as it had for years and years and years.

"Now look what you've gone and done!" Desert Princess screamed. "Just *look* what you've done!"

"Now *you* look, girl," the Town Marshal said. "You look and you listen to me. I'm a lot more to you than just the fifty-one percent controlling co-owner of this here lunchroom. I'm your uncle, girl, and don't you forget it. And I raised you up from the time you was a three-years-old orphan. And even besides all that—me bein' the law here—it's up to me to keep a little order . . ."

"Order!" she said scornfully, "what do you know about order?" She gazed wistfully for a moment at Boss, still hanging over the shoulder of Watusi Chief. When she spoke again her voice was softer. "Nobody ever made me like that before. Why, for a minute there, I knew the way I really was. The way I really am . . ."

"Trouble!" the Town Marshal broke in. "Trouble. From the moment I laid eyes on you two out on the highway this morning, I could smell trouble." The anger was rising in the Town Marshal's voice, the red flush working itself up into his face. "Didn't I tell you two to keep moving? Didn't I? Didn't I tell you two to keep agoin' right through my town, and not to stop for nothin'?"

Boss said, "Scope." Then he said, "You got seventy-five cents left, Watusi Chief?"

"Scope? What's he mean by scope?" the Town Marshal demanded.

"With the exception of seven cents, Boss," Watusi chief said, "we're broke."

"I'll bet I know what he wants," Desert Princess said, "Another Havana Panatela."

"I guess so," Watusi Chief said. "When things get bad, mints just ain't enough."

"I asked you what you meant by *scope*," the Town Marshal shouted, "and by God I want an answer!"

"Before you start talkin' that way, uncle, maybe you ought to kind of remember that I'm a Sunday school teacher," Desert Princess said. "What would my class think, do you think, if they heard my own uncle atalkin' like that?"

"Maybe so," the Town Marshal said, breathing hard, "and maybe you ought to remember it too—that you're a Sunday school teacher—when you're having all these dirty pictures made on your ceiling. My ceiling." He paused and looked up at Boss. "But I still ain't found out what you mean by . . ."

"There's no call at all to look at him with them mean, accusing eyes of yours . . ."

"I wasn't doing anything of the sort," the Town Marshal said, "I was just trying to find out . . ."

"And what's more," Desert Princess said, "I'm going to give him a Havana Panatela, even if it is fifty-one percent yours. After what he showed me about myself, why it's little enough to do."

The Town Marshal stared at her in silence for a moment. When he spoke his voice was lower, placating. "Honey," he said, "you don't know what you're saying. I raised you up and I loved you and took care of you all these years. I slaved and sacrificed for you so you'd have all the advantages. I even took this here thankless Town Marshal's job, to make the money so's you could have a nice little business of your own and a place where you could meet nice young fellers. And now, after all that, you stand up there, defying me, mocking me like a jaybird. And for what? For a good-for-nothing, no good at all *stranger*. A *maker*. That you never even laid eyes on before . . ."

He paused for breath. Desert Princess was staring down at her feet and there was a blush of guilt on her face.

"I guess," she said, "I guess what you say—well—I guess you're right." Her voice was small, subdued.

"You *guess* I'm right?" the Town Marshal said, louder now and with more of his old confidence. "You *know* I'm right. What I said to you, why, it's just plain common-sense facts. And there's no disputin' facts, is there, honey?"

"No," she said, her voice even smaller and quieter, "I guess not."

"Boss is gonna get kinda disturbed if he don't get a Havana Panatela pretty soon," Watusi Chief said.

"Oh, he *is*, is he?" the Town Marshal said.

"Well, goddam. That just about does it. First thing, you two come into my town, without even a by-your-leave. Then, you try to turn the head of my own niece, the little girl I raised up from a baby—as good a girl as you could ask for—teaches in the Sunday school every Sunday. Next, you grow trees in the ceiling of my lunchroom. And now—to top it all off—you go 'round demandin' Havana Panatelas. Okay. Now I'll tell you what I'm goin' to do. I'm gonna run you both in. Let's go!"

"You mind telling me what the charge is?" Watusi Chief asked.

"Charge? I'll give you plenty of charges. Vagrancy . . ."

"They still got seven cents!" Desert Princess said. "It ain't as if they was broke!"

". . . And vagrancy's only the beginning," the Town Marshal went on. "Apple trees in the ceiling without a permit. Pornography. Disturbance of the peace—why, what do you think the other folks in this town would think? Supposing they was to come into this respectable lunchroom and see a apple tree growing out of the ceiling?"

"But, Uncle!" Desert Princess said, "these boys ain't bums. They're willing to work. Why, just before you came in here and made such a ruckus, they was on their way to the state employment office. And I'll bet they was goin' there to get jobs!"

"Boss ain't gonna be in a good mood *at all* if he don't get a Havana Panatela pretty quick," Watusi Chief said.

"He sure *ain't* gonna be in a good mood, where I'm taking him," the Town Marshal said, "and neither are you. Lessen you like bars, chilled steel bars. And you're gonna stay right there behind 'em, too—till the judge gets back from deer hunting."

"Bars ain't so bad," Watusi Chief said, "not when Boss gets through with 'em."

"Oh—maybe you think my bars won't hold you, huh? Chilled steel . . ."

"Oh yeah, they'll *hold* all right. Boss he got a lot of respect for reality, including bars. I don't think he's about to bust out through 'em. But he'll kind of decorate 'em—so you'll be able to see what they *really* look like—what they *feel* like. And then maybe you won't be able to stand the sight of 'em yourself . . ."

"Oh, bars, bars, *bars!*" Desert Princess said. Why can't you men ever talk sense? Chilled steel! I never heard so much nonsense in all my life. Bars or no bars, Uncle, you just can't lock these men up when they're honestly looking for work. You just can't! It ain't fair!"

"I can't, huh? What makes you think I can't?" The Town Marshal's face was livid now and he was shouting. "I'll show you what I can do and what I can't do."

"You can't lock 'em up," Desert Princess said, calmly, quietly, positively, "not if you expect to get any peace at home for the next month or two of Sundays."

The Town Marshal stared at her. "After all I've done, after all I've said you're still taking up for these strangers . . ."

"Fair's fair!" Desert Princess said, "and it was you taught me to be fair!"

"Okay. *Okay.* I'll tell you what I'll do. I'll escort these two around to the state employment office myself. Right now. If they get themselves jobs, I'm all done with them. But if they don't, I'm locking 'em both up!"

"Unless he gets a Havana Panatela, Boss is gonna feel . . ."

"Boss can damn well *earn* his Havana Panatela," the Town Marshal broke in, "provided he gets a job. And if you ask me, that's a pretty big provided."

The skinny man with the straw-colored hair toyed nervously with the painted wedge on his desk that said INTERVIEWER. His worried eyes shifted from the two men seated beside his desk to the fat Town Marshal standing behind both of them.

It was pretty obvious the Town Marshal didn't want these two to get jobs—but the Interviewer was determined not to let that sway him. It was up to him to match men to jobs, come hell or high water. That was *his* job and he took pride in doing it well. Of course, it was a small town and a man had to live with his neighbors. And he did owe the Marshal a few favors. And the Marshal did have one of the prettiest girls in town for a niece . . .

But naturally, he wasn't going to be influenced by any of these considerations. If there had been a job for these two—the maker and his assistant—he wouldn't hesitate a minute. But of course, in a town like this, there just weren't any jobs for makers.

"I sure wish I *did* have something in your line," he said, his voice trembling a little with sincerity, "but the honest truth of the matter is that we haven't had a call for a maker in all the three years I've been holding down this desk."

"Scope," Boss said. His moist eyes blinked as he stared at the plain, blank, ivory-colored wall at the back of the state employment office. His voice was indistinct because of the five mints he was sucking.

"What in hell do you mean by *scope?*" roared the Town Marshal.

"Don't let it excite you, Marshal," the Interviewer said hastily. "Makers often say things that seem—uh

—a little obscure to folks." He turned to the two seated men. "Isn't there—uh—something else you could do? Short order cooking? Certified Public Accounting?"

"He's tried 'em," Watusi Chief said, "but his mind sort of wanders. And then he'll put bacon fat into the coffee or coffee into the frying pan. Or he'll use the wrong set of books to make out the income tax forms. Things like that. And I've got to work with him to kind of watch out for him."

"Scope," Boss said. He was still staring at the back wall and it was beginning to shimmer a little now and didn't look quite so ivory as it had a moment before.

"I'll scope you when I get you locked up, the Town Marshal said. And it's time we were going right now. You heard what the man said, didn't you? He ain't got a thing for you!"

And then the Interviewer's phone rang.

He smiled and talked into the phone and listened and when he put it down he looked like a man who's just squared a circle or filled an inside straight.

"That was your niece," he said to the Town Marshal. "Says she needs a maker and maker's assistant. Right away."

"What the hell do you mean!" the Town Marshal said. "Without my say-so she can't hire any . . ."

"O Desert Princess," said the Boss, "O wild heart of desert honey. Golden goddess of Havana Panatelas . . ."

"Shut up, you! I'm the controlling co-owner of that lunchroom . . ."

"It isn't for the lunchroom," the Interviewer said. "It's for the Sunday school. Remember, way back last fall, when the Sunday School Board voted fifty dollars for an Audio-Visual Training Aid? Well, she's scouted around and never found nothing decent for that price. But she thought, maybe, now with a maker right here in town and all . . ."

"Fifty bucks," Watusi Chief said, "will buy one hell of a mess of Havana Panatelas. We'll take it."

"What do you mean—we'll take it?" the Town Marshal demanded. Who the hell asked you?"

"I got his power of attorney," said Watusi Chief. "Want I should show it to you?"

"Nah. Nah. Never mind. But I'll tell you one thing. You'd better deliver the goods, because every one of those charges is still hanging over both your heads. I'm giving you till Sunday to get this Audio-Visual thing done and done right!"

"But that's only a third the usual time for a job like this," Watusi Chief said. "Think you can handle it, Boss?"

"Scope," Boss said.

"Where's the man responsible for this?" the Mayor asked as he strode up to Watusi Chief and the Town Marshal. It was Sunday morning. The mayor had just finished his dedication speech for the new Audio-Visual Aid.

"That's him, out there." Watusi Chief pointed out through the Sunday school window.

For a moment, the Mayor continued to stare in wonder at the enormous Audio-Visual Aid which filled the air of the Sunday school, hanging over the class that Desert Princess was now teaching. Then the Mayor looked out the window. The Boss was stretched out on the grass, flat on his back, eyes closed, a box of Havana Panatelas for a pillow. One of the cigars was lit and between his teeth. He was blowing pink smoke rings. Sometimes he would blow a green figure eight. Once in a while a dancing girl, all colors.

"Looks kinda beat, don't he?" the Town Marshal said.

"It takes it out of a man, making as big an Audio-Visual Aid as that with such a close deadline," Watusi Chief said. "And when a maker gets through working, he's put so much of himself into what he's done that there just ain't very much left over."

"Well, he's certainly made something that'll boost this town," the Mayor said. "Tourist business alone that it'll bring in—just that alone oughta pay off the bonded debt in two-three years. This sure was a damn fine idea of yours, Marshal."

"Hell, Mr. Mayor, it was mainly just using a little persuasion at the right moment," the Town Marshal said.

The man on the grass stirred. In a lazy circle, one hand swung up and took the cigar from his mouth. Gently, with the other hand, he thumbed his nose at the Marshal and the Mayor. He winked at Watusi Chief. Then he turned his face back up to the sky. He smiled wearily, happily. "Scope," he said.

Sunday school was over but the Smallest Girl was still there, staring in wonder—the stars in her eyes as bright as the millions and tens of millions of stars that shone out of the Audio-Visual Aid, above and all around her.

At random, she picked out one, a medium-sized yellow star with nine tiny dots revolving around it. Pointing to it, she turned toward Desert Princess.

"Do you really think there are people like us on this one?"

"Sure," Desert Princess said with a smile. "Audio-Visual Aids can't exist without people, any more than you can rightly say that people can exist without Audio-Visual Aids. Leastways, that's what the Boss said. And seein' how he's the maker, I guess he knows."

"Do you think they're as good as us? Or better? Or worse?"

"From what Boss says, I'm afraid they're just about as bad. He told me he figured they'd have just as much trouble with money and cheating and bombs and plain ignorance and fancy cussedness as us."

"But why couldn't he make 'em *better*, while he was at it?"

"Well—they're supposed to be a kind of model for us and of us. And if they're too much better, then they ain't no model at all, is they? And besides, Boss says he can only make 'em as good as his own vision is good. And I guess it sounds kind of funny, but he says his vision was none too good when he made this one, on account of he didn't have no Havana Panatelas to keep him calm."

"But why didn't he, if that was all he needed?" the Smallest Girl asked.

"Folks was a little stiff-necked, I guess, child. And you know what? Boss says he figures something like that was what happened when *we* was made. Any time, he says, that a maker gets a real big job, why, it just doesn't seem as if things are set up so he'll be in a peaceful mood. Or he'll have a close deadline to meet. All kinds of things."

"Gee, you talked to him a whole *lot*," the Smallest Girl said. "Are you going to get yourself married up to him?"

"No, course not. It's been wonderful knowing him and someday when you're big you'll know *how* wonderful. But makers just ain't very good husband material. I'll always remember him, though, I always will. Because it was him showed me who I really am. And that's the most important thing can happen to anybody ever. Even after I'm married to the Interviewer—and it isn't going to be long now before he asks me, but don't you dare tell him—I won't ever forget how the Boss showed me who I really was."

But the Smallest Girl was no longer really listening. She had turned back to the Audio-Visual Aid. Across the whole ceiling of the Sunday school it stretched. In the center a great, slowly revolving pinwheel of stars, throwing off little sparks of stars. And stretching out in every direction were the smaller pinwheels and clusters.

It was funny, the Smallest Girl thought. If you looked straight at the walls of the Sunday school, there they were, looking solid and real.

But if you focused your eyes on the Audio-Visual Aid, it wasn't like that at all. Your eyes started at the great star cloud in the center, your eyes caught by its foams and whirlpools and running rivulets of stars, all in motion, millions of stars. And as you looked there was a sound, a sound that your eyes seemed to hear, a new sound, a music that you knew had always been there but was always new.

Your eyes followed the sound out from the center, out to the other stars, whole islands of stars. Into the distance and distance so far that the islands themselves, each with millions of stars, were nothing but faint and winking points of light, no brighter than single stars. And finally even these points of light winked out completely. You couldn't see them any more at all.

And then suddenly you remembered that you hadn't seen the Sunday school at all. No walls and no roof. You just didn't see them at all, unless you made a funny kind of effort and really *tried* to see them.

The Smallest Girl looked back once more to the medium-sized yellow star with its nine tiny circling dots. She went closer to it. It grew bigger the closer she approached. And each of the circling dots was a world. And the sun and its worlds kept growing bigger. Or was she getting smaller, smaller the closer she approached the growing sun, the growing worlds. Bigger or smaller . . . closer and closer? And closer still and then it was she knew that she had made this star and its worlds her own, of her adoption, always hers.

"Do you think this one has people?" she asked without taking her eyes from the growing star. "Does it have a maker like Boss? Do you suppose it really does?"

But there was no answer from the world that was already almost another world. And the Smallest Girl did not hesitate but took another step and another, out of that world away from the Desert Princess and her Interviewer and the others, and none of them saw through her eyes her new world grow bigger, filling space as she grew smaller . . .

Till finally came the soft, final closing of a door. The darkness. The blaze of light.

And the Smallest Girl was in the world of her choice. And before her was a maker . . .

Accusing. Two green eyes set in unhealthy magenta, staring up at him. And a slosh of gin, a bare finger of gin in the bottle before his eyes.

He drank the gin in one gulp. Then he turned the empty bottle upside down, letting the last drop drip on the counter.

"Scope," he said.

"Did you speak to me, sir?" the waitress behind the wavering counter asked.

"Scope!" he said again, savagely. He looked up at

her. "If I had scope enough, if I could only do once, just once, what I'm trying to do, I could build whole universes. Endless islands of universes!"

In sudden anger he jabbed the neck of the bottle he held into one of the accusing green eyes on the plate before him and then into the other. Green ichor spurted across his shirt, over the counter, onto the skirt of the waitress.

"Scope!" he cried, and the shells at his back tinkled with a faint music. The tall sunburnt white man was coming toward him. Trader Horn.

He turned back to the waitress and regarded her. A gazelle of the far veldt she was, and in her eyes the moon of the eastern sea. "Enough scope," he said,

"O Moon of the Eastern Sea, and I'd make a dozen island universes for you, just for you, for you—and string them in a bracelet for your wrist . . ."

"Come on, Chief, let's go," Trader Horn said, his big sun-blistered hand on Chief's shoulder, "we gotta make the employment office before it closes, if we're gonna get a gig for tomorrow."

The Smallest Girl felt the sad tears coming and she let them come and she cried for a long time after the two men had left—but the stars in her eyes, the stars of wonder, the stars of her passage, they stayed bright through the tears.

►► **William Carlos Williams**

The High Bridge Above the Tagus River at Toledo

A young man, alone, on the high bridge over the Tagus which was too narrow to allow the sheep
     driven by the lean, enormous dogs whose hind legs worked slowly on cogs
to pass easily . . .
     (he didn't speak the language)

Pressed against the parapet either side by the crowding sheep, the relentless pressure of the dogs
     communicated itself to him also
above the waters in the gorge below.

They were hounds to him rather than sheep dogs because of their size and savage appearance, dog
     tired from the day's work.
The stiff jerking movement of the hind legs, the hanging heads at the shepard's heels, slowly
     followed the excited and crowding sheep.

The whole flock, the shepard and the dogs, were covered with dust as if they had been all day on
     the road. The pace of the sheep, slow in the mass,
governed the man and the dogs. They were approaching the city at nightfall, the long journey
     completed.

In old age they walk in the old man's dreams and will still walk in his dreams, peacefully continuing
     in his verse forever.

Sappho

That man is peer of the gods, who
face to face sits listening
to your sweet speech and lovely
    laughter.

It is this that rouses a tumult
in my breast. At mere sight of you
my voice falters, my tongue
    is broken.

Straightway, a delicate fire runs in
my limbs; my eyes
are blinded and my ears
    thunder.

Sweat pours out: a trembling hunts
me down. I grow
paler than grass and lack little
    of dying.

PARIS LA NUIT
A Portfolio of Photographs by Brassaï

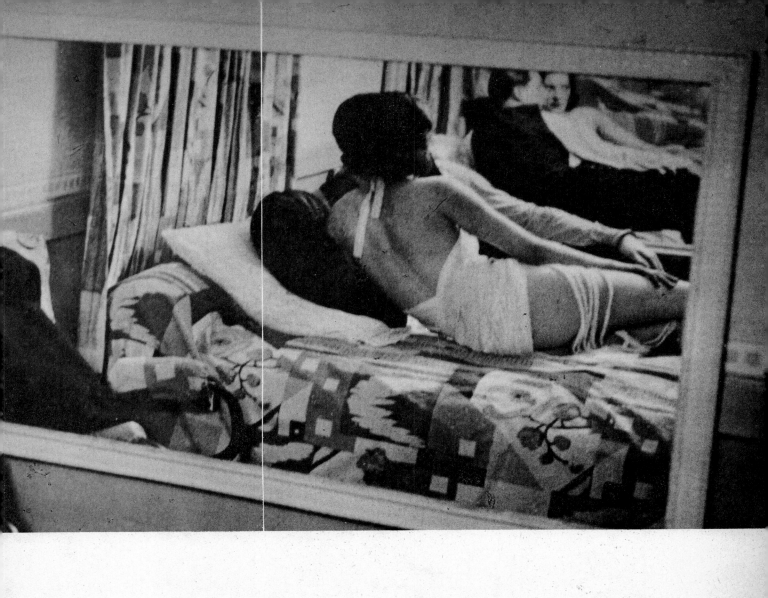

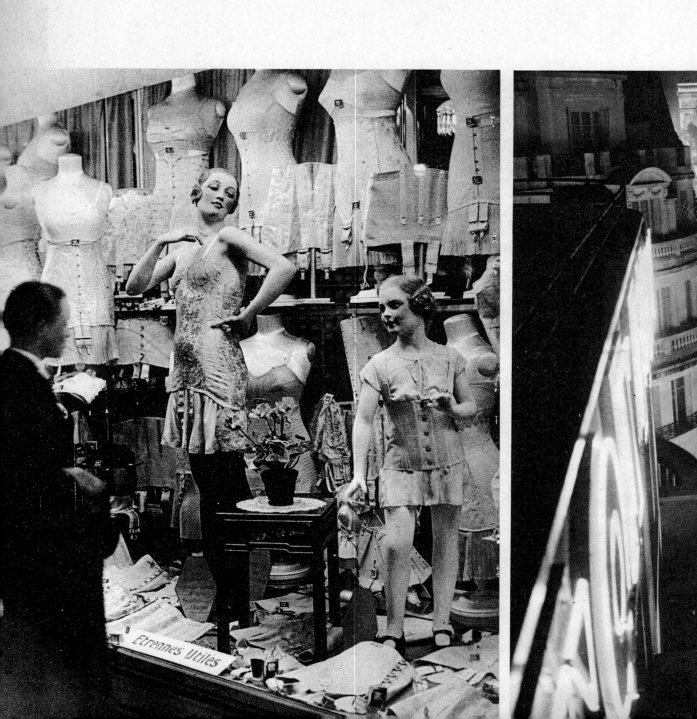

Etrennes Utiles

Horn on "Howl"

Fahrenheit 451, the temperature at which books burn, has finally been determined not to be the prevailing temperature at San Francisco, though the police still would be all too happy to make it hot for you. On October 3 last, Judge Clayton Horn of Municipal Court brought in a 39-page opinion finding Shigeyoshi Murao and myself not guilty of publishing or selling obscene writings, to wit Allen Ginsberg's *Howl and Other Poems* and issue 11 & 12 of *The Miscellaneous Man*.

Thus ended one of the most irresponsible and callous police actions to be perpetrated west of the Rockies, not counting the treatment accorded Indians and Japanese.

When William Carlos Williams, in his Introduction to *Howl*, said that Ginsberg had come up with "an arresting poem" he hardly knew what he was saying. The first edition of *Howl*, Number Four in the Pocket Poets Series, was printed in England by Villiers, passed thru Customs without incident, and was published at the City Lights bookstore here in the fall of 1956. Part of a second printing was stopped by Customs on March 25, 1957, not long after an earlier issue of *The Miscellaneous Man* (published in Berkeley by William Margolis) had been seized coming from the same printer. Section 305 of the Tariff Act of 1930 was cited. The San Francisco *Chronicle* (which alone among the local press put up a real howl about censorship) reported, in part:

Collector of Customs Chester MacPhee continued his campaign yesterday to keep what he considers obscene literature away from the children of the Bay Area. He confiscated 520 copies of a paperbound volume of poetry entitled Howl and Other Poems. . . . *"The words and the sense of the writing is obscene," MacPhee declared. "You wouldn't want your children to come across it."*

On April 3 the American Civil Liberties Union (to which I had submitted the manuscript of *Howl* before it went to the printer) informed Mr. MacPhee that it would contest the legality of the seizure, since it did not consider the book obscene. We announced in the meantime that an entirely new edition of *Howl* was being printed within the United States, thereby removing it from Customs jurisdiction. No changes were made in the original text, and a photo-offset edition was placed on sale at City Lights bookstore and distributed nationally while the Customs continued to sit on the copies from Britain.

On May 19, book editor William Hogan of the San Francisco *Chronicle* gave his Sunday column to an article by myself, defending *Howl*. (I recommended a medal be made for Collector MacPhee, since his action was already rendering the book famous. But the police were soon to take over this advertising account and do a much better job—10,000 copies of *Howl* were in print by the time they finished with it.) In defense of *Howl* I said I thought it to be "the most significant single long poem to be published in this country since World War II, perhaps since T. S. Eliot's *Four Quartets*." To which many added "Alas." Fair enough, considering the barren, polished poetry and well-mannered verse which had dominated many of the major poetry publications during the past decade or so, not to mention some of the "fashionable incoherence" which has passed for poetry in many of the smaller, *avant-garde* magazines and little presses. *Howl* commits many poetic sins; but it was time. And it would be very interesting to hear from critics who can name another single long poem published in this country since the War which is as significant of its time and place and generation. (A reviewer in the *Atlantic Monthly* recently wrote that *Howl* may well turn out to be *The Waste Land* of the younger generation.) The central part of my article said:

. . . It is not the poet but what he observes which is revealed as obscene. The great obscene wastes of Howl are the sad wastes of the mechanized world, lost among atom bombs and insane nationalisms. . . . Ginsberg chooses to walk on the wild side of this world, along with Nelson Algren, Henry Miller, Kenneth Rexroth, Kenneth Patchen, not to mention some great American dead, mostly in the tradition of philosophical anarchism. . . . Ginsberg wrote his own best defense of Howl in the poem itself. Here he asks:

"What sphinx of cement and aluminum bashed open their skulls and ate up their brains and imagination?

Moloch! Solitude! Filth! Ugliness! Ashcans and unobtainable dollars! Children screaming under stairways! Boys sobbing in armies! Old men weeping in the parks!"

A world, in short, you wouldn't want your children to come across. . . . Thus was Goya obscene in depicting the *Disasters of War*, thus Whitman an exhibitionist, exhibiting man in his own strange skin.

On May 29 Customs released the books it had been holding, since the United States Attorney at San Francisco refused to institute condemnation proceedings against *Howl*.

Then the police took over and arrested us, Captain William Hanrahan of the juvenile department (well named, in this case) reporting that the books were not fit for children to read. Thus during the first week in June I found myself being booked and fingerprinted in San Francisco's Hall of Justice. The city jail occupies the upper floors of it, and a charming sight it is, a picturesque return to the early Middle Ages. And my enforced tour of it was a dandy way for the city officially to recognize the flowering of poetry in San Francisco. As one paper reported, "The Cops Don't Allow No Renaissance Here."

The ACLU posted bail. Our trial went on all summer, with a couple of weeks between each day in court. The prosecution soon admitted it had no case against either Shig Murao or myself as far as *The Miscellaneous Man* was concerned, since we were not the publisher of it, in which case there was no proof we knew what was inside the magazine when it was sold at our store. And, under the California Penal Code, the willful and lewd *intent* of the accused had to be established. Thus the trial was narrowed down to *Howl*.

The so-called People's Case (I say so-called, since the People seemed mostly on our side) was presented by Deputy District Attorney Ralph McIntosh whose heart seemed not in it nor his mind on it. He was opposed by some of the most formidable legal talent to be found, in the persons of Mr. Jake ("Never Plead Guilty") Ehrlich, Lawrence Speiser (former counsel for the ACLU), and Albert Bendich (present counsel for the ACLU)—all of whom defended us without expense to us.

The critical support for *Howl* (or the protest against censorship on principle) was enormous. Here is some of what some said:

Henry Rago, editor of Poetry (Chicago)—

. . . I wish only to say that the book is a thoroughly serious work of literary art. . . . There is absolutely no question in my mind or in that of any poet or critic with whom I have discussed the book that it is a work of the legitimacy and validity contemplated by existing American law, as we know it in the statement of Justice Woolsey in the classic *Ulysses* case, and as we have seen

it reaffirmed just recently by the Supreme Court in the Butler case. . . . I would be unworthy of the tradition of this magazine or simply of my place as a poet in the republic of letters . . . if I did not speak for the right of this book to free circulation, and against this affront not only to Allen Ginsberg and his publishers, but to the possibilities of the art of poetry in America. . . .

William Hogan of the San Francisco Chronicle:

. . . Howl and Other Poems, according to accepted, serious contemporary American literary standards, is a dignified, sincere and admirable work of art. . . .

Robert Duncan and Director Ruth Witt-Diamant of the San Francisco (State College) Poetry Center:

. . . Howl is a significant work in American poetry, deriving both a spirit and form from Walt Whitman's Leaves of Grass, from Jewish religious writings. . . . It is rhapsodic, highly idealistic and inspired in cause and purpose. Like other inspired poets, Ginsberg strives to include all of life, especially the elements of suffering and dismay from which the voice of desire rises. Only by misunderstanding might these tortured outcryings for sexual and spiritual understanding be taken as salacious. The poet gives us the most painful details; he moves us toward a statement of experience that is challenging and finally noble.

Thomas Parkinson (University of California):

. . . Howl is one of the most important books of poetry published in the last ten years. Its power and eloquence are obvious, and the talent of Mr. Ginsberg is of the highest order. Even people who do not like the book are compelled to testify to its force and brilliance. . . .

James Laughlin (New Directions):

I have read the book carefully and do not myself consider it offensive to good taste, likely to lead youth astray, or be injurious to public morals. I feel, furthermore, that the book has considerable distinction as literature, being a powerful and artistic expression of a meaningful philosophical attitude. . . .

Kenneth Patchen:

The issue here—as in every like case—is not the merit or lack of it of a book but of a Society which traditionally holds the human being to be by its very functional nature a creature of shameful, outrageous, and obscene habits. . . .

Eugene Burdick (novelist and critic):

The poem Howl strikes me as an impressionistic, broadly gauged, almost surrealistic attempt to catch the movement, color, drama, and inevitable disappointments of life in a complex, modern society. Howl is a pessimistic, and indeed, almost a tragic view of life. . . . It is my impression that the total impact of the poem is far from lascivious or obscene. It is depressing, but not licentious or extravagant in its use of harsh words. . . .

Northern California Booksellers Association:

It may or may not be literature but it does have literary merit. . . . The proposition that adult literature must meet the standards of suitability for children is manifestly absurd. . . . To quote Supreme Court Justice Frankfurter in a similar case— ". . . the effect of this is to reduce the adult population to reading only what is fit for children . . . surely this is to burn the house down to roast the pig."

Barney Rosset and Donald Allen, editors of the Evergreen Review (in which Howl was reprinted during the trial):

The second issue of Evergreen Review, which was devoted to the work of writers in the San Francisco Bay Area, attempted in large part to show the kinds of serious writing being done by the postwar generation. We published Allen Ginsberg's poem Howl in that issue because we believe that it is a significant modern poem, and that Allen Ginsberg's intention was to sincerely and honestly present a portion of his own experience of the life of his generation. . . . Our final considered opinion was that Allen Ginsberg's Howl is an achieved poem and that it deserves to be considered as such. . . .

At the trial itself, nine expert witnesses testified in behalf of *Howl*. They were eloquent witnesses, together furnishing as good a one-sided critical survey of *Howl* as could possibly be got up in any literary magazine. These witnesses were: Mark Schorer and Leo Lowenthal (of the University of California faculty), Walter Van Tilburg Clark, Herbert Blau, Arthur Foff, and Mark Linenthal (all of the San Francisco State College faculty), Kenneth Rexroth, Vincent McHugh (poet and novelist), and Luther Nichols (book editor of the San Francisco Examiner). A few excerpts from the trial transcript—

DR. MARK SCHORER: The theme of the poem is announced very clearly in the opening line, "I saw the best minds of my generation destroyed by madness, starving hysterical naked." Then the following lines that make up the first part attempt to create the impression of a kind of nightmare world in which people representing "the best minds of my generation," in the author's view, are wandering like damned souls in hell. That is done through a kind of series of what one might call surrealistic images, a kind of state of hallucinations. Then in the second section the mood of the poem changes and it becomes an indictment of those elements in modern society that, in the author's view, are destructive of the best qualities in human nature and of the best minds.

Those elements are, I would say, predominantly materialism, comformity and mechanization leading toward war. And then the third part is a personal address to a friend, real or fictional, of the poet or of the person who is speaking in the poet's voice—those are not always the same thing—who is mad and in a madhouse, and is the specific representative of what the author regards as a general condition, and with that final statement the poem ends. . . .

MR. MCINTOSH (later in cross-examination): I didn't quite follow your explanation to page 21, "Footnote to Howl." Do you call that the second phase?

MARK SCHORER: I didn't speak about "Footnote to Howl." I regard that as a separate poem.

MR. MCINTOSH: Oh, I'm—

MARK SCHORER: It is not one of the three parts that make up the first poem. It's a comment on, I take it, the attitude expressed in Howl proper, and I think what it says—if you would like my understanding of it—is that in spite of all of the depravity that Howl has shown, all of the despair, all of the defeat, life is essentially holy and should be so lived. In other words, the footnote gives us this state in contradistinction to the state that the poem proper has tried to present.

MR. MCINTOSH (later): Did you read the one in the back called "America"? . . . What's the essence of that piece of poetry?

MARK SCHORER: I think that what the poem says is that the "I," the speaker, feels that he has given a piece of himself to America and has been given nothing in return, and the poem laments certain people who have suffered at the hands of—well, specifically, the United States Government, men like Tom Mooney, the Spanish Loyalists, Sacco & Vanzetti, the Scottsboro boys and so on.

MR. MCINTOSH: Is that in there?

MARK SCHORER: That's on page 33. In other words, that is the speaker associating himself with those figures in American history whom he regards as having been martyred. He feels that way about himself.

MR. MCINTOSH: Well, "America" is a little bit easier to understand than Howl, isn't it? . . . Now [referring to shorter poems in the back of the book]—you read those two? You think they are similar, in a similar vein?

MARK SCHORER: They are very different. Those are what one would call lyric poems and the earlier ones are hortatory poems.

MR. MCINTOSH: What?

MARK SCHORER: Poems of diatribe and indictment, the mood is very different, hortatory.

MR. MCINTOSH: That's all.

DR. LEO LOWENTHAL: In my opinion this is a genuine work of literature, which is very characteristic for a period of unrest and tension such as the one we have been living through the last decade. I was reminded by reading Howl of many other literary works as they have been written after times of great upheavals, particularly after World War One, and I found this work very much in line with similar literary works. With regard to the specific merits of the poem Howl, I would say that it is structured very well. As I see it, it consists of three parts, the first of which is the craving of the poet for self-identification, where he roams all over the field and tries to find allies in similar search for self-identification. He then indicts, in the second part, the villain, so to say, which does not permit him to find it, the Moloch of society, of the world as it is today. And in the third part he indicates the potentiality of fulfillment by friendship and love, although it ends on a sad and melancholic note actually indicating that he is in search for fulfillment he cannot find.

KENNETH REXROTH: . . . The simplest term for such writing is prophetic, it is easier to call it that than anything else because we have a large body of prophetic writing to refer to. There are the prophets of the Bible, which it greatly resembles in purpose and in language and in subject matter. . . . The theme is the denunciation of evil and a pointing out of the way out, so to speak. That is prophetic literature. "Woe! Woe! Woe! The City of Jerusalem! The Syrian is about to come down or has already and you are to do such and such a thing and you must repent and do thus and so." And Howl, the four parts of the poem—that is including the "Footnote to Howl" as one additional part—do this very specifically. They take up these various specifics seriatim, one after the other. . . . And "Footnote to Howl," of course, again, is Biblical in reference. The reference is to the Benedicite, which says over and over again, "Blessed is the fire, Blessed is the light, Blessed are the trees, and Blessed is this and Blessed is that," and he is saying, "Everything that is human is Holy to me," and that the possibility of salvation in this terrible situation which he reveals is through love and through the love of everything Holy in man. So that, I would say, that this just about covers the field of typically prophetic poetry. . . .

HERBERT BLAU: The thing that strikes me most forcefully about Howl is that it is worded in what appears to be a contemporary tradition, one that did not cause me any particular consternation in reading, a tradition most evident in the modern period following the First World War, a tradition that resembles European literary tradition and is defined as "Dada," a kind of art of furious negation. By the intensity of its negation it seems to be both resurrective in quality and ultimately a sort of paean of possible hope. I wouldn't say that the chances for redemption or chances for salvation in a work of this kind are deemed to be very extensively possible but, nonetheless, the vision is not a total vision of despair. It is a vision that by the salvation of despair, by the salvation of what would appear to be perversity, by the salvation of what would appear to be obscene, by the salvation of what would appear to be illicit, is ultimately a kind of redemption of the illicit, the obscene, the disillusioned and the despairing. . . .

VINCENT MCHUGH: In this case . . . we have a vision of a modern hell. Now, we have certain precedents for that, for example, the book that it makes me think of, or the work of literature that it makes me think of offhand, the work of literature which is ferociously sincere in the same way, is Mr. Pound's—some of Mr. Pound's Cantos, especially Canto XIV and Canto XV. These, for example, in turn derive certainly from Dante and from the famous so-called cantos in Dante, and Dante, in turn, derives from the Odyssey, and so on into all the mythologies of the world. . . .

The prosecution put only two "expert witnesses" on the stand—both very lame samples of academia—one from the Catholic University of San Francisco and one a private elocution teacher, a beautiful woman, who said, "You feel like you are going through the gutter when you have to read that stuff. I didn't linger on it too long, I assure you." The University of San Francisco instructor said: "The literary value of this poem is negligible. . . . This poem is apparently dedicated to a long-dead movement, Dadaism, and some late followers of Dadaism. And, therefore, the opportunity is long past for any significant literary contribution of this poem." The critically devastating things the prosecution's witnesses could have said, but didn't, remain one of the great Catholic silences of the day.

So much for the literary criticism inspired by the trial. Cross-examination by the Prosecutor was generally brilliant, as in the following bit:

MR. MCINTOSH: Does Mr. Ferlinghetti attend your poetry writing workshop?
DR. MARK LINENTHAL: He does not.
MR. MCINTOSH: Do you attend his?
DR. LINENTHAL: I do not.
MR. MCINTOSH: You haven't been over there hearing him read poetry?
DR. LINENTHAL: No, I haven't.
(etc.)

Legally, a layman could see that an important principle was certainly in the line drawn between "hard core pornography" and writing judged to be "social speech." But more important still was the court's acceptance of the principle that if a work is determined to be "social speech," the question of obscenity may not even be raised. Or, in the words of Counsel Bendich's argument:

"The first amendment to the Constitution of the United States protecting the fundamental freedoms of speech and press prohibits the suppression of literature by the application of obscenity formulae unless the trial court first determines that the literature in question is utterly without social importance." (Roth v. U.S.)

. . . What is being urged here is that the majority opinion in Roth requires a trial court to make the constitutional determination; to decide in the first instance whether a work is utterly without redeeming social importance, before it permits the test of obscenity to be applied. . . .

. . . The record is clear that all of the experts for the defense identified the main theme of Howl as social criticism. And the prosecution concedes that it does not understand the work, much less what its dominant theme is.

Judge Horn agreed, in his opinion:

I do not believe that Howl is without even "the slightest redeeming social importance." The first part of Howl presents a picture of a nightmare world; the second part is an indictment of those elements in modern society destructive of the best qualities of human nature; such elements are predominantly identified as materialism, conformity, and mechanization leading toward war. The third part presents a picture of an individual who is a specific representation of what the author conceives as a general condition. . . . "Footnote to Howl" seems to be a declamation that everything in the world is holy, including parts of the body by name. It ends in a plea for holy living. . . .

And the judge went on to set forth certain rules for the guidance of authorities in the future:

1. If the material has the slightest redeeming social importance it is not obscene because it is protected by the First and Fourteenth Amendments of the United States Constitution, and the California Constitution.
2. If it does not have the slightest redeeming social importance it may be obscene.
3. The test of obscenity in California is that the material must have a tendency to deprave or corrupt readers by exciting lascivious thoughts or arousing lustful desire to the point that it presents a clear and present danger of inciting to anti-social or immoral action.
4. The book or material must be judged as a whole by its effect on the average adult in the community.
5. If the material is objectionable only because of coarse and vulgar language which is not erotic or aphrodisiac in character it is not obscene.
6. Scienter must be proved.
7. Book reviews may be received in evidence if properly authenticated.
8. Evidence of expert witnesses in the literary field is proper.
9. Comparison of the material with other similar material previously adjudicated is proper.
10. The people owe a duty to themselves and to each other to preserve and protect their constitutional freedoms from any encroachment by government unless it appears that the allowable limits of such protection have been breached, and then to take only such action as will heal the breach.
11. Quoting Justice Douglas: "I have the same confidence in the ability of our people to reject noxious literature as I have in their capacity to sort out the true from the false in theology, economics, politics, or any other field."
12. In considering material claimed to be obscene it is well to remember the motto: Honi soit qui mal y pense (Evil to him who thinks evil).

At which the Prosecution was reliably reported to have blushed.

Under banner headlines, the Chronicle reported that "the Judge's decision was hailed with applause and cheers from a packed audience that offered the most fantastic collection of beards, turtle-necked shirts and Italian hair-dos ever to grace the grimy precincts of the Hall of Justice." The decision was hailed editorially as a "landmark of law." Judge Horn has since been re-elected to office, which I like to think means that the People agree it was the police who here committed an obscene action.

►► Charles Olson

The Lordly and Isolate Satyrs

The lordly and isolate Satyrs—look at them come in
on the left side of the beach
like a motorcycle club! And the handsomest of them,
the one who has a woman, driving that snazzy
convertible

        Wow, did you ever see even in a museum
such a collection of boddisatvahs, the way
they come up to their stop, each of them
as though it was a rudder
the way they have to sit above it
and come to a stop on it, the monumental solidity
of themselves, the Easter Island
they make of the beach, the Red-headed Men

        These are the Androgynes,
the Fathers behind the father, the Great Halves

Or as that one was, inside his pants, the Yiddish poet
a vegetarian. Or another—all in his mouth—a snarl
of the Sources. Or the one I loved most, who once,
once only, let go the pain, the night he got drunk,
and I put him to bed, and he said, Bad blood.

        Or the one who cracks and doesn't know
that what he thinks are a thousand questions are suddenly
a thousand lumps thrown up where the cloaca
again has burst: one looks into the face and exactly as suddenly
it isn't the large eyes and nose but the ridiculously small mouth
which you are looking down as one end of

        —as the Snarled Man
is a monocyte
        Hail the ambiguous Fathers, and look closely
at them, they are the unadmitted, the club of Themselves,
weary riders, but who sit upon the landscape as the Great
Stones. And only have fun among themselves. They are
the lonely ones

        Hail them, and watch out. The rest of us,
on the beach as have previously known it, did not know
there was this left side. As they came riding in from the sea
—we did not notice them until they were already creating
the beach we had not known was there—but we assume
they came in from the sea. We assume that. We don't know.

        In any case the whole sea was now a hemisphere,
and our eyes like half a fly's, we saw twice as much. Everything opened, even if the newcomers just sat, didn't,
for an instant, pay us any attention. We were as we had been,
in that respect. We were usual, the children were being fed pop

and potato chips, and everyone was sprawled as people are
on a beach. Something had happened but the change
wasn't at all evident. A few drops of rain
would have made more of a disturbance.

There we were. They, in occupation of the whole view
in front of us and off to the left where we were not used to look.
And we, watching them pant from their exertions, and talk to each other,
the one in the convertible the only one who seemed to be circulating.
And he was dressed in magnificent clothes, and the woman with him
a dazzling blond, the new dye making her hair a delicious
streaked ash. She was as distant as the others. She sat in her flesh too.

These are our counterparts, the unknown ones.

They are here. We do not look upon them as invaders. Dimensionally

they are larger than we—all but the woman. But we are not suddenly

small. We are as we are. We don't even move, on the beach.

It is a stasis. Across nothing at all we stare at them.
We can see what they are. They don't notice us. They have merely
and suddenly moved in. They occupy our view. They are between us
and the ocean. And they have given us a whole new half of beach.

As of this moment, there is nothing else to report.
It is Easter Island transplanted to us. With the sun, and a warm
summer day, and sails out on the harbor they're here, the Contemporaries. They have come in.

Except for the stirring of the leader, they are still
catching their breath. They are almost like scooters the way
they sit there, up a little, on their thing. It is as though
the extra effort of it tired them the most. Yet that just there
was where their weight and separateness—their immensities—
lay. Why they seem like boddisatvahs. The only thing one noticed
is the way their face breaks when they call across to each other.
Or actually speak quite quietly, not wasting breath. But the face
loses all containment, they are fifteen year old boys at the moment
they speak to each other. They are not gods. They are not even stone.
They are doubles. They are only Source. When they act like us
they go to pieces. One notices then that their skin
is only creased like red-neck farmers. And that they are all
freckled. The red-headed people have the hardest time
to possess themselves. Is it because they were over-
fired? Or why—even to their beautiful women—do the red ones
have only that half of the weight?

We look at them, and begin to know. We begin to see
who they are. We see why they are satyrs, and why one half
of the beach was unknown to us. And now that it is known,

now that the beach goes all the way to the headland we thought
we were huddling ourselves up against, it turns out it is the
same. It is beach. These Visitors—Resters—who, by being there,
made manifest what we had not known—that the beach fronted wholly
to the sea—have only done that, completed the beach.

The difference is
we are more on it. The beauty of the white of the sun's light, the
blue the water is, and the sky, the movement of the painted landscape, the boy-town the scene was, is now pierced with angels and
with fire. And winter's ice shall be as brilliant in its time as
life truly is, as Nature is only the offerer, and it is we
who look to see what the beauty is.

These visitors, now stirring
to advance, to go on wherever they do go restlessly never completing
their tour, going off on their motorcycles, each alone except for
the handsome one, isolate huge creatures wearing down nothing as
they go, their huge third leg like carborundum, only the vault
of their being taking rest, the awkward boddhas

We stay. And watch them
gather themselves up. We have no feeling except love. They are not
ours. They are of another name. These are what the gods are. They
look like us. They are only in all parts larger. But the size is
only different. The difference is, they are not here, they are not
on this beach in this sun which, tomorrow, when we come to swim,
will be another summer day. They can't talk to us. We have no desire
to stop them any more than, as they made their camp, only possibly
the woman in the convertible one might have wanted to be familiar
with. The Leader was too much as they.

They go. And the day

► ► **Mark Schorer**

On LADY CHATTERLEY'S LOVER

[In October 1926, after his final visit to England, D. H. Lawrence began work on his last novel, his "English novel," Lady Chatterley's Lover, at the Villa Mirenda, Scandicci, Florence, and he completed the first version in February 1927. After an expedition to a number of Etruscan tombs in April, he wrote a second version which was completed before summer. Late in 1927 and during January of 1928, after a long and desperate siege of illness, he wrote the third and present version. With the help of Mrs. Aldous Huxley, a typescript was prepared for private publication under the imprint of the Florentine bookseller, Giuseppe Orioli; and on March 9, 1928, Lawrence and Orioli delivered the work to a printer who could not read English and some of whose assistants could not read at all. By March 15, Lawrence was sending out subscription forms (one thousand copies were to be printed and sold at two pounds each) to friends in England, France, and the United States. He began reading proofs in early April and the last were finished on May 24; the book was in press at the very end of that month. Finished books were being mailed out by the end of the first week in July 1928, and before the end of the year, Orioli had published a second edition of two hundred copies, printed "on common paper, to be sold at a guinea." The novel *was immediately and frequently pirated in the United States and France, and to bring this theft to an end, Lawrence published a popular edition ("The Author's Unabridged Popular Edition") in Paris in May 1929. This edition carries an introductory essay called "My Skirmish with Jolly Roger," which Lawrence subsequently lengthened and enriched in the essay called "A Propos of Lady Chatterley's Lover," posthumously published in June 1930. Two years after Lawrence's death in 1930, an abridged version was issued by Alfred A. Knopf in New York and by Martin Secker in London, and this version has been widely distributed in inexpensive reprints since. It is not, of course, the novel as Lawrence wrote it, and cannot be so judged. The complete version has been published in English in many continental countries and in translation in most. In 1944, the Dial Press published Lawrence's first manuscript version under the title The First Lady Chatterley. The second manuscript version has never been published except in an Italian translation issued by Mondadori in Milan. The third and final version has never been published in Great Britain, and never legally in the United States. The three manuscripts, beautiful in themselves and beautifully preserved, are in the possession of Angelo Ravagli in Taos, New Mexico, and it was only through his great kindness and that of the late Frieda Lawrence Ravagli that the present essay was made possible.—MARK SCHORER.]*

Lady Chatterley's Lover came into being under the umbrella pines of an Italian wood where Lawrence liked to sit writing beside a spring of San Eusebio, before the cave where the saint had lived. The air was golden, wild flowers embroidered the ground, nightingales sang to him. He wrote: "Civilized society is insane." He had put himself at last as far as possible "outside the made world" in order to deliver this last judgment upon it, and yet, writing his condemnation of industrial society in the peace of this Tuscan *pinèta*, he was also closing a circle.

As is known to all who read, D. H. Lawrence was born, the son of a coal miner and a schoolteacher, in the village of Eastwood in the English midlands of Nottinghamshire where they edge on Derbyshire. What the life of that countryside was like at the end of the last and the beginning of the present century, and what Lawrence's youth, lived in that countryside, was like, is best told in his novel *Sons and Lovers*. The background of that novel, as of his first, *The White Peacock*, is a slow cultural convulsion about to reach its end, a convulsion in which the ancient pastoralism of the yeoman way of life yields to the

new mechanization of the industrial way of life, and in which, incidentally, a lovely landscape yields itself to an iron horror. What was lovely and peaceful in that older life and landscape was Lawrence's peculiar treasure; what was ugly and new, his special anathema. Just before his death (and very shortly after he had published *Lady Chatterley's Lover*), as with a gasp of nearly desperate nostalgia, he wrote to a boyhood friend, J. D. Chambers, the younger brother of that girl "Miriam" who is at the center of the conflict in *Sons and Lovers*.

Dear David,—

I hardly recognized you as J. D.—and you must be a man now, instead of a thin little lad with very fair hair. Ugh, what a gap in time! it makes me feel scared.

Whatever I forget, I shall never forget the Haggs—I loved it so. I loved to come to you all, it really was a new life began in me there. The water-pippin by the door—those maiden-blush roses that Flower would lean over and eat and Trip floundering round.—And stewed figs for tea in winter, and in August green stewed apples. Do you still have them? Tell your mother I never forget, no matter where life carries us.—And does she still blush if somebody comes and finds her in a dirty white apron? Or doesn't she wear work-aprons any more? Oh, I'd love to be nineteen again, and coming up through the Warren and catching the first glimpse of the buildings. Then I'd sit on the sofa under the window, and we'd crowd round the little table to tea, in that tiny little kitchen I was so at home in.

Son' tempi passati, cari miei! quanto cari, non saprete mai!—I could never tell you in English how much it all meant to me, how I still feel about it.

If there is anything I can ever do for you, do tell me. —Because whatever else I am, I am somewhere still the same Bert who rushed with such joy to the Haggs.

This recollection is in sharp contrast to a fresher one that appears in the second version of *Lady Chatterley*. There, late in the novel, Lawrence has his lovers go to the Eastwood country; they meet in the church at Hucknall where "the pinch of dust that was Byron's heart" (Byron, "that fat lad"!) is enshrined, and they survey the old Lawrence landscape—Haggs Farm now deserted, Felley Mill still and abandoned, everything "dead as Nineveh," all life sacrificed to "coal and iron." This bitterly personal scene disappears from the final version of the novel, but here we have a comparable episode in the long motor trip that Constance Chatterley makes through Derbyshire:

The car ploughed uphill through the long squalid straggle of Tevershall, the blackened brick dwellings, the black slate roofs glistening their sharp edges, the mud black with coal-dust, the pavements wet and black. It was as if dismalness had soaked through and through everything. The utter negation of natural beauty, the utter negation of the gladness of life, the utter absence of the instinct for shapely beauty which every bird and beast has, the utter death of the human intuitive faculty was appalling. The stacks of soap in the grocers' shops, the rhubarb and lemons in the greengrocers'! The awful hats in the milliners'! All went by ugly, ugly, followed by the plaster-and-gilt horror of the cinema with its wet picture announcements. "A Woman's Love!" . . . Tevershall! That was Tevershall! Merrie England! Shakespeare's England! No, but the England of to-day, as Connie had realized since she had come to live in it. It was producing a new race of mankind, over-conscious in the money and social and political side, on the spontaneous, intuitive side dead, but dead. Half-corpses, all of them: but with a terrible insistent consciousness in the other half. There was something uncanny and underground about it all. It was an underworld. . . . This is history. One England blots out another.

Constance Chatterley's drive, we may assume, duplicates in fact and feeling a drive through the same countryside that Lawrence made in 1925. "Been motoring all over my well-known Derbyshire," he wrote mildly enough to Martin Secker. "But I can't look at the body of my past, the spirit seems to have flown." The Lawrences had been living above Taos and in Oaxaca; now they had paused in England on their way to Italy again. For a few months they settled at Spotorno (where Angelo Ravagli, the "Tenente" of Lawrence's letters, was their landlord). Lawrence was weary and felt no incentive to write a long book, but he did, during this period, write in its rough form the novelette, *The Virgin and the Gypsy*, which returns him to the English setting and is in some ways a thematic anticipation of *Lady Chatterley* as well. Then they moved south to Florence and the Villa Mirenda. In the summer of 1926 they made one more visit to England, and late in that year, after the composition of *Lady Chatterley* was well under way, Lawrence wrote to Rolf Gardiner about this visit. In this letter he tells Gardiner in explicit detail of the familiar landmarks in Eastwood and its environs—the houses in which he lived as a boy, Haggs Farm and Felley Mill and other places that had figured prominently in the first half-dozen novels and in so many of his stories. "That's the country of my heart," he writes; but painfully, for he concludes as follows:

I was at my sister's in September, and we drove round —I saw the miners—and pickets—and policemen—it was like a spear through one's heart. I tell you, we'd better buck up and do something for the England to come,

for they've pushed the spear through the side of my England.

What he could do for "the England to come" was to write *Lady Chatterley*, and we are reminded of a letter from as far back as 1913:

Pray to your gods for me that Sons and Lovers shall succeed. People should begin to take me seriously now. And I do so break my heart over England when I read the New Machiavelli. And I am so sure that only through a readjustment between men and women, and a making free and healthy of this sex, will she get out of her present atrophy. Oh, Lord, and if I don't "subdue my art to a metaphysic," as somebody very beautifully said of Hardy, I do write because I want folk—English folk—to alter, and have more sense.

Fourteen years after his death, his widow said of Lawrence and *Lady Chatterley* and the English people, "he spoke out of them and for them, there in Tuscany, where the different culture of another race gave the impetus to his work."

Between the cottage on Walker Street in Eastwood, or Haggs Farm outside it, and the Villa Mirenda outside Florence, lay a long history. In that history, three items loom large: Lawrence's marriage to Frieda von Richthofen, the First World War, and travels all over the globe. His marriage is one of the most exploited subjects in our memoir literature, and all one need say of it here is that, whatever stresses it may have undergone, it had more of blessedness, and that without that blessedness, the lyrical portions of *Lady Chatterley*, which comprise a great hymn to true marriage, could not have been written. Lawrence's personal experiences in the war are the subject of the chapter called "The Nightmare" in the novel, *Kangaroo*, and the atmosphere of the war and of a war-made world hangs over all his works from 1916 on but is most prominent in the quality of that social world that threatens the lyrical world of *Lady Chatterley*, for Lawrence felt as early as 1916 what we all feel today, "the violence of the nightmare released now into the general air." The travels (southern and central Europe, the Far East, Australia, the United States and Mexico, Europe again) not only provided him with the series of settings through which his novels make their march and so lead him to their end at the Villa Mirenda, but also provided him with images of utopia (always smashed) that would give him the community relationship that he sometimes desperately felt he needed. It was only when he gave up that hope, and the programs that his novels sometimes developed out of that hope, that he could have come to rest in *Lady Chatterley*, where there is no program at all, only the inspired plea that the human being become what he already is, that is, human. The journey from the humanity and the inhumanity of his youth, to his discovery at the end of the essentially human as it could be defined in drama against that background—this is another circle that his last novel closes.

There were times in Lawrence's career when the whole beautiful line of it, as it was finally drawn, threatened to blow up completely. After the purely autobiographical novel, *Sons and Lovers*, Lawrence wrote his two most complex works, *The Rainbow* and *Women in Love*. These were novels that attempted to seize directly on the psychic realities. They end with regenerate heroes who have experienced visions of human felicity for which they can find no place either in this world or in the realistic convention of the novel. Then begins a period for which bitter, surely, is a mild word—bitter, galled, the withers wrung. And yet, in this period, where Lawrence tries to bring his characters into vital social relationships, we are at the center of the most fascinating and alarming elements in Lawrence, the artist.

Aaron's Rod (the novel that, in its first paragraph, announces the end of the war, the violence released now into the general air) was published in 1922, the year of Mussolini's *coup d'etat*; *Kangaroo*, in 1923; *The Plumed Serpent*, in January 1926. Unable to see any but negative virtues (that is, vices) in democracy, which seemed to Lawrence a means of freeing the individual to mediocrity and a numbed anxiety only, he was still fairly desperate to find some means of satisfying what he himself called his "societal impulse" and of making his novels end positively in this world. So he turned to undemocratic ideas, a part of the violence released now; and in these three novels, in three different ways, tried them out to see if they would work either for the novel or for life. They did not. This is the imaginative test of theoretical abstraction, and Lawrence's greatness of mind shows in the necessity he felt to reject the abstraction when it would not work for the imagination. The first two of these novels are fragmentary, implosive structures because the author, while he cannot prove the abstraction right, is unwilling to let his story prove it wrong and so lets the story jar to a stop in negation. The third is a unified work because the lives of the characters, in the actualities of the plot, prove that the abstraction is merely abstract, that is, wrong, and the novel ends in its rejection.

Aaron's Rod presents Lawrence in the character of Lilly, who assures Aaron Sisson that he will not find himself until he finds a greater man to whom he can submit his partial individuality; but in the end, Lilly can produce no such leader, not even himself. In *Kangaroo*, Lawrence puts himself in Aaron's position, as the man who seeks the leader; but, confronted by the alternative of the socialist, Struthers, and the fascist, Kangaroo, the Lawrentian hero departs for America, where he hopes to find a more plausible choice. Then, in *The Plumed Serpent*, Lawrence tries still another device: he transforms his seeker into a woman, a jaded European who has severed her connections with her own social past and seeks fulfillment in Mexico through the leadership of two men who are trying to institutionalize a primitive religion which is not in the least unlike Lawrence's own religion of "the dark gods"; but it will not work. As the two leaders fail her, so she fails them, and discovers, with Lawrence, that there are two kinds of power: the power to dominate others, and the power to fulfill oneself. "The leader-cum-follower relationship is a bore," Lawrence wrote then, in a letter. "And the new relationship will be some sort of tenderness, sensitive, between men and men, and between men and women." *Lady Chatterley's Lover*, the last novel, was first to be called *Tenderness*.

This is the final Lawrence, the Lawrence who kicked out, although with a dragging reluctance, the hypothetical fragments that he had tried to shore against the world's ruin and his own, and who was determined to attempt still to be free in the actualities of human relationship. He was an artist who had gone through a purgatorial period that sought escapes from freedom, and then settled with small content and no complacency into the paradise that knows what freedom is, or at least where it begins. This is the paradise that is allowed to human life when human beings can recognize that after all the sweat for something else, for something either more or less, the value of life exists in the act of living; that living means full living, or the life of the full and not the partial self, the self that realizes its powers rather than the self that seeks power or submits to it. And this is, after all, the beginning of the true democracy, as it is of the true marriage, because it is total integration, and therefore makes possible the only creative spontaneity, even though that be in isolation, in an Italian wood.

At the Villa Mirenda—a great square block of whitish-gray stone that stands, like the typical farm villa of Tuscany, alone on its hill, its clusters of cypresses thrusting up blackly green against the blue, its fields and vineyards falling away from it in all directions, and the matchstick dwellings of the *contadini* scattered here and there among the fields—here, the Lawrences saw few people. Chiefly they had the peasants and themselves. One reason that they took the place was because this was "a region of no foreigners." Lawrence knew quite well what he was facing ("Have you built your ship of death, oh, have you?") and he was trying to face it. ". . . people don't mean much to me, especially casuals; them I'd rather be without," he wrote; and, "the Florence society is no menace." He did not want what he could have, and he could not have what he felt that he needed. He took his isolation, then, with small content and no complacency. In July of 1926 he wrote to Rolf Gardiner (a British proto-fascist) as follows:

> I believe we are mutually a bit scared. I of weird movements, and you of me. I don't know why. But if you are in London even for a couple of days after the 30th, do come and see us, and we can talk a little, nervously. No, I shall ask you questions like a doctor of a patient he knows nothing about.
>
> But I should like to come to Yorkshire, I should like even to try to dance a sword-dance with iron-stone miners above Whitby. I should love to be connected with something, with some few people, in something. As far as anything matters, I have always been very much alone, and regretted it. But I can't belong to clubs, or societies, or Freemasons, or any other damn thing. So if there is, with you, an activity I can belong to, I shall thank my stars. But, of course, I shall be wary beyond words, of committing myself.
>
> Everything needs a beginning, though—and I shall be very glad to abandon my rather meaningless isolation, and join in with some few other men, if I can. If only, in the dirty solution of this world, some new little crystal will begin to form.

And even after he had finished the second version of Lady Chatterley (and among the truths that this novel most forcibly urges is the meaning and the necessity of isolation), he could still write as follows to Dr. Trigant Burrow:

> I suffer badly from being so cut off. But what is one to do? One can't link up with the social unconscious. At times, one is forced to be essentially a hermit. I don't want to be. But anything else is either a personal tussle, or a money tussle; sickening: except, of course, just for ordinary acquaintance, which remains acquaintance. One has no real human relations—that is so devastating.

Better to have no social relationships at all than to have them and pretend that they are real! So he wrote disgustedly to Huxley of Beethoven, whose letters he was reading, "always in love with somebody when he wasn't really, and wanting contacts when he didn't really—part of the crucifixion into isolated individuality—poveri noi." Every future holds only one final fact, and what Lawrence loved about Villa Mirenda was that it served to school him in that ultimate isolation.

> I never know what people mean when they complain of
>   loneliness.
> To be alone is one of life's greatest delights, thinking
>   one's own thoughts,
> doing one's own little jobs, seeing the world beyond
> and feeling oneself uninterrupted in the rooted connec-
>   tion
> with the centre of all things.

In those barely furnished rooms, in that quiet country landscape, the rooted connection might yet be found.

> There is nothing to save, now all is lost,
> but a tiny core of stillness in the heart
> like the eye of a violet.

Violets grew there in profusion, and Lawrence was dying among them. He was ill much of the time at the Mirenda, and his was an illness that could only be alleviated, not cured. If illness and the image of a black ship lay under his isolation, they also affected in a curious way Lawrence's attitude toward his work. During the months at Spotorno, after the English visit of 1925, he wrote only a few stories, his longest effort being that piece about an English girl called The Virgin and the Gypsy, which is preparatory to Lady Chatterley. At Villa Mirenda, the lethargic indifference, a weary kind of rest after all the high-strung battles, grew in him. He wrote his British publisher:

> In the real summer, I always lose interest in literature and publications. The cicadas rattle away all day in the trees, the girls sing, cutting the corn with sickles, the sheaves of wheat lie all afternoon like people dead asleep in the heat. E più non si frega. I don't work, except at an occasional scrap of an article. I don't feel much like doing a book, of any sort. Why do any more books? There are so many, and such a small demand for what there are. So why add to the burden, and waste one's vitality over it.

But news of the General Strike in England renewed the images of iron and of an "underground humanity" in his mind.

> I feel bad about that strike. Italian papers say: "The government will maintain an iron resistance." Since the war, I've no belief in iron resistances. Flesh and blood and a bit of wisdom can do quite enough resisting and a

bit of adjusting into the bargain—and with iron one only hurts oneself and everybody. Damn iron!

Then, once more, with the visit to England in the summer of 1926, mere images of iron became the monstrous realities of the senses, and soon after his return to Italy, he writes, "I've nearly done my novel."

2

The story of *Lady Chatterley's Lover* is among the simplest that Lawrence devised: Constance Chatterley, the frustrated wife of an aristocratic mine owner who has been wounded in the war and left paralyzed and impotent, is drawn to his gamekeeper, the misanthropic son of a miner, becomes pregnant by him, and hopes at the end of the book to be able to divorce her husband and leave her class for a life with the other man. Through all his career Lawrence had been concerned with the general theme of this book —the violation or the fulfillment of individuality in relationship—and many times he had handled the theme in the concrete terms here presented where fulfillment involves the crossing either of class or cultural lines, and often of both, where violation results from resisting this necessity. The familiar construction, then, is of a woman in a relatively superior social situation who is drawn to an "outsider" (a man of lower social rank or a foreigner) and either resists her impulse or yields to it. The two possibilities are embodied, of course, and respectively, in the situation into which Lawrence was born and in the situation into which he married. Inevitably, it became a favorite situation of his fiction.

Among the short stories, one might mention five as clear illustrations: one of his juvenile works, *A Fragment of Stained Glass*, deals with a medieval serf who flees his bondage with a miller's daughter; in *The Daughters of the Vicar*, one daughter chooses to defy her family in order to marry a miner; in *The Shades of Spring*, a Miriam-like girl reveals to her old, poetic lover that a gamekeeper has taken his place; in *Mother and Daughter*, the daughter chooses to upset her mother's values and her own by committing the absurdity of going off with an Armenian known to the mother as "the Turkish Delight"; in *None of That*, an enormously wealthy daughter of the jazz age invites an involvement (to her destruction) with a Mexican bullfighter.

Among the novelettes, one might again mention five. In *The Fox*, a constrictive relationship between two girls is shattered by the intrusion of a farmer-soldier and his passion for one of them; in *The Lady-bird*, an aristocratic Englishwoman yields to a mysterious central European, Dionys Psanek; in *St. Mawr*, Mrs. Witt and her daughter Lou are attracted by a Welsh groom and a half-breed Navajo; in *The Princess*, a New England virgin wishes to yield to a Mexican guide and discovers only too late that she cannot truly yield; in *The Virgin and the Gypsy*, an English virgin yields to a gypsy.

From the ten novels, we can once more choose five, although the situation is omnipresent. There is *Lady Chatterley's Lover* itself. In *Sons and Lovers*, the parental situation is not only an obvious example but the archetype. In *The Lost Girl*, a middle-class English girl leaves the comforts (and depredations) of home for a rigorous life with an Italian peasant. In *The Plumed Serpent*, Kate Forrester, a refined European, yields (temporarily) to the intellectual leadership of one Mexican and the physical leadership of another. And in the very first novel, *The White Peacock*, the situation not only presents itself in the Lettie-George relationship, but a gamekeeper, Annable, appears briefly but volubly as the earliest version of Parkin-Mellors, the gamekeeper of the last novel.

Such a catalogue as this takes two risks: it suggests a limited imaginative range, and it seems to denigrate the subject by a tone of frivolity. Neither risk is serious, for the theme itself, however badly one may state the situations that embody it, is pushed into every area that concerns us most seriously in this century. *Lady Chatterley's Lover*, like everything that Lawrence wrote, is an affirmation of life values as against the mechanization of human nature. This, his general subject matter, may be broken down into two major themes; the relation of men and women, and the relation of men and machines. In the works as they are written, the two are one, and his most subtle and penetrating perception, the knowledge that social and psychological conflicts are identical, is so firmly integrated in the structure of his books that it is almost foolhardy to speak of his having two themes when in fact he had one vision. But a vision has both a background and a foreground, and one may say, perhaps without distortion, that the men and machines relationship is the background, the man and woman relationship, the foreground. This division does not mean that the first determines the second, for it would be just as true to say that the second determines the first. They are, in fact, inextricable. We might say that one provides the scene, and the other, the drama enacted on that scene.

Who was Annable? One must remind oneself of the British novel as it was in the year 1911 to recognize what an extraordinary figure he is, standing there so clearly from the beginning, in that first novel, written when Lawrence was a very young man. Whether he had some prototype in actuality we will probably never know, and it is of no importance that we should know; certainly he had none in fiction. What is important is simply to observe that he was uniquely *there*—there from the beginning in Lawrence's imagination as the figure who asserts that modern civilized society is insane, and who without compromise rejects it. Nothing that one might say of ideas of primitivism and of the natural man as these had been used in the writing of the two preceding centuries would in any way reduce his uniqueness.

He was a man of one idea:—that all civilisation was the painted fungus of rottenness. He hated any sign of culture. I won his respect one afternoon when he found me trespassing in the woods because I was watching some maggots at work in a dead rabbit. That led us to a discussion of life. He was a thorough materialist—he scorned religion and all mysticism. He spent his days sleeping, making intricate traps for weasels and men, putting together a gun, or doing some amateur forestry, cutting down timber, splitting it in logs for use in the hall, and planting young trees. When he thought, he reflected on the decay of mankind—the decline of the human race into folly and weakness and rottenness. "Be a good animal, true to your animal instinct," was his motto. With all this, he was fundamentally very unhappy—and he made me also wretched.

Annable's difficulty is that he is not only an animal (as his name is not quite that word), but also a human being with a civilized experience behind him. The son of a prosperous father, he had been enrolled at Cambridge, had taken orders and served as curate to a fashionable rector, and had married (unhappily, in the end) a lady; yet now he lives in brutish squalor, amid a swarm of soiled children and a slatternly, illiterate woman, and strives not to lift his mind above these chosen circumstances. He does not manage to survive his choice. Yet he serves his function in providing a kind of choral emphasis in a novel that is concerned with the thinning out of human relationship amid a general deterioration of life. He serves no less to emphasize Lawrence's success in developing the character and situation of his last gamekeeper. His success with this figure is Lawrence's vindication of his crude attempt with Annable, just as it is the payment of his long-standing debt to the humanity of his own father. This is not so much a matter of psychological as it is of aesthetic maturity; Lawrence had found precisely the way that he wished to speak. For if *Lady Chatterley's Lover* concludes a long thematic history, it concludes no less a history of forms.

Lawrence was, of course, three things: he was a man in search of a life; he was a prophet in search of a revelation; and he was an artist in search of a convention. The first formed the second, and the second created the problems of the third, but it is only the third, finally—or the third as containing the others—that we can with much profit consider in the name either of criticism or of thought.

In a recent enthusiastic book on Lawrence by an Anglican priest who writes under the name of Father Tiverton, we are shown that the spirit of Lawrence's work was not at all inimical to much that is central in Christian thought, and also that this spirit makes him the kind of artist that he is. And how simply Father Tiverton puts it! "He reached the point in imaginative being at which the preacher and the poet coincide, since the poem is the sermon." The *whole* poem, of course, or the *whole* story, or the *whole* novel, not any set of extractable words or scenes that exist only as a portion of those wholes. This primary axiom of all reading and all criticism applies nowhere more drastically than to *Lady Chatterley's Lover*.

To reach the point where the preacher and the poet coincide *formally* was not a simple matter. We have already observed something of Lawrence's intellectual progress, how in novel after novel, the imaginative test qualifies the theoretical conviction. Thus Lawrence's mind constantly moved as each novel shrugged off its predecessor, at the same time that his techniques moved through a wide range of fascinating experimentation (still almost entirely unexamined by criticism) in his attempt to accommodate what was theoretically dear to him to the dearer forms of fiction. In both the broadest and the most special sense, Lawrence is first of all the artist: he gives primacy to the "living tissue" of imaginative experience, and his craft is constantly moving and moving always on a dynamic base.

All this is to say nothing at all about those sporadic bursts of "genius" ("A great genius, but no artist," runs the cliché.) that even the unfriendliest critics grant, those "fitful and profound insights" that even Mr. Eliot, for example, finds it possible to allow; it is only to say that in the one important way that a man is an artist, Lawrence was an artist: that he knew where his real life was lived. Once this obvious matter can be established (and Father Tiverton went far in doing just that), we can begin to analyze the spurts of genius and their place in the whole art, or even, conceivably, to describe the constant artist.

Lawrence, the constant artist, made constant demands on the forms of fiction that had not been made in the past. "It is the way our sympathy flows and recoils that really determines our lives," he wrote in the famous ninth chapter of *Lady Chatterley's Lover*.

And here lies the vast importance of the novel, properly handled. It can inform and lead into new places the flow of our sympathetic consciousness, and it can lead our sympathy away in recoil from things gone dead. Therefore, the novel, properly handled, can reveal the most secret places of life; for it is in the passional secret places of life above all, that the tide of sensitive awareness needs to ebb and flow, cleansing and freshening.

Among the "things gone dead" (and it is only one) is the conventionalized, the calcified ethic of Christianity, and it was Lawrence's belief that the human consciousness was capable of regeneration if only it could be led away from the rubble into "new places." ". . . for wide masses of people," John Lehmann wrote in 1947, in a plea for a renewal of "the world of love,"

the Christian symbols as they have known them have ceased to be significant, and their desperate need is to find new symbols—even if those symbols should lead us back to a rediscovery of the central meaning of Christianity, restored through the discarding of outworn and corrupted images, and irrelevant accretions of fact.

Although Mr. Lehmann himself found the mass of Lawrence's symbols inadequate to this end, one can argue—and so Father Tiverton argued—that this attempt was precisely Lawrence's. His wish was to take the sacraments out of their merely institutional bindings and to reassert the sacramental nature of life itself.

The old Church knew best the enduring needs of man, beyond the spasmodic needs of today and yesterday. . . . For centuries the mass of people lived in the rhythm, under the Church. And it is down in the mass that the roots of religion are eternal. When the mass of a people loses the religious rhythm, that people is dead, without hope. But Protestantism came and gave a great blow to the religious and ritualistic rhythm of the year, in human life. Non-conformity almost finished the deed. Now you have a poor, blind, disconnected people with nothing but politics and bank-holidays to satisfy the eternal human need of living in ritual adjustment to the cosmos in its revolutions. . . . Mankind has got to get back to the rhythm of the cosmos, and the permanence of marriage.

"I am a profoundly religious man," Lawrence once said of himself, and when Father Tiverton comes to the concluding point in his discussion where he wishes to state the central fact about Lawrence's

view and his art, he writes: "I should claim that one of the great virtues of Lawrence was his sense of the ISness rather than the OUGHTness of religion . . . he believed in his dark gods not because they 'worked,' but because they were true."

But how, in the realistic tradition of the British novel, was the artist to communicate the "ISness of religion"? Of the first three novels, where the content is suited to the realistic convention, *Sons and Lovers* is successful even though it is in that work that Lawrence discovers that what he wants his work to communicate is a more essential reality than "that hard, violent style full of sensation and presentation" (as Lawrence himself described it was capable). *The Rainbow* and *Women in Love* are his extended attempt at a form that will accomplish this end. The first begins as a traditional family chronicle and ends in a Blakean vision; the second consolidates the visionary and the hallucinatory effects of the first, and they dominate the whole. Neither is a novel in any traditional sense, not even a "psychological novel." They are psychic dramas in which primary human impulses rather than human personalities struggle and embrace, and they end with heroes who have made a journey of the soul and whose regeneration puts them beyond the conditions of that social world out of which the novel as we have known it has always come and in which it has always been rooted. In *Aaron's Rod* and *Kangaroo* the strenuous formal attempt is relinquished; these are rather rough chronicles of real journeys in which the soul's journey is *discussed* but in which no attempt is made to embody its destination in the drama. In *The Plumed Serpent*, an extremely ambitious work, the myth of the soul's journey coalesces happily with the primitive Mexican myth that the heroes are attempting to revitalize in Mexican political life and that makes up the bulk of the story; it ends with the European heroine's conclusion that the Mexican myth may be good for the Mexicans but that it is of small use to her, and she lapses back into the condition of her social world, saying, "But I can fool them so they shan't find out." She will take from them what is of use to her, for as long as may be.

In many of his short stories and in his short novels, Lawrence managed to maintain a realistic framework within which rich symbolic modulations that far transcend realism could be beautifully contained. In the shorter fiction, too, he could break into pure symbolic forms, as in *The Woman Who Rode Away*, or into splendid fable, as in *The Man Who Died*. But even as he managed more and more successfully to handle action that in itself was ritualistic and prose that was liturgical, the convention of the realistic novel could not be made wholly to yield. The progress from the first through the third version of *Lady Chatterley* is the history of an effort to make the events at once maximumly plausible in realistic terms and maximumly meaningful in psychic terms. The result in the third version is a novel in a solid and sustained social context, with a clear and happily developed plot, in which the characters function fully and the author allows them to speak for themselves; at the same time it is a novel in which everything is symbolic, in which "every bush burns," and which in itself finally forms one great symbol, so that one can easily remember it as one remembers a picture. In the background of this picture black machinery looms cruelly against a darkening sky; in the foreground, hemmed in and yet separate, stands a green wood; in the wood, two naked human beings dance.

3

The first *Lady Chatterley* is a relatively short, dark, and above all rough sketch written under the pall of recently experienced English gloom; the second, written after the Etruscan adventure, is much longer and leaps out of the dreariness of the first, with a strong infusion of lyric feeling and natural vitality that must derive from Lawrence's experience of the brilliantly sensuous tomb paintings at Tarquinia and elsewhere; the third, written after a hard and alarming illness, is about the same length as the second, but there is a sharpening of intellectual issues and a deepening of pathos. These are the large general changes, and if we add to them the fact that in each version as it succeeds an earlier, the treatment of the sexual act becomes more and more explicit, a development as necessary to the achievement of the four qualities just listed as it was to the full dramatization of Lawrence's theme, we have encompassed the major changes in tone and feeling. At the other end of the scale of revision are thousands of alterations in technical detail, and a systematic analysis of these changes would tell us a great deal about Lawrence the writer, but the place and time for such an analysis is a scholarly monograph that could best be published when all three texts of the novel are available to interested readers. Between these two extremes of

revisionary method are a variety of changes in dramatic structure, many of which have been observed by E. W. Tedlock, Jr., in an appendix to his *The Frieda Lawrence Collection of D. H. Lawrence Manuscripts* (1948). It is in the interest of the present account to observe a few of these.

Lawrence's first problem in revision seems to have been to tell his story in such a way as to achieve maximum plausibility within the terms of his own aspiration: he had to make the love of the lady and the gamekeeper convincing, and he had also to give their love a chance for survival in the world as he saw it. If we follow the alterations in the character of the keeper, in the character of Constance, and finally, in the nature of the resolutions, we will be able to see how he achieved his end.

In all three versions, the gamekeeper (called Parkin in the first two, Mellors in the third) is a man of about forty, a miner's son who has misanthropically withdrawn from the industrial world into work in the wood. In the first and second versions, he is of medium height, with reddish-brown eyes and a shaggy mustache; in the third, he is taller, with blue eyes. In the first version he is physically strong; in the second, not so strong; in the third, sometimes rather frail. The Parkin of the first version speaks only in the vernacular; the second uses the Derbyshire dialect in scenes of affection and the king's English when he wishes; Mellors speaks more or less like the second Parkin but is capable of much more conceptual language. The Parkin of the first version has least motivation for his misanthropy but is the most violent in asserting it. He delights in trapping poachers and getting summonses for them; to Mellors, this is an unpleasant part of his work. Where Parkin is positively churlish with Constance, Mellors is ironical and mildly derisive. The first Parkin's motivation lies in a smashed marriage with a brutish woman; the second Parkin's motivation lies in the same marriage, but with a background of an awkward sexual trauma that unfits him for any other woman and yet does not fit her for him. In Mellors, the sexual background is amplified but the traumatic experience disappears: he has had love affairs with young women drawn exactly on the models of Miriam and the Helena of Lawrence's second and third novels— romantic, "spiritual" women who offended his manhood, and from these he had turned to the "common" girl, Bertha, whom he married, but who revealed at once a ferocious sexual will under the force of which the marriage passed swiftly into brutish deterioration. From this marriage, Mellors escaped into the world, and the world of gentlemen: he had become an officer's aide in India. Now, in his

cottage, he has books that he can read and talk about, and he is Constance's equal in all but birth. The original Parkin is something of a clown as well as a boor: "The skirts of his big coat flapped, his brown dog ran at his heels. He was once more going to take the world by the nose. . . . He strode with a grand sort of stride, baggy coat-tails flapping. The son of man goes forth to war! She smiled to herself grimly." The second Parkin still has "a rather sticking-out brown moustache," but "His bearing had a military archness and resistance that was natural to him." Mellors has not only the military background itself, but, along with "a certain look of frailty," natural gentility, and when Constance sees him in town, "tall and slender, and so different, in a formal suit of thin dark cloth," she reflects that "he could go anywhere. He had a native breeding which was really much nicer than the cut-to-pattern class things."

In Constance Chatterley, the changes are perhaps less drastic, but they are no less important to her motivation. In the first version, she has had a certain continental experience but it has hardly made her worldly; in the second version, she has had a continental education; in the third version, she has not only had a continental education but also a series of casual, "intellectual" love affairs before her marriage. She is still "a ruddy, country-looking girl with soft brown hair and a sturdy body, and slow movements, full of unused energy," but she is also a woman whose experience has equipped her to take the full measure of her world. Her marriage ruined by Clifford's physical incapacity, she has, in her third figuration, a casual postmarital affair (and is encouraged in this conduct by her friends, her father, even her husband). In the third version, Lawrence introduces the character of Michaelis, a successful, trivial playwright, to put Constance at the very center of the full emptiness of this social-intellectual world. This motivation is of first importance, for it places Mellors and Constance in precisely the same situation: an experienced man and woman, both disillusioned with their experience, both capable of a better experience. With the minimization of the class barrier between Connie and Mellors and the amplification of their similar sexual defeat, Lawrence achieves the psychological realism of the final version.

If they are ready for one another, they still face the problem of finding a world that is ready for them. As only a glance at the variation in the three endings will show, Lawrence had solved this problem only in part by the alterations that we have already observed. In the first version, where class barriers are strongest, and where Lawrence is still hoping for some social role for his characters, Parkin ends as a worker in a

Sheffield steel mill and as the secretary of the local branch of the Communist party. Just before the end, after Constance is shown in an impossible scene in a worker's home, she and Parkin quarrel, and the likelihood of their finding any way out is small. In the final scene, she hopes to become his wife, simply his wife, living in his terms, sharing his interests, politics included; but our hope for her is small. In the second version, Parkin is no longer a political man and the Sheffield mills are an abomination to him; he plans to leave them for farm work. He is perhaps a little less unwilling to spend some of Connie's money in order to find a life for themselves, if she is so determined. The novel ends with his promising to "come to Italy" in her wake, when she needs him. But here Lawrence has tried to write out the class barrier by fiat. While Constance is visiting on the Continent, she has this revelation:

> Class is an anachronism. It finished in 1914. Nothing remains but a vast proletariat, including kings, aristocrats, squires, millionaires and working-people, men and women alike. And then a few individuals who have not yet been proletarianised. . . .
>
> It was a great relief to her that that vague, yet very profound class-mistrust which had laid like a negating serpent at the bottom of her soul, was now gone. Vitally, organically, in the old organic sense of society, there were no more classes. That organic system had collapsed. So she need not have any class-mistrust of Parkin, and he need have none of her.

This discovery presumably frees them to live in the world as it is, on their terms. The end of the second version is very explicitly uninterested in any retreat to the colonies. It is the world or nothing, this time. "To Connie, the wood where she had known Parkin in the spring had become the image of another world," but the implication is that she can make *that* world bloom in this one, probably in Italy. On this subject, Lawrence had taken his personal stand, and interested readers should examine his *Autobiographical Sketch*, written at this time and published posthumously in *Assorted Articles*. There he writes:

> Class makes a gulf, across which all the best human flow is lost. It is not exactly the triumph of the middle classes that has made the deadness, but the triumph of the middle-class thing. . . . the middle class is broad and shallow and passionless. Quite passionless. At the best they substitute affection, which is the great middle-class positive emotion. . . . Yet I find, here in Italy, for example, that I live in a certain silent contact with the peasants who work the land of this villa. I am not intimate with them . . . and they are not working for me; I am not their padrone. Yet it is they, really, who form

my ambiente. . . . I don't expect them to make any millennium here on earth, neither now nor in the future. But I want to live near them, because their life still flows.

But Connie and Mellors are not Frieda and D. H. Lawrence, and Lawrence has the dramatic tact to recognize as much in the third version. While the entire implication (underlined by the *rapport* that develops between Mellors and Connie's father) is that class is an anachronism, and that the moment we can make better assumptions about what we are in the potential human facts, this will be the first of many anachronisms to vanish from the actual social facts, Lawrence wisely allows the matter to remain in the realm of implication rather than forcing it to solve his dramatic problem. Again, with the question of marriage as it *is* versus marriage as it should be, the second version is as explicit as this:

> So it must be: a voyage apart, in the same direction. Grapple the two vessels together, lash them side by side, and the first storm will smash them to pieces. This is marriage, in the bad weather of modern civilisation. But leave the two vessels apart, to make their voyage to the same port, each according to its own skill and power, and an unseen life connects them, a magnetism which cannot be forced. And that is marriage as it will be, when this is broken down.

In the third version, the dramatic presentation of a true marriage is permitted to speak for itself, and the fact that this true marriage must exist in a wasteland leaves the end of the third version in some uncertainty, which is supremely right. The whole seems to slow down into a *decrescendo* as it begins to breathe out an uneasiness that is aesthetically fine, among Lawrence's really great effects. Political affirmations (and some impossible scenes) vanish, both the earliest assertions of class war and the middle assertions of the absence of class, and the novel ends with a long letter from Mellors to Constance, written from a farm where he is working, as both characters await their divorces and Connie awaits her child. Mellors hopes to find a farm of his own, perhaps in Canada, where they can make their life; but he does not hope for more, and he is hardly bold in the hope he has.

> . . . what I live for now is for you and me to live together. I'm frightened, really. I feel the devil in the air, and he'll try to get us. Or not the devil, Mammon: which I think, after all, is only the mass-will of people, wanting money and hating life. Anyhow I feel great grasping white hands in the air, wanting to get hold of the throat of anybody who tries to live, live beyond money, and squeeze the life out. There's a bad time coming! If things

go on as they are, there's nothing lies in the future but death and destruction, for these industrial masses. I feel my inside turn to water sometimes, and there you are, going to have a child by me. But never mind. All the bad times that ever have been, haven't been able to blow the crocus out: not even the love of women. So they won't be able to blow out my wanting you, nor the little glow there is between you and me. We'll be together next year. And though I'm frightened, I believe in your being with me. A man has to fend and fettle for the best, and then trust in something beyond himself. You can't insure against the future, except by really believing in the best bit of you, and the power beyond it. So I believe in the little flame between us. For me now, it's the only thing in the world. I've got no friends, not inward friends. Only you.

Earlier in the novel, we encounter this exchange between the lovers:

"I would like to have all the rest of the world disappear," she said, "and live with you here."

"It won't disappear," he said.

They went almost in silence through the lovely wood. But they were together in a world of their own.

In the end, Lawrence permits them to meet the world as it is with the only armor that they have: the courage of their own tenderness. But the reader remembers, perhaps, for his comfort and theirs, the echoing promise of Clifford himself, meant with such an ironic difference and delivered in the cadences of the later T. S. Eliot, that "every parting means a meeting elsewhere. And every meeting is a new bondage."

If Lawrence's first problem in revision was to achieve maximum plausibility within the terms of his aspiration, his second problem was to achieve maximum meaning through the amplification of his symbols. If the first problem involved him primarily in the solid realities of a class situation, the second involved him in the modulations of psychic reality. The basic contrast between life-affirming and life-denying values, between "tenderness" and the "insentient iron world" is the sole subject of Lawrence's symbolic amplifications, and nearly any line of revision, no matter how minor, that we chose to follow through the three versions of his novel would demonstrate the swelling connotative richness with which this contrast is presented.

Perhaps the most obvious development over the three texts is Lawrence's increase in descriptions of both the mechanical world and the wood on the Chatterley estate, for this juxtaposition in the setting of the novel is the first symbolic form of the basic thematic contrast of the novel. It is developed until the new consciousness of the lovers is itself like a wood in flower, and the shrinking consciousness of Clifford is itself like a machine in gear.

She was like a forest, like the dark interlacing of the oak wood, humming inaudibly with myriad unfolding buds. Meanwhile the birds of desire were asleep in the vast interlaced intricacy of her body.

But Clifford's voice went on, clapping and gurgling with unusual sounds.

Hardly less obvious is Lawrence's development of two kinds of scene—the intimate sexual scenes between the lovers in the wood and the intellectual and abstract discussions (including discussions of sex) inside Wragby Hall. This development is important not only in that it dramatizes the two ways of life but more especially in that it presents symbolically two ways of conceiving life. Incidentally, one might observe that in his amplification of the Wragby scenes, Lawrence also benefits the dramatic force of his novel, for insofar as the character of Clifford undergoes changes through these revisions, the physical barrier between him and his wife, which was the only real barrier in the first version, takes on relative unimportance as the temperamental and intellectual barrier between them becomes much more important. Again, in this whole growth, one might observe that changes in characterization are likewise in symbolic support of the basic thematic contrast of the book, for as Constance, in the third version, grows into the mature woman with a consciousness like a flowering wood, so Clifford, at the very height of his industrial efficiency, sags into a horrible infantilism, and the whole relationship of Clifford and Mrs. Bolton becomes an enormously subtle trope of class relations. Finally, one might view the alterations in Lawrence's language, from text to text, as integral to his symbolic intentions, and the contrast in language between the two kinds of scene as absolutely primary to the whole aesthetic purpose of the work. In the Hall, language is over-intellectualized, abstract, polite, and cynical; in the wood, it is intuitive, concrete, coarse, and earthy. "We have no language for the feelings," Lawrence wrote in his essay, *The Novel and the Feelings,* "because our feelings do not even exist for us." In a novel which attempts to direct the consciousness to its source in the feelings, Lawrence necessarily employed the only language that English convention provides.

Whatever one may feel as to Lawrence's success, one cannot for a moment question the purity of his intention. Lawrence, who is perhaps the only important puritan in his generation, is eloquent and complete in his remarks on this novel in *A Propos of*

Lady Chatterley's Lover. To those remarks one might add only a few observations that he made in other places. His purpose, he always asserted, was "to make the sex relation valid and precious, not shameful," and sex, he said, "means the whole of the relationship between man and woman." Given his intention, he could quite rightly say that "anybody who calls my novel a dirty sexual novel is a liar," and, "It'll infuriate *mean* people; but it will surely soothe decent ones."

With one friend, Lady Ottoline Morrell, who was apparently disturbed by the novel, he debated in calm protest:

About Lady C.—you mustn't think I advocate perpetual sex. Far from it. Nothing nauseates me more than perpetual sex in and out of season. But I want, with Lady C., to make an adjustment in consciousness to the basic physical realities. . . . God forbid that I should be taken as urging loose sex activity. There is a brief time for sex, and a long time when sex is out of place. But when it is out of place as an activity there still should be the large and quiet space in the consciousness where it lives quiescent. Old people can have a lovely quiescent sort of sex, like apples, leaving the young quite free for their sort.

The basic physical realities have, as any thoughtful reading of this novel will reveal, enormous reverberations throughout the whole of life. The urgency for the modern world no less than the precise descriptive relevance of Lawrence's vision is constantly brought home to us by psychologists. Eric Fromm, for example, in that notable book, *Escape from Freedom*, writes:

The word "power" has a twofold meaning. One is the possession of power over somebody, the ability to dominate him; the other meaning is the possession of power to do something, to be able, to be potent. The latter meaning has nothing to do with domination; it expresses mastery in a sense of ability. If we speak of powerlessness we have this meaning in mind; we do not think of a person who is not able to dominate others, but of a person who is not able to do what he wants. Thus power can mean one of two things, domination or potency. Far from being identical, these two qualities are mutually exclusive. Impotence, using the term not only with regard to the sexual sphere but to all spheres of human potentialities, results in the sadistic striving for domination; to the extent to which an individual is potent, that is, able to realize his potentialities on the basis of freedom and integrity of his self, he does not need to dominate and is lacking the lust for power. Power, in the sense of domination, is the perversion of potency, just as sexual sadism is the perversion of sexual love.

In the second version of *Lady Chatterley*, Lawrence, in the poetic terms of his novel, made the same distinction when he spoke of the two "energies"—"the frictional, seething, resistant, explosive, blind sort" and "the other, forest energy, that was still and softly powerful, with tender, frail bud-tips and finger-ends full of awareness."

The pathos of Lawrence's novel arises from the tragedy of modern society. What is tragic is that we cannot feel our tragedy. We have slowly grown into a confusion of these terms, the two forms of power, and, in confusing them, we have left almost no room for the free creative functions of the man or woman who, lucky soul, possesses "integrity of self." The force of his novel probably lies in the degree of intensity with which his indictment of the world and the consequent solitude of his lovers suggest such larger meanings. Certainly it is these meanings that make these characters, in Edmund Wilson's word, "heroic," and that give them the epic quality that was felt by no less a poet than Yeats. "These two lovers," he wrote to his friend, Mrs. Shakespear—

These two lovers the gamekeeper and his employer's wife each separated from their class by their love and by fate are poignant in their loneliness; the coarse language of the one accepted by both becomes a forlorn poetry, uniting their solitudes, something ancient humble and terrible.

Ancient, humble, and terrible. *Lady Chatterley's Lover* is all of those; but it is also this: triumphant. Lawrence sings in his novel, like Stephen Spender in a short poem of twenty years later, our first and final hymn.

Through man's love and woman's love
Moons and tides move
Which fuse those islands, lying face to face.
Mixing in naked passion,
Those who naked new life fashion
Are themselves reborn in naked grace.

Acknowledgment is made to these publishers for their kind permission to quote from the works of D. H. Lawrence: to Alfred A. Knopf, Inc., for quotation from "Autobiographical Sketch," in *The Later D. H. Lawrence*; to Twayne Publishers for quotation from *A Propos of Lady Chatterley's Lover*, in *Sex, Literature and Censorship*; and to The Viking Press, Inc., for excerpts from *The Letters of D. H. Lawrence* and *Last Poems*.

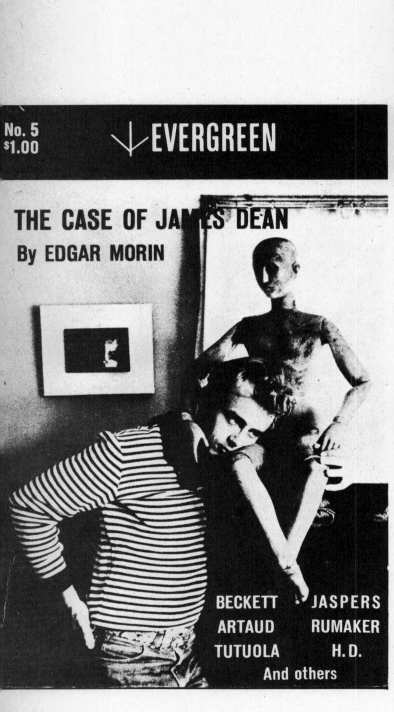

No. 5
$1.00

↓EVERGREEN

THE CASE OF JAMES DEAN
By EDGAR MORIN

BECKETT   JASPERS
ARTAUD   RUMAKER
TUTUOLA   H. D.
And others

No. 6
$1.00

↓EVERGREEN REVIEW

SUZUKI   LORCA   KLINE   REC
O'HARA   PIEYRE DE MANDIARGUES
CIORAN   SNYDER   Views & Revie

►► John Rechy

from CITY OF NIGHT

1958

Do you realize that a year ago in December I left New York and came to El Paso and went to Los Angeles and Pershing Square, then went to San Diego and La Jolla in the sun and returned to Los Angeles and went to Laguna Beach to a bar on the sand and San Francisco and came back to Los Angeles and went back to the Orange Gate and returned to Los Angeles and Pershing Square and went to El Paso and the sleepy alligators and stopped in Phoenix one night and went back to Pershing Square and on to San Francisco, again, and Monterey and the shadow of James Dean because of the movie, and Carmel where there's a house like a bird, and back to Los Angeles and on to El Paso where I was born, then Dallas with Culture, and Houston with A Million Population—and on to New Orleans where the world collapsed, and back, now, to El Paso grasping for God knows what?

And it seems (is it strange?) that I havent breathed all that time, that I was holding my breath —or had been, until Mardi Gras in New Orleans, when I was smashed in the stomach and forced not really to breathe but to explode, and once having been smashed and consequently having exploded, that now, in a way, Im dead, as dead as a corny balloon (I'll try for crazy by saying a corny green balloon)—because the ugliest things are still the corniest—punctured and shriveling up dead.

Because now that The Carnival is over (the clown on the float suddenly became an angel throwing me a silver star, and I jumped to catch it but someone else did too, and the cheap necklace the clown-angel had thrown spilled on Canal Street all pink and blue pieces of glass, my silver star), I can hardly sleep, and if I do I'll wake up and have to face myself in the mirror and that terrifies me because the mirror will stare at me, and I'll look for someone I knew (ages 15 to 20), and I wont see who I want to see. (Granted that this person never really existed, he existed for me until a few years ago, and I could fool others into believing he did exist (and some think still he does), and then he existed for me that much more.)

And when I do get up, now, the day will stand before me at attention like a private waiting to be told what to do, sir.

But all this is now, in El Paso. And I want to tell you about The Carnival.

From El Paso I went to New Orleans, riding on a sea of faces in an army of cars, and in the French Quarter I didnt sleep it seemed for days and days. Suddenly I would walk into the street, maybe from where supposedly I had been sleeping, and there was the sun. Or I would walk from somewhere else (and there was the sun) where a taxi took me with the kid in front bleeding where theyd hit him with a stick, and two others saying, "The dirty bastards, we're going to come back, the four of us—for sure," calling me Tony, which isnt my name, and asking was I with them and would we or wouldnt we kill the sons of bitches that had hit our buddy with a stick, while his back was turned, although our buddy—whom we had just met, the way we had met each other hustling the same queen (none of us made it that night) —had done nothing but flashed a mean switchblade on the other guy, ripping his hand at the thumb and the finger so that it opened like the webbed foot of a duck. Whether, as I said, I had been in someone's pad or that night in the taxi, or in a bar, where Chi-Chi the queen from Los Angeles dozed nightly perched like a blond owl on the bar—inevitably someone would open whatever door there was, and there was the sun pouncing on us like a hungry wild animal on food, and the door closed quickly.

It meant a day had gone by. But what good is a day going by so easily when, suddenly, there is the sun and another day, another stretch of time before you can hide again? It's better to wake up nights so you dont have to screw your eyes up and your dark self adjusting to the sun. So in the light I tried to sleep but couldnt make it, and it began again trying to fill the nothing with something which this time was goddamnit this.

The kid said, "See, you go and tell him—over there, see (and, man, that cat is loaded!)—that Sandy Lee wants to see him, and when he comes outside you come with him and shove him toward the stairs and me and my buddy'll grab his ass, and if he dont fork nice, we'll take it and break the bread in three." The man was drunk and I said, "Sandy Lee, outside, she wants to talk to you," and he got up and looked through the open door of the bar past Angel Face making love to the mike and into the courtyard leading to Sandy Lee's bar where his/her orange earring dangled for the tourists, and started to come with me and saw the two cats moving out and looked at me and sighed and understood and said, "You run along yourself, son, and you tell Sandy Lee I will see her later, hear?"

And the two cats outside prowled waiting, but he didnt show, thank God.

The boy-girls were bitchy to each other more than usual that night (the Vice had made them cut their hair, they looked so much like women—and that's against the law) over which queen would have which man at her pad that night, in case of didnt score, and I, and Us, we loved it, myself because, Christ, what the hell, and Sonny because he'd been run out of Miami for no visible legal means, and Jocko because the circus folded and where else is there a trapeze?— and who gives a damn anyway? Betti (who was Ben in Nebraska) said I was her new husband, and this pissed Vicki and Salli (Daniel and Bob in Atlanta) who grabbed Sonny and Jocko and said, "Well, honey, these are our husbands," almost at the same time in almost the same words and accents. Theyre sisters. And myself and the two other "husbands" felt ourselves so goddamned masculine, because to be desired by a queen—well, queens always say they want MEN. . . . And we kept on digging Pepper the most beautiful queen in the Quarter who looks like Kim Novak, trying to think we wished he was a she, because we dig real girls only—for love.

One day I took pill after pill someone handed out, and then heaven-puffs and spinach, and then beer and then whisky and then subversive vodka even and then something very strange that looked like a raisin (and was, plus), and the queen camping on Toulouse Street said, "Nothing like it, honey, wait and see." But, still dead sober, dead conscious, nothing could put me to sleep, and I saw Miss Bobbie and Whorina waving at me across the street asking did I have a place to stay?

They had short hair.

I stopped pretending once on St Peter not far from the Cathedral's bells next to the alley where the woman wanted to draw me for free because all the other portraitmakers were occupied at $2, $5, and $7 a head and she felt so lonesome and unwanted— stopped pretending as we walked along the hovering old houses that lead into the ugly courtyards and ugly dank places they call enchanting in the folders and on the tours but that only a horror movie could do justice, and into the house of the two lovers from New York and into bed with them in the middle. (Do they still go to bed in twos?) "Im going to surprise you," I said. "Im not dumb at all, like I look, like I try to look, and act, like you think I am, like you want me to be—or tough, really. That's just so I can make it. But what the hell. Im smart. Listen, I can quote Rimbaud. 'Jadis si je me souviens bien, ma vie etait un festin. . . .' And Verlaine. 'It rains in the street, as it rains in my heart. . . .' In French and English, see! And Nietzsche and Christ and Shakespeare and Desdemona and Drusilla Drake," who are two queens in the Quarter, "and I wrote a novel when I was 18 and I dig music, and I even have heard of painting, my favorite being Modigliani's because of the eyes, man, the cool crazy hipsters' eyes." And guess what?

They loved me!

But guess what?

They lost Interest in me. I knew it: (On Sutton Place overlooking the East River I saw a copy of Colette and looked through it, and the man said, "Get out of here, you read, I dont want you anymore, really masculine men dont read!" and he gave me a couple of bucks.) Because to play this, youve got to be dumb, and if you aint dumb, dad, you aint from nowhere cause that means you aint Mas-Cu-Line, and they dont dig and your bread is coming from Never. . . .

Although my wallet was loaded now (I had made it with the cat from New York who thought it was so sad but loved it when I told him I dug girls), I had to steal as badly as some guys need to shoot their load sometimes—for nothing better to do, the way old women knit. The jaded middle-aged man from Houston in the tawdry pink Cadillac with the jaded younger man with the face like a blubbery mask— rather, like a fish if a fish was a man—and the tall lank dancer just as jaded, said, "Join us for breakfast?" but we went straight to the motel, and I had expected money, but no one said anything so I decided to use this for my excuse—because I still need excuses, Im that new.

We drank and drank, and do you know that liquor only makes me more sober, more lucid? I had been sober all that time.

Me and those three, and they dug it weird. "Hurt me, baby, please hurt me," begged the pink Cadillac. "And me, too!" said fishface caressing my belt. "Please," murmured the lank, "please, be *mean*. . . ." Then all three were exhausted. Out. I went through fishface's pockets first, and he had $50.00, more, and I took only half—then the others, and I took just half. Then I slept on the floor because I didnt want to be near them and woke up, and woke them, in the afternoon. Then! Laughing, smiling, being happy, they rode me into town through the blazing sun and the knowledge of myself, with the stolen money cozy in the pocket of my levis.

I went to the Y and over it all General Lee stood surveying Lee Circle, arms crossed, disapproving, and I thought he must still be looking at me through the window of the Y as the hot-water steam mushroomed about me, protecting.

Every day, religiously, I wrote my mother, in Spanish. *Mi querida* mommie. It's been snowing here in New Orleans for the first time in 27 years, I told her.

The snow covered the cemetery in back of the Church of Our Lady of Guadalupe, which is my mother's name, and everyone, even Us, looked pink and real in the white light. And if it had snowed more, it might have killed some of the cockroaches. For one day this rotten city was purified.

Someone even threw a snowball!

The snow melted, it rained, and there was slush. The sun came out. . . .

From St Charles the parade (The Parade) passed in front of the Mayor, who drank champagne, standing on a platform with a Negro in white gloves while the King of the parade smashed the wine glass into the street and the people screamed with joy as the floats passed opening and closing giant mechanical eyes insanely and the girls with rosy legs twirled their nervous batons and the Air Force marched by in military style playing a march and feeling much a part of something—the Parade, in military style. The crowds were staggering as if the door, the only door, to a snakepit had suddenly been opened, and I read that one man shot another over some beads. The parade passes by and the men in masks throw beads— necklaces and bracelets and one-inch elephants and Japanese parasols and whistles and the people jump up and get them, and since this was Mardi Gras Day, the day before no more parades, well, if you hadnt gotten a bracelet or a necklace you were frantic. (This was when my angel who was really a clown threw me a star which was really a pink and blue necklace sprinkling glass on the street.) The Negroes dressed in torn tunics over their pants jazzed it with flaming sticks crazily to an inside rhythm—they must have, because the only music I could hear was the white band playing Dixie and the southunn laaadddii iies and genelmens in southunn voices saying, "Aint that gorjus, all them coluhs?" and, "Yall come rought on back," to the stray children, "this instant, heuh?"

Later, along Royal, the redwigged woman in the tight candystriped skirt leaned toward the half-naked blond Indian covered with rouge and whispered, "Screw me please, dear," where the cats hung on Jackson Square re-emptying their empty Hurricane glasses watching the tourists anxious to wait anxiously in line to have coffee and donuts at the Market before cruising Royal Street (Roo Rowyall) for gay antiques and pralines that are clean, where the stuffed black-mammy was punctured in the breast revealing very white cotton innards which you would have insulted many a southunn laaaaddddy, you believe it, not caring that the plainclothes had said if I was still in town theyd have me for novisiblelegalmeansofsupport, while around me in this sea of colors drowning the plainclothes, Marie Antoinette and Robin Hood were chased into the Cathedral by a band of cannibals that later caught on fire and got their picture in the paper ignoring Tarzana posing for the newsreel camera with her scarlet-painted nails, while dejectedly (the saddest single sight I saw) at Pirate's Alley, Scarlett OHara, her skirt high up revealing hairy man's legs, wailed to no one, "Tara *burned!* And I ain't got the money to pay the *taxes!*" And another phony Indian, much more cunning and much more naked, danced outside the Bourbon House while cameras clicked, flashed and rolled until the fat bald man whispered in the Indian's ear, would he consider giving a private performance?

At the Masquerade in the afternoon, the man in the ballet tights said to me, "You dare me?" And I did. And he went down. "I dare you again," I said. And he went down again. And they all started saying, "*I* dare you!" "I dare you, *too!*" Then to each other, "I dare *you!*" And the Masquerade had quite a bash, not caring that down Bourbon Sally Rand, who "made three World's Fairs famous" ("Well, how old *is* she?" said Salli as we passed the sign), was making quite a breeze, creating quite a storm (to go all the way), and Alouette twirled her giant breasts like windmills—but then what's the difference when Patti Waggin must have been doing the same somewhere on Main Street in way far-off Los Angeles?—which was nothing compared to what happened at Dixie's although Fat Herself moved chaperonely nervously sighing, "Please, boys, be *nice.*"

Then, *smash!*

Smash! Smash! Smash!

It burst, erupted, exploded, *what I cant tell you,* and I folded up at Walter's on Toulouse and wailed, broken up, and cried and cried and nearly fell. Suddenly, I was dead-drunk, worth all those days and nights of sober, because it had smashed, the world caved in—and it had happened, what I cant tell you, although it's the real subject of all this—it had happened with a single knowing smile as I sat with the $10-john (for 15 minutes, he dug me that much). It happened with that smile and Jerry's "Oh babe, I'll just have to tell you later." Later came. I broke up laughing, myself. "But, wait," I said, "you dont know the half of it," and because he, and then they, wouldnt understand the truth, the truth, the truth, because for them to feel the immensity of it for me, I had to extend the years of terror. Because you know but they didnt that the terror of ten lifetimes can be contained in a single moment, and although this moment was years long, still it was necessary to extend

it. And even so, did they understand? Well, how can I know? Well, some, I think, did. The world whirled and I vomited, and someone came to the head where I was folded over. "Are you my friend?" "Why else would I be here?" Yes, he was my friend, but goddamnit at that time I wanted to smash someone else, out there, someone who had been preferred over the image in the mirror, ages 15 to 20, of the me that had never existed really, that had stared for hours, not knowing he really didnt exist—preferred over me, and I was just as lonesome and ugly As You Please.

Don't let anyone tell you it doesnt happen like this except in phony stories, because it happens in life, dad-o, exactly like Im going to tell you—happened to me exactly like this, *exactly,* it happened like this—

Suddenly, in one moment, just like Im saying now, IN ONE SINGLE SOLITARY CRAZY ONE-UNIT MOMENT, I was sober. And more than before. As if I had been two people and one had gotten drunk, thank God, but the other, now, the sober one, could look on, and it's terrifying when the sober you sees the drunk you so ugly, beaten and scared, sitting next to Jocko at the Poor Boys saying himself, "I hate this goddamned city, too—Im heading for Miami tomorrow" ("Where the Vice'll bug you till you shag," said the sandy-haired boy), sitting with the mean-looking little girl hovering behind the counter like a vulture who, that night before the cab, said to my buddy of just a few moments, "Man, if you ever come around, I'll get you with my blade, and, man, dont think like I cant use it!" and the fat man making sandwiches with his hairy hands out of the long phallic bread like they use in the Village and North Beach and in all the other endless places where they have Poor Boys.

Out on the street—miracle of miracles!—for the first time, it was still dark.

The first church I phoned was St Patrick's, because there's one in El Paso where I used to go to Confession. "I cant see you," said the priest, "not until 8, we are closed now." "Like a drugstore?" He hung up. I called St Louis Cathedral because that is so big. "I cant see you—of course not—I get these calls all the time." A third one—youd think I would have given up. "Dont hang up, Father, Im in trouble, Im desperate," and he hung up. And I called the Church of Eternal Succor thinking they meant it, and the Church of Our Lady of Guadalupe because Im Mexican, because my mother's name is Guadalupe, and they all said, "No." "Go to sleep," so we can. "Come tomorrow," to the Confessional. "Sometime else." "When we are open." One even said, "God bless you," before he hung up.

And I was thinking that although there is no God,

never was a God, and quite possibly never will be One, it is possible to understand Him—or that part of Him that had forbidden tasting Knowledge, because, Christ! at that moment I longed for innocence more than anything else, and I would have given away all the frantic knowing for a return to Grace, which is only the state of, idiot-like, Not Knowing.

I called the last church listed in the yellow pages of the New Orleans Telephone Directory under Catholic (if I had one now I would look it up, but I will certainly go to the Telephone Company to find it), and a young priest answered who is Italian, and he didnt hang up and he was whom I had tried to reach and I was glad the others had hung up who couldnt have understood anyway, and he spoke to me because I said to him, "All I want is for you to say something to me—but I dont know what." Because what had really happened after I ran out of the Poor Boys was this. I tried to go to sleep at the Avenue Theater where they show three movies till five in the morning, but I felt something on my arm, which was three well-fed cockroaches, and something on my thigh, which was the man next to me's hungry hot hand, and in the head the gaunt-faced men and boys —theyre gaunt even when theyre fat—stood pretending to be smoking, licking their lips—but I couldnt sleep, because when I closed my eyes, the recurrent nightmare I had had as a very little boy came again that I was being crushed by WOODEN stones, over which, or between which, or among which, there was a thin, thin draping like cheesecloth, and each time I

closed my eyes, it was there, and I tried to push it or them, away. But when I opened my eyes the stones and cheesecloth were gone but the cockroaches were there all over the wall and me. (We had giant brown cockroaches at home, and when we left, in the afternoon, sometimes, in the hot fierce Texas summer, and returned at night, turning on the light, they flew at us—they had wings almost two inches wide—from all directions, making funny noises as they crashed like miniature planes against the wall—splut!) So I spoke to the real priest and I told him what I cant tell you and he talked to me and talked, and finally it was light again, this time thank God.

I left New Orleans that morning.

And I came to El Paso my hometown.

But it's windy here now. The clouds storm angrily across the sky rushing at each other like to battle. You know how it is in Texas every year before spring. One moment the painful awareness that soon spring is coming, with the yellow-green clusters of leaves budding on the trees—and the next moment the fierce wind with the needlepointed dust whirling and howling.

And the fierce wind is an echo of angry childhood and of a very scared boy looking out the window seeing my fat dog Winnie, dead, outside by the house, and the gray Texas dust gradually covering her up— and thinking, It isnt fair! WHY CANT DOGS GO TO HEAVEN????

►► **William Eastlake**

Portrait of an Artist with Twenty-Six Horses

With eyes wet and huge the deer watched. The boy watched back.

The boy crouched over a spring as though talking to the ground. The water plumed up bright through his turquoise-ringed hand, then eddied black in the bottomless whorl it had sculptured neat and sharp in the orange rock. The rock retreated to a blue, then again to an almost chrome yellow at the foot of the deer. The deer was coy, hesitant and greasewood-

camouflaged except for the eyes that watched. The boy watched back. Now the boy raised his ringed hand from the spring. The deer wheeled and fled noiselessly.

All around, above, and far beyond where the boy crouched at the spring the earth was on fire with beauty from a setting sun. The sky was on fire too and the spring water, tossing down the mesa, was ablaze. The long Jemez Range to the east had not caught fully. Soon it would catch. Not long after, in maybe half an hour, the world would go out.

The boy rose from his crouch over the spring and slung on a pack roll. Before the world went out he would have to go some distance. He could waste no more time talking to the ground.

Far off to the east and down in a valley, but still at an altitude of 7,500 feet, ran the town of Cuba. It was a collection of adobe shacks on the long wobble of asphalt going someplace else. A dark and handsome Navaho woman, disguised in the costume of city people, was stirring outside a restaurant labeled The Big Deal. She was hanging a sign that began, REAL LIVE WHITE PEOPLE. The Queen of Cuba City finished hanging the sign and went back inside. All of the sign said: REAL LIVE WHITE PEOPLE IN THEIR NATIVE COSTUMES DOING NATIVE DANCES.

"I don't think that's funny," James said. James, otherwise known as Twenty-six Horses, was her husband but he never came around the restaurant much.

James had a rough and weathered face and he had a purple ribbon which knotted his hair in the back of his head, a custom that the young Navahos had abandoned.

"You can't compete with people by imitating their methods." James sat at the end of the counter and looked unhappy.

The Queen of Cuba City had begun her restaurant by excluding Navahos. That didn't seem to do much good so she refused service to Christians, Jews, Seventh Day Adventists, Apaches, and people from Florida, in about that order. Two weeks ago she put up a sign: WE RESERVE THE RIGHT TO REFUSE SERVICE TO EVERYBODY. That didn't seem to help business either.

"White people don't put up those signs to help business," James had said. "They put them up because they're sick."

"I'm not sick. I want to make an extra buck," the Queen of Cuba City said.

"An Indian who wants to make an extra buck is sick," James said.

"I should go back to those hogans a hundred miles from nowhere and die?"

"And live," James said. "An Indian dies in the city."

"An Indian can learn to live," she said. "Soon the hogans will not be a hundred miles from nowhere. What you going to do then?"

"Come back and we'll figure it out."

"I got a business," she said.

A customer came in and James went back to looking unhappy, sitting at the end of the counter.

"That's a good sign you got out there," the white man said and then he ordered a hamburger. "Did you ever see the sign: Your Face Is Honest But We Can't Put It In The Cash Register?"

The Queen of Cuba City was frying the hamburger and didn't hear the white man so the white man turned to James and said, "Did you ever see that sign: Women Don't—. Oh, you're an Indian," the white man said. "I was trying to explain a gag to an Indian," the white man hollered back to the Queen of Cuba City. James got up and walked out.

When the Queen of Cuba City brought the white man his hamburger the white man said, "He doesn't speak any English I hope. I hope I didn't hurt his feelings."

"Not much," the Queen of Cuba City said.

"You let Indians in here?"

"That was my husband."

"I'm sorry," the white man said, putting down the hamburger gently and examining it carefully. "You look white. You talk white. I hope I didn't hurt your feelings."

"Not much," she said. "I'm trying to make a buck."

"Oh," the man said, relaxing. "And you will, too." He bit into the hamburger and swallowed a mouthful. "You've got what it takes," he said.

On the outside of the Big Deal Cafe Ike Woodstock was standing near the steps talking to Rudy Guterriez about uranium and Evelyn and Tap Patman were standing in front of their service station beneath a sign that said Gulf Pride Motor Oil and between the STOPS-NOX and BE KIND TO YOUR ENGINE signs. Across the street Arpacio Montoyo was talking to the priest beneath a CLEAN REST ROOMS sign. They were talking about how many angels could stand on the head of a pin.

James looked around for his horse but a car was standing where he had left it. Mr. Patman came over and said, "I put your horse around back, James. Out here it's liable to get hit."

"What did you tell James, Tappy?" Evelyn asked.

"That I moved his horse. Liable to get hit."

"It got hit."

"By what?"

"That Olds 88."

"It's a 98."

"When I can't tell an 88 from a 98!"

Evelyn and Tap Patman walked over and identified the car as an 88 with 98 hub caps.

"There now, what is our world coming to?"

James saw at a glance that the horse was favoring his left hind leg. He examined the leg carefully, going down on one knee while the horse swung his great neck to examine James' head. The leg was not too bad, nothing broken, but he would have to lead it home, twenty miles through the back country. Not too bad.

He had ridden into Cuba City every week now for the last four months and at first he thought it would not be too bad. She would come home. Each time he was certain she would come home. Both of them had been certain too their boy would come, home from the army, and he had—slightly damaged, but he had come home. He had stood around the hogan a few hours afraid to sit down on the rugs as though bugs would get him. He had kept standing in the middle of the hogan as though looking around the walls for windows, around the rough room for chairs and tables, a radio, a bed that stood on legs, a familiar white face. And then he was gone for Gallup. Outside the hogan he had taken a big deep breath, stuck his head back inside the hogan heavy with smoke, repeated something pleasant in English and then was gone for Gallup. He left, she said, because an artist can make a living there. "We got to make a living for him here," she said.

When James' wife came to Cuba City the first thing she did was refuse to speak Navaho. She leased the restaurant next to the Gulf Station from Tap Patman—sixty-eight dollars a month plus five per cent of the gross—hired four Spanish-Americans, fired a slovenly Anglo cook that was supposed to come with the place, stippled the rest rooms with neon, hung out a lot of white man's signs and concentrated on not speaking Navaho.

"You speak Navaho and soon the place is full of Indians. Indians haven't any money and they come in and play chants on the juke box, look under things, ask what the signs mean, bring their wives in to show off their jewelry, make big talk about the kids their wives stack on cradle boards along the counter, make jokes about the whites—and they haven't any money. I left the reservation, I came to Cuba City, to open a restaurant because it's a white man's world and you have to make it the white man's way. Anything else is talking to the ground. The white man came, saw, stole; the Indian only smiled. Okay, make a joke, but the white man is Chee Dodge. Even if the white man wanted to stop pushing us under the table, and sometimes he wants to stop, he can't. All right, so our boy came home from the army. What is he? A weaver. All right, he is the best weaver in the checkerboard area. All right, on the reservation too. All right, he is what the trader calls him—an artist. But listen, Twenty-six Horses, the white man has a machine and listen, Twenty-six Horses, by the time it takes our boy to set his loom, listen, the white man has a thousand rugs. Listen, the white man has a machine. All right, the trader

says the machine has the white man but that's Indian talk. The white man has a machine. Maybe he can't stop it, Twenty-six Horses, but he has a machine. Any way else is talking to the ground. It's a white world."

Twenty-six Horses had walked in front of his horse to the edge of Cuba City. Now no one would call him James. It was all right to call him James. James Trijillo, a good machine name, that's the way he made his mark in the government book. Twenty-six Horses was the name The People had given him when he had twenty-six horses. Now he had twenty-four, twenty-five, sometimes—once—he had thirty-four, but when they gave him the name he had twenty-six horses. That was a good name. It meant he was a big Chee Dodge.

The Indians named his wife the Queen of Cuba City when she moved into town and refused to speak Navaho. It was not a good name, it meant she was worse than an Apache—a Pueblo almost.

James had got the horse now to the top of the hill that overlooked Cuba. So they said his boy was an artist. Artist. What does their calling him an artist exactly mean? They meant nice by it he could tell by the tone, but it certainly had something to do with not being able to sell what you make. That was clear. It had something to do with not wanting to sell, too. The trader at Nargeezi had gotten the boy an order from a nice tribe of whites called the Masons. The Masons had even drawn the picture for him and left a ring with the same picture on it. Orders would follow from other nice tribes, the Kiwanis, the Elks, who wanted to help. They pay big. No, the boy had said. I do not feel it. James felt the Mason ring and he could feel it. "Here," the boy had said, touching just below his chest.

So an artist is a person who feels things just below his chest. All right, but he must feel something below that in his stomach too. Maybe that was why the boy left. Maybe his wife had been right. Maybe he wasn't looking around the hogan for a TV set or a bed with legs. Maybe the army had gotten him accustomed to three meals a day. Maybe an artist on the outside can make three meals a day.

"Can an artist on the outside make three meals a day?"

James had come upon a white man leaning on the side of his car on the Cuba Hill and he figured he might as well ask him as another.

"No," the white man said. "Tell me, what town is that?"

James told him it was Cuba City.

"You're an Indian, aren't you?"

"Yes," James said.

"Well, I can tell you I paid ten thousand dollars for this car," the man said. "It's got nearly three hundred horses. I've been busting to tell somebody but on the outside you're not supposed to tell anybody. I can tell an Indian I guess."

"Ten thousand dollars! I didn't know it was possible," James said.

"Since last month it's been possible," the man said. "The Caddie people did it. Tell me, are you going to sell some paintings on the outside?"

"No. It's my boy," James said.

"That's too bad," the man said. "If there's anything I can do to help, outside of buying one—?"

"I guess not," James said.

"Buying one would make it worse," the man said. "He'd only go through life under the delusion that he'd sell another."

"Maybe," James said.

"Everyone," the man said, "has been sane at one time or another in his life. He wants to create something, then he sees the way the world is going and decides he better go with it."

"Not even three meals a day?"

"Three meals a day is a lot of meals to give a man who will not go along."

Now that the man had made his speech and James had asked what he wanted, he pulled on his horse.

"Wait," the man said. "I can tell this to an Indian. Keep your boy here in the world. Don't let him get out there on the reservation. Out there we think we're on the outside looking in, but it's just the opposite, we're on the inside looking out. We are in there seeing who can be the biggest failure and we got a system of checking. We can always tell who wins. It's the man with the biggest car." The man leaning against the car hesitated. "Did you ever see a child's drawing?" the man said. "We have all got it and we all give it up."

The man had made two speeches now and James felt he could move on without being rude. He did, going on down the Cuba Hill pulling the horse after him.

The man continued leaning against the car watching the flowing sunset behind the purple rocks. He was one of the many vice-presidents of an oil company that was working the area. He always stopped where he could to enjoy a beautiful sight like this. Now he got back in the car and started her up. It was good to sound off. It wasn't often you got a chance. It wasn't often you could find someone like an Indian. And it would never get around. No one of his friends would ever suspect for a moment that he was sane.

James continued down the hill and wondered how a man like that was permitted out in the big reservation. It can only be that, like all the others, he never tells anyone.

But what the man had told him about artists was bad news for his boy. I wonder how you go about looking for someone out there? James had seen a television play in Arpacio Montoyo's bar. He had made his beer last to the end. It was about a girl who left home and the ending was that you should buy this soap. The man kept holding the soap up and hollering about the soap. It made a kind of exciting ending and probably a lot of sense too, if you grew up on the big reservation. The play might have been a solution to his problem. Certainly, James thought, if buying the soap of the man who was hollering would get his boy home he would buy all that man's soap the trader had. James was very worried about his boy.

James had reached the bottom of the north side of the Cuba Hill and started up the slight rise that had the only aspen grove at this altitude that anyone had ever heard of. The aspen leaves had ceased turning yellow and were waiting to fly into Ben Helpnell's porch when the wind blew. Ben Helpnell was out working on his new Monkey Ward pump beneath his abandoned wind mill. The new pump was the latest thing, later than the jet pump. It worked on the theory that "it is easier to push water than it is to pull it. It is a hermetically sealed, self-contained unit and without any fuss or bother or expensive plumbers or electricians, you just drop the whole thing in the well." Ben had done that yesterday and ever since he had been looking for it.

Ben saw James coming up and said, "I'm well shut of the damn thing." Ben was a horse-and-cattle trader and he saw now that James' horse was limping. But he had to work around to the subject gradually.

"I'm just as well shut of it," he repeated, but his heart had gone out of it. It was in the horse.

Suspecting a trade, James said nothing.

"Your wife's got some good signs out there," Ben said.

James did not want to talk about that.

"I ain't seen you by for a time," Ben said.

"My boy is gone," James said.

Ben studied over this for a while, looking down the well, then he looked over at the horse but his heart was no longer in the horse. It was involved now with James' grief.

"I tell you what, James," Ben said, studying the well again. "Take a horse, leave it off when you come back through."

Another day James would not have taken the horse first off. He would have hunched down, snapping sticks in his fingers and drawing pictures on the ground until they made a trade. It would have taken four or five hours, and Ben's wife might have changed clothes two or three times to impress the Indian. And James would choose his jewelry from the saddle bags to impress everyone and Ben would do a dance he picked up in Chihuahua that impressed even horses—all this to relieve the tension of the dealing when the excitement or the danger of closing became too real.

But now James' grief was in all their hearts and Mary would not want to change clothes three times, Ben would find no joy to do his dance nor James to show his jewelry. They would have only stumbled through a city deal with nothing to show for it except the grieving that James had brought.

"Take the blaze colt," Ben Helpnell said.

James transferred his saddle to the little blaze in the near corral while Ben Helpnell continued to stare down the well to figure the meaning of the lost pump.

"I should of tooken it back," he said, and finally standing up, "it's nothing against Monkey Ward. I must have done something wrong."

"You chunked it down the well," Mary said from where she watched behind a screen door.

"It said in the book—," and then Ben ceased, knowing that women will even contradict the book, and walked over to James at the corral.

James was weaving the cinch strap through its final gyrations before pulling good.

"Lots of horse," Ben Helpnell said. James swung into the saddle and started off leading his own horse with a rope in his dark right hand.

"When you get home he could be there," Ben Helpnell said.

"He could be there," James agreed, but he was not heard. He was already going up the road that led past the sawdust rotting remains of Girt Maxey's sawmill.

Two hours later he was going up the trail that led past the trading post then up on to the top of the piñon- and pine-studded mesa that looked out on his hogan below. His hogan below was smoking.

"He could be there."

No. He would shut his eyes and take another look. When he opened his eyes again a thin stream of blue cedar smoke still poured a fine column straight up from the middle of the conical hogan. He touched his horse and both of his horses flew off the mesa bearing straight down at the hogan with the long blue smoke.

No. This was not good. It would be pushing his luck too fast. He swung his horse in a great circle around the hogan and then stopped. Both of his

horses were breathing hard and the long blue cedar smoke still came out of the hogan. Now a quiet wind started and bent the long blue smoke until it curled heavy around James and the two horses. It was real smoke. But it would not do to go straight at the hogan. If luck was there it might be surprised away. Perhaps to call gently? James made a cup of his hands and called the boy's name toward the smoking hogan. Nothing happened but he did not want anything to happen so suddenly. He patted the blaze horse and looked back at his own horse at the end of the string.

"He could be there."

Now James cupped his dark hands again and called just a little more this time but still gently. And then he dropped his hands and watched quietly, careful that no move was made to disturb anything. The horses were very quiet too, as a hand pushed back the sheep flap at the hogan door and his boy stepped outside.

James waved. The horses began to move and the boy held both hands above his head.

The boy and James ate meat, coffee, and bread for a long time. When they had finished the meat and coffee and bread they had some more coffee with James not saying much, not wanting to push any of his luck away. The boy had been talking all along at a good pace without saying anything, but watching the heavy wooden loom on which he had begun to weave a picture. Finally he stopped and said, after a big pause and in English, "There, now, what's the world coming to when an artist won't settle for twenty-six horses?"

"No English spoken here," a voice said in Navaho. "The trader saw the smoke and sent a message that someone was home. I took down my signs in my restaurant and threw away the key. I finished with the restaurant. What's the world coming to when an Indian won't let the whites fight each other?"

James did not think it was time to recognize his luck but he looked around the round room and recognized everything in it that was all gone yesterday and all here now. And outside, too, there were twenty-six horses.

"What's wrong with talking to the ground?"

This, James knew, was his wife called Married-To-The-Man-With-Twenty-six-Horses talking. It was not the Queen of Cuba City.

"What's wrong," the woman repeated, "with talking to the ground? The Navaho People talked to the ground before the white man came. We could do worse than be with our own People even when we are talking to the ground."

James knew now that Married-To-The-Man-With-Twenty-six-Horses and the son of Twenty-six Horses had all made their speech and were waiting for him to say the end. The end, he knew, must have some style. It must not be the endless speeches of the white man. It must have style. It should be about three words. It should be in the best manner of The People. He looked over at the powerfully simple mountains and rocks, abstract, in quiet beauty woven on the big loom. And yet The People seemed to be worried about talking to the ground.

"The earth understands," he said gently for the end.

▶▶ **Amos Tutuola**

The Animal That Died but His Eyes Still Alive

The big gun that stops the voices of the soldiers
Animals are surplus in the town in which the people have no teeth

As I [Adebisi, the African huntress] was travelling along in this jungle it was so I was killing all the wild animals that I was seeing on the way. When I saw that the night was approaching I shot one small animal to death. I made a big fire and I roasted this animal which was an antelope, in the fire. Before I ate it to my satisfaction it was about ten o'clock in the night. But anyhow I ate out of it as I could and I kept the rest of it near the fire which I would eat in the morning. After that I lay down near this fire and then I slept but there was nothing which was happened to me throughout this night.

When I woke up in the morning by the crying of birds and when the dove gave the sign of eight o'clock, then I ate the rest of that roasted animal. After that I hung my gun and hunting bag on my

shoulder having checked the gun and saw that it was in good order. Then I started to look for the wild animals to be killed. And within three days I nearly killed the whole of the wild animals of this jungle. It was very scarcely to see one or two and I was very happy about this, but it still remained three big troubles—how to drive away all the pigmies from this jungle as they used to detain hunters in their custody. How to kill the dangerous animals who had light on eyes and how to kill a very curious and dangerous boa constrictor which was very dangerous to the hunters as well.

After I nearly killed the whole of the wild animals, I did not travel more than seven days when I came across a big wild animal. It was as big as an elephant. I had never seen the kind of this animal before. Because he had a very big head. Several horns were on his forehead. Each of the horns was as long and thick and sharp as cows' horns. Very long black and brown hairs were full this head and they were fallen downward, they were also very dirty. All the horns were stood upright on his forehead as if a person carried a bunch of sticks vertically. His beard was so plenty and long that it covered his chest and belly as well. The teeth of his mouth were so plenty and long that whenever he was eating a person who was in two miles away would be hearing the noises which they were making. Even as the teeth and the horns of his mouth and head were so fearful many of the wild animals who saw him when he was coming to kill them with all these things were dying for themselves before he would reach them instead to kill them with his teeth and horns, because they were too fearful to them.

He had two curious eyes which were as accurate as full moon of the dry season. Both were on the right part of his head as the other animals did, but each was bigger and could see everywhere without moving head. The powerful light that these eyes were bringing out could not go far or straight but they were bringing out the clear and round light. The ray of this light was always round him and it could be seen clearly from a long distance.

He had a kind of a terrible shout with which he was frightening the animals and his humming was also terrible to hear. All the rest animals were so hated and feared him that they never went near the place that he travelled for one week.

There was none part of his body which was not terrible and which was not frightened neither human being nor other creature of this world.

Immediately I saw this "super-animal" as I could call him, in that morning through the round clear light of his eyes, was that I stopped in one place and I first breathed out heavily with great fear. Because I could not escape again, I had already approached him too closely before I saw him. And at the same moment that he too saw me, although I was still quite aloof when he first saw me. He first sighted all his horns towards me and then he was running to me as fast as he could. But when I thought within myself that if I stood on the ground and shot him, he would kill me instantaneously, because my "shaka-bullah" gun would not be able to kill him in one shot, therefore I hastily climbed a tree to the top.

But when he ran to the place that I had stood before and he did not meet me there again. He was going round and round until when he saw me on top of this tree. As I was on top of this tree I thought that I was saved but not at all. Because at the same moment that he saw me on top of this tree, he started to bite the tree at the bottom. And to my fear within two minutes he had nearly bitten the whole bottom of this tree. When I saw that the tree was just toppling to the ground, just to safe my life, I hastily jumped from there to the top of another mighty tree which was nearby. And when he saw me on top of this mighty tree again, he started to bite the bottom of it as well and he was in great anger this time because he wanted to eat me without much trouble as this.

And when I saw that this mighty tree was toppling down as well, then I hastily sold my "death," I said within myself that before this "super-animal" would kill me I must first defend myself perhaps I would be saved. Then without hesitation I shot him. But when the gun-shots hit him on the chest and hurt him as well on the hind legs. It was this time this "super-animal" became more powerful and more dangerous than ever. And it was this day that I believed that—the half-killed snake is the most dangerous. Because this animal was then shrieking and shouting and humming more terribly with angry voice than ever. His fearful humming was hearing all over the jungle.

He was jumping and dashing to the trees, rocks, etc. and within a few minutes he had broken down all the trees of that area and scattered everything in disorder with great anger. When he came back to the tree on top of which I was he started to bite the bottom of this tree until it fell down. This tree hardly fell down when he jumped on me, but I was so lucky that immediately this tree fell on hard ground, it sprang up again before it lay down quietly, I fell off from it to a little distance, so by that he missed me to grip with his paws. Of course I hit my back on another tree which was near that spot and that gave me much pain. And as I was hastily standing up he had jumped high up and as he was coming down just to cover the whole of me, I hastily lay flatly on the ground and then he simply rolled along on the ground instead. Before he stood up again I had taken my cutlass and I was waiting for him at once.

Within one second he had stood up, but he did not attempt to bite me this time, he wanted to hit me to death with his horns. But at the same moment that I saw what he wanted to do this time, I hastily leapt to my left when he was about to butt me with his horns and I cut him several times with my cutlass within this moment, so he simply butted a heavy rock instead when he missed me. He hardly missed me when he turned to his back and as he was coming again with great anger, I hastily leaned my back on the stump of the big tree which he had cut down, and I exposed my chest and belly in such a deceived way that he believed that he would not miss me as before. So as he was running furiously towards me with all his power and when he was about to reach me, I hastily leapt again to my right unexpectedly and unfortunately he simply butted the stump of that tree. So all his horns pierced this stump of tree, he could not pull them out but he was held up there helplessly, except his hind legs with which he was scattering the ground very roughly.

After I rested for a few minutes then I started to beat him with my poisonous cudgel until when he was completely powerless and then he died after some minutes. It was like that I killed this "super-animal" as I could call him. But to my surprise was that as he had already dead the light of his eyes was still shining clearly and thus it was when I left there.

After I had killed this animal I started to look about for the fearful boa constrictor which my father had told me about his news that he (boa) was also very dangerous. As I was looking for this boa constrictor it was so I was killing all the wild animals which I was seeing on the way. And in a few days' time I killed the whole of them. So this time there was no more the fear of the wild animals again in this jungle except the fears of this terrible boa constrictor and the pigmies. I roamed about for several days but I did not come across this boa until one day when I travelled back to the place where I had killed "super-animal" unnoticed. But it was still a great surprise to see that the light of the eyes of this animal was still shining clearly. The flesh of his body was already decayed and the bones were already scattered on the ground but the eyes which brought out this light was still alive, the light was as clear as when the animal was still alive. So the eyes and the long hairs which were covered the skull were still on this skull as well and all the horns were still on the skull but they were still pierced the stump of that tree since the day that the animal had butted it (stump) himself.

In the first instance that I came there unexpectedly and when I saw this head with the clear light I thought that the animal had become alive after I had left there the other day. I stood before this head and I started to think of what to do with it, because the clear light which came out from the eyes was very attractively. When I thought what to do with it for a few minutes and I did not know yet so I pulled the head out of the stump. I first trimmed the hairs of the head very short then I cut those long horns very short too after that I trimmed the inside of the skull very neatly. But to my surprise when I put this skull or head on my head it was to my exact size and it seemed on my head as a cock helmet. I was seeing clearly through the eyes and the light of the eyes travelled far away in the jungle but I was then so fearful that there was not any living creature which would see me would not run away for fear because I was exactly as when that animal was alive. So when I believed that it would help me in future I wrapped it with the skin of animal and I kept it in my hunting bag. As from that day I was using it in the night as my light and I was wearing it on the head whenever I was hunting. So this wonderful head became a very useful thing at last.

►► Robert Creeley

The Three Ladies

I dreamt. I saw three ladies in a tree,
and the one that I saw most clearly
showed her favors unto me,
and I saw up her leg above the knee!

But when the time for love was come,
and of readiness I had made myself,
upon my head and shoulders
dropped the other two like an unquiet dew.

What were these two but the one?
I saw in their faces, I heard in their words,
wonder of wonders! it was the undoing of me
they came down to see!

Sister, they said to her who upon my lap
sat complacent, expectant:
He is dead in his head, and we
have errands, have errands . . .

Oh song of wistful night! Light shows
where it stops nobody knows, and two
are one, and three, to me—and to look
is not to read the book.

Oh one, two, three! Oh one, two, three!
Three old ladies sat in a tree.

Exit 3

The tractor-and-trailer rolled slowly off the shoulder and onto the turnpike, its red and yellow lights blinking. Jim stood a minute watching it go, then leaned down and picked up his suitcase and started walking briskly along the exit road, past the brightly lighted toll booths. He walked faster, tucking his scarf tightly about his throat as a cold wind sprang up. The exit road made a sweeping curve downward, joining the main highway a hundred yards on. He shifted his suitcase to the other hand and headed toward the highway.

As he walked along a Chevrolet convertible pulled up beside him, the motor idling. The horn blew. Jim turned, staring blindly into the headlights, and kept on going. The horn blew again, the car inching alongside him. The window on the driver's side rolled down and a head poked out.

"Hey, buddy. C'mere."

Jim hesitated a moment, then stopped and swung around, staring past the headlights and squinting his eyes to see better. He saw a sailor's white cap.

"C'mere a sec', buddy."

"Whatta you want?"

"C'mere, c'mere," the sailor persisted.

"I'm in a hurry," said Jim, swinging his suitcase to the other hand.

"It'll only take a minute."

Jim walked over to the car, stooping down and peering at several dark shapes in the back seat.

"Whatta you want?"

"Little favor," said the sailor, turning and smiling up at him, his arm slung loosely over the wheel. "Just a weensy favor," he grinned, crooking his thumb and forefinger small.

There was a commotion in the backseat. Two of the dark shapes were wrestling with a third. The third was shouting and swearing at the other two.

"Lemme alone! Ouch, you bastards! I don' wanta go!"

"G'wan, get outa here," snarled one of the dark shapes. "You're pissy-eyed."

"C'mon, soldier, this is where you check out," snapped the other. "Exit 3, soldier."

"Don't call me no soldier, goddamn it, don't you call me no soldier!"

"So, okay, marine boy. Hop to it. Here's harbor, baby."

"Just don't soldier me, goddamn it. Just watch what you call me."

"Now's that the way to treat a buddy?"

"Okay, buddy, okay, babydoll."

"You see," grinned the sailor, reaching out and taking Jim by the arm, "he's a little looped."

"So what's that got to do with me?"

"Now look, mate," said the sailor. "He lives around here somewhere, see? Gotta get a bus to get home'n see his folks. You know."

"Look, sailor, I don't want the responsibility," Jim said, backing away. "I plan on getting home myself sometime tonight."

The sailor clutched his arm firmly. "Take him off our hands, will you? We're sick of him. He's been driving us nuts all the way up from Carolina. Come on, be a pal."

"You better take him to a bus stop yourself."

"Buddy, we don't know nothing about this burg. We're heading for Boston."

The two were struggling with the drunken marine, trying to push him out of the car on the other side.

"I don't wanta go!" shouted the marine. "Lemme alone! Damn you, stop shoving me!"

"Out you go, Pluto." They each gave a violent shove and the marine flew out of the car, hitting the asphalt on his backside and folding up in a heap. He sat there stunned, his head swinging from side to side.

"Hey, don't think you're gonna dump him on me!" Jim shouted.

"Toss out his bag," said the sailor.

"Alley-oop!" A leather suitcase was pitched out the back window and landed in the grass off the shoulder of the road.

"Get this crate rolling!"

"Boston, here we come!"

"Hey! Wait a minute!"

"Thanks, matie!" the sailor called, stepping on the gas. "You're an angel, baby!"

The car leaped forward, shooting around the wide curve bending out to the highway, the tires screaming.

Jim threw down his suitcase. He plonked his hands on his hips and spat furiously over his shoulder, as the taillights of the convertible disappeared in the traffic. He glared over at the dark heap a little distance away. It was swaying back and forth on the road.

"Who the hell are you?" he said, taking a step toward him.

"Buddies . . . yeah . . . some buddies . . ." came a voice out of the dark heap. Jim kicked his suitcase onto the shoulder and advanced toward the marine. The marine was moaning to himself, buried in the folds of his raincoat.

"Come on." Jim leaned down and grabbed him under the arms. "Before you get run over."

"Let 'em run me over."

"Can you stand up?" Jim slapped him on the cheek.

"You're goddamned right, buddy. I'm a fucking american marine, remember that."

"Okay, stand up." Jim stepped back, watching him. The marine's head popped out of the collar of his raincoat and jerked from side to side. He looked up blearily at Jim in the darkness.

"You a doggie?" he said thickly.

"Get yourself up off the pavement."

"I'm a fucking american marine," he growled. "I can take the cold."

"Come on, get up." He reached down and grabbed him under the arms. "You gotta walk, don't you?"

"I can walk."

Jim strained and grunted as he pulled him up. He managed to get the marine on his feet, then clasped both arms around his middle, supporting him.

"Can you stand alone?" he said.

"I'm a fucking marine, I tell you."

"I know, I know. Can you stand alone?"

"I can stand alone."

Jim released his hold and took him by the arm. The marine swayed back and forth, his heavy boots scraping into the cinders as he struggled to get his footing.

"I'll never forget this, buddy. You're a peach, real peach."

He reached around, lifting his hand to touch Jim's cheek. The hand was crudely wrapped in a dirty handkerchief damp with blood. His knees buckled and he grinned, his eyes rolling loosely in his head, as he placed the hand on Jim's shoulder.

"What'd you do?" Jim said, trying to push the hand away.

"Window!" laughed the marine, his head flopping

TONY MUNZLINGER

on his chest. "Doggie. Only he was on'a other side'a window . . . smashed . . ." His head flew back and he shouted, "Smashed the fucking doggie!"

"Hey, cut that out. Look at yourself."

"I'm a slob. I don't give a shit."

"You can't go out on the street like this. Tuck in your shirt tail, fix your tie."

"Okay, buddy, you're pretty swell, buddy."

He began fumbling with the front ends of his shirt with his one good hand. The shirt was streaked with vomit down the front. He gave up trying to stuff the shirt ends into his trousers, and the bad hand moved up, clawing dumbly over his tie, smearing it with blood.

"I can't do it, buddy," he said, letting his hands fall heavily at his sides.

Jim squinted his eyes, then spit over his shoulder.

"Why them guys had to dump you on me I don't know."

He took the shirt ends and pushed them down inside the trousers. He had soiled his hands from the vomit and he took out his handkerchief and wiped them, muttering to himself. Then he straightened the marine's tie and squared his cap straight on his head, pushing the mop of oily black hair under the stiff crown. He pulled the coat together and buttoned it.

"I'll never forget this, baby, I never will, honest." He tried to put his arm around Jim.

"Okay, okay. Just stand still."

The belt of the raincoat was twisted in back. Jim straightened it out, evening the lengths, then buckled it tightly in front. He held the marine at arms length, and looked him up and down.

"You're okay, buddy," said the marine, raising his hand and wiping his nose on the bloody handkerchief. "You're okay." He tried to touch Jim, but Jim pushed the hand away.

"You puked all over your tie."

"In Virginia it was. Vomited all over Virginia."

Jim pulled the lapels of the coat together and buttoned them, hiding the tie.

"We're going down there," he said, pointing to the highway. "See?"

"Okay, babydoll. Anything you say. Anything." The marine leaned over suddenly and kissed Jim clumsily on the mouth.

"I thought you were a marine," Jim said, looking around for the suitcases.

"I'm a red white and blue marine, fucking american marine, true blue."

"Can you carry your bag?"

"I'm not helpless."

Jim steadied him, then walked over into the grass and picked up the leather suitcase belonging to the marine. When he got back he found him squatting on the asphalt.

"Whatta you trying to do?" He thrust the bag at him. "Let's get outta here. It's colder'n hell."

"Damned col'," muttered the marine.

Jim pulled him to his feet, slipping his arm into his and grasping it firmly. "Take this." He handed the marine his suitcase.

"Okay, baby. Anything. Anything you say."

Jim picked up his own suitcase and they started walking arm in arm, the marine stumbling clumsily, bumping at his side, down the exit road toward the highway.

"Tell me where you live."

"Nowhere." The marine tried to spit, but the saliva plopped on the shoulder of his coat and dribbled down the sleeve.

"Tell me where you live so I can put you on the right bus."

"My old man's gonna meet me exit 3."

"This is exit 3." Jim looked down toward the highway. "I don't see no car waiting."

"Call . . ."

"Call what?"

The marine stopped, pressing a hand to his forehead.

"Call . . . 2477 . . ."

"That your phone number?"

"Yeah."

Jim said the number to himself a couple of times. "You're sure that's right?"

"I wouldn't kid you, baby."

"We'll find the telephone. I'll call him. How'd he know what time you'd get here?"

"He knows. Right now. Mr. Stark, my father, you ask for him. He knows me. Tell him I'm home . . ."

The marine dropped his suitcase and fell on his knees, clutching his stomach.

"What's the matter with you?" Jim cried, bending down beside him. "You feel sick?"

The marine was crying.

"Hey," Jim said, shaking his arm. "You gonna vomit? Make it snappy."

The marine didn't say anything.

"Come on, get the hell up outta there. We gotta get moving." He pulled him by the shoulders, but he wouldn't budge. He swayed back and forth, weeping.

"I smashed his face," he moaned. "Cut it all up. I showed him. Cut his face to ribbons. Ground his face in the broken glass. He won't make faces anymore. I ground his pretty face to bits."

"Quit talking like that. You'll get locked up."

"Let them lock me up. I fought in it. I know what it's all about."

A car came along the exit road, slowed down as it

passed the two men, then stopped. A window slid down and a man's voice called, "Hey, soldier, can I give you a lift? Always glad to help our boys. Can only take one. How about it, soldier?"

The marine straightened up slowly, then sprang forward and cupping his hands to his mouth, shouted, "You go stick that ride! You gook, I know you." He started running for the car, stumbling and sliding over the asphalt. Jim started after him.

"Gook! Gook! Kill 'em!"

"I don't take no drunk," the man snarled. "Soldier or no." He stepped on the gas and the car tore off, gathering speed as it raced toward the highway.

"You keep your junky car, you goddamned gook!" shouted the marine, standing in the middle of the road and shaking his fist at the retreating automobile. "I know you. Know everything about you!"

He leaned forward, folding his arms over his chest and rocking back and forth, began to weep again.

"Whatta you want to do that for?" Jim said, hurrying up to him. "Guy wants to give you a ride and you act like that. Come on, here's your suitcase. Let's get to a telephone."

"Let him stick his car."

"Look, I'm getting pretty sick of you."

"Okay. Okay, babydoll. You're okay. You're a real buddy." He put his arm around Jim's shoulder.

"Will you do like I say?"

"Sure, baby, sure."

"You start acting funny again, I'm gonna leave you here cold and flat."

"Don't do that, buddy," the marine said, squeezing him tightly. "I'll do what you say, buddy. Honest I will."

"Okay. Grab your bag and come on."

They came down to the highway and walked into the blue light of the tall roadlamps standing at intervals along the way. Turning right they followed a narrow dirt path running alongside the concrete shoulder. The four-lane highway was crowded with traffic moving swiftly in either direction. The marine was having difficulty walking and he leaned heavily on Jim's shoulder.

"You walk too fast," he choked.

Jim slowed down, keeping his eye on the neon signs of some gas stations farther up the highway.

"Look," he said, "when we get to one of them stations I want you to behave yourself. You got me? No blabbing about gooks or anything. You understand? Clean up your mouth. People don't like to hear that kinda talk. This isn't the army."

"Goddamn it, I ain't in the army. I ain't no goddamned doggie."

"Okay. You just hold yourself up and talk straight. You hear?"

"I hear you, baby," said the marine, coming to a dead halt under a roadlamp. "I hear you talking all the time."

"Now what?" said Jim, dropping his suitcase.

The marine lifted both hands, holding them close to his face, clenching and unclenching his fists. He winced, staring at the bloody hand as though he hadn't seen it before.

"I did this, buddy. I killed a doggie in Virginia. Killed 'im through a window," he said, slowly uncoiling the sticky fingers. The blood-clotted handkerchief slipped to the ground, was picked up by the wind and carried off in the darkness.

"Now look what you done," Jim said.

The marine sighed and leaned heavily on Jim's shoulder.

"I ain't feeling no pain," he said, gruffly, trying to stuff the hand in his pocket. "It don't hurt me."

"It's damned near cut through to the bone. Here." Jim pulled his handkerchief from his pocket and took the hand.

"Aw, buddy, I don't wanta do that. That's your clean handkerchief."

"It's not so clean." Jim took the hand and wrapped the handkerchief around it to form a crude tourniquet.

"That's mighty white of you, buddy. Mighty white."

"Yeah, now come on. We gotta get moving."

A little farther on, in a flat open area on the other side of the highway, stood a glowing telephone booth, red white and blue plastic and glassed in on three sides.

Jim jerked the marine by the arm. They crossed the highway, Jim keeping a tight hold on the marine as they dodged their way through the traffic. When they got to the booth, Jim made the marine sit down on the suitcase.

"Stay put now. What was the number again?"

"What?"

"Your phone number. I wanta call your father."

"I forget."

"Come on, don't get funny."

"Okay, buddy, I wouldn't get funny with you."

"What is it then?"

"Wait a minute . . ." He shut his eyes tight and after a moment said slowly, "2477."

"Okay. Now you just sit here."

"Buddy . . ." The marine tried to get up.

"Stay there for godssakes." Jim made him sit down again.

"Buddy . . ."

"What?"

"If he ain't there, try the Columbia Café. That's . . ." He paused a moment, shutting his eyes again. "I know it. A minute. I know it. Yeah . . . 8191. You call there he ain't home, huh, buddy?"

"Okay. Don't move. I'll be out in a minute."

Jim stepped into the booth, pulling the door closed after him. He fumbled in his pocket for some change, found a dime, and dropped it in the slot. He dialed the first number. The phone rang again and again, one long, one short. There was no answer. He swung around to check how the marine was and saw only the leather suitcase overturned outside the booth. He looked quickly around the vacant lot to one side, then spotted him staggering out toward the middle of the highway in the midst of the traffic. The hand wrapped in the handkerchief was lifted, a bent cigaret hung loosely between his lips. He was pointing to the cigaret and motioning to a Negro sailor who stood on the opposite side of the highway, thumbing a ride. Jim flew out of the booth and ran over to the edge of the highway.

"Hey, get back here!" he shouted.

"Buddy, you got a match? Yo, dinge!" the marine was calling in a slurred voice over the roar of the traffic. "Yo, buddy-dinge," he howled. He lurched toward the Negro, pointing to the cigaret.

"Hey, sailor!" Jim shouted.

The Negro was waving his arms, motioning the marine back. There was a screech of brakes as a car bore down on him. The driver swerved to one side, narrowly missing him. He slowed down long enough to shout out a few curses, then sped on.

"Hey, sailor, stop that guy, will you?" Jim started across the highway. "He's drunk!"

The Negro lifted his bag and dodging a tractor-and-trailer, ran out to meet the marine. Both Jim and the Negro got to the marine at the same time and each took an arm and led him back across the highway.

"Wanta match," said the marine, as soon as they got to the telephone booth.

"I gotta match. Whyn't you ask me?"

"You was busy."

"You coulda got killed."

"Yeah, man, you shouldn't go bumming lights on a busy street the shape you're in." The Negro pulled a lighter from the pocket of his pea jacket and cupped the flame, holding it out to the marine.

"Much obliged, buddy," he said, puffing hard on the cigaret. He swung away and slumped against the booth. "Mighty fine, dinge, mighty fine of you."

"Look, sailor, you stay here a minute and keep an eye on him, will you? I'm trying to call his folks."

"I wanta get to New York before midnight," said the sailor.

"This'll only take a minute, pal. Honest."

"Hey, dinge, come on over here and talk to me," growled the marine. "Pretty nice for a boogie. Saved my life. Give the dinge the purple ticker."

"Don't you call me that."

"Lay off that stuff," Jim said to the marine. "He saved your life. He gave you a light, didn't he?"

"A spade's a spade. He's a good old spade." The marine slid down the booth and slumped in a sitting position at the base of it.

"Look, will you stay here a minute?" Jim said, taking the sailor by the arm.

"Boy, I told you I wanta get to New York. I ain't got no time to mess around."

"Just a minute, huh?"

The Negro glanced down at the marine, who sat propped against the plate-glass wall of the booth, his face buried in the lapels of his raincoat.

"Well, okay," he said slowly. "But I don't mean to stay around here much longer. I probably missed a dozen rides by now. You hurry up and make that call."

"That's swell of you," Jim said. He stepped into the booth, sliding the door to after him. He dialed the number of the Columbia Café and there was a long wait as the phone buzzed on and off at the other end. He kept glancing down to where the marine sat slouched against the glass, his knees drawn up to his chin. The Negro stood off a little, his hands thrust deep in his pockets, his collar turned up. He was looking down the highway in the direction of New York, watching the cars speed by.

Finally the receiver clicked at the other end, there was a hum of voices, and the straggly tail end of a blues being sung in a drunken wavering voice.

"Hello, hello, Columbia Café?"

A shrill giggle hurt his ear.

"That's right, kiddo. Whadda you want?"

It was a woman's voice.

"Is Mr. Stark there? I gotta talk to Mr. Stark right away."

"Who?"

"Stark—Mr. Stark—his son—"

"How do you spell that, kiddo?"

"S-t-a-r-k, I guess."

"You guess? What you want him for? Hey, Harry, make mine VO with soda, if you're buying!"

"Listen, is he there?"

"Who?"

"Mr. Stark."

"Say, what's your name?"

"What's that got to do with it? All I wanta know is if Mr. Stark's there. I gotta talk to him about something important. His son . . ."

"Geez, I sure wisht they had television on phones. You got an awful cute voice."

"Look . . ."

There was a rapping at the door of the booth. Jim glanced up and saw the Negro motioning toward his watch. Jim nodded quickly and held up his finger. "A minute . . . just one minute."

"Who's that knocking? Who're you talking to, cutie? Ouch, Harry, don't get so fresh! Hello . . ."

"Look, this is awful urgent. Could you please get me Mr. Stark. His son is drunk . . ."

"His son? Who's his son? I don't know his son. What's your name?"

"Look, that don't matter. I gotta talk to Mr. Stark 'cause his son's laying outside here stone drunk and I want Mr. Stark to come and pick him up."

"What's wrong with being stony drunk, I'd like to know? You should be happy. Whatta you say me and you get stony drunk, huh?" She tittered. "Where do you live?"

"Look, lady, all I want is a little simple information. Now don't get funny with me . . ."

"Who's getting funny? I like that."

"Is Mr. Stark there?"

"Who?"

"Oh, goddamn it to hell!"

"Look, kiddo, don't think you can use that kind of language with me, just 'cause I can't see you. I ain't truck."

The Negro started rapping on the door again.

"Just a minute! Just a minute, please!"

The Negro shook his head firmly and picking up his canvas bag started walking quickly toward the highway.

"Look, lady!" Jim blurted in the mouthpiece.

"You're hurting my ear! And quit calling me 'lady.'"

"I'm sorry. For the last time, is Mr. Stark there?"

"Who's that you're talking to?"

"Nobody."

"You talk to yourself?"

"Look, once and for all, is Mr. Stark there?"

"No, he ain't here."

"Jesus H. Christ!"

"Where're you calling from, kiddo? Whyn't you and your friend come on over? Hey, Harry, put my drink there . . . hey, kiddo . . . hello . . ."

Jim slammed down the receiver and shoving open the door, got up and jumped outside. He stood over the marine, hands on hips, scowling. He looked up and down the highway. The Negro was nowhere in sight. He leaned down and slapped the marine hard on top of the head.

"Wha . . . ? Wha . . . ?"

"Come on, you. Get up. We're getting out of here."

He pulled the marine to his feet.

"Wha . . . wha'sa matter?"

"Come on. We're gonna find a taxi station. I'm gonna put you in a cab and goodbye, baby. You're getting to be a real pain in the neck."

"Okay, buddy, anything," mumbled the marine. He yawned loudly and stared around stupidly with sleepy eyes, leaning on Jim. "Anything you say . . ."

Jim handed him his suitcase and flung one arm around him and they started walking toward a cluster of neon signs ahead.

"I couldn't get your folks."

"My folks?"

"Yeah, there wasn't any Mr. Stark at the Columbia Café."

"He must be somewhere else," the marine said thickly, as he stumbled along trying to keep up with Jim. "May be at the Silver Star."

"Well, I'm not going into that again. I had enough trouble making that call as it was. I'm putting you in a taxi and sending you home."

"Okay, baby. I'll never forget this. Honest."

They crossed tree-lined streets, the trees slender and bare in winter, and on either side, stretching down the blocks, low bungalows with warm yellow lights glowing in the windows.

"Pretty. Awful pretty," croaked the marine, swinging his head from left to right. "Ain't it pretty, buddy?"

"Huh?"

"The lights . . . awful pretty."

"I don't see no taxi station," Jim said, looking around. "I thought there was a taxi station along here."

They walked on. In the next block they came to a drugstore facing on a side street off the highway. The front of the store was one sheer wall of plate-glass window, adorned with flickering neon signs. Inside the cold white light of the place Jim spotted a row of telephone booths. A woman wearing steel-rimmed glasses stood behind a chrome counter, reading a newspaper. The store was empty.

"Look, I can get the number of a taxi from here," Jim said. He hesitated a moment. "Now look, you stay out here. Sit down on your suitcase and behave yourself. You understand me?"

"Sure, buddy, sure, I understand you."

Jim let go of the marine to take his suitcase from

him and the marine fell back, bumping his full weight against the window. The woman inside glanced up sharply from her newspaper.

"Be careful," Jim said. "You don't wanta bust this thing. That lady's watching us."

"I'll bust it. Bust any window I see," growled the marine. "Bust the doggie."

"Pipe down," Jim said, looking quickly around. "People might hear you. Cop or something."

"Hate the cops."

"For pete's sake, don't start that again."

"Kill every one of the bastards. Grind 'em up."

"You just sit down here and forget all that."

He set the suitcase against the window and helped the marine to sit down on it. He put his own suitcase beside him.

"Now, keep an eye on this bag while I'm inside. I don't want anybody stealing it."

"Nobody'll steal it, baby doll. I'll kill them."

"Okay. Now you just sit there and be quiet. I'll be back in a minute."

"Where you going, buddy?"

"I'm gonna call a taxi for you."

Jim stared at him.

"Didn't you call my father, buddy? I told you Columbia Café. He's gonna meet me exit 3."

"Look, he wasn't there. I told you already."

"You didn't tell me nothing. You getting funny with me, buddy?"

"I'm not getting funny with you. For christsake, I . . ."

"Just don't you get funny, that's all. Nobody gets funny with me. I'm a fucking american marine. Remember that. I don't take no shit from nobody. Smashed a window."

His head fell forward. The woman behind the counter had taken off her steel-rimmed glasses and was staring intently at the two outside.

"Look, I'm trying to help you out," Jim said. "I won't do you dirt. Now sit here and be quiet. I'm gonna get you a taxi so you can get home."

"Okay, baby. You're okay, baby." The marine began roughly fondling him. "I can trust you, baby, I know that."

"Well, okay. Just sit here now till I get back."

"Right you are, I got you, babydoll."

Jim straightened up, adjusting his scarf and smoothing his hair with one gloved hand. He glanced a moment at the woman behind the counter, then strode over to the full-length glass door, pushed it open and went inside. He walked straight up to the woman.

"I need a taxi right away. I . . ."

"Auburn 7-0801," she said crisply, her eyes trained on the marine sitting outside, his back against the window.

"Thank you."

He stepped into one of the booths and dialed the number. The phone on the other end buzzed once, there was a click, and a thick voice said, "Hummingbird cab."

"Listen, I want a taxi . . ."

"Where are you?"

"Where am I? I don't know. Wait a minute. I'll find out."

He pushed open the door and called, "Lady, hey, lady, what address is this?"

"Black Horse Pike, Burr Drugs," she said, not looking at him, her eyes still riveted outside the window. "He knows."

"Burr Drugs," Jim said, swinging back to the mouthpiece. "Black Horse . . ."

"I got you. Be there in a couple of minutes."

The phone clicked at the other end. Jim stared at the receiver a moment, then slowly put it back on the hook. As he was stepping out of the booth, there was a shrill scream from the woman at the counter, and turning toward the window Jim saw the marine standing facing them, his face twisted, his eyes bulging from his head, and the bloody hand lifted high over his head, clenched in a fist.

"Stop him! For godssake, stop him!" screamed the woman, her fingers pressed at her temples. "I knew he'd do something! I knew it!"

"Hey, don't do that!" Jim shouted, running for the door. "Hey!"

The marine walloped the window with his fist. The glass shuddered under the impact. He threw back his arm and pounded the window a second time, leaving a smear of blood where his fist struck.

The woman covered her mouth with her hand and hurried out the door after Jim.

"Stop him! What is he, nuts?" she cried, once outside.

Jim grabbed hold of the marine and pulled him away from the window.

"What're you trying to do? You said you wouldn't do anything. Look at you!"

"Smash the fucking window! Kill the bastards!" choked the marine, flailing his arms about high in the air. He was panting for breath and trembling, his face flushed red. Jim held him tightly in his arms.

"Are you crazy or something? Drop them arms! Drop them! Now look what you done to your hand. You got it bleeding all over again. Come on now. Calm yourself."

The marine let his arms fall heavily at his sides. He began to cry, his mouth flapping open and shut as he gulped for air; a string of saliva swung from his chin. He pressed his fists into his eyes.

"Smash it!" he gasped. "Smash it all!"

"Settle down," Jim coaxed. "You're getting yourself all worked up over nothing."

"You get him outa here," snapped the woman, polishing her glasses on one corner of her apron. "I'll call the police."

"Don't do that, lady. He's had a little to drink . . ." He lifted his hand awkwardly to her. "You know."

"A little huh? Why he's drunk as a hoot-owl. Must have the dt's to carry on like that. He busts that window, I'll make plenty trouble for him. And I'll hold you responsible." She snapped the glasses back on her nose. "Look at the mess he made," she said, pointing to the bloodstain. "I just had them windows cleaned."

"He won't bust your window, lady."

"Well, you get him away from there and hold on to him. That's not no ordinary cheap glass," she said rapping the window with her knuckles. "He busts that it'll cost him a pretty penny."

"He won't bust it, lady."

"Well, I'm telling you."

"Okay, lady, good night, lady."

"You hold him over by the curb. He comes close to this window again, I'm calling the cops, and I don't mean maybe."

"I got you, lady. Come on, boy. Come over here with me. Do like I say."

The marine would not move, but kept his fists knuckled over his eyes, his body shaking with dry sobs.

"What's he blubbering about? He got the crying jags?"

"I guess so," said Jim, leading the marine away. "He don't feel so good."

"I should think not, all he's had to drink."

She stared at the marine, pursing her lips and folding her arms beneath her apron. Jim led the marine to the curb and held him there with both arms around him.

"You just better keep an eye on him, I'm telling you," she said, scratching her arms under the apron.

"I will, lady."

She looked quickly up and down the street then turned and pushing open the glass door went back into the store.

"Now you see what can happen? You see? She coulda had you pinched."

"Don't care," choked the marine.

"You're acting like a baby. Tough guy, huh?"

"Bust her window," he said, rubbing his eyes. "Grind her face in it. Show her."

"Just behave yourself."

"Cut off her tits with the broken glass."

"Stop that."

"Dried up whore. Let me go talk to her," he muttered, struggling to break free.

"You stay right here. Haven't you caused enough trouble? The taxi'll be here in a minute. And, listen, don't you give the cabbie no trouble. You lay back and get some shuteye riding home. Don't you bother the taxi driver."

"I'll kill him, cut off her balls."

"Lean over and strangle him when you're skimming eighty an hour down Black Horse Pike," Jim whispered hoarsely in his face. "Go on and do that. I'm tired of the whole monkey business."

"I'll strangle him."

Three soldiers appeared at the corner, walking arm in arm, laughing and talking loudly. They stopped in front of the drugstore and then turned and stared at each other in amazement.

"This here ain't no bar," said one.

"I be damned if I want an ice-cream soda," said another, and he burst out laughing.

"Fi-yoo!" wheezed the third. "All this shoe leather burnt for nothing, and're my dogs in heat!"

They roared with laughter. The marine cocked his head up and glared over at them.

"Hey!" he shouted.

The three soldiers looked over to where Jim and the marine were standing.

"You an MP?" shouted the soldier in the middle, squinting and bending forward, hanging loosely on the arms of the other two.

"Come over here," snarled the marine.

"Who you shouting orders at, duckboy?" said one of the soldiers. "This ain't the army out here, buddy."

"Don't 'buddy' me. I ain't no goddamned soldier," said the marine, working to pry himself loose from Jim's arms. "I'll show you who the hell I am."

"G'wan, you guys, get going," Jim called. "He don't know what he's saying. He's drunk."

"I ain't so goddamned drunk I can't take care of three doggies," snapped the marine, freeing one arm and thrusting Jim aside. He stood with his legs apart, his hands held loosely on his hips, glowering at the soldiers.

"C'mere, doggies."

"Get *him!*" said one of the soldiers.

The three laughed, nudging each other.

"Go on, you guys," Jim said. "He don't know what he's saying."

"No marine scares us."

"Here's one'll make you shit razor blades," said the marine, taking a step forward.

"Come and try it."

Jim came up to the marine and took him by the arm. "Look, that taxi's gonna be here in a minute. You don't wanta make no trouble."

"Who's making trouble? Keep the hell outa my way." He stiff-armed Jim square in the chest and Jim pitched back, landing heavily in the gutter, the wind knocked out of him.

"Nobody kills a fucking american marine."

The woman in the store walked quickly to one of the telephone booths. She stepped inside, pulling the door shut after her.

"Come on, you guys," said one of the soldiers, reeling toward the marine. "Let's make short work of this bird."

The three of them advanced abreast, staggering a little, crouching low, their knees bent, their arms crooked, and hands clenched into fists. The marine scraped his feet into the grass plot, digging in for footing. He stooped low, thrusting his head out, his lips curled in a snarl, the white hard teeth clamped tight together, his eyes glistening, narrowed to slits.

"Come on, you doggie bastards, come to papa, come on, you fucking doggies, to papa."

He swayed his outthrust arms from side to side and crouched lower. One of the soldiers let out an earsplitting rebel yell and the three pounced on the marine, shouting and snarling, kicking him, beating at him with their fists. The marine's one good hand shot up, swiping wildly at the air. There was the hard smack of knuckles on flesh and breathless choked curses. The marine's knees began to buckle, his one hand disappeared in the tangle of swiftly flying arms and legs. The soldiers clung to him and the marine began to topple, lurching from side to side, and, groaning, sank to the ground beneath the weight of the men. He lay moaning. There was the sound of hoarse heavy breathing.

Jim picked up his suitcase and started walking down the dark street, kicking at the tufts of dead grass in the cracks of the pavement.

The woman had come out of the telephone booth and was standing behind the counter, staring at the men.

The soldiers untangled themselves, piling off the marine, and started hopping around from one foot to the other, laughing loudly, and snorting clouds of steam from their mouths.

"That settles the big-mouthed duckboy!" hooted one, panting for breath.

"Big shot marine! Ho, boy!"

They helped brush each other off, then each started setting his clothes right. One poked around in the grass, hunting for their caps.

The marine lay stretched full length on the grass plot, one arm thrust over his chest, the other pinned beneath him. His mouth was half open, a strangling noise came up from the depths of his throat.

"Come on, men. Let's go find that bar," said one.

"Celebrate the victory!" shouted another.

"Fi-yoo! I hope to Christ this ain't a dry town. No-o-o-o Sahara Mary! Yipeeeeee!"

They took arms and walked away, laughing and shouting, glancing back now and then to boo the prostrate figure of the marine until they rounded the corner and were gone.

At the end of the street Jim stopped beneath a streetlamp, set down his suitcase, and looked back. He could see the marine stretched out a little distance from the drugstore, and beyond that the headlights of the cars hurtling back and forth on the highway. He coughed up some phlegm in his throat, rolled it around on his tongue, then spit it over his shoulder into the gutter. He pulled up the collar of his overcoat and, rubbing his gloved hands together, looked again toward the other end of the street.

The woman in the drugstore came out, carrying a sponge in one hand and a little tin of water in the other. She glanced sharply at the marine, then turned to the plate-glass window. Dipping the sponge in the water, she began rubbing at the stain of blood on the glass. She rubbed briskly, pausing once to dip the sponge again in the water and wring it out, then polished the glass clean with a corner of her apron. She emptied the tin of water in the alley alongside the building and came back and stood in front of the window, one hand on her hip, giving a careful inspection of the glass. She walked over to one corner and rubbed at it with her sponge, then stepped back a pace to survey what she had done. Satisfied, she turned and stood regarding the marine for a moment. She went to him in quick short steps and bent over him, reaching one hand out from beneath her apron and slapping his cheek again and again. The low wail of a siren sounded somewhere along the highway. The woman snapped up her head and listened, thrusting her hands under her apron and rubbing them briskly. She stared down at the marine a moment, then her eyes darted up and down the street. The approaching siren grew louder. She spotted Jim standing at the corner and her mouth began to move, to shape words, as though she were calling to him. Jim turned his back on her. He began to shiver and took out a pack of cigarets from the pocket of his coat and lit one. He stuck the cigaret between his lips and, picking up his suitcase, stepped off the curb and started over the street at a brisk pace, heading across town.

Travel With Flora

COLLISION

Maiden Voyage

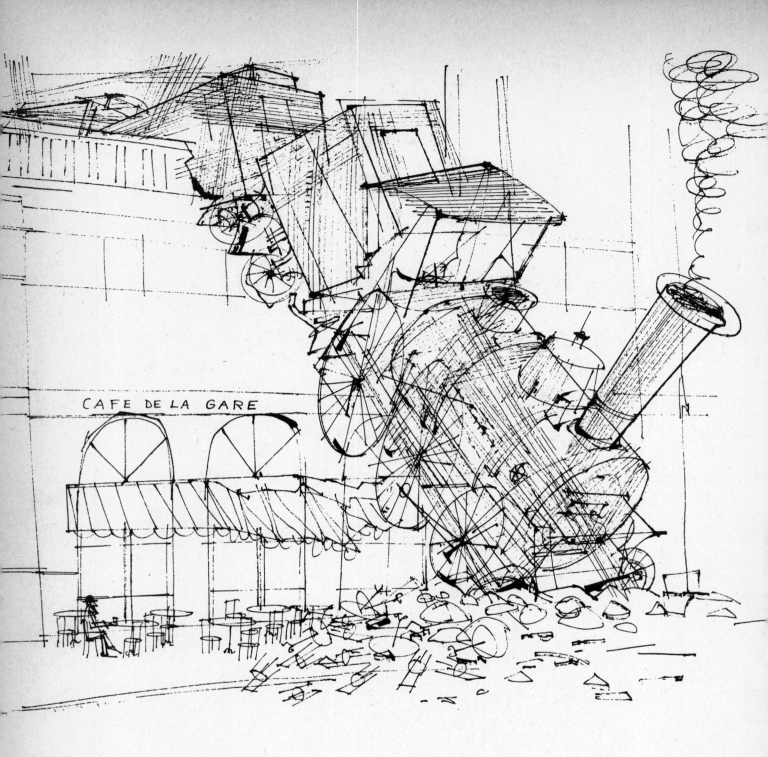

CAFE DE LA GARE

GARE MONTPARNASSE, OCTOBER 21, 1895

ARRIVAL OF THE REBELS

No More Masterpieces

One of the reasons for the asphyxiating atmosphere in which we live without possible escape or remedy—and in which we all share, even the most revolutionary among us—is our respect for what has been written, formulated, or painted, what has been given form, as if all expression were not at last exhausted, were not a point where things must break apart if they are to start anew and begin fresh.

We must have done with this idea of masterpieces reserved for a self-styled elite and not understood by the general public; the mind has no such restricted districts as those so often used for clandestine sexual encounters.

Masterpieces of the past are good for the past: they are not good for us. We have the right to say what has been said and even what has not been said in a way that belongs to us, a way that is immediate and direct, corresponding to present modes of feeling, and understandable to everyone.

It is idiotic to reproach the masses for having no sense of the sublime, when the sublime is confused with one or another of its formal manifestations, which are moreover always defunct manifestations. And if for example a contemporary public does not understand *Oedipus Rex*, I shall make bold to say that it is the fault of *Oedipus Rex* and not of the public.

In *Oedipus Rex* there is the theme of incest and the idea that nature mocks at morality and that there are certain unspecified powers at large which we would do well to beware of, call them *destiny* or anything you choose.

There is in addition the presence of a plague epidemic which is a physical incarnation of these powers. But the whole in a manner and language that have lost all touch with the rude and epileptic rhythm of our time. Sophocles speaks grandly perhaps, but in a style that is no longer timely. His language is too refined for this age, it is as if he were speaking beside the point.

However, a public that shudders at train wrecks, that is familiar with earthquakes, plagues, revolutions, wars; that is sensitive to the disordered anguish of love, can be affected by all these grand notions and asks only to become aware of them, but on condition that it is addressed in its own language, and that its knowledge of these things does not come to it through adulterated trappings and speech that belong to extinct eras which will never live again.

Today as yesterday, the public is greedy for mystery: it asks only to become aware of the laws according to which destiny manifests itself, and to divine perhaps the secret of its apparitions.

Let us leave textual criticism to graduate students, formal criticism to esthetes, and recognize that what has been said is not still to be said; that an expression does not have the same value twice, does not live two lives; that all words, once spoken, are dead and function only at the moment when they are uttered, that a form, once it has served, cannot be used again and asks only to be replaced by another, and that the theater is the only place in the world where a gesture, once made, can never be made the same way twice.

If the public does not frequent our literary masterpieces, it is because those masterpieces are literary, that is to say, fixed; and fixed in forms that no longer respond to the needs of the time.

Far from blaming the public, we ought to blame the formal screen we interpose between ourselves and the public, and this new form of idolatry, the idolatry of fixed masterpieces which is one of the aspects of bourgeois conformism.

This conformism makes us confuse sublimity, ideas, and things with the forms they have taken in time and in our minds—in our snobbish, precious, aesthetic mentalities which the public does not understand.

How pointless in such matters to accuse the public of bad taste because it relishes insanities, so long as the public is not shown a valid spectacle; and I defy anyone to show me *here* a spectacle valid—valid in the supreme sense of the theater—since the last great romantic melodramas, i.e., since a hundred years ago.

The public, which takes the false for the true, has the sense of the true and always responds to it when it is manifested. However it is not upon the stage that the true is to be sought nowadays, but in the street; and if the crowd in the street is offered an occasion to show its human dignity, it will always do so.

If people are out of the habit of going to the theater, if we have all finally come to think of theater as an inferior art, a means of popular distraction, and to use it as an outlet for our worst instincts, it is because we have learned too well what the theater has been, namely, falsehood and illusion. It is because we have been accustomed for four hundred years, that is since the Renaissance, to a purely descriptive and narrative theater—storytelling psychology; it is because every possible ingenuity has been exerted in bringing to life on the stage plausible but detached beings, with the spectacle on one side, the public on the other—and because the public is no longer shown anything but the mirror of itself.

Shakespeare himself is responsible for this aberration and decline, this disinterested idea of the theater which wishes a theatrical performance to leave the public intact, without setting off one image that will shake the organism to its foundations and leave an ineffaceable scar.

If, in Shakespeare, a man is sometimes preoccupied with what transcends him, it is always in order to determine the ultimate consequences of this preoccupation within him, i.e., psychology.

Psychology, which works relentlessly to reduce the unknown to the known, to the quotidian and the ordinary, is the cause of the theater's abasement and its fearful loss of energy, which seems to me to have reached its lowest point. And I think both the theater and we ourselves have had enough of psychology.

I believe furthermore that we can all agree on this matter sufficiently so that there is no need to descend to the repugnant level of the modern and French theater to condemn the theater of psychology.

Stories about money, worry over money, social careerism, the pangs of love unspoiled by altruism, sexuality sugar-coated with an eroticism that has lost its mystery have nothing to do with the theater, even if they do belong to psychology. These torments, seductions, and lusts before which we are nothing but Peeping Toms gratifying our cravings, tend to go bad, and their rot turns to revolution: we must take this into account.

But this is not our most serious concern.

If Shakespeare and his imitators have gradually insinuated the idea of art for art's sake, with art on one side and life on the other, we can rest on this feeble and lazy idea only as long as the life outside endures. But there are too many signs that everything that used to sustain our lives no longer does so, that we are all mad, desperate, and sick. And I call for us to react.

This idea of a detached art, of poetry as a charm which exists only to distract our leisure, is a decadent idea and an unmistakable symptom of our power to castrate.

Our literary admiration for Rimbaud, Jarry, Lautréamont, and a few others, which has driven two men to suicide, but turned into café gossip for the rest, belongs to this idea of literary poetry, of detached art, of neutral spiritual activity which creates nothing and produces nothing; and I can bear witness that at the very moment when that kind of personal poetry which involves only the man who creates it and only at the moment he creates it broke out in its most abusive fashion, the theater was scorned more than ever before by poets who have never had the sense of direct and concerted action, nor of efficacity, nor of danger.

We must get rid of our superstitious valuation of texts and *written* poetry. Written poetry is worth reading once, and then should be destroyed. Let the dead poets make way for others. Then we might even come to see that it is our veneration for what has already been created, however beautiful and valid it may be, that petrifies us, deadens our responses, and prevents us from making contact with that underlying power, call it thought-energy, the life force, the determinism of change, lunar menses, or anything you like. Beneath the poetry of the texts, there is the actual poetry, without form and without text. And just as the efficacity of masks in the magic practices of certain tribes is exhausted—and these masks are no longer good for anything except museums—so the poetic efficacity of a text is exhausted; yet the poetry and the efficacity of the theater are exhausted least quickly of all, since they permit the *action* of what is gesticulated and pronounced, and which is never made the same way twice.

It is a question of knowing what we want. If we are prepared for war, plague, famine, and slaughter we do not even need to say so, we have only to continue as we are; continue behaving like snobs, rushing en masse to hear such and such a singer, to see such and such an admirable performance which never transcends the realm of art (and even the Russian ballet at the height of its splendor never transcended the realm of art), to marvel at such and such an exhibition of painting in which exciting shapes explode here and there but at random and without any genuine consciousness of the forces they could rouse.

This empiricism, randomness, individualism, and anarchy must cease.

Enough of personal poems, benefiting those who create them much more than those who read them.

Once and for all, enough of this closed, egoistic, and personal art.

Our spiritual anarchy and intellectual disorder is a function of the anarchy of everything else—or rather, everything else is a function of this anarchy.

I am not one of those who believe that civilization has to change in order for the theater to change; but I do believe that the theater, utilized in the highest and most difficult sense possible, has the power to influence the aspect and formation of things: and the encounter upon the stage of two passionate manifestations, two living centers, two nervous magnetisms is something as entire, true, even decisive, as, in life, the encounter of one epidermis with another in a timeless debauchery.

That is why I propose a theater of cruelty.—With this mania we all have for depreciating everything, as soon as I have said "cruelty," everybody will at once take it to mean "blood." But "theater of cruelty" means a theater difficult and cruel for myself first of all. And, on the level of performance, it is not the cruelty we can exercise upon each other by hacking at each other's bodies, carving up our personal anatomies, or, like Assyrian emperors, sending parcels of human ears, noses, or neatly detached nostrils through the mail, but the much more terrible and necessary cruelty which things can exercise against us. We are not free. And the sky can still fall on our heads. And the theater has been created to teach us that first of all.

Either we will be capable of returning by present-day means to this superior idea of poetry and poetry-through-theater which underlies the Myths told by the great ancient tragedians, capable once more of entertaining a religious idea of the theater (without meditation, useless contemplation, and vague dreams), capable of attaining awareness and a possession of certain dominant forces, of certain notions that control all others, and (since ideas, when they are effective, carry their energy with them) capable of recovering within ourselves those energies which ultimately create order and increase the value of life, or else we might as well abandon ourselves now, without protest, and recognize that we are no longer good for anything but disorder, famine, blood, war, and epidemics.

Either we restore all the arts to a central attitude and necessity, finding an analogy between a gesture made in painting or the theater, and a gesture made by lava in a volcanic explosion, or we must stop painting, babbling, writing, or doing whatever it is we do.

I propose to bring back into the theater this elementary magical idea, taken up by modern psychoanalysis, which consists in effecting a patient's cure by making him assume the apparent and exterior attitudes of the desired condition.

I propose to renounce our empiricism of imagery, in which the unconscious furnishes images at random, and which the poet arranges at random too, calling them poetic and hence hermetic images, as if the kind of trance that poetry provides did not have its reverberations throughout the whole sensibility, in every nerve, and as if poetry were some vague force whose movements were invariable.

I propose to return through the theater to an idea of the physical knowledge of images and the means of inducing trances, as in Chinese medicine which knows, over the entire extent of the human anatomy, at what points to puncture in order to regulate the subtlest functions.

Those who have forgotten the communicative power and magical nemesis of a gesture, the theater can reinstruct, because a gesture carries its energy with it, and there are still human beings in the theater to manifest the force of the gesture made.

To create art is to deprive a gesture of its reverberation in the organism, whereas this reverberation, if the gesture is made in the conditions and with the force required, incites the organism and, through it, the entire individuality, to take attitudes in harmony with the gesture.

The theater is the only place in the world, the last general means we still possess of directly affecting the organism and, in periods of neurosis and petty sensuality like the one in which we are immersed, of attacking this sensuality by physical means it cannot withstand.

If music affects snakes, it is not on account of the spiritual notions it offers them, but because snakes are long and coil their length upon the earth, because their bodies touch the earth at almost every point; and because the musical vibrations which are communicated to the earth affect them like a very subtle, very long massage; and I propose to treat the spectators like the snake charmer's subjects and conduct them *by means of their organisms* to an apprehension of the subtlest notions.

At first by crude means, which will gradually be refined. These immediate crude means will hold their attention at the start.

That is why in the "theater of cruelty" the spectator is in the center and the spectacle surrounds him.

In this spectacle the sonorization is constant: sounds, noises, cries are chosen first for their vibratory quality, then for what they represent.

Among these gradually refined means light is interposed in its turn. Light which is not created merely to add color or to brighten, and which brings its power, influence, suggestions with it. And the light of a green cavern does not sensually dispose the organism like the light of a windy day.

After sound and light there is action, and the dynamism of action: here the theater, far from copying life, puts itself whenever possible in communication with pure forces. And whether you accept or deny them, there is nevertheless a way of speaking which gives the name of "forces" to whatever brings to birth images of energy in the unconscious, and gratuitous crime on the surface.

A violent and concentrated action is a kind of lyricism: it summons up supernatural images, a bloodstream of images, a bleeding spurt of images in the poet's head and in the spectator's as well.

Whatever the conflicts that haunt the mind of a given period, I defy any spectator to whom such violent scenes will have transferred their blood, who will have felt in himself the transit of a superior action, who will have seen the extraordinary and essential movements of his thought illuminated in extraordinary deeds—the violence and blood having been placed at the service of the violence of the thought—I defy that spectator to give himself up, once outside the theater, to ideas of war, riot, and blatant murder.

So expressed, this idea seems dangerous and sophomoric. It will be claimed that example breeds example, that if the attitude of cure induces cure, the attitude of murder will induce murder. Everything depends upon the manner and the purity with which the thing is done. There is a risk. But let it not be forgotten that though a theatrical gesture is violent, it is disinterested; and that the theater teaches precisely the uselessness of the action which, once done,

is not to be done, and the superior use of the state unused by the action and which, restored, produces a purification.

I propose then a theater in which violent physical images crush and hypnotize the sensibility of the spectator seized by the theater as by a whirlwind of higher forces.

A theater which, abandoning psychology, recounts the extraordinary, stages natural conflicts, natural and subtle forces, and presents itself first of all as an exceptional power of redirection. A theater that induces trance, as the dances of Dervishes induce trance, and that addresses itself to the organism by precise instruments, by the same means as those of certain tribal music cures which we admire on records but are incapable of originating among ourselves.

There is a risk involved, but in the present circumstances I believe it is a risk worth running. I do not believe we have managed to revitalize the world we live in, and I do not believe it is worth the trouble of clinging to; but I do propose something to get us out of our marasmus, instead of continuing to complain about it, and about the boredom, inertia, and stupidity of everything.

Translated by Mary Caroline Richards

► ► **Karl Jaspers**

The Atom Bomb and the Future of Man

1. *The Present Situation*

New destructive weapons have always been denounced as criminal when they first appeared. At one time cannon, and more recently the submarine—during World War I. But their existence came to be accepted soon enough. However, the atom bomb (hydrogen bomb, cobalt bomb) is a fundamentally new development. It confronts mankind with the possibility of its own total destruction.

Only experts understand the technical details, but each of us grasps the fact that America and Russia

(and England, lagging a bit behind) have mobilized enormous resources to increase their stores of such bombs and to intensify their destructive power. The bomb dropped on Hiroshima on August 6, 1945, was the first (160,000 dead; three days later the second bomb was dropped on Nagasaki). Before such destructive power, Japan capitulated. But these first bombs, frightening as they were, are insignificant beside the bombs that have since then been dropped experimentally in desert areas, and that develop more than 600 times the energy developed by the Hiroshima bomb. Even then the world, despite its horror, was not truly aroused until it learned that the extent and kind of destruction of life eluded exact calculation. We are told that survivors exposed to radioactive air waste away for years before they finally die. We are told quite flatly by the experts that it is possible today to destroy all life on earth by human action. Whether the already existing bombs, if they were all dropped within a short time, would suffice to contaminate the atmosphere with radioactivity to such an extent that all life would cease, has not been disclosed.

The great physicists whose brains have brought about this new situation have told us how things stand. Einstein, in 1955, shortly before his death, joined with others in signing an appeal which contains the following sentence: "In the event of massive use of hydrogen weapons, we must expect sudden death for some fraction of mankind, along with painful diseases and the final destruction of all living creatures."

Such is the disquieting situation today, with respect to the future of mankind, which is threatened as never before. Before this there had only been unrealistic ideas about the end of the world. Expectation of an impending end of the world was the morally and religiously effective terror which John the Baptist, Jesus, and the early Christians communicated to their contemporaries. But now we are confronted with the real possibility of such an end—if not the end of the world, or even of our planet, at least of human life.

2. *What Is Politically Desirable?*

All thinking people desire the abolition of atomic weapons. All states declare themselves willing. But abolition is trustworthy only if mutual control is instituted at the same time.

Another line of thought is: Even if atom bombs are not abolished, no one will dare to use them. Even Hitler, despite his mass production of poison gas, did not resort to it, not even when he was faced with disaster. When a weapon must inevitably destroy both warring factions, it has become unusable.

A third line of thought is: Because atomic war is impossible, all war has become impossible. In a world war waged over the meaning of the political order, at the price of life or death, resort to the atom bomb must intervene at some point, and therefore no great power will dare to start a war. Since it would be a war of annihilation to all parties, it cannot occur. Total

danger brings about total salvation. The extremity of the predicament imposes a form of political existence which, with the atom bomb, makes war as such impossible. We are really very lucky. The era of wars is behind us. We ought now to cope with the new and quite different serious problems that arise out of the elimination of war.

3. *The Actual Situation*

Because mutual control is not agreed upon, atom bombs continue to be produced.

And despite the atom bomb we still have wars. Measured by the standard of a world war these wars are local, to be sure; but they are fearfully destructive nevertheless. Instead of saying: There will be no wars because there are atom bombs, we should rather say: There can be wars today *with* atom bombs. Should the small states enjoy the terrible privilege of waging war? They commit violent actions in order to alter their status. They threaten small adversaries in order to impose their will by brute force, according to the age-old formula. They threaten the great powers with the danger of another world war. This danger acts as a deterrent. When the small states break treaties, the great powers do not dare to enforce respect for law by violent means. But this privilege of the small sovereign states is possible only because the great powers do not agree among themselves as to how the law and the treaties are to be defended. Rather, they exploit the actions of the small states to extend or consolidate their own positions of power. Thus, the threat of the atom bomb becomes part of the old policy of blackmail, cunning, and deceit. It is said that a good policy consists in carrying things to the brink of war without actually getting into war. Propagandistic appeals are made to moral motives, and a mass of evasive arguments serves to conceal the naked will to power which is proclaimed no longer to exist. In short, there is no desire to use the atom bomb, but it is kept ready as a threat. Hence the curious result: the more powerful the states are thanks to the bomb, the more they appear paralyzed for the time being, while the small states indulge in acts of violence.

What are the further prospects? The great powers strive to make peace between the small warring states, but not without ulterior motives. They take sides, and are almost always opposed to each other. In this way they remain exposed to the danger of a world war, while the small states fight among themselves under their partial protection. Since the idea of a common order is absent, all this amounts merely to postponement of world conflict. Because each little war is actually a disguised war between the great powers, each implies the danger of a world war.

4. The Crucial Point: International Control

Salvation seems close at hand. Since all states are willing to renounce the atom bomb, it should be sufficient for the three powers possessing the bomb to conclude a treaty and carry out its provisions. All existing bombs would be destroyed, and new ones would no longer be produced. But so far Russia has refused to agree to mutual control, without which there would be no guarantee that such a treaty would actually be carried out.

This would save the day. But international control would at once entail consequences going beyond elimination of the atomic threat. For international control would inevitably be associated with world-wide political change, namely, the transition from a state of affairs in which the nations confront one another like beasts in a jungle, to a community of nations based upon law, whose observance is secured by common institutions. It would mean the transition from a state of mere coexistence which an act of violence can change into war at any moment, to a state of co-operation in which the freedom of all would depend on effective international agreements. This would be the beginning of world peace.

The first consequence of such control would be that the powers would gain insight into all aspects of all situations, which must of itself lead to mutual frankness, and finally to the collective spirit indispensable for peace. The second consequence of control would be the voluntary restriction of state sovereignty by treaties, whose enactment, as with all laws, must not be based on trust alone, but on an effective controlling agency. Such an agency would be set up by the contracting parties themselves. Only in this way can the freedom arbitrarily to violate treaties be eliminated.

The setting up of such a mutual international control would mark the first and probably crucial step toward a situation in which the atom bomb could, with relative certainty, be ruled out. For the atom bomb can be abolished with certainty only if war as such is made impossible.

5. Political Principles of International Peace

World peace would be based on the following principles:

(1) Treaties are recognized as legally binding, unless they are changed by new negotiations. Even in the event of profound differences of opinion, the verdict of legal agencies is to be accepted. But just as a state cannot abolish its police force, so the peaceful international order cannot renounce all use of force. How to constitute an international police force under the control of the supreme legal authorities, is one great problem.

(2) The supremacy of law requires renunciation of absolute sovereignty. This implies that the decisions of the appointed officials would be determined by a majority of votes and that the right to veto would be renounced. Instead, it should be possible, after a lapse of time, to submit every verdict of the juridical authorities to review, new negotiation, and eventual revision. The setting up of supranational officials appointed by the states and endowed with such unprecedented great powers, is the second great problem.

(3) The actual conclusion of peace implies unrestricted exchange of news reports, and the free and public confrontation of ideas, without any censorship in either instance. The achievement of a change for the better requires world-wide publicity. This does not present any special difficulty.

(4) The nations will be concerned with each other's internal affairs. Injustice must be condemned by the whole world. Reparation of internal wrongs—for instance, when human rights are violated—would be made possible through the international courts.

(5) Unjust political divisions and treaties, originating in the past, would be subject to revision. Subjugated nations are to be freed, if they so desire, by an international agency. Free and secret ballots are the means for ascertaining the people's will.

6. These Principles Are in Effect Repudiated Today

The formulation of these principles has always aroused skeptical smiles. However, since the majority of mankind wants peace even political leaders today proclaim principles of peace. But these are the exact opposite of the principles of a really peaceful world order. We are told that the following principles are and must forever remain untouchable: the absolute sovereignty of individual nations, and hence the principle of noninterference in internal affairs, and the right to veto in international bodies; equality of all nations with regard to their right to arbitrary acts; peaceful coexistence of mutually exclusive political and social forms, which are mutually exclusive because they are based on totally different basic constitutions, with prohibition of free communication by means of iron curtains; finally, there is even complete renunciation of violence on the ground that force must not be resisted by force.

Let us take a closer look at these principles.

Absolute sovereignty and noninterference must be recognized today as at best necessary evils, because they prevent the inevitable abuse of interference and, thus, postpone war. They would be intolerable in a truly peaceful world order. For, by legal standards, the claims of absolute sovereignty and noninterference are identical with the claim to be entitled to commit wrongs. They imply readiness to violate treaties and to wage war whenever resort to such means is possible and profitable. The right to exercise a veto within the institutions that make decisions makes it impossible to subject the nations to a supranational legal principle. Noninterference prevents the spirit of legality from developing on an international basis. Just as every citizen of one state must feel personally wronged by any injustice done another citizen elsewhere in it, so every state must regard every wrong done to a citizen of another state as a wrong done to itself. Neither a state nor a community of states can subsist if the citizens are indifferent toward wrongs done to others. Those states which exercise terroristic violence against their subjects thereby violate their internal peaceful order, and threaten the peace of the world as well, because they are always ready to extend such violence over all mankind. Equality of rights makes peace impossible if it implies equal rights to act arbitrarily. Those who reject mutual control, who permit no free exchange of news and ban the free public discussion of all questions in their own states, and who do not tolerate the struggle among parties for decision by free elections, prove that they strive to assert themselves unconditionally, although they cannot show this openly without danger to themselves.

7. *The Breathing Space*

So long as the plan for a treaty abolishing the atom bomb and establishing international control has not moved forward, so long as the way to a world order has not actually been embarked upon, we face extreme alternatives: it seems that our present situation must lead either to a world order or to a world war and the probable destruction of mankind.

All that political leaders are doing for peace today is nothing but trying to gain time. Such efforts have always produced respites—valuable breathing spaces —in the continual advance of evil. Today, more is at stake. If the present respite, merely one respite in the

march toward ever-threatening war, does not become definitive, mankind is probably doomed, and history as we conceive of it at an end.

8. *What Does the Public Think?*

Let us see what is going on in the realm of public opinion and expression.

The behavior of the scientists reveals helplessness. Einstein, who induced Roosevelt to produce the atom bomb from fear that Hitler and the German physicists might produce it first, warned the world after the war that it was doomed if it continued to follow along this path. But once the intelligence of scientists and technologists has been set in motion, and enormous resources placed at their disposal, a well-intentioned warning can scarcely change anything. As skilled workers the scientists have become instruments of the state power, which strives always to possess the most destructive instruments in order to be superior to its enemies. Some scientists have scruples of conscience; they hesitate; but most remain imprisoned in the technical tasks set before them. Unmindful of the whole, they do what they are asked. There is a gulf between the ingenuity of their technological work and the naïveté of their political thinking. Frightened by the mischief they have already brought about, they demand peace as a solution, while going right ahead with their labors. These highly intelligent men both do and do not want it; they behave like children, and then bemoan the tragedy.

Everywhere people are protesting. Proposals are advanced that the bomb as such be declared criminal. But just as societies of pacifists have not in the least contributed to the prevention of war, all efforts to condemn the atom bomb merely as such, without realizing its function within the actual behavior of nations and the obvious motives of most people, are vain and dangerous. For they do not go to the root of human evil; they do not go beyond the symptoms. Because they divert attention from the essentials they contribute to their obfuscation; nothing can be achieved by indignation and appeals. Behind this façade of opinions and emotions, whether the protestors are pacifists or not, they preserve the way of life, the kind of thinking, which taken as the ground of human reality, produces just such terrors in consequence. Adjurations based upon indignation and anxiety are essentially as untrue in this connection as in any other, serving merely to veil the actuality of life. But reality is ignorant of such meaningless opinions. For self-complacency is opposed by "the truth allied to reality" (Hegel). This means: For truth to be effective one must not deal with symptoms, but go to the roots, to the origin of the evil.

Finally, there are those who prefer to close their eyes to the danger. They say that no policy, no plans are possible under the threat of total disaster. We want to live, not to die: should the disaster come to pass, it will be the end of everything. It is pointless to think about it.

What a deliberately blind outlook, what a stultifying policy this is! To push aside possibility in this fashion offends the dignity of reason. A man who is himself wants to know what is knowable. Ineluctably, we stand today in the shadow of great disaster. To treat a real possibility, one that has by no means been fully explored, as if it would disappear were we to exclude it from consciousness, is to behave like the ostrich. Continually to keep that catastrophe before one's eyes as a possibility—indeed, as a probability— is today the only hope for reflection, for political renewal, for averting the catastrophe.

It would be pleasant to think: This catastrophe can never be; if it were possible, every government and every church would be proclaiming this fact daily. While it is true that every man must die, that nations too must pass, and that history records the irresistible destruction of the most magnificent things it has produced, yet mankind itself, the soil of life from which new life has always sprung, will not be destroyed. We should like to think that things won't be so bad as that; surely, somehow a way will be found to remove the threat of destruction.

But arguing against all such reassurances is the fundamental experience of life, of which every older man is aware today: the seemingly impossible has come true several times in his lifetime. We were sure that certain things were impossible, or that they would come to pass only in some remote future which would not affect us. But we have ourselves witnessed these things: the First World War with its consequence that Europe ceased to be the center of the world; National Socialism with its murder of six million Jews. In the nineteen twenties, when we first heard about atomic energy, it was as pure theory. We felt that such extraordinary insights were most interesting for their bearing upon our notions of matter; they seemed to have no practical significance. Today they are reality.

To those who draw comfort from the feeling that the catastrophe is impossible because it would be monstrous—extraordinary in the absolute sense of the term—because it lies so far beyond the bounds of our habitual thinking, it is necessary to point out in all seriousness: Why should it be impossible for mankind to be destroyed, and destroyed quite soon?

After all it is no more extraordinary than the fact that man produces cosmic energy, the very energy of the sun—here on earth by releasing it from the earth's matter.

The survival of man depends on our response, by our thoughts and deeds, to the real possibility. The situation creates a responsibility of which we can become aware only if we are completely sincere.

9. *The Ideal of a Moral and Political Conversion*

The foregoing considerations have been political: Inasmuch as mankind refuses to perish, the states will have to accept restrictions on their sovereign powers. What took place within limited areas when the original states were founded, must take place again: a voluntary association of states must be formed. The possibility of extreme disaster, which superior intelligence has brought about, is to be eliminated by a technique of institutional arrangements for the effective enforcement of treaties. If this could be done, mankind would not have to change. Intelligently devised institutions would, by the common will of all, prevent any individual from making malevolent use of man's fundamental impulses—his drive to violent acts, his pleasure in violence and recklessness, his drive to sacrifice himself in the pursuit of violence, to risk his life in conquest, his drive to go on and on to ever greater adventures, to escape the shallowness of actual existence. Under collective rule these impulses would have to be gratified in ways that do not imperil the whole of mankind.

But all this has not been achieved so far. Political considerations tending toward such a goal are certainly the right ones. We must never give up trying to follow that path—the only practicable one; here planning is possible, and perhaps we can make some headway. But it is not enough. We have to ask whether treaties and institutions suffice to get rid of evil. May they not, rather, develop into sham entities, behind which each state will simply go on strengthening its own power positions, preparing for the worst?

In the meantime, tremendous resources and the best minds available today are being used to increase the numbers and the effectiveness of atom bombs, to make total death more possible. The eventuality draws closer day by day and year by year. It was the Second World War that enabled this to come to pass. Such enormous sums of money would not have been spent on anything so problematical of accomplishment, so totally unprofitable over a long stretch of time; in America it was fear of Hitler that set the thing in motion. What keeps it going is that war is still possible. It will stop only when war itself becomes impossible—war, which has existed as long as mankind, and the end of which seems impossible precisely because human nature is what it is.

Malice and stupidity, hitherto limited in their consequences, are today dragging all mankind to its destruction. Unless we henceforward live all for one and each for all, we shall perish together. This unprecedented situation requires a response to scale.

The response was given long ago. It looks beyond politics, and it has often been repeated since the prophets of the Old Testament first daringly uttered it and passed it on to all future ages. Because it has so often been repeated in vain, sometimes seriously and sometimes unseriously over the centuries, many have become weary of it. Now, however, we must face the extraordinary challenge of an extraordinary situation urgently imposed: we must transform our outlook and our ways of thinking, our moral-political will.

An idea that has long been present in individuals, but has so far remained powerless, has become the condition of the survival of mankind. I believe I am not exaggerating. Those who go on living just as they lived before have not grasped the danger. Merely to conceive it intellectually does not mean that it has been absorbed into the reality of one's life. Without a change of heart the life of mankind is lost forever. To survive, man must change. If he thinks only of the moment, everything will come to an end, almost certainly, the day the atom war breaks out.

So long as the political forces do not reach far enough, no real change of motivations can be claimed. Man remains what he has always been: the same violence, ruthlessness, reckless bellicosity; the same love of ease and refusal to see clearly; the same need for repose and improvidence in those who enjoy security, who are always outwitted by the bold go-getters; the same shameless blackmailing and the same submissiveness to it; the same hiding of all behind legal arguments and a merely fictitious authority, which some despise in secret, and others regard as insuring their comfort, but which all join in throwing overboard at the moment of crisis.

We should cease taking life as a great adventure that ends in death, thus enhancing the attractiveness of the extraordinary, and stimulating the will to power and domination. And we should cease living in passivity, voicing our complaints and accusations from the sidelines.

The work of building, of shaping the environment, of attaining, for the present generation and for posterity, life's fulfillment in peaceful competition, in contemplation of the beautiful, and in thinking truth, ought not to be hindered by the disastrous race to destroy life's accomplishments. The situation in which the criminal acts of a small minority can be applauded by the multitude, which only too soon—but still too late—finds itself under the rule of terror, exploited and enslaved, must come to an end.

The change can only be brought about by each and every man in his own conduct of life: first within himself, and then in the realization that he is not alone. Every tiniest deed, every smallest word, every nuance of behavior among the millions and billions who are alive, is important. What takes place on the large and public scale is merely a symptom of that which is done in private by the many. Every action by every statesman must be judged by its fidelity to the spirit that alone can assure the survival of mankind. The statesman who makes a highly moral appeal at the conference table and then behaves disloyally at home, shares in the responsibility for the continuation of the evil he warns against. If in his official capacity he displays tolerance for the human and all-too-human, while careless in the conduct of his own life, he undermines the spirit of the whole upon which we all count. The man who strives to bring about the miracle of a moral transformation in all mankind and yet contributes with his whole intelligence to the essentially thoughtless continuation of the existing state of affairs—perhaps by recourse to statements that have become empty the better to veil the truth—that man casts suspicion on morality itself.

When everything that can be projected in thought moves into the political arena, something will surely happen that cannot be foreseen. At this point the question, What are we to do? can no longer be answered by directions as to how it is to be done: the question can only be answered by an appeal to slumbering possibilities. Conversion is not enforceable. All we can do is to point to realities and make articulate the voices that for centuries have been calling for a change of heart. All that men can know of the possibilities of the future should be incorporated in the curricula of our schools. Whether the individual will be affected thereby is a matter we must leave to the freedom of the young. Once the fundamental facts of our political existence today are made clear, and the consequences of the various modes of possible behavior have been developed, the answer is up to each individual, not as a matter of opinion, but in the full context of his life.

10. Political and Moral Considerations Are Insufficient

Politically, it has become clear that only world peace can remove the threat of the atom bomb. To imagine that it will eventually be possible to wage wars without recourse to the atom bomb, to use it merely as a deterrent, is a delusion.

However, since a state of world peace can scarcely be realized by political means alone, this idea inevitably arose: Man seems doomed unless he experiences an inner change through his freedom. But such a conversion cannot be the object of a new politics: it can only be the prerequisite of a new politics.

Thus, although the political solution appears meaningful, it will be futile unless it is supplemented by something more. But the moral solution does not lie within the scope of our planning. Hence it appears unreal to the political realist. The realist points to the nature of man as it has always been and always will be. He is absolutely pessimistic regarding the long range prospects (which can quickly become short range). He shapes his policies for the moment only. The moralist, on the other hand, basing his thought upon the idea of a future regeneration of mankind, raises unfulfillable demands. Because his thought goes beyond the present reality, he is not listened to.

We must continue our questioning. Is there anything that goes beyond both realism and moralism and endows both with effectiveness? Both realism and moralism are superficially correct; this correctness becomes truth only if they are guided by something that is subordinate to neither. Left to themselves, realism is solely concerned with the present moment—the attitude of wait and see—and idealism merely condemns events in the name of its demands. In this way both prove that they do not dare to face extreme possibilities.

Political and moralistic thinking has forgotten the meaning of risking one's life, of dying, of sacrifice. The task of politics is to make life secure. This task demands sacrifices. But it leaves unanswered the question as to what sacrifice and death mean in themselves. For they can never be adequately justified in worldly terms.

The something without which both realism and moralism ring hollow eludes precise formulation. The question bearing on it is answered by the religious doctrines and the so-called beliefs or convictions that serve as substitutes for religion and are put forward as though taken for granted in public expression. The realists operate with the idea of an inevitable course of history (whether they conceive of it along Hegelian, Marxist, Spenglerian, or other lines). The moralists assume that in the end justice and truth will triumph (even though they continually commit unacknowledged violations of both justice and truth). Such fundamental beliefs, crystallized into conventions, produce an atmosphere of unreasoned confidence. But the fact that such confidence exists at all is evidence that we must look beyond realistic politics and idealistic morality to the other thing, the ground of all. Our theme, the atom bomb, leads us to this limit by way of the question most disquieting to our conscience: if man's action can result in the total destruction of mankind is it absolutely evil? Has the venture of a life a limit? Ought we to renounce the atom bomb, even before we have achieved world peace, to renounce it unconditionally, before there is international control of the production of atomic energy? Is it possible that we must return to the spirit of Einstein's decision when, under the threat of Hitler's totalitarian domination of the world, he advised in favor of producing the atom bomb? Is it possible that the decision taken at that time was at bottom taken in unawareness of the consequences, and that it faces us again in a new, more conscious form?

11. A Possible Alternative

This question cannot be answered by an analysis of possible events, but only in the conscience of him who will act or fail to act at the moment of crisis. It is this: Can there be a situation which might justify the use of the atom bomb for political or moral reasons?

In effect, the answer to this question is given today only too clearly: namely, that in given circumstances the bomb will be used. For the production of atom bombs is not condemned unconditionally, but only on the condition of mutual control. Moreover, it would be a mistake to think that we are dealing with a mere threat or with threats that cancel each other out. A threat that is not meant seriously is not a threat.

Should we endorse this actual answer, or should we condemn the atom bomb as such, unilaterally, even in the absence of controls, on the ground that it signifies, not just war, but the destruction of mankind?

Before going further we must characterize the political situation. Within the shadow of the atom bomb the danger grows that the totalitarian powers will rob the world of freedom. In a war waged with masses of men and the old weapons, with all technological resources short of the atom bomb, the totalitarian powers would be victorious today. In such a war, therefore, events would reach a point where the free states would be faced with the question: Are we to use the atom bomb or to accept totalitarianism? To risk the destruction of mankind or to give up our freedom? In view of our failure to outlaw the atom bomb by means of mutual control, protection of the free world by means of the old weapons would mean the continual sacrifice of the population in the form of military training and preparations for war. In view of the further failure to organize a politically reliable union of the free states, the moment can very well come, probably very suddenly, when to use or not to use the atom bomb will have to be decided by whatever men are then in power through the ordinary conditions and mechanisms of political ascension. It will then be too late for anything else.

To be sure, everyone agrees that the atom bomb must be abolished. But there is no agreement on this rarely discussed question: What are we to do when the life or death of freedom is at stake? If the atom bomb were resorted to very often, it would probably —though not certainly—destroy all life. However, loss of freedom as a result of a totalitarian victory would make life not worth living—although we cannot be sure that this would be for all time to come. The atom bomb's threat to all life would thus be matched by the totalitarian threat to all freedom. A time of momentous decision may come—no one can make it in advance. But discussion of the problem of conscience it involves is meaningful, if we are not to be caught unawares. Thought in anticipation of future possibilities may influence the ultimate decision. At least we can learn what is at stake. Deceptively reassuring ideas may be unmasked. The extreme situation is disclosed in all its rigor, is shown to be unresolvable by finite thinking. Such a disclosure may influence even the present policies.

12. Is There Still Hope?

At this point we are once again confronted with the question of what constitutes the common ground of politics and morality and makes them meaningful? The question being unanswerable in terms of finite thinking, how is it possible to conceive of a course of action in which we can have confidence?

Every variety of false hope must be done away with. We have had it in all its guises, time and again. We Germans saw that the lawful order of free life could be destroyed overnight because the forces of resistance were far too insignificant. In the situation that arose suddenly our political leaders acted thoughtlessly. They did not know what was actually going on, they missed the essentials. Diverted by secondary issues, which were exaggerated out of all proportion, they allowed themselves to be driven by the dark forces and capitulated to them. The peace that we once knew for years on end—before 1914, and before 1933—twice proved deceptive. Is the cycle to be forever repeated?

Do we even grasp what was necessity in our irresistible fall into the abyss? Certain factors in our hopeless headlong plunge were clear to us long ago, as well as the opposite possibilities of a magnificent forward development toward a richer life.

The rational man refuses to recognize such factors as inevitable. Schematic views which threaten or reassure need not necessarily fetter us; they may underline the fact that our future partly depends on ourselves, even though we cannot know how our deeds affect the larger course of events.

This is the appeal to our reason, but reason in all its range and depth, which includes good will. This reason is the only and ultimate thing on which we can base ourselves.

Therefore we must forgo every variety of hope that diverts us from this crucial recognition:

For instance, can we hope to find a technological escape from the technological evil on the general grounds that each new danger automatically creates new means of escape? Can we hope to escape into outer space? Can we gain a foothold on some as yet uninhabited planet? No, such fantasies reflect the arrogance of technological overconfidence. Even if such extremely improbable possibilities should one day come true, they are more remote than the imminent threat of atomic destruction.

Or can we have confidence in spontaneous, unforeseen, quasi-magical, sudden changes in the history of mankind, of life on earth, of the universe? In salvation by the intervention of the transcendent at the moment of catastrophe? No, for even if some such thing were possible, our expectation of it could not be made a motive for action; it would be madness.

Or does it make sense to expect new prophets to appear, divine revelations to be given, to raise the moral energy of mankind to a higher level? No, even if such events were possible on the basis of abstract intellectual analogies, they are nevertheless inconceivable to us. To entertain false expectations of such events would be very dangerous. For we cannot act meaningfully in expectation of the unintelligible. Such an expectation would make us prisoners of our own deception, and as a result we would throw away such opportunities as are actually open to us.

Today, defense against total evil depends solely on

our real actions, on our present reason. We can act and plan responsibly only on the basis of known data and guided by rational ideals. To be rational we must have confidence in human reason. Are we justified in trusting it? If this confidence may be put in question by our awareness of how irrational we often are, by the predominance of unreason and anti-reason in the majority of men, experience also teaches us how reason is awakened and how it can grow. While we cannot rely safely on mankind's rational responses, nevertheless everything good occurs in the confidence that rational men do respond to reason.

But what if this confidence, too, fails? We cannot accept the final defeat of reason by the superior strength of anti-reason. To be sure, human existence will in some very remote time probably come to an end as a result of cosmic processes. But today men themselves can bring about that end by their own unreason. This leads us to the question: What do we think of such a possibility? What form does hope take, when even confidence in reason is shaken?

Total destruction was often mentioned by the ancient prophets. The "day of Yahweh" will come when everything will be destroyed. The early Christians spoke of an impending end of the world. Today, such perspectives have once again become unavoidable, this time in consequence of technological developments. Except for those who live thoughtlessly from day to day, they must once again become the central preoccupation of our life.

Even though we cannot safely rely on reason in men, is there nonetheless some basis left for confidence? When despair says: Nothing avails—let us not think about it—let us live for the present—what lies in store for us is death in any case—is this really the last word, is there really nothing left after that? No, was Jeremiah's reply to his despairing disciple Baruch, when the state and the nation and even the religion of the Jews, become worshipers of Isis, lay in ruins: "The Lord saith thus; Behold, that which I have built will I break down, and that which I have planted I will pluck up. . . . And seekest thou great things for thyself? seek them not: for, behold, I will bring evil upon all flesh." What Jeremiah meant was that God is enough.

This, and this only, is the ultimate horizon, in the perspective of which everything falls into its right place. It is here that courage grows out of confidence in the ultimate ground of Being, which no worldly shipwreck can destroy, not even the shipwreck of reason. Then wings are given to the will, our will to achieve, to venture, to see purpose in the process of building within human existence so long as human existence lasts, even if we do not know how long our achievements will endure.

Reason teaches us that it is not courageous to pass judgments on the final end and the inevitable decline. It is only courageous to do that which is possible, in knowledge and non-knowledge, and never to give up hope as long as one lives.

Nor is it a courageous philosophy, but rather a petrifying one, to look on at the allegedly certain decline until it swallows one up. It takes courage to be shaken to one's depths, and to learn what the extreme situation reveals.

To us it is left to regard the splendor of the world, to love men, to keep hold of the present so long as it is granted us. In our love for one another we become aware of our origin and of eternity. Here is the ground and assurance of our hope, which will enable us to live in our world by reason, not merely by finite understanding, but by reason in the broadest sense of the word, and to direct our thoughts, impulses, efforts, beginning with our own everyday life, toward averting the final disaster that threatens.

For if we, if everyone, if some of us, not only now and again, but with our whole lives, come to reason; if this reason, once kindled among some of us, spreads like a purifying flame—only then may we hope to overcome the threatening total disaster.

Translated by Norbert Guterman

►► Kenneth Koch

Desire for Spring

Calcium days, days when we feed our bones!
Iron days, which enrich our blood!
Saltwater days, which give us valuable iodine!
When will there be a perfectly ordinary spring day?
For my heart needs to be fed, not my urine
Or my brain, and I wish to leap to Pittsburgh
From Tuskegee, Indiana, if necessary, spreading like a flower
In the spring light, and growing like a silver stair.
Nothing else will satisfy me, not even death!
Not even broken life insurance policies, cancer, loss of health,
Ruined furniture, prostate disease, headaches, melancholia,
No, not even a ravaging wolf eating up my flesh!
I want spring, I want to turn like a mobile
In a new fresh air! I don't want to hibernate
Between walls, between halls! I want to bear
My share of the anguish of being succinctly here!
Not even moths in the spell of the flame
Can want it to be warmer so much as I do!
Not even the pilot slipping into the great green sea
In flames can want less to be turned into an icicle!
Though admiring the icicle's cunning, how shall I be satisfied
With artificial daisies and roses, and wax pears?
O breeze, my lovely, come in, that I mayn't be stultified!
Dear coolness of heaven, come swiftly and sit on my chairs!

►► André Pieyre de Mandiargues

Childishness

For some time, a long time now, Jean de Juni had been toiling over a girl with dyed-blond hair whom he had approached in the street for this purpose, taken by the hand, led to the hotel, pushed ahead of him from the doorway to the desk and to the foot of the staircase between walls of pink and black tile, then up the red-carpeted steps, before making her enter a bedroom where the shutters were closed by iron bars permanently fixed deep in the wood, as if across a cell window in some ancient lunatic asylum. Outside, the sun prevailed oppressively, turning the stones fiery, the asphalt soft. There was no one in the streets where just before there had been only a dazed girl and Jean de Juni. Not a dog, not a cat, not a bird, not even a rat or a little mouse among the rubbish of the market place. It would be late afternoon before the first human noises could be heard in the streets, along with the strident sound of the shop-grilles being raised and the clatter of the water buckets that would be used to cool off the sidewalks in front of grocery stores. The hotel, like the city, was silent, dedicated to the siesta. The clerk, scarcely rousing himself to hand over the key, must have gone back to sleep on the couch behind the desk.

The girl's attitude and conduct were on the whole similar to those of a big doll made of some elastic material, had a doll been subjected to the same operation. She did not speak, she did not move any more than a doll would have, and her eyes stayed obstinately shut beneath the short bangs, in the hollow of the pillow into which her face had sunk rather deep. If the girl wasn't asleep too, it would have been no different if she were. Furthermore, Jean de Juni did not attempt to draw words from a witless mouth, nor to provoke signs of emotion which would have given him only the annoyance of having to respond. He arched the upper part of his body a little and rested one elbow on the hard bolster, above the pillow, holding his chin in his hand in order not to press with all his weight on the patient girl beneath him; unless, without so much courtesy, he assumed this position to limit to the indispensable, that is, to the lower areas, the points of contact between his body and his partner's. The noise of the bed sounded like a printing press, but one in an old-fashioned printshop that might have run off some local gazette, in the south or on an island, with typography of an oddly modern-style face. By its very perseverance and regularity, this sound, again recalling that of a machine, managed to become a part of the silence. Rather than disturbing the sleep of the hotel's occupants, it must have soothed them, and perhaps they would awaken when they no longer heard it. Jean de Juni felt himself capable of continuing until nightfall, in order to prolong his neighbors' siesta in the surrounding rooms, on condition that the girl persisted in her indifference and her apathy. "I'm making love," he told himself with no satisfaction, at a certain point. And he thought how inadequate the little sentence was, its laughable modesty giving no indication whatever to an ignorant listener or an uninitiated reader of the task virility had set itself. French, Spanish, or Italian would have furnished him with briefer, more expressive forms whose sense is generally that of thrusting in a tool or, better still, pounding home a nail. Then was he working at driving a nail (his nail) into this girl? He would have answered no, that it was more of a question of something like the slow passage across a warm sea on an old piston-driven steamer, the S.S. *Eros*, the archipelago mailboat, flying, as well it might, the blue and white flag inherited by Greece from the royal house

of Bavaria. The air in this shuttered room perfectly recalled the oily smell of the ship's corridor, the smell of lice in the woodwork of the cabins below decks. And as for love?

Well, love, a giant of salt raised in limitless expectation, a crystalline colossus shaped like a mantis, an empusa, a white statue loftier than the highest Himalayan peak, a terrifying personage creating its own solitude, "Above all," Jean de Juni thought, "I hope I never meet love; even in dreams I hope it never turns its hideous, flat, triangular head toward me; I hope I shall never be subject to its greedy gaze!" Then he smiled at such alarms without having interrupted his pumping nor hastened or retarded its rhythm. The girl's eyelids had remained closed, and she did not know that he had smiled; she was unaware he had imagined this monster.

The word in other forms, as a verb, for instance, was related to images and objects that were not so formidable. It suggested oily water, almost stagnant and rather tepid. Doubtless Jean de Juni had loved his mother, whose memory remained linked to a certain mauve dressing gown she wore in the morning, and he still remembered a swamp tortoise, or, as it was called, a mudder, that had been bought for him from an old man who was selling them in front of the Cathedral porch of Modena. With the others crawling around at the bottom of a basket, his tortoise must have been caught in the canals of the Po. It was an extremely large male which little Jean de Juni fed with strips of raw meat, preferably chicken or veal, or else liver, and which he cared for with a tenderness whose mysterious origin was somehow identified with the name "mudder" which the dictionary had revealed to him. The tortoise had escaped into the *campagna*, profiting from a command shouted to Jean de Juni that he go make his bow to some visitors, one afternoon, and then, a few days later, how horrible it was! he had recognized its lovely black and yellow carapace in some scraps scattered by the roadside, crushed under the wheel of a truck perhaps, if not by bricks (there were some fragments nearby) thrown by some cruel child.

To a child, other children are the executioners of everything he loves.

Yet the worst moment of his life, all the same, had been when he witnessed the butchering of a hog he had adopted on a mountain farm in Switzerland. Whenever he disappeared and they came to look for him, that summer, he could always be found in front of the little sty where the animal lived, adjoining the farmer's chalet. He brought the creature rapseed and potatoes, hard pears and all kinds of garbage, amazed by its prodigious gluttony. Then the day of its death had come, and the farmer, despite the child's entreaties and tears, had refused, of course, to spare it. Laughing besides, explaining that the animal had reached the desired point for meat and lard, and that any delay would cost a lot of money. So Jean de Juni had decided he would watch this hog die, since it was not within his power to save it.

Less tragically, more dimly, he also remembered loving an axolotl during the last years of his childhood. The pudgy little batrachian, muffled in its own gills like some precious and indecent pink foliage, clumsily maneuvering among the aquarium plants, diving to the bottom to dig a worm out of the mud, rising to gulp down the mites he tossed on the surface of the water, had given him long moments of happiness before giving him the grief of its death. Since then, as well as he could remember, Jean de Juni had not loved anyone or anything again. Strangely, death had pillaged his childhood with a kind of fury, and then, the plunder made, had seemed to turn away from those around him in order to make all its raids on other circles. Perhaps the reason for this was that for a very long time he had had around him only creatures and objects he regarded with such indifference that it was as if he were living in complete solitude, absolute penury, as if he had chosen some eremitic discipline.

And now, once more after so many other times, here he was, as the phrase had it, "thinking about his dead." "I've chosen a funny moment for it," he reminded himself.

For he was still pumping with the same imperturbable rhythm, as exact at that of a Swiss clock, as if a mechanism had been set in his loins to measure by the tempo of his thrusts the erosion of life and the approach of that death which he had just evoked with a touch of humor. He realized that these measurements were of an equivalent importance for the girls as well, and that (did she know it?) what they were doing together had the curious property of aligning each of their tempi against the other's in imitation of their superimposed bodies, until the instant, doubtless still far off, when the mechanism would stop by itself and the coincidence cease. It was of no consequence whatever that the girl refused or neglected to participate in the movement, since she submitted to it and since either by consent or by force she felt the regular strokes of the controlling organism. Jean de Juni thought how she was the matrix of this common tempo of theirs, and how he was playing the part of the die punch. Thus the machine was well defined; it could function, with the help of the gods, until the end of time itself. The word matrix carried no connotation for him, as it

should have, of a possible birth. In truth, the past and death prevailed upon him so tyrannically that life, in his meditation, reduced itself to its own decay, and he gave no heed to the future.

He wondered whether it was with a prostitute that he was beguiling the passage of the hours. Without being able to decide, for if she had followed him docilely enough at his first invitation, and if she had agreed to come to the hotel and walk upstairs into a bedroom with him, there had not once come up between them the question of the "little present." Nor of anything else, furthermore, no more of what they were about to do (of what they were doing now) than of hunger, or thirst, or of satiety, of sadness, of gaiety, or of eternal damnation. Judging her character from the reactions she displayed, it was not unjust to see in his partner a creature infinitely approaching nullity, furnished with an agreeably irregular little face, all the same, with a firm body and a smooth epidermis. What more could he hope for in such an adventure? He thought again (the case being a little less ordinary than that of a prostitute) that perhaps he was dealing with a victim of sunstroke, or with a girl so stupefied by the heat that she was no longer capable of walking by herself, of protecting herself. The cities of the south, when everyone takes his siesta and the streets are empty, provide such prey as a recompense for the wolf that persists in hunting despite the heat and the sultriness. He recalled many such encounters, and how he had exploited them.

Later, his thoughts blurred. His mind tended toward a kind of zero point, as if for some mystical union with his companion's nullity. This point was situated rather precisely in space; it was in front of him, to the left, on the copper ball that decorated the enameled iron bedpost here as at the other three corners. The bed being in the corner, Jean de Juni had walls on his right and in front of him, the window on his left, slightly behind. His sense of position resisted a while before leaving him, a last lamp blown out (and the smoke sucked up by the wind), but disappeared at last, and our man was nothing more than rhythm, active trepidation, the sound of a spring mattress dominating a silent country, a movement of loins coming and going in the half-light.

Now the sun, outside, had reached the hotel's façade. When it struck the shutter, a nick close to the hinge let in a ray of light that made a luminous spot on the wall in the shape of a banana or a scythe blade. Jean de Juni paid no attention, absorbed as he was in body by his pumping and in mind by his vacancy point, and he also did not notice that this sickle of light was very slowly changing position and moving nearer the bed. Suddenly it reached the gilded copper ball which immediately glowed beneath his unconscious eyes; it was like a flare which burst within his memory and awakened it, illuminating and reviving recollections so remote they had not occurred to him for thirty years or more. Passing over the copper (which might just as well have cast him among the Cyprian antiquities), he recognized a great ball which was a bouquet of mountain buttercups, carefully rounded and held in two hands on a long black skirt, before a severe blouse closed at the neck with a little garnet brooch, and behind the bouquet, above the brooch he found the face of his nurse Nina, whom he had called Criticona, in imitation of his mother, ever since the first words he had stammered and until the beginning of his age of forgetfulness and unreason. Nina Criticona, the old Triestine governess, whom he had loved, he remembered it perfectly, more than his parents, more than his tortoise, more than that hog, and more than his axolotl! Nina who adored him even while she scolded him, and who, in the vain hope of making him put on weight, cooked him rose jellies in the Dalmatian fashion.

Everything fell into place again, starting from the yellow sphere, as if there had been an electromagnet inside, and once the current was on the fragments of a great mobile dial mounted on iron legs had leaped into position and were beginning to function, each attached to another by magnetic attraction. Jean de Juni, without ceasing to be a kind of metronome beating time against the impassible girl's belly, and without once losing track of what he was doing, saw again the child he had been, three years old perhaps, four at the most, a child whom he had believed as completely obliterated from his own memory as from anyone else's (excepting Nina's, if she was not dead). A sickly child, looking still thinner because of the long chestnut curls that reached almost to his shoulders, wearing a white velvet overcoat and an ermine bonnet more like a woman's or a girl's hat than any boy's, his legs encased in pale-green woolen stockings that made him look, according to old Criticona, like a marsh bird she called "Sir Dotterel." Another avatar: he discovered himself in this child, and when he lifted his head it was through those childish eyes that he contemplated Nina Criticona's somewhat leonine, tender face, her blue gaze, both sad and gay at once, her round, palely mottled cheeks, her gray hair beneath a black plush hat fastened to her bun by jade hatpins. She was keeping a close watch on him, careful that he did not play too near the edge of the road behind which the ground fell steeply away, and that he did not fall a victim to the clumsiness habitual to the scions of very rich families.

For they were together on a road leading down the mountainside from the village where they visited the little shops, one expensive, one cheap, passing before the rest home where they were staying, winding sharply before joining the highway at the bottom of the valley. It had rained all night, all the day before, and the only place that was at all dry was this turn in the road, a natural balcony or landing worked into the mountain, with a bench on the stony ground where you could sit and look at the view. Nina Criticona, whenever the weather was clear enough, led the *bambino* in her charge up here. She had persuaded him, perhaps to make him take more exercise, that their walks must always furnish some windfall, at least a bouquet, worthy of being enshrined in their bedroom, and on the way home, disregarding the municipal placards in defense of the alpine flora, they rarely refrained from picking flowers.

As for this last word "flowers," still fresh from childhood despite so many years wasted in a life of trivial debauch, Jean de Juni would have liked to hide it away, and with a powerful movement of his loins he thrust it deep into the oozing bowels of the girl beneath him, who did not even wince, though the brutality of the stroke nearly broke the rhythm she was patiently enduring. But it was too late to return to a reality so commonplace; the old images triumphed all down the line. Again he saw the curve in the road where he had played as a child, again saw the pebbles of the slope down which the seepages had washed the loose soil into the stream, and in the stream itself, on a bank of black sand or mud, he saw what looked like a bed of slender, yellow-flowered asparagus, which were actually tussilagos, still without their broad leaves that come after the flowers and which account for the plant's common name of "coltsfoot." He saw the pinkish cowslips clustered at the foot of the slope on a rich mound, the brilliant green of their leaves spreading over the wet soil. While he was poking among them with the tip of a tiny horn-handled cane (the horn was chamois, silver-ringed), bought for him in the expensive shop, Criticona had stood up from the bench, leaving behind her umbrella and her workbag, but taking up the bouquet they had picked and which a breath of wind might have blown away. The child crossed the road. He was near her, beneath the bunch of buttercups, and she was holding him with her other hand because they were at the cliff's edge.

A few curves farther down, between the larches that were beginning to turn green again, a big covered cart drawn by a team of oxen was climbing toward them with a calm power that seemed to unroll the road like a ribbon, smoothing it out as they advanced before leaving it behind to trail all the way down to the valley floor. The cart would disappear and come into view again two or three times before reaching the top, it would turn, pressing close against the slope, it would continue at the same lumbering pace until it reached the village, and would not stop there. "It's a Piedmontese wagon," Criticona had said. "Poor people coming from the other side of the mountains to work on the new dam. They live under that canvas roof with their wives and their children, their animals too, dogs and maybe chickens. The cart is their house, like the gypsies. It's better for them than the cabins in the construction camps, and they don't have to pay the builders." A very dark man was guiding the team, walking ahead of the oxen and occasionally touching one or the other with a long stick, speaking to them in a voice whose rough accent and gentle intonation could be heard despite the noise of the waterfalls.

Little Jean de Juni could not take his eyes off this man leading the great horned beasts. "A Piedmontese," he repeated after Criticona, to fix the mysterious name in his head and to be sure not to forget it. The man was wearing a rather dirty red shirt, open despite the cold air to show a tanned chest, and a black handkerchief around his neck; his wild hair was a dazzling black. Little Jean thought he should describe this man to Criticona, who did not see very well even with glasses, so she could share his admiration; then he decided he would say nothing and keep the marvelous spectacle for himself. Nevertheless he resisted his governess who was trying to pull him away from the edge. Then the terrible thing happened (which left on the child's mind an indelible impression, since it would re-emerge down to the least detail, like a lithograph sprinkled with water, so many years after the event).

This is how it was. At the end of the wooded zone, the Piedmontese wagon had entered an area where there were larches and brushwood above the road only, and stunted besides, while the slope below ran almost vertically downward for over a hundred yards. A stream fell which in normal weather a few gutters made of hollow logs almost managed to contain, but which was everywhere overflowing after the recent showers. The roadway was dark in color, without visible pebbles or gravel, probably consisting of many seasons' deposit of rotten pine needles. Little Jean de Juni, when the wagon was at the narrowest point of the dark passage between the slope and the precipice,

saw that one of the oxen, the one pulling on the left, had suddenly shied and was throwing itself against its yokefellow as if it had gone wild. The creature had felt the ground, saturated by the overflowing gutters, give way beneath its weight; it was trying to gain a surer foothold and doubtless would have succeeded, aided by the other, which had instinctively understood the danger, if the team had been alone or yoked to a less clumsy, lighter load. But when the lumbering vehicle's wheels reached the place where the stream's cleft was, the ground caved in altogether, as if it had been mined. Then little Jean saw the wagon's hood wobble and capsize completely, and the wagon, sliding backwards, fell over the edge with the crumbled earth while the whole shaft rose up into the air, carrying the poor oxen with it, moving their heads and feet ridiculously for a moment, like great beetles wriggling in agony on a pin. There were no cries or bellowings; the waterfalls' racket had drowned them out, if there had been any. The black man, the leader, was safe. He had thrown himself flat on his face, he was rolling over the ground, it looked as if he were biting it. Then the child could no longer see, a slightly roughened hand covered his eyes. "Little Jean, don't look," Nina Criticona said. "You are too young to see death."

Jean de Juni continued to pump as he might have winnowed grain or broken stones, the rhythmic brutality of the operation leaving his imagination free rein. He thought how he had just lived again (or rather seen again in imagination, which is almost the same thing) the earliest episode to leave a mark on his deepest consciousness. The notion of a "first memory" is curious, forever disturbing to reflection. Jean de Juni had the idea, suggested perhaps by his old Criticona's words and her affectionately protective gesture, that the ring of his existence was within an inch of closing ("a slipknot!" he mused), and that he would find himself in danger of death if he slackened his labor or failed to distribute its regular pulsations with the same exactitude. This idea soon vanished, but it had still further attenuated (if that was possible) the long travail of love.

The gilded copper ball opposite him was still shining in the sunbeam with as much brilliance as before, while his loins were moving mechanically, driving up and down the flail (or the stonebreaker's hammer) with the same force still, and in the proper cadence. Instead of drawing closer to an erotic pleasure, he knew that he was moving from it now, as if the old Greek steamer evoked at the beginning of his revery had changed its course in order to return to its port of embarkation. At the same time Jean de Juni was vaguely satisfied, he had to admit, that there was no longer any question of attaining such pleasure, nor of landing in that wearisome country which was its destination. He attempted to revive the terrifying memory (which was already less so), and again recalled, voluntarily this time, the catastrophe on the mountain road. As he attempted to reconstruct it, and the Piedmontese wagon and the oxen falling together into the chasm were reconstituted before his eyes, he felt singularly exalted, experiencing (without being able to account for it in any other reasonable way except by some play of equilibriums, the operation of a pair of balances) a kind of grandiose elevation, glorious, even solar, sustained neither more nor less than his childhood climbs up a haystack or a heap of stones had been by Nina Criticona's firm hand. During this radiant course that lifted him high on the recoil from the accident into the very heaven of his childhood, the rather leonine features of his governess etched themselves as if superimposed, with unmistakable clarity, upon the face of the sun. Jean de Juni discovered once more the benevolent expression that was habitually in her eyes when she looked at him, and was moved as he had not been for a long, long time. Was this, finally, love? "Father sun . . ." he said in a very low voice, at the moment when the old nurse's countenance totally eclipsed the globe of fire.

So high did he feel that he let his arms bend a moment, since there was no longer any need for support, and his chest fell against the girl's breasts. She opened her eyes and seeing how remote he was, called to him as if she wanted him closer to her. "Come," she said to him, "haven't you gone far enough? Where do you think you're heading for, galloping hard enough to break down your poor horsey? Stop and come here now. Stop, get down, put your head on my shoulder, rest a little. You need it, and I'm worn out too." But he did not hear what she was saying, and she had become invisible to him, although she was directly beneath his gaze. He had stiffened his arms again, his whole body was rigid and in a state of utter insensibility, his mind entirely free of that obsession with death which habitually dominated him and left the haggard man in peace only when his steps led him to this questionable adventure, this disreputable hotel bedroom, this delusive bed. A dreamer recalled (perhaps afflicted with some tetanic infection), he found himself at the zenith of a clear sky and mounting still higher, proceeding toward a warm good sun which was also the face of Nina Criticona, leaning on a support which was the hand she gave him as she used to in the past. The girl was silent now, she had closed her eyes again, patient as before since it was impossible to have the least communication with him. Although she had been, on the whole, the instrument of his ecstasy, he had quite forgotten her, flung her back into the shadow with the vanished wagon, and the persistent rhythm of his loins henceforth had no other purpose than to bear him always further and higher into this admirable recovered purity, this sky, this luminous crystal where there was nothing to fear unless the sun should withdraw. "Criticona, old Criticona, don't leave me alone . . ." he repeated softly, like a child about to fall asleep.

Translated by Richard Howard

FRANZ KLINE, *Corinthian* (1958)

►► Frank O'Hara

Franz Kline Talking

[FRANK O'HARA: *Franz Kline's is one of the most out-standing achievements in contemporary painting. As a leader of the movement which is frequently called "American-type painting" abroad and is described as Abstract Expressionism or Action Painting here, his work embodies those qualities of individuality, daring and grandeur which have made the movement a powerful influence. The painters of this movement, so totally different from each other in aspect, so totally without the look of a school, have given us as Americans an art which for the first time in our history we can love and emulate, aspire to and understand, without provincial digression or prejudice. The Europeanization of our sensibilities has at last*

been exorcized as if by magic, an event of some violence which Henry James would have hailed as eagerly as Walt Whitman and which allows us as a nation to exist internationally. We have something to offer and to give besides admiration on the one hand and refuge on the other.

Kline's role in this achievement has been a compelling one. His work does not represent an esthetic "stand" for or against a past or present style, nor has he sought the absolute of a pure esthetic statement. These personages which are at the same time noble structures (Cardinal, Elizabeth, Siegfried), these structures which are at once tragic personages (Wanamaker Block, Bridge, C & O), seem both to

FRANZ KLINE
Photo by James Mitchell

express and to live by virtue of the American dream of power, that power which shuns domination and subjection and exists purely to inspire love.

Kline's studio is high-ceilinged and light and bare, with tall north windows facing on West 14th Street from the second floor. It is a floor through, and the south windows (French) give onto a terrace which is the roof of the store beneath (or is it a bar?). At the edge of this terrace, which has only two sun chairs and is bare like the studio, a little forest of trees-of-heaven partly hides a small tin building, apparently the rear of a 13th Street restaurant. Inside again, there are three or four painting walls of various sizes and early and recent paintings are stacked casually about. To see some of the paintings shown at the Egan Gallery in the late forties and early fifties is to take part in one of art's great dramas, the reaffirmation of value, a drama which has the added poignance of meeting again someone you once loved and who is more beautiful than ever. Near them are several recent works employing more color; side by side with the earlier works they state the inexorability of change in the environment of truly living forms: "This is our life yesterday, this our life today." Kline is one of those lighthouses toward which Baudelaire directed our gaze: what is thrilling is that they are shining here, in our very time.

He is an ardent conversationalist but in his studio he is quiet. Everything is clear there, as it is at his exhibitions. We went to my place for the talk which follows.]

FRANZ KLINE: That's Bill's isn't it? Terrific! You can always tell a de Kooning, even though this one doesn't look like earlier ones or later ones. It's not that style has a particular look, it just adds up. You become a stylist, I guess, but that's not it.

Somebody will say I have a black-and-white style, or a calligraphic style, but I never started out with that being consciously a style or attitude about painting. Sometimes you do have a definite idea about what you're doing—and at other times it all just seems to disappear. I don't feel mine is the most modern, contemporary, beyond-the-pale, gone kind of painting. But then, I don't have that kind of fuck-the-past attitude. I have very strong feelings about individual paintings and painters past and present.

Now, Bonnard at times seems styleless. Someone said of him that he had the rare ability to forget from one day to another what he had done. He added the next day's experience to it, like a child following a balloon. He painted the particular scene itself: in form, the woman can't quite get out of the bathtub. And he's a real colorist. The particular scene itself?

Matisse wouldn't let that happen, he didn't let himself get too entranced with anything.

In Braque and Gris, they seemed to have an idea of the organization beforehand in their mind. With Bonnard, he is organizing in front of you. You can tell in Léger just when he discovered how to make it like an engine, as John Kane said, being a carpenter, a joiner. What's wrong with that? You see it in Barney Newman too, that he knows what a painting should be. He paints as he thinks painting should be, which is pretty heroic.

What with the drying and all, you can tell immediately pretty much whether a painting was done all at once or at different intervals. In one Picasso you can see it was all immediate, spontaneous, or in another that he came back the next day and put on the stroke that completed it. Sometimes you get one of those dark Ryders; it's the top one and it's all spontaneous and immediate, done all at once, and there are seven or eight others underneath it you can't tell about.

Now I'm not saying that doing it all at once implies an idea of the organization beforehand or that you like it when it's done all at once or that you like it when you've had the idea before you began. You instinctively like what you can't do. I like Fra Angelico. I used to try all the time to do those blue eyes that are really blue. Someone once told me to look at Ingres. I loved Daumier and Rembrandt at the time and I was bored when I looked at Ingres. Before long I began to like it. You go through the different phases of liking different guys who are not like you. You go to a museum looking for Titian and you wind up looking at someone else. But the way of working before Cézanne is hidden. Cézanne is like an analyst and he seems to be right there, you can see him painting the side of a nose with red. Even though he wanted to paint like Velasquez.

They painted the object that they looked at. They didn't fit out a studio and start painting without a subject. I find that I do both. Hokusai painted Fuji because it was there. He and others remembered it and drew from their imagination of how they had tried to paint it when it was in front of them. When he paints Fuji with a brush—birds, mist, snow, etc.—it's not the photographic eye but his mind has been brought to the utter simplification of it, and that doesn't bring it into symbolism. With Hokusai it was more like Toulouse-Lautrec drawing dancers and wanting to draw like Degas who wanted to draw like Ingres. It has something to do with wanting to see people dance. Or like Rembrandt going to see Hercules Seghers' landscapes.

Malevitch is interesting to me. Maybe because you are able to translate through his motion the endless wonder of what painting could be, without describing an eye or a breast. That would be looking at things romantically, which painters don't do. The thing has its own appeal outside of the white-on-white, this-on-that idea. With Mondrian, in a way you see that the condition is that he's a guy who solves his own problems illogically. He's done it with paint illogically to himself—which makes it logical to some other people. I was at the studio of one of these people one day and he said he was going to put red in one of the squares to improve it and what did I think? I said try it out and see if you like it, not if it improves it.

There's this comedian I know in the borscht circuit. They had a theater group and everything up there and my friend asked me to go there and teach painting. I told him I didn't have the money to get there and he said he'd send it to me. I got up there and talked with this comedian. He had studied with Raphael Soyer and painted, but he never could sell anything, so he took this job as a comedian and never got back to painting. He loved Jackson Pollock and had such marvelous heart about it all that he could never have been popular at either painting or comedy. He cared so much. Somebody did an imitation of my drawing on a napkin, laughing, six lines, and said, "That's all there is to it." My friend said, "That's why I like it."

Then of course there are reviewers. I read reviews because they are a facet of someone's mind which has been brought to bear on the work. Although if someone's against it, they act as if the guy had spent his life doing something worthless.

Someone can paint *not* from his own time, not

FRANZ KLINE, *Elizabeth* (1957)

even from himself. Then the reviewer cannot like it, maybe. But just to review, like a shopper, I saw one this, one that, good, awful, is terrible. Or he may be hopelessly uninterested in what it is anyway, but writes about it. I read Leonard Lyons in the john the other day and he said every other country picked out the best art for the Venice Biennale, but we didn't. Then someone in the government went to Brussels and said painters should have to get a license for buying brushes. Lyons went on to say he hoped that there will be a day when abstractions are not supposed to be made for a child's playroom.

Criticism must come from those who are around it, who are not shocked that someone should be doing it at all. It should be exciting, and in a way that excitement comes from, in looking at it, that it's *not* that autumn scene you love, it's *not* that portrait of your grandmother.

Which reminds me of Boston, for some reason. You know I studied there for a while and once later I was up there for a show and met this Bostonian who thought I looked pretty Bohemian. His definition of a Bohemian artist was someone who could live where animals would die. He also talked a lot about the 8th Street Club and said that Hans Hofmann and Clem Greenberg run it, which is like Ruskin saying that Rowlandson and Daumier used up enough copper to clad the British Navy and it's too bad they didn't sink it. Why was he so upset about an artists' club in another city? You get classified as a New York painter or poet automatically. They do it in Boston or Philadelphia, you don't do it yourself.

Tomlin. In a way, they never did much about him and I think it's sad. He didn't start an art school, but he had an influence—his statements were very beautiful. When Pollock talked about painting he didn't usurp anything that wasn't himself. He didn't want to change anything, he wasn't using any outworn attitudes about it, he was always himself. He just wanted to be in it because he loved it. The response in the person's mind to that mysterious thing that has happened has nothing to do with who did it first. Tomlin, however, did hear these voices and in reference to his early work and its relation to Braque, I like him for it. He was not an academician of Cubism even then, he was an extremely personal and sensitive artist. If they want to talk about him, they say he was supposed to be Chopin. He didn't knock over any tables. Well, who's supposed to be Beethoven? Braque? I saw Tomlin's later work at the Arts Club in Chicago when he was abstract and it was the most exciting thing around—you look up who else was in the show.

If you're a painter, you're not alone. There's no way to be alone. You think and you care and you're with all the people who care, including the young people who don't know they do yet. Tomlin in his late paintings knew this. Jackson always knew it: that if you meant it enough when you did it, it will mean that much. It's like Caruso and Bjoerling. Bjoerling sounds like Caruso, but if you think of Caruso and McCormack you think of being in the world as you are. Bjoerling sounded like Caruso, but it turned out to be handsome. Bradley Tomlin didn't. Unless . . . Hell, if you look at all the painting in the world today it will probably all turn out to be handsome, I don't know.

The nature of anguish is translated into different forms. What has happened is that we're not through the analytical period of learning what motivates things. If you can figure out the motivation, it's supposed to be all right. But when things are "beside themselves" what matters is the care these things are given by someone. It's assumed that to read something requires an ability beyond that of a handwriting expert, but if someone throws something on a canvas it doesn't require any more care than if someone says, "I don't give a damn."

Like with Jackson: you don't paint the way someone, by observing your life, thinks you *have* to paint, you paint the way you have to in order to *give*, that's life itself, and someone will look and say it is the product of knowing, but it has nothing to do with knowing, it has to do with giving. The question about knowing will naturally be wrong. When you've finished giving, the look surprises you as well as anyone else.

Of course, this must be an American point of view. When Delacroix talks about the spirit, it must be French. It couldn't be Russian or Japanese. But writing his journals doesn't make him knowledgeable or practical. Delacroix was more interesting than that. That isn't the end in relation to his paintings. If it had been the end, people would have thought it interesting. Some people do think so.

Some painters talking about painting are like a lot of kids dancing at a prom. An hour later you're too shy to get out on the floor.

Hell, half the world wants to be like Thoreau at Walden worrying about the noise of traffic on the way to Boston; the other half use up their lives being part of that noise. I like the second half. Right?

To be right is the most terrific personal state that nobody is interested in.

►► **Daisetz T. Suzuki**

Aspects of Japanese Culture

1

When we look at the development of Japanese culture we find that Zen Buddhism has made many important contributions. The other schools of Buddhism have limited their sphere of influence almost entirely to the spiritual life of the Japanese people; but Zen has gone beyond it. Zen has entered internally into every phase of the cultural life of the people.

In China this was not necessarily the case. Zen united itself to a great extent with Taoist beliefs and practices and with the Confucian teaching of morality, but it did not affect the cultural life of the people so much as it did in Japan. (Is it due to the racial psychology of the Japanese people that they have taken up Zen so intensely and deeply that it has entered intimately into their life?) In China, however, I ought not omit to mention the noteworthy fact that Zen gave great impetus to the development of Chinese philosophy in the Sung dynasty and also to the growth of a certain school of painting. A large number of examples of this school were brought over to Japan beginning with the Kamakura era in the thirteenth century, when Zen monks were constantly traveling between the two neighboring countries. The paintings of Southern Sung thus came to find their ardent admirers on our side of the sea and are now national treasures of Japan, while in China no specimens of this class of painting are to be found.

Before proceeding further, we may make a few general remarks about one of the peculiar features of Japanese art, which is closely related to and finally deducible from the world conception of Zen.

Among things which strongly characterize Japanese artistic talents we may mention the so-called "one-corner" style, which originated with Bayen (Ma Yüan, fl. 1175-1225), one of the greatest Southern Sung artists. The "one-corner" style is psychologically associated with the Japanese painters' "thrifty brush" tradition of retaining the least possible number of lines or strokes which go to represent forms on silk or paper. Both are very much in accord with the spirit of Zen. A simple fishing boat in the midst of the rippling waters is enough to awaken in the mind of the beholder a sense of the vastness of the sea and at the same time of peace and contentment—the

Zen sense of the Alone. Apparently the boat floats helplessly. It is a primitive structure with no mechanical device for stability and for audacious steering over the turbulent waves, with no scientific apparatus for braving all kinds of weather—quite a contrast to the modern ocean liner. But this very helplessness is the virtue of the fishing canoe, in contrast with which we feel the incomprehensibility of the Absolute encompassing the boat and all the world. Again, a solitary bird on a dead branch, in which not a line, not a shade, is wasted, is enough to show us the loneliness of autumn, when days become shorter and nature begins to roll up once more its gorgeous display of luxurious summer vegetation.[1] It makes one feel somewhat pensive, but it gives one opportunity to withdraw the attention toward the inner life, which, given attention enough, spreads out its rich treasures ungrudgingly before the eyes.

Here we have an appreciation of transcendental aloofness in the midst of multiplicities—which is known as *wabi* in the dictionary of Japanese cultural terms. *Wabi* really means "poverty," or, negatively, "not to be in the fashionable society of the time." To be poor, that is, not to be dependent on things worldly—wealth, power, and reputation—and yet to feel inwardly the presence of something of the highest value, above time and social position: this is what essentially constitutes *wabi*. Stated in terms of practical everyday life, *wabi* is to be satisfied with a little hut, a room of two or three *tatami* (mats), like the log cabin of Thoreau, and with a dish of vegetables picked in the neighboring fields, and perhaps to be listening to the pattering of a gentle spring rainfall. The cult of *wabi* has entered deeply into the cultural life of the Japanese people. It is in truth the worshiping of poverty—probably a most appropriate cult in a poor country like ours. Despite the modern Western luxuries of comforts of life which have invaded us, there is still an ineradicable longing in us for the cult of *wabi*. Even in the intellectual life, not richness of ideas, not brilliancy or solemnity in marshaling thoughts and building up a philosophical system, is sought; but just to stay quietly content with the mystical contemplation of Nature and to feel at home with the world is more inspiring to us, at least to some of us.

[1] For pictures of a similar nature, see my Zen Essays, II and III.

However "civilized," however much brought up in an artificially contrived environment, we all seem to have an innate longing for primitive simplicity, close to the natural state of living. Hence the city people's pleasure in summer camping in the woods or traveling in the desert or opening up an unbeaten track. We wish to go back once in a while to the bosom of Nature and feel her pulsation directly. Zen's habit of mind, to break through all forms of human artificiality and take firm hold of what lies behind them, has helped the Japanese not to forget the soil but to be always friendly with Nature and appreciate her unaffected simplicity. Zen has no taste for complexities that lie on the surface of life. Life itself is simple enough, but when it is surveyed by the analyzing intellect it presents unparalleled intricacies. With all the apparatus of science we have not yet fathomed the mysteries of life. But, once in its current, we seem to be able to understand it, with its apparently endless pluralities and entanglements. Very likely, the most characteristic thing in the temperament of the Eastern people is the ability to grasp life from within and not from without. And Zen has just struck it.

In painting especially, disregard of form results when too much attention or emphasis is given to the all-importance of the spirit. The "one-cornered" style and the economy of brush strokes also help to effect aloofness from conventional rules. Where you would ordinarily expect a line or a mass or a balancing element, you miss it, and yet this very thing awakens in you an unexpected feeling of pleasure. In spite of shortcomings or deficiencies that no doubt are apparent, you do not feel them so; indeed, this imperfection itself becomes a form of perfection. Evidently, beauty does not necessarily spell perfection of form. This has been one of the favorite tricks of Japanese artists—to embody beauty in a form of imperfection or even of ugliness.

When this beauty of imperfection is accompanied by antiquity or primitive uncouthness, we have a glimpse of sabi, so prized by Japanese connoisseurs. Antiquity and primitiveness may not be an actuality. If an object of art suggests even superficially the feeling of a historical period, there is sabi in it. Sabi consists in rustic unpretentiousness or archaic imperfection, apparent simplicity or effortlessness in execution, and richness in historical associations (which, however, may not always be present); and, lastly, it contains inexplicable elements that raise the object in question to the rank of an artistic production. These elements are generally regarded as derived from the appreciation of Zen. The utensils used in the tearoom are mostly of this nature.

The artistic element that goes into the constitution of sabi, which literally means "loneliness" or "solitude," is poetically defined by a tea master thus:

As I come out
To this fishing village,
Late in the autumn day,
No flowers in bloom I see,
Nor any tinted maple leaves.[2]

Aloneness indeed appeals to contemplation and does not lend itself to spectacular demonstration. It may look most miserable, insignificant, and pitiable, especially when it is put up against the Western or modern setting. To be left alone, with no streamers flying, no fireworks crackling, and this amidst a gorgeous display of infinitely varied forms and endlessly changing colors, is indeed no sight at all. Take one of those sumiye sketches, perhaps portraying Kanzan and Jittoku (Han-shan and Shi'h-tê),[3] hang it in a European or an American art gallery, and see what effect it will produce in the minds of the visitors. The idea of aloneness belongs to the East and is at home in the environment of its birth.

It is not only to the fishing village on the autumnal eve that aloneness gives form but also to a patch of green in the early spring—which is in all likelihood even more expressive of the idea of sabi or wabi. For in the green patch, as we read in the following thirty-one-syllable verse, there is an indication of life impulse amidst the wintry desolation:

To those who only pray for the cherries to bloom,
How I wish to show the spring
That gleams from a patch of green
In the midst of the snow-covered mountain village! [4]

This is given by one of the old tea masters as thoroughly expressive of sabi, which is one of the four principles governing the cult of tea, cha-no-yu. Here is just a feeble inception of life power as asserted in the form of a little green patch, but in it he who has an eye can readily discern the spring shooting out from underneath the forbidding snow. It may be said to be a mere suggestion that stirs his mind, but just the same it is life itself and not its feeble indication. To the artist, life is as much here as when the whole field is overlaid with verdure and flowers. One may call this the mystic sense of the artist.

Asymmetry is another feature that distinguishes

[2] Fujiwara Sadaiye (1162-1241).
[3] Zen poet-recluses of the T'ang dynasty who have been a favorite subject for Far Eastern painters. [Gary Snyder's translations of some of the Han-shan poems are printed in this anthology.]
[4] Fujiwara Iyetaka (1158-1237).

Japanese art. The idea is doubtlessly derived from the "one-corner" style of Bayen. The plainest and boldest example is the plan of Buddhist architecture. The principal structures, such as the Tower Gate, the Dharma Hall, the Buddha Hall, and others, may be laid along one straight line; but structures of secondary or supplementary importance, sometimes even those of major importance, are not arranged symmetrically as wings along either side of the main line. They may be found irregularly scattered over the grounds in accordance with the topographical peculiarities. You will readily be convinced of this fact if you visit some of the Buddhist temples in the mountains, for example, the Iyeyasu shrine at Nikko. We can say that asymmetry is quite characteristic of Japanese architecture of this class.

This can be demonstrated *par excellence* in the construction of the tearoom and in the tools used in connection with it. Look at the ceiling, which may be constructed in at least three different styles, and at some of the utensils for serving tea, and again at the grouping and laying of the steppingstones or flagstones in the garden. We find so many illustrations of asymmetry, or, in a way, of imperfection, or of the "one-corner" style.

Some Japanese moralists try to explain this liking of the Japanese artists for things asymmetrically formed and counter to the conventional, or rather geometrical, rules of art by the theory that the people have been morally trained not to be obtrusive but always to efface themselves, and that this mental habit of self-annihilation manifests itself accordingly in art—for example, when the artist leaves the important central space unoccupied. But, to my mind, this theory is not quite correct. Would it not be a more plausible explanation to say that the artistic genius of the Japanese people has been inspired by the Zen way of looking at individual things as perfect in themselves and at the same time as embodying the nature of totality which belongs to the One?

The doctrine of ascetic aestheticism is not so fundamental as that of Zen aestheticism. Art impulses are more primitive or more innate than those of morality. The appeal of art goes more directly into human nature. Morality is regulative, art is creative. One is an imposition from without, the other is an irrepressible expression from within. Zen finds its inevitable association with art but not with morality. Zen may remain unmoral but not without art. When the Japanese artists create objects imperfect from the point of view of form, they may even be willing to ascribe their art motive to the current notion of moral asceticism; but we need not give too much significance to their own interpretation or to that of the critic. Our consciousness is not, after all, a very reliable standard of judgment.

However this may be, asymmetry is certainly characteristic of Japanese art, which is one of the reasons informality of approachability also marks to a certain degree Japanese objects of art. Symmetry inspires a notion of grace, solemnity, and impressiveness, which is again the case with logical formalism or the piling up of abstract ideas. The Japanese are often thought not to be intellectual and philosophical, because their general culture is not thoroughly impregnated with intellectuality. This criticism, I think, results somewhat from the Japanese love of asymmetry. The intellectual primarily aspires to balance, while the Japanese are apt to ignore it and incline strongly toward imbalance.

Imbalance, asymmetry, the "one-corner," poverty, simplification, *sabi* or *wabi*, aloneness, and cognate ideas make up the most conspicuous and characteristic features of Japanese art and culture. All these emanate from one central perception of the truth of Zen, which is "the One in the Many and the Many in the One," or better, "the One remaining as one in the Many individually and collectively."

2

That Zen has helped to stimulate the artistic impulses of the Japanese people and to color their works with ideas characteristic of Zen is due to the following facts: the Zen monasteries were almost exclusively the repositories of learning and art, at least during the Kamakura and the Muromachi eras; the Zen monks had constant opportunities to come in contact with foreign cultures; the monks themselves were artists, scholars, and mystics; they were even encouraged by the political powers of the time to engage in commercial enterprises to bring foreign objects of art and industry to Japan; the aristocrats and the politically influential classes of Japan were patrons of Zen institutions and were willing to submit themselves to the discipline of Zen. Zen thus worked not only directly on the religious life of the Japanese but also most strongly on their general culture.

The Tendai, the Shingon, and the Jōdō[5] contributed greatly to imbue the Japanese with the spirit of Buddhism, and through their iconography to develop their artistic instincts for sculpture, color painting, architecture, textile fabrics, and metalwork. But the philosophy of Tendai is too abstract and abstruse to be understood by the masses; the ritualism of Shin-

[5] These, with the Shin and the Nichiren, are the principal schools of Buddhism in Japan.

gon is too elaborate and complicated and consequently too expensive for popularity. On the other hand, Shingon and Tendai and Jōdō produced fine sculpture and pictures and artistic utensils to be used in their daily worship. The most highly prized "national treasures" belong to the Tempyō, the Nara, and the Heian periods, when those two schools of Buddhism were in the ascendancy and intimately involved with the cultured classes of the people. The Jōdō teaches the Pure Land in all its magnificence, where the Buddha of Infinite Light is attended by his retinue of Bodhisattvas, and this inspired the artists to paint those splendid pictures of Amida preserved in the various Buddhist temples of Japan. The Nichiren and the Shin are the creation of the Japanese religious mind. The Nichiren gave no specifically artistic and cultural impetus to us; the Shin tended to be somewhat iconoclastic and produced nothing worth mentioning in the arts and literature except the hymns known as *wasan* and the "honorable letters" (*gobunsho* or *ofumi*) chiefly written by Rennyo (1415-99).

Zen came to Japan after Shingon and Tendai and was at once embraced by the military classes. It was more or less by a historical accident that Zen was set against the aristocratic priesthood. The nobility, too, in the beginning felt a certain dislike for it and made use of their political advantage to stir up opposition to Zen. In the beginning of the Japanese history of Zen, therefore, Zen avoided Kyoto and established itself under the patronage of the Hōjō family in Kamakura. This place, as the seat of the feudal government in those days, became the headquarters of Zen discipline. Many Zen monks from China settled in Kamakura and found strong support in the Hōjō family—Tokiyori, Tokimune, and their successors and retainers.

The Chinese masters brought many artists and objects of art along with them, and the Japanese who came back from China were also bearers of art and literature. Pictures of Kakei (Hsia Kuei, fl. 1190-1220), Mokkei (Mu-ch'i, fl. c. 1240), Ryōkai (Liang K'ai, fl. c. 1210), Bayen (Ma Yüan, fl. 1175-1225), and others thus found their way to Japan. Manuscripts of the noted Zen masters of China were also given shelter in the monasteries here. Calligraphy in the Far East is an art just as much as *sumiye* painting, and it was cultivated almost universally among the intellectual classes in olden times. The spirit pervading Zen pictures and calligraphy made a strong impression on them, and Zen was readily taken up and followed. In it there is something virile and unbending. A mild, gentle, and graceful air—almost feminine, one might call it—which prevailed in the

periods preceding the Kamakura, is now superseded by an air of masculinity, expressing itself mostly in the sculpture and calligraphy of the period. The rugged virility of the warriors of the Kwanto districts is proverbial, in contrast to the grace and refinement of the courtiers in Kyoto. The soldierly quality, with its mysticism and aloofness from worldly affairs, appeals to the will power. Zen in this respect walks hand in hand with the spirit of Bushido ("Warriors' Way").

Another factor in the discipline of Zen, or rather in the monastic life in which Zen carries out its scheme of teaching, is this: as the monastery is usually situated in the mountains, its inmates are in the most intimate touch with nature, they are close and sympathetic students of it. They observe plants, birds, animals, rocks, rivers which people of the town would leave unnoticed. And their observation deeply reflects their philosophy, or better, their intuition. It is not that of a mere naturalist. It penetrates into the life itself of the objects that come under the monks' observation. Whatever they may paint of nature will inevitably be expressive of this intuition; the "spirit of the mountains" will be felt softly breathing in their works.

The fundamental intuition the Zen masters gain through their discipline seems to stir up their artistic instincts if they are at all susceptible to art. The intuition that impels the masters to create beautiful things, that is, or express the sense of perfection through things ugly and imperfect, is apparently closely related to the feeling for art. The Zen masters may not make good philosophers, but they are very frequently fine artists. Even their technique is often of the first order, and besides they know how to tell us something unique and original. One such is Musō the National Teacher (1275-1351). He was a fine calligrapher and a great landscape gardener; wherever he resided, at quite a number of places in Japan, he designed splendid gardens, some of which are still in existence and well preserved after so many years of changing times. Among the noted painters of Zen in the fourteenth and fifteenth centuries we may mention Chō Densu (d. 1431), Kei Shoki (fl. 1490), Josetsu (fl. 1375-1420), Shūbun (fl. 1420-50), Seshū (1421-1506), and others.

Georges Duthuit, the author of *Chinese Mysticism and Modern Painting*, seems to understand the spirit of Zen mysticism. From him we have this: "When the Chinese artist paints, what matters is the concentration of thought and the prompt and vigorous response of the hand to the directing will. Tradition ordains him to see, or rather to feel, as a whole the work to be executed, before embarking on anything. 'If the ideas of a man are confused, he will become the slave of exterior conditions.' . . . He who deliberates and moves his brush intent on making a picture, misses to a still greater extent the art of painting. [This seems like a kind of automatic writing.] Draw bamboos for ten years, become a bamboo, then forget all about bamboos when you are drawing. In possession of an infallible technique, the individual places himself at the mercy of inspiration."

To become a bamboo and to forget that you are one with it while drawing it—this is the Zen of the bamboo, this is the moving with the "rhythmic movement of the spirit" which resides in the bamboo as well as in the artist himself. What is now required of him is to have a firm hold on the spirit and yet not to be conscious of the fact. This is a very difficult task achieved only after long spiritual training.[6] The Eastern people have been taught since the earliest times to subject themselves to this kind of discipline if they want to achieve something in the world of art and religion. Zen, in fact, has given expression to it in the following phrase: "One in All and All in One." When this is thoroughly understood, there is creative genius.

It is of utmost importance here to interpret the phrase in its proper sense. People imagine that it means pantheism, and some students of Zen seem to agree. This is to be regretted, for pantheism is something foreign to Zen and also to the artist's understanding of his work. When the Zen masters declare the One to be in the All and the All in the One, they do not mean that there is a thing to be known as the One or as the All and that the One is the other and *vice versa*. As the One is in the All, some people suppose that Zen is a pantheistic teaching. Far from it; Zen would never hypostatize the One or the All as a thing to be grasped by the senses. The phrase "One in All and All in One" is to be understood as an expression of absolute *prajñā*-intuition and is not to be conceptually analyzed. When we see the moon, we know that it is the moon, and that is enough. Those who proceed to analyze the experience and try to establish a theory of knowledge are not students of Zen. They cease to be so, if they ever were, at the very moment of their procedure as analysts. Zen always upholds its experience as such and refuses to commit itself to any system of philosophy.

Even when Zen indulges in intellection, it never subscribes to a pantheistic interpretation of the world. For one thing, there is no One in Zen. If Zen ever speaks of the One as if it recognized it, this is a kind of condescension to common parlance. To Zen

students, the One is the All and the All is the One; and yet the One remains the One and the All the All. "Not two!" may lead the logician to think, "It is One." But the master would go on, saying, "Not One either!" "What then?" we may ask. We here face a blind alley, as far as verbalism is concerned. Therefore, it is said that "If you wish to be in direct communion [with Reality], I tell you, 'Not two!'"

The following *mondo*[7] may help to illustrate the point I wish to make in regard to the Zen attitude toward the so-called pantheistic interpretation of nature.

A monk asked Tōsu (T'ou-tzu), a Zen master of the T'ang period: "I understand that all sounds are the voice of the Buddha. Is this right?" The master said, "That is right." The monk then proceeded: "Would not the master please stop making a noise which echoes the sound of a fermenting mass of filth?" The master thereupon struck the monk.

The monk further asked Tōsu: "Am I in the right when I understand the Buddha as asserting that all talk, however trivial or derogatory, belongs to ultimate truth?" The master said, "Yes, you are in the right." The monk went on, "May I then call you a donkey?" The master thereupon struck him.

It may be necessary to explain these *mondo* in plain language. To conceive every sound, every noise, every utterance one makes as issuing from the fountainhead of one Reality, that is, from one God, is pantheistic, I imagine. For "He giveth to all life, and breath, and all things" (Acts 17:25); and again, "For in Him we live, and move, and have our being" (Acts 17:28). If this be the case, a Zen master's hoarse throat echoes the melodious resonance of the voice flowing from the Buddha's golden mouth, and even when a great teacher is decried as reminding one of an ass, the defamation must be regarded as reflecting something of ultimate truth. All forms of evil must be said somehow to be embodying what is true and good and beautiful, and to be a contribution to the perfection of Reality. To state it more concretely, bad is good, ugly is beautiful, false is true, imperfect is perfect, and also conversely. This is, indeed, the kind of reasoning in which those indulge who conceive the God-nature to be immanent in all things. Let us see how the Zen master treats this problem.

It is remarkable that Tōsu put his foot right down against such intellectualist interpretations and struck his monk. The latter in all probability expected to see the master nonplused by his statements which logically follow from his first assertion. The masterful Tōsu knew, as all Zen masters do, the uselessness of

[6] Cf. Takuan on "Prajñā Immovable."

[7] This and what follows are all from the *Hekigan-shu, Case* 79.

making any verbal demonstration against such a "logician." For verbalism leads from one complication to another; there is no end to it. The only effective way, perhaps, to make such a monk as this one realize the falsehood of his conceptual understanding is to strike him and so let him experience within himself the meaning of the statement, "One in All and All in One." The monk was to be awakened from his logical somnambulism. Hence Tōsu's drastic measure.

Secchō[8] here gives his comments in the following lines:

Pity that people without number try to play with the tide;
They are all ultimately swallowed up into it and die!
Let them suddenly awake [from the deadlock],
And see that all the rivers run backward, swelling and surging.

What is needed here is an abrupt turning or awakening, with which one comes to the realization of the truth of Zen—which is neither transcendentalism nor immanentism nor a combination of the two. The truth is as Tōsu declares in the following:

A monk asks, "What is the Buddha?"
Tōsu answers, "The Buddha."
Monk: "What is the Tao?"
Tōsu: "The Tao."
Monk: "What is Zen?"
Tōsu: "Zen."

The master answers like a parrot, he is echo itself. In fact, there is no other way of illumining the monk's mind than affirming that what is is—which is the final fact of experience.

Another example[9] is given to illustrate the point. A monk asked Jōshu (Chao-chou), of the T'ang dynasty: "It is stated that the Perfect Way knows no difficulties, only that it abhors discrimination. What is meant by No-discrimination?"

Jōshu said, "Above the heavens and below the heavens, I alone am the Honored One."

The monk suggested, "Still a discrimination."

The master's retort was, "O this worthless fellow! Where is the discrimination?"

By discrimination the Zen masters mean what we have when we refuse to accept Reality as it is or in its suchness, for we then reflect on it and analyze it into concepts, going on with intellection and finally landing on a circulatory reasoning. Jōshu's affirmation is a

final one and allows no equivocation, no argumentation. We have simply to take it as it stands and remain satisfied with it. In case we somehow fail to do this, we just leave it alone, and go somewhere else to seek our own enlightenment. The monk could not see where Jōshu was, and he went further on and remarked, "This is still a discrimination!" The discrimination in point of fact is on the monk's side and not on Jōshu's. Hence "the Honored One" now turns into "a worthless fellow."

As I said before, the phrase "All in One and One in All" is not to be analyzed first to the concepts "One" and "All," and the preposition is not then to be put between them; no discrimination is to be exercised here, but one is just to accept it and abide with it, which is really no-abiding at all. There is nothing further to do. Hence the master's striking or calling names. He is not indignant, nor is he short-tempered, but he wishes thereby to help his disciples out of the pit which they have dug themselves. No amount of argument avails here, no verbal persuasion. Only the master knows how to turn them away from a logical impasse and how to open a new way for them; let them, therefore, simply follow him. By following him they all come back to their Original Home.

When an intuitive or experiential understanding of Reality is verbally formulated as "All in One and One in All," we have there the fundamental statement as it is taught by all the various schools of Buddhism. In the terminology of the Prajñā school, this is: sūnyatā ("emptiness") is tathātā ("suchness"), and tathātā is sūnyatā: sūnyatā is the world of the Absolute, and tathātā is the world of particulars. One of the commonest sayings in Zen is "Willows are green and flowers red" or "Bamboos are straight and pine trees are gnarled." Facts of experience are accepted as they are, Zen is not nihilistic, nor is it merely positivistic. Zen would say that just because the bamboo is straight it is of Emptiness, or that just because of Emptiness the bamboo cannot be anything else but a bamboo and not a pine tree. What makes the Zen statements different from mere sense experience, however, is that Zen's intuition grows out of prajñā and not out of jñā.[10] It is from this point of view that when asked "What is Zen?" the master sometimes answers "Zen" and sometimes "Not-Zen."

We can see now that the principle of sumiye painting is derived from this Zen experience, and that directness, simplicity, movement, spirituality, completeness, and other qualities we observe in the

[8] Secchō (Hsüeh-tou, 980-1052) was one of the great Zen masters of the Sung, noted for his literary accomplishment. The Hekigan-shu is based on Secchō's "One Hundred Cases," which he selected out of the annals of Zen.
[9] Hekigan-shu, Case 57.

[10] Prajñā may be translated "transcendental wisdom," while jñā or vijñāna is "relative knowledge." For a detailed explanation, see my Studies in Zen Buddhism, pp. 85 ff.

sumiye class of Oriental paintings have organic relationship to Zen. There is no pantheism in sumiye as there is none in Zen.

There is another thing I must not forget to mention in this connection, which is perhaps the most important factor in sumiye as well as in Zen. It is creativity. When it is said that sumiye depicts the spirit of an object, or that it gives a form to what has no form, this means that there must be a spirit of creativity moving over the picture. The painter's business thus is not just to copy or imitate nature, but to give to the object something living in its own right. It is the same with the Zen master. When he says that the willow is green and the flower is red, he is not just giving us a description of how nature looks, but something whereby green is green and red is red. This something is what I call the spirit of creativity. Sūnyatā is formless, but it is the fountainhead of all possibilities. To turn what is possible into an actuality is an act of creativity. When Tōsu is asked, "What is Dharma?" he answers, "Dharma"; when asked, "What is Buddha?" he answers "Buddha." This is by no means a parrot-like response, a mere echoing; all the answers come out of his creative mind, without which there is no Zen in Tōsu. The understanding of Zen is to understand what kind of mind this is. Yakusan's meeting with Rikō will illustrate this.[11]

[11] Dento-roku ("Transmission of the Lamp"), fasc. 14.

Yakusan (Yao-shan, 751-834) was a great master of the T'ang era. When Rikō (Li Ao), governor of the province, heard of his Zen mastership, he sent for him to come to the capital. Yakusan, however, refused to come. This happened several times. Rikō grew impatient and came in person to see the master in his own mountain retreat. Yakusan was reading the sutras and paid no attention whatever to the arrival of the governor. The attendant monk reminded the master of the fact, but he still kept on reading. Rikō felt hurt and remarked, "Seeing the face is not at all like hearing the name." By this he meant that the person in actuality was not equal to his reputation. Yakusan called out, "O Governor!" Rikō echoed at once, "Yes, Master." The master then said, "Why do you evaluate the hearing over the seeing?" The governor apologized and asked, "What is Tao?" Yakusan pointed up with his hand and then down, and said, "Do you understand?" Rikō said, "No, Master." Thereupon Yakusan remarked, "The clouds are in the sky and water in the jar." It is said that this pleased the governor very much.

Did Rikō really understand what Yakusan meant? Yakusan's is no more than a plain statement of the facts as they are, and we may ask, "Where is Tao?" Rikō was a great scholar and philosopher. He must have had some abstract conception of Tao. Could he so readily reconcile his view with Yakusan's? Whatever we may say about this, Yakusan and Tōsu and other Zen masters are all walking the same track. The artists are also required to strike it.

►► Gary Snyder

The Cold Mountain Poems of Han-shan

In the Japanese art exhibit that came to America in 1953 was a small sumi sketch of a robe-tattered windswept long-haired laughing man holding a scroll, standing on a cliff in the mountains. This was Kanzan, or Han-shan, "Cold Mountain"—his name taken from where he lived. He is a mountain madman in an old Chinese line of ragged hermits. When

he talks about Cold Mountain he means himself, his home, his state of mind. He lived in the T'ang dynasty—traditionally A.D. 627-650, although Hu Shih dates him 700-780. This makes him roughly contemporary with Tu Fu, Li Po, Wang Wei, and Po Chü-i. His poems, of which three hundred survive, are written in T'ang colloquial: rough and fresh. The ideas are Taoist, Buddhist, Zen. He and his sidekick Shih-te (*Jittoku* in Japanese) became great favorites with Zen painters of later days—the scroll, the broom, the wild hair and laughter. They became Immortals and you sometimes run onto them today in the skid-rows, orchards, hobo jungles, and logging camps of America.—G.S.

Preface to the Poems of Han-shan by Lu Ch'iu-yin, Governor of T'ai Prefecture

No one knows just what sort of man Han-shan was. There are old people who knew him: they say he was a poor man, a crazy character. He lived alone seventy li west of the T'ang-hsing district of T'ien-t'ai at a place called Cold Mountain. He often went down to the Kuo-ch'ing Temple. At the temple lived Shihte, who ran the dining hall. He sometimes saved leftovers for Han-shan, hiding them in a bamboo tube. Han-shan would come and carry it away; walking the long veranda, calling and shouting happily, talking and laughing to himself. Once the monks followed him, caught him, and made fun of him. He stopped, clapped his hands, and laughed greatly—Ha Ha!—for a spell, then left.

He looked like a tramp. His body and face were old and beat. Yet in every word he breathed was a meaning in line with the subtle principles of things, if only you thought of it deeply. Everything he said had a feeling of the Tao in it, profound and arcane secrets. His hat was made of birch bark, his clothes were ragged and worn out, and his shoes were wood. Thus men who have made it hide their tracks: unifying categories and interpenetrating things. On that long veranda calling and singing, in his words of reply Ha Ha!—the three worlds revolve. Sometimes at the villages and farms he laughed and sang with cowherds. Sometimes intractable, sometimes agreeable, his nature was happy of itself. But how could a person without wisdom recognize him?

I once received a position as a petty official at Tan-ch'iu. The day I was to depart, I had a bad headache. I called a doctor, but he couldn't cure me and it turned worse. Then I met a Buddhist Master named Feng-kan, who said he came from the Kuo-ch'ing Temple of T'ien-t'ai especially to visit me. I asked him to rescue me from my illness. He smiled and said, "The four realms are within the body; sickness comes from illusion. If you want to do away with it, you need pure water." Someone brought water to the Master, who spat it on me. In a moment the disease was rooted out. He then said, "There are miasmas in T'ai prefecture, when you get there take care of your-

self." I asked him, "Are there any wise men in your area I could look on as Master?" He replied, "When you see him you don't recognize him, when you recognize him you don't see him. If you want to see him, you can't rely on appearances. Then you can see him. Han-shan is a Manjusri hiding at Kuo-ch'ing. Shih-te is a Samantabhadra. They look like poor fellows and act like madmen. Sometimes they go and sometimes they come. They work in the kitchen of the Kuo-ch'ing dining hall, tending the fire." When he was done talking he left.

I proceeded on my journey to my job at T'ai-chou, not forgetting this affair. I arrived three days later, immediately went to a temple, and questioned an old monk. It seemed the Master had been truthful, so I gave orders to see if T'ang-hsing really contained a Han-shan and Shih-te. The District Magistrate reported to me: "In this district, seventy li west, is a mountain. People used to see a poor man heading from the cliffs to stay awhile at Kuo-ch'ing. At the temple dining hall is a similar man named Shih-te." I made a bow, and went to Kuo-ch'ing. I asked some people around the temple, "There used to be a Master named Feng-kan here. Where is his place? And where can Han-shan and Shih-te be seen?" A monk named Tao-ch'iao spoke up: "Feng-kan the Master lived in back of the library. Nowadays nobody lives there; a tiger often comes and roars. Han-shan and Shih-te are in the kitchen." The monk led me to Feng-kan's yard. Then he opened the gate: all we saw was tiger tracks. I asked the monks Tao-ch'iao and Pao-te, "When Feng-kan was here, what was his job?" The monks said, "He pounded and hulled rice. At night he sang songs to amuse himself." Then we went to the kitchen, before the stoves. Two men were facing the fire, laughing loudly. I made a bow. The two shouted HO! at me. They struck their hands together—Ha Ha!—great laughter. They shouted. Then they said, "Feng-kan—loose-tongued, loose-tongued. You don't recognize Amitabha, why be courteous to us?" The monks gathered round, surprise going through them. "Why has a big official bowed to a pair of clowns?" The two men grabbed hands and ran out of the temple. I cried, "Catch them"—but they quickly ran away. Han-shan returned to Cold Mountain. I asked the monks, "Would those two men be willing to settle down at this temple?" I ordered them to find a house, and to ask Han-shan and Shih-te to return and live at the temple.

I returned to my district and had two sets of clean clothes made, got some incense and such, and sent it to the temple—but the two men didn't return. So I had it carried up to Cold Mountain. The packer saw Han-shan, who called in a loud voice, "Thief! Thief!" and retreated into a mountain cave. He shouted, "I tell you man, strive hard!"—entered the cave and was gone. The cave closed of itself and they weren't able to follow. Shih-te's tracks disappeared completely.

I ordered Tao-ch'iao and the other monks to find out how they had lived, to hunt up the poems writ-ten on bamboo, wood, stones, and cliffs—and also to collect those written on the walls of people's houses. There were more than three hundred. On the wall of the Earth-shrine Shih-te had written some *gatha*. It was all brought together and made into a book.

I hold to the principle of the Buddha-mind. It is fortunate to meet with men of Tao, so I have made this eulogy.

Twenty-Four Poems by Han-shan

1

The path to Han-shan's place is laughable,
A path, but no sign of cart or horse.
Converging gorges—hard to trace their twists
Jumbled cliffs—unbelievably rugged.
A thousand grasses bend with dew,
A hill of pines hums in the wind.
And now I've lost the shortcut home,
Body asking shadow, how do you keep up?

2

In a tangle of cliffs I chose a place—
Bird-paths, but no trails for men.
What's beyond the yard?
White clouds clinging to vague rocks.
Now I've lived here—how many years—
Again and again, spring and winter pass.
Go tell families with silverware and cars
"What's the use of all that noise and money?"

3

In the mountains it's cold.
Always been cold, not just this year.
Jagged scarps forever snowed in
Woods in the dark ravines spitting mist.
Grass is still sprouting at the end of June,
Leaves begin to fall in early August.
And here am I, high on mountains,
Peering and peering, but I can't even see the sky.

4

I spur my horse through the wrecked town,
The wrecked town sinks my spirit.
High, low, old parapet-walls
Big, small, the aging tombs.
I waggle my shadow, all alone;
Not even the crack of a shrinking coffin is heard.
I pity all these ordinary bones,
In the books of the Immortals they are nameless.

5

I wanted a good place to settle:
Cold Mountain would be safe.
Light wind in a hidden pine—
Listen close—the sound gets better.
Under it a gray-haired man
Mumbles along reading Huang and Lao.
For ten years I haven't gone back home
I've even forgotten the way by which I came.

6

Men ask the way to Cold Mountain
Cold Mountain: there's no through trail.
In summer, ice doesn't melt
The rising sun blurs in swirling fog.
How did I make it?
My heart's not the same as yours.
If your heart was like mine
You'd get it and be right here.

7

I settled at Cold Mountain long ago,
Already it seems like years and years.
Freely drifting, I prowl the woods and streams
And linger watching things themselves.
Men don't get this far into the mountains,
White clouds gather and billow.
Thin grass does for a mattress,
The blue sky makes a good quilt.
Happy with a stone underhead
Let heaven and earth go about their changes.

8

Clambering up the Cold Mountain path,
The Cold Mountain trail goes on and on:
The long gorge choked with scree and boulders,
The wide creek, the mist-blurred grass.
The moss is slippery, though there's been no rain
The pine sings, but there's no wind.
Who can leap the world's ties
And sit with me among the white clouds?

9

Rough and dark—the Cold Mountain trail,
Sharp cobbles—the icy creek bank.
Yammering, chirping—always birds
Bleak, alone, not even a lone hiker.
Whip, whip—the wind slaps my face
Whirled and tumbled—snow piles on my back.
Morning after morning I don't see the sun
Year after year, not a sign of spring.

10

I have lived at Cold Mountain
These thirty long years.
Yesterday I called on friends and family:
More than half had gone to the Yellow Springs.
Slowly consumed, like fire down a candle;
Forever flowing, like a passing river.
Now, morning, I face my lone shadow:
Suddenly my eyes are bleared with tears.

11

Spring-water in the green creek is clear
Moonlight on Cold Mountain is white
Silent knowledge—the spirit is enlightened of it-
self
Contemplate the void: this world exceeds stillness.

12

In my first thirty years of life
I roamed hundreds and thousands of miles.
Walked by rivers through deep green grass
Entered cities of boiling red dust.
Tried drugs, but couldn't make Immortal;
Read books and wrote poems on history.
Today I'm back at Cold Mountain:
I'll sleep by the creek and purify my ears.

13

I can't stand these bird-songs
Now I'll go rest in my straw shack.
The cherry flowers out scarlet
The willow shoots up feathery.
Morning sun drives over blue peaks
Bright clouds wash green ponds.
Who knows that I'm out of the dusty world
Climbing the southern slope of Cold Mountain?

14

Cold Mountain has many hidden wonders,
People who climb here are always getting scared.
When the moon shines, water sparkles clear
When wind blows, grass swishes and rattles.
On the bare plum, flowers of snow
On the dead stump, leaves of mist.

At the touch of rain it all turns fresh and live
At the wrong season you can't ford the creeks.

15

There's a naked bug at Cold Mountain
With a white body and a black head.
His hand holds two book-scrolls,
One the Way and one its Power.
His shack's got no pots or oven,
He goes for a walk with his shirt and pants askew.
But he always carries the sword of wisdom:
He means to cut down senseless craving.

16

Cold Mountain is a house
Without beams or walls.
The six doors left and right are open
The hall is blue sky.
The rooms all vacant and vague
The east wall beats on the west wall
At the center nothing.

Borrowers don't bother me
In the cold I build a little fire
When I'm hungry I boil up some greens.
I've got no use for the kulak
With his big barn and pasture—
He just sets up a prison for himself.
Once in he can't get out.
Think it over—
You know it might happen to you.

17

If I hide out at Cold Mountain
Living off mountain plants and berries—
All my lifetime, why worry?
One follows his karma through.
Days and months slip by like water,
Time is like sparks knocked off flint.
Go ahead and let the world change—
I'm happy to sit among these cliffs.

18

Most T'ien-t'ai men
Don't know Han-shan
Don't know his real thought
& call it silly talk.

19

Once at Cold Mountain, troubles cease—
No more tangled, hung-up mind.
I idly scribble poems on the rock cliff,
Taking whatever comes, like a drifting boat.

20

Some critic tried to put me down—
"Your poems lack the Basic Truth of Tao"
And I recall the old-timers
Who were poor and didn't care.
I have to laugh at him,
He misses the point entirely,
Men like that
Ought to stick to making money.

21

I've lived at Cold Mountain—how many autumns.
Alone, I hum a song—utterly without regret.
Hungry, I eat one grain of Immortal-medicine
Mind solid and sharp; leaning on a stone.

22

On top of Cold Mountain the lone round moon
Lights the whole clear cloudless sky.
Honor this priceless natural treasure
Concealed in five shadows, sunk deep in the flesh.

23

My home was at Cold Mountain from the start,
Rambling among the hills, far from trouble.

Gone, and a million things leave no trace
Loosed, and it flows through the galaxies
A fountain of light, into the very mind—
Not a thing, and yet it appears before me:
Now I know the pearl of the Buddha-nature
Know its use: a boundless perfect sphere.

24

When men see Han-shan
They all say he's crazy
And not much to look at—
Dressed in rags and hides.
They don't get what I say
& I don't talk their language.
All I can say to those I meet:
"Try and make it to Cold Mountain."

Translated by Gary Snyder

NOTES

The preface:

Feng-kan is reckoned in the traditional line of Zen Masters, but in mid-T'ang the Zen people did not yet constitute a separate Buddhist sect. They were rather a "meditation group" living in the mountains or the monasteries of the T'ien-t'ai (Japanese Tendai) sect, and the Vinaya (discipline) sect.

Manjusri is the Bodhisattva of wisdom, Samantabhadra the Bodhisattva of love, Amitabha the Bodhisattva of boundless compassion.

A *gatha* is a short Buddhist poem.

A doggerel eulogistic poem, also by Lu Ch'iu-yin, follows the biography. I have not translated it.

The poems:

4—a rare example of a poem in the literary manner. Han-shan usually writes in the colloquial, as very few Chinese poets have done.

5—the gray-haired man is Han-shan himself. Huang is "The Book of the Yellow Emperor" and Lao is Lao-tzu, the *Tao Te Ching*.

15—the Way and its Power, i.e., the *Tao Te Ching*.

22, 23—the full moon, the pearl. Symbols of the Buddha-nature inherent in all beings.

Most of Han-shan's poems are written in the "old-song" (*ku-shih*) style, with five or seven characters to a line.

►► E. M. Cioran

On a Certain Experience of Death

Some men make their way from affirmation to affirmation, their life a series of acceptances. . . . Forever applauding reality or what passes for it in their eyes, they accept the universe and are not ashamed to say so. There is no contradiction they cannot resolve or relegate to the category of "the way things turn out." The more they let themselves be contaminated by philosophy, the more they pride themselves, faced with the entertainments of life and death, on being a *good audience*.

For others, habitual nay-sayers, affirmation demands not only deliberate self-deception, but self-sacrifice as well: how much effort the merest nod to existence can cost! What repudiations must be renounced! They know there is never just one "yes": each assent implies another, perhaps a whole parade —who can afford to take such risks lightly? Yet the security of negation aggravates the nay-sayers too, and hence they conceive the necessity and the interest of affirming something—anything.

It is true that negation is the mind's first freedom, yet a negative habit is fruitful only so long as we exert ourselves to overcome it, adapt it to our needs; once *acquired* it can imprison us—a chain like any other. And slavery for slavery, the servitude of existence is the preferable choice, even at the price of a certain self-splintering: it is a matter of avoiding the contagion of nothingness, the comforts of the abyss. . . .

For centuries theologians have told us that hope is the daughter of patience. And of modesty as well, one might add; the man of pride has no *time* for hope. . . . Unwilling and unable to wait for their culmination, he violates events as much as he violates his own nature; bitter, tainted, when he exhausts his rebellion he abdicates his existence—for him there is no intermediate formula. His lucidity is undeniable, but let us remember that lucidity is a condition peculiar to those who by their incapacity to love are as isolated from others as from themselves.

The assent to death is the greatest one of all. It can be expressed in several ways. . . .

There are among us daylight ghosts, devoured by their absence, for whom life is a long aside. They walk our streets with muffled steps, and look at no one. No anxiety can be discovered in their eyes, no haste in their gestures. For them an outside world has ceased to exist, and they submit to every solitude. Careful to keep their distance, solicitous of their detachment, they inhabit an undeclared universe situated somewhere between the memory of the unimaginable and the imminence of certainty. Their smile suggests a thousand vanquished fears, the grace that triumphs over all things terrible: such beings can pass though matter itself. Have they overtaken their own origins? Discovered in themselves the very sources of light? No defeat, no victory disturbs them. Independent of the sun, they are self-sufficient: illuminated by Death.

We are not in a position to identify the moment when the operations of erosion occur within us at the expense of our human substance. We know only that the result of such operations is a void, into which the idea of our own destruction gradually settles. A vague, faintly outlined idea: as if the void were aware of itself. Then from the furthest reaches of the self, in sonorous transfiguration, may be heard a noise, a sound, a *tonality* which by its very insistence must either paralyze us forever or preserve our life anew. We may find ourselves captives of fear or of nostalgia; lower than death or on its own level. Captives of fear, if this tonality merely perpetuates the void in which it occurs; and of nostalgia, if it converts the void to plenitude. According to our structure, we shall discern in death either a deficit or a surplus of being.

Before affecting our perception of duration—acquired relatively late—the fear of death attacks our sense of dimension, of immediacy—our illusion of what is *solid:* space shrinks, shoots from our grasp, turns into thin air, becomes entirely transparent. Our fear replaces space, welling up until it obscures the very reality that provoked it—until it substitutes itself for death. All experience is suddenly reduced to an exchange between the self and this fear, which as an autonomous reality isolates us in such unmotivated terrors, such gratuitous shudders that we run the risk of forgetting we are going to . . . die. Yet fear can supplant our real problems only to the extent that we—unwilling either to assimilate or to exhaust it—perpetuate it within ourselves like a temptation and enthrone it at the very heart of our solitude. One step further and we shall become debauchees not of death but of the fear of death. Such is the history of all the fears we have not been able to overcome: no longer subservient to motivation, they grow into independent, tyrannical idols. "We live in fear, and therefore we do not live." Buddha's words may be taken to mean that instead of keeping ourselves at the stage of being where fear opens out onto the world, we make it an end in itself, a closed universe, a substitute for *space.* If fear controls us, it must distort our image of the world. The man who can neither master nor exploit his fear ultimately ceases to be himself, loses his identity, for fear is valuable only if one defends oneself against it; the man who surrenders to it can never recover, but must proceed, in all transactions with himself, from treason to treason until he smothers death itself beneath his fear of it.

The attraction of certain problems derives from their lack of rigor, and hence from the contradictory solutions they provoke: so many more difficulties to entice the amateur of the Insoluble.

In order to "document" myself on the subject of death, a biological treatise is of no more use than the catechism: as far as *I* am concerned, it is a matter of indifference whether I am going to die because of original sin or the dehydration of my cells. Entirely independent of our intellectual system, death, like every individual experience, can be confronted only by knowledge without *information*. Hence many uneducated men have spoken more pertinently of it than this or that metaphysician; once experience had detected the agent of their destruction, such men devote all their thoughts to it, so that death becomes no mere impersonal "problem," but a reality all their own, *their death.*

Yet among all those who, uneducated or not, think continually of death, most do so only because they are terrified by the prospect of their final agony, not realizing that even if they were to live centuries, millennia, the *reasons* for their fear would remain entirely unchanged, agony being merely an accident in the process of our annihilation, a process that is, after all, coextensive with our duration. Life, far from being what Bichat once called an ensemble of functions for resisting death, is rather an ensemble of functions for bearing us toward it. Our substance diminishes with every step, yet it is of this very diminution that all our efforts should tend to make a stimulant, a principle of efficacity. Those who cannot benefit from their possibilities of nonexistence are strangers to themselves: puppets, objects "furnished" with a self, numbed by a neutral time that is neither duration nor eternity. To exist is to profit by our share of unreality, to be quickened by each contact with the void that is within us. To this void the puppet remains insensible, abandons it, permits it to decay, to die out. . . .

A kind of germinative regression, a return to our roots, death destroys our identity only to permit us a surer access to it—a reconstitution; for death has no meaning unless we accord it all the attributes of life.

Although at our first, our primary perceptions of its quality, death presents itself as a dislocation, a loss, it subsequently produces, by revealing the nullity of time and the infinite worth of each separate moment, certain tonic effects: if it offers us only the image of our own inanity, by the same token it converts the inanity into an absolute, inviting us to commit ourselves to it. And by thus rehabilitating our "mortal" aspect, death institutes itself as a day by day dimension of our life, a triumphal agony.

What is the good of fastening our thoughts upon some tomb or other, staking anything upon our eventual rot? Spiritually degrading, the macabre confronts us with exhaustion of our glands, the stinking garbage of our dissolution. We can claim to be alive only to the degree that we slight or circumvent the idea of our eventual corpse. Nothing of value results from reflections on the material fact of dying. If I permitted the flesh to dictate its philosophy, to impose its conclusions upon me, I might as well do away with myself before knowing them. For everything the flesh has to teach me annihilates me without recourse: does it not refuse all illusion? Does it not, as the interpreter of our ashes, continually contradict our lies, our fantasies, our hopes? Let us therefore proceed beyond its arguments, and force it to join battle against its own evidence.

To rejuvenate ourselves at the contact of death is a matter of investing it with all our energies, of becoming, like Keats, "half in love with easeful death" or, like Novalis, of making of death the principle that "romanticizes" life. If Novalis was to carry his nostalgia for death to the point of sensuality, it was Kleist who was to derive from it a completely inner "felicity." *"Ein Strudel von nie geahnter Seligkeit hat mich ergriffen . . ."* (a whirlpool of undreamed-of felicity has seized me), he writes, before committing suicide. Neither defeat nor abdication, his death was a rage of happiness, an exemplary and concerted madness, one of the rare successes of despair. Schlegel's remark that Novalis was the first man to experience death "as an artist" seems to me to apply more exactly to Kleist, who was better equipped for death than anyone has ever been. Unequalled, perfect, a masterpiece of tact and taste, his suicide makes all others unnecessary.

A vernal annihilation, culmination rather than chasm, death dizzies us only to raise us all the more readily above our customary selves, with the same privilege as love's, to which it is related in more than one respect: both love and death, applying an explosive pressure upon the framework of our lives, disintegrate us, fortify us, ruin us by the distractions of plenitude. As irreducible as they are inseparable, their elements constitute a fundamental equivocation. If, to a certain point, love destroys us, with what sensations of expansion and pride it does its work! And if death destroys us altogether, what *frissons* does it not employ! Sensations, shudders by which we transcend the *man* within us, and the accidents of the self.

Since both love and death define us only to the degree that we project our appetites and impulses upon them, that we co-operate wholeheartedly with their equivocal nature, they are necessarily beyond our grasp as long as we regard them as exterior realities, accessible to the operations of the intellect. We plunge into love as into death, we do not reflect upon them: we savor them as accomplices, we do not measure them. For that matter, every experience that is not converted into a voluptuous one is a failure. If we had to limit ourselves to our sensations as they were, they would appear intolerable for being too distinct, too dissimilar from our essence. Death would not be the Great Human Experiment That Failed if men knew how to assimilate it to their nature or how to transform it into pleasure. But death remains within them as an experience *apart*, different from what they are.

And it is still another indication of the double reality of death—its equivocal character, the paradox inherent in the manner we experience it—that it presents itself to us as a *limit* and at the same time as a *datum*. We rush toward it, and yet we are already there. Thus even as we are incorporating it within our lives, we cannot keep ourselves from positing it in the future. By an inevitable inconsistency, we interpret death as the future which destroys the present, our present. If fear assisted us in defining our sense of space, it is death which reveals the true meaning of our temporal dimension, since without death, being in time would mean nothing to us, or, at the most, the same thing as being in eternity. Hence the traditional image of death, despite all our efforts to elude it, obstinately haunts us, an image for which sick men are chiefly responsible. In such matters we agree to recognize their qualifications; a prejudice in their favor automatically accords them a kind of "profundity," although most of them give every evidence of a disconcerting futility. We have all known *operetta incurables*.

More than anyone else the sick man is expected to identify himself with death; yet he does his utmost to detach himself from it, to project death outside himself. Since it is easier for him to run away from it than to confess its presence in himself, he uses every artifice to rid himself of death. He makes a practice, even a doctrine out of his defensive reaction. The ordinary man, in good health, is delighted to imitate him in every detail. And only the ordinary man? The mystics themselves employ subterfuges, practice every form of evasion, flight tactics: for them death is only an obstacle to be surmounted, a barrier which separates them from God, a last step in duration. In this life, they sometimes manage—thanks to ecstasy, that springboard—to leap beyond time: an instantaneous trajectory by which they achieve only "fits" of beatitude. They must disappear for good if they would attain the object of their desires; hence they love death because it permits them to realize these desires, and they hate death because it delays so long in coming. The soul, according to Theresa of Avila, aspires only to its creator, but "it sees at the same time that it is impossible to possess its creator if it does not die; and since it is impossible for the soul to put itself to death, it dies of the desire to die, until it is actually in danger of death." Always this need to make death into an accident or a means, to reduce it to a disappearance instead of regarding it as a presence—always this need to dispossess death. And if religions have made of it only a pretext or a scarecrow—a weapon of propaganda—it is the duty of the unbelievers to see that justice is done, to re-establish death and restore all its rights.

Each being *is* his sentiment of death. It follows that the experiences of sick men and mystics cannot be discarded as false, although we may question their interpretations of these experiences. We are on ground where no criterion functions, where certitudes swarm, where everything is a certitude, because our truths here coincide with our sensations, our problems with our attitudes. Furthermore, what "truth" can we claim, when at every moment we are engaged in another experience of death? Our "destiny" itself is only the development, the phases of this primordial and yet changing experience, the translation into apparent time of that *secret time* in which the diversity of our ways of dying is elaborated. To explain a destiny, biographers should abandon their usual procedure, should give up examining this apparent time, this readiness of their subject to deteriorate his own essence. The same thing is true for a whole epoch: to know its institutions and its dates is less important than to divine its intimate experience of which these are the signs. Battles, ideologies, heroism, sanctity, barbarism—all so many simulacra of an interior world which alone should solicit our attention. Every culture dies out in its own way, every culture perfects several rules of extinction and imposes them upon its members: even the best among them could not change or evade such rules. A Pascal, a Baudelaire circumscribe death: one reduces it to our search for salvation, the other to our physiological terrors. If death overwhelms man, crushes him, it remains no less, for them both, *within* man. Quite the contrary, the Elizabethans or the German Romantics made of death a cosmic phenomenon, an orgiastic metamorphosis, a vivifying nothingness—ultimately a *force* in which man was to steep himself and with which it was important to maintain direct relations. For the Frenchman, what counts is not death in itself—an evidence of Matter's absentmindedness or merely an impropriety—but our behavior in the eyes of our fellow men, the strategy of *adieux*, the countenance which the calculations of our vanity impose upon us—in short, *attitude*; not our quarrel with ourselves, but with others: a spectacle in which it is essential to observe the details and the motives. The whole of French art consists of knowing how to die *in public*. Saint-Simon describes not the agony of Louis XIV, of Monsieur, or of the Regent, but the *scènes* of their agony. The customs of the Court, an awareness of its ceremony, its ostentation, have been inherited by a whole people enamored of display and anxious to associate a certain brilliance with the last breath. In this regard Catholicism has been useful to the French: does it not maintain that the way we die is essential to our salvation, that our sins can be redeemed by a "good death"? A questionable notion, but one entirely adapted to a nation's histrionic instinct, and which, in the past more than today, is related to conceptions of honor and dignity, to the style of the *honnête homme*. It was then a question, setting God aside, of saving face in front of an audience, in front of the elegant strollers and gapers and the worldly confessors; not of perishing, but of *officiating*, preserving one's reputation before witnesses and asking extreme unction of them alone. . . . Even the worst libertines died decorously, so much did their respect for opinion prevail over the irreparable, so much did they conform to the usages of an epoch in which to die signified, for man, to renounce solitude and privacy alike, to go on parade one last time, and in which the French were the greatest of all specialists in agony.

It is nevertheless doubtful that by relying on the "historical" aspect of the experience of death we shall manage to penetrate further into its original character, for history is merely an inessential mode of being, the most effective form of our infidelity to ourselves, a metaphysical refusal, a mass of events with which we confront the only event which matters. Everything that aims at affecting man—religions included—is tainted with a crude sentiment of death. And it is to seek a true, purer sentiment of this kind that the hermits took refuge in the desert, that negation of history which they rightly compared to the angels, since—they maintained—both were unaware of sin and the Fall into the realm of time. The desert, in fact, provides the image of duration translated into coexistence: a motionless flow, a metamorphosis bewitched by space. The solitary retires there less to expand his solitude and enrich his absence than to produce within himself the tonality of death.

In order to hear this tonality we must institute a desert within ourselves. . . . If we succeed, certain harmonies flow through our blood, our veins dilate, our secrets and our resources appear upon the surface of ourselves where desire and disgust, horror and rapture mingle in obscure and luminous festivity. The dawn of death breaks within us: cosmic trance, the bursting of the spheres, a thousand voices! We are death, and everything is death—death seduces us, sweeps us away, carries us aloft, casts us to earth, or hurls us beyond the bounds of space itself. Death, forever intact, unworn by all the ages of our history, makes us accomplices in its apotheosis; we feel its immemorial freshness, and its time unlike any other . . . death's time, which ceaselessly creates and decomposes us. To such a degree does death hold us, immortalize us in agony, that we shall never be able to indulge ourselves in the luxury of dying; and although we possess the very science of destiny, although we are a veritable encyclopedia of fatalities, we nevertheless know nothing, for it is death that knows everything within us.

I often remember how, at the end of my adolescence, emmeshed in mortuary considerations, enslaved by a single obsession, I apprenticed myself to every force that invalidated my existence. My other thoughts no longer interested me: I knew too well *where* they led me, upon what they converged. From the moment I had only one problem, what was the use of concerning myself with *problems*? Ceasing to live in terms of a self, I gave death enough rope for my own enslavement; in other words, I no longer belonged to myself. My terrors, even my name were borne by death, and by substituting itself for my own eyes, death revealed to me in all things the marks of its sovereignty. In each man I passed I discerned a cadaver, in each odor a rot, in each joy a last grimace. Everywhere I stumbled against future victims of the noose, against their imminent shadows: other men's lives wore no mystery for The One who scrutinized them through my eyes. Was I bewitched? I preferred to think so. From now on what was I to do? The Void was my eucharist: everything within me, everything exterior to me was transubstantiated into a ghost. Irresponsible, at the antipodes of consciousness, I ended up by delivering myself to the anonymity of the elements, to the drunkenness of indivisibility, determined not to re-integrate my being nor to become again a colonist of chaos.

Unable to see in death the positive expression of the void, the agent that awakens the creature from itself, the summons resounding in the ubiquity of drowsiness, I knew nothingness by heart, and I accepted my knowledge. Even now, how could I mistake the autosuggestion that produced the universe?

Yet I protest against my own lucidity. I must have Reality at any price. I have feelings only out of cowardice; very well, I wish to be a coward, to impose a "soul" upon myself, to let myself be devoured by a thirst for immediacy, to destroy all my evidence and find myself a world whatever the cost. And if I could not find a world, I would content myself with a shard of being, with the illusion that something exists, whether before my eyes or somewhere else. I would be the conquistador of a continent of lies. To be duped or die: there was no other choice. Like those who have discovered life by the detours of death, I would hurl myself upon the first deception, upon anything that might restore my lost reality.

After the banality of the abyss, what miracles in being! Existence is the unheard of, *what cannot happen*, a state of exception. And nothing can engage it save our desire to accede to it, to force an entrance, to take it by assault.

To exist is a habit I do not despair of acquiring. I shall imitate the others, the cunning ones who have managed it, the turncoats of lucidity; I shall rifle their secrets, even their hopes, quite happy to snatch with them at the indignities that lead to life. Denial is beyond my strength, or my patience; assent tempts me. Having exhausted my reserves of negation, and perhaps negation itself, why should I not run out into the street shouting at the top of my lungs that I am on the verge of discovering a truth, the only one that is worth anything? But I do not know yet what that truth is; I only know the joy which precedes it, the joy and the madness and the fear.

It is this ignorance—and not fear of ridicule—that robs me of the courage of rousing the world with my news, of observing the world's terror at the spectacle of my happiness, of my definitive assent, my fatal yes.

Since we derive our vitality from our store of madness, we have only the certitudes and therapeutics of delirium with which to oppose our dread and our doubt. By dint of unreason, let us become a source, an origin, a starting point—let us multiply by all possible means our *cosmogonic moments*. We actually exist only when we radiate time itself, when suns rise within us and we dispense their light, illuminating the hours. . . . It is then that we share in the volubility of things which are so astonished to have come into being and so impatient to broadcast their surprise in the metaphors of light. Everything swells and dilates to acquire the habit of the unexpected. A generation of miracles: everything converges upon us, for everything radiates from us. But can this really

be us—ourselves? Of our own will? Can the mind conceive so much of day, time suddenly made eternal? And what brings to birth within us this quivering space, these roaring equators?

To think we could free ourselves of our penchant for agony, of our oldest evidence, would be to deceive ourselves about our capacity for aberration. In fact, after the favor of a few bits of being, we relapse into panic and disgust, into the temptations of melancholia and the cadaver, into the deficit of being that results from the negative sentiment of death. However serious our fall, it may nevertheless be useful to us if we turn it into a discipline that can induce us to reconquer the privileges of delirium. The hermits of the first centuries of Christianity will serve us again as an example. They will teach us how, in order to raise our psychic level, we must join a permanent combat with ourselves. It is with singular appropriateness that one Father of the Church has called them "athletes of the desert." They were warriors whose state of tension, whose relentless struggles against themselves we can scarcely imagine. There were some who recited up to seven hundred prayers a day; they kept track by dropping a pebble after each one. . . . A mad arithmetic which made me admire them all the more for their matchless pride. They were not weaklings, these obsessed saints at grips with the dearest of all their possessions: *their temptations*. Living only in their behalf, they exacerbated these temptations to have still more to struggle against. Their descriptions of "desire" comprise such violence of tone that they scrape our senses raw and give us shudders no libertine author succeeds in inspiring. They were ingenious at glorifying "the flesh" in reverse. If it fascinated them to such a degree, what merit in having fought against its attractions! They were titans, more frenzied, more perverse than those of mythology; for the latter would never have been able, in their simplicity of mind, to conceive, for the accumulation of energy, all the advantages of self-loathing.

Our unprovoked natural sufferings being far too incomplete, it is up to us to augment, to intensify them, to create others for ourselves—artificial ones. Left to itself, the flesh encloses us within a narrow horizon. Only if we put it to the torture will it sharpen our perceptions and enlarge our perspectives: the mind is the result of the torments the flesh undergoes or inflicts upon itself. The anchorites knew how to remedy the insufficiency of their ills. . . . After having joined battle with the world, they had to declare war against themselves. What tranquillity for their neighbors! Does our ferocity not derive from the fact that our instincts are all too interested in other people? If we attended more to ourselves and became the center, the object of our own murderous inclinations, the sum of our intolerances would diminish. We shall never be able to estimate the number of horrors which those primitive monkish colonies spared humanity. Had all those hermits remained in the secular world how many excesses would they not have committed! For the greatest good of their time, they had the inspiration to exercise their cruelty upon themselves. If we would moderate our manners, we must learn to turn our claws upon ourselves, to develop the technique of the desert. . . .

Why, you ask, exalt this leprosy, these repulsive exceptions with which ascetic literature has gratified us? We must cling to whatever we have. At the same time that I execrate the monks and their convictions, I cannot help but admire their extravagances, their willful character, their asperity. There must be a secret in so much energy: the secret of religions themselves. And although they are perhaps not worth troubling about, the fact remains that everything that lives, every rudiment of existence, participates in a religious essence. Let us speak plainly: everything which keeps us from self-dissolution, every lie which protects us against our unbreathable certitudes is religious. When I grant myself a share in eternity, when I conceive of a permanence which includes me, I trample underfoot the evidence of my friable, worthless being, I lie to the others as to myself. Were I to do otherwise, I should disappear within an hour. We last only as long as our fictions. When we see through them, our capital of lies, our religious holdings collapse. To exist is equivalent to an act of faith, a protest against the truth, an interminable prayer. . . . As soon as they consent to live, the unbeliever and the man of piety are fundamentally the same, since both have made the only decision that defines a *being*. Ideas, doctrines—mere façades, decorative fantasies, accidents. If you have not resolved to kill yourself, there is no difference between you and the others, you belong to the faction of the living, all—no matter what their convictions—great believers. Do you deign to breathe? You are approaching sainthood, you deserve canonization. . . .

Moreover, if you are dissatisfied with yourself, if you want to change your nature, you engage yourself twice over in an act of faith: you desire two lives within one. Which is precisely what our ascetics are attempting when, by making of death a means of not dying, they take pleasure in their vigils, their cries, their nocturnal athleticism. By imitating their excesses, even outstripping them, the day will come, perhaps, when we shall have mistreated our reason as much as they did. "I am guided by whoever is madder than myself"—thus speaks our thirst. Only our flaws, the opacities of our clairvoyance, can save us: were that transparence perfect, it would strip us of the senseless creature which inhabits us, the self to whom we owe the best of our illusions and our conflicts.

Since every form of life betrays and corrupts Life, the man who is genuinely alive assumes a maximum of incompatibilities, works relentlessly at pleasure and pain alike, espousing the nuances of the one as of the other, refusing all *distinct* sensations and every unmingled state. Our inmost aridity results from our allegiance to the rule of the *definite*, from our plea in bar of imprecision, that innate chaos which by renewing our deliriums keeps us from sterility. And it is against this beneficent factor, against this chaos, that every school of thought, every philosophy reacts. And if we do not succor it with all our solicitude, we shall waste our last reserves: those which sustain and stimulate our death within us, preventing it from growing old.

After having made of death an affirmation of life, having converted its abyss into a salutary fiction, having exhausted our arguments against the evidence, we are ambushed by stagnation, depression: it is the revenge of our accumulated bile, of our nature, of this demon of common sense which, allayed for a time, awakens to denounce the ineptitude and the absurdity of our will to blindness. A whole past of merciless vision, of complicity with our ruin, of accustoming ourselves to the venom of truth, and so many years of contemplating our remains in order to extract from them the principle of our knowledge! Yet we must learn to think against our doubts and against our certitudes, against our omniscient humors, we must above all, by creating for ourselves *another* death, one that will be incompatible with our carrion carcasses, consent to the undemonstrable, to the idea that something exists. . . .

Nothingness may well have been more convenient. How difficult it is to *dissolve* oneself in Being!

Translated by Richard Howard

Michael McClure

►► **Michael McClure**

Ode to Jackson Pollock

Hand swinging the loops of paint—splashes—drips—
    Chic lavender, duende black, blue and red!

Jackson Pollock my sorrow is selfish. I won't meet
    you here. I see your crossings of paint!
We are all lost in the cloud of our gestures—

    —the smoke we make with our arms. I cry
        to my beloved too. We are lost
        in lovelessness. Our sorrows
    before us. Copy them in air! We
make their postures with our stance.

            They grow before us.
The lean black she-wolves on altars of color.
    We search our remembrance for memories
        of heroic anguish. We put down
        our pain as singing testimony.
Gouges, corruptions, wrinkles, held loose

    in the net of our feelings and hues—
we crash into their machinery making it
        as we believe. I say

    we. I—you. You saw the brightness
of pain. Ambition. We give in to the lie
        of beauty in the step of creating.
Make lies to live in. I mean you. Held
        yourself in animal suffering.
        You made your history. Of pain.

Making it real for beauty, for ambition
    and power. Invented totems from teacups
        and cigarettes. Put it all down

    in disbelief—waiting—forcing.

    Each gesture painting.—Caught on
        to the method of making each motion
your speech, your love, your rack

and found yourself. Heroic—huge—burning
    with your feelings. Like making money

    makes the body move. Calls you to action
swirling the paint and studying the feeling

    caught up in the struggle and leading it.
For the beauty of animal action
        and freedom of full reward.

To see it down—and praise—and admiration
    to lead, to feel yourself above all others.

NO MATTER WHAT—IT'S THERE! NO ONE
        can remove it. Done in full power.
Liberty and Jackson Pollock the creator.
        The mind is given credit.

            You strangled
        the lean wolf beloved to yourself—
            Guardians of the secret
        —and found yourself the secret
            spread in clouds of color

burning yourself and falling like rain

transmuted into grace and glory, free
        of innocence

    containing all, pressing experience
        through yourself onto the canvas.
Pollock I know you are there! Pollock
    do you hear me?!! Spoke to himself
        beloved. As I speak to myself
to Pollock into the air. And fall short

of the body of the beloved hovering
        always before him. Her face
not a fact, memory or experience
        but there in the air

    destroying confidence.
The enormous figure of her mystery

always there in trappings of reason.

    Worked at his sureness. Demanding
        Her place beside him. Called

    from the whirls of paint, asked for
a face and shoulders to stand naked
        before him to make a star.

He pulling the torn parts of her body
            together
    to make a perfect figure—1951.
Assembled the lovely shape of chaos.
    Seeing it bare and hideous, new
        to the old eye. Stark
black and white. The perfect figure
    lying in it peering from it.
And he gave her what limbs and lovely face
        he could
from the squares, angles, loops, splashes, broken shapes
    he saw of all with bare eye and body.

"10 — 9 — 8 — 7 — 6 — 5 ...

The Life Line

It was a March night in 1913. The moonlit air tasted of dust as Enrique Cepeda, Governor of the Federal District, arrived at the Belén prison. Thirty armed men climbed out of the cars, wiping their noses on their sleeves, lighting ragged cigarettes, polishing their leather boots against their trouser legs. Islas shouted to the prison guard, "Here comes the District Governor!" and Cepeda swaggered up to the first official and belched: "Here comes the District Governor . . ."

Gabriel Hernández was asleep in a cell. His bleared eyes opened and his obsidian mask cracked into a scowl at the kick of a black boot.

"Come on, you, get dressed."

Hernández stood up, and from the corner of his eye he saw the guards posted outside his cell. "Take him to the patio," the Subwarden ordered.

The purple air, the gray walls of Belén . . . the great riddled wall of the patio with its gunpowder blossoms. . . . Cepeda, Islas and Casa Eguía offered each other cigarettes, roaring with laughter at their complicity. The guards approached the patio wall with General Hernández in their midst.

"If I'd had a gun you wouldn't be able to murder me."

Cepeda's fat hand struck him in the face.

The five guards fired, among the echoes of the Governor's laughter. He stopped laughing with the last shot and pointed to the ground. "Burn him right here," he said, and leaned against the wall.

While the fire was consuming the General's body, while the smoke from his charred flesh was blackening Cepeda's features, Gervasio Pola and three other prisoners escaped from Belén by hiding in the garbage wagon.

During the trip from Belén to the dump, Pola thought that this was how a dead man must feel, wanting to shout to the burial party that he was still alive, had not died at all, had merely suffered a fainting spell; that they should not nail shut the coffin, should not heap dirt on him. The four men, face down under the load of garbage, pressed their nostrils to the cracks in the wooden floor, breathing the loose dust of the streets. One of them punctuated his hoarse gasping with deep sighs, and Pola would have liked to steal that lost air. His lungs were clogging up with the odors of rotten garbage when the wagon

1959

finally stopped. He nudged the man next to him and they all waited for the doors to open, for the crew to begin shoveling the refuse onto the dump.

Then they were out in the fields near San Bartolo. The two garbage men had not put up any resistance, and now they were tied to the wheels of their wagon. The mounds of gray filth, swarming with flies, spread from the road to the foot of the nearest mountain. Pola felt discouraged when he glanced at the smeared faces and wet clothing of his companions.

One of them said, "We have to reach the nearest Zapata camp by morning."

Pola looked down at the man's bare feet. Then, still looking down, he stared at the feeble naked legs of the second, the oozing fetter-sores on the ankles of the third. The mountain wind began to stir the heaps of rubbish. They had to decide on their route, on which way to flee among the rocks and thorns.

Gervasio began the march, heading toward the mountain, and the others fell in behind him Indian file. At first, as they crossed the field, their feet sank in the mud and deep weeds; later they were scratched and bloody from the daggers of the dry scrub. Gervasio slackened his pace at the foot of the sierra. A cold wind creaked in the bushes.

"We'll have to separate," he murmured without raising his eyes. "We'll keep together until just outside Tres Marías. Then Pedro and I will turn off . . . we'll take the easier route, but we'll have to dodge the Federal outpost. You and Sindulfo turn off to the left, Froilán, because you know the way to Morelos better than we do. If we don't find the camp before dark, we'll separate again, each man on his own, and hide until daybreak or hope that a Zapata detachment goes by so we can join it. If this doesn't work out . . . well, we'll see each other in Belén."

"But Sindulfo can't make it with his bad leg," Froilán Reyero said, "and the road to the left is the hardest. It would be better for Sindulfo to go with you, Gervasio, and Pedro with me."

"It would be better to keep together," Sindulfo said, "no matter what happens."

Pola raised his eyes. "You heard the plan. At least one of us can save his hide. It's better for one to escape alone than for all of us to die together. We'll follow the plan."

The cold wind that rises before dawn whipped their tired bodies, and Gervasio led the way along the path that wound up the cliffs.

Sometimes the immensities of nature do not make one feel small. Gervasio felt that his little band was a heroic army, and that their bleeding feet would sound like the marching of a throng, would ring like metal hoofs, until they had conquered the grandeur of the sierra and made it a slave to their triumph. The dawning sun revealed the dark pines along their ascent. They climbed slowly, without speaking.

Then Pola said, "Look, Froilán, who could have told you that you'd feel even lonelier up here than you did in Belén, and even more like a prisoner? I remember the first night I heard the cries. There were so many first nights, and first mornings . . . all of them the same, and all new. Like the first morning I heard the drums and the shots in the patio. But I was never the first, or the next, or the last. It was never time for me to get up and tell them I was ready and wasn't afraid, they didn't have to blindfold me. I wanted them to get mad at me, so I could show them who I was. But they never did. You know how some died weeping and thrashing and begging for mercy. They didn't know I was there in solitary waiting for the chance to spit their mercy in their faces. Every one that went to the wall left me waiting there, wanting to go in his place with my head held up. I could have taken the place of any one of them on the march to the patio. They never let me."

"I don't care what happens," Pedro said, "as long as you don't leave me alone out here. We're better off together. They caught us together and they'll catch us again and shoot the four of us at once. But I don't want to be left alone out here on the mountain."

Sindulfo said nothing, merely reached down with his arms, trying to touch his festering ankles without stopping walking.

They halted at noon among the highest peaks, where they were to separate, and sat down in the shadow of a pine.

"There isn't any water here to wash Sindulfo's sores," Froilán Reyero said.

"Don't think about water," Sindulfo said.

"Or about food," Gervasio said with a laugh.

"Food," Pedro murmured.

"I said, don't think about it."

"We're getting near Tres Marías."

"I know. It's time to split up."

"I don't like it, Gervasio."

"You know the country better than any of us. Don't complain. I'm the one who's going to have a hard time."

"I don't want to be alone."

"There was an old man back home in the village who wanted to die all alone. He'd thought about death for a long time, so that it wouldn't take him by surprise. When he thought it was near he told everybody to get out of the house and let him meet it by himself. He wanted to enjoy it alone because he'd waited for it for so long. That night, when he knew it was almost time, he got out to the door somehow, with his eyes staring, and tried to tell the others what dying was like. I saw the whole thing because I'd sneaked into the yard to steal oranges. I was grateful I could see him die."

Pedro was silent.

"But there won't be anybody to say anything to . . . before. The moment before."

"You can tell it to one of the Federals."

"They don't give you time. If you're alone, that's the end. If you're with others, you can exchange a look with your friends before you die."

"And there won't be anybody to pardon you," Pedro said.

Gervasio thought that the vultures pardon us, the earth pardons us, even the worms pardon us at the end of their feast. He stood up under the tree and looked out across the valley. Suddenly he knew that somewhere, far away, far from the wounds of his companions, from the sorrow of this land in chains, from the ruined mountainsides and the sound of murders, somewhere on the shore of Mexico's vast and indifferent world, there would be room for the salvation of a man like himself, a man stained with filth and weariness, forgotten by the rest of Mexico, but faithful, and most faithful to Mexico when he was most faithful to himself. *I must save myself now, to save others later. They want me to die with them: it would be a comfort to my men to know we are dying together. They would even prefer to have me die first, to make their own deaths easier. I want to save them if they will let me. But first I must save myself.*

"You know how they shot General Hernández," Froilán was saying. "And then they burned his body. He was all alone. That's what'll happen to us if they capture us again. We're better off here in the sierra, the four of us together."

"I don't want to die alone here," Sindulfo said. "Or in the prison either."

Pola hit him across the shoulders with a dry branch. The dawn light from the valley softened the anger in his eyes. "You fool! Why do you have to blubber? You've given us enough trouble already, hauling you along with that damned foot of yours. Why can't you keep your mouth shut?"

"All right, boss, all right . . ."

Froilán grasped Pola's arm. "Don't hit him again, Gervasio." Spirals of smoke were rising from the forest below them, smelling of burnt leaves and dry pine-boughs.

"Let's go, then. They're cooking down there, look at the smoke. It can mean friends or enemies. If you just think about how hungry you are, and walk straight in to the first . . ."

They separated at Tres Marías, Froilán holding up Sindulfo, clutching him around the waist, and Gervasio with Pedro behind him, rubbing his arms against the chill mountain mist. They had to avoid the Federal outpost with its numbed soldiers, its smell of fried beans, that stood between them and the first Zapata camp. Gervasio led him through the damp firs and rocks. The earth felt cold and dead under their feet. At sunset Pedro grasped his stomach with both hands and fell to his knees. Then he began to vomit. The shadows of twilight spread through the dark tangle of the forest. Pedro looked at Gervasio, his mouth twitching, and silently begged a rest, a moment to breathe.

"It's almost dark, Pedro. We've got to keep on for a while longer, then we'll separate. Come on, get up."

"Like General Hernández, the way Froilán said. First shot and then burned. That's what's ahead of us, Gervasio. It's better to stay here in the mountains and die alone, with God. Where are we going? Tell me, Gervasio, where are we going?"

"Don't talk. Give me your hand and get up."

"Yes, you're the boss, the strong man, you know we have to keep walking and walking. What you don't know is where. If we join up with Zapata, then what?"

"You don't think in a war, Pedro. You fight."

"But what's the use of fighting if you don't know what's going to come out of it? Do you think it makes any difference if we fight or not? Here we are all alone, where nobody will find us, and I've got this fever, so stop and think. What can we do, the two of us? What difference does it make what we do or say? Whatever's going to happen will happen anyway. We've done enough already. Let's go away, Gervasio, let's get out of it as fast as we can. It won't make any difference."

"What do you want to do?"

"Let's go to Cuautla and see if we can find some decent clothes or some money. Then each one to his own home."

"They'll hunt you down, they'll catch you, Pedro. You can't get out of it now. Besides, there's no place to go. Mexico doesn't have any hiding places. It's the same for everybody."

"And afterwards?"

"Then we go home."

"To the same as before?"

"Don't ask questions. When you get into a revolution you stop asking questions. You just do what you have to do, that's all."

"But seriously, who's going to win? Have you ever thought about that?"

"We don't know who's going to win. Everyone'll win, Pedro. Everyone who stays alive. We're still alive. Come on, stand up."

"It's that fever, Gervasio. As if I had rats eating me in my stomach."

"Let's go. It's almost night."

"We ought to sleep here. I can't go any farther."

The air was loud with the whirr of the cicadas, and a cold wind came up the slope. Pedro was still on his knees, rubbing his arms again. It grew darker.

"Don't leave me, Gervasio, don't leave me. . . . You're the only one who knows where we should go. . . . Don't leave me, for the love of God . . ."

He reached down and clawed the earth. "Please come up close . . . I'm cold . . . we can warm each other . . ." He pitched forward with his face in the dust. "Talk to me, Gervasio. Don't bury me here all alone . . ." He wanted to look at his hands, to see if he was still alive, but the night was black now, and full of terrors. "Take me away," he shouted, "take me away, Gervasio. Let's go back to prison. I'm afraid of this mountain. I don't want to be free, I want my fetters back. I want them back on, Gervasio. Gervasio! . . ."

Pedro clasped his ankles and for a moment he felt that he was a prisoner again. *But I want to be in the real prison, not a prisoner of the cold and the darkness. Dear God, tell them to put my fetters back on. I don't want to be free. I wasn't born free . . .* "Gervasio! Don't leave me alone. You're the boss, Gervasio, take me away. . . . Gervasio . . ."

His words echoed among the rocks. Gervasio Pola was running down the mountainside, toward the yellow bonfire in the valley of Morelos.

General Inés Llanos wiped his fingers on his stomach and sat down near the fire. The broad, pale sombreros of the soldiers, and their Indian eyes, shone in the firelight.

"Speak up, don't be afraid. You say you escaped from Belén?"

"Yes, sir. I escaped by myself and crossed the mountain in one day." He blew on his chilled hands. "Now I want to join Zapata and keep on fighting."

The General laughed and took another tortilla from the brazier. "You're so stupid I almost pity you. Don't you know how to read? What does the *Plan de Ayala* say? It says that Madero was too weak. And who kicked him out? General Victoriano Huerta, our new boss . . ."

"But Zapata?"

"Piss on Zapata. You're talking to Inés Llanos, your humble servant. I represent the legitimate government, and tomorrow you'll be back in Belén. So eat a few tortillas, because it's a long hard trip."

Gervasio Pola entered the gray walls of Belén for the second time. The black splotch in the patio showed where the body of General Hernández had been burned. Pola walked across the ashes, and his knees trembled. In solitary he wanted to sleep, but two officials came into his cell.

"I don't need to tell you," the blond Captain said, "that we're going to take you out to the wall." He stared at the ceiling. "But first you're going to tell us where to find the prisoners that escaped with you. Pedro Ríos, Froilán Reyero, and Sindulfo Mazotl."

"You'll catch them anyhow . . ."

"Of course. But we want to shoot the four of you together, as an example. So tell us where or tomorrow you'll stand against the wall all alone."

The cell door creaked shut, and Gervasio heard their footsteps fading away on the stones of the long gallery. A cold wind blew in through the bars. Gervasio lay down on the stone floor. *Tomorrow . . . against the wall. Alone. Tomorrow. And my knees trembled when I walked across those ashes. . . . We're going to be a bridge of ashes: Pedro will cross mine, and Sindulfo will cross Pedro's, and Froilán will cross Sindulfo's. We won't be able to say goodbye to each other except with our footsteps. Against the wall, alone. Trying to forget what I know, and remember what I've forgotten. We were going to be heroes, but what does it feel like when a bullet hits you in the guts . . . and then another one . . . and then another one? . . . You won't see the blood running out of you. There won't be time. You won't see the Captain either, he'll come up to you with his pistol to shoot you again, right between the eyes, to make sure you're dead, but you won't be able to speak to him, to beg him to have pity on you. I'm afraid. Dear God, I'm afraid, I'm afraid . . . and You aren't going to die with me. I'm going to die alone. I can't tell You about it, You wouldn't understand, You aren't going to die tomorrow. But my friends would understand. We could talk about it, about dying, and then stop talking at the right moment, and then die together. . . . Together, together . . .*

Gervasio stood up and shouted to the guard, "Tell the Captain to come back . . ."

(Pedro stopped in the mountains beyond Tres Marías, just beyond the Federal outpost. He was sick, he would still be there. Froilán and Sindulfo went left and the trail was bad and Sindulfo was a cripple, they could not have gone very far. Besides, they had not eaten for days, and with the cold weather . . .)

On a Sunday morning, before the church bells had begun to ring, Gervasio walked sleepily down the hollow gallery of Belén. He felt of his shoulders, his face, his stomach, his testicles: they had a better right to live than he did, but they were going to die. He wanted to remember everything that had ever happened to him, but all he could remember was a bird wetting its wings in a river down in the lowlands. He tried to think of other things, of women, of his parents, but he could only see that wet bird. The guards halted and Froilán, Pedro, and Sindulfo came out of another cell. He didn't see their faces but he knew they were his friends. They were going to die together, then, all four of them. The dawning sun bathed his face. He felt as he had felt in the mountains, not small but great, a hero. They marched up the wall and gave a half-turn, so as to face the firing squad.

"We'll go to heaven together," Gervasio murmured to his companions.

"What a bitch of a way to die," Sindulfo said.

Gervasio filled his lungs with air. "We'll fall together. Give me your hand. Tell the others to join hands."

Then he saw the eyes of his companions, and felt that death would appear to them first. He closed his own eyes so that life would not leave him before it was time. The bird, torn to pieces, fell into the river, and the Captain stepped forward to give the *coup de grâce* to the four men writhing in the dust.

"Next time, see if you can't kill them yourselves," he said to the firing squad. Then he walked away, looking at the lines on the palm of his hand.

Translated by Lysander Kemp

►► Juan Rulfo

from PEDRO PÁRAMO

I came to Comala because I was told that my father, a certain Pedro Páramo, was living here. My mother told me so, and I promised her I would come to see him as soon as she died. I pressed her hand so that she'd know I would do it, but she was dying and I was in the mood to promise her anything. "Be sure you go and visit him," she told me. "I know he'll be pleased to know you." So all I could do was to keep telling her I would do it, and I kept on saying it until I had to pry my hand loose from her dead fingers.

Before that she told me, "Don't ask him for anything that isn't ours. Just for what he should have given me and didn't. Make him pay for the way he forgot us."

"All right, Mother."

I didn't intend to keep my promise. But then I began to think about what she told me, until I couldn't stop thinking and even dreaming about it, and building a whole world around that Pedro Páramo. That's why I came to Comala.

It was in the dog days, when the hot August wind is poisoned by the rotten smell of the saponaria, and the road went up and down, up and down. They say a road goes up or down depending on whether you're coming or going. If you're going away it's uphill, but it's downhill if you're coming back.

"What's the name of that village down there?"

"Comala, sir."

"You're sure it's Comala?"

"Yes, sir."

"Why does it look so dead?"

"They've had bad times, sir."

I expected it to look the way it did in my mother's memories. She was always sighing for Comala, she was homesick and wanted to come back but she never did. Now I was coming back in her place, and I remembered what she told me: "There's a beautiful view when you get to Los Colimotes. You'll see a green plain . . . it's yellow when the corn is ripe. You can see Comala from there. The houses are all white, and at night it's all lighted up." Her voice was soft and secret, almost a whisper, as if she were talking to herself.

"And why are you going to Comala?" I heard him ask me.

"To see my father."

"Oh," he said.

And we were silent again.

We were walking downhill, hearing the steady trot of the burros. Our eyes were half-closed, we were so tired and sleepy in the August heat.

"They'll give you a fine party," he said. "They'll be glad to see somebody again. It's been years since anybody came here."

Then he added: "It's you, so they'll be glad to see you."

The heat shimmered on the plain like a transparent lake. There was a line of mountains beyond the plain, and beyond that, nothing but the distance.

"What does your father look like?"

"I don't know," I said. "I just know that he's called Pedro Páramo."

"Oh."

But the way he said it, it was almost like a gasp. I said, "At least that's what they told me his name was."

I heard him say, "Oh," again.

I met him in Los Encuentros, where three or four roads come together. I was just waiting there, and finally he came by with his burros.

"Where are you going?" I asked him.

"That way, señor," he said, pointing.

"Do you know where Comala is?"

"That's where I'm going."

So I followed him. I walked along behind, keeping up with his steps, until he understood I was following him and slowed down a little. After that we walked side by side, almost touching shoulders.

He said, "Pedro Páramo is my father too."

A flock of crows flew across the empty sky, crying caw, caw, caw.

After we crossed the ridge we started downhill again. We left the warm air up there and walked down into pure heat without a breath of air in it. Everything looked as if it were waiting for something.

"It's hot here," I said.

"This is nothing. Just wait, you'll be a lot hotter when you get to Comala. That town's the hottest place in the world. They say that when somebody dies in Comala, after he arrives in hell he goes back to get his blanket."

"Do you know Pedro Páramo?" I asked him.

I dared to ask him questions because I had an idea I could trust him.

"Who is he?" I asked.

"He's hate. He's just pure hate."

He lashed the burros even though he didn't need to, because they were keeping ahead of us down the slope.

I had my mother's picture in my shirt pocket and I could feel it warming my heart, as if she were sweating too. It was an old picture, all frayed at the edges, but it was the only one I knew about. I found it in the kitchen in a box full of herbs, and I've kept it ever since. My mother hated to have her picture taken. She said pictures were for witchcraft, and maybe she was right, because the picture was full of holes, like needle holes. Near the heart there was a hole so big you could put your middle finger into it.

It's the same picture I have with me now. I hope it'll help me with Pedro Páramo when he recognizes who it is.

"Look," he said, stopping. "See that mountain, the one that looks like a pig's bladder? Good. Now look over there. See the ridge of that mountain? Now look over here. See that mountain way off there? Well, all that's the Media Luna, everything you can see. And it all belongs to Pedro Páramo. He's our father, but we were born on a petate on the floor. And the real joke is that he took every one of us to be baptized. He took you, didn't he?"

"I don't know."

"You go to hell."

"What did you say?"

"I said we're almost there, señor."

"I know. But what about the village? It looks deserted."

"That isn't how it looks. It is. Nobody lives there any more."

"And Pedro Páramo?"

"Pedro Páramo died a long time ago."

It was the hour when the children play in the streets in every village, filling the afternoon with their shouts. When the walls still reflect the yellow light of the sun.

At least that's what I saw in Sayula yesterday at the same hour. I also saw the doves flying in the still air. They circled around and disappeared over the roof tops, and the shouts of the children flew up like birds.

Now I was here in this silent village. I heard the sound of my footsteps on the fieldstones that paved the streets. A hollow sound, echoing against the walls.

I was walking down the main street, past the empty houses with their broken doors and their weeds. What did what's-his-name call that weed? "Captain's wife, señor. It's a pest that just waits till a house is empty, then it moves in. You'll see what it's like."

When I was passing a corner I saw a woman wrapped up in a rebozo, but she disappeared as if she didn't even exist. I kept on walking, looking into the open doorways. Suddenly she crossed the street in front of me.

"Good evening," she said.

I followed her with my eyes. "Where does Doña Eduviges live?" I called to her.

And she pointed: "There. The house next to the bridge."

I knew that her voice was a living human voice. That she had teeth in her mouth, and a tongue that moved when she talked, and eyes like the eyes of everybody else on earth.

It was growing dark.

She called out, "Good night!" to me. There weren't any children playing, or any doves, but I felt that the village was still alive, and that if I didn't hear anything except the silence, that was because I wasn't used to silence, with my head still so full of noises and voices.

Especially voices. And here where the air was so dead, they sounded even louder. I remembered what my mother told me: "You'll hear me better there, better than now. I'll be nearer to you there." My mother . . . living.

I'd wanted to tell her, "You made a mistake, you didn't give me the right directions. You told me where this was and that was, and here I am in a dead village, looking for somebody who doesn't even exist."

I found the house at the bridge by walking toward the sound of the river, and knocked on the door. Or I tried to. But my hand just knocked on empty air, as if the wind had opened the door. A woman stood there. She said: "Come in."

And I went in.

I stayed in Comala. Before he left me, the man with the burros said: "I'm going farther on. My house is over there, where the mountains come together. If you want to come along, you'll be welcome. But if you want to stay here, go ahead, even if it's just to take a look at the village. Maybe you'll find somebody living."

I stayed. That's what I came to do.

"Where can I find a place to stay?" I called to him. I almost had to shout.

"Look for Doña Eduviges, if she's still alive. Tell her I sent you."

"What's your name?"

"Abundio . . ." But I couldn't hear his last name.

"I'm Eduviges Dyada. Come in."

It looked as if she'd been waiting for me. She said everything was ready, and I followed her through a long row of dark rooms. They seemed empty at first, but when I got used to the darkness and the narrow thread of light that followed us, I could see shadows on both sides. I thought we must be walking through a passageway between piles of bundles.

"What have you got in here?" I asked.

"Junk," she said. "The whole house is full of junk. All those that went away picked this house to keep their furniture and belongings in, and they don't come back for them. But the room I've kept for you is at the rear. I always keep the junk out of it, in case somebody comes back. And so you're her son, then?"

"Whose?"

"Doloritas'."

"Yes . . . but how do you know?"

"She told me you were coming. She said you'd arrive today."

"Who? My mother?"

"Yes."

I didn't know what to think, and she didn't explain.

"This is your room," she said.

There wasn't any door, just an opening, and when she lit the candle I could see it was empty.

"It doesn't have any bed," I told her.

"Don't worry about that. You're tired, and just being tired is enough of a mattress. You can sleep on the floor, and I'll fix your bed tomorrow. You ought to know it isn't easy to furnish a room on the spur of the moment. You have to know in advance, and your mother didn't let me know till just today."

"My mother . . . my mother is dead."

"Oh, then that's why her voice sounded so weak. As if she were a long way away. Now I understand. And when did she die?"

"Seven days ago."

"Poor Dolores. She must have felt deserted. We promised each other we'd die together. So that we could give each other courage on the way, in case it was necessary. In case there were any difficulties. We were very close friends. Didn't she ever talk to you about me?"

"No, never."

"That's strange. We made that promise when we were girls. And it was just after she was married. But we were very fond of each other. Your mother was so pretty, so . . . well, let's say so sweet, you couldn't help loving her. But I'm sure I'll catch up with her. I know how far away heaven is, all right, but I know the shortcuts. You just die, God willing, when you want to, not when He arranges it. Or if you want you can make Him arrange it earlier. Excuse me for talking to you like this, but I can't help thinking of you as my son. Yes, I've said many times, 'Dolores' son should have been mine.' I'll tell you why later. The only thing I want to tell you right now is that I'll catch up with her on one of the roads to heaven."

I thought the woman must be crazy. Then I didn't think anything at all, except that I must be in some other world. My body seemed to be floating, it was so limp, and you could have played with it as if it were a rag doll.

"I'm tired," I said.

"First come and eat something. A little something or other."

"I will. But later."

The water that dripped from the roof tiles was making a hole in the sand in the patio. It fell drip, drip, drip on a laurel leaf, and the leaf bowed down and bobbed up again. The storm had already passed. Now and then, when the wind shook the branches of the pomegranate tree, there was a little shower under the tree, printing the ground with brilliant drops for a moment until they sank in and blurred. During the storm the chickens were all hunched up as if asleep, but now they stretched their wings and strutted out into the patio, gobbling up the earthworms the rain brought out. The sun glowed on the stones, lit everything up with colors, drank up the water from the earth, played with the shining air that played with the leaves.

"What are you doing in the toilet so long?"

"Nothing, Mamma."

"If you stay there, a snake'll come and bite you."

"Yes, Mamma."

I was thinking of you, Susana. In the green hills. When we flew kites in the windy season. We heard the sounds of the village down below us while we were up there, up on the hill, and the wind was tugging the string away from me. 'Help me, Susana.' And gentle hands grasped my hands. 'Let out more string.'

The wind made us laugh; our glances met while the string paid out between our fingers; but it broke, softly, as if it had been struck by the wings of a bird. And up there the paper bird fell in somersaults, dragging its rag tail, until it was lost in the green of the earth.

Your lips were moist, as if they had been kissing the dew.

"I told you to come out of the toilet."

"Yes, Mamma. Right away."

I was remembering you. When you were there looking at me with your sea-green eyes.

He looked up and saw his mother in the doorway.

"Why are you taking so long? What are you doing?"

"I'm thinking."

"Can't you think somewhere else? It isn't good for you to spend so much time in the toilet. Besides, you ought to be working at something. Why don't you go to your grandmother's to help with the corn?"

"All right, Mamma. Right away."

"Grandmother, I'm going to help with the corn."

"We've already finished . . . but we're going to make some chocolate. Where have you been? We were looking for you all during the storm."

"I was in the other patio."

"What were you doing? Praying?"

"No, Grandmother. I was just watching it rain."

His grandmother looked at him with those eyes of hers, half-yellow and half-gray, that seemed to look inside a person and read his thoughts.

"Well, then, go and clean the mill."

Susana, you are miles and miles away, above all the clouds, far away above everything, hidden. Hidden in His immensity, behind His Divine Providence, where I can never find you or see you. Where my words can never reach you.

"Grandmother, the mill's broken."

"That Micaela must have broken it. She breaks everything in the house, and she just won't learn. But there's no help for it."

"Why don't we buy a new one? This one's so old it isn't worth fixing."

"I suppose you're right. But it cost so much to bury your grandfather, and then all these tithes to the church, I don't think there's a centavo in the house. Well, we'll simply have to sacrifice ourselves and buy a new one. Go see Doña Inés Villalpando and ask her to give us one on credit until October. We can pay her out of the harvest."

"Yes, Grandmother."

"And while you're at it, tell her to lend us a sifter and a pruning knife. The way all these plants are growing, pretty soon they'll crowd us out into the street. If I still had my big house with the land out back and all, I wouldn't complain, but your grandfather sold it when we came here. God knows nothing ever comes out the way you want it to. Tell Doña Inés that we'll pay her what we owe her out of the harvest."

"Yes, Grandmother."

There were hummingbirds in the patio. It was that time of year. They were buzzing among the jasmine flowers.

He went past the doorway of the Sacred Heart and found twenty-four centavos. He left four centavos and kept the twenty.

Before he left, his mother asked him: "Where are you going?"

"To Doña Inés Villalpando's, to buy a new mill. The old one's broken."

"Tell her to give you a yard of black taffeta and put it on our bill."

"All right, Mamma."

"And on your way back, buy me some aspirins. There's some money in the flowerpot in the entry."

He found a peso. He left his twenty centavos and took the peso.

"Now," he thought, "I've got more than enough money, no matter what happens."

"Pedro!" they shouted at him, "Pedro!"

But he didn't hear them. He was far away.

It rained again in the night. He listened to the drumming of the water for a long while, but then he fell asleep, and when he woke up all he could hear was a quiet drizzle. The windowpane was glazed with water, and the heavy drops ran down it like tears. *I was watching the drops fall, Susana, in the glare of the lightning, and every breath I breathed was a sigh, and every thought was a thought of you.*

The rain turned into a breeze. He heard: "The forgiveness of our sins and the resurrection of the flesh. Amen." That was inside, where the women were finishing the Rosary. They stood up, bolted the door, and put out the light.

All that was left was the night light, and the sound of the rain, like the chirping of crickets . . .

"Why didn't you come to the Rosary? You know we're still praying for your grandfather."

His mother stood there in the shadow of the doorway, with a candle in her hand. Her shadow quivered on the ceiling. It was long and spread out, and the beams broke it up into pieces.

He said: "I don't feel well."

She went away. She put out the candle. When she closed the door and went away, the sobs came, mingled with the sob of the rain.

The church clock rang the hours, one after another, one after another, as if somehow time had shriveled.

"As I said, I almost was your mother. Didn't she tell you about it?"

"No. She never told me anything like that. I heard about you from somebody named Abundio. I didn't catch his last name, but he drives burros."

"Of course, Abundio. So he still remembers me! I used to give him a tip for every person he brought to the house. But everything's different now, with the village so poor, and nobody ever comes here. You say he recommended me to you?"

"He told me to be sure to look for you."

"I can't help being grateful to him. He was a good man, Abundio. Dependable, you know. He used to carry the mail, even after he went deaf. I remember the day it happened. We all felt sorry for him, because we liked him, he used to carry the mail and tell us what was happening out there in the world. I expect he told them out there what was going on back here. He was a great one to talk. And then he stopped talking, just like that. He said it wasn't any use talking if you couldn't hear what you were saying. What happened was that one of those skyrockets, the kind that explodes, went off right over his head. After that he didn't talk, even though he still could. But he was a good man, Abundio, even so."

"The man I told you about wasn't deaf."

"No? Then it couldn't be the same one. Besides, Abundio's dead. I'm sure he must be dead. Didn't he tell you? It couldn't be the same one."

She shook her head.

"But to get back to your mother," she said. "I was going to tell you . . ."

I listened, but I also looked at her closely. I thought she must have suffered a lot at some time in her life. Her face was so pale, you would think there wasn't any blood in her body, and her hands were all wrinkled and withered up. You couldn't see her eyes. She had on an old white dress with a lot of lace, and a medal of the Virgin on a piece of twine, with the words *Refuge of Sinners.*

". . . And as I was saying, he was the man who tamed horses in the Media Luna. His name was Inocencio Osorio but everybody called him The Jumpingjack because he was so light on his feet. Pedro said he was good at breaking in colts, but he was good at something else, too, and it wasn't taming, it was stirring things up. I mean at stirring up dreams, and that's the truth. He had an affair with your mother, and with lots of others. Including myself. One time when I was sick he came to the house and said, 'I'm going to examine you, so you'll get better.' When he said that it always meant he'd handle you all over, first just your fingertips, then rubbing your hands, then your arms, until finally he got to your legs, rubbing and rubbing, so that if they were cold before, pretty soon they were hot. And all the time he'd be telling you your fortune. He'd go into a sort of trance and roll his eyes like a gypsy, and sometimes he'd end up stark naked because he said that's what we wanted. Sometimes he'd be right, too. He couldn't be wrong every time.

"But what I wanted to tell you is that when this Osorio went to see your mother he told her she shouldn't have anything to do with any man that night, because the moon was very unfavorable.

"So Dolores came to tell me she didn't know what to do. She said she couldn't go to bed with Pedro Páramo, even though it was their wedding night. I tried to tell her not to pay any attention to Osorio, he was nothing but a liar and a swindler.

" 'I can't do it,' she said. 'You go in my place. He'll never know the difference.'

"Of course I was a lot younger than she was, and not quite so dark-skinned, but he wouldn't be able to tell in the darkness.

" 'I can't do it, Dolores. You've got to sleep with him yourself.'

" 'Please do me this one favor. I'll pay you back with others.'

"In those days your mother was a girl with meek eyes. If there was anything really beautiful about her, it was her eyes. And she knew how to talk you into anything.

" 'Please go in my place,' she said.

"And I went.

"The darkness helped me, and so did something she didn't know, which was that I liked Pedro Páramo too.

"I got into bed with him, full of love, and embraced him, but he'd been out on a spree the day before and was all tired out. He coughed and coughed but all he did was put his legs between mine.

"I got up before dawn and went to see Dolores. I said:

" 'Now you go. It's another day.'

" 'What did he do with you?' she asked.

" 'I don't know yet,' I said.

"You were born the next year, I wasn't your mother, but I almost was.

"I suppose your mother was embarrassed to tell you about all this."

My mother. ". . . Green fields. You can see the horizon rise and fall when the wind moves in the wheat, or when the rain ruffles it in the afternoon. The color of the earth, the smell of alfalfa and bread. A village that smells of new honey . . ."

"She always hated Pedro Páramo. 'Doloritas! Have you told them to fix my breakfast?' And your mother would get up before dawn to light the fire. The cats would wake up and follow her around, a whole parade of them. 'Doña Doloritas!'

"How many times did your mother hear that?

'Doña Doloritas, I can't eat this, it's cold.' How many times? And even though she was used to the worst, those meek eyes of hers began to harden."

". . . And everything had the flavor of orange blossoms in the warmth of the season . . ."

"Finally she began to sigh.

" 'Why are you sighing, Doloritas?'

"I was with them that afternoon. We were out in the fields watching the flocks of little birds, and there was one buzzard circling in the sky.

" 'Why are you sighing, Doloritas?'

" 'I'd like to be a buzzard like that one, so I could fly to where my sister is.'

" 'All right, Doña Doloritas. You can go see her right now, today. Let's go back to the house so you can pack your suitcase.'

"And your mother went.

" 'Goodbye, Don Pedro.'

" 'Goodbye, Doloritas.'

"She left the Media Luna for good. A few months afterward I asked Pedro Páramo about her.

" 'She likes her sister better than me. She's probably happy now. Anyway, I was getting tired of her. I'm not going to inquire about her, if that's what you're thinking.'

" 'But what will they live on?'

" 'Let God help them out.' "

". . . But make him pay you for having abandoned us . . ."

"And until now when she told me you were coming to see me, we didn't hear another thing about her."

"We went to live with my Aunt Gertrudis in Colima," I told her. "She kept saying what a burden we were. 'Why don't you go back to your husband?' she'd ask my mother.

" 'Has he sent for me? No. I won't go back if he doesn't send for me. I came here because I wanted to see you. Because you're my sister, that's why.'

" 'I understand. But it's time you went back. . .' "

I thought that woman was listening to me, but she had her head cocked as if she heard some faraway murmur. Then she said:

"When are you going to get some rest?"

The day you went away, I knew I would never see you again. Your face was dark in the blood-red light of the setting sun. You were smiling. You left the village behind you, and how often you had told me: "I like it because of you, but I hate it for everything else. Even for having been born in it." I thought: "She is not coming back." And I told myself many times: "Susana is not coming back. Susana is never coming back."

"What are you doing here? Aren't you working?"

"No, Grandmother. Rogelio wants me to watch the baby, and I'm taking him for a walk. It's a hard job to watch both the telegraph and the baby, with Rogelio just drinking beer in the billiard parlor. Besides, he doesn't pay me anything."

"You aren't there to get paid, you're there to learn. When you know a little something, then you can start asking for pay. Right now you're just an apprentice. Maybe tomorrow or the day after you'll be the boss. But you've got to have patience, and learn how to take orders. If he tells you to take the baby for a walk, then do it, for the love of God. You've got to resign yourself."

"That's all right for other people, Grandmother. Not for me."

"You and your ideas! I'm afraid you're going to turn out bad, Pedro Páramo."

Translated by Lysander Kemp

Sports

On the Beach

Music

Gastronomy

The Good Life

The End

Gentlemen from Franz Hals Paintings (1957). Drawing
by José Luis Cuevas

Todos Santos, Día de Muertos

The solitary Mexican loves fiestas and public gatherings. Any occasion for getting together will serve, any pretext to stop the flow of time and commemorate men and events with festivals and ceremonies. We are a ritual people, and this characteristic enriches both our imaginations and our sensibilities, which are equally sharp and alert. The art of the fiesta has been debased almost everywhere else, but not in Mexico. There are few places in the world where it is possible to take part in a spectacle like our great religious fiestas with their violent primary colors, their bizarre costumes and dances, their fireworks and ceremonies, and their inexhaustible welter of surprises: the fruit, candy, toys and other objects sold on these days in the plazas and open-air markets.

Our calendar is crowded with fiestas. There are certain days when the whole country, from the most remote villages to the largest cities, prays, shouts, feasts, gets drunk and kills, in honor of the Virgin of Guadalupe or Benito Juárez. Each year on the 15th of September, at eleven o'clock at night, we celebrate the fiesta of the *Grito*[1] in all the plazas of the Republic, and the excited crowds actually shout for a whole hour . . . the better, perhaps, to remain silent for the rest of the year. During the days before and after the 12th of December,[2] time comes to a full stop, and instead of pushing us toward a deceptive tomorrow that is always beyond our reach, offers us a complete and perfect today of dancing and revelry, of communion with the most ancient and secret Mexico. Time is no longer succession, and becomes what it originally was and is: the present, in which past and future are reconciled.

But the fiestas which the Church and State provide for the country as a whole are not enough. The life of every city and village is ruled by a patron saint whose blessing is celebrated with devout regularity. Neighborhoods and trades also have their annual fiestas, their ceremonies and fairs. And each one of us—atheist, Catholic, or merely indifferent—has his own saint's day, which he observes every year. It is impossible to calculate how many fiestas we have and how much time and money we spend on them. I remember asking the mayor of a village near Mitla, several years ago, "What is the income of the village

government?" "About 3,000 pesos a year. We are very poor. But the Governor and the Federal Government always help us to meet our expenses." "And how are the 3,000 pesos spent?" "Mostly on fiestas, señor. We are a small village, but we have two patron saints."

This reply is not surprising. Our poverty can be measured by the frequency and luxuriousness of our holidays. Wealthy countries have very few: there is neither the time nor the desire for them, and they are not necessary. The people have other things to do, and when they amuse themselves they do so in small groups. The modern masses are agglomerations of solitary individuals. On great occasions in Paris or New York, when the populace gathers in the squares or stadiums, the absence of people, in the sense of a people, is remarkable: there are couples and small groups, but they never form a living community in which the individual is at once dissolved and redeemed. But how could a poor Mexican live without the two or three annual fiestas that make up for his poverty and misery? Fiestas are our only luxury. They replace, and are perhaps better than, the theater and vacations, Anglo-Saxon weekends and cocktail parties, the bourgeois reception, the Mediterranean café.

In all of these ceremonies—national or local, trade or family—the Mexican opens out. They all give him a chance to reveal himself and to converse with God, country, friends or relations. During these days the silent Mexican whistles, shouts, sings, shoots off fireworks, discharges his pistol into the air. He discharges his soul. And his shout, like the rockets we love so much, ascends to the heavens, explodes into green, red, blue and white lights, and falls dizzily to earth with a trail of golden sparks. This is the night when friends who have not exchanged more than the prescribed courtesies for months get drunk together, trade confidences, weep over the same troubles, discover that they are brothers, and sometimes, to prove it, kill each other. The night is full of songs and loud cries. The lover wakes up his sweetheart with an orchestra. There are jokes and conversations from balcony to balcony, sidewalk to sidewalk. Nobody talks quietly. Hats fly in the air. Laughter and curses ring like silver pesos. Guitars are brought out. Now and then, it is true, the happiness ends badly, in quarrels, insults, pistol shots, stabbings. But these too are part

[1] Padre Hidalgo's call-to-arms against Spain, 1810.
[2] Fiesta of the Virgin of Guadalupe.

of the fiesta, for the Mexican does not seek amusement: he seeks to escape from himself, to leap over the wall of solitude that confines him during the rest of the year. All are possessed by violence and frenzy. Their souls explode like the colors and voices and emotions. Do they forget themselves and show their true faces? Nobody knows. The important thing is to go out, open a way, get drunk on noise, people, colors. Mexico is celebrating a fiesta. And this fiesta, shot through with lightning and delirium, is the brilliant reverse to our silence and apathy, our reticence and gloom.

According to the interpretation of French sociologists, the fiesta is an excess, an expense. By means of this squandering the community protects itself against the envy of the gods or of men. Sacrifices and offerings placate or buy off the gods and the patron saints. Wasting money and expending energy affirms the community's wealth in both. This luxury is a proof of health, a show of abundance and power. Or a magic trap. For squandering is an effort to attract abundance by contagion. Money calls to money. When life is thrown away it increases; the orgy, which is sexual expenditure, is also a ceremony of regeneration; waste gives strength. New Year celebrations, in every culture, signify something beyond the mere observance of a date on the calendar. The day is a pause; time is stopped, is actually annihilated. The rites that celebrate its death are intended to provoke its rebirth, because they mark not only the end of an old year but also the beginning of a new. Everything attracts its opposite. The fiesta's function, then, is more utilitarian than we think: waste attracts or promotes wealth, and is an investment like any other, except that the returns on it cannot be measured or counted. What is sought is potency, life, health. In this sense the fiesta, like the gift and the offering, is one of the most ancient of economic forms.

This interpretation has always seemed to me to be incomplete. The fiesta is by nature sacred, literally or figuratively, and above all it is the advent of the unusual. It is governed by its own special rules, that set it apart from other days, and it has a logic, an ethic and even an economy that are often in conflict with everyday norms. It all occurs in an enchanted world: time is transformed to a mythical past or a total present; space, the scene of the fiesta, is turned into a gaily decorated world of its own; and the persons taking part cast off all human or social rank and become, for the moment, living images. And everything takes place as if it were not so, as if it were a dream. But whatever happens, our actions have a greater lightness, a different gravity. They take on other meanings and with them we contract new obligations. We throw down our burdens of time and reason.

In certain fiestas the very notion of order disappears. Chaos comes back and license rules. Anything is permitted: the customary hierarchies vanish, along with all social, sex, caste and trade distinctions. Men disguise themselves as women, gentlemen as slaves, the poor as the rich. The army, the clergy and the law are ridiculed. Obligatory sacrilege, ritual profanation is committed. Love becomes promiscuity. Sometimes the fiesta becomes a Black Mass. Regulations, habits and customs are violated. Respectable people put away the dignified expressions and conservative clothes that isolate them, dress up in gaudy colors, hide behind a mask, and escape from themselves.

Therefore the fiesta is not only an excess, a ritual squandering of the goods painfully accumulated during the rest of the year; it is also a revolt, a sudden immersion in the formless, in pure being. By means of the fiesta society frees itself from the norms it has established. It ridicules its gods, its principles and its laws: it denies its own self.

The fiesta is a revolution in the most literal sense of the word. In the confusion that it generates, society is dissolved, is drowned, insofar as it is an organism ruled according to certain laws and principles. But it drowns in itself, in its own original chaos or liberty. Everything is united: good and evil, day and night, the sacred and the profane. Everything merges, loses shape and individuality, and returns to the primordial mass. The fiesta is a cosmic experiment, an experiment in disorder, reuniting contradictory elements and principles in order to bring about a renascence of life. Ritual death promotes a rebirth; vomiting increases the appetite; the orgy, sterile in itself, renews the fertility of the mother or of the earth. The fiesta is a return to a remote and undifferentiated state, prenatal or presocial. It is a return that is also a beginning, in accordance with the dialectic that is inherent in social processes.

The group emerges purified and strengthened from this plunge into chaos. It has immersed itself in its own origins, in the womb from which it came. To express it in another way, the fiesta denies society as an organic system of differentiated forms and principles, but affirms it as a source of creative energy. It is a true "re-creation," the opposite of the "recreation" characterizing modern vacations, which do not entail any rites or ceremonies whatever and are as individualistic and sterile as the world that invented them.

Society communes with itself during the fiesta. Its members return to original chaos and freedom. Social structures break down and new relationships, unexpected rules, capricious hierarchies are created. In the general disorder everybody forgets himself and enters into otherwise forbidden situations and places. The bounds between audience and actors, officials and servants, are erased. Everybody takes part in the fiesta, everybody is caught up in its whirlwind. Whatever its mood, its character, its meaning, the fiesta is participation, and this trait distinguishes it from all other ceremonies and social phenomena. Lay or religious, orgy or saturnalia, the fiesta is a social act based on the full participation of all its celebrants.

Thanks to the fiesta the Mexican opens out, participates, communes with his fellows and with the values that give meaning to his religious or political existence. And it is significant that a country as sorrowful as ours should have so many and such joyous fiestas. Their frequency, their brilliance and excitement, the enthusiasm with which we take part, all suggest that without them we would explode. They free us, if only momentarily, from the thwarted impulses, the inflammable desires that we carry within us. But the Mexican fiesta is not merely a return to an original state of formless and normless liberty: the Mexican is not seeking to return, but to escape from himself, to exceed himself. Our fiestas are explosions. Life and death, joy and sorrow, music and mere noise are united, not to re-create or recognize themselves, but to swallow each other up. There is nothing so joyous as a Mexican fiesta, but there is also nothing so sorrowful. Fiesta night is also a night of mourning.

If we hide within ourselves in our daily lives, we discharge ourselves in the whirlpool of the fiesta. It is more than an opening out: we rend ourselves open. Everything—music, love, friendship—ends in tumult and violence. The frenzy of our festivals shows the extent to which our solitude closes us off from communication with the world. We are familiar with delirium, with songs and shouts, with the monologue . . . but not with the dialogue. Our fiestas, like our confidences, our loves, our attempts to reorder our society, are violent breaks with the old or the established. Each time we try to express ourselves we have to break with ourselves. And the fiesta is only one example, perhaps the most typical, of this violent break. It is not difficult to name others, equally revealing: our games, which are always a going to extremes, often mortal; our profligate spending, the reverse of our timid investments and business enterprises; our confessions. The somber Mexican, closed up in himself, suddenly explodes, tears open his breast and reveals himself, though not without a certain complacency, and not without choosing a stopping-place in the shameful or terrible mazes of his intimacy. We are not frank, but our sincerity can reach extremes that horrify a European. The explosive, dramatic, sometimes even suicidal manner in which we strip ourselves, surrender ourselves, is evidence that something inhibits and suffocates us. Something impedes us from being. And since we cannot or dare not confront our own selves, we resort to the fiesta. It fires us into the void; it is a drunken rapture that burns itself out, a pistol shot in the air, a skyrocket.

Death is a mirror which reflects the vain gesticulations of the living. The whole motley confusion of acts, omissions, regrets and hopes which is the life each one of us finds in death, not meaning or explanation, but an end. Death defines life; a death depicts a life in immutable forms; we do not change except to disappear. Our deaths illuminate our lives. If our deaths lack meaning, our lives also lacked it. Therefore we are apt to say, when somebody has died a violent death, "He got what he was looking for." Each of us dies the death he is looking for, the death he has made for himself. A Christian death or a dog's death are ways of dying that reflect ways of living. If death betrays us and we die badly, everyone laments the fact, because we should die as we have lived. Death, like life, is not transferable. If we do not die as we lived, it is because the life we lived was not really ours: it did not belong to us, just as the bad death that kills us does not belong to us. Tell me how you die and I will tell you who you are.

The opposition between life and death was not so absolute to the ancient Mexicans as it is to us. Life extended into death, and vice versa. Death was not the natural end of life but one phase of an infinite cycle. Life, death and resurrection were stages of a cosmic process which repeated itself continuously. Life had no higher function than to flow into death, its opposite and complement; and death, in turn, was not an end in itself: man fed the insatiable hunger of life with his death. Sacrifices had a double purpose: on the one hand man participated in the creative process, at the same time paying back to the gods the debt contracted by his species; on the other hand he nourished cosmic life and also social life, which was nurtured by the former.

Perhaps the most characteristic aspect of this conception is the impersonal nature of the sacrifice. Since their lives did not belong to them, their deaths lacked any personal meaning. The dead—including warriors killed in battle and women dying in childbirth, companions of Huitzilopochtli the sun god—disappeared at the end of a certain period, to return to the undifferentiated country of the shadows, to be melted into the air, the earth, the fire, the animating substance of the universe. Our indigenous ancestors did not believe that their deaths belonged to them, just as they never thought that their lives were really theirs in the Christian sense. Everything was examined to determine, from birth, the life and death of each man: his social class, the year, the place, the day, the hour. The Aztec was as little responsible for his actions as for his death.

Space and time were bound together and formed an inseparable whole. There was a particular "time" for each place, each of the cardinal points, and the center in which they were immobilized. And this complex of space-time possessed its own virtues and powers, which profoundly influenced and determined human life. To be born on a certain day was to pertain to a place, a time, a color and a destiny. All was traced out in advance. Where we dissociate space and time, mere stage sets for the actions of our lives, there were as many "space-times" for the Aztecs as there were combinations in the priestly calendar, each one endowed with a particular qualitative significance, superior to human will.

Religion and destiny ruled their lives, as morality and freedom rule ours. We live under the sign of liberty, and everything—even Greek fatality and the grace of the theologians—is election and struggle, but for the Aztecs the problem reduced itself to investigating the never-clear will of the gods. Only the gods were free, and only they had the power to choose—and therefore, in a profound sense, to sin. The Aztec religion is full of great sinful gods—Quetzalcóatl is the major example—who grow weak and abandon their believers, in the same way that Christians sometimes deny God. The conquest of Mexico would be inexplicable without the treachery of the gods, who denied their own people.

The advent of Catholicism radically modified this situation. Sacrifice and the idea of salvation, formerly collective, became personal. Freedom was humanized, embodied in man. To the ancient Aztecs the essential thing was to assure the continuity of creation; sacrifice did not bring about salvation in another world, but cosmic health; the universe, and not the individual, was given life by the blood and death of human beings. For Christians it is the individual who counts. The world—history, society—is condemned beforehand. The death of Christ saved each man in particular. Each one of us is Man, and represents the hopes and possibilities of the species. Redemption is a personal task.

Both attitudes, opposed as they may seem, have a common note: life, collective or individual, looks forward to a death that in its way is a new life. Life only justifies and transcends itself when it is realized in death, and death is also a transcendence, in that it is a new life. To Christians death is a transition, a somersault between two lives, the temporal and the otherworldly; to the Aztecs it was the profoundest way of participating in the continuous regeneration of the creative forces, which were always in danger of being extinguished if they were not provided with blood, the sacred food. In both systems life and death lack autonomy, are the two sides of a single reality. They are references to invisible realities.

Modern death does not have any significance that transcends it or that refers to other values. It is rarely anything more than the inevitable conclusion of a natural process. In a world of facts, death is merely one more fact. But since it is such a disagreeable fact, contrary to all our concepts and to the very meaning of our lives, the philosophy of progress ("Progress toward what, and from what?" Scheller asked) pretends to make it disappear, like a magician palming a coin. Everything in the modern world functions as if death did not exist. Nobody takes it into account, it is suppressed everywhere: in political pronouncements, commercial advertising, public morality and popular customs; in the promise of cut-rate health and happiness offered to all of us by hospitals, drugstores and playing fields. But death enters into everything we undertake, and it is no longer a transition but a great gaping mouth that nothing can satisfy. The century of health, hygiene and contraceptives, miracle drugs and synthetic foods, is also the century of the concentration camp and the police state, Hiroshima and the murder story. Nobody thinks about death, about his own death, as Rilke asked us to do, because nobody lives a personal life. Collective slaughter is the fruit of a collectivized way of life.

Death also lacks meaning for the modern Mexican. It is no longer a transition, an access to another life more alive than our own. But although we do not view death as a transcendence, we have not eliminated it from our daily lives. The word death is not pronounced in New York, in Paris, in London, because it burns the lips. The Mexican, in contrast, is familiar with death, jokes about it, caresses it, sleeps with it, celebrates it; it is one of his favorite toys and his most steadfast love. True, there is perhaps as much fear in his attitude as in that of others, but at least death is not hidden away: he looks at it face to face, with impatience, disdain or irony. "If they are going to kill me tomorrow, let them kill me right away." [3]

The Mexican's indifference toward death is fostered by his indifference toward life. He views not

[3] From the popular folk song *La Adelita*.

only death but also life as nontranscendent. Our songs, proverbs, fiestas and popular beliefs show very clearly that the reason death cannot frighten us is that "life has cured us of fear." It is natural, even desirable, to die, and the sooner the better. We kill because life—our own or another's—is of no value. Life and death are inseparable, and when the former lacks meaning, the latter becomes equally meaningless. Mexican death is the mirror of Mexican life. And the Mexican shuts himself away and ignores both of them.

Our contempt for death is not at odds with the cult we have made of it. Death is present in our fiestas, our games, our loves and our thoughts. To die and to kill are ideas that rarely leave us. We are seduced by death. The fascination it exerts over us is the result, perhaps, of our hermit-like solitude, and of the fury with which we break out of it. The pressure of our vitality, which can only express itself in forms that betray it, explains the deadly nature, aggressive or suicidal, of our explosions. When we explode we touch against the highest point of that tension, we graze the very zenith of life. And there, at the height of our frenzy, suddenly we feel dizzy: it is then that death attracts us.

Another factor is that death revenges us against life, strips it of all its vanities and pretensions and converts it into what it really is: a few neat bones and a dreadful grimace. In a closed world where everything is death, only death has value. But our affirmation is negative. Sugar-candy skulls, and tissue-paper skulls, and skeletons strung with fireworks . . . our popular images always poke fun at life, affirming the nothingness and insignificance of human existence. We decorate our houses with death's-heads, we eat bread in the shape of bones on the Day of the Dead, we love the songs and stories in which death laughs and cracks jokes, but all this boastful familiarity does not rid us of the question we all ask: What is death? We have not thought up a new answer. And each time we ask, we shrug our shoulders: Why should I care about death if I have never cared about life?

Does the Mexican open out in the presence of death? He praises it, celebrates it, cultivates it, embraces it, but he never surrenders himself to it. Everything is remote and strange to him, and nothing more so than death. He does not surrender himself to it because surrender entails a sacrifice. And a sacrifice, in turn, demands that someone must give and someone receive. That is, someone must open out and face a reality that transcends him. In a closed, nontranscendent world, death neither gives nor receives: it consumes itself and is self-gratifying.

Therefore our relations with death are intimate—more intimate, perhaps, than those of any other people—but empty of meaning and devoid of erotic emotion. Death in Mexico is sterile, not fecund like that of the Aztecs and the Christians.

Nothing is more opposed to this attitude than that of the Europeans and North Americans. Their laws, customs, and public and private ethics all tend to preserve human life. This protection does not prevent the number of ingenious and refined murders, of perfect crimes and crime waves, from increasing. The professional criminals who plot their murders with a precision impossible to a Mexican, the delight they take in describing their experiences and methods, the fascination with which the press and public follow their confessions, and the recognized inefficiency of the systems of prevention, show that the respect for life of which Western civilization is so proud is either incomplete or hypocritical.

The cult of life, if it is truly profound and total, is also the cult of death, because the two are inseparable. A civilization that denies death ends by denying life. The perfection of modern crime is not merely a consequence of modern technical progress and the vogue of the murder story: it derives from the contempt for life which is inevitably implicit in any attempt to hide death away and pretend it does not exist. It might be added that modern technical skills and the popularity of crime stories are, like concentration camps and collective extermination, the results of an optimistic and unilateral conception of existence. It is useless to exclude death from our images, our words, our ideas, because death will obliterate all of us, beginning with those who ignore it or pretend to ignore it.

When the Mexican kills—for revenge, pleasure or caprice—he kills a person, a human being. Modern criminals and statesmen do not kill: they abolish. They experiment with beings who have lost their human qualities. Prisoners in the concentration camps are first degraded, changed into mere objects; then they are exterminated en masse. The typical criminal in the large cities—beyond the specific motives for his crimes—realizes on a small scale what the modern leader realizes on a grand scale. He too experiments, in his own way: he poisons, destroys corpses with acids, dismembers them, converts them into objects. The ancient relationship between victim and murderer, which is the only thing that humanizes murder, that makes it even thinkable, has disappeared. As in the novels of Sade, there is no longer anything except torturers and objects, instruments of pleasure and destruction. And the nonexistence of the victim makes the infinite solitude of the murderer even more intolerable. Murder is still a relationship in Mexico, and in this sense it has the same liberating significance as the fiesta or the confession. Hence its drama, its poetry and—why not say it?—its grandeur. Through murder we achieve a momentary transcendence.

At the beginning of his eighth Duino Elegy, Rilke says that the "creature," in his condition of animal innocence, "beholds the open" . . . unlike ourselves, who never look forward, toward the absolute. Fear makes us turn our backs on death, and by refusing to contemplate it we shut ourselves off from life, which is a totality that includes it. The "open" is where contraries are reconciled, where light and shadow are fused. This conception restores death's original meaning: death and life are opposites that complement each other. Both are halves of a sphere that we, subjects of time and space, can only glimpse. In the prenatal world, life and death are merged; in ours, opposed; in the world beyond, reunited again, not in the animal innocence that precedes sin and the knowledge of sin, but as in innocence regained. Man can transcend the temporal opposition separating them (and residing not in them but in his own consciousness) and perceive them as a superior whole. This recognition can take place only through detachment: he must renounce his temporal life and his nostalgia for limbo, for the animal world. He must open himself out to death if he wishes to open himself out to life. Then he will be "like the angels."

Thus there are two attitudes toward death: one, pointing forward, that conceives of it as creation; the other, pointing backward, that expresses itself as a fascination with nothingness or as a nostalgia for limbo. No Mexican or Spanish-American poet, with the possible exception of César Vallejo, approaches the first of these two concepts. The absence of a mystic—and only a mystic is capable of offering insights like those of Rilke—indicates the extent to which modern Mexican culture is insensible to religion. But two Mexican poets, José Gorostiza and Xavier Villaurrutia, represent the second of these two attitudes. For Gorostiza life is a "death without end," a perpetual falling into nothingness; for Villaurrutia it is no more than a "nostalgia for death."

The phrase that Villaurrutia chose for his book, *Nostalgia de la Muerte*, is not merely a lucky hit. The author has used it in order to tell us the ultimate meaning of his poetry. Death as nostalgia, rather than as the fruition or end of life, is death as origin. The ancient, original source is a bone, not a womb. This statement runs the risk of seeming either an empty paradox or an old commonplace: "For thou art dust, and unto dust shalt thou return." I believe that the poet hopes to find in death (which is, in effect, our origin) a revelation that his temporal life has denied him: the true meaning of life. When we die,

The second hand
will race around its dial,
all will be contained in an instant . . .
and perhaps it will be possible
to live, even after death.[4]

A return to original death would be a return to the life before life, the life before death: to limbo, to the maternal source.

Muerte sin Fin, the poem by José Gorostiza, is perhaps the best evidence we have in Latin America of a truly modern consciousness, one that is turned in upon itself, imprisoned in its own blinding clarity. The poet, in a sort of lucid fury, wants to rip the mask off existence in order to see it as it is. The dialogue between man and the world, which is as old as poetry and love, is transformed into a dialogue between the water and the glass that contains it, between the thought and the form into which it is poured and which it eventually corrodes. The poet warns us from his prison of appearances—trees and thoughts, stones and emotions, days and nights and twilights are all simply metaphors, mere colored ribbons—that the breath which informs matter, shaping it and giving it form, is the same breath that corrodes and withers and defeats it. It is a drama without personae, since all are merely reflections, the various disguises of a suicide who talks to himself in a language of mirrors and echoes, and the mind also is nothing more than a reflection of death, of death in love with itself. Everything is immersed in its own clarity and brilliance, everything is directed toward this transparent death: life is only a metaphor, an invention with which death—death too!—wants to deceive itself. The poem is a variation on the old theme of Narcissus, although there is no allusion to it in the text. And it is not only the consciousness that contemplates itself in its empty, transparent water (both mirror and eye at the same time, as in the Valéry poem): nothingness, which imitates form and life, which feigns corruption and death, strips itself naked and turns in upon itself, loves itself, falls into itself: a tireless death without end.

If we open out during fiestas, then, or when we are drunk or exchanging confidences, we do it so violently that we wound ourselves. And we shrug our shoulders at death, as at life, confronting it in silence or with a contemptuous smile. The fiesta, the crime

[4] Quoted from Xavier Villaurrutia's poem *Décima Muerte*.

of passion and the gratuitous crime reveal that the equilibrium of which we are so proud is only a mask, always in danger of being ripped off by a sudden explosion of our intimacy.

All of these attitudes indicate that the Mexican senses the presence of a stigma both on himself and on the flesh of his country. It is diffused but nonetheless living, original, and ineradicable. Our gestures and expressions all attempt to hide this wound, which is always open, always ready to catch fire and burn under the rays of a stranger's glance.

Now, every separation causes a wound. Without stopping to investigate how and when the separation is brought about, I want to point out that any break (with ourselves or those around us, with the past or the present) creates a feeling of solitude. In extreme cases—separation from one's parents, matrix or native land, the death of the gods or a painful self-consciousness—solitude is identified with orphanhood. And both of them generally manifest themselves as a sense of sin. The penalties and guilty feelings inflicted by a state of separation can be considered, thanks to the ideas of expiation and redemption, as necessary sacrifices, as pledges or promises of a future communion that puts an end to the long exile. The guilt can vanish, the wound heal over, the separation resolve itself in communion. Solitude thus assumes a purgative, purifying character. The solitary or isolated individual transcends his solitude, accepting it as a proof or promise of communion.

The Mexican does not transcend his solitude. On the contrary, he locks himself up in it. We live in our solitude like Philoctetes on his island, fearing rather than hoping to return to the world. We cannot bear the presence of our companions. We hide within ourselves—except when we rend ourselves open in our frenzy—and the solitude in which we suffer has no reference either to a redeemer or a creator. We oscillate between intimacy and withdrawal, between a shout and a silence, between a fiesta and a wake, without ever truly surrendering ourselves. Our indifference hides life behind a death mask; our wild shout rips off this mask and shoots into the sky, where it swells, explodes, and falls back in silence and defeat. Either way, the Mexican shuts himself off from the world: from life and from death.

Translated by Lysander Kemp

►► Boris Pasternak

Icefloe

Although of stripling shoots it wouldn't hazard
Any dreams as yet, the spring earth's just
Expelled through snow an adam's apple black
As river banks. The sunset's burrowed

Like a tick and stuck its head so deep
Into the gulf, you'd have to pull out Evening
From that swamp with meat attached. How fond
Of Flesh is Spaciousness in the sinister

North!—It strangles, gulping on the sun;
It hales that burden down the quaggy shore;
It slams it down upon the ice and shreds
It up like rosy salmon flesh.

For all those leaning and voracious lulls;
For all the twilight reeling of intemperate
Shades—the ice-cake knives are now unsheathed;
The clatter of green blades prevails.

The greedy, dull, and unabating screech;
That baleful clank and shock of blades; the grind
And click of blocks that yawn and clench and lock
Like heavy, vast, and masticating jaws.

Translated by R.A. Gregg

Stuart Davis Photo by Dan Budnik

►► Pierre Gascar

The Spider-Child of Madras

I had not seen him coming. He must have crept out of the shadows in the courtyard of the Chinese restaurant, where the light from the windows was dim. Not that I saw anything at eye level—only the noise of furtive scuttling over gravel revealed his presence. And then I could advance no farther: he blocked my path. I had no coins left. I tried to dodge him by taking a few steps to one side, but he followed so quickly that I was again, at bay. He made me think of a giant spider, partly becuse of his noiseless speed and the thin arms that supported him on either side of his body, but also because of the long, dead legs he dragged behind him across the gravel, like a bug only partly squashed, or hampered by too many limbs.

He was still a child, a child whose body was emaciated by paralysis and malnutrition, the bony nakedness of his chest showing through the torn shirt, his thighs about the size of a man's wrist. Ten years old?

"Come on!" exclaimed the English doctor who was with us. "I gave something to that one over there —they divided it up among themselves." He pointed to one of the chattering beggar children who surrounded us. In them, poverty became almost cheerful. Why had the paralyzed child chosen me? He did not speak; still leaning on his hands, he stretched his sharp, attentive face toward me. He did not beg, he lay in wait.

I tried to outflank him again, almost running this time. The spider-child resumed his rapid, spineless gait and sank down in front of me once more. No, he did not need to beg; he was besieging me.

I was turning out my pockets when the beggar child the English doctor had given coins to shouted something in Hindu. The spider-child moved away. I made my escape and rejoined my friends at the foot of the stairs leading up to the restaurant.

It was the best Chinese restaurant in Madras (moreover, anywhere in Asia, except for Chinese food . . .), but it was best not to be seen from the street while you were eating. Chopsticks are difficult enough to handle, even without a sense of guilt . . .

The beggar child the English doctor had given coins to was watching us eat. He had found us again in the restaurant. The eyes of hunger do not have that black intensity, the tragic depths attributed to them. The beggar child merely seemed interested in what we were doing. In Asia, eating is so remarkable

an act that people will watch you at dinner with as much attention as if you were repairing a watch.

"You take one from me?" the beggar child asked in English, turning to the English doctor. He had managed to get hold of some newspapers.

"You're picking on me," the doctor said. "But where have you been these last few days? We haven't seen you at all."

"I went to Bombay to find something. But there was nothing for me, in Bombay," the child explained. "So I have come back. . . . You take one from me?"

"You went there alone?"

"Sure," the child answered.

The doctor turned to me. "You realize what he's saying? All of eight years old. . . ." He held out a coin to the child. "Here. Now go away. We want to eat in peace."

"What a beautiful little boy," said the doctor's wife, staring after the beggar child as he moved away. She had taken too long a sunbath on her terrace that afternoon. She had not yet learned to mistrust the secret strengh of the deceptively overcast sky. Only a month before she had come out to India to be with her husband; they had been married in London some time before.

She had the girlish cast of countenance that some dark Englishwomen retain for a long time, though she was too red tonight. A little sad as well, perhaps. The doctor would leave early in the morning. The young wife went out on the terrace. Around her lay the city, white here, gray over there toward the tangle of huts. She could hear nothing from the terrace, except at night, when muffled shouts rose from around the fires below.

The rest of the time, on the terrace, there was the silence of the pale sky and the silence of nearly two million human beings made vigilant by hunger. Famine threatened the city. Each year there were thirty thousand more inhabitants, but no additional means of feeding them. The second Five-Year Plan provided for the establishment of new industries, though not tomorrow. Meanwhile, the birth rate must be lowered. It was the municipal authorities' constant concern. They urged the use of contraceptives. My God, it wasn't witchcraft! Some cotton— nothing but a little cotton. They distributed it free to the women who came to the clinics. But the population immured itself in the mute frenzy of its own multiplication, and its silence became a little more of a threat every day.

The doctor's young wife knew this silence quite well now. She knew the weight it carried. She lay out on the terrace in the sun for a long time. Then, idly, she walked back into the house that was haunted by the prowling silence of barefoot servants and, dazed by the sun, feverish, she wandered all day long from room to room, carrying her burning boredom with her.

"And look at that mischief in his eyes," she continued, nodding toward the beggar child.

He had approached a neighboring table. Three men were sitting around it—Scandinavians, probably. Dead drunk. Prohibition was severely enforced in Madras, as almost everywhere in India: they must have been sailors on shore leave. They stared at the Chinese food with gloomy detachment. The beggar child waited, his newspapers in his hand, standing on one leg in order to scratch the back of his knee with the other foot.

One of the sailors took a five-rupee note out of his pocket, stared at it, and turned it over without seeming to make any sense out of this piece of paper; he gave it to the child, whose eyes shone. The young wife was right: he was beautiful. He passed near us on his way out.

"Well, my friend, business is good tonight," the doctor said to him.

The child smiled and ran down the stairs.

"One rupee is the daily handout I give to my patients," the doctor said.

"Just enough to keep them from dying of hunger. It's what the ones who are lucky enough to work can earn. The coolies, for instance. And our *dhobies* too."

The *dhobies* did the city's washing, and they were a numerous profession. They beat the linen on big flat stones along the river bank at the city's gates. We had spent the morning among them. But on this particular morning, the doctor and his Indian nurse had not found the *dhobie* they were looking for.

She was tubercular. The British doctor who belonged to the World Health Organization was conducting, along with his Indian colleagues, an experimental anti-tuberculosis campaign based on the Isoniazide P.A.S. treatment. They had selected seventy patients from the poorest classes. Certainly there was all too wide a field to choose from. On certain days they gave these patients Isoniazide tablets. And they waited. Watched. If the results were favorable, they would try to apply this treatment to all the other tuberculosis sufferers, who numbered in the tens of thousands. So they would have to act fast. The imminence of famine complicated everything. Already they were obliged to subsidize the patients under treatment to keep them from dying of hunger. Some lived leaning aginst the trunk of a tree. There were 200,000 persons in the city with no fixed residence.

The tubercular *dhobie* and her family had been living under a porch. Behind this fact lay a whole history: among the inferior social classes of India, tuberculosis is considered a shameful disease; the *dhobie* had been driven out of her own neighborhood and had taken refuge among the untouchables, but they had expelled her in their turn; since then she had drifted all day long, and returned to her porch only at night.

When the time came for her tablets, it was not always possible to find her. The doctor and his nurse wandered through the tremendous *dhobie* quarter, partitioned into white labyrinths of drying linen.

"Why don't you ever take me with you?" the doctor's young wife asked. "I could help you, make myself useful. . . ."

The doctor did not answer. He was young too. Still very much in love. His hobby was ancient Indian painting, the kind with a Persian elaboration of detail. He had initiated his wife into its mysteries. He probably wanted to keep this soft woman lolling on the white terrace, this cool house gleaming with the discreet gilt of Indian paintings as something of himself set apart from this city whose sufferings he lived through every day.

The young wife now seemed even sadder than before, and still very red. She was thirsty, but her husband caught her arm. "Look, you know quite well how dangerous this water is. I'll order some tea. Oh, here they are again."

The beggar child had just come into the room behind one of his older comrades. They headed for the table where the sailors were sitting, still as drunk and listless as before.

"That one's their leader," the doctor said. "I wonder what's going on. . . ."

The older boy spoke to the sailors. Was it true they had given this beggar five rupees? The sailors were not sure any more, and answered with great weariness.

"He probably thinks the boy stole it from them," the doctor said. "If they commit thefts in the neighborhood, they can't stay here long, and this is their territory. They protect it against the other beggars. Their life is here, the sidewalk belongs to them, and this is where they sleep."

Later, when we left the restaurant, we found the beggar children on the sidewalk where they were settling down for the night. Hoping for more handouts, they accompanied us for quite a distance. One of them was carrying the paralyzed child on his back.

The handsome boy who had been given the five rupees was in front of us, walking backwards. He was still begging, but as if it were a game, pretending to cry, then bursting into laughter. He knew we weren't going to give him anything more. The doctor and his wife watched him with amused fondness: and that was what he was begging for.

"What if we were to adopt him?" the young wife asked her husband with choked eagerness.

"He wouldn't stay with us," the doctor replied. "They're children of the streets. They love their freedom."

I looked at the little paralytic on his comrade's back, the spider-child with the sharp face. I turned to the young wife: "What about that one? If you adopted him, do you think he would run away?"

Translated by Richard Howard

►► **Denise Levertov**

The 5-Day Rain

The washing hanging from the lemon tree
in the rain
and the grass long and coarse.

Sequence broken, tension
of bitter-orange sunlight
frayed off.
        So light a rain

fine shreds
pending above the rigid leaves.

Wear scarlet! Tear the green lemons
off the tree! I don't want
to forget who I am, what has burned in me,
and hang limp and clean, an empty dress—

►► **Henry Miller**

Defense of the Freedom to Read

On May 10th, 1957, the book Sexus (The Rosy Crucifixion), by the world-famous American author, Henry Miller, was ordered by the Attorney General [of Norway] to be cofiscated on the grounds that it was "obscene writing."

Volume I of the Danish edition of the book had at this stage been available for over eight months on the

Norwegian market, and was on sale in a considerable number of the most reputable book shops in the country.

Copies of the book were confiscated in a total of 9 book shops. Proceedings were instituted against two of these booksellers, chosen at random. . . .

In a judgment pronounced by the Oslo Town

Court on June 17th, 1958, the two booksellers were found guilty of having "offered for sale, exhibited, or in other ways endeavored to disseminate obscene writing," and this judgment has now been appealed to the Supreme Court.

It is and has been my pleasure and privilege to act as defending counsel. As a result of my official association with this case I have enjoyed a certain measure of personal contact, through the medium of correspondence, with that eminent author and warm-hearted and talented fellow human, Henry Miller.

The letter addressed to myself which is reproduced in this document, and which constitutes Henry Miller's ardent appeal to the tribunal of the Norwegian Supreme Court, is intended by him to assist in the defense of the most important bastion of freedom, democracy, and humanism: the freedom to read.

Trygve Hirsch
Barrister-at-Law

Big Sur, California
February 27th, 1959

Mr. Trygve Hirsch
Oslo, Norway

Dear Mr. Hirsch:

To answer your letter of January 19th requesting a statement of me which might be used in the Supreme Court trial to be conducted in March or April of this year. . . . It is difficult to be more explicit than I was in my letter of September 19th, 1957, when the case against my book *Sexus* was being tried in the lower courts of Oslo. However, here are some further reflections which I trust will be found à propos.

When I read the decision of the Oslo Town Court, which you sent me some months ago, I did so with mingled feelings. If occasionally I was obliged to roll with laughter—partly because of the inept translation, partly because of the nature and the number of infractions listed—I trust no one will take offense. Taking the world for what it is, and the men who make and execute the laws for what they are, I thought the decision as fair and honest as any theorem of Euclid's. Nor was I unaware of, or indifferent to, the efforts made by the Court to render an interpretation beyond the strict letter of the law. (An impossible task, I would say, for if laws are made for men and not men for laws, it is also true that certain individuals are made for the law and can only see things through the eyes of the law.)

I failed to be impressed, I must confess, by the weighty, often pompous or hypocritical, opinions adduced by scholars, literary pundits, psychologists, medicos and such like. How could I be when it is precisely such single-minded individuals, so often wholly devoid of humor, at whom I so frequently aim my shafts?

Re-reading this lengthy document today, I am more than ever aware of the absurdity of the whole procedure. (How lucky I am not to be indicted as a "pervert" or "degenerate," but simply as one who makes sex pleasurable and innocent!) Why, it is often asked, when he has so much else to give, did he have to introduce these disturbing, controversial scenes dealing with sex? To answer that properly, one would have to go back to the womb—with or without the analyst's guiding hand. Each one—priest, analyst, barrister, judge—has his own answer, usually a ready-made one. But none go far enough, none are deep enough, inclusive enough. The divine answer, of course, is—first remove the mote from your own eye!

If I were there, in the dock, my answer would probably be—"Guilty! Guilty on all ninety-seven counts! To the gallows!" For when I take the short, myopic view, I realize that I was guilty even before I wrote the book. Guilty, in other words, because I am the way I am. The marvel is that I am walking about as a free man. I should have been condemned the moment I stepped out of my mother's womb.

In that heartrending account of my return to the bosom of the family which is given in *Reunion in Brooklyn*, I concluded with these words, and I meant them, each and every one of them: "I regard the entire world as my home. I inhabit the earth, not a particular portion of it labeled America, France, Germany, Russia. . . . I owe allegiance to mankind, not to a particular country, race, or people. I answer to God, not to the Chief Executive, whoever he may happen to be. I am here on earth to work out my own private destiny. My destiny is linked with that of every other living creature inhabiting this planet—perhaps with those on other planets too, who knows? I refuse to jeopardize my destiny by regarding life within the narrow rules which are laid down to circumscribe it. I dissent from the current view of things, as regards murder, as regards religion, as regards society, as regards our well-being. I will try to live my life in accordance with the vision I have of things eternal. I say "'Peace to you all!' and if you don't find it, it's because you haven't looked for it."

It is curious, and not irrelevant, I hope, to mention at this point the reaction I had upon reading Homer recently. At the request of the publisher, Gallimard, who is bringing out a new edition of *The*

Odyssey, I wrote a short Introduction to this work. I had never read *The Odyssey* before, only *The Iliad*, and that but a few months ago. What I wish to say is that, after waiting sixty-seven years to read these universally esteemed classics, I found much to disparage in them. In *The Iliad*, or "the butcher's manual," as I call it, more than in *The Odyssey*. But it would never occur to me to request that they be banned or burned. Nor did I fear, on finishing them, that I would leap outdoors, axe in hand, and run amok. My boy, who was only nine when he read *The Iliad* (in a child's version), my boy who confesses to "liking murder once in a while," told me he was fed up with Homer, with all the killing and all the nonsense about the gods. But I have never feared that this son of mine, now going on eleven, still an avid reader of our detestable "Comics," a devotee of Walt Disney (who is not to my taste at all), an ardent movie fan, particularly of the "Westerns," I have never feared, I say, that he will grow up to be a killer. (Not even if the Army claims him!) I would rather see his mind absorbed by other interests, and I do my best to provide them, but, like all of us, he is a product of the age. No need, I trust, for me to elaborate on the dangers which confront us all, youth especially, in *this* age. The point is that with each age the menace varies. Whether it be witchcraft, idolatry, leprosy, cancer, schizophrenia, communism, fascism, or what, we have ever to do battle. Seldom do we really vanquish the enemy, in whatever guise he presents himself. At best we become immunized. But we never know, nor are we able to prevent in advance, the dangers which lurk around the corner. No matter how knowledgeable, no matter how wise, no matter how prudent and cautious, we all have an Achilles' heel. Security is not the lot of man. Readiness, alertness, responsiveness—these are the sole defenses against the blows of fate.

I smile to myself in putting the following to the honorable members of the Court, prompted as I am to take the bull by the horns. Would it please the Court to know that by common opinion I pass for a sane, healthy, normal individual? That I am not regarded as a "sex addict," a pervert, or even a neurotic? Nor as a writer who is ready to sell his soul for money? That, as a husband, a father, a neighbor, I am looked upon as "an asset" to the community? Sounds a trifle ludicrous, does it not? Is this the same *enfant terrible*, it might be asked, who wrote the unmentionable *Tropics, The Rosy Crucifixion, The World of Sex, Quiet Days in Clichy*? Has he reformed? Or is he simply in his dotage now?

To be precise, the question is—are the author of these questionable works and the man who goes by the name of Henry Miller one and the same person? My answer is yes. And I am also one with the protagonist of these "autobiographical romances." That is perhaps harder to swallow. But why? Because I have been "utterly shameless" in revealing every aspect of my life? I am not the first author to have adopted the confessional approach, to have revealed life nakedly, or to have used language supposedly unfit for the ears of schoolgirls. Were I a saint recounting his life of sin, perhaps these bald statements relating to my sex habits would be found enlightening, particularly by priests and medicos. They might even be found instructive.

But I am not a saint, and probably never will be one. Though it occurs to me, as I make this assertion, that I have been called that more than once, and by individuals whom the Court would never suspect capable of holding such an opinion. No, I am not a saint, thank heavens! nor even a propagandist of a new order. I am simply a man, a man born to write, who has taken as his theme the story of his life. A man who has made it clear, in the telling, that it was a good life, a rich life, a merry life, despite the ups and downs, despite the barriers and obstacles (many of his own making), despite the handicaps imposed by stupid codes and conventions. Indeed, I hope that I have made more than that clear, because whatever I may say about my own life which is only a life, is merely a means of talking about life itself, and what I have tried, desperately sometimes, to make clear is this, that I look upon life itself as good, good no matter on what terms, that I believe it is we who make it unlivable, we, not the gods, not fate, not circumstance.

Speaking thus, I am reminded of certain passages in the Court's decision which reflect on my sincerity as well as on my ability to think straight. These passages contain the implication that I am often deliberately obscure as well as pretentious in my "metaphysical and surrealistic" flights. I am only too well aware of the diversity of opinion which these "excursi" elicit in the minds of my readers. But how am I to answer such accusations, touching as they do the very marrow of my literary being? Am I to say "You don't know what you are talking about"? Ought I to muster impressive names—"authorities"—to counterbalance these judgments? Or would it not be simpler to say, as I have before—"Guilty! Guilty on all counts, your Honor!"

Believe me, it is not impish, roguish perversity which leads me to pronounce, even quasi-humorously, this word "guilty." As one who thoroughly and sincerely believes in what he says and does, even when wrong, is it not more becoming on my part to admit "guilt" than attempt to defend myself against those who use this word so glibly? Let us be honest. Do those who judge and condemn me— not in Oslo necessarily, but the world over—do these individuals truly believe me to be a culprit, to be "the enemy of socety," as they often blandly assert? What is it that disturbs them so? Is it the existence, the prevalence, of immoral, amoral, or unsocial behavior, such as is described in my works, or is it the exposure of such behavior in print? Do people of our day and age really behave in this "vile" manner or are these actions merely the product of a "diseased" mind? (Does one refer to such authors as Petronius, Rabelais, Rousseau, Sade, to mention but a few, as "diseased minds"?) Surely some of you must have friends or neighbors, in good standing too, who have indulged in this questionable behavior, or worse. As a man of the world, I know only too well that the appanage of a priest's frock, a judicial robe, a teacher's uniform provides no guarantee of immunity to the temptations of the flesh. We are all in the same pot, we are all guilty, or innocent, depending on whether we take the frog's view or the Olympian view. For the nonce I shall refrain from pretending to measure or apportion guilt, to say, for example, that a criminal is more guilty, or less, than a hypocrite. We do not have crime, we do not have war, revolution, crusades, inquisitions, persecution and intolerance because some among us are wicked, mean-spirited, or murderers at heart; we have this malignant condition of human affairs because all of us, the righteous as well as the ignorant and the malicious, lack true forbearance, true compassion, true knowledge, and understanding of human nature.

To put it as succinctly and simply as possible, here is my basic attitude toward life, my prayer, in other words: "Let us stop thwarting one another, stop judging and condemning, stop slaughtering one another." I do not implore you to suspend or withhold judgment of me or my work. Neither I nor my work is that important. (One cometh, another goeth.) What concerns me is the harm you are doing to yourselves. I mean by perpetuating this talk of guilt and punishment, of banning and proscribing, of whitewashing and blackballing, of closing your eyes when convenient, of making scapegoats when there is no other way out. I ask you point-blank—does the pursuance of your limited role enable you to get the most out of life? When you write me off the books, so to speak, will you find your food and wine more palatable, will you sleep better, will you be a better man, a better husband, a better father than before? These are the things that matter—what happens to you, not what you do to me.

I know that the man in the dock is not supposed to ask questions, he is there to answer. But I am unable to regard myself as a culprit. I am simply "out of line." Yet I am in the tradition, so to say. A list of my precursors would make an impressive roster. This trial has been going on since the days of Prometheus. Since before that. Since the days of the Archangel Michael. In the not too distant past there was one who was given the cup of hemlock for being "the corrupter of youth." Today he is regarded as one of the sanest, most lucid minds that ever was. We who are always being arraigned before the bar can do no better than to resort to the celebrated Socratic method. Our only answer is to return the question.

There are so many questions one could put to the Court, to any Court. But would one get a response? Can the Court of the Land ever be put in question? I am afraid not. The judicial body is a sacrosanct body. This is unfortunate, as I see it, for when issues of grave import arise the last court of reference, in my opinion, should be the public. When justice is at stake responsibility cannot be shifted to an elect few without injustice resulting. No Court could function if it did not follow the steel rails of precedent, taboo, and prejudice.

I come back to the lengthy document representing the decision of the Oslo Town Court, to the tabulation of all the infractions of the moral code therein listed. There is something frightening as well as disheartening about such an indictment. It has a medieval aspect. And it has nothing to do with justice. Law itself is made to look ridiculous. Once again let me say that it is not the courts of Oslo or the laws and codes of Norway which I inveigh against; everywhere in the civilized world there is this mummery and flummery manifesting as the Voice of Inertia. The offender who stands before the Court is not being tried by his peers but by his dead ancestors. The moral codes, operative only if they are in conformance with natural or divine laws, are not safeguarded by these flimsy dikes; on the contrary, they are exposed as weak and ineffectual barriers.

Finally, here is the crux of the matter. Will an adverse decision by this court or any other court effectively hinder the further circulation of this book? The history of similar cases does not substantiate such an eventuality. If anything, an unfavorable verdict will only add more fuel to the flames. Proscription only leads to resistance; the fight goes on underground, becomes more insidious therefore, more difficult to cope with. If only one man in Norway reads the book and believes with the author that one has the right to express himself freely, the battle is won. You cannot eliminate an idea by suppressing it, and the idea which is linked with this issue is one of freedom to read what one chooses. Freedom, in other words, to read what is bad for one as well as what is good for one—or, what is simply innocuous. How can one guard against evil, in short, if one does not know what evil is?

But it is not something evil, not something poisonous, which this book *Sexus* offers the Norwegian reader. It is a dose of life which I administered to myself first, and which I not only survived but thrived on. Certainly I would not recommend it to infants, but then neither would I offer a child a bottle of *aqua vite*. I can say one thing for it unblushingly—compared to the atom bomb, it is full of life-giving qualities.

Henry Miller

[*Ed. note: The final decision of the Norwegian Supreme Court found the defendants not guilty, but upheld the ban on the book.*]

▶▶ **Jerry Tallmer**

The Seven Deadly Sins

The most *complete* event of theater in this past season occurred neither on Broadway nor off Broadway nor, strictly speaking, in the theater. It occurred at the ballet, at the New York City Center, and it was the American première of Kurt Weill and Bertolt Brecht's *The Seven Deadly Sins*, presented seventeen times during the winter repertory—only four performances had originally been planned—and now being repeated as I write in June.

The funny thing is, it isn't actually a ballet either. It's unidentifiable, a new species (circa 1933, Hitler in Germany, Weill in Paris). It is, however, clearly identifiable as a classic. Which, along with its completeness—the number of arts it brings to fullest pitch in fullest co-ordination—is what ranks it even above what were, for me, the only two other real events of theater this past season, *Epitaph for George Dillon* and *A Raisin in the Sun*.

So many arts, so many heroes! Let us begin by talking about the Minnie Mouse whore shoes of Lotte Lenya. Here the hero is Rouben Ter-Arutunian, but he will be a hero a thousand times throughout this production for some of the most penetrating sets and costumes any branch of our theater has ever known. The mode is German Expressionist and thereafter, the prime sources are Kirchner and Grosz, the work is economical, unified, exact, and of a mingled ferocity and compassion that is almost more than the heart can bear.

They are white, those shoes, or maybe black-and-white, but from where I sat on two occasions you could mostly only see the white. They bulge up at the toes like Dutchboy shoes, and backward from the heels like the stern of a Chinese junk. They are about two sizes too large for Miss Lenya, and at least a couple of half-inches too high in uplift. She cannot really walk in them, she can only either clop or shamble, poor crafty little Miss Minnie Mouse on the make, her flanks hobbled again as much by her short shiny skirt in some blue silk 1933 Berlin equivalent of day-glo; above that, clashing violently, a blouse in blatant checkers of orange and white.

In she comes, diagonally, Anna all alone, no, not all alone, there's someone with her, from a corner in the farthest reaches of the dark stage. Clop, clop, heels in the night, a city, a bench, a park, a sidewalk. The person with her is a girl dressed precisely the same way, same shoes, same shiny blue skirt, same blouse, same problems. It is herself, her "sister," her better self, Anna II, Allegra Kent. Miss Lenya is singing, Miss Kent will dance. And both will act: but that means *act!*

Miss Lenya, Anna I, has her arm protectively around the other's shoulder. She is going to take care of her sister, see that she makes good, stays good, that they both get along in this great wide world. Kurt Weill's irresistibly lovely prussic acid—isn't that the one with the scent of almonds?—is welling forth from the only throat in the world that God designed for the express purpose of emitting it. "*She's the one with the looks,*" sings Lenya, "*I'm realistic. She's just a little mad, my head is on straight. You may think that you can see two people, but in fact you see only one, and both of us are Annie.*" A man enters. The Annies go into action, Annie I showing Annie II what to do. Approach him and accost him. Get him on the bench, get him to make love. Then, with this little camera, I take a picture. Then we threaten him with blackmail and we take his money.

The first of the seven deadly sins is Idleness. This girl (these girls) is not going to disappoint her family. She (they) will not be idle, at any rate. She'll make good. She'll show the family, and help them, send them money, send them back enough to build that little home they dream of. I forgot or had no chance yet to say that meantime the family itself has become apparent, sitting there, waiting, silent, sullen, on a platform down at the left, under what may well be the single most effective piece of stage scenery I have ever seen: a green-glass, purple-glass, hanging lamp shade out of mid-America (by way of Bavaria) in the mid-nothings, huge, puritanical, grotesque, deathly oppressive. The family are four: mama, papa, the two brothers, sung and acted (i.e., excellently burlesqued) by the members of a male quartet, one of the barrel-chested bassos doing mama in a mustache. I see I also so far forgot to say that *The Seven Deadly Sins* takes place not in Germany or Paris but in America, an America that never was and never will be yet always was and ever shall be: the America of the dreams of distant geniuses, the feed-back America of those who have never yet been here, in all its surreal gigantism, mechanization, menace, and in all its dark unspoiled promise. The America, if I may go a little dreamy myself, of the raw frontier crossed with Sinclair's jungle crossed with Hollywood crossed with James Fenimore Cooper crossed with Dashiell Hammett crossed with Amelia Earhart crossed with Veblen crossed, for all I know, with Melville's *Confidence-Man* and much, much more, not to mention Kafka, Marx, and everyone on *that* team. Says Lotte Lenya today, thinking back to Paris and 1933: "We had none of us been there, Weill, Brecht, Balanchine, or myself. But we had a *fantastic* curiosity of this country. We read all the literature. We saw every American movie. We heard every American record that came out. We soaked it up."

What is most astonishing, and thrilling, to me, now, about *The Seven Deadly Sins*, is the way that it continues to cut back and forth into time and space with multiple, and multiplying, lines of force. A whole war and Reich and quarter of a century after its origin, it still—and I strongly suspect more than ever—invokes a nostalgia with a miraculous three-way stretch into past, present, and future; fact, fiction, and fantasy; old world, new world, and worlds beyond the corruptions or liberations of either. It is, in short, a construct of poetic vision, whatever the remaining intentions of its author, Bertolt Brecht. If they were to teach us something as we sit there in detachment, he has utterly failed. If they were to keep us from feeling so that we might think and learn, he has failed. But he has not failed, even if we feel as we learn. He is a hero in the company of heroes, not least of whom are his translators, W. H. Auden and Chester Kallman, who have honored and enhanced all those multiple lines of force by just barely edging their sprung-English version with incredibly subtle tinges of alienisms, Germanisms, anachronisms, jazzisms, Bible Belt-isms, pop-song lyricisms, and, where appropriate, plain bone-bare bitter-end *New Masses* sarcasm, filtered through a magic glass of time.

But our Annies are still in the park, resisting Idleness, and the family is still waiting there for cash and grace, back home in little old Louisiana ("*Where the moon on the Mississippi is a-shining ever, like you've heard about in the songs of Dixie.*"). Every time the Annies confront another sin, the family starts praying her gloomily back from perdition—that plural-singular usage is the only one possible—and there are six big sins to go. And six cities to go, Memphis, Philadelphia, Los Angeles, Boston, Baltimore, San Francisco—what a Mitteleuropa road map of America!—with degradation and tension mounting at each stop. Annie performs in a cabaret and finds that fine art isn't what's wanted; Annie gets in the circus as a bareback rider (stunning sugar cane background and prop pony) but is thrown out when she strikes the boorish ringmaster in anger; Annie wins a contract for a "solo turn," but it means starving herself half to death (the sin is Gluttony) while the other Annie, Lotte Lenya, slurps on ice-cream cones; Annie finds a Daddy Warbucks in Boston, but wrecks it all by tossing herself away on a handsome pimp; Annie drives many men to suicide in Baltimore but her practical-minded sister coolly appropriates her ill-gotten gains.

All this while, between prayers, injunctions, tears, the family mansion has been going up brick by brick, back home in Louisiana. All this while the beautiful little Allegra Kent has been flying back and forth across the stage in one desperation after another, one costume (or nudity) after another, quiet as a tomb in her own voice, but hearing always, from every corner, without letup, the iron-hard instructions and corrections of Anna I. And everywhere, whatever Miss Kent's own deshabille or frenzy, those Minnie Mouse shoes are wading along beside her, that blue day-glo skirt, that blouse, that presence, reminder, reality. "*And the last big town we came to was San Francisco,*" Miss Lenya sings as the music lifts toward its most melodic, and suddenly the whole back wall is one huge shimmering sheet of Reynolds Wrap, and out from an endless row of sentry box doorways comes marching a terrifying clockwork army of man-dolls and girl-dolls, all in evening clothes, all puppet-jointed, all pink-faced, doll-faced, identical. Little Anna II dodges them, flees them, dashes frantically against and among them; they march on, through her, over her, as if she did not exist. "*Sister,*" shrieks Anna I, "*you know, when our life here is over, those who were good go to bliss unalloyed, those who were bad are rejected forever.*" From within what is now a fully built brick house, the family morosely chants: "*Who fights the Good Fight and all Self subdues, wins the Palm, gains the Crown.*" Light suddenly smashes on the aluminum backdrop with a glare as fierce as the sun's, the music smashes to climax, and, with a final unloosed scream

of agony—did one hear it or self-generate it?—the dancing Anna dives straight into the blazing white-hot heart of that sun, and through it, and out of this life.

But life is life, and life remains. Lotte Lenya sings: "*Now we're coming back to you, Louisiana,*" and on the instant everything is back where it began, two trudging Annas, two sets of Minnie Mouse shoes, two blue skirts, and the long, slow, painful—even grateful—trek home. Don't worry, the family is still there, the family is doing fine, the family will always do fine. That's what families are for. Overhead the lamp shade dangles, looming over the whole stage, looming over all Louisiana, all America, all Paris, all Berlin. We are finished, exhausted, fulfilled. It is complete. But this article is not quite complete, for there is one hero as yet unnamed. He is George Balanchine of Les Ballets 1933 and the New York City Ballet 1959, the director, choreographer, and fundamental activating energy of *The Seven Deadly Sins,* now as once before. If everything bears the stamp of genius in its creation and execution, the personal imprint of Balanchine is what wakes it into life and sculpts it, down to the last perfect detail, into unforgettable form.

Photographs Taken at Rodez

Antonin Artaud
Photo Pastier

►► John Wieners

A Poem for Early Risers

I'm infused with the day
even tho the day may destroy me.
I'm out in it.
Placating it. Saving myself
from the demons
who sit in blue
coats, carping
at us across
the table. Oh they
go out the doors,
I am done with them,
I am done with faces
I have seen before.

For me now the new:
the unturned tricks
of the trade. The place
of the heart where man
is afraid to go.

It is not doors. It is
the ground of my soul
where dinosaurs left
their marks. Their tracks
are upon me. They
walk flatfooted.
Leave heavy heels
and turn sour the green
fields where I eat with
ease. It is good to
throw them up. Good
to have my stomach growl.
After all, I am possessed
by wild animals and
long haired men and
women who gallop
breaking over my beloved
places. Oh put down

thy vanity man the
old man told us under
the tent. You are over-
run with ants.

2

Man lines up for his
breakfast in the dawn
unaware of the jungle
he has left behind
in his sleep. Where
the fields flourished
with cacti, cauliflower,
all the uneatable foods,
where the morning man
perishes, if he remembered.

3

And yet, we must remember.
The old forest, the wild
screams in the backyard
or the cries in the bedroom.
It is ours to nourish.
The nature to nurture.
Dark places where the
woman holds, hands
us, herself handles an
orange ball. Throwing it
up for spring. Like
the clot my grandfather
vomited months before he
died of cancer. And
spoke of later in terror.

►► **William Eastlake**

Three Heroes and a Clown

Two bronc riders and one clown were sitting in a café four miles out of Montrose, Colorado, all watching another bronc man, Ralph Clearboy, watching and listening, listening but not quite catching until Clearboy removed a battered cigar, replacing this, to a bright, cut lip, with a clear bourbon, then he held the fragmented cigar and the empty bourbon glass in either hand and confronted the others with a pure, blank stare.

"What was you fixin' to say?" Willard Moss said.

"A white Lincoln," Clearboy said.

"What about it?"

"I bought one," Clearboy said. "I bought a white Lincoln."

"And what is the moral of that?" the clown said. "What does the Good Book say about that?"

"I wonder."

"Wonder no longer my boy. We are off."

"Where to?"

"To Gunnison," the clown said. "Where else? The rodeo's at Gunnison." The clown stood up. He had a sign on his back and he waved his arms as though he might fly away but before he took off he would make a speech. The clown pounded the table for attention and embarrassed everyone in the café.

"And we will pay a visit to Maria's joint. We will be the first cowboys to ride from Montrose to Gunnison in three hours including a two-hour stopover at Maria's. The first."

Clearboy remained seated. "In a white Lincoln," Clearboy said quietly.

The clown was talking to Clearboy, a professional bronc rider. A clown seems to be only the comic character that entertains you between the rodeo acts but actually his main purpose in the arena is to entice, cajole or pull the Brahma bull or the bronc horse off the rider after the rider has been thrown, to keep those sharp raging hooves of the bronc or the needle horns of the bull from killing the cowboy. The clown is, of course, a contract man, different from a bronc rider. A bronc rider shows up at any show he shows up at and if he shows at no show it makes no difference, it is only his entry fee that allows him to compete for the money anyway. His entry fee and his card in the R.C.A., the Rodeo Cowboys Association. The cowboys got a union too.

"Do you know this cowboy's got a sore rear end?"

The clown did not say this. They were in the white Lincoln now, where you go over Blue Mesa just before Cimarron between Montrose and Gunnison, and Clearboy, Ralph Clearboy, said it and stuck one foot out the window whilst the white Lincoln was going one hundred miles an hour. The clown never said anything funny. His name was Morg or Morgan Beltone and all the stuff he said and did at the show was written for him. What was most appealing about the clown was that, as a contract man he drew a regular salary. The white Lincoln used a great deal of gasoline. Hi-test Flite-fuel, forty-one cents a gallon in Aztec. At these prices you can't ride with a better man than a contract clown.

Four men on a trip to Gunnison in a white Lincoln, including a colored cowboy and a clown. The colored cowboy's name was Willard Moss. Moss is the only colored cowboy who belongs to the R.C.A. outside of Marvel Rogers. If he draws a good horse Marvel is worth the admission price. Willard Moss, the colored bronc man who rode in the rear seat of the Lincoln is not quite so good as Marvel Rogers but Willard Moss is very good.

Ralph Clearboy was the best. He drove and owned the Lincoln and was the best. Together with the finance company he owned the Lincoln, but he was still the best.

"We are doing one hundred and ten miles an hour," Ralph Clearboy announced to the saddle sitting beside him in the front seat.

"I don't get paid for this," Willard Moss said.

"You don't get paid for anything if we don't make Gunnison in time," Abe Proper said. Abe Proper sat near the right window alongside the clown and Willard Moss in the back seat. That made four cowboys in the car plus a saddle that couldn't fit in the trunk with the other saddles. They all wore tight Levi's and tight bright Miller shirts and twisted Stetsons and Justin boots. Except the clown who had a sign embroidered on his shirt back announcing Lee Rider Wear.

Abe Proper made a cigarette at a hundred and ten miles an hour. He was the only cowboy in the bunch who rolled his own, maybe because he was brought up in New York and found making them exotic, an accomplishment, a badge. Proper had not gotten into bronc riding until he was fifteen, nine years ago, but he was pushing Ralph Clearboy for total points or total dollars earned for the All Around Champion Prize. Actually Abe Proper was ahead right now since Montrose where Abe took first money in the second bareback go round. But no one expected it to last. Proper did not expect it to last.

"One hundred and twelve miles an hour," Ralph Clearboy announced.

The white Lincoln mounted by four cowboys from the Spanish Trails Fiesta at Durango, from Colorado Springs, from Butte, Montana, and Cheyenne, from the Rodeo de Santa Fe, from the Monte Vista Roundup and back to Durango and then Albuquerque and now bent for the Cattlemen's Days at Gunnison. Four cowboys in bat-winged hats, orange and red shirts, mounting a white Lincoln, their flowing chrome horse a high, white streak on dark Blue Mesa above the Black Canyon of the Gunnison.

"Like as not——"

"Like as not what?" Abe said.

"Like as not," the clown said, "we'll make it into Gunnison okay."

"If we don't make it into the Gunnison."

"One hundred fourteen," Clearboy said.

"The turn!" Willard Moss said.

"Too late!"

The white Linclon did not even try for the turn, did not even seem to know its front wheels were turned but continued to go straight, even to gain some altitude, to zoom out in flight, hang there in the quiet, high sky an endless moment before it began to fall off on one tail fin, not as though the car were not made to fly but as though the pilot, the cowboy at the controls, had quit and lost control and she went into a long slanting dive down the mountain, began to clip clip the pointed spruce trees with an awful whack whack whack, then the white car fell off on her left tail fin, crump crumped into some scrub oak, made a weak attempt to become airborne again, then slithered to final rest in weird and abrupt silence at the exact edge of another black cliff where there was a fall to infinity to the river, the last slide down into the Black Canyon of the Gunnison. The white Lincoln hung there.

"I was just fixing to make a cigarette," Abe Proper said. Proper wiped the blood and tobacco from the side of his face.

"Is everyone here?" Clearboy said.

"I think the clown stepped out," someone said.

"Without a chute?" Clearboy felt around for his saddle.

"It's back here," Willard Moss said. "And I've found the clown under the saddle."

"Did I make a good ride?" the clown said.

"We're not even at Gunnison yet."

"I reckon we missed. We missed a turn on the road," Clearboy said.

"Again?" the clown said.

"You'd think I made a practice of trying to fly this thing."

"One of us should take lessons." Willard Moss discovered now that the Lee Rider ad on the back of the clown's shirt was being vandalized with blood, Proper's blood. He ceased suddenly however his attempt at humor as he made another discovery. Now he said gently, "No one move."

"Why?"

"No one even talk."

"Why?"

"Because this thing is balancing on the edge of a cliff."

"Oh?"

"Yes," Willard continued gently. "Any movement, even vibration——."

"If we could," Clearboy whispered, "Slip out each door without almost breathing."

"But the clown's in the middle," someone whispered.

"Then suddenly. All climb out suddenly."

"I think it's beginning to move."

"She's moving."

"She's going."

"Everybody out!"

They all tore out and fell into the oak brush except the clown. He stayed put. The car moved slightly then hung delicately on the final edge balancing lightly, waving there, a seesaw with the clown sitting in the car on the pivot, reading something.

"Get out!" Moss hollered to the clown. "She's going to go!"

The clown looked up from his reading. "I can't seem to move," he said.

"You mean you're hurt?"

"No. I seem frozen."

"Something broken?"

"No, scared. Kind of frozen. Scared."

"Then relax," Abe Proper said, holding up a red hand. "Relax. Forget where you are. The car has just drove up to the front of Madison Square Garden. They're waiting for you in there. Get out. Come on, get out."

"No," the clown said. "I can't get out."

"Listen," Willard Moss said. "The car has just drove up in front of Maria's joint. They're waiting for you in there. Get out."

"No," the clown said. "I can't get out."

"If you don't get out you're a dead clown."

"I can't get out."

"You yellow?"

"I still can't move. If I move I know the car will go."

Willard now tried to think of something else. "We will all grab the car and try to hold it."

"Don't! Don't touch the car!" the clown said. "If you touch the car the car will go."

The clown and everyone else were silent for a while and then the clown said, "Clearboy was driving fast because he didn't want to get to Gunnison because he knew Proper would take him at Gunnison like he took him at Durango, like he took him at Santa Fe," the clown said evenly. Everyone was quiet and then the clown said, "Clearboy lost his nerve at Santa Fe when War Paint nearly killed him but he didn't know he'd lost anything till Proper took him three in a row. He didn't know he lost anything until suddenly he was going one hundred fourteen miles an hour and he didn't really know what he was up to then, didn't know he was trying to cash out the easy way because he'd lost his nerve."

Clearboy was down on one knee searching for his hat. Now he found the remains of a hat and looked up at the clown.

"If you've got any nerve," Clearboy said, "just get out of that car before she goes."

"I never had any nerve," the clown said. "That's why I never took up bronc riding, never thought of riding War Paint. Jumping off a building either. Never thought of riding War Paint."

"You started riding me in Montrose."

"I started riding you in Durango," the clown said. "I started riding you when you stopped riding horses." The clown could not resist adding, "Properly."

Abe Proper got up now from a scrub oak and said, "For God's sake get off Clearboy and get out of the damn car before she goes."

"She's going," the clown said.

And she was too, very slowly at first as though the seesaw car were being tilted downward by an invisible hand toward the invisible void. Now the car picked up a slight momentum then it hesitated before it made the long slow bounce down the cliff as though in a dream. The clown in a white car down a black canyon as in a dream or a very slow-motion film with no reality at all except that finally now the car and the clown were gone. The three bronc riders were left standing there on a lonely slope horseless—carless anyway, and without the clown—clownless and breathless too.

"I was just saying—and there I was left talking to the air," Willard Moss said.

"I saw the car enter the water," Clearboy said.

"And like as not," Abe Proper pulled down the shapeless remnants of a cowboy hat. "Like as not——. Well, I can't believe it."

"Believe what?"

"That the clown would do it."

"He didn't."

"Oh, yes he did."

"I mean a purpose."

"I don't care how he did it, he did it."

"That's true."

"He was quite a clown."

"Yes, he was."

"What do you mean, was?" Clearboy said. "I am fixin' to go down and get him."

"That's impossible."

"It's impossible that anyone can call me a coward." Clearboy knelt down to study the canyon wall. "And die to get away with it."

They all thought about this a while.

"You mean he's still alive?"

"Of course he is," Clearboy said. "I've seen him dive off a high platform without a river, into only fifty gallons of water, without no river at all and without a car, without any car to protect him." Clearboy looked down carefully into the dark shadows of the canyon. "Without my car," Clearboy said, and then he spit and said quickly, "I see a path down."

"He didn't call you a coward, Clearboy."

"He said I lost my nerve. It's one and the same thing."

"Well, you have been looking bad lately."

"I been drawing bad horses."

"But why don't you spur them out of the chute?"

"Because I don't want to make bad horses look worse."

"Oh?"

"Yes," Clearboy said.

"You want to take all the blame?"

"Yes," Clearboy said. "And yes, well, maybe I'm not doing too good myself but that's not why I tried to kill the clown."

"All of us."

"Well, the clown thought I was trying to kill him particular," Clearboy paused, "because he was riding me. I was not trying to kill nobody. I was only trying to get to Gunnison on time."

"He said you didn't really know it. It was your sub something," Willard said.

"Your subconsciousness was driving the car while he was riding you," Abe Proper said.

"It's all those books the clown reads," Clearboy said. "And he's reading one of them right now." Clearboy stood up. "In my car."

They all followed behind Clearboy until he got to the path he had spotted and then they continued to follow him but far back and cautiously. After fifteen minutes of awful descent, lost down there, hidden from the blaze of noon above, Clearboy suddenly halted and they all bunched into him.

"This is as far down as the path goes," Clearboy said. "The deer or whatever made it must have quit here."

"Or committed suicide."

"Yes," Clearboy said, invisible and canyon-lost, his voice quickly lost too in river noise.

"Out there and down there," Clearboy said louder. "The car. My car."

They could make out, after studying ahead and down, a white car shape all right.

"But we can't get to it," the voice of Abe Proper said.

"It's only about a fifteen foot drop," the voice of Clearboy said from somewhere. "He made it sixty feet in my car."

"But you can't."

There was rushing noise and then a splash.

"But he did," Willard Moss finished.

"I reckon we better get back up."

"Yes," Willard Moss said. "We better get back up and hold some kind of a funeral or something."

"Yes," Abe Proper said. "Something nice. Something to——," Proper paused, invisible and hushed, climbing up ahead somewhere to the sun. "Yes, a funeral," the voice of Abe Proper continued. "Something to make it legal."

"We didn't have to jump to prove anything."

"No."

"All we've got to do," Willard Moss said, greeting the torch of noon with upturned face, "is to hold something to make it legal."

They lay down on the mesa top as though thrown there on the dark igneous rock, two bright-costumed and beaten cowboys beneath a wild sun. Abe Proper tried to pull his remnant of Stetson over his eyes.

"And, oh God——," Proper said weakly.

"What?" Willard said.

"I just remembered."

"What?"

"Both of our saddles are buried down there."

"Oh," Willard Moss said and then he said, laying a dark hand on darker rock and wincing quickly, "Amen."

When Ralph Clearboy hit the water he hit just above the car and allowed himself to drift down to it. He went through an open door, felt all through the car including the front seat. He felt a saddle, nothing more. No clown. He went out through the open window of the other door and got up on the roof which was well above water to think. Where was the clown hiding?

The clown was not hiding. He was sitting on a sand bar fifty yards below the car holding the unreadable remains of a book. He had made it down okay by wedging himself in a ball between the front of the rear seat and the back of the front seat before the car took its first bounce. He was banged up quite a bit and was bleeding red from his ear but the clown was okay. The book he held was an awful mess.

"Down here!" the clown hollered.

"Where?"

"Down here!"

Clearboy started to drop off the car and drift down to where the clown was sitting but the car moved until it got stuck again on the clown's sand bar.

"Well, you haven't lost your nerve then, Clearboy," the clown said, watching Clearboy dismount.

"And you didn't lose your book," Clearboy said, only now barely able to see the clown.

"I didn't know I had it," the clown said, letting it drop. "It was only something to hold on to, I guess."

"I guess," Cearboy said, his teeth chattering from the icy water. "How do you guess we are going to get out of here?"

"I've fished below here," the clown said. "It's not too far down to a boat landing near Maria's place."

"I guess you've done everything," Clearboy said, still iced and chattering.

The clown thought about Maria's place and then he looked up toward the tall canyon wall he had come down. "Now I guess I have," the clown said. The clown paused and added, "Except——."

"Except what?"

"Ride War Paint."

"You still riding me?"

"No, I'm not," the clown said standing up. "You will ride War Paint. Let's get down to Maria's place."

"You think so?"

"Of course we'll get to Maria's place," the clown said. "Follow me."

And Clearboy did and regretted it. Even when they were sitting on the dry boat landing he still regretted it. He regretted following a crazy clown. The moral is you don't follow a crazy clown to prove nothing. The moral is you ride a horse when you have to ride a horse but you don't invent a ride to please a clown. Until he met War Paint again Clearboy would settle for this. War Paint and himself would make it together, uninfluenced by nobody.

"I wonder what happened to the other two cowboys?"

"Willard and Proper?"

"Yes."

"They're probably having a funeral over us."

"Well," Clearboy said, beginning to warm in the sun, "the next guy who has a funeral over me when I'm having bad luck is going to be tied to War Paint and throwed in this canyon, then you will be the first dead clown to ride down the Gunnison River on a horse. Do you understand?"

"I think I understand," the clown said weakly.

They sat there on the dock in the sun, resting and nursing their wounds.

"Look," the clown said, "there's the car. The current must have freed it and brought it down. That makes us the——," the clown paused and stood up. "That makes us the first two cowboys to go down the Gunnison River in an automobile."

Clearboy remained sitting watching with a blank, enchanted fixity where the clown watched, watching as children must watch an empty gondola emerge from the tunnel of love.

"Anyway I reckon we was the last ones down in a white Lincoln," Clearboy said.

The clown thought about this a long while without being able to top it. The clown had a button nose and small red cheeks and now, standing all oozing wet with his Lee Rider ad running red, he pointed his finger to the sky.

"Someone's been praying for me. Here I am all alive because a cowboy got the nerve to jump down a canyon to rescue a clown."

"To rescue——." Clearboy got up, placed a yellow square of tobacco into his square, hard face still

blued from the water and began to wade out toward the huge, slow-turning object. "My white Lincoln," Clearboy finished.

The clown, Morgan Beltone, watched Clearboy guide the white car onto the beach. He decided no help was needed and moved off toward Maria's place.

"Here you are," Maria said, across the mahogany bar. "Here you are supposed to be at the rodeo in Gunnison and here you been swimming. Where's Clearboy? Where's Proper? Where's Moss? Where's your partners?"

Morgan Beltone wiped some water off his face. "We decided to fly in the car to Gunnison this time and we came down near here a little bit ago," the clown said. "Will you give me a drink?"

Maria, her wide Spanish face puzzled, poured the drink.

"To all the bronc men I saved from getting killed in the arena and never got no appreciation from. To all those cowboy heroes and to progress," Morgan Beltone said, raising the glass. "Today I have pioneered a new route in a new kind of machine, cutting off half the distance across Blue Mesa. Why, perhaps some day I will be appreciated very much."

The clown drank the drink down and looked plaintively through the window at all the big world he had not conquered. The clown—and so wrongly so, Morgan Beltone thought—had never been loved or appreciated very much.

"Honey, save it for the show," Maria said. "You want another drink?"

"Why not?" the clown said.

Hans Nordenström

What is 'Pataphysics?

$1.00
U.K.: 5/-
Canada: $1.20
EVERGREEN REVIEW

No.15
$1.00
U. K.: 5/-
Canada: $1.20
↓ EVERGREEN REVIEW

No.14
$1.00
U.K.: 5/-
Canada: $1.20
↓ EVERGREEN REVIEW

REPORT OBSCENE
MAIL TO
YOUR POSTMASTER

U.S. POST

ON, 5
1A&15
7-PM
1960
MASS.

►► **Terry Southern**

Red-Dirt Marihuana

1960

The white boy came into the open-end, dirt-floor shed where the Negro was sitting on the ground against the wall reading a Western Story magazine.

In one hand the boy was carrying a pillowcase that was bunched out at the bottom, about a third filled with something, and when the Negro looked up it appeared from his smile that he knew well enough what it was.

"What you doin', Hal', bringin' in the crop?"

The white boy's name was Harold; the Negro pronounced it *Hal'*.

The boy walked on over to one side of the shed where the kindling was stacked and pulled down an old sheet of newspaper which he shook out to full size and spread in front of the Negro. He dumped the gray-grass contents of the pillowcase onto the paper and then straightened up to stand with his hands on his hips, frowning down at it. He was twelve years old.

The Negro was looking at it, too; but he was laughing. He was about thirty-five, and he laughed sometimes in a soft, almost soundless way, shaking his head as though this surely were the final irony, while his face, against very white teeth, gleamed with the darks of richest pipebriar. His name was C.K.

"*Sho'* is a lotta gage," he said.

He reached out a hand and rolled a dry pinch of it between his thumb and forefinger.

"You reckon it's dried out enough?" the boy asked, nasal, sounding almost querulous, as he squatted down opposite. "Shoot, I don't wannta leave it *out* there no more—not hangin' on that dang sycamore anyway—it's beginnin' to *look* too funny." He glanced out the end of the shed toward the big white farmhouse that was about thirty yards away. "Heck, Dad's been shootin' *dove* down in there all week—I was down there this mornin' and that damned old dog of Les Newgate's was runnin' around with a piece of it in his *mouth!* I had to git it away from 'im 'fore they seen it."

The Negro took another pinch of it and briskly crushed it between his flat palms, then held them up, cupped, smelling it.

"They wouldn't of knowed what it was noway," he said.

"You crazy?" said Harold, frowning. "You think my Dad don't know *Mex'can loco-weed* when he sees it?"

"Don't look much *like* no loco-weed now though, do it?" said the Negro flatly, raising expressionless eyes to the boy.

"*He's* seen it dried out, too, I bet," said the boy, loyally, but looking away.

"*Sho'* he is," said C.K., weary and acid. "Sho', I bet he done *blow* a lot of it too, ain't he? Sho', you daddy pro'bly one of the biggest ole hop-heads in Texas—why I bet he *smoke* it an' *eat* it an' jest anyway he can git it into his ole haid! Hee-hee!" He laughed at the mischievous image. "Ain't *that* right, Hal'?"

"You crazy?" demanded Harold, frowning terribly; he took the Negro's wrist. "Lemme smell it," he said.

He drew back after a second.

"I can't smell nothin' but your dang sweat," he said.

"'Course not," said C.K., frowning in his turn, and brushing his hands, "you got to git it jest when the *flower* break—that's the *boo*-kay of the plant, you see; that's what we call that."

"Do it again," said Harold.

"I ain't goin' *do* it again," said C.K., peevish, closing his eyes for a moment, ". . . it's jest a waste on you—I do it again, you jest say you smell my *sweat*. You ain't got the nose for it noway—you got to know you business 'fore you start foolin' round with *this* plant."

"I can do it, C.K.," said the boy earnestly, ". . . come on, dang it!"

The Negro sighed, elaborately, and selected another small bud from the pile.

"Awright now when I rub it in my *hand*," he said sternly, "you let out you breath—then I *cup* my hand, you put your nose in an' smell strong . . . you got to suck in *strong* thru you nose!"

They did this.

"You smell it?" asked C.K.

"Yeah, sort of," said Harold, leaning back again.

"That's the *boo*-kay of the plant—they ain't no smell like it."

"It smells like tea," said the boy.

"Well, now that's why they calls it that, you see—but it smell like somethin' *else* too."

"What?"

"Like mighty fine gage, that's what."

"Well, whatta you keep on callin' it *that* for?" asked the boy crossly, ". . . that ain't what that Mex'can called it neither—he called it '*pot.*' "

"That ole *Mex*," said C.K., brushing his hands and laughing, "he *sho'* were funny, weren't he? . . . thought he could pick *cotton* . . . told *me* he use to *pick-a-bale-a-day!* I had to laugh when he say that . . . oh, sho', you didn't talk to that Mex'can like I

did—he call it *lotta* things. He call it '*baby*,' too! Hee-hee. Yeah, he say: 'Man, don't forgit the *baby* now!' He mean bring a few *sticks* of it out to the field, you see, that's what he mean by that. He call it '*charge*,' too. Sho'. Them's *slang* names. Them names git started people don't want the *police* nobody like that to know they business, you see. Sho', they make *up* them names, go on an' talk about they business nobody know what they *sayin'*, you see what I mean."

He stretched his legs out comfortably and crossed his hands over the magazine that was still in his lap.

"Yes indeed," he said after a minute, staring at the pile on the newspaper, and shaking his head, "I tell you right now, boy—that sho' is a lotta gage."

About two weeks earlier, on a day when C.K. wasn't helping Harold's father, they had gone fishing together, Harold and C.K., and on the way back to the house that afternoon, Harold had stopped and stood looking into an adjacent field, a section of barren pasture-land where the cows almost never went, but where there was a cow at that moment, alone, lying on its stomach, with its head stretched out on the ground in front of it.

"What's wrong with that dang *cow?*" he demanded, not so much of C.K., as of himself, or perhaps of God—though in a sense C.K. *was* responsible for the stock, it being his job at least to take them out to pasture and back each day.

"Do look like she takin' it easy, don't it?" said C.K., and they went through the fence and started toward her. "*Look* like ole Maybelle," he said, squinting his eyes at the distance.

"I ain't never seen a cow act like *that* before," said Harold crossly, ". . . layin' there with her head on the ground like a damned old hound-dog."

The cow didn't move when they reached it, just stared up at them; she was chewing her cud, in a rhythmic and contented manner.

"*Look* at that dang cow," Harold muttered, ever impatient with enigma, ". . . it is old Maybelle, ain't it?" He felt of her nose and then began kicking her gently on the flank. "Git up, dang it."

"Sho' that's ole Maybelle," said C.K., patting her neck, "what's the matter with you, Maybelle?"

Then C.K. found it, a bush of it, about twenty feet away, growing in the midst of a patch of dwarf-cactus, and he was bent over it, examining it with great care.

"This here is a *full-growed* plant," he said, touching it in several places, gently bending it back, almost caressingly. Finally he stood up again, hands on his hips, looking back at the prostrate cow.

"Must be mighty fine gage," he said.

"Well, I ain't never seen loco-weed make a cow act like *that*," said Harold, as if that were the important aspect of the whole incident, and he began absently kicking at the plant.

"That ain't no ordinary loco-weed," said C.K., ". . . that there is *red-dirt marihuana*, that's what *that* is."

Harold spat, frowning.

"Shoot," he said then, "I reckon we oughtta pull it up and burn it."

"I reckon we oughtta," said C.K.

They pulled it up.

"Don't gen'lly take to *red-dirt*," C.K. remarked, casually, brushing his hands, ". . . they say if it *do*, then it's might fine indeed—they reckon it's got to be *strong* to do it, you see."

"Must be pretty dang *strong* awright," Harold dryly agreed, looking back at the disabled cow, "you think we oughtta git Doc Parks?"

They walked over to the cow.

"Shoot," said C.K., "they ain't nothin' wrong with *this* cow."

The cow had raised her head, and her eyes followed them when they were near. They stared down at her for a minute or two, and she looked at them, interestedly, still chewing.

"Ole Maybelle havin' a *fine* time," said C.K., leaning over to stroke her muzzle. "Hee-hee. She *high*, that's what she is!" He straightened up again. "I tell you right now, boy," he said to Harold, "you lookin' at a *ver'* contented cow there!"

"You reckon it'll ruin her milk?"

"Shoot, that make her milk all the more *rich!* Yeah, she goin' give some Grade-A milk indeed after *that* kinda relaxation. Ain't that right, Maybelle?"

They started back to the fence, Harold dragging the bush along and swinging it back and forth.

"Look at the ole *root* on that plant," said C.K., laughing, ". . . big ole juicy root—sho' would make a fine soup bone I bet!"

He had twisted off a branch of the plant and plucked a little bunch of leaves from it which he was chewing now, like mint.

"What's it taste like?" asked Harold.

C.K. plucked another small bunch and proffered it to the boy.

"Here you is, my man," he said.

"Naw, it jest makes me sick," said Harold, thrusting his free hand in his pocket and making a face; so, after a minute, C.K. put that piece in his mouth too.

"We could dry it out and smoke it," said Harold.

C.K. laughed a short derisive snort.

"Yes, I reckon we could."

"Let's dry it out and sell it," said the boy.

C.K. looked at him, plaintive exasperation dark in his face.

"Now Hal' don't go talkin' without you knows what you talkin' *about*."

"We could sell it to them Mex'can sharecroppers over at Farney," said Harold.

"Hal', what is you *talkin'* about—them people ain't got no money."

They went through the fence again, silent for a while.

"Well, don't you wantta dry it out?" Harold asked, bewildered, boy of twelve, aching for action and projects—*any* project that would bring them together.

C.K. shook his head.

"Boy, you don't catch me givin' no advice on that kinda business—you daddy run me right off this place somethin' like that ever happen."

Harold was breaking it up.

"We'd have to put it some place where the dang stock wouldn't git at it," he said.

So they spread the pieces of it up in the outside branches of a great sycamore, where the Texas sun would blaze against them, and then they started back on up to the house.

"Listen, Hal'," said C.K. about halfway on. "I tell you right now you don't wanta say nothin' 'bout this to nobody up at the house."

"You crazy?" said the boy, "you don't reckon I *would* do you?"

They walked on.

"What'll we do with it when it's dried *out*, C.K.?"

C.K. shrugged, kicked at a rock.

"Shoot, we find *some* use for it I reckon," he said, with a little laugh.

"You think it's dried *out* enough?" Harold was asking, as they sat with the pile of it between them, he crumbling some of it now in his fingers, scowling at it.

C.K. took out his sack of *Bull Durham*.

"Well, I tell you what we goin' have to do," he said with genial authority, ". . . we goin' have to *test* it."

He slipped two cigarette papers from the attached packet, one of which he licked and placed alongside the other, slightly overlapping it.

"I use *two* of these papers," he explained, concentrating on the work, "that give us a nice *slow-burnin'* stick, you see."

He selected a small segment from the pile and crumpled it, letting it sift down from his fingers into the cupped cigarette paper; and then he carefully rolled it, licking his pink-white tongue slowly over the whole length of it after it was done. "I do that," he said, "that seal it in good, you see." And he held it up then for them both to see; it was much thinner than an ordinary cigarette, and still glittering with the wet of his mouth.

"That cost you a half-a-*dollah* in *Dallas*," he said.

"Shoot," said the boy, uncertain.

"Sho' would," said C.K., ". . . oh you git you three for a dollah, you *know* the man—'course that's mighty good gage I'm talkin' 'bout you pay half-a-dollah . . . that's you *quality* gage. I don't know how good quality this here is yet, you see."

He lit it.

"Sho' *smell* good though, don't it?"

Harold watched him narrowly as he wafted the smoking stick back and forth beneath his nose.

"*Taste* mighty good too! Shoot, I jest bet this is *ver'* good quality gage. You wanta taste of it?" He held it out.

"Naw, I don't want none of it right now," said Harold. He got up and walked over to the kindling stack, and drew out from a stash there a package of Camels; he lit one, returned the pack to its place, and came back to sit opposite C.K. again.

"Yeah," said C.K. softly, gazing at the thin cigarette in his hand, "I feel this gage awready . . . this is *fine*."

"What does it feel like?" asked Harold.

C.K. had inhaled again, very deeply, and was holding his breath, severely, chest expanded like a person who is learning to float, his dark brow slightly knit in the awareness of actually *working* at it physically.

"It feel *fine*," he said at last, smiling.

"How come it jest made me *sick?*" asked the boy.

"Why I tole you, Hal'," said C.K. impatiently, "'cause you tried to fight *against* it, thats' why . . . you tried to *fight* that gage, so it jest make you *sick!* Sho', that was *good* gage that ole Mex had."

"Shoot, all I felt besides gittin' sick at my stomach was jest right *dizzy*."

C.K. had taken another deep drag and was still holding it, so that now when he spoke, casually but without exhaling, it was from the top of his throat, and his voice sounded odd and strained:

"Well, that's 'cause you *mind* is young an' unformed . . . that gage jest come into you mind an' cloud it over!"

"My *mind?*" said Harold.

"Sho', you *brain!*" said C.K. in a whispery rush of voice as he let out the smoke. "You brain is young an' unformed, you see . . . that smoke come in, it got no where to go, it jest *cloud* you young brain over!"

Harold flicked his cigarette a couple of times.

"It's as good as any dang nigger-brain I guess," he said after a minute.

"Now boy, don't *mess* with me," said C.K., frowning, ". . . you ast me somethin' an' I tellin' you! *You* brain is young an' *unformed* . . . it's all *smooth*, you brain, smooth as that piece of shoeleather. That smoke jest come in an' cloud it over!" He took another drag. "Now you take a full-*growed* brain," he said in his breath-holding voice. "it *ain't* smooth—it's got all *ridges* in it, all over, go this way an' that. Shoot, a man know what he doin' he have that smoke runnin' *up* one ridge an' *down* the other! He control his high, you see what I mean, he don't fight against it. . . ." His voice died away in the effort of holding breath and speaking at the same time—and, after exhaling again, he finished off the cigarette in several quick little drags, then broke open the butt with lazy care and emptied the few remaining bits from it back onto the pile. "*Yeah* . . ." he said, almost inaudibly, an absent smile on his lips.

Harold sat or half reclined, though somewhat stiffly, supporting himself with one arm, just staring at C.K. for a moment before he shifted about a little, flicking his cigarette. "Shoot," he said, "I jest wish you'd tell me what it *feels* like, that's all."

C.K., though he was sitting cross-legged now with his back fairly straight against the side of the shed, gave the appearance of substance wholly without bone, like a softly filled sack that has slowly, imperceptibly sprawled and found its final perfect contour, while his head lay back against the shed, watching the boy out of half-closed eyes. He laughed.

"Boy, I done *tole* you," he said quietly, "it feel good."

"Well, that ain't nothin', dang it," said Harold, almost angrily, "I awready feel good!"

"Uh-huh," said C.K. with dreamy finality.

"Well, I *do*, god-dang it," said Harold, glaring at him hatefully.

"That's right," said C.K., nodding, closing his eyes, and they were both silent for a few minutes, until C.K. looked at the boy again and spoke, as though there had been no pause at all: "But you don't feel as good now as you do at *Christmas*time though do you? Like when right after you daddy give you that new *Winchester?* An' then you don't feel as *bad* as that time he was whippin' you for shootin' that doe with it neither do you? Yeah. Well now that's how much difference they *is*, you see, between that cigarette you got in you hand an' the one I jest put out! Now that's what I tellin' *you*."

"*Shoot*," said Harold, flicking his half-smoked Camel and then mashing it out on the ground, "you're crazy."

C.K. laughed. "Sho' I is," he said.

They fell silent again, C.K. appearing almost asleep, humming to himself, and Harold sitting opposite, frowning down to where his own finger traced lines without pattern in the dirt floor of the shed.

"Where we gonna keep this stuff at, C.K.?" he demanded finally, his words harsh and reasonable, "we can't jest leave it sittin' out like this."

C.K. seemed not to have heard, or perhaps simply to consider it without opening his eyes; then he did open them, and when he leaned forward and spoke, it was with a fresh and remarkable cheerfulness and clarity:

"Well, now the first thing we got to do is to *clean* this gage. We got to git them *seeds* outta there an' all them little sticks. But the *ver'* first thing we do . . ." and he reached into the pile, "is to take some of this here *flower*, these here ver' small leaves, an' put them off to the side. That way you got you *two* kinds of gage, you see—you got you a *light* gage an' a *heavy* gage."

C.K. started breaking off the stems and taking them out, Harold joining in after a while; and then they began crushing the dry leaves with their hands.

"How we ever gonna git all them dang seeds outta there?" asked Harold.

"Now I show you a *trick* about that," said C.K., smiling and leisurely getting to his feet. "Where's that pilly-cover at?"

He spread the pillowcase flat on the ground and, lifting the newspaper, dumped the crushed leaves on top of it. Then he folded the cloth over them and kneaded the bundle with his fingers, pulverizing it. After a minute of this, he opened it up again, flat, so that the pile was sitting on the pillowcase now as it had been on the newspaper.

"You hold on hard to that end," he told Harold, and he took the other himself and slowly raised it, tilting it, and agitating it. The round seeds started rolling out of the pile, down the taut cloth and onto the ground. C.K. put a corner of the pillowcase between his teeth and held the other corner out with one hand; then, with his other hand, he tapped gently on the bottom of the pile, and the seeds poured out by the hundreds, without disturbing the rest.

"Where'd you learn all that at, C.K.?" asked Harold.

"Shoot, you got to know you business you workin' with *this* plant," said C.K., ". . . waste our time pickin' out them ole seeds." He stood for a moment looking around the shed. "Now we got to have us somethin' to *keep* this gage in—we got to have us a *box*, somethin' like that, you see."

"Why can't we jest keep it in that?" asked Harold, referring to the pillowcase.

C.K. frowned. "Naw we can't *keep* it in that," he said, ". . . keep it in that like ole sacka turnip . . . we got to git us somethin'—a nice little *box*, somethin' like that, you see. How 'bout one of you empty shell boxes? You got any?"

"They ain't big enough," said Harold.

C.K. resumed his place, sitting and slowly leaning back against the wall, looking at the pile again.

"They sho' ain't, is they," he said, happy with that fact.

"We could use two or three of 'em," Harold said.

"Wait a minute now," said C.K., "we talkin' here, we done forgit about this *heavy* gage." He layed his hand on the smaller pile, as though to reassure it. "One of them shell boxes do fine for that—an' I *tell* you what we need for this *light* gage now I think of it . . . is one of you momma's quart *fruit* jars!"

"Shoot, I can't fool around with them dang jars, C.K.," said the boy.

C.K. made a little grimace of impatience.

"*You* momma ain't begrudge you one of them fruit jars, Hal'—she *ast* you 'bout it, you jest say it got *broke!* You say you done *use* that jar put you fishin' minners in it! *Hee-hee* . . . she won't even *wanta* see that jar no more, you tell her *that*."

"I ain't gonna fool around with them jars, C.K."

C.K. sighed and started rolling another cigarette.

"I jest goin' twist up a few of these sticks now," he explained, "an' put them off to the side."

"When're you gonna smoke some of the other?" asked Harold.

"What, that *heavy* gage?" said C.K., raising his eyebrows in surprise at the suggestion. "Shoot, *that* ain't no workin'-hour gage there, that's you *Sunday* gage . . . oh you mix a little bit of that *into* you light gage now and then you *feel like* it—but you got to be sure ain't nobody goin' to mess with you 'fore you turn *that* gage full on. 'Cause you jest wanta lay back then an' take it easy." He nodded to himself in agreement with this, his eyes intently watching his fingers work the paper. "You see . . . you don't *swing* with you heavy gage, you jest *goof* . . . that's what you call that. Now you light gage, you *swing* with you light gage . . . you *control* that gage, you see. Say a man have to go out an' *work*, why he able to *enjoy* that work! Like now you seen me turn on some of this light gage, didn't you? Well, I may have to go out with you *daddy* a little later an' lay on that fence-wire, or work with my post-hole digger. Why I able to *swing* with my post-hole digger with my light gage on. Sho', that's you *sociable* gage, you light gage is—this here other, well, that's what you call you *thinkin'* gage. . . . Hee-hee! Shoot, I wouldn't even wanta *see* no post-hole digger I turn *that* gage full on!"

He rolled the cigarette up, slowly, licking it with great care.

"Yeah," he said half-aloud, ". . . ole fruit jar be *fine* for this light gage." He chuckled. "That way we jest look right in there, know how much we got on hand at all time."

"We got *enough* I reckon," said Harold, a little sullenly it seemed.

"Sho' is," said C.K., "mor'n the law allows at that."

"Is it against the law then sure enough, C.K.?" asked Harold in eager interest, ". . . like that Mex'can kept sayin' it was?"

C.K. gave a soft laugh.

"I jest reckon it *is*," he said, ". . . it's against all kinda law—what we got here is. Sho', they's one law say you can't have *none* of it, they put you in the jailhouse you do . . . then they's another law say they catch you with more than *this* much . . ." he reached down and picked up a handful to show, "well, then you in *real* trouble! Sho', you got more than *that* why they say: 'Now that man got more of that gage than he *need* for his personal use, he must be *sellin'* it!' Then they say you a *pusher*. That's what they call that, an' boy I mean they put you *way* back in the jailhouse then!" He gave Harold a severe look. "I don't wanta tell you you business, nothin' like that, Hal', but if I was you I wouldn't let on 'bout this to nobody—not to you frien' Big Law'ence or *any* of them people."

"Heck, don't you think I know better than to do that?"

"You ain't scared though, is you Hal'?"

Harold spat.

"Shoot," he said, looking away, as though in exasperation and disgust that the thought could have occurred to anyone.

C.K. resumed his work, rolling the cigarettes, and Harold watched him for a few minutes and then stood up, very straight.

"I reckon I could git a fruit jar outta the cellar," he said, "if she ain't awready brought 'em up for her cannin'."

"That sho' would be fine, Hal'," said C.K., without raising his head, licking the length of another thin stick of it.

When Harold came back with the fruit jar and the empty shell box, they transferred the two piles into those things.

"How come it's against the *law* if it's so all-fired good?" asked Harold.

"Well, now I use to study 'bout that myself," said C.K., tightening the lid of the fruit jar and giving it a pat. He laughed. "It ain't because it make young boys like you sick, I tell you *that* much!"

"Well, what the heck is it then?"

C.K. put the fruit jar beside the shell box, placing it neatly, carefully centering the two just in front of him, and seeming to consider the question while he was doing it.

"I *tell* you what it is," he said then, "it's 'cause a man see too much when he git high, that's what. He sees right *through* ever'thing . . . you understan' what I say?"

"What the heck are you talkin' about, C.K.?"

"Well, maybe you too young to know what I talkin' 'bout—but I tell you they's a lotta trickin' an' lyin' go on in the world . . . they's a lotta ole *bull-crap* go on in the world . . . well, a man git high, he see right through all them tricks an' lies, an' all that ole bull-crap. He see right through there into the *truth* of it!"

"Truth of *what*?"

"*Ever'*thing."

"Dang you sure talk crazy, C.K."

"Sho', they *got* to have it against the law. Shoot, ever'body git high, wouldn't be nobody git up an' feed the chickens! Hee-hee . . . ever'body jest *lay in bed*! Jest lay in bed till they *ready* to git up! Sho', you take a man high on good gage, he got no use for they ole bull-crap, 'cause he done see right through there. Shoot, he lookin' right down into his ver' *soul*!"

"I ain't never heard nobody talk so dang crazy, C.K."

"Well, you young, boy—you goin' hear plenty crazy talk 'fore you is a growed man."

"Shoot."

"Now we got to think of us a good place to *put* this gage," he said, "a *secret* place. Where you think, Hal'?"

"How 'bout that old smokehouse out back—ain't nobody goes in there."

"Shoot that's a *good* place for it, Hal'—you sure they ain't goin' tear it down no time soon?"

"Heck no, what would they tear it down for?"

C.K. laughed.

"Yeah, that's right," he said, "well, we take it out there after it gits dark."

They fell silent, sitting there together in the early afternoon. Through the open end of the shed the bright light had inched across the dirt floor till now they were both sitting half in the full sunlight.

"*I* jest wish I knowed or not you daddy goin' to work on that south-quarter *fence* today," said C.K. after a bit.

"Aw him and Les Newgate went to *Dalton*," said Harold, ". . . heck, I bet they ain't back 'fore dark. You wanta go fishin'?"

"Shoot, that sound like a *good* idee," said C.K.

"I seen that dang drumhead jumpin' on the west side of the pond again this mornin'," said Harold, ". . . shoot, I bet he weighs seven or eight pounds."

"I think we do awright today," C.K. agreed, glancing out at the blue sky and sniffing a little, ". . . shoot, we try some calf liver over at the second log

—that's jest where that ole drumhead is 'bout now."

"I reckon we oughtta git started," said Harold. "I guess we can jest leave that dang stuff here till dark . . . we can stick it back behind that firewood."

"Sho'," said C.K., "we stick it back in there for the time bein'—I think I jest twist up one or two more 'fore we set out though . . . put a taste of this heavy in 'em." He laughed as he unscrewed the lid of the fruit jar. "Shoot, this sho' be fine for fishin'," he said, ". . . ain't nothin' like good gage give a man the strength of patience—you want me to twist up a couple for you, Hal?"

Harold spat.

"Aw I guess so," he said, ". . . you let *me* lick 'em though, dang it, C.K."

►► William S. Burroughs

Deposition: Testimony Concerning a Sickness

I awoke from The Sickness at the age of forty-five, calm and sane, and in reasonably good health except for a weakened liver and the look of borrowed flesh common to all who survive The Sickness. . . . Most survivors do not remember the delirium in detail. I apparently took detailed notes on sickness and delirium. I have no precise memory of writing the notes which have now been published under the title *Naked Lunch*. The title was suggested by Jack Kerouac. I did not understand what the title meant until my recent recovery. The title means exactly what the words say: NAKED Lunch—a frozen moment when everyone sees what is on the end of every fork.

The Sickness is drug addiction and I was an addict for fifteen years. When I say addict I mean an addict to *junk* (generic term for opium and/or derivatives including all synthetics from demerol to palfium. I have used junk in many forms: morphine, heroin, dilaudid, eukodal, pantapon, diocodid, diosane, opium, demerol, dolophine, palfium. I have smoked junk, eaten it, sniffed it, injected it in vein-skin-muscle, inserted it in rectal suppositories. The needle is not important. Whether you sniff it smoke it eat it or shove it up your ass the result is the same: addiction. When I speak of drug addiction I do not refer to

keif, marijuana or any preparation of hashish, mescaline, Bannisteria Caapi LSD6 Sacred Mushrooms or any other drug of the hallucinogen group. . . . There is no evidence that the use of any hallucinogen results in physical dependence. The action of these drugs is physiologically opposite to the action of junk. A lamentable confusion between the two classes of drugs has arisen owing to the zeal of the U.S. and other narcotic departments.

I have seen the exact manner in which the junk virus operates through fifteen years of addiction. The pyramid of junk, one level eating the level below (it is no accident that junk higher-ups are always fat and the addict in the street is always thin) right up to the top or tops since there are many junk pyramids feeding on peoples of the world and all built on basic principles of monopoly:

1—Never give anything away for nothing.

2—Never give more than you have to give (always catch the buyer hungry and always make him wait).

3—Always take everything back if you possibly can.

The Pusher always gets it all back. The addict needs more and more junk to maintain a human form . . . buy off the Monkey.

Junk is the mold of monopoly and possession. The

addict stands by while his junk legs carry him straight in on the junk beam to relapse. Junk is quantitative and accurately measurable. The more junk you use the less you have and the more you have the more you use. All the hallucinogen drugs are considered sacred by those who use them—there are Peyote Cults and Bannisteria Cults, Hashish Cults and Mushroom Cults—"the Sacred Mushrooms of Mexico enable a man to see God"—but no one ever suggested that junk is sacred. There are no opium cults. Opium is profane and quantitative like money. I have heard that there was once a beneficent non-habit-forming junk in India. It was called *soma* and is pictured as a beautiful blue tide. If *soma* ever existed the Pusher was there to bottle it and monopolize it and sell it and it turned into plain old time JUNK.

Junk is the ideal product . . . the ultimate merchandise. No sales talk necessary. The client will crawl through a sewer and beg to buy. . . . The junk merchant does not sell his product to the consumer he sells the consumer to his product. He does not improve and simplify his merchandise. He degrades and simplifies the client. He pays his staff in junk.

Junk yields a basic formula of "evil" virus: *The Algebra of Need*. The face of "evil" is always the face of total need. A dope fiend is a man in total need of dope. Beyond a certain frequency need knows absolutely no limit or control. In the words of total need: "*Wouldn't you?*" Yes you would. You would lie, cheat, inform on your friends, steal, do *anything* to satisfy total need. Because you would be in a state of total sickness, total possession, and not in a position to act in any other way. Dope fiends are sick people who cannot act other than they do. A rabid dog cannot choose but bite. Assuming a self-righteous position is nothing to the purpose unless your purpose be to keep the junk virus in operation. And junk is a big industry. I recall talking to an American who worked for the Aftosa Commission in Mexico. Six hundred a month plus expense account:

"How long will the epidemic last?" I enquired.

"As long as we can keep it going. . . . And yes . . . maybe the aftosa will break out in South America," he said dreamily.

If you wish to alter or annihilate a pyramid of numbers in a serial relation, you alter or remove the bottom number. If we wish to annihilate the junk pyramid, we must start with the bottom of the pyramid: *the Addict in the Street,* and stop tilting quixotically for the "higher ups" so-called, all of whom are immediately replaceable. *The addict in the street who must have junk to live is the one irreplaceable factor in the junk equation.* When there are no more addicts to buy junk there will be no junk traffic. As long as junk need exists, someone will service it.

Addicts can be cured or quarantined—that is allowed a morphine ration under minimal supervision like typhoid carriers. When this is done, junk pyramids of the world will collapse. So far as I know, England is the only country to apply this method to the junk problem. They have about five hundred quarantined addicts in the U.K. In another generation when the quarantined addicts die off and pain killers operating on a non-junk principle are discovered, the junk virus will be like smallpox, a closed chapter—a medical curiosity.

The vaccine that can relegate the junk virus to a landlocked past is in existence. This vaccine is the Apomorphine Treatment discovered by an English doctor whose name I must withhold pending his permission to use it and to quote from his book covering thirty years of apomorphine treatment of addicts and alcoholics. The compound apomorphine is formed by boiling morphine with hydrochloric acid. It was discovered years before it was used to treat addicts. For many years the only use for apomorphine which has no narcotic or pain-killing properties was as an emetic to induce vomiting in cases of poisoning. It acts directly on the vomiting center in the back brain.

I found this vaccine at the end of the junk line. I lived in one room in the Native Quarter of Tangier. I had not taken a bath in a year nor changed my clothes or removed them except to stick a needle every hour in the fibrous grey wooden flesh of terminal addiction. I never cleaned or dusted the room. Empty ampule boxes and garbage piled to the ceiling. Light and water long since turned off for nonpayment. I did absolutely nothing. I could look at the end of my shoe for eight hours. I was only roused to action when the hourglass of junk ran out. If a friend came to visit—and they rarely did since who or what was left to visit—I sat there not caring that he had entered my field of vision—a grey screen always blanker and fainter—and not caring when he walked out of it. If he had died on the spot I would have sat there looking at my shoe waiting to go through his pockets. Wouldn't you? Because I never had enough junk—no one ever does. Thirty grains of morphine a day and it still was not enough. And long waits in front of the drugstore. Delay is a rule in the junk business. The Man is never on time. This is no accident. There are no accidents in the junk world. The addict is taught again and again exactly what will happen if he does not score for his junk ration. Get up that money or else. And suddenly my habit began to jump and jump. Forty, sixty grains a day. And it still was not enough. And I could not pay.

I stood there with my last check in my hand and realized that it was my last check. I took the next plane for London.

The doctor explained to me that apomorphine acts on the back brain to regulate the metabolism and normalize the blood stream in such a way that the enzyme system of addiction is destroyed over a period of four or five days. Once the back brain is regulated apomorphine can be discontinued and only used in case of relapse. (No one would take apomorphine for kicks. *Not one case of addiction to apomorphine has ever been recorded.*) I agreed to undergo treatment and entered a nursing home. For the first twenty-four hours I was literally insane and paranoid as many addicts are in severe withdrawal. This delirium was dispersed by twenty-four hours of intensive apomorphine treatment. The doctor showed me the chart. I had received minute amounts of morphine that could not possibly account for my lack of the more severe withdrawal symptoms such as leg and stomach cramps, fever and my own special symptom, The Cold Burn, like a vast hive covering the body and rubbed with menthol. Every addict has his own special symptom that cracks all control. There was a missing factor in the withdrawal equation—that factor could only be apomorphine.

I saw the apomorphine treatment really work. Eight days later I left the nursing home eating and sleeping normally. I remained completely off junk for two full years—a twelve-year record. I did relapse for some months as a result of pain and illness. Another apomorphine cure has kept me off junk through this writing.

The apomorphine cure is qualitatively different from other methods of cure. I have tried them all. Short reduction, slow reduction, cortisone, antihistamines, tranquilizers, sleeping cures, tolserol, reserpine. None of these cures lasted beyond the first opportunity to relapse. I can say definitely that I was never *metabolically* cured until I took the apomorphine cure. The overwhelming relapse statistics from the Lexington Narcotic Hospital have led many doctors to say that addiction is not curable. They use a dolophine reduction cure at Lexington and have never tried apomorphine so far as I know. In fact, this method of treatment has been largely neglected. No research has been done with variations of the apomorphine formula or with synthetics. No doubt substances fifty times stronger than apomorphine could be developed and the side effect of vomiting eliminated.

Apomorphine is a metabolic and psychic regulator that can be discontinued as soon as it has done its work. The world is deluged with tranquilizers and energizers but this unique regulator has not received attention. No research has been done by any of the large pharmaceutical companies. I suggest that research with variations of apomorphine and synthesis of it will open a new medical frontier extending far beyond the problem of addiction.

The smallpox vaccine was opposed by a vociferous lunatic group of anti-vaccinationists. No doubt a scream of protest will go up from interested or unbalanced individuals as the junk virus is shot out from under them. Junk is big business; there are always cranks and operators. They must not be allowed to interfere with the essential work of inoculation treatment and quarantine. *The junk virus is public health problem number one of the world today.*

Since *Naked Lunch* treats this health problem, it is necessarily brutal, obscene and disgusting. Sickness is often repulsive details not for weak stomachs.

Certain passages in the book that have been called pornographic were written as a tract against Capital Punishment in the manner of Jonathan Swift's *Modest Proposal.* These sections are intended to reveal capital punishment as the obscene, barbaric and disgusting anachronism that it is. As always the lunch is naked. If civilized countries want to return to Druid Hanging Rites in the Sacred Grove or to drink blood with the Aztecs and feed their Gods with blood of human sacrifice, let them see what they actually eat and drink. Let them see what is on the end of that long newspaper spoon.

I have almost completed a sequel to *Naked Lunch.* A mathematical extension of the Algebra of Need beyond the junk virus. Because there are many forms of addiction I think that they all obey basic laws. In the words of Heiderberg: "This may not be the best of all possible universes but it may well prove to be one of the simplest." If man can *see.*

Post Script . . . . Wouldn't You?

And speaking *Personally* and if a man speaks any other way we might as well start looking for his Protoplasm Daddy or Mother Cell. . . . I Don't Want To Hear Any More Tired Old Junk Talk And Junk Con. . . . The same things said a million times and more and there is no point in saying anything because *Nothing Ever Happens* in the junk world.

Only excuse for this tired death route is THE KICK when the junk circuit is cut off for the nonpayment and the junk-skin dies of junk-lack and overdose of time and the Old Skin has forgotten the skin game simplifying a way under the junk cover the way skins will. . . . A condition of total exposure is precipitated when the Kicking Addict cannot choose but see smell and listen. . . . Watch out for the cars. . . .

It is clear that junk is a Round-the-World-Push-an-Opium-Pellet-with-Your-Nose-Route. Strictly for Scarabs—stumble bum junk heap. And as such report to disposal. Tired of seeing it around.

Junkies always beef about *The Cold* as they call it, turning up their black coat collars and clutching their withered necks . . . pure junk con. A junky does not want to be warm, he wants to be Cool-Cooler-COLD. But he wants The Cold like he wants His Junk—NOT OUTSIDE where it does him no good but INSIDE so he can sit around with a spine like a frozen hydraulic jack . . . his metabolism approaching Absolute ZERO. TERMINAL addicts often go two months without a bowel move and the intestines make with sit-down-adhesions—Wouldn't you?—requiring the intervention of an apple corer or its surgical equivalent. . . . Such is life in The Old Ice House. Why move around and waste TIME?

Room for One More Inside, Sir.

Some entities are on thermodynamic kicks. They invented thermodynamics. . . . Wouldn't you?

And some of us are on Different Kicks and that's a thing out in the open the way I like to see what I eat and visa versa mutatis mutandis as the case may be: *Bill's Naked Lunch Room*. . . . Step right up. . . . Good for young and old, man and bestial. Nothing like a little snake oil to grease the wheels and get a show on the track Jack. Which side are you on? Fro-Zen Hydraulic? Or you want to take a look around with Honest Bill?

So that's the World Health Problem I was talking about back in The Article. The Prospect Before Us Friends of MINE. Do I hear muttering about a personal razor and some bush league short con artist who is known to have invented The Bill? Wouldn't You? The razor belonged to a man named Occam and he was not a scar collector. Ludwig Wittgenstein *Tractatus Logico-Philosophicus* "If a proposition is NOT NECESSARY it is MEANINGLESS and approaching MEANING ZERO."

"And what is More UNNECESSARY than junk if You Don't NEED it?"

Answer: "Junkies, if you are not ON JUNK."

I tell you boys, I've heard some tired conversation but no other OCCUPATION GROUP can approximate that old thermodynamic junk Slow-DOWN. Now your heroin addict does not say hardly anything and that I can stand. But your Opium "Smoker" is more active since he still has a tent and a Lamp . . . and maybe 7-9-10 lying up in there like hibernating reptiles keep the temperature up to Talking Level: How low the other junkies are "whereas We—WE have this tent and this lamp and this tent and this lamp and this tent and nice and warm in here nice and warm nice and IN HERE and nice and OUT-SIDE ITS COLD. . . . ITS COLD OUTSIDE where the dross eaters and the needle boys won't last two years not six months hardly won't last stumble bum around and there is no class in them. . . . But WE SIT HERE and never increase the DOSE . . . never—never increase the dose never except TO-NIGHT is a SPECIAL OCCASION with all the dross eaters and needle boys out there in the cold. . . . And we never eat it never never never eat it. . . . Excuse please while I take a trip to The Source Of Living Drops they all have in pocket and opium pellets shoved up the ass in a finger stall with the Family Jewels and the other shit.

Room for one more inside, Sir.

Well when that record starts around for the billionth light year and never the tape shall change us non-junkies take drastic action and the men separate out from the Junk boys.

Only way to protect yourself against this horrid peril is come over HERE and shack up with Charybdis. . . . Treat you right kid. . . . Candy and cigarettes.

I am after fifteen years in that tent. In and out in and out in and OUT. *Over and Out.* So listen to Old Uncle Bill Burroughs who invented the Burroughs Adding Machine Regulator Gimmick on the Hydraulic Jack Principle no matter how you jerk the handle result is always the same for given co-ordinates. Got my training early . . . wouldn't you?

Paregoric Babies of the World Unite. We have nothing to lose but Our Pushers. And THEY are NOT NECESSARY.

Look down LOOK DOWN along that junk road before you travel there and get in with the Wrong Mob. . . .

STEP RIGHT UP. . . . Only a three Dollar Bill to use BILL's telescope.

A word to the wise guy.

►► André Hodeir

An Analysis of Alain Resnais' Film "HIROSHIMA MON AMOUR"

Works and works alone have the power to reveal the essence of an art. What is the cinema? Thousands of films have ascribed it to the novel, the theater, or to painting; some have suggested subtler affinities between the world of moving images and that of music. Alain Resnais' work *Hiroshima Mon Amour* strikes through the mask and shows us at last what the most popular expressive means of our time can achieve *as art*. This is because Resnais, a man of the cinema, has been able to create—has been inspired to create—a musician's film.

For the man who regards the movies as sheer entertainment but still insists on the quality of his amusement, *Hiroshima* satisfies a demand and resolves a contradiction. As an assiduous spectator at film-society screenings, at first-run houses, or at neighborhood theaters, I have received like so many others the poetic shock of Dreyer's *Passion of Joan of Arc* and seen the explosion of comic expression in *Duck Soup*. Despite such achievements, it must be admitted that the cinema has not found a specific language: from film to film we submit to the fascination—discredited on each occasion by critical reflection—of a sub-art. In fact I have never listened to movie-lovers in debate without having to acknowledge, beneath their *a priori* sympathetic enthusiasm, an inadequate sense of contemporary art in general. It is doubtless this failure to appreciate the evolution of Western sensibility which permits them an untempered enjoyment of a Rossellini film whose narrative technique would have condemned it in Stendhal's time, or an admiration of a Fritz Lang character whose insistent power the *Castle*'s surveyor had expressed—and with what force, what depth!—some fifteen years before. Works, fortunately, cancel out all culture lags: *Hiroshima Mon Amour* has raised the cinema to the level of the arts which authentically represent the movement of thought and the world of perception in the twentieth century. We shall see that it has thereby contested the fundamental rights to existence of some venerable expressive forms, and not the least among them.

2

Destined, apparently, to public indifference, *Hiroshima* received nothing but official hostility. Spurned by academicians, dismissed from the Festivals on the most unconvincing pretexts, Resnais' work is powerful enough to wait for a turn of fortune. A day will certainly come when it will be asked to minister to French prestige. The important thing is that the public has given this film an unhoped-for reception. Five months after its first showing, *Hiroshima* was still playing on the Champs-Elysées. Snobbery? Development of popular taste? If we regard this indisputable *succès d'opinion* in the light of the criticism which preceded it, it does not appear that the film's extraordinary originality has been discerned in any but the most superficial manner. French criticism, moreover, is traditionally leveling; given a press that accords Françoise Sagan a place among the major postwar writers and accords the same tepid approval—always approval!—to the music of Barraqué as to that of Luigi Nono, it was inevitable that Alain Resnais would be assimilated to the "Nouvelle Vague" of his young confreres in the French cinema. Apparently total blindness is disappearing among our specialized critics these days; on the other hand, there are few who are not myopic. Perhaps an elite public understands that *Hiroshima* has nothing to do with the absurd "revival" inspired by the "Nouvelle Vague" directors; but there is every reason to fear that among those whose support has been the warmest, many liked this film the way the ordinary music lover likes the Ninth Symphony: in its least essential aspects.

There has been a lot of discussion, for instance, of the film's "human" meaning. This deliberately undefined story of a young French actress making a film about peace in Hiroshima and becoming the mistress of a Japanese architect on the eve of her departure has provoked many disconcerting commentaries. These have immediately "placed" the work on the moral level, obviating any judgment from an aesthetic viewpoint. Yet Resnais and his scenarist Marguerite Duras have had the intelligence to present this situation as a *given fact*: the film's first images present the couple during their night of love; the die is cast. What is admirable is that everything is reexplored for reasons that are exterior to the couple but that have profoundly marked these two human beings who do not yet know each other. There is, first of all, the silent presence of the memory of Hiroshima; the entire first part of the film, in which the vague and virtually deformed images of the lovers alternate with pitiless documentary shots, is glossed by the woman in an expressionless voice: "stones, scorched stone, split stones, anonymous hair-pieces which the women of Hiroshima found just as they had fallen, whole, where they wakened in the morning" until she is interrupted by the calm, slightly hoarse voice of the Japanese man: "You have seen nothing in Hiroshima, nothing." A second element of memory appears a little later on, when the woman watches her sleeping lover: the recollection of her first love, a young German soldier whom she knew in Nevers, fifteen years before, during the occupation. A furtive analogy in the posture of the Japanese, lying with his arms alongside his body, reminds her fleetingly of the German's corpse: the shot is admirable for its devastating brevity, linking to this first, linear film a second, discontinuous one whose development is non-chronological, as anarchic as memory itself. From this point on, the woman cannot keep the past from troubling the surface of her consciousness: henceforth this second film gains supremacy over the first and invades it from all sides until it invests it completely. The power of the images released is such that the evocation of a traumatic past, producing a realistic and impersonal narrative in the first film (the Japanese architect greedily questions the evidently suffering Frenchwoman), is transformed in the parallel film into an oneiric meditation from which even the German soldier's face will gradually be eliminated. "You weren't quite dead . . . I've told our story . . . it could be told, you see . . . look how much I've forgotten you already": so that it is toward oblivion that this meditation is oriented, and we already know that we must take literally the woman's final cry to her Japanese lover: "I'll

forget you! I've forgotten you already!" that precedes this admirable exchange in the last shots: "Hi-ro-shi-ma . . . that's your name." "And yours is Nevers . . . Nevers-en-France," which reveals the film's deepest meaning and concludes it with a song of pain, a resonance the cinema has never before achieved.

3

I am not sorry *Hiroshima* is a *significant* film, rich with its authors' ideas and convictions. The ways of poetry are not those of the novel, and if an entire section of the film belongs to a purely poetic universe, the central narrative employs a novelistic narrative which justifies its transactions with the world. The problems are evoked here in a resolutely contemporary perspective; no references to God or Law vitiate the purity of this drama of individual liberty and the right to happiness confronting collective consciousness and the unavoidability of war. Fortunately, *Hiroshima* is not a *film-à-thèse*. Its authors have carefully developed their doctrine: man and man alone is in question; those who regard a love affair between a Frenchwoman and a German soldier as an insult to the Resistance lack as much understanding as those who are shocked by a Frenchwoman's liaison with an Oriental. If *Hiroshima* expresses anything, it is first of all the suffering of those human beings society frustrates in their most fundamental aspirations.

Reference has also been made to the film's psychoanalytic intentions, which implies that the concept of psychoanalysis has a virtually unlimited range: if there is a psychoanalytic tendency whenever there is

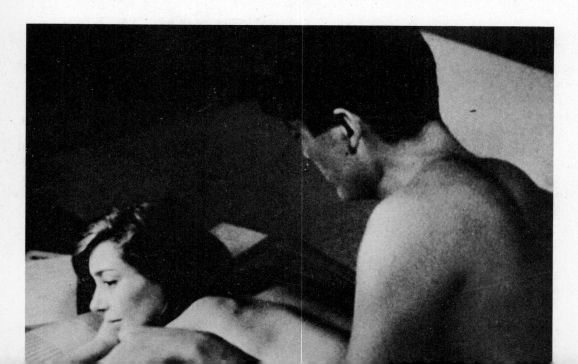

a dream or a reference to a voluntarily suppressed past ("Nevers is the city I dream about most at night; but, it's also the thing I think about least"), then *Hiroshima* is a film with psychoanalytic tendencies. But in that event, we must immediately point out that Alain Resnais does not regard psychoanalysis from the rather summary viewpoint to which certain products of the Hollywood industry have accustomed us. *Hiroshima* can be defined as the *exploration of a soul*. Actor-witness of the first film, the Japanese architect (admirably played by Eiji Okada) has no access to the second. His own suffering is revealed only in his stubborn returns to the young woman from whom he is continually separated ("I want to see you again . . . maybe you can stay . . . impossible not to come back . . ."). The already powerful love uniting these two human beings is threatened by life itself; we watch them hesitate as their paths diverge; yet these two people form a couple. Resnais has entirely isolated them from the exterior world. At the moment when the woman, reliving her former misery, speaks with the accents of madness, the Japanese slaps her: in the silence that follows, the heads of the neighboring diners turn toward them in a series of sudden close-ups, and we are startled to discover that *other people* exist around this couple. Thus the world, after the superbly frozen evocation of Hiroshima itself, makes only brief appearances: it is the extraordinarily seamed face of an old Japanese woman, it is a "sophisticated" dancer of distinguished vulgarity, it is a little boy in the peace parade who has been taught to march like a soldier (this last shot occurs in the only crowd sequence—lyrically handled—where Resnais shows us the shooting of the anti-H-bomb film his heroine is starring in).

4

Once we have said this much, it is evident that the film's beauty does not depend on its meaning. With the same script, with similar images, another director would have made an altogether different and perhaps uninteresting film. Hitherto *beauty* in the cinema has been synonymous with "striking images tastefully juxtaposed." The result was an elementary form, a necessarily weak sense of unity too readily and too immediately grasped. The conception of cutting Alain Resnais employs in *Hiroshima* introduces a notion of specifically musical discontinuity and thereby creates a complex relationship of time organizations. In the non-realistic sequences—and frequently even in the realistic ones—the text is used in a contrapuntal spirit. There would be no novelty in this if it were

a linear counterpoint, à *la* Hindemith, that was employed, but what is used instead is a kind of discontinuous, virtually *serial* counterpoint. Sometimes the text matches the images, sometimes it is ahead of them, or behind, sometimes it completely discards all visual support. The interior monologue declares its independence of the interior vision; the result is a dialectical language with which Resnais integrates the non-realistic use of the sound track. Everything is either foreshadowed or revealed later. After her lover wakes up, the woman exchanges a series of apparently unimportant remarks with him, while the recollection of Nevers haunts her; it is a distant bell tolling that informs us of this inner preoccupation: we will understand later (when she says: "The bells of Saint-Etienne were chiming . . . chiming") that this sound comes not from a nearby belltower but from the depths of time and consciousness.

These pre-evocations of the past have at times an extraordinary poetic force. When the woman tells the story of her love—in deliberately unexpressive terms ("then he died")—an unaccountable image appears on the screen, motionless, timeless—a kind of summerhouse, rather ugly and strangely flooded with light. This neutral and motionless shot has an incomparable beauty: we realize that it is aesthetically connected with the idea of death. Later on, as a matter of fact, the narrative returns to the situation previously referred to ("when I went down to the dock at noon, he wasn't quite dead . . .")—which the camera this time illustrates with a plunging movement (from the bridge toward the body on the dock)—and explains it: "someone had fired from a garden"—which the camera suggests with a brutal shot of the garden in which we recognize, motionless in the summer sunshine, the summerhouse we have seen before. There is a correspondence here between structure and poetic effect for which we would be hard put to find an equivalent outside the art of music. And if we were to point to some precursor, the dramatic innovations of Alban Berg (particularly in *Wozzeck*) come to mind rather than Orson Welles' hesitant attempts to explore time in *Citizen Kane*.

Another analogy with musical form is the division of the work into a certain number of parts. I make out ten: some, extremely brief, function as interludes, like the third movement of Beethoven's Fourteenth Quartet. Each is subject to its own tempo: Oddly enough, the tempo grows slower and slower after the lyrical sequence of the parade: we proceed from *andante* to *adagio* to *largo*. This predilection for slowness, which had already led Dreyer, in *Joan of Arc*, to the peak of cinematic expression, is not one of the film's least beauties. We need scarcely add that Alain Resnais "keeps to his tempo" with a rigor approaching Fürtwangler's in his great renditions of Beethoven. Certainly all this has been profoundly thought out as well as deeply felt.

The care Resnais has lavished on his sound track has permitted him to control certain effects generally left to chance. He has been able to give a poetic and occasionally dramatic significance to silence which I do not remember ever having noticed before. The few breaks in tempo, or rather "pedal points" which several times break up the large central "movement" are veritable *structures of silence* superbly integrated into the story and its incidents. For instance, when the girl, confined in a cellar after her German lover's death, stares with a no longer human expression at the cat (whose sudden appearance in a close-up is no less extraordinary for gratifying our expectation), the alternation of shots between her face and the cat's head is accompanied by a long silence: this is a moment of pure beauty in which the world of madness and the sentiment of eternity are identified, more perfectly, doubtless, than the text itself suggests.

One last correspondence in the film's conception, and a subtler one, with the domain of musical form is the notion of variations. I refer less to the last "movements," where the same situation is agonizingly repeated (the Frenchwoman tries to leave the Japanese; he comes toward her again), than to the four poems which Marguerite Duras has inserted in her text and which Resnais has put into images with a sense of structure more than one famous composer might envy. These poems are arranged in pairs: the first and the third are songs of carnal love; the other two are about forgetting. Resnais seems to have conceived the third poem as an "inversion" of the first: to a daylight traveling shot, fast and impersonal, in a shady Hiroshima street, corresponds a much slower inverse movement, fleetingly locating the character in the same setting seen, this time, by night. Is the first traveling shot, as some have suggested, a figuration of the act of love? Perhaps; whether or not it is significant, the relation of image to text is arresting; and even more so in the third poem, which culminates in the poetic identification of places with human beings, a concept whose cinematic validity is affirmed by the very style of the work. The poem is an invocation to men loved ("I meet you—I remember you"); then, gradually, these become only one man. The meditation assumes an exceptional *gravity* on the screen; it achieves, in its almost unendurable gentleness, an intensity—I might say, a purity—which reminds us of the loveliest pages of western poetic literature. During the long walk through the city, during which Hiroshima's nocturnal aspect is revealed, a new thematic element makes its appearance: the night; point of departure for that discontinuous polyphonic development in which the work in a sense recapitulates itself. Revery then takes the form—a marvelously simple device—of an alternation of lateral traveling shots at apparently equal speeds, so that Nevers melts into Hiroshima and Hiroshima into Nevers. In this uniform movement, the mournfully frozen façades of the old French town and the still sadder lights of the Japanese city are identified in order to form an oneiric world of an overpowering unity, which is exemplified by the handling of the images.

After this harrowing sequence, its poetic and formal apogee, the work is nothing but a slow, dying fall toward its final song. The third poem was a "grand variation" on the first; the last contradicts the second. The latter, treated dramatically (the young woman, in front of her mirror, talks to herself: "Fourteen years since I've lost all hope of an impossible love"), is not based on the true relation of image and text we find once more, in an intentionally simplified form, in the fourth poem, when a last flare of memories disturbs the heroine in her acceptance of death, when she finally leaves her past and "gives it to oblivion." The image, here, is a curious extension of the text: the "lovely poplars along the Nièvre" come in answer to the young woman's summons, but these motionless scenes of the Nivernaise landscape tinge her soul with a suggestion of detachment, even serenity, which she cannot yet be feeling. Perhaps this farewell alludes to a *subsequent* perception of things. Besides, the poetic *tonus* of this sequence heralds that of the penultimate section: the strangely Wellesian night club scene which immediately succeeds it. Here detachment gives way to indifference: nothing matters any more, everything has been said, save for love's last cry.

5

If I have been able to present an accurate image of *Hiroshima Mon Amour*, one free of any personal obsession, the esthetic *données* such an image implies should be evident. Just as the beauty of great musical work derives from the form—that is, from the relations the work sustains with musical space and time —similarly, authentic beauty cannot exist in the cinema beneath a certain formal level which this art, in Alain Resnais' film, has finally achieved. Only a form conceived as a dialectic of time and space can satisfactorily illuminate the human or philosophical meaning of a film; such form alone possesses, in its own extensions, the *raison d'être* of a non-signifying cinema which might relate itself to the pure poem and perhaps replace it.

Thanks to these formal attainments, it seems that the cinema is in a position to abandon the castoff properties of realism for good. Certainly realism will support a certain kind of cinema for a long time to come, as it supports a sub-literature which the masterpieces of Joyce and Broch have left undisturbed. But it seems impossible to me that a real artist can remain unaffected by the power of the oneiric world Resnais' film has released (an oneiric world quite different from Buñuel's surrealism, and still more alien to the nightmarish, constantly editorialized imagery of Ingmar Bergman). Not only does the foreshadowing-recollection complex assume a poetic value in the formal conception of the work, but this conception involves the spectator, makes him participate in the ambiguous interplay. Beneath the memories and the forebodings we accord to the characters lie our forebodings and our recollections: for anyone without imagination or memory (on the poetic level, I mean), *Hiroshima* may seem an esoteric, almost incomprehensible work.

When a film is as astonishing as this, one can afford to leave its weaknesses in obscurity. Nevertheless, these flaws exist. Hitherto, no film has been able to withstand time: will *Hiroshima* join those works which Jean Barraqué says are "no longer frozen in a sumptuous and distant past, but live on with their own energy of life and death"? A masterpiece today, is Resnais' film nevertheless condemned to be relegated to those film libraries where yesterday's "masterpieces" end their pathetic careers? For our children, raised on a "dialectical" and "discontinuous" cinema, will *Hiroshima* be anything more than an occasionally visible precursor?

It is difficult to answer such questions with any certainty. The work is not perfect: we can even discern the points where it will age. Perhaps the formal imagination which today compels our admiration masks a certain lack of formal rigor. Resnais has conceived his film in successive mutations: perhaps the last turns of the screw are thereby weakened. Furthermore, every film is dependent upon one factor extremely liable to "date": interpretation by its actors. Today we laugh at the visual or auditory evidence left by the woman who was the "divine," the "immortal" Sarah Bernhardt; what will we think, in twenty years, of the acting of Emmanuelle Riva? The actress plays an overpowering role; firmly directed by Resnais, she is not afraid to assume the

risks it involves. If she succeeds in being "like a thousand women at once" for us—thereby justifying the Japanese architect's passionate speeches—must she not, in order to do so, exceed the limits of a certain restrictive discipline which the screen seems to impose, and does she not thereby risk eventually provoking the same reactions as her illustrious predecessor?

The theater's one advantage over the cinema is that Sarah Bernhardt's acting does not affect the essence of *Phèdre*. In the cinema, as in jazz, interpretation is identified with the work itself. If there are errors in Emmanuelle Riva's conception of the role, nothing will efface them. Nor will anything obliterate the inadequacies of Marguerite Duras' text, whose importance is obviously capital. Certain inequalities in this text are already apparent. The French novelist has achieved some splendid moments; I have already referred to a number of them;

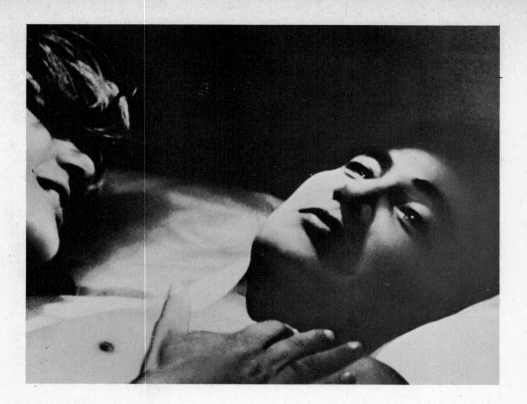

but she has also fallen into some of the worst literary traps. The ghost of Péguy makes occasional and unfortunate appearances ("Whole cities are in anger. Against whom, this anger of whole cities? The anger of whole cities, whether they wish it or not, . . ." etc.). Occasionally the influence is heavier still ("Time for what? To live? To die?" "The time to know." "That doesn't exist. Nor the time to live. Nor the time to die. So I don't care.")

Marguerite Duras and Alain Resnais might have avoided such dialogues, fortunately quite infrequent in *Hiroshima*. But for the film not to suffer from a disparity between image and text, Resnais would have had to secure the collaboration of a writer of genius. Does such a writer exist . . . ?

Similarly, one is led to wonder if the extremely weak score might not have been a good deal better. Certainly a mysterious curse pursues this most musical of directors in his quest of a composer worthy of the name. The species is virtually unknown in the world of the cinema where Resnais has mistakenly done all his prospecting. From *Van Gogh* to *Nuit et Brouillard* a pseudo-lyrical neoclassicism or the most out-and-out amateurishness has partially spoiled a number of admirable short films. But even if he had widened his horizon and turned to the masters of serial music to whom his own sense of structure relates him, I doubt if Resnais would have discovered the creator whose sensibility might have fruitfully corresponded to his own. Until he has found this *alter ego* so patiently pursued from film to film, Alain Resnais will be well advised to limit the composer's role as much as possible, as in *Hiroshima*.

6

Perhaps, then, this film which is sustained by neither a great poetic text nor a fine score is destined to date. For the moment, however, its most evident effect is the superannuation it has imposed on the films preceding it. *Hiroshima* has pushed toward oblivion the surest values in the history of the cinema. Not, of course, with the definitive power of Bach's work that obscures five centuries of polyphony; but with the evidence, perhaps, of Louis Armstrong's first great improvisations, which brought New Orleans pre-jazz to an end. In order for the cinema to exist as art, it has had to create a kind of discontinuous narrative (integrated, in this case, with a linear account) subject to permutations in space and time: the basis of a specific language. Above all, a true creator has had to give this conception—which is not the result of a doctrine—the dimensions of a work. Some may regret that Resnais' world is one of contemplation, from which violence seems missing; but this does not affect the purity of the work, nor diminish the power of its presence.

We have come this far. But let us look ahead. Can we estimate the significance of the formal attainments which have so radically reclassified the cinema in the hierarchy of contemporary art? The cinema is not yet the total art Wagner dreamed of; it may become so. In the light of the notions glimpsed along the way, the theater scarcely seems equipped, by its very structure, to assimilate itself to the formal universe now in gestation. Poetry, painting, and the novel are making tremendous efforts to redefine themselves; have they the means to do so? Only music seems to give an adequate account of the realities of the sensible world: because it has created them. Following music's lead, can the cinema regroup the other arts? If it achieves more and more extreme expressive heights than they, can it not even supplant them? Perhaps this is what Henri Michaux meant when he wrote several years ago: "Succession, the construction-destruction process is music's own. There are several musical genres which have thereby gained their reputation. In a painting, we are accustomed, indigently enough, to be content with the final state. But perhaps artists of genius exist whom we will discover only through the cinema, in a new kind of architecture uniquely apparent on film, artists capable of unheard-of works and monuments 'in time,' progressively demolished in magnificent 'declining trajectories.'"

It is time, it seems, to reconsider in their very essence these arts which—Michaux adds—"still take so much pleasure in their servitude." Norman McLaren has shown—though crudely—that a painting in movement is possible. What painter of genius will learn how to master the resources of the screen?

The profound relationships of the cinema with painting and poetry are still to be discovered. The historical importance of *Hiroshima Mon Amour* is that it has declared the analogies of cinematic construction and musical composition. Henceforth the meaning of the word *film* must change. There is no doubt about it: if genuine composers, used to advanced compositional techniques, could apply their spirit of variation to the cinema, further upheavals would result. We may hope that such a musician as Michel Fano, making his debut in the cinema with a short film full of promises, *Chutes de Pierres, Danger de Mort*, will confirm this prediction. Resnais' career, too, has reached only its first flowering. We may suppose that at thirty-seven, the creator of *Hiroshima* is just discovering his universe. Moreover, other directors will receive the impact of his film: works will appear on our screens which would not have been possible yesterday. The cinema is beginning; it is only beginning. It is up to the creators of the future to prove whether it can, in Mallarmé's prophetic phrase, "regain its true course from music."

Translated by Richard Howard

►► Roger Shattuck

What Is 'Pataphysics?

1. *'Pataphysics is the science of the realm beyond metaphysics; or, 'Pataphysics lies as far beyond metaphysics as metaphysics lies beyond physics—in one direction or another.*

Now, metaphysics is a word which can mean exactly what one wants it to mean, whence its continuing popularity. To Aristotle it meant merely the field of speculation he took up after physics. The pataphysician beholds the entire created universe, and all others with it, and sees that they are neither good nor bad but pataphysical. René Daumal, writing in the twentieth century, said that he proposed to do for metaphysics what Jules Verne had done for physics. 'Pataphysics, then, entering the great beyond in whatever direction it may lie, offers us a voyage of discovery and adventure into what Jarry called "ethernity." That, of course, is where we all live.

2. *'Pataphysics is the science of the particular, of laws governing exceptions.*

The realm beyond metaphysics will not be reached by vaster and vaster generalities; this has been the error of contemporary thought. A return to the particular shows that every event determines a law, a particular law. 'Pataphysics relates each thing and each event not to any generality (a mere plastering over of exceptions) but to the singularity that makes it an exception. Thus the science of 'Pataphysics attempts no cures, envisages no progress, distrusts all claims of "improvement" in the state of things, and remains innocent of any message. 'Pataphysics is *pure* science, lawless and therefore impossible to outlaw.

3. 'Pataphysics is the science of imaginary solutions.

In the realm of the particular, every event arises from an infinite number of causes. All solutions, therefore, to particular problems, all attributions of cause and effect, are based on arbitrary choice, another term for scientific imagination. Gravity as curvature of space or as electro-magnetic attraction—does it make any difference which solution we accept? Understanding either of them entails a large exercise of scientific imagination. Science must elect the solution that fits the facts—travel of light or fall of an apple. 'Pataphysics welcomes all scientific theories (they are getting better and better) and treats each one not as a generality but as an attempt, sometimes heroic and sometimes pathetic, to pin down one point of view as "real." Students of philosophy may remember the German Hans Vaihinger with his philosophy of *als ob*. Ponderously yet persistently he declared that we construct our own system of thought and value, and then live "as if" reality conformed to it. The idea of "truth" is the most imaginary of all solutions.

4. 'Pataphysics, all things are equal.

The pataphysician not only accepts no final scientific explanation of the universe, he also rejects all values, moral, aesthetic, and otherwise. The principle of universal equivalence and the conversion of opposites reduces the world in its pataphysical reality to particular cases only. All the more reason, indeed, that the pataphysician should enjoy "working," and in the most diverse ways, should respond to all the normal (and "abnormal") appetites of the flesh and the spirit, should sometimes behave with considerateness toward his neighbor and even fulfill a "responsible" role in society. 'Pataphysics preaches no rebellion and no acquiescence, no new morality nor immorality, no political reform, no reaction and certainly no promise of happiness nor unhappiness. What would be the use, all things being equal?

5. 'Pataphysics is, in aspect, imperturbable.

Jarry was regarded by most of his contemporaries as a joker or a lunatic. Here lie the first errors of incomprehension. 'Pataphysics has nothing to do with humor or with the kind of tame insanity psychoanalysis has drummed into fashion. Life is, of course, absurd, and it is ludicrous to take it seriously. Only the comic is serious. The pataphysician, therefore, remains entirely serious, attentive, imperturbable. He does not burst out laughing or curse when asked to fill out in quadruplicate a questionnaire on his political affiliations or sexual habits: on the contrary, he details a different and equally valid activity on each of the four sheets. His imperturbability gives him anonymity and the possibility of savoring the full pataphysical richness of life.*

6. All things are pataphysical; yet few men practice 'Pataphysics consciously.

No difference in value, only in state, exists between ordinary men and those who are consciously aware of the pataphysical nature of the world, including themselves. The College of 'Pataphysics is no better and no worse than the French Academy or than the Hilldale Garden Club Men's Auxiliary Committee of Three on Poison Ivy Extermination. The College, however, being aware of its own nature, can enjoy the spectacle of its own pataphysical behavior. And what science but 'Pataphysics can cope with consciousness, "self"-consciousness perpetually twisting out of itself into the reaches of ethernity? Père Ubu's monstrous *gidouille* or belly is represented by a spiral, which Dr. Faustroll's 'Pataphysics transposes into a symbol of ethernal consciousness circling forever around itself. Symbol? By now all words are pataphysical, being equal.

7. Beyond 'Pataphysics lies nothing; 'Pataphysics is the ultimate defense.

Like the sorcerer's apprentice, we have become victims of our own knowledge—principally of our scientific and technological knowledge. In 'Pataphysics resides our only defense against ourselves. Not that 'Pataphysics will change history: that great improvisation of the past already belongs to the Science of Sciences. But 'Pataphysics allows a few individuals,

* Imperturbability is not just a dignified version of "cool kicks." "Playing it cool" means indifference and is, at best, an indifferent game. The pataphysician is concerned; not through *engagement* in an attempt to create human values, but in the manner of the child looking through a kaleidoscope or the astronomer studying the galaxy.

beneath their imperturbability, to live up to their particular selves: Ubu or Faustroll, you or I. Outwardly one may conform meticulously to the rituals and conventions of civilized life, but inwardly one watches this conformity with the care and enjoyment of a painter choosing his colors—or perhaps of a chameleon. 'Pataphysics, then, is an inner attitude, a discipline, a science, and an art, which allows each man to live his life as an exception, proving no law but his own.

► ► Félix Fénéon

(1861–1944)
Soft Spoken Anarchist

"Impetuous Keeper of his peace," in the words of *Father Ubu's Little Almanach*: A disturbing peace for those impenitent men of letters, his contemporaries: offhandedly to have explored and exhausted the charms of the Gothic tale, to have made sport of the learned rarity of the symbolists' style in a few pages of bold and brilliant art criticism, in sum, to be a man *full of talent and promise*, and to give up writing anything other than snotty little reviews for the *Revue independante* and three-line news items in *Le Matin*—could all this be taken seriously? Enigmatic, impenetrable Fénéon, with the look of "an American Mephistopheles," according to Remy de Gourmont; canonized, moreover, by his indictment for anarchism in the trial known as the Trial of the Thirty

(but in fact, there is no indication in his Works, edited by Jean Paulhan, that he wrote for the subversive *En-Dehors*). As editor of the *Revue Blanche*, to which he himself deigned to contribute only two translations, he backed Jarry, who, in turn, dedicated to him the thirty-sixth chapter of *Faustroll*. Who else besides Jarry could have understood that these brief notations, which the profane will take for an innocuous, superficial game, are in fact the epitome of the *exploits* and *opinions* of one of the most intelligent men of all time?

Michel Décaudin,
Regent of the History and
Exegesis of 'Pataphysics

Our Times

Scratching it with a hair-triggered revolver, Mr. Ed . . . B . . . removed the end of his nose, in the Vivienne police station.

Falling from a scaffolding at the same time as Mr. Dury, stone-mason, of Marseille, a stone crushed his skull.

Louis Lamarre had neither work nor lodging; but he did have a few coppers. He bought a quart of kerosene from a grocer in Saint Denis, and drank it.

A madwoman of Puéchabon (Hérault), Mrs. Bautiol, née Hérail, used a club to awaken her parents-in-law.

At finding her son Hyacinth, 69, hanged, Mrs. Ranvier, of Bussy-Saint-Georges, was so depressed she couldn't cut the rope.

In Essoyes (Aube), Bernard, 25, bludgeoned Mr. Dufert, who is 89, and stabbed his wife. He was jealous.

In Brest, thanks to a smoker's carelessness, Miss Ledru, all done up in tulle, was badly burned on thighs and breasts.

In Djiajelli, a thirteen-year-old virgin, propositioned by a lewd rake of ten, did him in with three knife-blows.

Scissors in hand, Marie le Goeffic was playing on a swing. So that, falling, she punctured her abdomen. In Bretonneau.

Not finding his daughter of 19 austere enough, the Saint-Etienne jeweler Jallat killed her. He still, it is true, has eleven other children.

"What! all those children perched on my wall!" With eight shots, Mr. Olive, a Toulon property-owner made them scramble down, covered with blood.

Marie Jandeau, a handsome girl well known to many gentlemen of Toulon, suffocated in her room last night, on purpose.

A Nancy dishwasher, Vital Frérotte, recently returned from Lourdes forever cured of tuberculosis, died, on Sunday, by mistake.

Miss Verbeau did manage to hit Marie Champion, in the breast, but she burned her own eye, for a bowl of vitriol is not an accurate weapon.

At skittles apoplexy felled Mr. André, 75, of Levallois. While his bowl was still rolling, he ceased to be.

Belles-Lettres

LAFORGUE (Jules). A plump and beardless youth. Sings to the moon: insidious amoral laments, incantatory litanies. This Selenite is reader to the Empress Augusta. Oh, the agonies of that good lady, if he should read her his poems!

TAINE (Hippolyte). Applies to literary history the techniques of scientific farming. For any given country, studies soil chemistry, topography, and climate, then treats a generation of artists as a crop of mushrooms, beets, and Brussels sprouts.

LARROQUE (Jean). *Pen and Sword in the Eighteenth Century.* (Ollendorff.) How tedious for Mr. Jean Larroque, conscientiously to have read every last publication of a whole century! He felt that he should not suffer alone.

BOYER D'AGEN. *Native Land.* (Victor Havard.) Mr. Boyer hoes through his memory, culling reminiscences of childhood and seminary years which he sets out in chunky, ill-assorted, haze-ridden, garlicky sentences. Were Athens, Sienna, Venice, and Haarlem to vie for Mr. Boyer, he would choose Agen.

Translated by Edward Morris

Eugène Ionesco
Photo courtesy of le Collège de 'Pataphysique

Foursome*

The Scene:
The entrance is to the left. Stage center, there is a table, and on it three potted plants are lined up side by side. Elsewhere, an armchair or a sofa.

The Characters:
DUPONT, *costumed like Durand*
DURAND, *costumed like Dupont*
MARTIN, *costumed in the same fashion*
THE PRETTY LADY, *wearing a hat, dress, shoes, cape or furs, and gloves, and carrying a handbag etc., at least on her entrance*

First and only scene
[*As the curtain rises an agitated* DUPONT, *his hands behind his back, is pacing around the table.* DURAND, *doing the same business, moves in the contrary direction. When* DUPONT *and* DURAND *meet and collide, they about-face and move in opposite directions.*]

DUPONT: . . . No . . .

DURAND: Yes . . .

DUPONT: No . . .

DURAND: Yes . . .

DUPONT: No . . .

DURAND: Yes . . .

DUPONT: I tell you no . . . Look out for the potted plants . . .

DURAND: I tell you yes . . . Look out for the potted plants . . .

DUPONT: And I tell you no . . .

DURAND: And I tell you yes . . . and I repeat to you yes . . .

DUPONT: You don't need to keep on saying yes to me. For it's no, no and no, thirty-two times no.

DURAND: Dupont, look out for the potted plants . . .

DUPONT: Durand, look out for the potted plants . . .

DURAND: You're pigheaded. My god, how pigheaded can you be . . .

DUPONT: Who, me? You're the one that's pigheaded, pigheaded, pigheaded . . .

DURAND: You don't know what you're talking about. Why do you say that I'm pigheaded? Look out for the potted plants. I am not pigheaded at all.

DUPONT: Do you still want to know why you're pigheaded . . . Oh, you do bug me, you know.

DURAND: I don't know whether I bug you or not. Maybe I do bug you. But I'd really like to know why you say I'm pigheaded. Because, in the first place, I'm not pigheaded . . .

DUPONT: Not pigheaded? Not pigheaded, when you refuse, when you deny, when you resist, when you insist, in short, after I've made it all perfectly clear to you . . .

DURAND: Perfectly unclear . . . you haven't convinced me. You're the one who's pigheaded. As for me, I'm not pigheaded.

DUPONT: Yes, you are pigheaded . . .

DURAND: No.

DUPONT: Yes.

DURAND: No.

DUPONT: Yes.

DURAND: I tell you no.

DUPONT: I tell you yes.

DURAND: But I just told you no.

DUPONT: And I just told you yes.

DURAND: You don't need to keep on saying yes to me, it's no, no . . . NO.

DUPONT: You are pigheaded, you can see very well that you are pigheaded . . .

DURAND: You're reversing our roles, my friend . . . Don't knock over the potted plants . . . You're reversing our roles. If you are acting in good faith, you ought very well to realize that you're the one who's being pigheaded.

DUPONT: How could I be pigheaded? Nobody's pigheaded when he's in the right. And as you will come to see, I am right, that's all, I'm just plain right . . .

DURAND: You can't be right because I am right . . .

DUPONT: I beg your pardon, I am.

DURAND: No, I am.

DUPONT: No, I am.

DURAND: No, I am.

DUPONT: No, I.

DURAND: No, I.

DUPONT: No.

DURAND: No.

DUPONT: No.

DURAND: No.

DUPONT: No.

DURAND: No.

DUPONT: No.

DURAND: No. Look out for the potted plants.

DUPONT: Look out for the potted plants.

MARTIN [entering]: Ah, at last you have come to an agreement.

DUPONT: Oh, no, far from it . . . I am not at all in agreement with him . . . [He points at Durand.]

DURAND: I'm not at all in agreement with him. [He points at Dupont.]

DUPONT: He denies the truth.

DURAND: He denies the truth.

DUPONT: He does.

DURAND: He does.

MARTIN: Oh . . . stop being so stupid . . . And look out for the potted plants. Characters in a play don't always have to be even more stupid than in real life.

DURAND: We're doing the best we can.

DUPONT [to Martin]: In the first place, you bug me, you and your big cigar.

MARTIN: And you think you two don't bug me, pacing around like this, with your hands behind your backs, neither one of you willing to make the least concession . . . You'll end up by making me dizzy and by knocking over the potted plants . . .

DURAND: Well, you and your disgusting smoking are going to make me vomit . . . It's absurd to go around smoking like a chimney all day long.

MARTIN: Chimneys aren't the only things that smoke.

DUPONT [to Martin]: You smoke like a chimney that's not been cleaned out.

MARTIN [to Dupont]: What a banal comparison . . . You've got no imagination.

DURAND [to Martin]: It's certainly true that Dupont has no imagination. But as for you, you haven't got any either . . .

DUPONT [to Durand]: And neither do you, my dear Durand.

MARTIN [to Dupont]: Nor do you, my dear Dupont.

DUPONT [to Martin]: Nor do you, my dear Martin.

DURAND [to Dupont]: Nor do you, my dear Dupont. And don't call me my dear Durand anymore, I'm not your dear Durand.

DUPONT [to Durand]: Nor do you, my dear Durand, you've got no imagination. And don't call me my dear Dupont.

MARTIN [to Dupont and Durand]: Don't call me your dear Martin, I'm not your dear Martin.

DUPONT [to Martin, overlapping Durand]: Don't call me your dear Durand, I'm not your dear Dupont.

DURAND [to Martin, overlapping Dupont]: Don't call me your dear Durand, I'm not your dear Durand.

MARTIN: In the first place, my cigar couldn't possibly bug you because I haven't got a cigar . . . Gentlemen, permit me to tell you that you both exaggerate. You exaggerate. I'm outside whatever is bothering you. So I can judge objectively.

DURAND: Good, judge . . .

DUPONT: Judge, then. Go ahead.

MARTIN: Permit me to tell you, freely, that you are not going about it in a way that will get you anywhere. Try to agree on one thing—find at least some basis for discussion, to make a dialogue possible.

DURAND [to Martin]: No dialogue is possible with Monsieur [he points at Dupont], under these conditions. The conditions he proposes are not admissible.

DUPONT [to Martin]: I'm not trying to get somewhere, at any cost. These are the conditions of Monsieur [he points at Durand] and they're dishonorable . . .

DURAND: Oh! what nerve . . . To pretend that my conditions are dishonorable . . .

MARTIN [to Dupont]: Let him explain.

DUPONT [to Durand]: Go ahead and explain.

MARTIN: Look out for the potted plants.

DUPONT: I shall explain. But I don't know if anyone will really listen to me, nor do I know if anyone will really understand me. However, understand me well, for if we're to understand each other, we have to understand each other, this is what Monsieur Durand doesn't manage to comprehend, and he's famous for his incomprehension.

DURAND [to Dupont]: You dare speak of my famous incomprehension. You know very well that it's your incomprehension that's famous. You're the one who has always refused to comprehend me.

DUPONT [to Durand]: Now you're going too far. Your bad faith is self-evident. A child of three months would understand me, that is if it were a baby in good faith.

DUPONT [to Martin]: You heard him, huh? You heard that . . .

DURAND [to Dupont]: That's going too far . . . You're the one who doesn't want to comprehend. [To Martin.] Did you hear what he had the nerve to claim?

MARTIN: Gentlemen, my friends, let's not waste time. Let's get down to it, you're talking but you're not saying anything.

DUPONT [to Martin]: Who, me? I'm talking without saying anything?

DURAND [to Martin]: What, you dare say that I'm talking without saying anything?

MARTIN: Excuse me, I didn't mean to say exactly that you were talking without saying anything, no, no, it wasn't entirely that.

DUPONT [to Martin]: How could you say that we were talking without saying anything, when you are the one who has just said that there was talking without saying anything, although it is absolutely impossible to talk without saying anything inasmuch as every time one says something, one talks and contrariwise every time one talks one says something.

MARTIN [to Dupont]: Let's grant that I said what I said about your talking without saying anything, now this doesn't mean that you always talk without saying anything. There are times, however, when one says more in saying nothing and when one says nothing in talking too much. This depends on the situation and on the people involved. Now just how much have you actually said during the last few minutes? Nothing, absolutely nothing. No matter who says so.

DURAND [interrupting Martin]: Dupont's the one who talks without saying anything, not me.

DUPONT [to Durand]: You're the one.

DURAND [to Dupont]: You're the one.

MARTIN [to Dupont and Durand]: You're the ones.

DUPONT [to Durand and Martin]: You're the ones.

MARTIN: No.

DUPONT: Yes.

DURAND [to Dupont and Martin]: You're talking without saying anything.

DUPONT: I, I'm talking without saying anything?

MARTIN [to Durand and Dupont]: Yes, exactly, you're talking without saying anything.

DUPONT [to Durand and Martin]: You too, you're talking without saying anything.

MARTIN [to Dupont and Durand]: You're the one who's talking without saying anything . . .

DURAND [to Dupont and Martin]: You're the one who's talking without saying anything . . .

DUPONT [to Durand and Martin]: You're the one who's talking without saying anything.

MARTIN [to Durand]: It's you.

DURAND [to Martin]: It's you.

DUPONT [to Durand]: It's you.

DURAND [to Dupont]: It's you.

DUPONT [to Martin]: It's you.

MARTIN [to Durand and Dupont]
DURAND [to Martin and Dupont]   : You . . . you
DUPONT [to Martin and Durand]   . . . you . . .

[Exactly at this moment, the PRETTY LADY enters.]

THE LADY: Good day, gentlemen . . . Look out for the potted plants. [The three men halt suddenly and turn toward her.] What are you squabbling about? [She simpers.] Come now, gentlemen . . .

DUPONT: Oh, dear lady, here you are at last and now you're going to rescue us from this impasse.

DURAND: Oh, dear lady, you're going to see where bad faith has brought us . . .

MARTIN [interrupting Durand]: Oh, dear lady, let me tell you just what's happened . . .

DUPONT [to the two other men]: I'm the one who will tell her what's happened, for this lovely lady is my fiancée . . .

[The PRETTY LADY remains standing and smiling.]

DURAND [to the other two men]: This lovely lady is my fiancée.

MARTIN [to the other two men]: This lovely lady is my fiancée.

DUPONT [to the Pretty Lady]: My dear, tell these gentlemen that you are my fiancée.

MARTIN [to Dupont]: You're mistaken, she is my fiancée.

DURAND [to the Pretty Lady]: Dear lady, tell these gentlemen that you are really . . .

DUPONT [to Durand, interrupting]: You're mistaken, she is mine.

MARTIN [to the Lady]: Dear lady, please tell . . .

DURAND [to Martin]: You're mistaken, she's mine.

DUPONT [to the Lady]: Dear lady . . .

DUPONT [to Martin]: You're mistaken, she's mine.

DURAND [to the Pretty Lady]: Dear lady . . .

DUPONT [to Martin]: You're mistaken, she's mine.

MARTIN [to the Lady]: Dear lady, please say that . . .

DURAND [to Dupont]: You're mistaken, she's mine.

DUPONT [to the Pretty Lady, violently pulling her toward him by her arm]: Oh, dear lady . . .

[The PRETTY LADY loses a shoe.]

DURAND [violently pulling the Lady by her other arm]: Let me embrace you.

[The LADY loses her other shoe, and one glove comes off in Dupont's hands.]

MARTIN [who has gone to pick up a potted plant, making the Lady turn toward him]: Please accept this bouquet.
[He sticks the potted plant in her arms.]

THE LADY: Oh, thank you.

DUPONT [turning the Lady toward him and putting another potted plant in her arms]: Do take these pretty flowers. [The LADY is jostled and loses her hat.]

THE LADY: Thank you, thank you . . .

DURAND [same business as Dupont]: These flowers belong to you, just as my heart belongs to you . . .

THE LADY: I'm delighted . . . [Her arms are loaded down with the potted plants and she's dropped her purse.]

MARTIN [violently pulling her toward him and shouting]: Embrace me, embrace me . . . [The LADY loses her cape and furs.]

DURAND [same business]: Embrace me.

DUPONT [same business]: Embrace me.
[They continue this business for several moments; the LADY drops the flowers, her skirt comes undone, and her clothes are rumpled. The three men alternatively tear her from each other's arms as they move about the table.]

THE LADY: Oh, shit . . . Leave me alone.

DUPONT [to Martin]: Leave her alone.

MARTIN [to Durand]: Leave her alone.

DURAND [to Dupont]: Leave her alone.

EACH OF THE MEN [to the other two]: It's you she's telling to leave her alone.

THE LADY [to the three men]: Leave me alone, all of you.

DURAND, DUPONT, MARTIN [astonished]: Me? me? me?

[All movement stops. The LADY, rumpled, unhooked, winded, half undressed, moves down to the footlights.]

THE LADY: Ladies and gentlemen, I agree with you entirely. This is completely idiotic.
Curtain.

Translated by Donald M. Allen

▶▶ René Daumal

(1908–1944)
Experimental Mystic

Poet, novelist, philosopher, Sanskrit scholar and specialist in Hinduism, could René Daumal have been a pataphysician to boot? One wonders. His translations include three volumes of Suzuki's writings on Zen Buddhism, Hemingway's *Death in the Afternoon*, and a collection of the earliest dramatic texts in Sanskrit. We are dealing, naturally, with a multiple personality that will not be easily pinned down: a grave and fantastical spirit, mystical and mysterious, an authentic magician who also dealt in jokes and games. One could almost believe he took pains in advance to evade the methods and classifications of pedantic critics.

Since 'Pataphysics is pure limitlessness, however, no one is diminished by being called a pataphysician. Daumal so recognized and proclaimed himself. In *The Great Carouse* he introduces Jarry into the action conversing with Rabelais and Léon-Paul Fargue; and in the Thirties he edited and contributed to a regular feature of the *Nouvelle Revue Française* entitled "'Pataphysics this month."

Daumal practiced a kind of experimental mysticism all his own—"just to see." Principally, he risked a series of semi-suicides by controlled inhalation of carbon-tetrachloride in order to test the frontiers of life. "I had entered another life far more intense than this one, a burning coal of reality and sheer evidence into which I had hurled myself as a butterfly into a candle flame." Daumal affirmed "the vision of the Absurd as the purest and most elementary form of metaphysical experience. Its cruel testimony sheds light on all experience, and thus it becomes a significant moment in the discovery of the world. I readily call this moment of knowledge 'Pataphysics because I recognize the same attitude in Jarry's book, *Exploits and Opinions of Dr. Faustroll, Pataphysician.*"

It is understandable that a pataphysician like Julien Torma should have reproached Daumal for thinking "'Pataphysics can be married to mysticism. . . . You're right to speak of chaos. But it's obvious you believe in it like a kind of God." Those, however, are merely differences between pataphysicians.

One can form one's own opinion of Daumal as magician and pataphysician from the story which follows, written shortly after *The Great Carouse* in 1936 or 1937, and a few years earlier than *Mount Analogue*, "A Novel of Symbolically Authentic, Non-Euclidean Adventures in Mountain Climbing." A good half-dozen symbolic interpretations of the story come to mind, none of them necessary for so limpid a text. And furthermore, there is no reason why any of these explanations should be the right one, nor that there should be a right one at all. That, of course, is in the nature of 'Pataphysics.

Luc Etienne,
Regent of Spoonerism (Contrepet),
Superintendent of Versification,
Holorhymes, Palindromes and
Jingles, DSOGG

The Great Magician

There was once a powerful magician who lived in a garret in the Rue Bouffetard. He lived there in the guise of a little old clerk, tidy and punctual, and worked in a branch of the Araganais Bank on the Avenue des Gibelins. With the wave of a magic toothpick he could have transmuted all the tiles of the roof into bars of gold. But that would have been immoral, for he believed that work ennobles man. And—to some extent—even woman, he would add.

When his Aunt Ursula, an old shrew who had just been ruined by the collapse of Serbian-Bulgarian stocks, came to live with him and demanded that he take care of her, he could have transformed her at will into a pretty young princess, or into a swan harnessed to his magic chariot, or into a soft-boiled egg, or into a ladybug, or into a bus. But that would have broken with good family tradition, the backbone of society and morality. So he slept on a straw mat and would get up at six o'clock to buy Aunt Ursula her rolls and prepare her coffee; after which, he listened patiently to the daily broadside of complaints: that the coffee tasted of soap, that there was a cockroach baked into one of the rolls, that he was an unworthy nephew and would be disinherited. "Disinherited of what?" you might well wonder. But he let her talk on, knowing that if he wanted to . . . But Aunt Ursula must never suspect that he was a powerful magician. That might give birth to thoughts of lucre and close the gates of Paradise to her forever.

After that, the great magician would go down his six flights, sometimes almost breaking his neck on the murderously slippery stairs. However, he would pick himself up with a faint smile, thinking that if he wished he could change himself into a swallow and take wing through the skylight. But the neighbors might see, and so wondrous a feat would shake the very foundation of their naive but wholesome faith.

When he reached the street, he would brush the dust off his alpaca jacket at the same time taking care not to pronounce those words which would have instantly turned it into a brocade vestment. Such an act would have planted a sinister doubt in the hearts of the people passing and shaken their innocent belief in the immutability of the laws of nature.

He had his breakfast at the counter in a café, taking only some ersatz coffee and a bit of stale bread. Ah, if he wanted to . . . but in order to stop himself from making use of his supernatural powers, he would swallow five cognacs in rapid succession. The alcohol, dulling the edge of his magic powers, brought him round to a salutary humility and to the feeling that all men, including himself, were brothers. If the cashier repulsed him when he tried to kiss her, pretending it was because of his dirty beard, he would tell himself that she had no heart and understood nothing of the spirit of the gospels. At a quarter of eight, he was in his office, his sleeve-protectors on, a pen behind his ear, and a newspaper spread before him. With only a slight effort of concentration he could have known straight off the present, past, and future of the entire world, but he restrained himself from using this gift. He made himself read the paper so as not to lose touch with the common language; it allowed him to communicate over an *apéritif* with his equals—in appearance—and guide them in the right direction. At eight o'clock, the paper scratching began, and if he made a mistake now and then, it was in order to justify the reprimands of his superiors, who otherwise would be guilty of the serious sin of having made a false accusation. And so, all day long the great magician, in the guise of an average employee, carried on his task as humanity's guide.

Poor Aunt Ursula! Whenever he returned at noon having forgotten to buy some parsley, that dear lady, instead of cracking the basin over his head, would certainly have behaved differently had she known who her nephew really was. But then she would never have had the opportunity of discovering to what extent anger is a momentary madness.

If he had wanted to! . . . Instead of dying in a hospital of an unknown disease in barely Christian fashion, leaving no more trace on earth than a moth-eaten coat in the wardrobe, an old toothbrush, and mocking memories in the ungrateful hearts of his colleagues, he could have been a pasha, an alchemist, a wizard, a nightingale, or a cedar of Lebanon. But that would have been contrary to the secret designs of Providence. No one made a speech over his grave. No one suspected who he was. And who knows—perhaps not even he himself.

Still, he was a most powerful magician.

Translated by Charles Warner,
Emphyteutic Correspondent

The year of Our Lord 1895, the twenty-second of the Pataphysical Era, Paul Valéry published *Introduction to the Method of Leonardo da Vinci;* a year later Alfred Jarry staged and published *Ubu Roi.* Valéry, aged twenty-five, and Jarry, aged twenty-three, dedicated their respective works—situated at opposite literary poles—to the same person, Marcel Schwob, aged twenty-nine. In an era of astonishing careers, Schwob's was one of the richest and most varied. He was born into a Jewish family of journalists and intellectuals, achieved vast erudition before he reached twenty in a variety of fields including Villon and Rabelais studies and English literature, and then plunged into the world of letters and the theater. He became a close associate of the *Mercure de France* in its early symbolist years and held the influential post of literary editor of the *Echo of Paris Illustrated Monthly.* After collaborating with Lugné-Poe at the Théâtre de L'Œuvre, he produced two translations for Sarah Bernhardt, including the famous *Hamlet* that she played herself *en travesti.* Schwob was married to the actress, Marguerite Moréno, and died at the age of thirty-eight.

Schwob's writings are usually assimilated to Symbolism or to the kind of intellectualized decadence we call *fin de siècle.* Yet his best works display an originality of technique such as one rarely finds in the prose of the era. In *The Children's Crusade,* he probes the dimensions of a simple action by relating it from several intersecting points of view, a narrative device still judged revolutionary when employed by Faulkner or Lawrence Durrell. *Imaginary Lives,* a collection of hypothetical biographies of real figures such as Captain Kidd and Cyril Tourneur, opens up a promising literary genre halfway between the prose poem and the historical novel. The text translated below on the obsolescence of laughter comments obliquely on the relationship between 'Pataphysics and the comic, a subject generally misunderstood.

Valéry and Jarry knew what they were about. Marcel Schwob nurtured within him the double soul of *père* Ubu and Monsieur Teste.

Pascal Pia, Satrap,
GMOOG

Laughter

Laughter is probably destined to disappear. With so many animal species extinct, why should a tic peculiar to one of them persist? This coarse physical proof of our sense of a certain disharmony in the world will have to go by the board in the face of complete skepticism, absolute knowledge, universal pity and respect for all things.

To laugh is suddenly to find oneself disregarding laws: did we then really believe in the world order and a magnificent hierarchy of final causes? And when all anomalies have been linked up with some cosmic mechanism, men will laugh no longer. One can only laugh at individuals. Generalizations do not affect the glottis.

To laugh is to feel superior. When we come to kneeling and making public confessions at crossroads and humbling ourselves the better to love, then we shall have no understanding of the grotesque.

And those who, apart from any grasp of relativity, have made much of the equivalent value of their own existence and that of any dependent or solitary cell, will, without the understanding of it all, begin to hold things and objects in respect. The recognition of the equality of every individual in the universe will never send people's lips curving over their bicuspids.

Then, when this movement has vanished from the human face, this is perhaps the interpretation that will be placed on it:

"This kind of contraction of the zygomatic muscles was peculiar to man. It was his means of showing at one and the same time his imperfect grasp of the system of the world and his conviction that he was superior to everything else."

The religion, science and skepticism of the future will contain only a very small part of our labored thinking on these subjects. Furthermore, it is certain that the contraction of the zygomatic muscles will have no place in them. And, to those who in the future will fall in love with the things of the past, I should like to point out the plays of Georges Courteline (1860-1929) that in our barbaric age provoked the greatest amount of laughter, which will by then have disappeared. I know that men will be astonished by our convulsed mouths and tear-filled eyes, our shaking shoulders and twitching bellies, just as we ourselves are astonished by the odd practices of the earliest men; but I earnestly beg enlightened persons to bear in mind how very important is any historical document, of whatever kind it may be. . . .

The biographers of the poet Walt Whitman say that he was never once seen to laugh in his life. He was a gentle, cheerful man, and one who understood all things. Anomalies were not miracles of the absurd to him. He thought himself superior to no living being. Philemon, who died laughing on seeing a donkey eating figs, may be placed at the opposite pole of humanity to the great poet Walt Whitman. Observe that all that made Philemon laugh to such excess was that he was sure he, being a poet, was superior to a donkey; and yet this donkey, supposedly so different from Philemon, was eating the same dessert as he.

We possess a portrait of Walt Whitman in which the old poet, paralyzed and grave-faced, is compounding the error of a butterfly which has lighted on his arm as on a dead tree trunk.

The tics of humanity are not immutable. Even the gods sometimes change. We have already changed our manner of laughing; you must learn to look with equanimity on the prospect of an age when men will not laugh at all. Those who then want to shape their own lips into such a contraction will get a very good idea of this bygone habit by reading the books of Georges Courteline. And those who wish to laugh now should make haste to do so. We are not yet at the stage of seeking out the pedestal of the Laughter God among ruins. He lives among us. When our statues have fallen and our customs have been swept away, when men number the years in some new era, they will tell each other this simple little legend of him who gave us so much joy:

"He was a charming little divinity of subtle wit and kind heart, who dwelt in Montmartre. He wrote with such grace that coarse words, seeking an indestructible sanctuary, found it in his work."

(Extract)   *Translated by Ross Chambers,*
Proveditor-Propagator in Australia and the
Antipodal Islands, GMOGG

▶▶ Julien Torma

(1902–1933)
Author by Neglect

"The greatest pataphysician of the 20th century, and the purest." This is André Rousseaux's description of Julien Torma. His strange drama, *Le Bétrou*, has been called the "*Faust* of the 20th century," and his collection of notes, *Euphorismes*, the most important work of the last fifty years. Yet Torma remains little known—so little known that several writers have not hesitated to borrow from him.*

His work is indeed brief. Four slim volumes: *The Dark Lamp* (1920), *The Big Tuft* (1925), *Euphorismes* (1926), *Cuts* (1926), published during the author's life, and the uncollected works carefully published by the Collège de 'Pataphysique since 1951.

* Sartre found the subject of *No Exit* in *Euphorismes*.

But this offhand and apparently neglected literary work, in which genius reveals itself in its own failure, turns out to be an audacious and perfectly deliberate enterprise. Torma consciously began his literary venture where Rimbaud, Lautréamont and Jarry had left off. It is here that Torma differs from the surrealists who were his contemporaries (he stayed wholly aloof from the movement though a close friend of Robert Desnos and René Crevel, both of whom he profoundly influenced). Now, at a distance of thirty years, it is clear to us that the surrealists, even while they professed not to be artists and men of letters, were esthetes above all else: and they must not be reproached for something that their ultimate development has perfectly justified. Torma who had seen them as "consummate men of letters," "the sons of Dada,"* was infinitely better able than they to create a work beyond art and literature. His nature and his tastes played their part in this: his tendency to mystification, his way of life so unstable as to be still partially unknown, his incredible negligence. His attitude of detachment from his poems and other writings was free of all affectation: and we owe our knowledge of the part of his work that has survived to the miracle of Jean Montmort's friendship for him. His life and attitude toward his own creation is not less significant than the creation itself. These poems—without descending to the facile ornamentation of "automatic writing"—definitively galvanize language, and his theater, with naïveté and a formidable ingenuity, reverses the sets and reveals the machinery: that's all there is, on stage and in life. Psychology is turned inside out like a glove.

L. Barnier,
Proveditor-Inquisitor General,
Administrator of Aberrances,
Hereditary Stator OGG

* The French reads "fils à Dada," a play on the expression "fils à papa," i.e., young men whose fathers assure their material prosperity. [Translator's note.]

The Experiment of the Musical Jet

Letter to René Daumal

Lille
October 20, 1929

My Dear Daumal,†

Don't make excuses for having sent me the number of *Bifur*. *Bifur* is *Bifur*, and you can write on the walls if you feel like it. If you hadn't sent it, I wouldn't have read your essay—and learned that 'Pataphysics can be married to mysticism. That still interests me. Out of all the readings that chance has tossed in my way—and that good old divinity has always humored me—the scraps of Jarry that I've read have annoyed me the least. I see through them. There are people who see through H. Bordeaux or Gide. Do we blame them? As for me, I see better through Sengle or Emmanuel Dieu. A question of taste and ambition. It's this in fact which makes some books still possible, for I haven't sunk—despite your past protests—to gardening or to gnosticism. And I'm glad that you see through the same bodies of smoke.

But I'm dragging my heels again.

You probably suspect that I don't much appreciate being slapped with the absolute, believing in no other absolute than that of the slap. Isn't this the one and only? Your article annoys me, because everything in it is true. But the tone is missing. Precisely, the word true means nothing here and is a patsy for a pataphysical pat. You're right to speak of chaos. But it's obvious that you believe in it like a kind of God. In spite of all your finesse, dear René, you're on a pilgrim's progress. Let me be malicious. You're playing with the absolute.

Your 'Pataphysics laughs too much. And with a laugh much too comic and cosmic. Putting metaphysics behind 'Pataphysics is like making a belief into a mere façade. When in fact the real nature of 'Pat. is to be a façade which is only a façade, with nothing behind it.

I can't see Dr. Faustroll laughing. I don't have a copy of the book at the moment. But I know what I'm saying—eh?—you write, "Faustroll sneers." You're frightfully out of date. We've passed Mephisto. And evil and a bad conscience, and conscience itself. If Faustroll played at being Mephistophelean it could only be for the pataphysic hell of it. Because Mephistopheleanism is still part of their

† Daumal had just published an important article in the review *Bifur* (July 1929), on " 'Pataphysics and the Revelation of Laughter" and sent it to Torma with a cordial letter, since published by Gallimard in *Correspondence of René Daumal.* Torma's reply is dated three years after his last published work.

cookery, as we say. Faustroll is imperturbable. Or not even. He seems natural and isn't natural. Because nature is only a gag neither more nor less interesting than any other. He doesn't choose. He makes no distinction, he has no preferences. He navigates upside down. But even his navigation doesn't exist. These characters and their adventures aren't real. You can see this in the death and resurrection of Bosse-de-Nage. Still, they aren't imaginary like heroes of novels and fantastic tales. For in the case of these characters we suppose, at least temporarily and extravagant as the hypothesis may seem, that they could without too much unlikelihood exist. So I see what you're driving at when you say that all defined existence is a scandal. With the One and Co. But why not say—that undefined existence is a scandal, even though the word scandal is unnecessary. Fau-

stroll says: I am God, and he certainly has as much right to say it as God himself. But it's going a bit far—or not far enough—to take him seriously.

Writing nothing—holy or impious—No time. Doing nothing, vague jobs—and vagueness in the jobs. It'll last while it lasts . . . probably until the hour of our death. Amen—Don't consider that an allusion.

Yours, with the customary reservations.

J. Torma

R.D. did the other one tell you that I almost spoke badly of you six months ago? He wrote me that he has broken with the brain-washers.*

Translated by Neal Oxenhandler

* Robert Desnos, leading surrealist poet, had severed relations with André Breton. [Editor's note.]

►► Léon-Paul Fargue

(1876–1947)
Explorer

The most sedentary poet of the century was its most untiring explorer of the imagination. Born March 4, 1876 in the center of Les Halles, the market district of Paris, Léon-Paul Fargue scarcely ever left the capital; here he met his numerous friends (les "potassons"—the "grinds"). He died there in 1947, after four years of retirement caused by paralysis—years particularly rich in final voyages and discoveries. An individual with "twelve thousand senses, wharves of ideas, colonies of feeling, and a memory of three million acres" (*Haute Solitude*) could easily consider the travels and experiences of a tourist vain and valueless.

In 1894 his first verses appeared in the review "Art Littéraire" together with Jarry's *Minutes de Sable Mémorial.* This conjunction was not accidental—schoolmates at the lycée Henri IV and bound by strong affection, they had gone off together on scandalously amusing expeditions on the upper decks of the Paris buses. Later, while Jarry's Dr. Faustroll was assaulting the great pataphysical islands of time, the

opinionated Fargue, prowling with half-closed eyes, departed day after day to explore and re-create the lost islands of his past. He couples a bent for discovery with a flair for creating a style suited to these astonishing circumnavigations, with their uncertain, hilarious or deceptive endings, to these ambiguous "dead ends cluttered with butterflies" where we observe the pataphysical creation of imaginary memories. The *Ludions* (1929), set to music by Erik Satie, whose childlike "counting" style matches Fargue's taste for mystification, re-create with frequently invented and distorted words an eerie and vital world, more immediate than the present. The past disappears—and with it, once and for all, every type of poetry which concerns itself with the past.

Fargue was as little inclined to follow a literary school (he quickly dissociated himself from the surrealist poets, whom he referred to as "false witnesses") as to seek out the public, and it was often necessary to take his manuscripts away from him. *Sous la lampe* (1930), *Le Piéton de Paris* (1939) and especially *Haute Solitude* (1941) stake out his tireless and solitary prospecting of the imaginary.

At the end of his voyaging, like Jules Verne's polar captain, he arrives finally at "Destiny" (*Saison en Astrologie*—1945 and *Les Quat' Saisons*—1947): in his role as director of the obsequies of the universe—to the tune of his "Danse Mabraque" (*Haute Solitude*)—Fargue unveils his mystification; everything has been foreseen in the ineluctable, delectable disorder of that grandiose and final voyage. At the crossroads of the breakdown of twenty centuries of civilizations, Fargue calmly watches the universal chaos roll by.

H.P. Bouché,
Proveditor-General of Animal and Vegetable Affairs,
Administrator of Quincunxes,
Grand Anallagmatic Deferent OGG

Danse Mabraque

I was lost in a forest of strange protozoae—in a city without props, that hung like a buzzard over the stampede below. I recognized everything and recognized nothing. My soul was running on ahead in zigzags, like a dog happy to be free of his kennel. Grasses and metaphors, blue mice, furies and pebbles burned like dribblings of powder. We saw fade and disappear in the air, like schools of nautiluses, numbers out of our heads, grammatical rules, first names and insults. A kind of sharp-clawed autumn, sparkling with animal suns, ripped everything out of us, laid everything bare. The vacuum cleaners of astral Mythology were engulfing both matter and mind. And our eyes were watching all this—our ears were hearing it all!

—"Our eyes, our ears, our sensibilities—bah!" the old hermaphrodite from the Conservatory kept saying, pestering me—"bah! Shells, shards, peelings—nothing. Spoiled brats' diapers, barnacles, spondulae, calyptrates, glistening dung-beetles!"

Above our heads thundered flotillas of 3's and of 9's; Mary Anns, Rhones, +'s and %'s whirled about mixed with Charleses, goddams, springs and flies, with foot/feet, goose/geese, moose/. . . . . . . The ether grew humpbacked, for the stuff of the world was pouring out of its perfect and imagined form. It was no more the orange or the round rush stem they once used to teach us in high school, but a stained glass window of caramels melting into men's guts stuck with toothbrushes and butterfly wings. Our beards sprouted enormously during those months of collapse. But to look for a barber, a knife or the top of a tin can was asking for the height of the ridiculous. My cheeks were covered with fish scales. And yet, strangely enough, I hadn't the least desire to scratch. All furious urgings had left us like hunger

. . . and in fact, this is true—neither of us was hungry. Yet, since the devil is everywhere, even in the heart of the Apocalypse when he is no longer needed, we kept seeing restaurants! . . . No more notaries, no more glasses, no more matches, no more sickness, no more soap . . . but the restaurants remained, as bizarre in their blinding solitude as fringes of snow were once, lying in an already green and flowery meadow, in the middle of April. April, I say . . . that's it! March, April, May, June, Jamestown, Nashville, Baltimore, Trenton, this is the forest primeval, the murmuring pines and the Bowery, 27th street, the Washington Heights uptown local, Adams, Jefferson, Madison Avenue . . . he, she, we, you, add seven, carry two. . . . !

Here it is then.

It is better to die like an army of candles. To have known the world, to have had gold, sight, sperm and sense, and to finish in such stupidities, is really too much. This is all we have found—

Adultery, cocktails, pimps, Jewish finance, quickie whorehouses, author's rights, expense accounts, the rule of three. And these dog-faced lovers who boast of making miracles!

We must agree to die, without insolence, without brilliance. But let us keep our places on the gleaming toboggan—puffing and fatherly as a suburban locomotive—and let ourselves slide into the ultimate dust of this sooty factory: If we are enough to constitute another world, and if we find ourselves toe over teakettle in a finer civilization, more lasting than our own, we may still consider ourselves happy. But this present one is finished—Everybody out! Closing time! Exits at the back of the hall!

(Extract)   *Translated by Paul Schmidt*

► ► **Jacques Prévert**

Satrap

. . . It Droppeth as the Gentle Rain[*]
a ballet

First Tableau

A large town.

A hostess is welcoming her guests.

They discuss the latest news in the papers, reading them and reading aloud from them.

How strange.

It says that the most extraordinary storms have broken out all over the world—in California, Japan, Spain and Guatemala—and are already spreading a little bit everywhere else too.

Peculiar cloud formations, diluvian and foul-smelling showers.

Fully documented and highly scientific articles describe how the specialists, whose torrent of words must never be doubted, agree that the clouds filling the skies are themselves filled with excreta!

The gentlemen are all rather intrigued and just a little worried, and the ladies are all very skeptical but extremely curious.

—Just imagine what a splash it would make if it were really true!

—And that's putting it mildly!

And all the guests who are going to go, leave the room.

One monsewer, standing on the threshold with a sheepish grin, stretches out his hand the way people do stretch out their hands to see if perhaps it might have stopped raining.

Suddenly he draws back his hand and dolefully holds it under the noses of the others as a silent witness of his affliction.

The newspapers were telling the truth after all, the evidence cannot be denied.

—But who do you think will ever believe such rubbish?

—It smells like the end of the world—and ours in particular!

—How divine—after us the deluge—and what a shower!

* At first glance this ballet's original title *Les Fausses Sceptiques* (*The Skeptical Impostors*) looks like a pastiche of a typically classic title by Molière or Marivaux; but at second hearing it sounds *exactly* like *Les Fosses Septiques* (*The Septic Tanks* or *The Cess Pits*).

With these words on their lips, the ladies take dainty little deep breaths as they delicately pass out.

And one of them, as she departs, adds, smiling:

—All the same, it could have the most madly amusing possibilities!

The curtain falls.

So does the shit.

Bonnard

Second Tableau

Time has passed, and the weather has gone from bad to worse.

The hostess is still there welcoming guests at another of her eternal receptions.

Some come back, others go.

The gentlemen are wearing their best draincoats and the ladies arrive with their sweet little parashits.

As the sewage-scrapers are on strike and prying no further than their own privies, the rowdy young folk with their shittzle-sticks are beating it up everywhere.

But everybody goes on talking in the same old way about the wind and the weather and the good old days.

—It was bound to happen, say the ladies, they told you it would!

And as the ballet takes place in present-day France, and in the neighborhood of Paris, the conversation is extremely witty and everybody is quoting the latest gossip from the Barber of Seville's Literary Supplement.

—The smell of what falls in foreign fields is nowhere near as foul as ours.

—The only genuine, original shit falls in Paris! But nobody mentions Father Ubu who
SHITE
had forecast and foretold the lot.

perched high on their pilgrims' staffs which with perfect and exquisite taste they have converted into stilts, go on their way singing.

Following the musicians, they pray for the assuagement of the floods, and for the advent of the rainbum of the Lord.

Singing and parading they wend their way along the Boulevard des Crapucines.

Translated by Stanley Chapman, V.D.C.D.R.

Third and Final and Highly Edifying Tableau

Apotheosis to end all apotheoses—in which the whole world ends up crappy ever after, and in which we let the people sing.

One or two bits of wall that are almost white can still be seen on a smeared and smothered Sacré-Coeur in the middle of the backdrop.

For we are in Montmartre where already it will soon be spring, although like snow in winter the shit falls inexorably.

And along comes a religious parade of pious souls —yet it is still the same gay, elegant, carefree and joyful Paris of old.

And the pilgrim fathers and the pilgrim mothers,

►► Raymond Queneau

Satrap

A Fish's Life

Strange life, a fish's life! . . . Sturgeonstrange! minnow . . . I've never been able to understand how anyone could live like that. The aiguesistence of life in that form disturbs me marsh more than any other reason for tears that the world may impose on me. For me an aquarium foments a concatenation of red-hot pincers. This afternoon I went to see the one that is the pride of the Zoological Gardens of the Foreign City. I stayed there in a stupor until the attendants turned me out.

The fact that they are prisoners emphasizes still more the strangeness of this life. I noticed one of these animals, it had black stripes, swimming up and down with perfect regularity. As these beasts don't sleep, such at least is my opinion, I therefore suppose that at this late hour at which I am now writing, my zebra is still running down and up, still as radically unoccupied. Even when he eats he doesn't need to stop moving, no more than he does when he reproduces himself. This latter occupation takes place, so they say, in so impersonal a fashion that there is clearly no need to stop flapping your fins in order to indulge in it.

Then what does he think about, my fish? Of course I don't expect him to reflect, to indulge in rational activity, to construct syllogisms and to refute sophisms, no, of course not, but doesn't my fish ever look at what's going on on the other side of the thick glass window that separates him from the human world? In everybody's opinion, the answer is: no, my fish doesn't think, his intellectual activity is equal to zero. This is what I find atrocious. It isn't possible to have a human relationship with a fish. Fishermen, it seems to me, tell certain anecdotes. But they are people one rarely meets in my Native City; for me these anecdotes are fables and hear-at-a-distance-say. Outside his aquarium the animal comes back to life. You can ascribe a meaning to his aiguesistence: he comes and goes in the river (I have seen some rivers in the Foreigners' country), slips in between the weeds beaten down by the current, lies in wait for his prey, allows himself to be tempted by the bait. Yes, the river fish, one can still understand. But the seafish? the sardine? the herring? the cod? A sardine is stupefying. In a cinematograph in the Foreign City where I recently strayed, I saw, flat, some sardines, layer upon layer of them, innumerable and maritime, a compact crowd, familiarly rubbing scales with each other. A sardine, though, is a living being. And the cod! the herring! They bring tears to my eyes. Daddy! Mamma! It's really too atrocious, the life of a fish in a shoal! If you tried to think about it for long, you'd run the risk of bursting open your skull. We get born in a crowd, by millions, then all together we go off, we fraternal herrings, to cross the boundless Ocean, jostling each other's fins and falling into all the nets. That's how it is, the life of us herrings. And what about the one who happens to be in the middle of the shoal? Millions of his congeners surround him and here one day, only he doesn't distinguish day or night, here one day he suddenly feels giddy, the central herring. Yes, giddy. Then what would be his fate? Oh, it's really too dismal! Daddy! Mamma! it's really too atrocious, the life of a fish in a shoal.

This is becoming intolerable. It's made my scales all ruffled. The salt is cracking my gums. The ocean foam comes and bursts its last bubbles under my window. I am so alone in this town where I am laboriously studying the foreign language. But that's the last-born of my worries. It doesn't interest me. My Native City has bestowed a Special Scholarship on me to enable me to acquire a thorough knowledge of this language. The only part my father thinks me capable of playing is that of professor of gibberish. I shouldn't like to disappoint him; I shall prove myself worthy of this favor that he managed to get for me; I have a heart and I'm grateful; but why does my father think me stupid? I'll be a professor of macaronics, right. I defer, I don't say anything, but I can't stop myself having other anxieties, and which concern the science of life. Life! I shall devote my life to studying life! I swear it on oath, here and now, in front of my window which looks out on one of the quadrilateral streets of the Foreign City. I stood up, I held out my arms to the air of the street and I said:

I, et cetera, life. Then I sat down again. Now it's done. My eggsistence has a meaning now and I think if a person gives his life a meaning while he is still young, this enables him to increase his possibilities and intensify his development, in short: to build himself a destiny. It seems to me that the star is rising that will lead me toward the heights that I want to attain and that I shall attain. For I have my pride. It is the heights of the science of life that I shall reach, and to hell with the mumbo-jumbo lingo of these Foreigners whom we only know in the guise of Tourists, rare at that. What's the good of talking to them?

Today I went back to the aquarium. I saw the moray. Each one is alone in its cage. They are ferocious. They eat meat. In the days when the nations had an emperor, they used to eat slaves, so the journalists say. They differ a great deal from other fish, and the thing that thus exalts them is ferocity. Now ferocity is one of the cardinal categories of man's life in society. There are great mysteries in it. That ferocity should save certain fish from the atrocity of the life common to their genus is yet another reason for anxiety. The moray seems to be an autonomous individual solely by virtue of the power of its ferocity!

There is something else that causes me distress: the skate. The anatomical construction of this fish wrings my heart: to have your head on your back or on your belly, I can't tell which, this pains me. Its gills I take for eyes. And its eyes, they are underneath it! and it has a nose! and a small, cruel mouth. I nearly wept with grief when I was deciphering this appalling face, and this apparition flew off toward the surface of the water, beating its fins as if they were wings, suddenly having turned into some marine bird, the reflected image of the albatross with its great feathers. No. It's not possible, the existence of the skate. To have your eyes in such a place, and to fly in the water, and to do nothing. No.

That's how it is. I started too low on the ladder of the living. The abyss is so deep. A monkey's life one can concede; a cow's, not too bad; a bird's, well, all right. But what I cannot bring myself to understand with all these animals is that they do nothing, and that they care even less. Pish. Fish. This morning I had two letters, one from my father and the other from Paul. The former writes: "Our town is preparing for the Festival. I am sorry you won't be able to be there; there won't have been a finer one for years and years. I shall make considerable sacrifices which will consecrate my wealth and my glory.

"I hope you are working zealously and that you will prove worthy of the Special Scholarship which I

Photo by Jean Weber

had so much trouble in getting for you. It is fortunate that I managed to wangle you this meritorious distinction which guarantees you a brilliant, respectable and hitherto unheard of situation: certificated guide interpreter dragoman of the Native City. Is this not glorious? What a future, my boy! What a debt of gratitude you owe me! Without me, what would you be? For me, what should you not do? Make yourself worthy of my great name. Work."

Right. The second writes: "Thanks for the means of locomotion on two wheels that you sent me. I can use it now and I astonish the populace, which is a thing I had no desire to do. Everybody says that this year the Festival will surpass in splendor anything that has so far been seen. It's a pity you won't be there. But that isn't the most interesting thing. Jean is making some strange discoveries; he's on a really very odd track. We're waiting to be sure of ourselves before we tell you this extraordinary news. The velocipede is very useful to me." A discovery is a discovery, a track isn't a discovery. My brothers? just children.

I really live like a foreigner in this Foreign City: without the slightest contact with its population. I hardly know anyone but the Landlady, the Professor and the Keeper. I do not even have with its inhabitants that intermediate and massitudinarian contact which is engendered by the use of public transport, for I move from place to place only by means of birotation. My bicycle transports me from the place where my landlady watches to the place where my professor teaches and from there, most often, to the place where the keeper reigns. I ride through the Foreign City, without any other relation with the compact mass that throngs the streets than the abuse, which I don't understand, of the bus drivers and the reprimands of the vigilant urban militiamen watching over the even flow of the traffic. The only existing relationships are those that I construct for myself and by myself. In other words, among the real ones, I see none that are feminine. My virginity I believe necessary to the intensity of my thought. That was how a Foreigner imagined the law of the falling apple. I ought not to lose in semen what rises to my brain for my future glory. My life is dedicated to life, I've sworn it on oath. Life, I observe in the lobster. Then it's appalling. He, the lobster, finds satisfaction in it. At least you'd think so. I've just written to my father telling him what I think of the life of the lobster. I'm quite aware that my father has no ideas on that subject, but I do want to keep him up to date with the progress of my thought.

It seems at first sight that there is hardly any difference between a fish's life and that of the crustaceans. The day before yesterday I saw a lobster meandering about in the middle of some turbot and sole. They all seemed to belong to the same world. But on further reflection I perceive that there are plenty of differences between these people. A lobster is *quite* different from a fish! The sole is not so far removed from man, after all: that's what I think now. But the lobster! To live in a shell, in other words to have your bones all around you, what a radical alteration that must cause in your way of understanding life! To have the entire sea perpetually around you; to move your pincers; to see the others pass by; to lie in wait for your prey: those, no doubt, are the prolegomena to any reflection on the part of the lobster.

As for fish, I persist in regarding theirs as a bitch of a life, a cow of an aiguesistence, and devoid of personality. But that doesn't make the ogresistence of the lobster any less distressing. Is that life, then? That silence, that shadow, that seaweed, that kind of ferocity on the end of pincers, that avid armor? One should meditate upon life when one thinks of the lobster in his osscurity. And how do they die, those who don't finish up boiled in the housewifely pan? Do they depart this life of old age, lobsters? Do they "pass on" quite peacefully, or do they resist death with pincers hardened by arthritis on which little annelida have become encrusted? Does he have any suspicion of his defunction, the lobster? Wouldn't he prefer to be a skate, for instance, with eyes on his belly and white wings? Would he prefer to climb trees and devour their fruit like his colleague the coconut-palm crab, that swift and jagged animal? And when I say that an animal is this or that, I certainly don't intend to make a subjective judgment. Not even a human one. But to define the very meaning of its eksistence.

I haven't had any letters from the Native City. I've been working very hard. The streets seem to me so lifeless when I go home in the evenings. I thought of my father, of my mother, of my brothers; and then of the cheetah I met the other day in the Zoo. It may seem odd, but he belongs to the nobility. What a vast distance from the cheetah to the lobster, even though the latter also wears armor.

I imagine what it would be like if a man and a cheetah were the only beings left in the world. Both would walk on the surface of the earth, proud and free companions. It would probably be so. Now let's postulate a man and a lobster as the sole survivors of some catastrophe. Flames obscure the horizon. The exhausted man divests himself of his tattered shoes, of his torn socks. He immerses his bleeding feet in the sea to find some comfort therein. Then up comes the lobster and crushes his big toe. The man, who has lost the habit of howling, leans over the surface of the water and says to the lobster: "We are the only creatures alive in the universe, we are alone in the fight against universal disaster, shall we enter into an alliance, lobster?" But the contemptuous animal turns his carapace on him and makes his way toward other oceans. For do we know what a lobster dreams of? And what can we think of his incomprehensible hatesistence? The image of the inflexible and imperturbable lobster pierces the humans' sky with its unintelligible pincers. Above the foggy roofs, from my open window, I suddenly seem to see its two threatening paws rise up, opening and shutting their gigantic nippers to dissect the constellations.

I am making hardly any progress in the Foreign Language. My professor has informed me of this and, if I understand him aright, I shall return to my Native City not very much more bilingual than before, a bit less, perhaps. And then what will my father, and the entire city with him, say? This could cause me some anxiety, if I didn't have other and more important things to worry about.

Would animal life be perpetual happiness? And once again I go to the aquarium to look at the sole and the dorado. I look at them impartially, objectively. Well! the fish don't appear to be specially happy; they don't give that impression. Here is one more category that doesn't apply itself to this animal and maritime life. It doesn't participate in happiness. But in unhappiness? Congers, turbot and sole couldn't answer me. So I didn't deign to pay any more attention to them, and made my way toward a quarter I didn't yet know and which serves as a refuge for tropical fish. There were the cancerous and the capricornous, and others that came from the eels'

sea. There were feathery ones and mustached ones, and others which had dogs' faces or truncated bodies. Millimetric individuals, absolutely transparent, were moving at lunatic speed. Other, bigger ones, allowed themselves variegated ornaments, zebra stripes, stippling, color. These little fish started my entire mind off on a new track, one which was as confusing as the first; it seemed to me, however, that these minute beasts, probably devoid of any even slightly coherent view of the world, or so I imagined then, showed, at least in a certain sense, all the signs of gaiety. Their abrupt and absurd convolutions, the lightning flashes they described in the water, no matter how unjustifiable they might be from the point of view of any sort of system, however incoordinate, the hazards of these broken trajectories seemed to me to manifest a certain joy which, I felt, could only be tropical.

This discovery of a little humanity in the behavior of these tiny beasts, or, to communicate my impressions otherwise, but in a practically identical fashion, this discovery of a true vitality corresponding to the human idea of life, had to some extent assuaged the anguish that every visit to the aquarium inflicts on me, when I noticed not far from the exit a poorly lit corner where a glass cage seemed to be sleeping. I didn't know what was in it. I went to see.

In a sense it was a good thing that I went: in the interests of the science of life. But I could perfectly well have done without that frightful sight. The solitary tank contained (contained!) a few white worms: they were fish: to be absolutely precise, cave fish. Cut off from the sun, they have lost their eyes. They have forgotten all about color and their fins are now no more than minute, vermiform appendices. The silence and osscurity of the sea is still a phosphorescence and an echo. In the subterranean caves, where pockets of pure water stagnate, it is a mineral silence and osscurity. It's still possible to live there. There are living beings, but what living beings: those whitish larvae that claim the name of fish. Their ancestors, so it says in the essplanatory card, were gallant fish with lively eyes and nimble fins, and colored, like everything that the light caresses. But living in the shadows has transformed them, and here they are. They're alive! They're alive! There are people who see that as a testimony to the power, the adaptability, the perenniality of life. But I wept at the sight of the acuatic, living cave fish, at the thought of the atrocious life they lead. It's difficult to imagine it: to be born, to endure, to die perhaps: osscure, blind. And they reproduce themselves. What a terebrant mystery, this persistency in subsistence in such wretched conditions. Yes, wretched, they are wretched! And if, even so, they had a way . . . I don't say of thinking but if, even so, they had . . . I don't say a consciousness . . . but if they had a way of transcending themselves? Yes, exactly that: a way of transcending themselves. There is nothing there that resembles human life. It would be perfectly inhuman and without any possible interpretation; and yet, there would be some sense in living like that: blind, osscure.

Blind . . . Osscure . . . I wept indeed.

My mother has written to me. Jean is making long excursions into the Arid Mountains, those harsh and violent mountains where nobody ever adventures. He has been gone for several days, so perhaps he has gone as far as the Petrifying Spring, perhaps to the top of the Grand Mineral, the highest of these mountains. All this worries my mother. She's afraid he'll never come back. But my father never reproaches him in any way. As for me, I must work and make myself worthy of the great honor that has been done me. Yes, I'm very willing to make myself worthy, but this foreign language seems so little made for me. I am not making the slightest progress. My professor reprimands me, and complains. Could some echoes of my lack of ability already have reached the Native City? Could the fellow have written to them? Sometimes I imagine that my landlady is a spy. Ah! why am I not delivered from the obsession with these cockeyed words the Foreigners use to express what they imagine to be thoughts; and to see them again, these Foreigners, under the guise of Tourists, with their foolish questions, their stupid interests, their asinine sightseeing; and to talk to them, lathering with my saliva the globulous vocables of their hyperdialect! Pooh! Misery! And all of a sudden I remembered, but why that memory? one winter day. The wind was bellowing behind the windows: alone in my room I was initiating myself into the springgame; I must have been eleven. It was already dark. My father came in suddenly, looked at me for a few moments and his eyes seemed to me to be made of stone; then, without a word, very quietly, he shut the door and went away. I stopped playing and started thinking; and understood that later on I should become . . . Silence. It isn't the memory of a happy moment, but an uneasy impression, a premonition of something extraordinary.

When I'm back in the Native City I'm afraid my father, and the people under his jurisdiction too, will judge me severely at first, for my knowledge of the foreign language will perhaps seem to them to be insufficient, even though few of them are connoisseurs, unless it is Le Busoqueux, the traditory. But their opinion on this matter won't worry me, for I shall have other treasures to present to them, treasures won from the depths, treasures for whose discovery I ventured into the most secret caves, got mixed up with the lobster, and embroiled myself with the innumerable sardines of the Ocean. My meditations on life, that's what I shall offer them, and it is then, and then alone, that the Native City will be able to pride itself on being such for me.

It is when I lose life such as man understands it that I achieve the object of my research, and this object manifests itself in an absolutely pure and lancinating fashion in the guise of the cave fish. Today I shall go back and see them. I did think that if they were capable of transcending themselves, what inhumanity this transcendence would be! But look here, was it possible? I looked at them. The tank that contains them (contains!) isn't specially big. A horizontal bulb lights them up, but faintly, as is proper. The water seems to stagnate, as is also proper. There they are, four, no more. Perhaps some others are hiding more radically from the light. They don't do much. Most of the time they remain motionless. When they do bestir "themselves," it's a sort of whitish flow, a pallid belly that lightly brushes the sand and, a few "steps" further on, ceases to move. I wonder when they eat and what they eat. Yes, what do they eat? And the lobster, what does he consume? fish, I suppose; that can still give the illusion of penetrating into the lobster's world since man also eats sea food. But these livid beings? What do they eat? Some weed as devoid of all color as themselves? Perhaps they don't eat? Or perhaps something which isn't food.

What interested me only a month ago now leaves me completely cold. It is life and not its baroque translation into a barbaric dialect, it's life itself which is the meaning of my activity: it's toward the comprehension of life that all my intelligence is tending. And what is still finer is that the immediate result of this passionate study is the contrary affirmation of the non-comprehensibility of animal life, of its inhumanity. How can one claim to have enclosed the universe within a series of interconnected concepts, what I mean is: within a system, if the meaning of the life of the lobster or of the cave fish is completely beyond the grasp of the human spirit? The only categories in which one can discern this life are those of Terror, of Silence, and of the Shadows. For the cave fish, perhaps one should add that of Discoloration.

Two in the morning is striking. From my window I can see a room opposite lit up. Its shutters are closed. This room lit up late at night, like mine . . . The light goes out . . . Was it a mirror?

Translated by Barbara Wright,
Regentess of Shakesperian Zozology, GFCOGG

from EXPLOITS AND OPINIONS OF DOCTOR FAUSTROLL, PATAPHYSICIAN

8: Definition

An epiphenomenon is that which is superinduced upon a phenomenon.

Pataphysics, whose etymological spelling should be ἔπι (μετὰ τὰ φυσικά) and actual orthography 'pataphysics, preceded by an apostrophe so as to avoid a simple pun,[1] is the science of that which is superinduced upon metaphysics, whether within or beyond the latter's limitations, extending as far beyond metaphysics as the latter extends beyond physics. Ex: an epiphenomenon being often accidental, pataphysics will be, above all, the science of the particular, despite the common opinion that the only science is that of the general. Pataphysics will examine the laws governing exceptions, and will explain the universe supplementary to this one; or, less ambitiously, will describe a universe which can be—and perhaps should be—envisaged in the place of the traditional one, since the laws that are supposed to have been discovered in the traditional universe are also correlations of exceptions, albeit more frequent ones, but in any case accidental data which, reduced to the status of unexceptional exceptions, possess no longer even the virtue of originality.

DEFINITION. *Pataphysics is the science of imaginary solutions which symbolically attributes the properties of objects, described by their virtuality, to their lineaments.*

Contemporary science is founded upon the principle of induction: most people have seen a certain phenomenon precede or follow some other phenomenon most often, and conclude therefrom that it will ever be thus. Apart from other considerations, this is true only in the majority of cases, depends upon the point of view, and is codified only for convenience—if that! Instead of formulating the law of the fall of a body toward a center, how far more apposite would be the law of the ascension of a vacuum

[1] A simple pun in French, e.g., "patte à physique."

toward a periphery, a vacuum being considered a unit of non-density, a hypothesis far less arbitrary than the choice of a concrete unit of positive density such as water?

For even this body is a postulate and an average

Bonnard

man's point of view, and in order that its qualities, if not its nature, should remain fairly constant, it would be necessary to postulate that the height of human beings should remain more or less constant and mutually equivalent. Universal assent is already a quite miraculous and incomprehensible prejudice. Why should anyone claim that the shape of a watch is round—a manifestly false proposition—since it appears in profile as a narrow rectangular construction, elliptic on three sides; and why the devil should one only have noticed its shape at the moment of looking at the time? —Perhaps under the pretext of utility. But a child who draws a watch as a circle will also draw a house as a square, as a façade, without any justification, of course; because, except perhaps in the country, he will rarely see an isolated building, and even in a street the façades have the appearance of very oblique trapezoids.

We must, in fact, inevitably admit that the common herd (including small children and women) is too dimwitted to comprehend elliptic equations, and that its members are at one in a so-called universal assent because they are capable of perceiving only those curves having a single focal point, since it is easier to coincide with one point rather than with two. These people communicate and achieve equilibrium by the outer edge of their bellies, tangentially. But even the common herd has learned that the *real* universe is composed of ellipses, and tradesmen keep their wine in barrels rather than cylinders.

So that we may not abandon, through digression, our usual example of water, let us reflect, in this connection, upon the irreverence of the common herd whose instinct sums up the adepts of the science of pataphysics in the following phrase:

9: Faustroll Smaller than Faustroll

To William Crookes

Other madmen cried ceaselessly that the figure one was at the same time bigger and smaller than itself, and proclaimed a number of similar absurdities as if they were useful discoveries.

The Talisman of Oramane

Doctor Faustroll (if one may be permitted to speak from personal experience) desired one day to be smaller than himself and resolved to explore one of the elements, in order to examine any disturbances which this change in size might involve in their mutual relationship.

For this purpose he chose that substance which is normally liquid, colorless, incompressible and horizontal in small quantities; having a curved surface, blue in depth and with edges that tend to ebb and flow when it is stretched; which Aristotle terms heavy, like earth; the enemy of fire and renascent from it when decomposed explosively; which vaporizes at a hundred degrees, a temperature determined by this fact, and in a solid state floats upon itself—water, of course! And having shrunk to the classic size of a mite, as a paradigm of smallness, he traveled along the length of a cabbage leaf, paying no attention to his fellow mites or to the magnified aspect of his surroundings, until he encountered the Water.

This was a globe, twice his size, through whose transparency the outlines of the universe appeared to him gigantically enlarged, whilst his own image, reflected dimly by the leaves' foil, was magnified to his original size. He gave the orb a light tap, as if knock-ing on a door: the deracinated eye of malleable glass "adapted itself" like a living eye, became presbyopic, lengthened itself along its horizontal diameter into an ovoid myopia, repulsed Faustroll by means of this elastic inertia and became spherical once more.

The doctor, taking small steps, rolled the crystal globe, with some considerable difficulty, toward a neighboring globe, slipping on the rails of the cabbage-leaf's veins; coming together, the two spheres sucked each other in, tapering in the process, until suddenly a new globe of twice the size rocked placidly in front of Faustroll.

With the tip of his boot the doctor kicked out at this unexpected development of the elements: an explosion, formidable in its fragmentation and noise, rang out following the projection all around of new and minute spheres, dry and hard as diamonds, that rolled to and fro all along the green arena, each one drawing along beneath it the image of the tangential point of the universe, distorting it according to the sphere's projection and magnifying its fabulous center.

Beneath everything, the chlorophyll, like a shoal of green fishes, followed its charted currents in the cabbage's subterranean canals . . .

Sir William Crookes, F.R.S.: his presidential address to the Society for Psychical Research in London on January 29, 1897, is largely responsible for the theme and some of the phraseology of this chapter. The address was translated into French and printed in the *Revue Scientifique*, Paris, May, 1897.

17: Concerning the Fragrant Isle

To Paul Gauguin

The Fragrant Isle is completely sensitive, and fortified by madrepores which retracted themselves, as we landed, into their coral-red casemates. The skiff's mooring line was fastened around a great tree that swayed in the wind like a parrot rocking itself in the sunshine.

The king of the islands was naked in a boat, his loins girded with his white and blue diadem. He was clad, too, in sky and greenery like a Caesar's chariot race, and as redheaded as if he were on a pedestal.

We drank to his health in liquors distilled in vegetable hemispheres.

His function is to preserve for his people the image of their gods. He was fixing one of these images to the mast of his boat with three nails, and it was like a triangular sail, or the equilateral gold of a dried fish brought back from the septentrion. And over the doorway of his wives' dwelling place he has captured the ecstasies and contortions of love in a divine cement. Standing apart from the interlacing of young breasts and rumps, sibyls record the formula of happiness, which is double: *Be amorous*, and *Be mysterious*.

He possesses also a zither with seven strings of seven colors, the eternal colors; and, in his palace, a lamp nourished from the fragrant wellsprings of the earth. When the king sings, moving along the shore as he plays his zither, or when he prunes with an axe, from images of living wood, the young shoots which would disfigure the likeness of the gods, his wives burrow into the hollow of their beds, the weight of fear heavy upon their loins from the vigilant gaze of the Spirit of the Dead, and from the perfumed porcelain of the great lamp's eye.

As the skiff cast off from the reefs, we saw the king's wives chasing from the island a little legless cripple sprouting green seaweed like a wizened crab; on his dwarfish trunk a fairground wrestler's tunic aped the king's nakedness. He pushed himself forward jerkily with his cestus-covered fists, and with a rumbling from the casters under his base attempted to pursue and clamber aboard the platform of the *Omnibus de Corinthe*, which was just crossing our route; but such a leap is not within everyone's power. And he fell miserably short, cracking his posterior lavatory pan with a fissure less obscene than ludicrous.

Paul Gauguin: Jarry and Gauguin were together at Pont-Aven in 1894 and probably knew each other previously, since both were contributors to the review *Essais d'Art Libre* (1892-94), edited first by Rémy de Gourmont, subsequently by Léon-Paul Fargue and Jarry.

The unfortunate Pierre Loti makes his first (anonymous) appearance in *Faustroll* at the end of this chapter, as the legless cripple ("cul de jatte"). The *Omnibus de Corinthe* on which he fails to get a footing was a short-lived quarterly satirical review, edited by Marc Mouclier, describing itself as an "illustrated vehicle of general ideas," the title of which was doubtless derived from the Latin proverb *Non licet omnibus adire Corinthum*.

Bonnard

19: Concerning the Isle of Ptyx

To Stéphane Mallarmé

The isle of Ptyx is fashioned from a single block of the stone of this name, a priceless stone found only in this island, which is entirely composed of it. It has the serene translucency of white sapphire and is the only precious stone not ice cold to the touch, for its fire enters and spreads itself like wine after drinking.

Other stones are as cold as the cry of trumpets; this has the precipitated heat of the surface of kettle-drums. It was easy for us to land there, since it was cut in table form, and we had the sensation of setting foot on a sun purged of the opaque or too dazzling aspects of its flame; as with the torches of olden times. One no longer noticed the accidents of things but only the substance of the universe, and this is why we did not care whether the flawless surface was a liquid equilibrated according to eternal laws, or a diamond, impervious except under a light falling directly from above.

The lord of the islands came toward us in a ship: the funnel puffed out blue halos behind his head, magnifying the smoke from his pipe and imprinting it on the sky. And as the ship pitched and tossed, his rocking chair jerked out his welcoming gestures.

From beneath his traveling-rug he drew four eggs with painted shells, which he handed over to Doctor Faustroll after first taking a drink. In the flame of the punch we were drinking, the hatching of the oval embryos broke out over the island's shore: two distant columns, the isolation of two prismatic trinities of Pan pipes, splayed out in the spurt of their cornices the quadridigitate handshake of the sonnet's quat-

rains; and our skiff rocked its hammock in the new-born reflection of the triumphal arch. Dispersing the hairy curiosity of the fauns and the rosy bloom of the nymphs aroused from their reverie by this mellifluous creation, the pale motor vessel withdrew its blue breath toward the island's horizon, with its jerking chair waving good-by.

Mallarmé: another of the six among the twenty-seven "equivalents" to whom a chapter is also dedicated. The title of this chapter is inspired by Mallarmé's sonnet based on the ending —yx. In a letter, addressed to Lefebvre and Casalis, Mallarmé writes: ". . . I only have three rhymes in *ix*, do your best to send me the real meaning of the word *ptyx*: I am assured that it does not exist in any language, which I would far prefer so that I may have the pleasure of creating it through the magic of rhyme." To answer Mallarmé's query: the word is, in this nominative singular form, unknown in ancient Greek, but is found often in its conjugation, *ptykos, ptyki*, etc. In the nominative, the alternative *ptykhê* was used (from which we derive "triptych"), the sense being a *fold* or *thickness*.

41: Concerning the Surface of God

God is, by definition, without dimension; it is permissible, however, for the clarity of our exposition, and though he possesses no dimensions, to endow him with any number of them greater than zero, if these dimensions vanish on both sides of our identities. We shall content ourselves with two dimensions, so that these flat geometrical signs may easily be written down on a sheet of paper.

Symbolically God is signified by a triangle, but the three Persons should not be regarded as being either its angles or its sides. They are *the three apexes* of another equilateral triangle circumscribed around the traditional one. This hypothesis conforms to the revelations of Anne-Catherine Emmerich,* who saw the cross (which we may consider to be the *symbol* of the Verb of God) in the form of a Y, a fact which she explains only by the physical reason that no arm of human length could be outstretched far enough to reach the nails of the branches of a Tau.

Therefore, POSTULATE:

Until we are furnished with more ample information and for greater ease in our provisional estimates,

let us suppose God to have the shape and symbolic appearance of three equal straight lines of length a, emanating from the same point and having between them angles of 120 degrees. From the space enclosed between these lines, or from the triangle obtained by joining the three farthest points of these straight lines, we propose to calculate the surface.

Let x be the median extension of one of the Persons a, 2y the side of the triangle to which it is perpendicular, N and P the extensions of the straight line $(a + x)$ in both directions *ad infinitum*.

Thus we have:

$$x = \infty - N - a - P.$$

But

$$N = \infty - 0$$

and

$$P = 0.$$

Bonnard

Which conforms to the dogma of the equivalence of the three Persons between themselves and in their totality.

We can say that a is a straight line connecting o and ∞, and can define God thus:

DEFINITION: *God is the shortest distance between zero and infinity.*

In which direction? one may ask.

We shall reply that His first name is not Jack, but *Plus-and-Minus.* And one should say:

± *God is the shortest distance between o and ∞, in either direction.*

Therefore

$$x = \infty - (\infty - o) - a - o = \infty - \infty + o - a - o$$
$$x = -a.$$

In another respect, the right triangle whose sides are a, x, and y give us

$$a^2 = x^2 + y^2.$$

By substituting for x its value of $(-a)$ one arrives at

$$a^2 = (-a)^2 + y^2 = a^2 + y^2.$$

Whence

$$y^2 = a^2 - a^2 = o$$

and

$$y \sqrt{o}.$$

Therefore the surface of the equilateral triangle having for bisectors of its angles the three straight lines a will be.

$$S = y (x + a) = \sqrt{o}\,(-a + a)$$
$$S = o \sqrt{o}.$$

COROLLARY: At first consideration of the radical $\sqrt{-\bar{o}}$, we can affirm that *the surface* calculated is *one line at the most*; in the second place, if we construct the figure according to the values obtained for x and y, we can determine:

That the straight line $2y$, which we now know to be $2\sqrt{-\bar{o}}$, has its point of intersection on one of the straight lines a in the opposite direction to that of our first hypothesis, since $x = -a$; also, that the base of our triangle coincides with its apex;

That the two straight lines a make, together with the first one, angles at least smaller than 60°, and what is more can only attain $2\sqrt{oo}$ by coinciding with the first straight line a.

Philippe Dumarçay, Regent of Omphalology

Which conforms to the belief in the two principles; but it is more correct to attribute the sign + to that of the subject's faith.

But God being without dimension is not a line.

—Let us note, in fact, that, according to the formula

$$\infty - o - a + a + o = \infty$$

the length a is nil, so that a is not a line but a point.

Therefore, *definitively*:

GOD IS THE TANGENTIAL POINT BETWEEN ZERO AND INFINITY. Pataphysics is *the* science . . .

* Anne-Catherine Emmerich: an unlettered mystical fantasist, who produced some highly imaginative revelations of the life of Christ (e.g. *La Douloureuse Passion*) under the influence of divine inspiration.

The final sentence, "Pataphysics is *the* science . . .": In the original, "La Pataphysique est le science . . ." The French may be translated with important differences in nuance; either as the beginning of a deliberately unfinished sentence ("Pataphysics is the science . . .") or, if one takes it to be a complete sentence, it might equally well read "Pataphysics is science . . ." Let this remain, textually, the final pataphysical mystery.

In the original MS of *Faustroll*, the last words of the book are followed by the word END in the center of the page, and, underneath this, Jarry's remark: "This book will not be published integrally until the author has acquired sufficient experience to savor all its beauties in full."

Translated by Simon Watson Taylor

►► Dr. I. L. Sandomir

Opus Pataphysicum Inaugural Harangue

pronounced on 1 Décervelage 76 P.E.
by *His Magnificence Dr. I. L. Sandomir,* Vice-Curator-Founder of the College, on the occasion of the College's first meeting, which brought together almost all those who were Optimates or Members at that time.

Beloved Proveditors,
Beloved Satraps,
Beloved Regents,
and you all, beloved Auditors of the College of 'Pataphysics,

Seeing before us such a closely packed Assembly, gathered together for these solemn and inaugural Assizes, we nevertheless cannot ignore altogether certain doubts (*sensation*) which might cloud the general sense of enthusiasm.

That the College of 'Pataphysics, after a long gestation, should at last have presented itself to the World and that the World should have presented itself to the College (*applause*), does that not in itself represent a fall from grace and a kind of dilution of its pataphysical excellence? (*new sensation*) We do not fear to say aloud, as you can hear (*bravo, bravo!*) what some people may perhaps be thinking surreptitiously. And since for a College such as ours existence can evidently be little more than a barely necessary evil, we would not be reluctant to share their opinion if precisely this necessary evil—especially by virtue of the contradictions which it implies—did not appear capable of perfecting in depth the pataphysical character of this College: for it still would be an unwarrantable limitation of 'Pataphysics if one should wish to confine it within the domain of nonexistence under the pretext of withdrawing it to the very frontiers of existence. (*applause*) 'Pataphysics transcends both equally, and, in our Statutes affirm, the existence of a College could have no authority to restrain or cramp it in any manner, since it is illimitation itself. (*The audience rises and applauds the Vice-Curator-Founder.*)

It was not necessary for the College to be born in order that 'Pataphysics should exist. Ontologically, if I may use such a vulgar adverb, 'Pataphysics precedes Existence. A priori, this is obvious because Existence has no more reason to exist than reason has to exist. A posteriori, it is equally obvious because the manifestations of existence are aberrant and their necessity entirely contingent.

In the infinite glittering of pataphysical light, existence is a mere ray of light, and by no means the brightest, among all those which emerge from this inexhaustible sun. And he whom human infirmity calls the Creator was only, as our Unremovable Curator Doctor Faustroll (*ovation*) has made clear, the first in time or in ethernity of all pataphysicians. When the Scriptures depict newborn Wisdom proclaiming: *Nondum erant abyssi et jam concepta eram*, there is no doubt that it is 'Pataphysics which is being referred to, save in the one particular that Wisdom was not created by God *ante secula*, but on the contrary, as everything tends to show, he created it *ipsum et secula*, among other pataphysical objects. The World is but one of these objects and human beings—since custom demands that we mention them—are pataphysical concretions. (*Murmurs of agreement.*)

The present era has had the privilege of recalling this fact to us with brilliant clarity. Since the apparent death of Alfred Jarry, it seems that humanity has unconsciously taken upon itself the task of incarnating—not indeed *more really* for that would be impossible, but more openly and more fulgeratingly—the explosive fullness and undefinable profusion of 'Pataphysics. (*Profound silence revealing complete attentiveness.*) Our first World Unbraining and the peace which followed it, our prosperities and our crises, our combined overproductions and famines, our morale and our defeatism, a vivificatory spirit and an assinatory literature, our scientific mythologies and our mystics, our civic or military virtues and our revolutionary faiths, our platonic and other despairs, our fascist and democratic furies, our occupation and our liberation, our collaboration, just as much as our resistance (*the audience remains motionless*), our triumphs and our immolations, the translucency of our emaciations like the blackness of our markets, then, again, the imperturbable and inevitable resumption of ranting from the forum, our radios, our newspapers, our national and international organisms, our court orders and disorders, our padagogies of all complexions, our illnesses and our manias, everything written, everything sung, everything said and everything done, this whole mass of priceless seriousness, this whole inexorable buffoonery, this Coliseum of blablabla seems to have been planned with an admirable application so that no false note may intrude to mar this universal and impeccable Pataphysical Harmony. (*Thunderous applause.*)

It is for this reason that, turning toward you, my dear young listeners, we say to you: Open your eyes and you shall see (*signs of approval*). More fortunate than St. Paul who could only envisage the deity in terms of an enigma and through a glass darkly, you are privileged to regard 'Pataphysics face to face. Thus the teaching of these learned Regents, the example of these incorruptible Satraps, the counsel of

these most serene Proveditors cannot instruct you any more effectively than can the spectacle now spread before your eyes. And we feel it appropriate to recall at this juncture the words uttered by a great pataphysician who was unfortunately unaware of the fact—we refer to Dr. Pangloss: Pataphysically one can say that all is for the best in the most pataphysical of all possible worlds. There could not be more 'Pataphysics in this World than there is because already it is the sole ingredient. The World in all its dimensions is the true College of 'Pataphysics. (*Bursts of applause. Choruses of approval.*)

In any case, the role of this College here assembled will be far more modest. And at this point I can appropriately examine a fresh doubt (*some movement among the audience*) which I divined in your thoughts. Have you not, in short, even if only momentarily and despite the inestimable guarantees which the pataphysically unsuspectable personality of these Optimates assured you, have you not experienced almost a hesitation at the threshold of the College (*hesitation*)? Does not the word College imply teaching? Does not the word teaching imply usefulness or pretensions to usefulness? Does not the word usefulness imply seriousness? Does not the word seriousness imply antipataphysics? All these terms are equivalent (*profound sensation*). And it would be too simple to retort that nothing could be antipataphysics, since all and even those things beyond all are pataphysical. This is pataphysically evident but by no means prevents this Antipataphysics from existing. For it exists: it exists fully; it exists formally; it exists aggressively. And in what does it consist? Ah! this is where the argument runs full circle (*general sigh of relief*): it is precisely ignorance of its own pataphysical nature and it is this ignorance which is its pugnacity, its power, its plenitude and the root of its being. The seriousness of God and of mankind, the usefulness of services and works, the gravity and weight of teachings and systems are only antipataphysical because they will not and cannot proclaim themselves to be pataphysical; for as far as *being* is concerned they cannot be otherwise than they are (*general approval*). *Ducunt volentem fata* (i.e. *pataphysica*) *nolentem trahunt.* (*bravo!*) And so the College is pataphysically founded (*acclamations*).

For it is within the College that the unique and fundamental distinction is made between 'Pataphysics as the substance, if one may say so, of being and non-being, and 'Pataphysics as the science of this substance: or in other terms, between the 'Pataphysics that one is and the 'Pataphysics that one does. For this reason there are, as our Statutes announce, two sorts of pataphysicians: on one hand, those who are pataphysicians without wanting to be and without knowing and, above all, without wanting to know—which is, must necessarily be, will always be the immense mass of our contemporaries; on the other hand, those who recognize themselves to be pataphysicians, affirm themselves as such, demand to be considered as such, and in whom 'Pataphysics is superabundant. In them resides the true Pataphysical Privilege, for "'Pataphysics is the only science." (*Prolonged cheering*.)

It is these then whom our College reunites in its useless Ark which drifts and plunges upon the flood of usefulness. Should we regret that it can never have a democratic nature, nor address itself to all? In a flood, are not the waves of the many necessary to bear up the Noetic skiff?* Can you believe that an enterprise which takes neither seriousness nor laugh-

* Cf. the skiff in which Dr. Faustroll set out on his terrestrial navigation of the "imaginary" world. [*Editor's note*.]

ter—that shameful seriousness—seriously, an enterprise that refuses to be lyrically lyrical, to serve any kind of purpose, indeed that refuses to save mankind or, what is even more unusual, the World, could possibly have oecumenical pretensions? (*Cries of: no, no!*) The College is not a Church. It is not concerned with winning as many "souls" as possible. In addition, the majority could gain no satisfaction in its ranks, for, in their pataphysically naïve misunderstanding of 'Pataphysics (which they incarnate nevertheless) they find a sort of mediocre stimulant which they could never do without. (*Disapproving murmurs*.)

Minority members by vocation (*approving murmurs*), we are so much the more alert and ready to undertake our epigenic navigation in this new appropriately paraffined skiff which is the College of 'Pataphysics. (*Applause, cheers and acclamations. The Assembly rises and sings the Palotins' Hymn.*)

[*stenographic record*]

'Pataphysics is the only science.

► ► **Martin Williams**

Charlie Parker: The Burden of Innovation

It now seems possible to discuss Bix Beiderbecke as if he were a musician—but Bix Beiderbecke has been dead for thirty years. Charlie Parker has been dead only five years, and although they speak of him often, it is becoming more and more unusual for anyone to discuss his music. They speak of him as a god, perhaps because it saves the trouble of reflection on his playing. Some pray to him as a saint, but surely a saint must have a clear self-knowledge and acceptance of his destiny. Some say, in paranoid *non sequiturs* that pass for insight, that he was destroyed by big business and advertising. An uptown barkeep mutters, "I got no use for a man who abuses his talent." They proclaim, "Bird never practiced." (Indeed? And what if he had practiced?) They say of the more careless performances, the squeaks, "He was a man in a hurry." Perhaps he said it better, "I was always in a panic." His friends say, "You had to pay your dues to know him." In a sense you have to

pay them even to listen to him. Perhaps that is as it should be.

Like Louis Armstrong before him, Charlie Parker was called on to change the language of jazz, to reinterpret its fundamentals, and give it a way to continue. That way to continue was not just a matter of new devices—it had also to be a change even in the function of the music. His work implied, with an irrevocable brilliance, that jazz could no longer be thought of as only an energetic background for the barroom, as a kind of vaudeville, or as a vehicle for dancers. From now on, it was (as many of its followers had said it should be) a music to be listened to. We will make it that, he seemed to say, or it will perish. The knowledge that he was sending it along that road must have been an awesome burden to bear.

There has been a great deal of nonsense written about the "modern jazz" or "bebop" movement. It has been said that the beboppers made their compositions by adopting the chord sequences of standard popular songs and writing new melody lines on them. So they did, and so had at least two generations of jazzmen before them. It has been said that they started the similar practice of improvising only with reference to a chord sequence and with none to a theme proper—in classical terms "harmonic variation," in the term of jazz critic André Hodeir "chorus phrase"—the practice was a norm and commonplace by the late thirties and in the work of men like Teddy Wilson, Lester Young, Roy Eldridge, Coleman Hawkins, Charlie Christian, Ben Webster, had reached a kind of deadlock of perfection.

Both practices are, basically, as old as the blues. (Certainly King Oliver's three classic 1923 choruses on *Dippermouth Blues* have no thematic reference to the melody of that piece.) One might even say that the jazzman spent the late twenties and the thirties discovering that he also could "play the blues" on the chords of *I Got Rhythm, Digga Digga Do, Tea For Two, Exactly Like You, Rose Room,* and the rest.

What was needed and what bebop and Charlie Parker provided, was a renewed musical language with which the old practices could be replenished and continued.

It came, in part, as have all innovations in jazz, from an assimilation and transformation of devices from the tradition of European music. But a deliberate effort to import classical harmony or melodic device might have led to all sorts of affectation and spuriousness. (It nearly had done so in Beiderbecke's work, and it does for others every day.) The crucial thing about the bebop style is that its real basis came from the resources of jazz itself, and it came in much the same way that innovation had come in the past. That basis is rhythmic and it is based on rhythmic subdivision. Any other way would surely have been disastrous. And we should not talk about passing chords, polytonality and the rest before we have talked about rhythm.

The rhythmic impulse in the so-called "cakewalk" style, the earliest formal pre-jazz style we know of, is a half-note pulse. (It is a bit difficult to be dogmatic about this since we depend on printed scores for evidence and many old cakewalks were revised to conform to later styles, but it is a safe enough statement.) The rhythmic basis of ragtime is a syncopated half-note. In the New Orleans style, apparently, syncopation gradually divided the pulse until it became an even four in Armstrong's work. The rhythmic basis of bebop is an eighth-note.

To say that is to reduce the marvelous rhythmic flexibility of Charlie Parker and Max Roach to the most mundane level, and, for that matter, to speak of rhythm, melodic line, and harmony as if they were entities is a critic's necessary delusion. But such separations can clarify much. To many ears attuned to the music of a Hawkins or a Buck Clayton and the rhythmic conceptions they use, Parker's music seemed at first pointlessly fussy, decorative—a flurry of technique. But once one is in touch with Parker rhythmically, every note becomes a direct and functional expression.

It is fitting that Parker's first recorded solo, on *Swingmatism,* owes so much to Lester Young, for whatever his debt to others (and to himself) for the genesis of his style, he had obviously absorbed Young's language soundly and thoroughly, and between Armstrong and Parker, Lester Young was probably the most gifted and orginal improviser that jazz produced. Significantly, Young's style depended on a brilliantly flexible use of the 4/4 pulse which was perfected in the Count Basie orchestra in which he worked. His solo at the end of *Doggin' Around* is the handiest example, and one of the best. He begins actually in the final bar of Basie's piano chorus and his own chorus starts with only one note in his first bar—any reed player and probably any horn player at the time would have used four times as many at a minimum. The second musical phrase of his chorus begins at the second bar and dances gracefully through the seventh, unbroken. The eighth bar is silent; in nine he begins his third phrase, logically off the second. But Young's basic contribution is not in the innovation of a melodic unit of eight bars (most players before him would have phrased four bars at a time), nor in the daring symmetry of balancing one casual note at its beginning against a silence at its end. It is in the meter and organization of his melodies. Young's heavy accents may fall on "weak" beats, and a freely moving rhythmic impulse seems to dictate the way his melodic line moves.

Harmonically, what Lester Young did was show how original one could be with whatever materials were at hand. By a marvelous ear and a refusal to allow a literal reading of harmony and melodic structures to inhibit him, he could freely, casually, and tantalizingly phrase several beats ahead of a coming tonic chord and the arrival of the chord shows he was right all along. His opening chorus on *Taxi War Dance* contains a bold enough use of this kind of linear phrasing to have captivated a whole generation of reed players.

Charlie Parker's second recorded solo is also indicative—brilliant and exasperating, perhaps ominous. On *Hootie Blues* he played what might have been a beautifully developed and rhythmically original chorus—one which does introduce almost everything he was to spend the rest of his life refining—but he interrupts it in the seventh bar to interpolate a very trite swing riff figure, granted that there is the sound intuition that a contrasting and simple figure was precisely right at that moment in his melody, a simply commonplace one was not.

No one who has listened with receptive ears to Charlie Parker play the blues could doubt that aspect of his authenticity as a jazzman, nor could one fail to understand after hearing much of him that the emotional (even technical) basis of his work is the urban, southwestern blues idiom that we also hear running through every performance by the Basie orchestra of the late thirties. *Parker's Mood* (especially take 1) is as indigenously the blues as a Bessie Smith record, and, in its way, perhaps more basically so than several James P. Johnson records or even Leroy Carr records. But what one also senses is the increase in emotional range that Parker's technical innovations make possible in the idiom. One also knows that his innovations represent a truly organic growth for jazz and, as I have said, have nothing to do with the spurious impositions of many self-consciously "progressive" jazzmen. On the other hand, for every *Laird Baird*, with its childlike but daring shifts from introspection to shimmering dance, intuitively held together in their own secret order and directness, there are half a dozen records of exuberant, brilliant disarray. One cannot call such disorder evidence of the wisdom of the young artist discovering his talent before he begins to censure it, for Parker obviously had the conception very much in hand by 1940 and spent the rest of his days developing it and, some say, destroying it as well.

There is an improvisation on *Lady Be Good* that is in some ways the great Charlie Parker solo, and in others is too good to be typical. It was made under the really unbelievable circumstances of a Jazz at the Philharmonic concert in the spring of 1946 in Los Angeles; it thereby refutes what is patently true, that Parker's playing really belonged only in the small improvising quintets which he established as the norm. The circumstances were made even more trying by the fact that as Parker begins to swing further away from the conventions of the period in his style, he is rewarded with a conventional background riff from the other musicians who were on the stage at the time. The solo is apt to sound conventionally conceived at first (at least it did to me) but it is not. The first four notes are Gershwin's but what follows them makes Parker's a strikingly reorganized echo of that well-known ditty. Then there is an immediate

reversal and he fills four bars by developing a simple riff figure. The following phrase overtakes it as a return to more complex melody, yet grows out of the riff and, we realize, is also a kind of reverse echo of his opening phrase. A dancing descent of short notes next predicts the direction of the rest of his solo. He gradually transforms the advanced "swing" style he had begun with into the style he was offering to replace it. The movement of the melodies is masterful, and within it, the structure (some of it continuing the echo patterns) is superb.

Yet, this solo is delivered with a kind of personal and technical strain and pressure that is so foreign to the fluent ease of a Lester Young or the dramatic stances of a Roy Eldridge—and to Parker at his best—that it may even prevent one from hearing its coherent brilliance. Even in the midst of such order as this, we may have to return to the proposition that a lot of Parker's work is oddly incomplete; it leaves us with no feeling of order restored—or even passion spent, lacking sometimes even the sense of emotional completeness that gives much jazz playing its special kind of order. Parker fulfilled a mission, surely, to salvage a music and set it on its course. Perhaps he was also the victim of that mission. In any case, one may even wonder if he really fulfilled his talent; one wonders it especially when one hears recordings on which he did seem to fulfill himself, and recordings where his passionate failures are so brilliant.

Almost opposite to the "classic" development of a *Lady Be Good* is another public recording made with a far more appropriate group, the Carnegie Hall concert of 1947 with Dizzy Gillespie. Here is Parker the daring romantic: passing and altered harmonies, complex movements and counter-movements of rhythm, unexpected turns of melody—and much of it is delivered with an emotional directness that itself makes the complexity necessary and functional. The celebrated stop-time break on *A Night In Tunisia* shows Parker's intuitive sense of balance at its most complete: an alternation of tensions and releases so rapid, terse, and complete that it may seem to condense all of his best work into one melodic leap of four bars. Yet, in the recordings of that concert there is at other times an edge to his tone, an apparent strain, and occasionally even a gratuitous showiness in his notes.

The rhythmic impulse in his work was crucial, but Parker also had one of the most fertile harmonic imaginations jazz has known; in this respect one can mention only Art Tatum in the same paragraph with him. Tatum must have been an enormous influence, one feels sure, harmonically and even perhaps in rhythm and note values. But Tatum's imagination was almost exclusively harmonic, and as an improvisor Parker was perhaps the greatest *inventor* of melodies jazz has seen. Also, although surely not a jazz composer in the sense that Morton, Ellington, and Monk are jazz composers, he wrote some enduring lines which perhaps themselves give the best introduction to his improvising. One should acknowledge first the simpler blues-riffs, however, like *Now's The Time, Bluebird* or even *Cool Blues*. On the other hand, players at first found the sophisticated blues lines like *Relaxin' At Camarillo* and *Billie's Bounce* almost impossible to play, not because of their notes but because their strong melodic lines demanded so fresh a way of phrasing. The fulfillment of this more complex side of Parker's compositional talent is in pieces like *Anthropology* (*Thriving From A Riff*) and *Confirmation. Confirmation*, a marvelous creation, is in the "popular song" thirty-two bar form, but flows without the usual melodic repeats until its last eight bars thus: ABCA—again a drastic expansion of traditional material. *Confirmation* is apt to confuse and delight us all at once on first hearing but we should also notice that there is a subtle inner pattern to it, even to the detail that the phrase ending of B is drawn from A.

One problem with Parker's work is that although there is now available an abundance of riches (a sometimes quite confusing one), the brilliant series of records, those made for the Dial label is not fully available. If it were not so, we would not have to stop at the two current LPs that use the Dial masters (and it is possibly the best single Parker set available). If it were not so, and if the material were edited well, we could hear *Bird of Paradise* evolving from three takes of *All the Things You Are* and we could hear those different brilliant variations on alternate takes of *Embraceable You, Scrapple from the Apple, Klactoveedsedsteen, Dexterity, Moose the Mooch* and *Cheers*, if they were placed together the way they happened originally. Verve has issued most of its material that way, but the Savoy recordings have appeared, with one exception, haphazardly, and different versions of one piece may be scattered across as many as four LP collections.

However, what is available currently from the Dial catalogue is some of the best of it. There was a far better take of *Quasimodo* than the one now included, but the leaping solo on *Crazeology* tells as much as any single performance about the ease with which Parker handled harmony, rhythm, and line. *Klactoveedsedsteen* would be a wonder if only for Max Roach's drumming, but it has a breathtaking Parker solo that seems suspended above the chord changes for sixteen bars not really establishing its tonality until he slides into the bridge. From that point

he builds form simply by increasing complexity, but with an originality of line entirely his own. The beautiful melody Parker creates on *Embraceable You* is justly celebrated (but one wonders how many listeners really follow it beyond the first few bars). The improvised bridge of the opening chorus on *Scrapple from the Apple* might in itself be enough to announce the likelihood of a major talent, and the performance confirms it with that chorus of surpassingly fluent invention which follows.

The group that made those records was, at least in its raw materials, a fine collection of foils and counterfoils to Parker. The talent of a then still-developing and sometimes faltering Miles Davis, was, in its detached lyricism, sonority, and lack of virtuosity an excellent contrast. What is perhaps more important is that in a growing capacity for asymmetry and displacement, Davis was able to carry and refine a part of Parker's rhythmic message in a unique manner, quite opposite from Dizzy Gillespie's virtuoso playing. Pianist Duke Jordan is a really classic and balanced melodic improviser. Bud Powell or John Lewis replace him on some of the Savoys, and with the former at least, the whole group quality changes: Powell's ideas are perhaps too much like Parker's. Max Roach was at the peak of his early career in the mid-forties. The simplest way to put it is to say that he could *play* the rhythms that Parker used and implied, and he knew exactly when and how to break up his basic pulse to complement what the soloists were doing with it. To call what he does interfering or decorative is perhaps to misunderstand not only the whole basis of this music but the function of all jazz drumming from Baby Dodds forward. Hear Roach on *Crazeology* behind J. J. Johnson, then Miles Davis—and throughout.

Surely one of the most interesting documents in jazz is the Savoy LP which preserves all the recorded material from the record date that produced *KoKo, Now's The Time*, and *Billie's Bounce*. (When one thinks that with a little more organization in its reissues, Savoy might have given us several more such instructive collections. . . .) It might be enough just to hear the various final performances gradually shape and reshape themselves (there are still dubious shifts of personnel—could Dizzy Gillespie really be playing all that piano on *Meandering?*) but the session was one of Parker's best, and its climax was *KoKo. KoKo* may seem only a fast-tempo showpiece at first, but it is not. It is a precise linear improvisation, for one thing, which has exceptional melodic content, and, incidentally, at times almost an atonality in its handling of the chord changes from *Cherokee*. It is also an almost perfect example of virtuosity *and* economy: following a pause, notes fall over and between this beat and that beat—breaking them asunder, robbing them of any vestige of monotony—rests fall where heavy beats once came, now "heavy" beats come between beats and on weak beats. It has been a source book of ideas for fifteen years, and no wonder; now that its basic innovations are more familiar, it seems even more a great performance in itself.

Parker's career on records after 1948 is a wondrous, a frustrating, and finally a pathetic thing. It was perhaps in some search for form and for refuge from the awful dependency on the inspiration and intuition of the moment that he took on the mere *format* of strings, the *doo-wah* vocal groups, the Latin percussive gimmicks. A major artist can find an inspiration in odd places, but what Miles Davis makes out of an Ahmad Jamal is, happily, not Ahmad Jamal; Charlie Parker with strings still includes the strings and the banal writing for them. What a perversion of "success" to place a major jazzman in such a setting, whatever he thought about it or would admit feeling about it. (Yet, hasn't Louis Armstrong had worse, and often?) There is an arrangement of *What Is This Thing Called Love* whose triteness is gross indeed, yet Charlie Parker plays brilliantly on it: in effect a great creative musician battling pseudo-musical pleasantries. Then there is a *Just Friends* which is the only one of his records he would admit to liking, and a *In the Still of the Night* where he shimmers and slithers around tritely conceived choral singing like a great dancer in front of a chorus doing time-steps. The Latin gimmickry is not as bad, and on *Mongo Monque* Parker adjusts his own phrasing admirably, but to what end? One cannot hear Dizzy Gillespie improvise without realizing that his phrasing often depends on his experience in rhumba bands, but Parker's is always a development of jazz and jazz rhythms. It was perfectly natural for Gillespie to use Chano Pozo as a second drummer; for Parker such things remain extrinsic effects however well he adapts himself.

What remains otherwise from those years is often an expansive and expanding excellence. One cannot hear the fluent sureness of *Chi Chi*, the easy conservatism of *Swedish Schnapps*, the developed virtuosity of *She Rote* without knowing that a major talent is extending and perfecting his language. And there is the celebrated excitement of *Bloomdido* and *Mohawk* on the "reunion" recordings with Gillespie. (Even on several of these personal successes, what a careless misunderstanding of Parker's music to involve him with a compulsive and rhythmically inappropriate drummer like Buddy Rich!)

Perhaps to Charlie Parker invention simply came too easily or perhaps he was tortured by the constancy of his invention. Perhaps, on the other hand, he did rely too completely on the intuitive impulse of the moment; it was his strong point and he may therefore have come to believe it was his only point. Perhaps, when he could blow everyone else away just by standing up and playing, he admitted hearing no call to any other kind of challenge, and was thereby persuaded to take on the spurious challenge of flirting with popularity by standing in front of those strings. In his utter dependency night after night on the inspiration of the act of playing itself, in his refusal to coast or merely embellish and determination always to invent, he may have given himself the kind of challenge that no man of sensitivity could carry without inviting disaster.

Charlie Parker is called the great "modernist" in jazz. He was certainly the most brilliant improviser after Armstrong, but perhaps like Armstrong he was as much the heir to a heritage as he was an innovator within it. And hearing Sonny Rollins put many of Parker's ideas into an order, and hearing the innovations of Ornette Coleman, one wonders if Parker and his associates were not perhaps the *last* major jazz improvisers to borrow nineteenth century harmony and make melodies over chord changes.

DISCOGRAPHY Lester Young's *Doggin' Around* solo is on Decca DXB-170; *Taxi War Dance*, along with some of his best playing, is on Epic LG 3107.

Dial recordings by Charlie Parker are on Roost 2210, and the 1947 Carnegie Hall concert is on one side of Roost 2234.

The full recording date that produced *Billie's Bounce*, *Now's The Time*, *Thrivin' From a Riff*, and *KoKo* is on Savoy 12079. The several 1945 quintets on Savoy 12020 have Dizzy Gillespie and were the first recordings to show the essentially lean and functional quality of the bebop style, and the way that Parker and Gillespie play the unisons on *Salt Peanuts* and *Hot House* is still exemplary. (It is a shame that Parker's *Shaw Nuff* from the same recording session was not included.) Perhaps the best single Savoy collection is 12001 with *Bluebird* (take 1), *Bird Gets The Worm* (take 1), *Parker's Mood* (take 1), *Constellation* (take 1) and *Buzzy* (take 5). Savoy 12001 has *Donna Lee* (take 3), *Chasing The Bird* (take 1), *Cheryl*, and interesting 1944 solos on the several versions of *Tiny's Tempo* and *Red Cross*. The superb *Parker's Mood* (original take) is on Savoy 12009 as is *Donna Lee* (take 3). On Savoy 12014, are the originally released versions of *Barbados*, *Bird Gets The Worm*, *Bluebird*, and *Chasing The Bird*.

The concert *Lady Be Good* was last issued on Clef MG Vol. 1, but Parker's solo from it is included in the three-record set Verve MG V-8100-3, a cross-section of Parker's recordings after 1948 and including *Laird Baird*, *Confirmation*, *Mohawk*, and *She Rote*. Among the separate collections on Verve, *Diverse* is on MG V-8009; *Bloomdido*, *Mohawk* and the other Gillespie reunion selections (with alternate takes) are on MG V-8806; *Laird Baird*, *Confirmation*, and other quartets are on MG V-8005; and *Swedish Schnapps*, *She Rote*, *Au Privave* and two other good blues are on MG V-8010.

Bank Day

During the night he dreamt that someone gave him $15, not for anything he had done but for the sport, and now he tried in various ways to relive the ecstasy of his acceptance. He could not do it, because awake he knew too much, as that nobody ever got anything for it is better to a giver be. One thing he did not know was what time it was, yet he had himself so placed that he did not have to listen to the clock tick off its superior knowledge in the dark. He lay with his head, and his impatience, buried beneath the cover, waiting for the alarm (which did not know that it was set) to sound. Oh, he might easily have imagined that he lay thus fortified against Martha's soft respiration, or against the shocking knowledge that a wife of his could on this day be so tranquilly asleep, but he tried not to permit her innocent failings to make of him a bully or a nag. Neither could he admit the intolerable truth, that what had kept him so long alert was pain. Being a lesser kind of realist he had proposed that everything, even a brutal alarm clock, must one day break down, and being by press of circumstances a pessimist had decided it would choose to break down today. Thus when at last it did sound off he was already halfway over Martha, halfway over her incredible baby which even as late as last week they had both imagined to be a persistent gas, and Martha was grunting quietly. Thank God I love you, he thought, kissing her somewhere as he passed by.

Now steadying himself on the slippery linoleum he had himself working fairly well, alarm going off, lights going on, almost at once, and in the long-desired morning saw that the clock's amputated hands approximated his own opinion of the time. In fact he knew so well their vagaries that he corrected them, aiming the silver stub straight up toward twelve, the other, Wild Pink as Martha's nails, toward five. Whenever possible he liked to do two things simultaneously, and turning freed the cat from the bathroom with his left hand while scratching a kitchen match with the thumbnail of his right. "Pret-ty Kit-ty, Pret-ty Kit-ty." Stooping stiffly he stroked her supple back while lighting the burner under the coffee pot. But now he had to remain there squatting, watching the cat spring onto the bed to knead Martha's uneasy mountains with her paws. And somehow he did not cry aloud as he lunged with

grinding vertebrae into the bathroom to comb his hair and brush his teeth. (He had shaved the night before, while reading the help wanted ads for the final futile time.) Back in the room again, he cleverly combined a proper kiss on Martha's cheek with stooping for his polished shoes. What stunned him was how, on such a diet, anyone could smell so sweet. "Martha, Martha," he softly called. "Bank day today."

"Un?" Frowning she partly opened her blue eyes, and rolled sidewise onto the sleeping cat. He kissed her on the other cheek, at the same time groping cautiously.

"John?"

He held up the ruffled, delighted cat.

"Oh, did I squash Pretty Kitty!" Smiling ruefully, she enfolded it. "Aren't I a Humpty Dumpty though?" she asked.

He kissed her mouth this time. "You're a damn beauty, but it's becoming unsafe to sleep with you . . . I'm sorry, I didn't mean that," he said, and wincing erected himself again. He turned his tight-skinned face from her. "Why don't you get up," he snapped.

Now he imagined Martha's smooth white forehead inventing pain, for both of them. "You get back in bed," she said.

"I'd love to—we might get hungry around supper time."

"I don't care," she said, but at the same time she was quaking the bed, rolling out of it onto her hands and knees, muzzily cursing the slippers which eluded her and which he at last shied toward her with his toe. "Oh, there. What did you mean you didn't mean just now?"

"Nothing," he said. The coffee water was boiling, and he shook coffee in, set out coffee cups.

"Tell me. You always mean something, John," she begged, but suddenly heaved to her slippered feet, confronting him all humpty-dumptyish in white. "Ah, you oughtn't to have said that, John."

"I apologized long ago."

"Still, you're right," she said, and sighed. "You're so right, you know."

"I'll sleep in the cat's room from now on," he said, seeing her start for it. They still had the radio, and passing she flicked it on. He leaped after, furling the sudden flag music that threatened to smother him. Soon music stopped, and a man's voice announced that MUZ was on the air again. This man asked all his friends to leave for work five minutes early today, as a light frost on their windshields might hamper visibility. "Turn it down, Martha, turn it down," he implored, on her return.

Martha did so without complaint, but placing their toast on the burner, spreading oleo, he heard how unhappily she opened the catfood can. And she looked unhappily askance as she handed the can to him. "We should never have kept that cat," she said.

"I know," he said, spooning only a modest portion for Pretty Kitty, for himself a giant one. He selected several condiments from their large supply, basil, savory, sage, shallot, added them freely with flourishes. That was their extravagance, whenever they had pennies to spare they bought a seasoning. "Tonight I'll barbecue you some frankfurters," he said, cracking the egg she passed to him and dropping it one-handed onto the meat in the frying pan. "A pound of them."

"With refried beans," she said.

"And beer?"

She nodded a festive yes, but, "I still wish you wouldn't go," she said.

"You've lost your appetite?"

"Let me go instead. Now that we know I'm not really sick."

"You? They wouldn't take you like that."

Looking down, "I'll tell them I've been eating well."

"Aha." It was not that he thought her incapable; in fact he fancied she would make the sacrifice with a certain swagger which he himself could not pretend. Certainly he detected no deficiency of blood in her! What he cowered from was the picture of her standing in the dark in that ghoulish line, listening to those sanguinary jokes, and then competing meanly for that frightful prize. "No, what is it they say? I still have some pride," he said.

"Let me go with you then."

"What is it they say again?"

"Think of the extra money though."

"No," he said. All dripping sounds made him feel weak, and he crossed to bang the leaky sink. "Will I get enough for us to pay up my insurance and live until my check arrives?"

She nodded. "Just."

"Then that's enough."

"If they take you, yes."

"Oh, they'll take me," he mumbled, giddily watching her pour tomato juice: "Please, Martha, not today."

"It's good for you."

"Not today."

Now that he had their breakfast ready, he stood aside and allowed her the little pleasure of serving it. He did not sit down until she told him to, and then only because he knew how it distressed her to see him prowl the floor while snatching mouthfuls from the ice box top. Doubling up, he wondered if having a baby was like sliding cramp-backed into a breakfast nook. At least she did not watch, but looked at the calendar above his head.

"Gene Autry was born today."

"Thank God!" he said, swilling coffee before he ate.

"I wonder if anyone was born on my birthday. Shall I see?"

"Maybe some other great man," he said fiercely through clenching teeth. "Maybe he left $15 to every female born that day, out of sentiment. Whimsical, he stipulated in his will that no one was to get her inheritance until she turned thirty-five. All pregnant women get a double share, of course."

But she sank sighing opposite. "Battle of the Alamo."

"Ah, then I should have been an insurance agent after all," he admitted readily, "now retired on the policies I'd sold myself, buying new ones with my dividends. Or I would have made a fine shattered disc jockey," he proposed, and glared at the whispering radio. "Right now I could be lying in bed warning all my friends of light frosts on their way to work, warning them to buy new windshields on their way back again." Briefly he paused, washing down his cat pourri with a third or fourth cup of black coffee sloshed from the tremendous pot. "What I really should have done," he said, "was re-enlist in the army for forty years. That way they'd have had to invest in a new back for me, instead of leaving me to subsist on thirty-five a month and pain. Well, thank God anyway I was carrying that ice cream freezer in the line of duty, rather than throwing it at some dyspeptic officer." He paused to laugh. "What is it they say, an army is only as good as its bloody cook? I'll never forget that big one I worked with in India. Neither will you, I've told you about him often enough. Babu? He used to sit cross-legged on a huge table, Buddha-esque, supervising his two dozen native cooks. They'd bring him a taste of each dish they cooked, if they left out one of their twenty or thirty curries he'd know and remonstrate. Needless to say, he thrived. Three hundred and forty pounds of him, and never moved from his table for twelve hours a day except to leak. Now there's the job for me. The only difference would be that I would lie down on my table, my cooks would specialize in sautéed snails and bouillabaisse. I myself would never lift anything heavier than a very young squab, plucked of course." He paused to glance at her, then quickly away again. "I know what you're going to say," he said, "I should have been born to the baronetcy of Upper-Aultby-by-the-Sea or Sweet-Sweet-Puke, but the answer is no— let's be practical."

She did not laugh or smile at any of this, but did shake her head occasionally as he in order not to howl aloud explained on and on to her his views. That he had spent half his life cooking for men who despised his dishes but greedily devoured him. That the sense of gratitude, like his food, was a passing thing. That if he could lay his hands on any one of several men there would be no frankfurters for dinner tonight, roast pig au jus instead. That the ugliest man in the world was an unused cook, was he, was him. At last he could endure it no longer but straightened cursing to his feet to stride the floor, lift their miserable frying pan and slam it on their miserable stove. He wheeled on her asking, "Well, aren't you going to make me up," appalled.

She mumbled some mild apology, squeezing past him to the bureau top. He followed her, but by the time she had her rouge uncapped he was pacing the room again. "Stand still," she ordered, cornering him, and under her soft finger tips his nerves did quiet a little bit. He closed his eyes and pretended that she was caressing him. In truth she was, of course, and he wished that she would never stop. Yet a moment later he broke roughly away from her. "Well, how do I look?"

Martha stretched to look at him closely, too closely, and it seemed to him that her considered judgment was, "You look, you look."

"What!" Very ugly indeed, he thought, when your wife speaks to you of love and only the nerves respond.

"Come here," she said.

"I can't understand a word you say," he said, stooping to receive her kiss. "How do I look?"

"You're a damn beauty," she said. "Have you everything? Here's your shopping list, your firewood, your matches and cigarettes."

"Thanks, thanks, thanks," he said, taking everything at once.

"I gave you both the cigarettes."

"You'll need one."

"Not as much as you will two."

But he, flinging her cigarette onto the bed, denied her any sacrifice. He strode sharply to the door, which she unlocked for him. "I'm a son-of-a-bitch," he said.

"Don't tell me your troubles," she said, and as he passed by she turned his jacket collar up.

Groping down the narrow passage between the two facing rows of cabins, he believed that he had never seen the world so dark before. It was not until he reached the sidewalk that he glanced up at their palm tree and realized their neon sign was out. This vastly pleased him, for he could stare back at the darkness he had left and almost imagine a home was there, a well-tended little home that drew milkmen, ministers, and paperboys. Well, he was on his way to work, and unseen he swung out his piece of wood almost jauntily: for the first time this day his thoughts did not twinge with pain. Walking did this for his back, almost made a citizen of him. And almost he returned to leave Martha a gentle word, but knew too well that by the time she had nervously unlocked the door he would have thought of something else. Thus he contented himself with remarking to a passing cur, "Oh, aren't I one?"

Now he wished he had that second cigarette. More strongly he wished he had four miles to walk, instead of blocks. He wished he were a mailman, with a full-time watchman's job at night. But already he was approaching a lighted street, where the jobholders did not appear to be allowing frosty windshields to slow them much. He felt anger rise again, for each one carried a box of kleenex on the rear window ledge, and he could always be sure the skinny queen up front would stare out at him from her limp embrace to ask, "Hey, mister, don't you wish you had me?" Thus he became sensitive about his piece of wood, tucked it under his right arm now, away from the street. Cold though he was, he turned his collar down. "Well now, ma'am," was his reply.

So it did not displease him to be turning the final corner into blackness now, even though it meant that he was almost there. In fact he could already see their puny fire, see the boys bent over it like thin frozen fingers over a glowing ember held in the palm, Winston shorter and broader and a little apart, like a stubby thumb. If at first he only imagined Winston's fast anxious gabble coming through to him over the receding traffic noise, a step or two later he could hear nothing else. Surely it was the most comical sound in the world, being at this distance wholly unintelligible, yet somehow he could not smile. For $15 he would have turned around and toted an ice-cream freezer the four long blocks that he had come. Receiving no offers of any kind he approached the fire in a circumspect way, on grass. Winston, however, was not surprised.

"Hey, Johnny! Johnny! (It's Johnny.) Hey, you're late, Johnny," he cried.

John bowed stiffly to the group, extended his hands with the others over the fire. "Gentlemen." He looked from one to another of the boys, and some returned his look. Oliver alone did not face the fire, nor mingle his hands with theirs. He watched the darkness warily, but glanced back just long enough to grin at John. John looked at Winston last. "Winston, it takes a while for the three of me to get ready a morning, you understand."

"Ah ah ah!" Winston shouted laughter down, leaned close to peer at John. "What are you going to make, a deposit or a withdrawal today, Johnny?"

"I thought I'd cash in a few frozen assets today," John said, blinking faster than Winston could.

"Ah ah ah! Come on up to the fire then, Johnny. We'll warm those assets up for you, Johnny. We'll warm them up," Winston cried, his thick hands like bracelets on John's thin arms. "Anyway I see you brought your firewood, Johnny. Here, give it here. I'll put it on the pile here. That's a nice one, Johnny. We'll use that one any minute now. We'll need plenty of wood before we're through." Winston reached into his loose pants for a large gold watch he had, bent to read it at the fire. A flame was licking at his hands, and like scientists they watched while Winston appeared to read the number of seconds it took him to feel the burn. Hearing laughter, he pocketed his watch, kicked the barrel wrathfully with his big black boot. "It's those goddam palm fronds, they snap at you. You ever notice that, Johnny? You notice the gutter when you came up, how neat it was? They like that, don't they Johnny, the way I clean it up for them? And it helps us too. They have a clean gutter and it keeps us warm. That way everyone wins, Johnny? Am I right?"

"Winnie, why don't you stop whinnying," the carpenter said. Whenever he spoke to anyone he cocked his head and screwed up one eye, his left, as though aligning nails, and his voice had a metallic ring: "Why don't you save your strength, you'll need it in a little while."

"Ah ah ah," Winston warned, moving to the carpenter's side. He clenched a fist and held up a hard arm to him. "By any chance what you're looking for?"

The carpenter ignored the arm, but reached behind Winston to rap the wooden brace instead. "Hell, I could make a better man than you out of knotty pine."

Winston hearing their laughter smiled. He stood nodding and blinking at the carpenter. "You you you," he said.

"Man offered me a job yesterday," the carpenter said over Winston's head to John. "He called it a little Sunday job. Ten bucks for the day, hanging doors. Bastard would have had to pay three times that much to any man with a card. I told him I'd wait and let them bleed me here, it don't take so long."

John nodded. "It leaves no scab," he said. He enjoyed watching the carpenter rolling one, for he tucked the brown paper into the creases of his fingerless hand as though this were some sort of newfangled machine he had. He sprinkled the tobacco casually, used a patented twist and a lick, and when he was done he put his machine away. "Carpenter, why don't you give up and go back home?"

Lighting up, the carpenter cocked his head at John. A spark was feeding on his thin grey sweater, already pocked with tobacco burns. "Maybe I will in a gallon or two."

Winston, tittupping around the barrel, leaned close to John. "I had muscular spasmatisms, Johnny," he whispered. He paused to throw in a stick. Then he nudged John toward the barrel, looking up at him. "The wife was sick this weekend, Johnny. Figure it out for yourself: the weekend is the only time you can sell ice cream, the kids are home. That's a sure twenty I lost right there. Then I had to give her twenty-five Friday for the license plates. The state tax was seventeen. Figure it for yourself, that took care of the bank account. I had $1100 in the bank before I got sick, after I sold the store. You've seen my bankbook, haven't you, Johnny?"

"I've seen it, yes."

Winston's hand came out of his pocket, clamped John again. "I guess you'd be surprised if the wife kicked me out one of these days, wouldn't you, Johnny?" he asked. "Well, I wouldn't be surprised, Johnny. I'm ready for her, Johnny." He looked down at his shoes. "I have to have my shoes made special, Johnny. Look at that arch. Look at that toe, Johnny. Steel." Winston gave the barrel a ringing kick. "Dr. Bastard, you better take me today, you son-of-a-bitch. I was first man here."

"What time you get here, Winston?" Oliver was guarding the darkness still.

"Winnie spends his nights here," the carpenter said. "Then around midnight his wife drives by and gives him a ice-cream bar."

The little man with the cruddy vest opened his eyes. His name was Henry or Hank, Herman perhaps. "You should tell your wife to carry beer in her truck, I'll come over and keep you company."

"Hell, Howard, are you here?" Oliver wanted to know. "What were you last time they tested you, about 90 proof?"

"Sure, straight Kentucky bourbon. They pay me

extra for that. That's a hell of a lot better than a puking 3.2."

"Don't worry about me, I'm a sarsaparilla man."

Howard grinned redly at Oliver's back. "I always noticed you coons had queer names for that bathtub poison you like to make."

"Easy boy, Howard," Oliver said, and his voice was soft. "I'm liable to split your skull and light a match, we'll all blow up."

"Ah ah ah! Howie, you going to let him get away with that? Hey, Howie?"

Howard nodded a goodnatured yes.

"Hey, Larry! (There's Larry.) Hey, Larry! You've got your helmet on today."

"Larry forgot to take it off when he got up this morning," John said, turning his back to bake.

"Not hardly," grinning Larry said.

"We thought you went back East last week."

Larry shook his aluminum head. "Too goddam cold back there. They got twelve inches of snow at El Paso Friday night. Three feet in the drifts. Hell, I'm waiting for spring. A climate like this, a man's blood gets thin."

"You can say that again," the carpenter, spitting, said.

"Ah, ah, ah!"

"Amen."

"Hey, look at the size of that one," Winston whispered loudly, and they turned to look. "Look at that chest, look at that asseroo. Look at that tourist crease in his pants. What does the bastard do, sell it by the goddam barrel?"

The newcomer stepped among them now, spreading great hands to the fire. He did look as though he could get rich fast. "How do they pay here?" he asked. "Cash on the line?"

Looking askance, they nodded yes.

"I lost my wallet to a floozy last night, papers and everything. I need gas to get out of here."

"Gas." Everyone looked everywhere else, the carpenter whispering obscenities.

Flushing the big man drew in his hands, stepped back a step. "What time does the show start, anyway?"

He had to wait a minute for their reluctant "Eight."

"We better line up," said the carpenter, moving toward the bank, "before some tourist tries to bull in ahead of us. Oliver, you go first. I'll come after Winnie—after Winnie anyone looks good, ah ah ah." But he turned to look closely at John, as Martha had. "On second thoughts, maybe you better follow him."

"Thanks."

Even such a line as theirs, now started, grew, as though aimless passers-by tagged on out of curiosity. Yet there was a kind of sardonic knowledge on every face, wary eyes were large, and the sickly dawn showed complexions blue. The sense of watchful apathy survived bad jokes and expletives. It almost seemed that Winston himself had found a mood. He moved from line to fire, back again, without announcements of any kind, confronted John with unblinking eyes. "Dr. Bastard has it in for me, Johnny. You notice that? He'll try anything to pass me by."

"Winnie, why don't you give up?" the carpenter wished to know. "Last time they took you they were pumping it into your right arm faster than they could squeeze it out your left."

"I was sick that day."

"Hell, they couldn't get a pint out of you if they cut your throat, you know that."

"Ah, ah ah, out of you, you mean."

"Me, I'm a red-blooded American boy."

"The carpenter has it made," Oliver said. "He sells it Mondays—then Tuesdays his old lady comes down and gets it back."

"So?"

Winston gripped John and the carpenter: "Dr. Bastard goes for the black ones, you ever notice that? Johnny, you ever see him turn a black one down? What is he, a comminist?"

"Ah ah ah," the carpenter said.

"So maybe your old lady's half-full of the dark stuff now, you ever think of that?"

"Easy boy, Winnie," Oliver's calm voice said. "You're liable to lose that blood without getting paid for it."

But now small noises were made inside the bank— a thud, a word or grunt, the squeal of sliding furniture, a peevish laugh, a politic one—the line tensed forward to interpret them:

"Dr. Bastard must be knocking off a piece."

"They're finishing Winnie's coffin up."

"They're playing darts with our needles, men."

Here a blind was raised. They blinked, surprised to find that the sun was out, it lit up Marie's bright smile for them. She waved her fingers pluckily. Some smiled but no one waved at her, for she was too pink, too plump, too newly starched. Under present circumstances they would have preferred one of the little hairy ones. When a draft carried Winston's stinking smoke to them, they were glad at the chance to flail their arms and cough and curse. Why doesn't somebody pee on it, we'll use Winston's ass to plug it up, ah ah ah, there goes the lock.

"Hey, Marie. Marie! Is Dr. Bastard our doctor today?"

Marie nodded her head, but reprovingly. "You boys know the rules, just six at a time," she said.

Dr. Baxter did not look at them. He sat on the edge of his desk, his long thin legs crossed and braided intricately, his long thin fingers shuffling papers which his deep-set eyes seemed not to read. When Marie motioned to Oliver, Oliver glided forward to the doctor's desk. The deep grey eyes swept intimately over him, like smoke, the slender head jerked almost imperceptibly. "Thank you, doctor," Oliver said, but Dr. Baxter seemed not to hear. He waited for Marie to lead Oliver out.

The eyes had withdrawn again. The rustling papers seemed to converse with the little sounds of Winston's nervousness, the gaspish breaths, the twitching lids, the clenching and unclenching fists. Winston was sickened by what he heard: he looked wildly to John, for help.

"Winston," Dr. Baxter said in soft grieving voice, "do you remember what I said to you last week?"

"Doctor?"

"I said I did not want to see you here again."

"Doctor!"

"I want you to go home now, Winston, please."

"Doctor, you didn't even look at me!"

"Nor am I going to look at you."

"Doctor, doctor. . . ."

The doctor prepared to rise, and all stood watching him untwine his legs like sometimes useful things. Winston jerked forward now. "Dr. Bastard, Dr. Bastard!" he cried, grasping Dr. Baxter's arm.

Dr. Baxter shrugged Winston off, quickly closed a door on him. Winston stood shaking in front of it. John and the carpenter tried to hold onto the jerking arms, but just now Winston was too strong for them. "You've got to help me, you bastards," he cried. "Johnny, what will you do for me? What will you do?"

"Maybe we can get Marie to take a little from the rest of us."

"Sure, just two ounces apiece from eight of us."

They turned to the opening door.

"Ask her, Johnny. Ask Marie!"

But Marie came out shaking her pretty head. "Don't bother to ask," she said.

Winston tore loose, stepped toward Marie. "Marie! Johnny!" he cried, turning back to him. "What will you do for me?"

John did not answer him. He watched Dr. Baxter in the doorway now, watched Winston jerk to the quiet voice. "Winston, I thought I asked you to get out of here?"

Turning, Winston glared at the boys, nodding his head, jerking his jaw at them. He moved to the door in this convulsive way. He looked hard at the boys as he went out, but instantly was in again to point a finger at the watching doctor across the room.

"You!" he cried, and the door slammed closed.

When Dr. Baxter was seated on his desk again, tightly screwed, he laughed, and Marie called out to John. John pinched his cheeks. Stepping smartly to the desk he fixed his eyes on the mournful face, willing, look at me, Dr. Bastard, look at me. But Dr. Baxter stubbornly spared himself. "John," he said softly, "I thought we agreed you would skip a week."

"Next week, doctor. You remember, I get my check next week." He felt the eyes sweep lightly over him, now briskly back and forth across his cheeks, while he stared back horrified. "*Doctor!*"

Looking away, the doctor almost laughed again. "Marie."

"Thank you, doctor," John said, following Marie out of the room. He paused at the foot of Oliver's bed. Oliver nodded at his bottle, already half-full, and smirking he winked at John. "I'll wait for you."

"Do."

Removing his jacket, John stepped into his cubicle and lay down on his clean bed. He smiled at Marie when she came in. Her fingers were warm as she puckered him. "You better stay home next week, you heard what the doctor said."

"Don't worry, Marie."

"Eat lots of red meat."

"Yes, nurse," John said.

As soon as she had gone, he opened his eyes. He fired up his cigarette and lay deeply inhaling it, watching his bottle fill. He was glad that Oliver would wait for him; he would need Oliver's steadiness on the long walk to the grocery store, and he knew Winston would be out there reviling them. He did not blame Winston at all. Yet he did not allow himself to brood long on tomorrow's uncertainties, but centered all his failing attention on the warm, smug feeling of the man who knows that for today at least he still has it, made.

►► **Yasar Kemal**

The Baby

He was walking so fast that the dust whirled up to his waist. The sun beat down on him dulling his senses. Now and again he reeled from side to side. The dust, hot as embers, penetrated his torn shoes and burned his feet.

Ismail was murmuring indistinctly all the while. In his arms was a baby wrapped in a multicolored sash. The baby's head lay unsupported over Ismail's right arm. Its face was flushed, red as raw liver, and covered with a layer of dust. Its eyes were closed, its little neck so thin.

The dust whirling up to his waist, Ismail kept on walking and muttering. The sweat had soaked through his striped shirt, turning into mud the dust that clung to it.

Everywhere in the fields along the road people were carrying sheaves to the threshing floor while harvesting machines filled the air with their noise.

Ismail swerved off the road into a field where a group of men and women were binding sheaves of wheat. He put the baby on the damp earth under a cart. Nearby a yellow dog was dozing, his tongue lolling out. Ismail climbed onto the cart, took a dipper of water from the barrel, and drank thirstily. He poured the rest over his bare hairy chest.

He sat down leaning against the wheel and stretched his legs. His big toe protruded from the torn shoe. The skin underneath was cracked and the nail long and jagged.

A woman with a pointed chin walked over to the cart for a drink. When she saw Ismail her expression changed. Her large dark eyes widened.

"Why, Ismail, brother, what brings you here?"

Her glance fell to the baby under the cart.

"Alas," she said, "alas, poor Zala. Alas, my dark-eyed one."

She bent down and took the child in her arms.

"Its neck has weakened," she said. "He won't live, brother. Alas, Zala, my dark-eyed Zala. There was no one like her."

She thrust her breast into the baby's mouth. The baby took it.

"Look, Ismail, brother! The child wants the breast, he's hungry. That's why he's so weak, the heat has sucked him dry. Let me get Hürü. She'll suckle him. Her breasts are full. What with her baby at home, she's been spilling her milk uselessly on to the ground since this morning."

She pulled her breast from the child's mouth.

"He won't let go, even though it's dry. Hey there, Hürü! Hürü, my girl, come here! Hurry!"

Hürü left the group of laborers.

"Look Hürü! Zala's child. Come here and suckle it."

Hürü took the child and turned her back to them.

"It's his luck, poor mite," she said. "My breasts were so swollen I just couldn't stand it any longer. There I was, just about to spill my milk on to the ground. It's his luck."

"There was no one like Zala," said the woman with the pointed chin. "No one like her. When we were girls we used to go hoeing together. She had a gay smiling face. And her hair! It was so thick and long. Black, almost purple. There was one thing though: she just couldn't go barefoot. When she could find nothing else, she would tie some rags round her feet. She just couldn't go barefoot . . ."

Hürü took the child from her breast. Its eyes were closed, and only its chin moved. There was milk smeared around its mouth.

"And I was just about to spill my milk on to the ground." She sighed. "Poor Zala! Who would have thought her child would be left like this among strangers?"

"Brother," asked the woman with the pointed chin, "how did Zala die?"

Some of the women, who had seen the baby in Hürü's arms, came toward the cart.

"What," cried Mother Hava, whose white hair hung out from her torn kerchief, "is it Zala's baby? Alas, poor Zala!" Her eyes filled with tears. "Alas, my dark-eyed Zala! My luckless child! How can it be she's dead, my poor girl? How did she die?"

"How did she die, Ismail?" asked Black Elif, a short hollow-cheeked querulous woman. "What did you do to her?"

Ismail kept murmuring indistinctly. His head was bent. Suddenly he got up, brushed his back with his hand, and took the child from Hürü.

"She died," he answered sharply. "I took her to the doctor, but she died. He gave her injections, but she died."

He walked away quickly. A large, torn, black *shalvar* swung about his long legs, his white drawers showing through the torn parts.

The women were left there staring after him.

Mother Hava's shriveled lips moved softly.

"How he grieves! The poor boy, you see his grief. . . . He's crying tears of blood. He couldn't look us in the face. As if it was he who killed her."

"Oh woman, for goodness sake," the hollow-cheeked woman began querulously, "he never looked after her properly, say he be struck down, damn him. Let him wander about with the child in his arms like this—through village after village. Let him! He didn't take her to the doctor, not for twenty days. They say the placenta didn't come out. Oh, I don't know, they say it stayed inside and rotted there. Was there anybody like Zala? Why if Big Emine hadn't died, would she have given her daughter to that Ismail who came from God knows where?"

"He's left to the mercy of strangers, the poor man," said Hürü. "He's a good plucky man, Ismail, he never did anybody any harm."

"Do you think he'll be able to find someone to look after the child?" asked Mother Hava.

"Who?" answered the woman with the pointed chin. "People can't even look after their own children. See Hürü here, she's had to leave her pretty child at home, where it whines all day long like a hungry animal while she spills her milk uselessly on the ground here. No, Hürü's child is in a bad way. She comes home in the evening . . . her milk like blood. . . ."

Hürü got up.

"Do you think I come here of my own free will?" she cried. "This cursed poverty! Do you think I enjoy coming here? We'd all go hungry if I didn't. We'd be left to the charity of strangers. It isn't as if you didn't know this, sister. . . . If I could help it . . ."

"It's hard," said Mother Hava. "To depend on charity is worse than death."

"And the old woman," continued the woman with the pointed chin, "she's blind. How does she look after your child? Isn't it true, Hürü my girl? She can't see. . . ."

"She adores the child. She hovers about it like a bird. You know, children never cry with her. If a child has been crying its eyes out and won't stop, just take him to her, it'll calm down immediately. She has such a way of singing lullabies . . ."

"That's true," said Black Elif, "but suppose the child's face is covered with flies, that he's been eaten by them? It has to cry or she won't know. What can she do, poor woman? She loves children but she's blind. They say that more often than not, she thrusts the milk bottle into the child's eye thinking it's his mouth."

She looked after Ismail.

"Where is Ismail going?" she wondered. "Where is he taking the child? Who will look after it? With all this work now, people can't look after their own children."

"There's his uncle," said Mother Hava. "His family will take care of it."

The woman with the pointed chin was making her way toward the laborers.

"Huh," she cried turning round, "and where's the woman to look after him there? God forbid that a baby live on after its mother!"

"Oh my God," said Mother Hava, "why didn't it die when its mother died? Why did you let it live after its mother, my God? Did you need this orphan to help fill the world? Alas, Zala. . . . And everyone busy in the fields. . . . What can Ismail do?"

The sun was high in the sky. Clouds of dust rose in the air. Farther away, near the village, a thin wisp of smoke rose toward the sky. The wheat stumps in the fields sparkled. The huge plain was ablaze, gleaming like a burnished tin plate under the sun.

The shining metal of a harvesting machine flashed nearby, dazzling Ismail. His eyes were burning with sweat. He saw a mulberry tree, white with dust, on one side of the road, and walked toward it. The child's head was hanging down over his arm, stretching its limp emaciated neck.

He set the child under the tree. He took off his shirt and wrung it out, laying it on a blackberry bush indistinct under the dust. Mud patches had formed on his *shalvar*. He shook them off.

The child was whining. Black flies were swarming over its face and eyes. With a swift motion, Ismail waved them away, but the child did not stop whining. Ismail rocked it softly to and fro.

"Hush, little one," he said. "Hush, hush-a-by."

The whining did not stop.

He snatched up the wet shirt from the bush, put it on quickly, and strode away. The dust whirled about him in a cloud up to his waist. The child's head was hanging down. It was crying continually, almost moaning, in a thin small voice.

A truck passed by them, raising dust over the whole road. When Ismail emerged from the cloud of dust, a pungent smell of swamps came to his nostrils. On his right a green rice paddy stretched to the village. The huge field was steaming under the burning sun. The ditch near the road was filled with stagnant water covered with a creamy film of dust.

On the edge of the rice paddy stood an old field hand, white-bearded and bent, an *aba* thrown over his shoulders and a hoe in his hands. The drops of perspiration on his face were visible from a distance. Ismail passed him quickly, bending his head toward the child, staring at it.

"Hey there, traveler," said the old laborer. "The child's head is hanging down."

Ismail did not hear him. His head bent, he strode on.

"God protect us," muttered the old laborer to himself. "Curse this misery. It's hard . . ."

Ismail entered the village without slowing his pace. The narrow dusty lanes were covered with huge dung heaps piled on top of each other. All around the dung-plastered earth huts, flocks of open-beaked hens, tongues sticking out, wings drooping, were wriggling in the dust. A few dogs with long red tongues lolling out were asleep. There was not a single tree in the village. Near the ditches, so smothered in dust it was impossible to distinguish them as trees, were some young elms. So small, they were bushes rather than trees.

Ismail's uncle's house was in the middle of the village: a hut made of reeds and covered with grass. Its right wall had caved in. Hens and dogs were lying under an old cart near the door, its paint peeled off and its wheels rusted. A duck was waddling about leading its brood.

The door was open. A large woman sat on the threshold fast asleep, her legs drawn up to her belly, her head resting on the doorjamb.

Ismail stood before the door, his head still inclined toward the baby, his face desolate. The child was crying. The woman slowly lifted her head, and a swarm of flies flew off. She rubbed her eyes. She did not recognize Ismail.

"What's that?" she said in a soft voice. "Why don't you come in? Don't stay there in the sun."

Ismail did not hear her. He just stood there, his head bent over the child. His shadow fell on the gray dust and the dung in front of the door: a dark shadow half the size of a man.

The woman got up, wide awake now.

"Why Ismail, my child, is it you?" she cried.

She took the child from him. Ismail still did not move. The child still cried.

"Hush, little one. Hush, don't cry. Ismail, come on in. You're boiling in the sun. It's sweltering out there. Come, come. Oh my poor unfortunate one!"

She laid the baby on a ragged mat. Then she turned to Ismail.

"Ismail, my son," she said, touching his arm, "I implore you, come in. You're drenched in sweat. Drenched."

Ismail was staring at her with glassy eyes.

He went in and sank down as if all the strength had left his knees.

The woman looked at Ismail.

"My child," she said, "don't torment yourself so.

Life is like this. You can't die with the dead. Zala was a good wife, but what can you do? Pull yourself together. You can't die with the dead. Where is the man who doesn't lose his wife, the wife who doesn't lose her husband? One in a thousand, my child. Stop tormenting yourself. Do you know what a state you're in? Have you any idea what you look like? You can't change what is. You must bear it. You must think of yourself now. We heard about you, and your uncle was so anxious. They said, he takes the baby in his arms, Ismail, and sings to him all the time. . . . Like one possessed he keeps singing lullabies. Your uncle was worried. Night and day, they told us, with the child in his arms, Ismail sits there singing to him. Don't do this, my son, don't do this to yourself."

Ismail's long face had become longer, darker. His eyes seemed to have turned in their sockets. He was sitting on the damp dirt floor near the shelves of dishes, his back leaning on the brush wall.

"Aunt," he said, "dear Aunt . . . he's killing me. Make him stop crying. Do something."

Old Jennet took the child in her arms. Jennet's hair was all white with a yellow strand here and there. She had small twinkling eyes. Her chin was large and strong and gave a masculine look to her face. Her slender bent waist was encircled with a worn-out sash who knows how many years old.

"Hush, little one, hush poor orphan. Hush my hapless one, hush-a-by . . ."

She walked up and down rocking the baby in her arms.

"Hush, my hapless one. Hush-a-by, my orphan, hush-a-by."

The child cried as if it had been wound up.

"They say, Ismail, that you didn't look after Zala properly. They say she died through want of proper care. They say you took her to the fields, heavy as she was with child, up to the last day. And when the pains started you threw her into a stable, with no one to assist her, to do something. All alone you left her. That's what they're saying about you, may they be punished for their gossiping lies."

A shadow fell across the door. It was Dondu, a young girl with narrow shoulders and large plump hips outlined under her black *shalvar*. Below her thick matted brows and lashes, her eyes were huge and the shadows of her lashes fell on her dimpled face. There was always a smile on her lips, showing her white teeth.

She took the baby from Old Jennet and turned her back to them. Baring her breast, she put it in the child's mouth, and he stopped crying.

Outside, two naked children stood near the door. Each held a knife in one hand and a branch in the other. Their bellies were large and swollen, their little necks thin as sticks. They were coated all over with dried cracked mud.

One of the children stuck his head in through the doorway and drew it back quickly.

"Hist," he said, "if you saw!"

He lifted his middle finger.

"Its neck is that thin. That thin!"

The other child also stuck his head in and looked.

"It's really that thin . . . thin as a straw. Little sister Dondu is suckling it."

"She's not really suckling it. She's just doing it to make it stop crying. Girls don't have milk. Not unmarried girls who don't go with a man. My mother says so. She's just making believe."

"Well, even if it is make-believe. . . . Who cares? The baby's not crying. It's suckling, isn't it?"

They walked away whittling their branches with their knives.

"That's what they're saying about you, Ismail. They say you locked her up in there with the child, and not a soul to give them even a drink of water, while you went to the fields. Ah Ismail, you know how tongues wag and distort everything. If one won't believe this, a thousand will. A man's mouth is not a sack you can shut by pulling a string. Why, they're just ready to tear you to pieces the minute you have troubles. They say that in that dark room the sick woman would take up her child in her arms and turn and turn around stark naked, like a mad person. May they be punished for their gossiping tongues! They say she became mad with grief, Zala. . . . Ah Ismail, ah, my child . . .'"

Ismail, who had seemed not to be listening to all this, suddenly sat up.

"Aunt," he said, "dear Aunt, for heaven's sake . . ." His voice was pleading but angry. "For God's sake Aunt. . . . Do you think I'd ever hurt Zala's little finger? She was the mainstay of my house. The mainstay. Ask me what happened! Ask me what I feel! Let them talk. You ask my heart. It's burning me inside like a live coal. How can I stop grieving for Zala, ever? Of what use am I now Zala's gone? Can I ever find another one like her even if I walk the whole world over? Can I? Ask me how I feel!"

Jennet's eyes filled with tears.

"There was no one like Zala," she said. "Never anyone like her in this world."

Ismail's voice seemed to come not from him, but from the wall, the floor, some other place. His eyes were half closed and strange.

"Aunt," he said, "you must believe me. It wasn't my fault. 'Woman,' I said, 'Zala, your time's drawing near . . . stop working in the field now. I'll work by myself,' I said to her, 'I'll do the threshing. Anyway there's so little left to be done. So little left!' She wouldn't listen to me. 'I've been waiting and waiting for this day,' she said. 'To be free to work for myself and not for strangers. I'll work till I drop dead, till my bones break. It is only this year,' she said to me, 'that you're not a field hand any more. How many years I have been waiting for this. . . . Isn't it better to work another's field as a partner than as a field hand? Even if half the crop is another's, the other half's mine.' Nothing I said would make her stay at home. She was already heavy, her belly was huge. It made my heart bleed to see her work. 'Zala,' I said to her, 'don't, don't do this.' But she persisted. 'This is what I've always wanted. How many times have I not said to myself, will I ever see the day when I'll work on my own and not for others? How many years have I toiled miserably in the houses of strangers?' She put all her heart and soul into her work. 'This is what I've been waiting for,' she kept saying. 'My father was a field hand, my mother a servant, and they died without seeing anything better. I'm not going to be like them.' Like one possessed, she kept repeating. 'This is what I've been waiting for.'

"That day, it was so torrid, Aunt, the birds just dropped, crack, from the skies, their tongues out. We were carrying our wheat to the threshing floor. The sun was high in the sky, boring into our heads like a nail and Zala was carrying a huge stack on her back. Two men would have been barely able to lift it. 'Woman,' I said, 'don't load yourself so.' But her eyes filled. 'This is what I've been waiting for.'

"Suddenly halfway to the threshing floor, she threw down the stack. 'What's the matter?' I asked. 'The pain,' she replied, 'it's getting worse. This morning it wasn't so bad, but now it's getting sharper. Like a knife. It's killing me. I'm going home. You mind your work. Don't stop! We mustn't let the ants get a share of our crop. This is a chance in a million. . . . To be working for ourselves . . . our own crop . . .' She turned toward the village, holding her belly with her hands. But after a few steps, she dropped down. I rushed to her side. 'You go right back,' she cried, 'do you want the ants to eat up our crop? I'll go by myself.' She got up and walked away.

"When I came home in the evening, she was lying down, and by her side, wrapped up in old rags and laid in a sieve, was the baby. She had cut the cord herself with a pair of blunt scissors. There wasn't a woman to assist her at the farm. She had washed the child all by herself, put salt over him, and laid him there.

"Well, Aunt, there they were, the *Agha* on one side, Zala on the other, biting my head off. 'Do you want the birds and ants to get our crop?' they cried. The *Agha* became angry and started shouting at me. Zala kept repeating, 'We've been lucky enough to get this chance, a chance in a million, to have a crop of our own. Don't leave it to rot there because of me. I'll look after myself.' She harried me so. There was nothing I could do about it. I had to go to work, leaving her there all by herself. I couldn't help it."

Old Jennet sighed quietly, a deep, deep sigh.

"All her life she worked for others. An orphan, miserable. . . . To have something of her own seemed to her something sweeter than life. She didn't live to see it. Alas, my poor Zala, she didn't live."

Ismail continued unheeding.

"She had been in bed for a week without being able to get up," when I said to her, 'Zala, you can't go on like this. You'll never get well this way. You'll die here without food or water in this empty place.' Her face was like wax, all yellow and drawn. Her bones jutted out. 'I'll wait by your side and look after you,' I said. 'And if you're not better I'll take you to the doctor. What do I care about the crop, what do I care about anything when you're like this.' She began to cry, begging me to go on with the work. 'I'll be all right in the morning, you'll see,' she said. And she sent me back to the field. She stayed in Zeki Agha's stable in the dark. All alone, nobody to bring food or water, in a wretched state. . . . If it weren't for the *Agha*, I would have got the better of her, but the *Agha*, curse him, was pressing me. 'I took you into partnership,' he would say, 'when you were a common hireling. You've no right to let my crop rot there in the fields.' In the evening I'd come home. 'Zala,' I'd beg her, 'you're not well. Let me stay beside you. Or let's go to the doctor.' And every time, she'd swear to God she was better. 'Today I feel a little better,' she would say. 'In the morning I'll get straight out of bed.' I'd come back in the evening and find her still lying there. And twenty days passed in this way. Zala had grown paper thin. Her eyes had sunk in their sockets. She was just skin and bones. . . . There was not so much work left now. But I had had enough. I couldn't bear it any more. I saw I was losing Zala, I was losing her . . ."

His lips began to tremble, but his voice hardened. It was under control now, strong and firm, no longer a murmur.

"I went and planted myself before the *Agha*. 'Agha,' I said, 'my wife is dying. I must take her to the doctor.' The *Agha* laughed. 'Ismail,' he said, 'don't you know our women? They lie and lie in bed, sick beyond hope you would think, but they always get up in the end. They don't need doctors. They're tempered in steel, they are. What are you worrying about? You go on with your work.' 'No,' I said, 'Agha, whatever I have let it be yours, yours as your mother's milk. My cotton, my sesame, my wheat, I give it to you freely. Let it be yours . . . but get me twenty-five liras.' He yielded finally and gave me the money. I got a cart and took her to the doctor, but he wasn't there, he had gone away on holiday. I searched the town from end to end. Finally I found a health officer, one of those who give quinine injections. He came out and looked at Zala, who seemed to be drawing her last breath.

"He leaned over to my ear. 'But she's done for,' he whispered. 'Let her be.' I said, 'It had to happen. You give her an injection.' 'I can't give an injection to one at the point of death,' he said. 'What's the use?' I put the money before him. 'Here,' I said, 'is your money. Give her the injection. I'm paying you, aren't I? You'd give an injection to this tree, to my horses if I paid you to. What is it to you? Is it your business? Give her this injection, brother,' I said, 'so that my conscience be at rest, so that people should not cover me with curses, so that friend and foe should see.' He was a good man and gave her an injection. I made him give another one. 'Give her another one, brother, I owe such a lot to Zala . . .' He gave it to her. Her skin was stuck to her bones, just skin and bones, Aunt. . . . That's what Zala had become. . . . You wouldn't believe it. If you'd seen her with your own eyes, you'd have said, 'This isn't Zala.'

"It was midday when I hitched the horses to the cart. The world was crackling in the heat as we started for home. If she's to die, I thought, let it be at the farm. It was so hot, so unbearably hot. The huge plain, the whole world was ablaze. We had hardly traveled halfway home when Zala sat up erect all of a sudden. She was going to say something, but she couldn't say it. Her head fell back. I heard her murmur, 'A chance in a million. . . . My child . . .' softly, so low I could hardly hear."

"A chance in a million she had, poor thing, to work on her own," said Old Jennet. "But fate . . . alas, alas, Zala! . . ."

"Her eyes turned," Ismail continued. "There was no sound, no breath. The child was in her arms. The sun was drilling into my head. I felt strange all of a sudden. . . . Then everything went black. When I came to myself, I was lying on the ground covered with dust, aching all over. Not a trace of the cart or the horses. . . . I started up and raced along the red-hot road. I thought if the horses have upset the cart into a stream. . . . Alive, all she ever had was misery and toil. Dead, I thought, let her body not be disgraced. The child, I thought, must not fall prey to birds and worms. If it must die . . . and it will. Can a baby live without its mother? Why, it's difficult enough to keep a baby alive even when it has its mother.

"As I ran, I looked about me to see if the child had not fallen somewhere along the road.

"I ran and ran. And then I saw a crowd gathered in the center of the village. What village? I still don't know which one. Just a village. . . . Such a crowd, throw a pin down and it wouldn't fall to the ground. I heard the word 'dead' and broke through the crowd. The cart was in the center. The child was still in Zala's arms, its face covered with dust . . . its eyes closed. The women were weeping.

"I climbed into the cart and drove away. They didn't ask me 'who are you, what is the dead woman to you.' They didn't ask me 'where are you going.' Not a word passed their lips. They just stood petrified, staring after me.

"I was left with the child. . . . It was harvest time, everybody was busy. I took the child to a nearby village where there was a woman called the Yellow-haired Girl, who had milk. I left the baby with her and went back home. Two days later they brought it back to me. The woman had refused to suckle it. 'I have hardly enough milk for my own child,' she had said. 'I can't kill my own child to feed a stranger's.' There isn't a nursing mother in the whole neighborhood that I didn't go to. Whomever I gave it to dumped it back into my arms. With all the work in the fields, there I was bound hand to foot. It doesn't take the bottle, it doesn't get milk any other way, it doesn't die and put an end to his agony. It's a wonder it doesn't die. On one side a child whining all the time like a hungry kitten, on the other the crops. I'm at my wit's end."

Ismail stood up. He was so tall his head touched the grass roof of the hut. He swayed and sank down again.

"So you see how it is," he said. "You are another mother to him. Help me! With all this work . . . I'm at a loss."

Old Jennet, her head bowed, sat motionless. After a while she slowly lifted her head.

"Ismail," she said, "this was a chance in a million to work for yourselves at last. She didn't live to see this day. That's what Zala wanted to say, isn't it, Ismail? 'Take care of my child' is what she was going to say . . ."

"She kept repeating it all the time," said Ismail.

"A chance in a million, a chance in a million. She was so happy that at last we would be free from working for others. She was mad with joy but she didn't live to see it. She couldn't bear to work as a servant, as a hireling, it killed her. And all her life was spent in drudgery. She didn't live to see anything better. You're another mother for this orphan. Do what you think best."

The young girl Dondu walked toward Jennet without taking her breast from the child's mouth. Her face was flushed like the flame of a live coal.

"Aunt Jennet," she said bending to her ear, "when the baby's sucking I feel all strange, pleasant. . . . I feel pleasant things down my back. I wish it would suck like this all day, I wish there were ten babies to suck like this. It's so pleasant . . ."

"Don't be silly," said Jennet. "It does that to all of us."

Toward evening Ismail's uncle came home. He was a large, hulking man. Bits of straw, husks of wheat, and dust clung to his sunburned face.

"Ismail!" he said. "They say, Ismail, that you take the child in your arms and rock him night and day. They say you've lost your mind."

The baby was lying on a blanket by the prop in the center of the hut. It was crying.

His wife made signs to him from behind and the old man checked himself.

"So that's how it is, Ismail? We heard what happened and our hearts bled for you."

"Man," said Jennet, "send for Musdulu. Let him come. His wife is suckling now. So is Emine, the lame woman. There's Hürü too, but she can't look after her own child, poor thing. Musdulu's wife has plenty of milk, and she's clean. Send somebody to Musdulu. His wife told me that if Musdulu agrees she'll suckle it."

A little later Musdulu arrived with the boy sent to fetch him. He was a short man. The large red kerchief tied over the collar of his navy-blue jacket caught the eye. He wore a new cap over his carefully combed hair. His *shalvar* also was new. On his feet, he had yellow shoes from Adana with the back folded down.

The uncle took Musdulu by the hand and made him sit down beside him.

"My son," he said, "my good Musdulu." He pointed to the baby crying on the ground beside the prop. "You see . . . God protect us all. Man is a creature of many woes, but if he were not in need, God wouldn't reach out to help him. Your wife has plenty of milk. Ismail will spare nothing. He will give unstintingly. Two instead of one, what do you say? A good deed is never lost. Do a good deed and throw it into the ocean, if the fish don't know it, God will. Do a good deed . . . God will know."

Musdulu's head was bowed, his thin lips pursed tightly. He was silent.

"My son," said Ismail's uncle again, "you know it's harvest time. No one at home. No woman, no children . . . that's Ismail's situation. Just imagine it: it would melt a heart of stone. . . . He's all alone, poor man. He's had a chance in a million to work on his own. He mustn't lose this chance because of the child. What do you say, Musdulu? Don't you have something to say, my son?"

Musdulu hadn't moved. He just sat very still, his head bowed.

"It isn't every day one has a chance to do a good deed," insisted the uncle. "You can be sure God will bless you for it. You'll be opening the gates of Paradise for yourself. If your wife doesn't give it milk, this child will die. It's a life you'll be saving. Thanks to you, he'll live. Look how it cries, poor mite . . . can a man's heart be deaf to it?"

Musdulu rose up and walked to the door. One foot over the threshold, he turned.

"Uncle," he burst out, "what made you take Musdulu's wife for a servant? My wife is not a servant!"

He went out in a fury.

Ismail sprang to the door, his hands stretched toward Musdulu.

"Brother," he cried, "brother, don't! It's wicked."

His uncle clutched his arm.

"Man," he said, "don't go begging this son of a bitch. Not even for your life you mustn't. Why, you're like a woman. What's come over you? Let it die, man." He pointed to his wife. "This woman has buried sixteen children. Not babies like this one, but healthy, fine babies."

"My child," said Old Jennet, "you're not yourself. A baby . . . not a month old! You'll marry. God will give you others. If it has to die, let it die. Sixteen I've given to this hard earth. How did I bear it? My hearth was barren. You'll marry again. God will give you others. Don't worry so, my child. You'll make yourself ill. With all the harvest work . . . you'll kill yourself."

Ismail's face was white. Old Jennet's expression changed as she looked at him.

"Wait a minute," she said, thinking aloud, "wait a minute. Emine the lame woman, one . . . Hürü, two . . . Emine, one . . . Hürü. . . . There just isn't anyone else." She kept muttering to herself. "But Emine's milk is poisoned. . . . Not one of her children ever lived. Why, as far back as I can remember she's been bearing children. She's like me, she can't keep them. Each year she bears one and each year it dies before it's a month old. She herself doesn't know how many children she's borne up to now. How can I give her the child? As for Hürü, she's over head and ears in her own troubles. She can't take care of her own child, he's sick with diarrhea after sucking and sucking his mother's hot milk. He's left to the blind woman. . . . Blind! How can she look after the child? It's his mother he needs."

"Woman," said the uncle impatiently, "what are you sitting there muttering about? Poisoned or not, there isn't anyone but this lame woman. . . . Let's give the child to her."

"Man," protested his wife, "it would be nothing better than killing it on the spot. You can't do that . . . in cold blood . . ."

Ismail broke in:

"Aunt," he said in a harsh voice, "if she'll take it, let's give it to her. Let it not die of hunger at least. Let people not cover me with their curses. . . . If it's going to die anyway, let it be like that. Look what a state he's in. Everybody's child dies. It will die, let it die . . ."

They sent for the lame woman. She came hobbling along, up down, up down, trailing her lame leg behind her. She was short and her body heaved to one side. It was a wonder she just didn't topple over. She wore a faded black *shalvar*, so old if one thread was pulled from it, it would certainly fall to pieces. The *shalvar*, loosely tied at the waist, hung down on the lame side and would have slipped down her legs if her large hips had not held it up. She was covered with dust and flour, and pieces of dough were stuck to her. Her black wrinkled breasts hung out of her torn blouse down to her belly. Her head was another sight: the eyes were hidden beneath a mop of wavy dirty hair, and huge moles sprouted all over her black wrinkled face.

She planted herself before the uncle.

"Veli Agha," she said, "you sent for me. Here I am."

"My daughter," said the old man, "you see this child: I sent for you to look after it. Ismail will do anything you want. He'll give to your heart's content. To your heart's content. It's a life you'll be saving, which is no little deed. God will love you all the more for it. On top of that you'll get your due, and more. What do you say, my daughter?"

Ismail broke in:

"Sister," he said pleadingly, "my sister Emine, whatever you want I'll give to you. Even if you ask me for bird's milk I'll find it for you."

Emine's face had become even more shriveled and dark.

"Veli Agha," she said, "my milk's not enough for my own child. Do I ever eat properly to have milk! . . ."

Ismail straightened.

"Look," he said, "my own sister Emine. Even if it's bird's milk you want, I'll find it for you. What do you say? Come on say yes."

"What can I say, brother," answered Emine. "When my man comes home this evening we'll see."

And without giving any milk to the baby crying on the ground, she turned and left.

The young girl Dondu came running in. She took up the child and, turning her back to them, she gave it the breast. The crying stopped.

"This mother of mine," she complained, "she won't let me go out. She just invents work for me out of nothing! This mother of mine . . ."

The croaking of frogs filled the night. The west wind, which had risen in the afternoon, had dropped now. There was not a breath of air. The air smelled of swamps and of fresh cow dung. It was sticky, but the sky was full of huge shining stars.

Farther away on the edge of a meadow stood a tall plane tree. At night, white storks settled on its branches. Rows and rows of white storks. The clatter of their beaks could be heard from time to time.

In front of the uncle's house a trellis was set on poles, the height of a man. Cows were lying under the trellis and all about it chewing cud.

On the right side of it, near Old Jennet, lay the baby, crying ceaselessly. Old Jennet was rocking the cradle and, with the cradle, the whole trellis shook on its poles. Uncle Veli, who had gone to sleep long ago, was snoring. After a while the rocking cradle was still. Old Jennet, too, must have fallen asleep. Mosquitoes were all over infesting the air.

It was long past midnight. The baby was crying again. Ismail kept turning convulsively from one side to the other, tossing on his mattress until the whole trellis shook.

"Aunt," he whispered at last, almost inaudibly. "Aunt Jennet!"

"Aunt," he said, "take him to that lame woman. He's killing me. He doesn't stop crying. He won't stop. He's killing me. Take him, take him."

The old woman got up rubbing her eyes. She took the child from its cradle.

All the women in the village were talking of Emine, the lame woman, and Ismail's baby. In the fields, in the streets, grazing their animals, weaving at their looms, whenever two women got together, they could speak of nothing else.

A group of women was gathered at Black Elif's door. They were twirling their hand spindles as they talked.

"Eh, my dear, this is what I call luck. Did you ever see the like of it? Zala's death was a boon for that sluttish Emine."

"Why, my dear, if at least she would look after the child, it wouldn't be so bad. It lies there whining like an abandoned puppy all day long. And she sits there like a lady stuffing herself with all the food Ismail brings. Why, he has emptied the market of sugar, of butter, the fool, and filled her home with goods. That lame woman's house has turned into a real shop."

"Eh, a real shop! . . ."

"The lame woman's house . . ."

"If at least she took care of the child . . ."

"I can't bear to pass her door. All day long, it cries and cries, the poor mite. . . . It breaks my heart. Like a little puppy, it whines . . ."

"Poor innocent babe . . . It breaks your heart!"

"If you saw Ismail! What a state he's in!"

"It breaks your heart."

"He's all pale and thin, poor man."

"It breaks your heart!"

"All he has, even the shirt on his back, will be swallowed by that lame woman. He'll soon find himself a field hand again, drudging like a dog."

"Like a dog!"

"That child's in a bad way."

"It'll die . . ."

"Why, rather than give it to the lame woman, he'd much better have left it under a tree!"

"To be carried away by the eagles!"

"Much better have thrown it into the river!"

"Buried it alive straight away . . ."

"Yes, my dear!"

"Every other day, Ismail comes with a sack on his back . . ."

"For the woman to eat, he says, for her to have more milk . . ."

"He sits by the cradle, his head bowed, staring at the child. Like a statue. He doesn't speak. He just sits there looking at it from the moment he comes till the moment he leaves, like a statue . . ."

"He just sits and stares at it . . ."

"His own flesh and blood . . ."

"He's heartbroken, poor man."

"Heartbroken . . ."

"Motherless . . ."

"How can a baby live without its mother?"

"Poor Ismail, all these efforts in vain!"

"Her milk's poisoned."

"If her own children lived, it would live too."

"It won't live . . ."

Ten days later after she had taken the child, Emine roused the whole village with her laments.

"Aaah, women," she screeched to whoever would listen to her, "I never saw such a thing. They've dumped that child on me. It never has its fill of milk, it's always hungry for more. I said I'd suckle it, but it's my own child who's getting the worse of it. He's got diarrhea now. Like water it's coming out. He'll die, my Duran. At least this one will live, I had said. And now because of the other one, he'll die. I'll take it and dump it right back on them, I will. Let him keep his gifts. What does he bring anyway? Here I am killing my own child, and he gives me two pounds of sugar. Two pounds of sugar in ten days! Yes, my dear, two pounds of sugar . . ."

"Take it back to Jennet," the listening women would say. "Take it back."

After Emine had gone trailing her lame leg behind her, they would turn to each other.

"The child won't live anyway."

"Let her take it back!"

"All day it whines like an abandoned puppy."

"Let her take it back!"

"Why, Emine will kill it before its time."

"Let her take it back!"

"Did you hear, my dear? She doesn't like what he brings her! . . ."

"Eh, the more one has . . ."

"Two pounds of sugar! Why, that slut hasn't had that much sugar since she came out of her mother's womb!"

"Not since she came out of her mother's womb!"

"That lame slut . . ."

"How I pity that man! . . . It's heart-rending."

"Let her take it back!"

"Let her take it back!"

Twelve days after he had given the lame woman the child, Ismail returned, carrying on his back a sack half-filled with goods. Without stopping at his uncle's, he walked straight to Emine's house. It was a one-room hut covered with rotted grass, the color of lead, its brush wall plastered with lumps of dung. Inside there was next to nothing: three sacks piled in a corner and a worn-out mattress shedding its cotton. A calf was tied in another corner. Next to it was the cradle, a cracked old thing all black with dirt. The two children were lying in it side by side, their little fists thrust into each other's face. The place was steeped in mud and smelled of fresh dung and urine.

Under the window, hardly larger than a hand, two moss-covered pine-wood jars were oozing water continually.

Ismail stopped dead at the foot of the cradle. He looked and looked . . .

"Sister," he said, "sister Emine, what's happened to the child?"

The baby's skin was stuck to its bones, its belly had swelled, its eyes were deep in their sockets.

He could stand it no longer. He went out.

Emine shook the sugar sack.

"Look," she said, "look, Elif, my girl, what he's brought. Look! What does this damned long ass think he's doing? And he has the cheek to stand there, giving himself airs and ask what's happened to the child. My foot's happened, that's what. The devil take him! Just two pounds of sugar! And he expects me to nurse it on that!"

As she spoke, she took the things from the sack and threw them all over the place.

"It'll die, my child will die. Diarrhea! It'll die, and everybody will blame me!"

"Well, take it back then!" exclaimed Black Elif. "Why don't you give it back to him?"

"My child will die. Everybody'll say she killed her own child in order to nurse a stranger's child."

Ismail straightened up from the brush wall he had been leaning against and drew a deep long breath.

"Bitch," he said, the word hissing through his lips. "Lame bitch!"

He walked off swaying as if drunk.

Two days later Emine, shouting and cursing at the top of her voice, brought back the baby to Old Jennet.

"What will people say," she kept repeating, "if my own child dies? What will people say?"

Old Jennet sent the child back to its father.

The wheat, heaped all around the threshing floor, reached the height of a man. Ismail had started threshing long before dawn. The sun was now quarter high and the mound in the center was rising steadily. Ismail threw his fork onto the stalks. He took a long drink from the jug which stood in the shady part of the threshing floor. On the threshing machine was a young boy with a slender neck and very long eyelashes. He kept lashing with a whip at the two lean bay horses before him, and leading them rapidly around over the yet unbroken stalks. The air was filled with a rank smell of straw, of dry grass, which pricked the nostrils.

Ismail leaned over to the baby, crying in the shade of the wheat rick, and put into its mouth a raki bottle filled with milk to which he had fixed a nipple.

The child stopped crying and started to suck weakly. Ismail's right knee was on the ground. His face was covered with straw and dust, which clung especially to the long scar down his left cheek. The collar of his torn, striped shirt was open and his hairy chest showed through. He was drenched in sweat.

He took off his shirt and stretched it out over the wheat stumps, then he came back, leaning his knee on the ground, and held the bottle. He was worn out; his breath came out in gasps as through a bellows.

He called to the boy at the threshing machine.

"Mehmet, come along," he cried. "Come and eat."

Mehmet left the horses near the wheat so that they could eat too. He came and opened his bundle of food.

Ismail was eating with one hand, while he held the bottle with the other. If he so much as made a move to pull the bottle away, the baby would begin to cry immediately, and Ismail could not bear that.

Mehmet kept talking all the time as he ate.

"Uncle Ismail, let me tell you something. There was a boy in our village." He pointed to the baby. "He was just like this one. His mother had died. And everywhere the father went, he had to carry the baby with him in his arms. He was poor, you see, and no one wanted to look after the baby. And the baby was dying of hunger, crying and crying, and it was dying. My mother said so! She said it was dying in its father's arms. Now, that child, you know, they call him the Kurd's son in the village. But my mother says his father wasn't a Kurd, or anything. One night, his father wrapped the baby up in an old sack, put it on the fountain stone in the middle of the village, and left it there. Then he just disappeared. A Kurdish girl found the child and brought it up. Now they call him the Kurd's son. A Kurdish girl. . . . His father just disappeared. He never set foot in the village again. No one knows where he went, no one ever saw him again. Oh I don't know! That's what my mother says, anyway."

Ismail suddenly straightened up. The bits of straw, stuck to the hairs of his chest, flashed in the sun. He took his shirt from the stubbles. He put it on quickly, took the child in his arms, and walked away.

The blind woman heard the sound of steps and turned her head toward the door.

"Who's that?" she cried. "Who is it? Have you got a baby with you? Isn't that a baby's voice I hear?"

"It's me," said Ismail. "It's me, mother."

"I'm sorry, my son," said the old woman. "I don't recognize your voice."

"It's me, mother," said Ismail. "It's Ismail of the Avshar's, Durmush Agha's old hireling . . ."

"Ah," said the blind woman. Her voice was soft, full of tears, but bitter as poison. "Every one of us grieved so for Zala. She didn't live to see better days, poor thing. May that sluttish lame woman be cursed. I've heard she's brought back the child, is it so? Aaah, if only my son were here. Hürü wouldn't go to work then. I'd look after the baby for Zala's dear sake. My son, it's crying there in your arms, lay it down in the cradle here, beside the child. . . . Have you done so? Hush, hush-a-by, my poor motherless lamb. Hush-a-by . . ."

down !

She rocked the cradle softly to and fro.

"Mother," Ismail said, "when will Mahmud's time be up? How much longer? . . ."

"Lulla-lulla-lullaby. Hush, hush, hush-a-by. Aaah," said the old woman with sudden vehemence, "ah, my poor son! When it comes to taxes, does the Government ever lay off? Lulla-lulla-lullaby, hush, hush . . . I am an old woman and I never heard such a thing happen, not once. Hush, my motherless lamb, hush-a-by. . . . It's the road tax, Ismail. He didn't pay it and it grew and grew. Hush, my poor babe, hush, hush-a-by, my little one. The Government says, let him give me my money, and I'll let him go. . . . Hush, my love, hush. It says, if he doesn't pay me, it's his business, he'll just rot in prison till he dies. Hush, my poor little one left among strangers, hush. . . . And it's no little sum, my son, it can't be saved. Hush, my poor orphan, hush. Hürü works, but what can one woman do alone? Hush, Zala's baby, hush-a-by. Time and time again, I've said, 'I'll go and throw myself at the Government's feet . . .' It's no use, they've told me, it's the money they must have. Hush, my luckless one, hush-a-by. Lulla-lulla-lullaby."

The hut was just large enough to hold two beds side by side. Its brush wall was unplastered. The grass roof had grown so thin that the sun pierced through. The room was spotlessly clean.

The blind woman was sitting near the door, her face turned toward the light. She was rocking the cradle very slowly and singing a lullaby all the while.

"Lulla-lulla-lullaby. . . . Motherless babies always cry like this without stopping. Lulla-lulla-lullaby. Oh dear! I feel strange myself. My time's drawing near, it seems. Since Mahmud went away, the fever's never left me, not a single day. Lulla-lulla-lullaby. The fever has me shaking all over. It leaves me limp, exhausted. Hush, my love, hush. Hush, pretty flower of the mountains, don't cry, hush. Aah, if only my Mahmud were here. Lulla-lulla-lullaby . . . would I have ever let Zala's baby be dragged miserably like this from door to door. Hush-a-by, hush." She stopped rocking the cradle. "On which side did you put it, Ismail? Where is Zala's baby?"

Ismail took her hand and placed it on the baby. The blind woman passed her hand over the baby's face, softly, caressingly.

"Alas," she said, "alas, the poor motherless thing! Skin and bones, it has become. Hürü has finished gathering her crop. Hush-a-by, hush. Now she's hoeing our cotton. Hush, hush-a-by, hush. Skin and bones. Hush-a-by."

The sun had set when Hürü came. She understood the situation immediately. The blind woman was lying down, groaning and shivering all over. The fever came over her like this every afternoon. Ismail was sitting by the cradle rocking it slowly to and fro.

Hürü appeared to be twenty years old. Her face was sunburned, almost black.

"Ismail, brother," she said. "What can I say now? My heart breaks for you, but what can I say? You see how it is, my breasts swell all day long till evening, but I cannot suckle my own baby. I just press out the milk on to the earth. What can I say, Ismail, brother? If Mahmud were here . . ."

"Sister," said Ismail, "sister Hürü! I'll give you anything you want. I'll do your threshing for you, as soon as I've finished mine. You're my last hope."

Sempé

"Mother," said Hürü, "what do you say? What can I say now? What can I say . . ."

"My daughter," said the old woman, moaning all the while, "my lovely black-eyed, golden-haired girl, we can't sit here and let it die, the poor little thing. Why, it's almost dead already. Zala's baby . . . what can I say? Zala's baby. What can I say . . . Zala's keepsake . . ."

Ismail straightened up as if a deadly weight had been lifted from him. He went out.

Hürü was carrying the babies, one on each arm. The blind woman followed, her hand on Hürü's belt. The dawn was just breaking when they came to the field.

Hürü made a little bed of grass and lay the children next to each other on it. Then she settled the blind woman near them.

The cotton field was about five acres wide. In the dim half-light it was not possible to distinguish the cotton from the other plants. As soon as it grew lighter, Hürü started hoeing. There was not a single tree or shady place in the field or anywhere near it. There was not even a bush on the whole plain. A smell of fresh earth rose at every blow of the hoe.

The sun was now high in the sky and heat enveloped the whole plain.

"My daughter," said the blind woman. "Hürü, my daughter, the children are burning. They'll die in this heat. Come, my pretty child, come and place them in my shadow."

The blind woman was sitting with her back to the sun. Hürü put the two babies in her shadow.

"But, mother," she said, "at midday, there'll be no shadow at all. What will we do then, mother?"

The blind woman's lips trembled.

Her mouth was thin and drawn and her lips disappeared among the wrinkles. Her face was as small as the palm of a hand and pockmarked. Her eyes had sunk in their sockets. Two little balls fluttered constantly under the closed eyelids. Her thin hands, just skin and bones with the veins jutting out, were dotted with large and small specks like sun spots. Sitting there, her silhouette was no larger than that of a small child. When the babies cried, she would call to Hürü in her soft voice full of goodwill and kindness to come and suckle them. Then swaying slowly from side to side, she would sing her lullaby.

"Sleep my pretty baby, sleep, lulla-lulla-lullaby,
In lovely gardens you shall grow, lulla-lulla-lullaby."

Such a gentle voice the old woman had. A voice to soothe crying babes, a voice so full of warmth, it penetrated to the heart.

As the sun rose higher and higher, she would call Hürü and make her place the children closer to her. She would lean over them. Every now and again she would ask Hürü if the children were in the sun or not.

When the sun is at its zenith, scorching the huge plain, it is impossible even to touch the soil with the hand or to walk on the ground. The plants droop, the cotton leaves becomes limp. The blind woman then settled the children on her lap and bent over them. One would have thought her asleep were it not for the lullaby she sang softly as she swayed slowly from side to side.

"Sleep my pretty baby, sleep, lulla-lulla-lullaby,
In lovely gardens you shall grow, lulla-lulla-lullaby,
From your little green cradle, hush, hush, hush-a-by,
I've taken you, my pretty one, lulla-lulla-lullaby.
Poor motherless little babe, hush, hush, hush-a-by,
Never felt a mother's warmth, lulla-lulla-lullaby."

As she sang she softly caressed Zala's baby, which was lying on her right side.

"Sleep my pretty baby, sleep, lulla-lulla-lullaby,
In lovely palaces you shall grow, lulla-lulla-lullaby."

The sun beat down on them, the sun burned and consumed them, but the old woman managed to protect the two babies until the afternoon. It was just about five o'clock, when the sun was going down, that the fever took her. She began to tremble and roll on the ground. She was shaking all over and writhing in long convulsions on the warm earth.

And so it went, day after day: the old woman keeping the two babies from the sun all through the long hot day, and in the afternoon . . .

They would continue in this way until the hoeing of the five acres was done. There was just one little corner left. Just one little patch, no larger than a hand . . . but there was no help for it.

Bad news travels quickly. Ismail had finished threshing his crop and was stacking his grain when he heard it. He was stunned.

He found Hürü lying down, her face yellow, her cheeks sunken.

Ismail's voice came out with difficulty.

"Sister," he said. "God help you, sister Hürü. I was so grieved. May she rest in peace. She didn't see the light in this world. May her grave be full of light."

"She's dead," said Hürü, in a tremulous voice. "It's two days since she died. She loved children, poor woman. She had such a way of singing lullabies, it broke your heart. No one could resist it."

"May her grave be filled with light," said Ismail softly. "She never saw the light . . ."

"We have no trellis, brother, you know," said Hürü in a moaning voice. "Mosquitoes swarmed all over us where we lay on the ground. They say it was because of that. Ah, how she sang! No one could resist her. When she sang her lullabies, it just broke your heart. Ah . . ."

She tossed her head sideways.

"I'm burning, brother," she said. "Burning all over, like a live coal!"

Ismail was looking at her silently. Then he said:

"Sister, I've brought you this."

He put the sugar near her pillow. The children were sleeping soundlessly in the cradle. He took up his baby and walked to the door. Then he turned.

"Sister," he said. "Sister Hürü, don't worry about your crop. I'll do the threshing for you. Don't have any fear in your heart for the crop. I'll do it. It isn't because I'm taking the child that . . ."

The shadow of a cloud passed over the dusty road where bits of straw gleamed. Far off toward the south, white clouds called sails were gathered in clusters over the Mediterranean.

As far as the eye could see, the huge level plain was turning blue under the afternoon sun, like a smooth calm sea. The dark shadows of the blue mountains far away were lengthening toward the east.

Ismail was up to his waist in whirling dust.

On his left, the green rice field stretched to the village. A pungent smell of swamps reached his nostrils. In the ditch along the road, the creamy film of dust covering the stagnant water broke into ripples as the wind swept over it.

The child's head rested on his right arm. Its sunken eyes were like two dark holes. Its neck was now so thin it was unable to support the head, and its skin all shriveled and black was stuck to the bones. Its jaw hung slack and its shriveled lips were drawn in. Flies were swarming in and out of its open mouth. Ismail's head was bent toward the child's head which rested on his right arm. He was looking at it. He kept looking at it as he walked.

Translated by Thilda Gokceli

►► Stig Dagerman

The Games of Night

Sometimes at night, when his mother was crying in the bedroom and only unknown steps clattered on the stairs, Åke had a game which he played instead of crying. He pretended that he was invisible and that he could wish himself anywhere, just by thinking it. On those evenings there was only one place to wish oneself, and so Åke was suddenly there. He never knew how he had arrived; he just knew that he was standing in a room. What it looked like he didn't know, because he hadn't the right eyes for it, but it was full of the smoke of cigarettes and pipes, and people laughed suddenly, frighteningly, for no reason, and women who couldn't talk clearly leaned across a table and laughed in just the same, dreadful way. It cut through Åke like knives, yet he was glad to be there. On the table around which everybody was sitting were a number of bottles, and as soon as a glass was empty a hand unscrewed the screw-stopper and filled it again.

Åke who was invisible lay down on the floor and crawled under the table without anybody who sat there noticing him. In his hand he carried an invisible drill and without a moment's hesitation he set the point of it against the underside of the table-top and started drilling upward. He soon got through the wood, but went on drilling. He drilled through glass, and suddenly, when he had pierced the bottom of a bottle, the brandy ran in a fine thin stream down through the hole in the table. He recognized his father's shoes under the table, and dared not think what would happen if he suddenly became visible again. But then with a thrill of joy he heard his father say, "Empty," and somebody else joining in, "Hell, so it is." Then everybody in the room got up.

Åke followed his father downstairs and when they reached the street he led him, though his father never noticed it, to a taxi-rank, and whispered the right address to the driver. During the whole journey he stood on the step to be sure they were really going in the right direction. When they were only a few blocks from home, Åke wished himself back—and there he lay again in the kitchen bench bed, listening to the car drawing up in the street. Not until it drove off again did he hear that it was not the right car: it had stopped next door. The right one must be still on the way; perhaps it had got into a traffic jam, perhaps it had stopped in front of a cyclist who had fallen off; lots of things can happen to cars.

But at last one came which sounded like the right one. A few doors beyond Åke's house it began slowing down; it drove slowly past the next-door house and stopped with a slight squeak exactly opposite the right gateway. A door opened, a door banged, and somebody whistled as he rattled his money. His father never whistled, but one never knew; why shouldn't he suddenly take to whistling? The car started up and turned the corner, and afterward the street was absolutely quiet. Åke strained his ears and listened down the stairs, but the front door never closed behind anybody coming in. The little click of the staircase light-switch never came. There was no muffled noise of footsteps on the way upstairs.

Why did I leave him so soon? Åke wondered. I might just as well have stayed with him all the way to the door, when we were so near. Now of course he's standing down there because he's lost his key and can't get in. Now perhaps he'll get angry and go away, and won't come back until the door's opened tomorrow morning. And he can't whistle, or he'd whistle to me or mum to throw down the key.

As noiselessly as he could Åke clambered over the edge of the creaking bed and bumped against the kitchen table in the darkness; he stiffened all over his body as he stood there on the cold linoleum; but his mother's sobbing was as loud and as regular as the breathing of a sleeper, so she had heard nothing. He went forward to the window, and when he reached it he pushed the roller blind gently aside and looked out. There was not a soul in the street, but the lamp above the gateway opposite was lit. It was lit at the same time as the staircase light, so it was like the lamp above Åke's own door.

Presently Åke grew cold and he padded back to the bench bed. To avoid bumping against the table he slid his hand along the draining board, until suddenly his finger tips touched something cold and sharp. For a while he let his fingers explore and then gripped the handle of the carving knife. When he crept back into bed he had the knife with him. He laid it beside him under the blanket and made himself invisible again. After that he was back in that same room, standing in the doorway and watching the men and women who held his father prisoner. He realized that if his father was to be free he must release him in the same way as the Viking released the missionary, when the missionary was bound to a stake to be roasted by cannibals.

Åke crept forward, raised his invisible knife and drove it into the back of the fat man next to his father. The fat man died and Åke went on round the table. One by one they slid down off their chairs without really knowing what had happened. When his father was free Åke took him down the many stairs and as he could hear no taxi about they walked very slowly down the steps, crossed the street and boarded a tram. Åke arranged it so that his father had a seat inside, hoping that the conductor wouldn't notice that his father had been drinking and hoping that his father wouldn't say anything out of place to the conductor, or suddenly laugh out loud, just like that, without having anything to laugh at.

The song of the night tram rounding a bend forced its way inexorably into the kitchen, and Åke who had already left the tram and was lying in bed again noticed that his mother had stopped sobbing during the short time he had been away. The roller blind in the next room flew up toward the ceiling with a fearful clatter, and when the clatter had died away his mother opened the window and Åke wished he could jump out of bed and run into their room and call out that she could quite well shut the window again, draw down the blind and go quietly to bed, for now he really was coming. "On that tram, because I helped him get on to it." But Åke knew it was no good doing that, as she would never believe him. She didn't know how much Åke did for her when they were alone at night and she thought he was asleep. She didn't know what journeys he made and what adventures he braved for her sake.

When later the tram stopped at the halt round the corner he stood by the window and looked out through the crack between the blind and the window frame. The first people to come round the corner were two youths who must have jumped off while the tram was still moving; they were pretending to box with each other. They lived in the new house diagonally across the street. Passengers who had alighted were making a noise round the corner, and when the tram peered out with its lamp and rattled slowly across Åke's street, little groups of people came in sight and then vanished in different directions. One man with an unsteady gait, carrying his hat in his hand like a beggar, made straight for Åke's gateway, but it wasn't Åke's father; it was the porter.

But still Åke waited. He knew there were several things round the corner that might delay a tram passenger: there were shopwindows, for instance—there was a shoe shop there. Here his father might be standing to choose a pair of shoes for himself before he came in; and the fruit shop had a window too, with hand-painted placards in it which lots of people stopped to look at because of the funny little men painted on them. But the fruit shop also had a slot machine that didn't work properly, and it might well be that his father had put in a twenty-öre piece for a packet of Läkerol for Åke, and now couldn't get the drawer open.

While Åke was standing by the window waiting for his father to tear himself away from the slot machine, his mother suddenly left the bedroom next door and went past the kitchen. As she was barefoot Åke hadn't heard her, but she couldn't have noticed him because she walked on into the hall. Åke dropped the blind and stood motionless in total darkness while his mother searched for something among the coats. It must have been a handkerchief, for after a little while she blew her nose and returned to her room. Although her feet were bare, Åke noticed that she was walking especially quietly so as not to wake him. She shut her window at once and drew down the blind with a hard, quick pull. Then she lay down hastily on the bed and the sobbing began again, exactly as if she could only sob lying down, or had to start sobbing as soon as she did lie down.

When Åke had looked out at the street once again and found it empty except for a woman being embraced by a seaman in the gateway opposite, he crept back to bed, thinking—as the linoleum suddenly creaked underfoot—that it sounded as if he had dropped something. Now he was terribly tired; sleep rolled over him like mists as he walked, and through these mists he caught the clash of steps on the stairs —but going the wrong way: coming downstairs instead of up. As soon as he slipped under the covers he glided reluctantly but swiftly into the waters of sleep and the last waves that beat over his head were as soft as sobs.

Yet sleep was so brittle that it could not keep him away from all that preoccupied him when awake. Certainly he had not heard the taxi drawing up in front of the gate, the switching on of the staircase light or the steps coming upstairs, but the key that poked into the keyhole poked a hole in his sleep; instantly he was awake and joy struck down in him like a flash of lightning, sending a wave of heat through him from toes to forehead. Then the joy vanished as quickly as it had come, in a smoke of questions. Åke had a little game which he played whenever he awoke in this way. He played that his father hurried straight through the hall and stood between the kitchen and bedroom so that both of them might hear him as he shouted,

"One of the chaps fell off a scaffolding and I had to take him to hospital; I've been sitting by him all night; I couldn't ring you because there wasn't a phone anywhere near." Or, "What do you know? We've won first prize in the lottery and I've come back late like this so's to keep you guessing as long as I could." Or, "What do you know? The boss gave me a motorboat today and I've been out trying her, and early tomorrow morning we'll push off in her all three of us. What do you say to that, eh?"

But reality always happened much more slowly and never so surprisingly. His father couldn't find the hall light-switch. At last he gave up and knocked down a coat hanger. He swore and tried to pick it up, but instead overturned a suitcase standing by the wall. Then he gave that up too, and tried to find a peg for his coat, but when he had found it the coat fell on the floor just the same, with a soft thud. Leaning against the wall his father walked the few steps to the lavatory, opened the door and left it open, and switched on the light; and as so many times before Åke lay quite rigid listening to the splashing on the floor. Then the man switched out the light, bumped into the door, swore and entered the room through the drawn curtain, which rattled as if it wanted to bite.

Then everything was quiet. His father stood in there without saying a word; there was a faint creaking from his shoes and his breathing was heavy and irregular, but these two things only made it all even more hideously quiet, and in this quietness another flash of lightning struck down in Åke. It was hatred, this heat that surged through him; he squeezed the handle of the knife until his palm hurt, but he felt no pain. The silence lasted only a moment. His father began to undress. Jacket and waistcoat. He threw them on a chair. He leaned back against a cupboard and let the shoes drop off his feet. His tie flapped. Then he took a few steps further into the room, that's to say toward the bed, and stood still while he wound up the clock. Then everything was quiet again, as horribly quiet as before. Only the clock crunched the silence, like a rat—the gnawing clock of the drunk.

Then the thing the silence was waiting for would happen. His mother threw herself desperately round in bed, and the scream welled out of her mouth like blood.

"You devil, you devil—devil-devil-devil!" she shrieked, until her voice died and all was silent. Only the clock nibbled and nibbled and the hand clutching the knife was quite wet with sweat. The fear in the kitchen was so great that it couldn't be endured without a weapon, but at last Åke grew so weary from his deadly fear that unresistingly he plunged headfirst into sleep. Far down in the night he woke for a moment and through the open door heard the bed in the other room creaking and a soft murmur filling the room, and didn't quite know what it meant except that these were two safe noises which meant that fear had yielded for that night. He was still holding the knife; he let it go and pushed it from him, filled with a burning lust for himself, and in the very moment of falling asleep he played the last game of the night—the one that brought him final peace.

Final—and yet there was no end. Just before six in the evening his mother came into the kitchen, where he was sitting at the table doing his homework. She just took the arithmetic book from him and pulled him up from the bench with one hand.

"Go to your dad," she said, dragging him out into the hall and standing behind him to cut off his retreat. "Go to your dad and tell him I said he was to give you the money."

The days were worse than the nights. The games of the night were much better than those of the day. At night one could be invisible and speed over the roofs to wherever one was wanted. In the daytime one was not invisible. In the daytime things took longer; it wasn't such fun to play in the daytime. Åke came out of the gateway and was not the slightest bit invisible. The porter's son pulled at his coat, wanting him to play marbles, but Åke knew his mother was standing up there at the window watching him until he should disappear round the corner, so he broke free without a word and ran away as if somebody were after him. But as soon as he turned the corner he began to walk as slowly as he could, counting the paving stones and the splashes of spittle on them. The porter's boy caught him up but Åke didn't answer him, for one couldn't tell people that one was out looking for one's father because he hadn't brought the wages home yet. At last the porter's boy tired of it, and Åke drew nearer and nearer to the place he didn't want to get nearer to. He pretended that he was getting further and further away from it, but it wasn't true at all.

The first time, though, he went right past the café, brushing so close by the doorman that the doorman muttered something after him. He turned up a little side street and stopped in front of the building where his father's workshop was. After a while he passed through the entrance into the yard, pretending that his father was still there and that he'd hidden himself somewhere behind the drums and sacks for Åke to come and look for him. Åke raised the lids of all the paint barrels, and each time he was just as much surprised not to find his father crouching inside. After hunting through the yard for half an hour at least, he realized at last that his father couldn't have hidden himself there, and he turned back.

Next to the café were a china shop and a watchmaker's. At first Åke stood looking in at the window of the china shop. He tried to count the dogs, first the pottery ones in the window, and then the ones he could see if he shaded his eyes and peered at the shelves and counters inside. The watchmaker came out just then and drew down the iron shutter in front of his window, but through the chinks in the shutter Åke could see the wrist watches ticking away inside. He looked also at the clock with the Correct Time and decided that when the second hand had gone round ten times he would go in.

While the doorman was shouting at a fellow who was showing him something in a newspaper, Åke stole into the café and ran straight to the right table before too many people noticed him. At first his father didn't see him, but one of the other painters nodded at Åke and said,

"Your nipper's here."

His father took Åke on his knee and rubbed his bristly chin against the boy's cheek. Åke tried not to look at his eyes, but now and again he was fascinated by the red lines in the whites of them.

"What d'you want, son?" his father asked, but his tongue was soft and slurry in his mouth and he had to say the same thing two or three times before he was satisfied.

"Money."

Then his father put him gently down on the floor, leaned back and laughed so loudly that the others had to hush him. Still laughing he took the purse from his pocket, clumsily drew off the rubber band round it and hunted about for a long time until he found the shiniest one-crown piece.

"Here you are then, Åke," he said. "Off you go and get some sweets for yourself."

The other painters were not to be outdone, and Åke was given a crown by each of them. He held the money in his hand as, overwhelmed with shame and confusion, he picked his way out between the tables. He was so afraid that someone might see him running out past the doorman and tell tales at school, and say, "I saw Åke coming out of a pothouse last evening." But he paused for a moment in front of the watchmaker's window, and while the second hand swept ten times round its center he stood pressed against the grille, knowing that he would have to play his games again tonight; but which of the two people he played for he hated more he couldn't tell.

Later, when slowly he turned the corner he met his mother's gaze from thirty feet up, and walked as lingeringly as he dared toward the gateway. Next to this was a wood merchant's, and he was bold enough to kneel for a little and stare through the window at an old man putting coal into a black sack. Just as the old man finished Åke's mother came and stood behind him. She jerked him to his feet and took his chin in her hand, to find his eyes.

"What did he say?" she whispered. "Did you funk it again?"

"He said he was coming back right away," Åke whispered back.

"What about the money?"

"Shut your eyes, mum," said Åke; and now he played the last of the day's games.

While his mother shut her eyes, Åke slipped into her outstretched hand the four crown pieces, and then dashed down the street on feet that slipped on the stones because they were so frightened. A rising shout pursued him along the houses, but did not stop him. On the contrary, it made him run all the faster.

Translated by Naomi Walford

►► **LeRoi Jones**

Cuba Libre

Along with a group of other American Negroes, LeRoi Jones, the poet and then-editor of Yugen magazine, went to Cuba late in July 1960 on a trip arranged by The Fair Play For Cuba Committee. While there, he went to Sierra Maestra in Oriente province to attend a mass anniversary rally of the July 26th movement. The following account records his impressions of his journey to Oriente and the happenings at the meeting:

It was late at night, and still Habana had not settled down to its usual quiet. Crowds of people were squatting around bus stops, walking down the streets in groups headed for bus stops. Truckloads of militia were headed out of the city. Young men and women with rucksacks and canteens were piling into buses, trucks, and private cars all over the city. There were huge signs all over Habana reading "A La Sierra Con Fidel . . . Julio 26." Thousands of people were leaving Habana for the July 26th celebration at Sierra Maestra all the way at the other end of the island in Oriente province. The celebration was in honor of Fidel Castro's first onslaught against Moncada barracks July 26, 1953, which marked the beginning of his drive against the Batista government. Whole families were packing up, trying to get to Oriente the best way they could. It was still three days before the celebration and people clogged the roads from Habana all the way to the Eastern province.

The night of our departure for Oriente we arrived at the train station in Habana about six P.M. It was almost impossible to move around in the station. *Campesinos* (peasant farmers), businessmen, soldiers, *militianas*, tourists—all were thrashing around trying to make sure they had seats in the various trains. As we came into the station, most of the delegates of a Latin American Youth Congress were coming in also. There were about nine hundred of them, representing students from almost every country in Latin America. Mexicans, Colombians, Argentines, Venezuelans, Puerto Ricans (with signs reading "For the Liberation of Puerto Rico"), all carrying flags, banners, and wearing the large, ragged straw hat of the *campesino*. We were to go in the same train as the delegates.

As we moved through the crowds toward our train, the students began chanting: "Cuba Si, Yanqui No . . . Cuba Si, Yanqui No . . . Cuba Si, Yanqui No." The crowds in the terminal joined in, soon there was a deafening crazy scream that seemed to burst the roof off the terminal. Cuba Si, Yanqui No! We raced for the trains.

Once inside the train, a long modern semi-air-conditioned "Silver Meteor," we quickly settled down and I began scribbling illegibly in my notebook. But the Latin Americans came scrambling into the train still chanting furiously and someone handed me a drink of rum. They were yelling "Ven-

ceremos, Venceremos, Venceremos, Venceremos."
("We will win.") Crowds of soldiers and militia on
the platform outside joined in. Everyone was screaming as the train began to pull away.

The young militia people soon came trotting
through the coaches asking everyone to sit down for
a few seconds so they could be counted. The delegates got to their seats and in my coach everyone began to sing a song like "two, four, six, eight, who do
we appreciate . . . Fidel, Fidel, Fidel!!" Then they
did Ché (Guevara), Raul, President Dorticos, etc. It
was about 1,000 kilometers to Oriente and we had
just started.

Young soldiers passed out ham sandwiches and
Maltina, a thick syrupy sweet beverage that only
made me thirstier. Everyone in the train seemed to
be talking excitedly and having a wild time. We were
about an hour outside Habana and I was alternating
between taking notes and reading about ancient
Mexican religion when Olga Finlay, our interpreter,
came up to my seat accompanied by a young woman.
"I told her you were an American poet," Olga said,
"and she wanted to meet you." I rose quickly and
extended my hand, for some reason embarrassed as
hell. Olga said, "Señora Betancourt, Señor LeRoi
Jones." She was very short, very blonde and very
pretty, and had a weird accent that never ceased to
fascinate me. For about thirty minutes we stood in
the middle aisle talking to each other. She was a
Mexican delegate to the Youth Congress, a graduate
student in Economics at one of the universities, the
wife of an economist, and a mother. Finally, I
offered her the seat next to mine at the window. She
sat, and we talked almost continuously throughout
the fourteen-hour ride.

She questioned me endlessly about American life,
American politics, American youth—although I was
jokingly cautioned against using the word American
to mean the U.S. or North America. "Everyone in
this car is American," she said. "You from the
North, we from the South." I explained as best I
could about the Eisenhowers, the Nixons, the Du-
Ponts, but she made even my condemnations seem
mild. "Everyone in the world," she said, with her
finger, "has to be communist or anti-communist.
And if they're anti-communist, no matter what kind
of foul person they are, you people accept them as
your allies. Do you really think that hopeless little
island in the middle of the sea is China? That is irrational. You people are irrational!"

I tried to defend myself, "Look, why jump on me?
I understand what you're saying. I'm in complete
agreement with you. I'm a poet . . . what can I do?
I write, that's all, I'm not even interested in politics."

She jumped on me with both feet as did a group of
Mexican poets later in Habana. She called me a
"cowardly bourgeois individualist." The poets, or at
least one young wild-eyed Mexican poet, Jaime Shel-
ley, almost left me in tears, stomping his foot on the
floor, screaming: "You want to cultivate your soul?
In that ugliness you live in, you want to cultivate
your soul? Well, we've got millions of starving people to feed, and that moves me enough to make
poems out of."

Around ten P.M. the train pulled into the town of
Matanzas. We had our blinds drawn, but the militia
came running through the car telling us to raise
them. When I raised the blind I was almost startled
out of my wits. There were about 1,500 people in the
train station and surrounding it, yelling their lungs
out. We pulled up the windows. People were all
over. They ran back and forth along the train screaming at us. The Mexicans in the train had a big sign
painted on a bedspread that read "Mexico is with
Fidel. Venceremos." When they raised it to the
windows young men leaped in the air, and women
blew kisses. There was a uniformed marching band
trying to be heard above the crowd, but I could
barely hear them. When I poked my head out of the
window to wave at the crowds, two young Negro
women giggled violently at first, then one of them ran
over to the train and kissed me as hard as she could
manage. The only thing to do I could think of was
to say "Thank you." She danced up and down and
clapped her hands and shouted to her friend, "Un
americano, un americano." I bowed my head gra-
ciously.

What was it, a circus? That wild mad crowd. Social ideas? Could there be that much excitement
generated through all the people? Damn, that people
still can move. Not us, but people. It's gone out of us
forever. "Cuba Si, Yanqui No," I called at the girls
as the train edged away.

We stopped later in the town of Colon. There
again the same mobs of cheering people. Camaguey.
Santa Clara. At each town, the chanting crowds. The
unbelievable joy and excitement. The same idea, and
people made beautiful because of it. People moving,
being moved. I was ecstatic and frightened. Something I had never seen before, exploding all around
me.

The train rocked wildly across and into the interior. The delegates were singing a "cha cha" with
words changed to something like "Fidel, Fidel, cha
cha cha, Ché Ché, cha cha cha, Abajo Imperialismo

Yanqui, cha cha cha." Some American students whom I hadn't seen earlier ran back and forth in the coaches singing "We cannot be moved." The young folk-song politicians in blue jeans and pigtails.

About two o'clock in the morning they shut the lights off in most of the coaches, and everybody went to sleep. I slept for only an hour or so and woke up just in time to see the red sun come up and the first early people come out of their small grass-roofed shacks beside the railroad tracks, and wave sleepily at the speeding train. I pressed my face against the window and waved back.

The folk singing and war cries had just begun again in earnest when we reached the town of Yara, a small town in Oriente province, the last stop on the line. At once we unloaded from the train, leaving most luggage and whatever was considered superfluous. The dirt streets of the town were jammed with people. Probably everyone in town had come to meet the train. The entire town was decorated with some kind of silver Christmas tree tinsel and streamers. Trees, bushes, houses, children, all draped in the same silver holiday tinsel. Tiny girls in brown uniforms and red berets greeted us with armfuls of flowers. Photographers were running amuck through the crowd, including an American newsreel cameraman who kept following Robert Williams, a member of our group. I told Robert that he ought to put his big straw hat in front of his face American gangster style.

From the high hill of the train station it was possible to see a road running right through Yara. Every conceivable kind of bus, truck, car, and scooter was being pushed toward the Sierra, which was now plainly visible in the distance. Some of the campesinos were on horses, dodging in and out of the sluggish traffic, screaming at the top of their lungs.

The sun had already gotten straight up over our heads and was burning down viciously. The big straw campesino hats helped a little but I could tell that it was going to be an obscenely hot day. We stood around for a while until everyone had gotten off our train, and then some of the militia people waved at us to follow them. We walked completely out of the town of Yara in about two minutes. We walked until we came to more railroad tracks; a short spur leading off in the direction of Sierra Maestra. Sitting on the tracks were about ten empty open cattle cars. There were audible groans from the American contingent. The cars themselves looked like movable jails. Huge thick bars around the sides. We joked about the American cameraman taking a picture of them with us behind the bars and using it as a *Life* magazine cover. They would caption it "Americans in Cuba."

At a word from the militia we scrambled up through the bars, into the scalding cars. The metal parts of the car were burning hot, probably from sitting out in the sun all day. It was weird seeing hundreds of people up and down the tracks climbing up into the cattle cars by whatever method they could manage. We had been told in Habana that this was going to be a rough trip and that we ought to dress accordingly. Heavy shoes, old clothes, a minimum of equipment. The women were told specifically to wear slacks and flat shoes because it would be difficult to walk up a mountain in a sheath dress and heels. However, one of the American women, a pretty young middle-class lady from Philadelphia, showed up in a flare skirt and "Cuban" heels. Two of the Cubans had to pull and tug to get her into the car, which still definitely had the smell of cows. She slumped in a corner and began furiously mopping her brow.

I sat down on the floor and tried to scribble in my notebook, but it was difficult because everyone was jammed in very tight. Finally, the train jerked to a start, and everyone in all the cars let out a wild yell. The delegates began chanting again. Waving at all the people along the road, and all the dark barefoot families standing in front of their grass-topped huts calling to us. The road which ran along parallel to the train was packed full of traffic, barely moving. Men sat on the running boards of their cars when the traffic came to a complete halt, and drank water from their canteens. The train was going about five miles an hour and the campesinos raced by on their plow horses jeering, swinging their big hats. The sun and the hot metal car were almost unbearable. The delegates shouted at the trucks "Cuba Si, Yanqui No," and then began their "Viva" shouts. After one of the "Vivas," I yelled "Viva Calle Cuarenta y dos" (42nd St.), "Viva Symphony Sid," "Viva Cinco Punto" (Five Spot), "Viva Turhan Bey." I guess it was the heat. It was a long slow ride in the boiling cars.

The cattle cars stopped after an hour or so at some kind of junction. All kinds of other coaches were pulled up and resting on various spurs. People milled about everywhere. But it was the end of any tracks going further toward Sierra. We stood around and drank warm water too fast.

Now we got into trucks. Some with nailed-in bus seats, some with straw roofs, others with just plain truck floors. It was a wild scramble for seats. The militia people and the soldiers did their best to indicate which trucks were for whom, but people staggered into the closest vehicle at hand. Ed Clarke, the young Negro abstract expressionist painter, and I ran and leaped up into a truck with leather bus seats in the back. The leather was too hot to sit on for a while so I put my handkerchief on the seat and sat lightly. A woman was trying to get up into the truck, but not very successfully, so I leaned over the rail and pulled her up and in. The face was recognizable immediately, but I had to sit back on the hot seat before I remembered it was Françoise Sagan. I turned to say something to her, but some men were already helping her back down to the ground. She rode up front in the truck's cab with a young lady companion, and her manager on the running board, clinging to the door.

The trucks reared out onto the already heavily traveled road. It was an unbelievable scene. Not only all the weird trucks and buses but thousands of people walking along the road. Some had walked from places as far away as Matanzas. Whole detachments of militia were marching, route step, but carrying rifles or .45's. Women carrying children on their shoulders. One group of militia with blue shirts, green pants, pistols and knives, was carrying paper fans, which they rippled back and forth almost in unison with their step. There were huge trucks full of oranges parked along the road with lines of people circling them. People were sitting along the edge of the road eating their lunches. Everyone going a la Sierra.

Our trucks sped along on the outside of the main body of traffic, still having to stop occasionally when there was some hopeless roadblock. The sun, for all our hats, was baking our heads. Sweat poured in my dry mouth. None of us Americans had brought canteens and there was no water to be had while we were racing along the road. I tried several times to get some oranges, but never managed. The truck would always start up again when we came close to an orange vendor.

There was a sign on one of the wood shack "stores" we passed that read "Niños No Gustan Los Chicle Ni Los Cigarros Americanos Ni El Rocan Rool." It was signed "Fondin." The traffic bogged down right in front of the store so several French photographers leaped off the truck and raced for the orange stand. Only one fellow managed to make it back to our truck with a hat full of oranges. The others had to turn and run back empty-handed as the truck pulled away. Sagan's manager, who had strapped himself on the running board with a leather belt, almost broke his head when the truck hit a bump and the belt snapped and sent him sprawling into the road. Another one of the correspondents suddenly became violently ill and tried to shove his head between the rough wooden slats at the side of the truck; he didn't quite make it, and everyone in the truck suffered.

After two hours we reached a wide, slow, muddy river. There was only one narrow cement bridge crossing it, so the trucks had to wait until they could ease back into the regular line of traffic. There were hundreds of people wading across the river. A woman splashed in with her child on her shoulders, hanging around her neck, her lunch pail in one hand, a pair of blue canvas sneakers in the other. One group of militia marched right into the brown water, holding their rifles high above their heads. When our truck got on the bridge directly over the water, one of the Cuban newspapermen leaped out of the truck down ten feet into the water. People in the trucks would jump right over the side, sometimes pausing to take off their shoes. Most went in shoes and all.

Now we began to wind up the narrow mountain road for the first time. All our progress since Yara had been upgrade, but this was the first time it was clearly discernible that we were going up a mountain. It took another hour to reach the top. It was afternoon now and already long lines of people were headed back down the mountain. But it was a narrow line compared to the thousands of people who were scrambling up just behind us. Fom one point where we stopped just before reaching the top it was possible to look down the side of the long hill and see swarms of people all the way down past the river seeming now to inch along in effortless pantomime.

The trucks stopped among a jumble of rocks and sand not quite at the top of the last grade. (For the last twenty minutes of our climb we actually had to wind in and out among groups of people. The only people who seemed to race along without any thought of the traffic were the campesinos on their broken-down mounts.) Now everyone began jumping down off the trucks and trying to re-form into their respective groups. It seemed almost impossible. Detachments of campesino militia (work shirts, blue jeans, straw hats and machetes) marched up behind us. Milicianas of about twelve and thirteen separated our contingent, then herds of uniformed, trotting boys of about seven. "Hup, hup, hup, hup," one little boy was calling in vain as he ran behind the rest of his group. One of the girls called out "Hup, hup, hup, hup," keeping her group more orderly. Rebel soldiers wandered around everywhere, some with long, full beards, others with long, wavy black hair pulled under their blue berets or square-topped khaki caps, most of them young men in their twenties or teen-agers. An old man with a full grey beard covering most of his face, except his sparkling blue eyes and the heavy black cigar stuck out of the side of his mouth, directed the comings and goings up and down this side of the mountain. He wore a huge red-and-black-handled revolver and had a hunting knife sewn to his boot. Suddenly it seemed that I was lost in a sea of uniforms, and I couldn't see anyone I had come up the mountain with. I sat down on a rock until most of the uniforms passed. Then I could see Olga about fifty yards away waving her arms at her lost charges.

There was a public address system booming full blast from what seemed the top of the hill. The voice (Celia Sanchez, Fidel's secretary) was announcing various groups that were passing in review. When we got to the top of the rise, we could see a large, austere platform covered with all kinds of people, and at the front of the platform a raised section with a dais where the speakers were. Sra. Sanchez was announcing one corps of militia and they marched out of the crowd and stopped before the platform. The crowd cheered and cheered. The militia was commended from the platform and then they marched off into the crowd at the other side. Other groups marched past. Young women, teen-age girls, elderly *campesinos*, each with their own militia detachment, each to be commended. This had been going on since morning. Hundreds of commendations, thousands of people to be commended. Also, since morning, the officials had been reading off lists of names of *campesinos* who were to receive land under the Agrarian Reform Law. When they read the name of some farmer close enough to the mountain to hear it, he would leap straight up in the air and, no matter how far away from the platform he was, would go barreling and leaping toward the speaker. The crowd delighted in this and would begin chanting "Viva Fidel, Viva Fidel, Viva Reforma Agraria." All this had been going on since morning and it was now late afternoon.

After we walked past the dais, introduced to the screaming crowd as "intellectual North American visitors," we doubled back and went up onto the platform itself. It was even hotter up there. By now all I could think about was the sun; it was burning straight down and had been since early morning. I tugged the straw hat down over my eyes and trudged up onto the platform. The platform itself in back of the dais was almost overflowing, mostly with rebel soldiers and young militia troops. But there were all kinds of visitors also, the Latin American delegates, newsmen, European writers, American intellectuals, as well as Cuban officials. When we got up on the platform, Olga led us immediately over to the speakers' dais and the little group of seats around it. We

were going to be introduced to all the major speakers.

The first person to turn around and greet us was a tall, thin, bearded Negro in a rebel uniform bearing the shoulder markings of a *Comandante*. I recognized his face from the papers as that of Juan Almeida, chief of the rebel army, a man almost unknown in the United States. He grinned and shook our hands and talked in a swift combination of Spanish and English, joking constantly about conditions in the United States. In the middle of one of his jokes he leaned backward, leaning over one man to tap another taller man on the shoulder. Fidel Castro leaned back in his seat, then got up smiling and came over to where we were standing. He began shaking hands with everybody in the group, as well as the many other visitors who moved in at the opportunity. There were so many people on the platform in what seemed like complete disorder that I wondered how wise it was as far as security was concerned. It seemed awfully dangerous for the Prime Minister to be walking around so casually, almost having to thread his way through the surging crowd. Almost immediately, I shoved my hand toward his face and then grasped his hand. He greeted me warmly, asking through the interpreter where I was from and what I did. When I told him I was a New York poet, he seemed extremely amused and asked me what the government thought about my trip. I shrugged my shoulders and asked him what did he intend to do with this revolution.

We both laughed at the question because it was almost like a reflex action on my part: something that came out so quick that I was almost unaware of it. He twisted the cigar in his mouth and grinned, smoothing the strangely grown beard on his cheeks. "That *is* a poet's question," he said, "and the only poet's answer I can give you is that I will do what I think is right, what I think the people want. That's the best I can hope for, don't you think?"

I nodded, already getting ready to shoot out another question, I didn't know how long I'd have. Certainly this was the most animated I'd been during the entire trip. "Uh," I tried to smile, "What do you think the United States will do about Cuba ultimately?" The questions seemed weird and out of place because everyone else was just trying to shake his hand.

"Ha, well, that's extremely difficult to say, your government is getting famous for its improvisation in foreign affairs. I suppose it depends on who is running the government. If the Democrats win it may get better. More Republicans . . . I suppose more trouble. I cannot say, except that I really do not care what they do as long as they do not try to interfere with the running of this country."

Suddenly the idea of a security lapse didn't seem so pressing. I had turned my head at a weird angle and looked up at the top of the platform. There was a soldier at each side of the back wall of the platform, about ten feet off the ground, each one with a machine gun on a tripod. I asked another question. "What about communism? How big a part does that play in the government?"

"I've said a hundred times that I'm not a communist. But I am certainly not an anti-communist. The United States likes anti-communists, especially so close to their mainland. I said also a hundred times that I consider myself a humanist. A radical humanist. The only way that anything can ever be accomplished in a country like Cuba is radically. The old has been here so long that the new must make radical changes in order to function at all."

So many people had crowded around us now that it became almost impossible to hear what Fidel was saying. I had shouted the last question. A young fashion model who had come with our group brushed by me and said how much she had enjoyed her stay in Cuba. Fidel touched his hand to the wide campesino hat he was wearing, then pumped her hand up and down. One of the Latin American girls leaned forward suddenly and kissed him on the cheek. Everyone milled around the tall young Cuban, asking questions, shaking his hand, taking pictures, getting autographs (an American girl with pigtails and blue jeans) and, I suppose committing everything he said to memory. The crowd was getting too large, I touched his arm, waved, and walked toward the back of the platform.

I hadn't had any water since early morning, and the heat and the excitement made my mouth dry and hard. There were no water fountains in sight. Most of the masses of Cubans had canteens or vacuum bottles, but someone had forgotten to tell the Americans (North and South) that there'd be no water. Also, there was no shade at all on the platform. I walked around behind it and squatted in a small booth with a tiny tin roof. It had formerly been a soda stand, but because the soda was free, the supply had given out rapidly and the stand had closed. I sat in the few inches of shade with my head in my hands, trying to cool off. Some Venezuelans came by and asked to sit in the shade next to me. I said it was all right and they offered me the first cup of water I'd had in about five hours. They had a whole chicken also, but I didn't think I'd be able to stand the luxury.

There were more speakers, including a little boy from one of the youngest militia units, but I heard them all over the public address system. I was too beat and thirsty to move. Later Ed Clarke and I went around hunting for water and finally managed to find a small brown stream where the soldiers were filling up their canteens. I drank two coca-cola bottles full, and when I got back to Habana came down with a fearful case of dysentery.

Suddenly there was an insane, deafening roar from the crowd. I met the girl economist as I dragged out of the booth and she tried to get me to go back on the front platform. Fidel was about to speak. I left her and jumped off the platform and trotted up a small rise to the left. The roar lasted about ten minutes, and as I got settled on the side of the hill Fidel began to speak.

He is an amazing speaker, knowing probably instinctively all the laws of dynamics and elocution. The speech began slowly and haltingly, each syllable being pronounced with equal stress, as if he were reading a poem. He was standing with the campesino hat pushed back slightly off his forehead, both hands on the lectern. As he made his points, one of the hands would slide off the lectern and drop to his side, his voice becoming tighter and less warm. When the speech was really on its way, he dropped both hands from the lectern, putting one behind his back like a church usher, gesturing with the other. By now he would be rocking from side to side, pointing his finger at the crowd, at the sky, at his own chest. Sometimes he seemed to lean to the side and talk to his own ministers there on the platform with him and then wheel toward the crowd calling for them to support him. At one point in the speech the crowd interrupted for about twenty minutes crying "Venceremos, venceremos, venceremos, venceremos, venceremos, venceremos, venceremos, venceremos." The entire crowd, 60- or 70,000 people all chanting in unison. Fidel stepped away from the lectern grinning, talking to his aides. He quieted the crowd with a wave of his arms and began again. At first softly, with the syllables drawn out and precisely enunciated, then tightening his voice and going into an almost musical rearrangement of his speech. He condemned Eisenhower, Nixon, The South, The Monroe Doctrine, The Platt Amendment, and Fulgencio Batista in one long, unbelievable sentence. The crowd interrupted again, "Fidel, Fidel, Fidel, Fidel, Fidel, Fidel, Fidel, Fidel, Fidel, Fidel, Fidel, Fidel." He leaned away from the lectern, grinning at the chief of the army. The speech lasted almost two-and-a-half hours, being interrupted time and again by the exultant crowd and once by five minutes of rain. When it began to rain, Almeida draped a rain jacket around Fidel's shoulders, and he re-lit his cigar. When the speech ended, the crowd went out of its head, roaring for almost forty-five minutes.

When the speech was over, I made a fast move for the platform. Almost a thousand other people had the same idea. I managed to shout something to Castro as he was being whizzed to the back of the platform and into a car. I shouted "A fine speech, a tremendous speech."

He shouted back, "I hope you take it home with you," and disappeared in a host of bearded uniforms.

We were told at first that we would be able to leave the mountain in about three hours. But it had gotten dark already, and I didn't really fancy shooting down that mountain road with the same exuberance with which we came . . . not in the dark. Clarke and I went out looking for more water and walked almost a mile before we came to a big pavilion where soft drinks and sandwiches were being served. The soft drinks were hot and the sandwiches took too long to get. We came back and lay down at the top of a hill in back of the speakers' platform. It drizzled a little bit and the ground was patently uncomfortable. I tried to go to sleep but was awakened in a few minutes by explosions. The whole sky was lit up. Green, red, bright orange: the soldiers were shooting off fireworks. The platform was bathed in the light from the explosions and, suddenly, floodlights from the rear. The public address system announced that we were going to have a show.

The show was a strange mixture of pop culture and mainstream highbrow "haute culture." There was a choral group singing a mildly atonal tone poem, a Jerome Robbinsesque ballet about Hollywood, Calypso dancers, and Mexican singers and dancers. The last act was the best, a Mardi Gras scene involving about a hundred West Indian singers and dancers, complete with floats, huge papier-mâché figures, drummers, and masks. The West Indians walked through the audience shouting and dancing, their many torches shooting shadows against the mountains. When they danced off and out of the amphitheater area up toward a group of unfinished school buildings, except for the huge floodlights on stage, the whole area was dark.

Now there was great confusion in the audience. Most Cubans were still going to try to get home that night, so they were getting themselves together, rounding up wives and children, trying to find some kind of transportation off the mountain. There were still whole units of militia piling into trucks or walk-

ing off down the hill in the dark. The delegates, our group and a couple more thousand people who didn't feel like charging off into the dark were left. Olga got all the Americans together and we lined up for what was really our first meal of the day: beans, rice, pork, and a small can of fruit juice. At that time, we still had some hopes of leaving that night, but soon word was passed around that we weren't leaving, and it was best that we slept where we were. "Sleep wherever you want," was what Olga said. That meant the ground, or maybe cement sidewalks around the unfinished school buildings and dormitories of the new "school city." Some of the Americans started grumbling, but there was nothing that could be done. Two of our number were missing because of the day's festivities: a young lady from Philadelphia had to be driven back to Habana in a station wagon because she had come down with diarrhea and a fever, and the model had walked around without her hat too often and had gotten a slight case of sunstroke. She was resting up in the medical shack now, and I began to envy her her small canvas cot.

It was a very strange scene, about 3- or 4,000 people wandering around in semi-darkness among a group of unfinished buildings, looking for places to sleep. The whole top of the mountain alive with flashlights, cigarette lighters, and small torches. Little groups of people huddled together against the sides of buildings or stretched out under new "street lamps" in temporary plazas. Some people managed to climb through the windows of the new buildings and sleep on dirt floors, some slept under long aluminum trucks used for hauling stage equipment and some, like myself and the young female economist, sat up all night under dim lights, finally talking ourselves excitedly to sleep in the cool grey of early morning. I lay straight back on the cement "sidewalk" and slept without moving, until the sun began to burn my face.

We had been told the night before to be ready by six A.M. to pull out, but when morning came we loitered around again till about eight o'clock, when we had to line up for a breakfast of hot milk and French bread. It was served by young militia women, one of whom wore a big sidearm in a shoulder holster. By now, the dysentery was beginning to play havoc with my stomach, and the only toilet was a heavy thicket out behind the amphitheater. I made it once, having to destroy a copy of a newspaper with my picture in it.

By nine no trucks had arrived, and with the sun now beginning to move heavily over us, the crowds shifted into the few shady areas remaining. It looked almost as if there were as many people still up on the mountain as there had been when we first arrived. Most of the Cubans, aside from the soldiers, stood in front of the pavilion and drank lukewarm Maltina or pineapple soda. The delegates and the other visitors squatted against buildings, talking and smoking. A French correspondent made a bad joke about Mussolini keeping the trains running on time, and a young Chinese student asked him why he wasn't in Algeria killing rebels.

The trucks did arrive, but there were only enough of them to take the women out. In a few minutes the sides of the trucks were almost bursting, so many females had stuffed inside. And they looked terribly uncomfortable, especially the ones stuck in the center who couldn't move an inch either way. An American newspaperman with our group who was just about to overstay his company-sanctioned leave began to panic, saying that the trucks wouldn't be back until the next day. But only a half-hour after the ladies pulled out, more trucks came and began taking the men out. Clarke, Williams, another member of our group, and I sat under the tin roof of an unfinished school building drinking warm soda, waiting until the last truck came, hoping it would be the least crowded. When we did climb up into one of the trucks it was jammed anyway, but we felt it was time to move.

This time we all had to stand up, except for a young *miliciano* who was squatting on a case of warm soda. I was in the center of the crowd and had nothing to hold on to but my companions. Every time the truck would stop short, which it did every few yards we traveled, everyone in the truck was slung against everyone else. When the truck did move, however, it literally zoomed down the side of the mountain. But then we would stop again, and all of us felt we would suffocate being mashed so tightly together, and from all the dust the trucks in front of us kicked up. The road now seemed like The Exodus. Exactly the same as the day before, only headed the opposite way. The trucks, the people on foot, the families, the militias, the *campesinos*, all headed down the mountain.

The truck sat one place twenty minutes without moving, and then when it did move it only edged up a few yards. Finally the driver pulled out of the main body of traffic and honking his horn continuously drove down the opposite side of the road. When the soldiers directing traffic managed to flag him down, he told them that we were important visitors who had to make a train in Yara. The truck zoomed off again, rocking back and forth and up and down, throwing its riders at times almost out the back gate.

After a couple of miles, about five Mexicans got off the truck and got into another truck headed for Santiago. This made the rest of the ride easier. The *miliciano* began opening the semi-chilled soda and passing it around. We were really living it up. The delegates' spirits came back and they started their chanting and waving. When we got to the train junction, the cattle cars were sitting, but completely filled with soldiers and farmers. We didn't even stop, the driver gunned the thing as fast as it would go and we sailed by the shouting soldiers. We had only a few more stops before we got to Yara, jumped down in the soft sand, and ran for the big silver train marked "CUBA" that had been waiting for us since we left. When we got inside the train we discovered that the women still hadn't gotten back, so we sat quietly in the luxurious leather seats slowly sipping rum. The women arrived an hour later.

While we were waiting in Yara, soldiers and units of militia began to arrive in the small town and squat all around the four or five sets of tracks waiting for their own trains. Most of them went back in boxcars, while we visitors had the luxury of the semi-air-conditioned coach.

The ride back was even longer than the fourteen hours it took us before. Once when we stopped for water, we sat about two hours. Later, we stopped to pick up lunches. The atmosphere in the train was much the same as before, especially the Mexican delegates who whooped it up constantly. They even made a conga line up and down the whole length of the train. The young Mexican woman and I did a repeat performance also and talked most of the fifteen or sixteen hours it took us to get back to Habana. She was gentler with me this time, calling me "Yanqui imperialist" only a few times.

Everyone in the train was dirty, thirsty, and tired when we arrived in Habana. I had been wearing the same clothes for three days and hadn't even once taken off my shoes. The women were in misery. I hadn't seen a pocket mirror since the cattle cars.

The terminal looked like a rear outpost of some battlefield. So many people in filthy wrinkled clothes scrambling wearily out of trains. But even as tired as I was I felt excited at the prospect of being back in the big city for five more days. I was even more excited by the amount of thinking the trip to the Sierra was forcing me to. The "new" ideas that were being shoved at me, some of which I knew would be painful when I eventually came to New York.

The idea of "a revolution" had been foreign to me. It was one of those inconceivably "romantic" and/or hopeless ideas that we Norteamericanos have been taught since public school to hold up to the cold light of "reason." That "reason" being whatever repugnant lie our usurious "ruling class" had paid their journalists to disseminate. The "reason" that allows that voting, in a country where the parties are exactly the same, can be made to assume the gravity of actual moral engagement. The "reason" that permits a young intellectual to believe he has said something profound when he says, "I don't trust men in uniforms." The *residue* has settled on all our lives, and no one can function comfortably in this country without it. That thin crust of lie we cannot even detect in our own thinking. That rotting of the mind which has enabled us to think about Hiroshima as if someone else had done it, or to believe vaguely that the "counterrevolution" in Guatemala was an "internal" affair.

The rebels among us have become merely people like myself who grow beards and will not participate in politics. A bland revolt. Drugs, juvenile delinquency, complete isolation from the vapid mores of the country—a few current ways out. But name an alternative here. Something not inextricably bound up in a lie. Something not part of liberal stupidity or the actual filth of vested interest. There is none. It's much too late. We are an *old* people already. Even the vitality of our art is like bright flowers growing up through a rotting carcass.

But the Cubans, and the other *new* peoples (in Asia, Africa, South America) don't need us, and we had better stay out of their way.

I came out of the terminal into the street and stopped at a newsstand to buy a newspaper. The headlines of one Miami paper read, "CUBAN CELEBRATION RAINED OUT." I walked away from the stand as fast as I could.

▶▶ **Kenneth Koch**

Bertha

Scene 1. *Oslo, the Ramparts.*

NOBLE:
The walls of our castles no longer withstand
The barbarian attack!

COUNSELOR:
       Seek BERTHA in her haven!

NOBLE:
Bertha! we are at the barbarians' mercy.

BERTHA:
Give the signal for attack!

NOBLE:
Attack? attack? How can we attack?
We are at the barbarians' mercy, they have surrounded our walls!

BERTHA:
Let me commune with my special gods a little.
Meanwhile, ATTACK!

NOBLE:
       Bertha commands attack!

COUNSELOR:
          Oh, the queen is mad!

NOBLE:
Mad, yes—but queen still. Never had Norway fairer or more brave.

OFFICER:
To the attack, as commanded by Queen Bertha!

OLD MAN:
Unhappy pagans! Soon the wrath of Bertha will be wreaked on them!
(*Bertha appears, clothed in a ring of white eagles.*)

BARBARIANS:
Help, help! Back! We are defeated!
       (*They scurry.*)

ALL:

Bertha has saved us from the barbarian menace.

(*Bertha retires.*)

Scene 2. *A Study in the Castle.*

TEACHER:

Yes it's a very interesting tale, that one you tell of the battle.

But why do you think you and your people yourselves are not Barbarians?

BERTHA:

Off with my teacher's head!

WHACK!

Let higher learning be disreinstated!

(*Banners are sent up all over the kingdom.*)

Scene 3. *Bertha's Summer Lodge.*

BERTHA:

Ah, how sweet it is to take the Norway air

And breathe it in my own lungs, then out again

Where it again mingles with the white clouds and blue Norwegian sky.

For I myself, in a sense, am Norway, and when Bertha breathes

The country breathes, and it breathes itself in,

And so the sky remains perfectly pure Norway.

MESSENGER:

Bertha, the land is at peace.

BERTHA:

Attack Scotland!

Scene 4. *A Little Scotch Frontier Town, on the Battle-Lines.*

SCOTCHMAN:

They say Queen Bertha's men rage to win all Scotland as a present for their mad queen.

2ND SCOTCHMAN:

No one has ever had Scotland defeated for very long. Let Queen Bertha try what she may!

3RD SCOTCHMAN:

Here come the armies of Bertha, Queen of Norway!

BERTHA (*At the head of her army, in a red and blue uniform; plants a banner*):

Here shall Bertha stay, nor all Scotland conquer!

Just to this flag's wave shall Bertha of Norway's kingdom reach!

No greed urges the just Norwegian nation to further spoils.

ALL SCOTCH:

Hurrah for Queen Bertha!

COMMON NORWEGIAN SOLDIER:

She is mad!

(*Trumpets, and dispersal of all troops; the flag alone remains standing on the snowy stage.*)

Scene 5. *The Council Chamber.*

COUNSELOR:

Queen Bertha, we are tired of useless wars.

BERTHA:

Useless! Do you call it useless to fight off an invader?

COUNSELOR:

I was not speaking of the Barbarian Wars.

BERTHA:

Well, I was! The council is dismissed.

(*Everyone leaves, including Bertha.*)

Scene 6. *A Rose Garden.*

GIRL:

If Queen Bertha knew we were here!

MAN:

She'd chop our two heads off, chip chap chop. There's no doubt about it.

GIRL:

Why does she forbid us young lovers to meet in the garden?

MAN:

A diseased mind, and the horrid fears of encroaching old age.

(*They embrace. Explosion. Both fall dead.*)

BERTHA (*From a castle window*):

Let there be no more garden meetings.

Scene 7. *Bertha on her Throne.*

BERTHA:

I am old, I am an old queen. But I still have the power of my childhood

Contained in my office. If I should lose my office, no more power would accrue

To my aged and feeble person. But even supposing I keep my power?

What chance is there that anything really nice will
  happen to me?
(*She plays with a flag, musing.*)
The flag of Norway! Once its colors drove my young
  heart wild
With dreams of conquest, first of the Norwegian flag,
  then of all the other nations in the world . . .
I haven't gotten very far—yet still Bertha is great.
  (*Ringing a bell.*) Call in the High Commissioners!

Scene 8. The Throne Room.

BERTHA:
We must give up the country to the barbarians! I
  wish to conquer Norway again!

COUNSELOR (*Aside*):
Bertha is mad! (*To Bertha:*) Yes, your Majesty.
(*Clarions are sounded.*)

Scene 9. A Public Place.

NORWEGIAN CITIZEN:
They say Bertha will give us up to the barbarians!

2ND NORWEGIAN CITIZEN:
Impossible!
(*The barbarian armies march in, with red and white
  banners.*)

BARBARIAN CHIEFTAIN:
On to the Castle! Norway is barbarian!
(*Sounds of cannon.*)

Scene 10. The Throne Room.

MESSENGER:
Bertha arrives, at the head of teeming troops!
On her arrival from Scotland all Norway has rallied
  to her banner!
Millions of Norwegians surround the castle shriek-
  ing, "Bertha, Queen of Norway!"

BARBARIAN CHIEFTAIN:
Let us be gone! We cannot withstand such force.
  Quickly, to the tunnel!
                    (*They disappear.*)
(*Bertha appears in regal splendor and walks to her
  throne, followed by applauding citizens. She as-
  cends the throne.*)

BERTHA:
Norway!
(*She falls from the throne and lies dead in front of
  it.*)

NOBLE:
Bertha is dead!

CITIZEN:
She was a great queen!

2ND CITIZEN:
She conquered her own country many times!

3RD CITIZEN:
Norway was happy under her rule!
(*Trumpets and sirens.*)

END

Picnic on the Battlefield

The Characters:
    ZAPO, a soldier
    MONSIEUR TÉPAN, the soldier's father
    MADAME TÉPAN, the soldier's mother
    ZÉPO, an enemy soldier
    FIRST CORPSMAN
    SECOND CORPSMAN

[SCENE: A battlefield. Barbed wire stretches from one end of the stage to the other, with sandbags piled against it.

Battle is in full swing. We hear bombs bursting, rifle shots and machine-gun fire.

Alone on stage, hidden flat on his belly among the sandbags, Zapo is very frightened.

The fighting stops. Silence.

From a knitting bag, Zapo takes out a ball of wool, knitting needles, and starts knitting a sweater that is already quite well along. The field telephone beside him suddenly rings.]

ZAPO: Hello . . . hello . . . yes, sir, Captain. . . . Yes, this is the sentry in Section 47. . . . Nothing new, Captain. . . . Excuse me, Captain, when are we going to start fighting again? . . . And what am I supposed to do with the grenades? Should I send them on up front or to the rear? . . . Don't get annoyed, I didn't say that to upset you. . . . And, Captain, I'm really feeling pretty lonesome. Couldn't you send me a companion out here? . . . Even the goat. [Evidently the Captain gives him a good dressing down.] Yes sir, Captain, yes sir! [Zapo hangs up. We hear him grumbling to himself.] [Silence.]

[Enter Monsieur and Madame Tépan, carrying baskets as though they are off on a picnic. Their son, who is sitting with his back turned, does not see them arriving.]

M. TÉPAN [ceremoniously]: My boy, get up and kiss your mother on the forehead. [Taken by surprise, Zapo gets up and, with a great deal of respect, gives his mother a kiss on the forehead. He is about to speak, but his father beats him to it.] Now give me a kiss.

ZAPO: My dear sweet parents, how did you ever dare come all the way out to a dangerous spot like this? You must leave here right away.

M. TÉPAN: Are you trying to tell your father what war and danger are all about? For me, all this is only a game. How many times do you think I've jumped off the subway while it was still moving?

MME. TÉPAN: We thought you were probably bored, so we came to pay you a little visit. After all, this war business must get pretty tiresome.

ZAPO: It all depends.

M. TÉPAN: I know perfectly well what goes on. In the beginning, it's all new and exciting. You enjoy the killing and throwing grenades and wearing a helmet; it's quite the thing, but you end up bored as hell. In my day, you'd have really seen something. Wars were a lot livelier, much more colorful. And then best of all, there were horses, lots of horses. It was a real pleasure: if the captain said "Attack!" before you could shake a stick we were all assembled on horseback in our red uniforms. That was something to see. And then we'd go galloping forward, sword in hand, and suddenly find ourselves hard against the enemy. And they'd be at their finest too, with their horses—there were always loads and loads of beautifully round-bottomed horses and their polished boots, and their green uniforms.

MME. TÉPAN: No, the enemy uniform wasn't green. It was blue. I remember perfectly well it was blue.

M. TÉPAN: And I say it was green.

MME. TÉPAN: When I was little I went out on the balcony any number of times to watch the battle, and I'd say to the little boy next door, "I'll bet you a gumdrop the Blues win." And the Blues were our enemies.

M. TÉPAN: All right, so you win.

MME. TÉPAN: I always loved battles. When I was little, I always said that when I grew up I wanted to be a Colonel in the Dragoons. But Mama didn't want me to. You know what a stickler she is.

M. TÉPAN: Your mother's a real nincompoop.

ZAPO: Forgive me, but you've got to leave. You just can't go walking into a war when you're not a soldier.

M. TÉPAN: I don't give a damn. We're here to have a picnic with you in the country and spend a nice Sunday.

MME. TÉPAN: I even made a lovely meal. Sausage, hard-boiled eggs, I know how much you like them! Ham sandwiches, red wine, some salad and some little cakes.

ZAPO: O.K., we'll do whatever you say. But if the Captain comes along he'll throw a fit. Plus the fact that he doesn't much go for the idea of visiting the battlefront. He keeps telling us :"War calls for discipline and grenades, but no visits."

M. TÉPAN: Don't you worry about it, I'll have a few words with your Captain.

ZAPO: And what if we have to start fighting again?

M. TÉPAN: You think that scares me, I've seen worse. Now if it was only cavalry battles! Times have changed, that's something you don't understand. [A pause.] We came on motorcycle. Nobody said anything.

ZAPO: They probably thought you were arbitrators.

M. TÉPAN: We did have some trouble getting through, though. With all those jeeps and tanks.

MME. TÉPAN: And the very minute we arrived, you remember that bottleneck because of the cannon?

M. TÉPAN: During wartime, you've got to be prepared for anything. Everybody knows that.

MME. TÉPAN: Well now, we're ready to start eating.

M. TÉPAN: Right you are, I could eat a horse. It's the smell of gunpowder that does it.

MME. TÉPAN: We'll eat sitting down on the blanket.

ZAPO: All right to eat with my rifle?

MME. TÉPAN: Let your rifle alone. It's bad manners to bring your rifle to the table. [A pause.] Why, child, you're filthy as a little pig. How did you manage to get in such a mess? Let's see your hands.

ZAPO [Ashamed, he shows them]: I had to crawl along the ground during maneuvers.

MME. TÉPAN: How about your ears?

ZAPO: I washed them this morning.

MME. TÉPAN: That should do then. Now how about your teeth? [He shows them.] Very good. Now who's going to give his little boy a great big kiss for brushing his teeth so nicely? [To her husband:] Well, give your son a kiss for brushing his teeth so nicely. [M. Tépan gives his son a kiss.] Because, you know, one thing I just won't allow is not washing, and blaming it on the war.

ZAPO: Yes, Mama. [They eat.]

M. TÉPAN: Well, my boy, have you been keeping up a good shooting score?

ZAPO: When?

M. TÉPAN: Why, the last few days.

ZAPO: Where?

M. TÉPAN: Right here and now. After all, you are fighting a war.

ZAPO: No, no great shakes. I haven't kept up a very good score. Practically no bull's-eyes.

M. TÉPAN: Well, what have you been scoring best with in your shooting, enemy horses or soldiers?

ZAPO: No, no horses. There aren't any horses anymore.

M. TÉPAN: Well, soldiers then?

ZAPO: Could be.

M. TÉPAN: Could be? Aren't you sure?

ZAPO: It's just that I. . . . I fire without taking aim [a pause] and when I fire I say an *Our Father* for the guy I shot.

M. TÉPAN: You've got to show more courage. Like your father.

MME. TÉPAN: I'm going to put a record on the phonograph. [She puts on a record: a Spanish paso-doble. Sitting on the ground, they all three listen.]

M. TÉPAN: Now that's real music. Yes, ma'am, I tell you. Olé!
[As the music continues, an enemy soldier, Zépo, enters. He is dressed like Zapo. Only the color of his uniform is different. Zépo wears green; Zapo wears gray.
[Standing unseen behind the family, his mouth agape, Zépo listens to the music. The record comes to an end. Zapo, getting up, spots Zépo.
[Both raise their hands in the air, while M. and Mme. Tépan look at them, startled.]

M. TÉPAN: What's going on?

[*Zapo seems about to act, but hesitates. Then, very decisively, he points his rifle at Zépo.*]

ZAPO: Hands up!

[*Zépo, more terrified than ever, raises his hands still higher. Zapo doesn't know what to do. All of a sudden, he hurriedly runs toward Zépo and taps him gently on the shoulder, saying:*]

ZAPO: You're it. [*Pleased as punch, to his father:*] There you are! A prisoner!

M. TÉPAN: That's fine. Now what are you going to do with him?

ZAPO: I don't know. But could be they'll make me a corporal.

M. TÉPAN: In the meantime, tie him up.

ZAPO: Tie him up? What for?

M. TÉPAN: That's what you do with prisoners, you tie 'em up!

ZAPO: How?

M. TÉPAN: By his hands.

MME. TÉPAN: Oh yes, you've definitely got to tie his hands. That's the way I've always seen it done.

ZAPO: All right. [*To the prisoner:*] Please put your hands together.

ZÉPO: Don't do it too hard.

ZAPO: Oh, no.

ZÉPO: Ouch! You're hurting me.

M. TÉPAN: Come on now, don't mistreat your prisoner.

MME. TÉPAN: Is that the way I brought you up? Haven't I told you over and over again that you've got to be considerate of your fellow man?

ZAPO: I didn't do it on purpose. [*To Zépo:*] Does it hurt the way it is now?

ZÉPO: No, like this it doesn't hurt.

M. TÉPAN: Speak right up and tell him if it does. Just pretend we're not here.

ZÉPO: This way it's O.K.

M. TÉPAN: Now his feet.

ZAPO: His feet too? How long does this go on?

M. TÉPAN: Didn't they teach you the rules?

ZAPO: Sure.

M. TÉPAN: Well?

ZAPO [*to Zépo, very politely*]: Would you kindly be good enough to please sit down on the ground?

ZÉPO: All right, but don't hurt me.

MME. TÉPAN: See! Now he's taking a dislike to you.

ZAPO: No. No he's not. I'm not hurting you, am I?

ZÉPO: No, this is fine.

ZAPO [*out of nowhere*]: Papa, suppose you took a snapshot with the prisoner down there on the ground and me standing with my foot on his stomach?

M. TÉPAN: Say, yes! That'll look classy.

ZÉPO: Oh, no you don't. Not that.

MME. TÉPAN: Let him. Don't be so stubborn.

ZÉPO: No. I said no and I mean no.

MME. TÉPAN: Just a little old snip of a snapshot. What difference could that possibly make to you? Then we could put it in the dining room right next to the Lifesaving Certificate my husband got thirteen years ago.

ZÉPO: No, you'll never talk me into it.

ZAPO: But why should you refuse?

ZÉPO: I've got a fiancée. And if she ever sees the snapshot, she'll say I don't know how to fight a war.

ZAPO: No, all you have to do is tell her it isn't you at all, it's a panther.

MME. TÉPAN: C'mon, say yes.

ZÉPO: All right, but I'm only doing it to please you.

ZAPO: Stretch all the way out.

[*Zépo stretches all the way out. Zapo puts one foot on his stomach and grabs his rifle with a military air.*]

MME. TÉPAN: Throw your chest out more.

ZAPO: Like this?

MME. TÉPAN: Yes, that's it. Don't breathe.

M. TÉPAN: Make like a hero.

ZAPO: How do you mean a hero, like this?

M. TÉPAN: It's a cinch. Make like the butcher when he was telling us what a lady-killer he is.

ZAPO: Like so?

M. TÉPAN: Yes, that's it.

MME. TÉPAN: Just be sure your chest is puffed way out, and don't breathe.

ZÉPO: Are you about finished?

M. TÉPAN: Have a little patience. One . . . two . . . three.

ZAPO: I hope I'll come out all right.

MME. TÉPAN: Oh yes, you looked very military.

M. TÉPAN: You were fine.

MME. TÉPAN: That makes me want to have my picture taken, too.

M. TÉPAN: Now there's a good idea.

ZAPO: All right. I'll take it if you want me to.

MME. TÉPAN: Give me your helmet so I'll look like a soldier.

ZÉPO: I don't want any more pictures. Even one was too much.

ZAPO: Don't feel that way. Come right down to it, what difference could it make?

ZÉPO: That's my final say.

M. TÉPAN [to his wife]: Don't push him. Prisoners are always very touchy. If we keep it up, he'll get mad and spoil all our fun.

ZAPO: Well now, what are we going to do with him?

MME. TÉPAN: We could ask him to eat with us. What do you think?

M. TÉPAN: I don't see any reason why not.

ZAPO [to Zépo]: All right then, how'd you like to eat with us?

ZÉPO: Uh . . .

M. TÉPAN: We brought along a nice bottle of wine.

ZÉPO: Well, in that case O.K.

MME. TÉPAN: Make yourself right at home. Don't be afraid to ask for things.

ZÉPO: Fine.

M. TÉPAN: Well now, how about you, have you been keeping up a good shooting score?

ZÉPO: When?

M. TÉPAN: Why, the last few days.

ZÉPO: Where?

M. TÉPAN: Right here and now. After all, you are fighting a war.

ZÉPO: No, no great shakes. I haven't kept up a very good score. Practically no bull's-eyes.

M. TÉPAN: Well, what have you been scoring best with in your shooting, enemy horses or soldiers?

ZÉPO: No, no horses. There aren't any horses any more.

M. TÉPAN: Well, soldiers then?

ZÉPO: Could be.

M. TÉPAN: Could be? Aren't you sure?

ZÉPO: It's just that I. . . . I fire without taking aim [A pause] and when I fire I say a *Hail Mary* for the guy I shot.

ZAPO: A *Hail Mary*? I'd have thought you'd say an *Our Father*.

ZÉPO: No. Always a *Hail Mary*. [A pause.] It's shorter.

M. TÉPAN: Come, my boy, you have to be courageous.

MME. TÉPAN [to Zépo]: If you like, we can untie you.

ZÉPO: No, leave me this way. It doesn't matter.

M. TÉPAN: You're not going to start putting on airs with us? If you want us to untie you, just say the word.

MME. TÉPAN: Please feel free.

ZÉPO: Well, if you really mean it, untie my feet. But it's just to please you people.

M. TÉPAN: Zapo, untie him. [Zapo unties him.]

MME. TÉPAN: Well now, feel better?

ZÉPO: Sure do. But listen, maybe I'm causing you too much trouble.

M. TÉPAN: Not at all. Make yourself right at home. And if you want us to undo your hands, just say so.

ZÉPO: No, not my hands, too. I don't want to overdo it.

M. TÉPAN: Not at all, my boy, not at all. I tell you, you don't disturb us one bit.

ZÉPO: All right, go ahead and untie my hands then. But just while we eat, huh? I don't want you to think when you give me an inch I'm going to take a mile.

Arrabal
Photos by Fred McDarrah

M. TÉPAN: Untie his hands, sonny.

MME. TÉPAN: Well, since our honorable prisoner is so nice, we're going to have a lovely day out here in the country.

ZÉPO: Don't call me "honorable" prisoner. Just say "prisoner" plain and simple.

MME. TÉPAN: You're sure that won't make you feel bad?

ZÉPO: No, not at all.

M. TÉPAN: Well, you're certainly unpretentious, anyway.

[*Sound of airplanes.*]

ZAPO: Airplanes. They're going to bomb us for sure.

[*Zapo and Zépo dive for the sandbags and hide.*]

ZAPO [*to his parents*]: Run for cover! The bombs are going to land right on you.

[*The sound of the planes drowns out everything. Immediately bombs start falling. Shells explode nearby. Deafening racket. Zapo and Zépo are crouching among the sandbags. M. Tépan goes on calmly talking to his wife, who answers him with equal calm. Because of the bombardment we cannot hear their conversation.*

[*Mme. Tépan heads for one of the picnic baskets, from which she takes an umbrella. She opens it. The Tépans take shelter under the umbrella as though it were raining. Standing there, they shift from one foot to the other, in rhythm, all the while discussing personal matters. The bombardment continues.*]

[*At last, the airplanes take off. Silence.*]

[*M. Tépan stretches one arm out from under the umbrella to make certain there is no longer anything coming down from the sky.*]

M. TÉPAN: You can close your umbrella now.

[*Mme. Tépan closes it. Together they go over to their son and prod him on the behind a couple of times with the umbrella.*]

M. TÉPAN: All right, come on out. The bombing's over.

[*Zapo and Zépo come out of their hiding place.*]

ZAPO: They didn't get you?

M. TÉPAN: You don't expect anything to happen to your father, do you? [*Proudly:*] Little bombs like that? Don't make me laugh.

[*From the left, a pair of Red Cross corpsmen enter, carrying a stretcher.*]

1ST CORPSMAN: Any bodies?

ZAPO: No, none here.

1ST CORPSMAN: You're sure you took a good look?

ZAPO: Absolutely.

1ST CORPSMAN: And there's not one single body?

ZAPO: Didn't I just say so?

1ST CORPSMAN: Not even someone wounded?

ZAPO: Not even.

2ND CORPSMAN: Well, we're really up the creek! [To Zapo, persuasively:] Take a good look all around here, see if you don't turn up a stiff someplace.

1ST CORPSMAN: Don't press the issue. They told you once and for all there aren't any.

2ND CORPSMAN: What a lousy deal!

ZAPO: I'm really very sorry. I swear I didn't plan it that way.

2ND CORPSMAN: That's what they all say. That there aren't any corpses, and that they didn't plan it that way.

1ST CORPSMAN: So let the man alone!

M. TÉPAN [obligingly]: If we can help you at all, we'd be delighted to. At your service.

2ND CORPSMAN: Well, I don't know. If we keep on like this, I really don't know what the Captain's going to say to us.

M. TÉPAN: What seems to be the trouble?

2ND CORPSMAN: Just that the others are all getting sore wrists carrying out the dead and wounded, while we still haven't come up with anything. And it's not because we haven't been looking.

M. TÉPAN: I see. That really is a bore. [To Zapo:] You're quite sure there are no corpses?

ZAPO: Obviously, Papa.

M. TÉPAN: You looked under the sandbags?

ZAPO: Yes, Papa.

M. TÉPAN [angry]: Why don't you come right out and say you don't want to have any part in helping these good gentlemen?

1ST CORPSMAN: Don't jump on him like that. Leave him alone. We'll just hope we have better luck in some other trench where maybe everybody'll be dead.

M. TÉPAN: I'd be delighted for you.

MME. TÉPAN: So would I. Nothing pleases me more than to see people who take their work seriously.

M. TÉPAN [indignantly, to anyone within hearing]: Well, isn't anyone going to do anything for these gentlemen?

ZAPO: If it was up to me, it'd be good as done.

ZÉPO: Same here.

M. TÉPAN: Look here now, isn't one of you at least wounded?

ZAPO [ashamed]: No, not me.

M. TÉPAN [to Zépo:] What about you?

ZÉPO [ashamed]: Me either. I never was lucky.

MME. TÉPAN [delighted]: I just remembered! This morning, while I was peeling onions, I cut my finger. How's that?

M. TÉPAN: Why of course! [Really in the swing of things:] They'll put you on the stretcher and carry you right off!

1ST CORPSMAN: Sorry, it's no good. Women don't count.

M. TÉPAN: Well, that didn't get us anywhere.

1ST CORPSMAN: It doesn't matter.

2ND CORPSMAN: Maybe we can get our fill in the other trenches. [They start to go off.]

M. TÉPAN: Don't you worry, if we find a corpse, we'll hang onto it for you. There's not a chance we'd give it to anybody but you.

2ND CORPSMAN: Thank you very much, sir.

M. TÉPAN: It's nothing, my boy. It's the very least I could do. [The corpsmen make their goodbyes. All four of the others reply in kind. The corpsmen exit.]

MME. TÉPAN: That's what's so pleasant about spending Sunday out in the battlefield. You always run into such nice folks. [A pause.] Come to think of it, why is it you're enemies?

ZÉPO: I don't know. I'm not too well educated.

MME. TÉPAN: I mean is it from birth, or did you become enemies after?

ZÉPO: I don't know. I don't know a thing about it.

M. TÉPAN: Well then, how did you come to go to war?

ZÉPO: One day I was home fixing my mother's iron and a man came by and said to me: "Are you Zépo?" . . . "Yes." . . . "Good, you've got to go to war." So I asked him, "What war?" And he said to me: "Don't you read the newspapers? You are a hick!" So I told him yes I did, but not all that war stuff . . .

ZAPO: That's just what happened to me; exactly what happened to me.

M. TÉPAN: Sure, they came after you, too.

MME. TÉPAN: No, it's not the same. You weren't fixing the iron that day, you were repairing the car.

M. TÉPAN: I was talking about the rest of it. [To Zépo:] Go on. Then what happened?

ZÉPO: Well then I told him that I had a fiancée, and if I didn't take her to the movies on Sunday, she wouldn't know what to do with herself. He said that that didn't matter.

ZAPO: Same as me. Exactly the same as me.

ZÉPO: Well, then my father came down and he said I couldn't go to war because I didn't have a horse.

ZAPO: Like my father said.

ZÉPO: The man said they didn't use horses any more, and I asked him if I could take along my fiancée. He said no. Then I asked him could I take along my aunt to make me custard every Thursday. I like custard.

MME. TÉPAN [realizing that she has forgotten something]: Oh! The custard!

ZÉPO: Again he said no.

ZAPO: The way he did to me.

ZÉPO: And ever since then, here I am, nearly always all alone in the trench here.

MME. TÉPAN: As long as you're so much alike, and both so bored, I think you and your honorable prisoner might play together this afternoon.

ZAPO: Oh no, Mama! I'm too scared. He's an enemy.

M. TÉPAN: Oh come on now, don't be scared.

ZAPO: If you knew what the general told us about the enemy.

MME. TÉPAN: What did he tell you?

ZAPO: He said the enemy soldiers are very mean.

When they take prisoners, they put pebbles in their socks so it hurts when they walk.

MME. TÉPAN: How horrible! What savages!

M. TÉPAN [indignantly, to Zépo]: Aren't you ashamed to be part of an army of criminals?

ZÉPO: I didn't do anything. I'm not mad at anybody.

MME. TÉPAN: He's trying to put one over on us, acting like a little saint.

M. TÉPAN: We should never have untied him. Probably all we have to do is have our backs turned for him to go putting pebbles in our socks.

ZÉPO: Don't be so mean to me.

M. TÉPAN: How do you expect us to be? I'm shocked. I know just what I'm going to do. I'm going to find the Captain and ask him to let me go into battle.

ZAPO: He won't let you. You're too old.

M. TÉPAN: Well then I'll go buy a horse and a saber and I'll go to war on my own.

ZÉPO: Please, madame, don't treat me like this. Besides, I was just going to tell you, our general said the same thing about you people.

MME. TÉPAN: How could he dare tell such a lie?

ZAPO: The very same thing, honest?

ZÉPO: Yes, the very same thing.

M. TÉPAN: Maybe it's the same one who talked to both of you.

MME. TÉPAN: Well, if it is the same general, the least he could do is use a different speech. Imagine telling everybody the same thing.

M. TÉPAN [to Zépo, changing his tone]: Can I fill your glass again?

MME. TÉPAN: I hope you enjoyed our little lunch.

M. TÉPAN: It was better than last Sunday, anyway.

ZÉPO: What happened then?

M. TÉPAN: Well, we went out to the country and laid all our chow out on the blanket. While we had our backs turned, a cow came along and ate the whole lunch, including the napkins.

ZÉPO: What a glutton, that cow!

M. TÉPAN: Yes, but then to get even, we ate the cow. [They laugh.]

ZAPO [*to Zépo*]: I bet they weren't hungry after that.

M. TÉPAN: To your health! [*They all drink.*]

MME. TÉPAN [*to Zépo*]: Tell me something, what do you do for amusement in the trenches?

ZÉPO: Just to pass the time and keep myself amused, I take odds and ends of rags and make little flowers out of them. See, I get bored a lot.

MME. TÉPAN: And what do you do with these rag flowers?

ZÉPO: At first I used to send them to my fiancée, but one day she told me that the cellar and the greenhouse were already filled with them, that she didn't know what to do with them any more, and would I mind sending her something else for a change?

MME. TÉPAN: And what did you do?

ZÉPO: I tried learning something else, but I couldn't do it. So, to pass the time, I just go on making my rag flowers.

MME. TÉPAN: And then do you throw them away?

ZÉPO: No, now I've found a way to make use of them: I furnish one flower for each of my buddies who dies. That way, I know that even if I make a whole lot, there'll never be enough.

M. TÉPAN: You found a good way out.

ZÉPO [*timidly*]: Yes.

ZAPO: Well, you know what I do so's not to get bored is knit.

MME. TÉPAN: But tell me, do all the soldiers get bored the way you two do?

ZÉPO: That depends on what they do for relaxation.

ZAPO: Same thing over on our side.

M. TÉPAN: Well then, let's stop the war.

ZÉPO: But how?

M. TÉPAN: Very easy. You tell your buddies that the enemy doesn't want to fight, and you tell the same thing to your comrades. And everybody goes home.

ZAPO: Terrific!

MME. TÉPAN: That way you can finish fixing the iron.

ZAPO: How come nobody ever thought of that before?

MME. TÉPAN: It takes your father to come up with ideas like that. Don't forget he's a Normal School graduate, and a philatelist, too.

ZÉPO: But what will all the field marshals and the corporals do?

M. TÉPAN: We'll give 'em guitars and castanets to keep 'em quiet.

ZÉPO: Excellent idea.

M. TÉPAN: See how easy it is? It's all settled.

ZÉPO: We'll wow 'em!

ZAPO: Boy, will my buddies be glad!

MME. TÉPAN: What do you say we celebrate and put on that pasodoble we were listening to before?

ZÉPO: Wonderful!

ZAPO: Yes, put on the record, Mama.
    [*Mme. Tépan puts on the record. She winds the phonograph and waits. Not a sound is heard.*]

M. TÉPAN: You can't hear anything.

MME. TÉPAN [*going to the phonograph*]: Oh! . . . I made a boo-boo! Instead of putting on a record, I put on a beret.

    [*She puts the record on. A lively pasodoble is heard. Zapo dances with Zépo; Mme. Tépan with her husband.*
    [*The field telephone rings. None of the group hears it. They go on dancing in a lively manner.*
    [*The phone rings again. The dancing continues. Battle breaks out once more with a great din of bombs, rifle fire and the crackle of machine guns. Having noticed nothing, the two couples keep on dancing gaily.*
    [*A sudden machine-gun blast mows them all down. They fall to the ground, stone dead. One bullet seems to have nicked the phonograph: the music keeps repeating the same strain over and over, like a record with a scratch in it. We hear this repeated strain for the remainder of the play.*
    [*From the left, the two corpsmen enter, carrying the empty stretcher.*]
    FAST CURTAIN

Translated by James Hewitt

A New Comic Style: Arrabal

Perhaps it is one characteristic of great works at their inception (and this must apply in every creative dimension) that they reach our sensibility by routes that are unexplored but whose direction, it seems, pre-existed in us as if on dotted lines. No one has spoken this language to us before, and yet we recognize it as our own. Hearing it, in fact, produces a kind of jubilation: a sense of a discovery that is simultaneously a "recognition" and a confirmation.

Is it premature to speak of the achievement of a playwright whose work has not yet been staged? Four plays have already been published together in a volume and a fifth, *Picnic On The Battlefield*, appeared separately in *Les Lettres Nouvelles* (four more plays are still unpublished). A novel, *Baal Babylone*, has just been published in France. To me, these works constitute enough of a dossier to bear witness to Arrabal's *presence* among us today.

Some will not be pleased by this "presence," others will be embarrassed, for poets always bring with them a certain necessary scandal. Many will look for—and find—the imperfections of this work still in its developmental stages; many will not hesitate to point out the influence of Strindberg, of Jarry, of Kafka, and of their lineage. Yet Arrabal's themes, his major obsessions, and above all his own manner of "being in the world" sharply distinguish him from any of these.

Arrabal is Spanish; until recently he lived in Spain. He was born at the beginning of the Spanish civil war, grew up under a military dictatorship, the definitive eradication of civil liberty, the terrorism of a church reinstated in its repressive functions, the torpor of a humiliated populace, the nightmare of a police state become a daily reality, the secret hatreds, the generalized corruption, the asphyxiation by boredom, unemployment and poverty in city and countryside alike, and the imbecile braggadocio of a General prospering behind the triple screen of army, police, and church. Such is the background this work is inscribed upon, and it is a fact we must never lose sight of.

Half crushed beneath the yoke of family and social prohibitions, this lonely "little man" (not so far from the early Chaplin), defenseless but endowed with an unfailing vitality, bursts into Ubuesque laughter and, almost with astonishment, realizes that he is thereby throwing off his chains, that the walls which confined him are crumbling, collapsing, falling into dust on all sides.

Arrabal's theater is a theater of deliverance, resolutely oriented—not by virtue of an explicit ideological choice, but by a simple reaction of self-defense—toward a liberation of man. There is in his work an incredible hunger for hope, an appetite we do not find, for example, in Beckett, or find no longer. Yet Arrabal is certainly locked in the lions' cage. And he is afraid. And he acts like children when they are afraid (like Chaplin), he laughs: both to *humor* the ferocious creatures and to escape his own fear. This rather creaky laugh, which forces the audience to confront a weakness too evident to be disguised, gradually becomes conscious of its own power and effectiveness. At first, in fact, it is enough merely to laugh, in any way at all, for that laughter—faint at first, growing more confident—ultimately to become a formidable weapon.

The two short one-act plays, *Orison* and *The Two Executioners*, provide us with Arrabal's fundamental themes which we shall again encounter, detailed and amplified, in the two full-length plays.

In *Orison*, a man and a woman of unspecified age and social condition speak to each other over a child's coffin, while a muted blues trumpet plays off-stage. A black backcloth, four candles, and an iron crucifix complete the decor, and it is against this tragically divested background that the dialogue begins: so innocent, stubborn, and cruel, even in its tenderness, between two beings (two ancient children or surviving J3's) who all of a sudden decide *to be good* the way you might decide to play hide-and-seek instead of hopscotch or marbles.

They are bored and they have committed a murder—for diversion. We find them watching over the body, apparently without remorse (they have not yet reached this stage or have passed quite beyond it), but determined to spend their time from now on altogether differently. And going back to the sources, stripping away the pious imagery corrupted by the centuries, they make direct contact with the arch-legend, the definitive type of the good man as he is established in the Gospels. After a brief moment of enthusiasm rich in well-intentioned promises, they find themselves again revolving in a colorless void:

"It's going to be boring," Lilbé points out. "It's going to be like the rest. . . . We're going to get tired of this too." And Fidio says: "We'll try," making a great effort not to lose everything. And that is the play's last line.

Between crime and sanctity they see no real qualitative difference. Neither the one nor the other resolves anything. Even when it is as good as new, the old Christian myth (it is comparably central in *The Automobile Graveyard*) reveals itself as unworkable, unusable. It is like a lost truth, a gold coin you happen to have found in the mud: nostalgically you watch it gleaming in the hollow of your hand though you know perfectly well it no longer can be used as currency, if it ever could. Profoundly maladjusted to the world and glowing with good will, Fidio and Lilbé are like the lovers in *Modern Times*, acting out the farce of perfect happiness while the hut they live in collapses upon them piece by piece, or like that image of Chaplin shivering in his striped bathing suit and flinging himself with great enthusiasm into three inches of brook water: how familiar the hero's belly-smacked bewilderment as he limps to his feet covered with mud . . . and the public's laughter. *Orison* will be laughed at, although it is perhaps the most poignant play of the entire group.

In *The Two Executioners* we participate in the degradation, the corruption of the myths, the morality, and the vocabulary of the respectable middle class (sin, pardon, sacrifice, guilt, suffering, altruism, etc.), cunningly perverted by a monstrous mother. She has just denounced her husband to the police and, accompanied by her two sons, settles down in the anteroom of the torture chamber to enjoy his agony. There is no certainty that this "melodrama in one act" will not also turn out to be comic on the stage, despite the horror of the situation. Enlarged out of all proportion, horror ends up as farce, becoming so intolerable that only laughter succeeds in assimilating it.

For the mother, the father's agony under the eyes of her two sons is the occasion for a wild display of self-glorification whose stages follow the progression of the martyrdom unfolding on the other side of the partition. Ultimately the mother disappears into the torture chamber itself to pour salt and vinegar on her husband's wounds, despite the protests of her "unnatural son" and with the encouragement of the other boy, who is totally deranged by the "maternal system"; finally the "unnatural son" lets himself be vanquished: he embraces his mother and knowing the truth—knowing he is betraying her *and* his father by this gesture—falls weeping to his knees and begs for forgiveness.

Emanu, the hero of *The Automobile Graveyard* and the counterpart of Fidio in *Orison*, is constantly obsessed by an irresistible desire to be good. He has learned all the rules of the game and takes pride in his mastery of them with just that mixture of complacency and kindness, that utter lack of adjustment to the world of traditional values (of which he nevertheless presents himself as the champion), which is the basis of Arrabal's comic style. In the long run the game becomes dangerous: betrayed by one of his companions, disavowed by the other, Emanu is tied to a policeman's bicycle and crucified against a lamp-post, but after his disappearance the world continues as before, neither better nor worse; a child is born and the sun rises.

While Emanu is modestly re-inventing the Passion for his own purposes, impelled by a fatality of which

Arrabal with Richard Seaver and Irving Rosenthal
Photo by Fred McDarrah

he is ignorant, the inhabitants of *The Automobile Graveyard*, crammed in the filthy jalopies that define the stage, adopt in their practical lives the manners of a *grand seigneur*—casual, blasé, cruel and capricious. A mismatched pair of athletes training for long-distance races tirelessly crosses the stage until the moment when, disguised as policemen and playing this new role with the same imbecile application, they arrest and execute Emanu. There is not one character here who is not displaced with regard to his true situation in society and even with regard to the action of the play, which follows its own foreseeable course without paying much attention to them, using them here and there like the gear-wheels of a machine for pulverizing reality.

It is in this displacement (itself a source of comedy) between what they are and what they pretend to be, what they supposedly say or think and what they objectively signify within the limits of a necessary action, that their inalienable share of freedom appears, nerve-racking but tireless, ridiculous but always renewed. From their first appearance on the earth, the weak and the small find before their very eyes, imposed or proposed, the typical examples of success in every genre: triumphs procured by Fame, Glory, Power, ideal Love, perfect Crime, Sanctity, etc. The truth is there ("a first-class truth," as

Beckett says, valid, unfortunately, only for travelers of the same class), one has only to choose. With frantic enthusiasm and lack of foresight they throw themselves into one or another of these exemplary courses and, of course, fall, hurt themselves, even destroy themselves altogether. Despite failure they persist, hardy and cheerful, cunning if need be, and dimly seeking, beyond the great models that darken the horizon, a way of living, a way of being, that will at last be the right one, that will at last establish a possible goodness among men.

Violent death occurs in all of Arrabal's plays, assuming for him the same obsessive quality as the stubborn search for goodness: Lilbé and Fidio in *Orison* keep watch over the black coffin of a child they have killed; Emanu, a parallel with the husband in *The Two Executioners*, is assassinated under our eyes, gradually and according to the rules, like a bull in the arena. In *Fando and Lis* crime is committed under an irresistible impetus profoundly related to the sexual act. For the criminal, murder is only a desperate way of taking possession of another person, of fixing him forever in a relation to oneself that is perfect and irreversible. Such is the crime Fando commits when, full of savage tenderness, he drags his beloved wife to the land of Tar in her little paralytic's wagon. Throughout the entire play he struggles to

less and less effect against the desire and the need to make her suffer. After each scene of violence, forgiveness is asked and accorded, but the equilibrium is increasingly unstable, the tenderness becomes shriller, while the anger grows more and more impatient, as though seeking in the darkness an answer which is not vouchsafed. "Talk to me, Lis, talk to me, say something to me," Fando never stops repeating, as if words still had the power of halting the pitiless tide of violence. And perhaps they might have this power, but Lis is terrorized, helpless, loving, clumsy: an exasperating victim who offers her neck to the executioner's knife even before he can demand it. Three chance comrades, the three men with the umbrella, also on their way to Tar, create a brief diversion: Fando introduces Lis to them in an extraordinary scene, raising her skirts, showing them her legs, and forcing them to kiss her.

In this way, for a while, Fando is able to share Lis with others, she assumes an existence in other eyes than his own, and he no longer suffocates in an inexorable dialogue of the deaf. But violence, postponed for a moment, comes to its logical conclusion—the answer sought for—which is Lis's death, and peace follows the crime, an ease like that which follows love. This is an absurd crime which obeys torture's complex dialectic: the executioner, bound to his victim, finds himself caught in an inescapable mesh (each torture requiring a greater one, the only one capable of appeasing the executioner's sense of his own guilt), where pleasure is produced by suffering and vice versa, where the individual finally and desperately attempts to violate his own limits. There is an element of Sade in Arrabal (one is explicitly reminded of that "excess of sensibility that borders on insensibility" Sade speaks of in *Aline and Valcour* and which often could define the behavior of Arrabal's heroes). It is this type of relationship—moreover absolutely reversible: the executioner becoming the victim of his victim who is in turn transformed into the executioner—which unites the two couples: Milos and Dilla, Lasca and Tiossido, in *The Automobile Graveyard*.

The universe Arrabal's characters inhabit is incontestably today's world, and our international James Deans will probably identify themselves with his heroes whose very existence is a challenge to the established moral values, to the Order which sets up the sclerosed structures under which our civilization is gently collapsing. The mockery of Justice is a frequently recurring theme in Arrabal, particularly in *The Automobile Graveyard*. In *Picnic On The Battlefield* the entire plot is based on the absurdity of

War: Zapo Tépan and his parents are picnicking in the middle of the battlefield. An enemy soldier, Zépo, wanders into the area and they conscientiously make him a prisoner of war:

Mme. Tépan: Come to think of it, why is it you're enemies?
Zépo: I don't know. I'm not too well educated.
Mme. Tépan: I mean, is it from birth, or did you become enemies after?
Zépo: I don't know. I don't know a thing about it.
M. Tépan: Well, then, how did you come to go to war?
Zépo: One day, home, I was in the middle of fixing my mother's iron and a man came by and said to me. "Are you Zépo?" . . . "Yes". . . . "Good, you've got to go to war." So I asked him, I did: "What war?" And he said to me: "Don't you read the newspapers? You are a hick!" I told him yes, I did, but not all that war stuff.
Zapo: That's just what happened to me, exactly what happened to me.

At the end of the play all four will be cut down by the same burst of machine-gun fire at the moment they least expect it.

In a more general way Arrabal's universe also derives from childhood (that misunderstood category of thought and language), which instinctively makes use of the values proposed by adult systems with the sole purpose of taking possession of the world, of measuring oneself against it with all one's strength and one's weakness, of sharpening upon it one's insatiable appetite for life. With an incomparable skill and accuracy Arrabal has seized upon the poetic truth of the language of childhood, a speech as direct as a shower of stones, a nakedness of diction with nothing *behind* it, no shadows, no implications, no ambiguity, and no false mystery. The extreme simplicity of this language (like the knowing simplicity of his dramatic construction) bears witness in Arrabal—who is an excellent mathematician—to a search for pure form which at its limit would achieve the abstract beauty of an algebraic formula or of the animated cartoons of a Norman McLaren. It is Arrabal's ambition to reach this point, though one may doubt that this is a possible course for the theater. At present his dramatic originality and effectiveness have inaugurated a comic style for which there seems to be an equivalent only in the cinema, in Chaplin's first films. We must wait for this theater to assume its true dimensions on the stage in order to appreciate in the proper light—that of the footlights—what an attentive and ardent reading permits us to discover here now.

Translated by Richard Howard

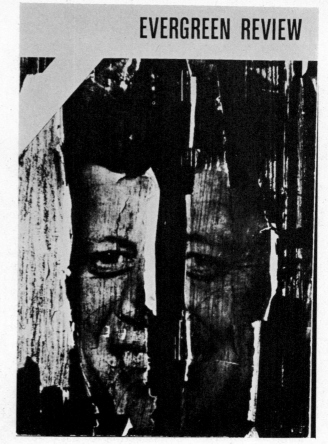

EVERGREEN REVIEW

No. 21
$1.00
U. K.: 5/-

Special This Issue:
THE GERMAN SCENE

EVERGREEN REVIEW

↓ EVERGREEN REVIEW

George Grosz

►► Robert Stromberg

A Talk with Louis-Ferdinand Céline

It is a very strange feeling, to be seeing Céline. Céline the terrible! Céline the outraged! Céline the put upon! Céline the *Fou!*

Céline lives in Meudon, on the fringe of Paris. He lives in a three-story nineteenth-century wood and mortar house with his wife Lucette Almanzor and about half-a-dozen dogs, as near as I could count. His wife, he says, is the owner of the house.

"I thought you were coming tomorrow . . . I wasn't expecting you . . . I haven't prepared . . . I thought tomorrow . . . come in, come in." Those were his first words.

He addressed his wife in French, telling her to take my coat, to get me a chair. He is a large man—but he is bent. He moved slowly, a shuffle—as if he were too weak to do anything else—to the other side of a large room that seemed to be a combination kitchen, dining area and writing room. He sat down at a large round table, pushing to one corner, and some of it to the floor, piles of books, papers and magazines and made room for us to talk.

"What is it you want? Who is this for? I don't want scandal! I've had enough." When I satisfied him finally, he settled more comfortably in his seat.

"There is a good deal of interest in you in America," I began. He dismissed this with a blow of air and a wave of his hand.

"What interest? Who is interested? People are interested in Marlene Dietrich and insurance—that's all!"

"How have you been feeling, are you still practicing medicine?"

"No, no more, I gave it up six months ago, I'm not well enough."

"Do the people here know you as Céline?" (Céline's real name is Louis-Ferdinand Destouches, M.D.)

"They know me well enough to be unpleasant about it."

He gave no further explanation.

"What do you do with most of your time?"

"I'm around the house always . . . the dogs . . . I have things to do . . . I keep busy . . . I don't see anyone . . . I don't go out . . . I'm busy."

"Are you writing?"

1961

"Yes, yes, I'm writing . . . I have to stay alive, so I write . . . No! I hate it. I have always hated it . . . it is the most terrible thing for me to do . . . I never liked it, but I'm good at it . . . it does not interest me in the least, the things I write—but I have to do it. It is torture, it is the hardest job in the world."

His face is bony, gaunt, and it is gray; and his eyes are terrible things to look into; he was angry at the thought of still having to work.

"I am almost 67—in May I shall be 67 . . . to do this torture, the hardest job in the world. . . ."

Gallimard, his publisher, recently brought out his latest book, *North*.

"It is about how the Germans suffered during the war," Céline said. "No one has written about that . . . no! no! you're not supposed to mention that, how they suffered . . . keep quiet . . . shhh!" He put his finger to his lips for quiet. "It isn't nice to talk about that . . . be still . . . NO! only the other side suffered . . . shh!"

Among Céline's books translated into English are *Death on the Installment Plan, Journey to the End of the Night* and *Guignol's Band.* Céline had been accused by many responsible people of having written inflammatory and anti-Semitic articles and pamphlets during the German occupation of France. They appeared in a number of French newspapers and were reportedly reprinted by the Germans for consumption in Germany. His books, however, were banned in Nazi Germany. As a result of these accusations he was forced to leave the country. He went to Denmark where he lived for six years, but spent two of those years in a Danish jail.

"Why did you go to Denmark?"

"I had money there. I had nothing here."

"Were you forced to leave France . . . did the government tell you to leave . . . did you leave of your own account?"

"They tore up my apartment in Montparnasse . . ."

"Who?"

"Madmen, that's who . . . they tore everything I owned, everything I had . . . I was out at the time, with my wife, when we came back the apartment was destroyed . . . ruined . . . everything murdered . . . I went to Denmark."

A few days following my talk with Céline I met a former member of the French resistance movement who happened to have been in on the raiding party Céline had spoken of. I was assured by this man that if Céline had been home when the raiders struck, he almost certainly would have been murdered.

"Why were you in jail in Denmark?"

"I was a criminal of war."

"Were you accused of collaboration?"

"I said criminal of war! Don't you understand! Criminal of war! I was not accused of collaboration . . . I was a criminal of war! Is that clear!"

"You were supposed to have written things against the Jews."

"I wrote nothing against the Jews . . . all I said was that 'the Jews are pushing us into war,' that's all. They had a fight with Hitler and it was none of our business, we shouldn't have mixed into it. The Jews have had a war of lamentation for two thousand years and now Hitler has given them more lamentations. I have nothing against the Jews . . . it is not logical to say anything good or bad about five million people."

That was the end of the discussion on this subject. Céline came back to France in 1950, after the six unhappy years in Denmark. Even when he came back a great cry was heard from many quarters of the French press and from many government officials who demanded that he be further punished. Nothing was done officially, however, but from Céline's own inferences, his neighbors made it quite plain what they thought of him.

I had the feeling, sitting in Céline's kitchen, watching and listening to him, that in spite of all he said, in spite of all his natural crankiness and apparent loathing of personal contacts, he was pleased to have someone come to him, someone listen to him and to ask questions of him; to recall the past, to show that he was not forgotten—people were still reading *Death on the Installment Plan* and *Journey to the End of the Night*.

He was being discussed in spite of all the difficulties and the hatreds and foul taste he left with many. If there is any kind of spirit left in him at all, and it seems doubtful, it is a spirit which says "I know what's the proper music . . . I know the right tune . . . they hear nothing . . ."

"You once said that you couldn't read modern books, that they were 'stillborn, unfinished, not written . . .' Do you read anything now?"

"I read the encyclopedia and *Punch*, that's all. *Punch* is not funny, they try to be funny but they are not."

"Is there anyone whom you consider to be a worthwhile writer today?" Before I could suggest anyone he snapped, "Who, Hemingway? He is a faker, an amateur . . . the French realists of the 19th century are a hundred times better." And he quickly rattled off a number of French writers, so quick that I did not get them. "Dos Passos had a good style, that's all."

"How about Camus?" I asked innocently.

"Camus!" I thought he would throw the vase at me.

"Camus!" he repeated, astonished.

"He is nothing . . . a moralist . . . always telling people what is right and what is wrong—what they should do and what they should not do . . . get married, don't get married . . . that is for the church to do . . . he is nothing!"

Then Céline volunteered the English novelist Lawrence Durrell. "A whole book about how a girl kisses, the different ways she can kiss and what this means . . . is that writing? That is not writing, it is nothing, a waste. I never had that in my books, my books are style, nothing else, just style. That is the only thing to write for.

"Who knows how many have tried to copy my style . . . but they can't. They can't keep it up for four hundred pages, just try it, they can't do it . . . that's all I have, just style, nothing else. There are no messages in my books, that is for the church!" He blew the air and waved his hand, dismissing it all.

"No, my books will soon be forgotten, they mean nothing, books don't change anything, it means nothing . . . I have been everything, a cowboy in America, a bootlegger in London, a shark, everything in fact. I have worked since I was eleven . . . I know what it's all about . . . I know the French language . . . I can write, that's all.

"Listen to the conversation in the street . . . it has nothing to do with books . . . it is always 'Then I said to him . . . and he said to me . . . and then I said'—actors, that's all. Everybody wants applause . . . the bishop says 'Yesterday I spoke before two thousand people, tomorrow I will speak before three thousand.' That's religion! Look at the Pope—when people see the Pope they want to eat him! He is so fat—he eats too much, he drinks too much . . . actors, that's all they are!

"People are interested in insurance and good times —that's all. Sex! That's all the fight is about . . . everybody wants to eat everybody else. That is why they are afraid of the Blacks. He is strong! Full of strength! He will take over. That is why they are afraid of him . . . it is his time now, there are too many of them, he is showing his muscle . . . the white man is afraid . . . he is soft. He has been too long on top . . . the smell stinks to the roof, and the Black, he feels it, he smells it, and he is waiting for the take-over . . . it won't be long now.

"It is time for the yellow color . . . the black and the white will mix and the yellow will dominate, that's all. It is a biological fact, when black and white mix the yellow comes out strongest, that is the only thing . . . in two hundred years someone will look at a statue of a white man and ask if such a strange thing ever existed . . . someone will answer, 'No, it must have been painted on.'

"That is the answer! The white man is a thing of the past . . . he is already finished, extinct! It is time for something new. They all talk here, but they know nothing . . . let them go over there and then talk . . . it is another song there, I was in Africa, I know what it is . . . it's very strong, they know where they are going . . . the white man buried his head too long in the womb . . . he let the church corrupt him, everybody was taken in . . . you're not allowed to say anything like that . . . the Pope is watching, be careful . . . say nothing! heaven forbid . . . NO! It is a sin . . . you'll be crucified . . . keep it still . . . be quiet . . . be a nice dog . . . don't bark . . . don't bite . . . here is your pap . . . shut up!

"There is nothing inside them . . . they are like bulls . . . wave something to distract them; tits, patriotism, the church . . . anything in fact, and they will jump. It doesn't take much, it is very easy . . . they want always to be distracted . . . nothing matters . . . life is very easy."

For what seemed a long time, Céline said nothing. Finally, I said that I had never met a woman who was not sickened by his books, they can never finish them.

"Of course, of course, what did you expect . . . my books are not for women . . . they have their own tricks . . . bed . . . money . . . their own little games . . . my books are not their tricks . . . they know how to go about it . . .

"No, I don't see anyone anymore . . . yes, my daughter is living, she lives in Paris, I never see her. She has five children. I have never seen them." A long silence again. And then ". . . There is no doubt—I am a persecuted man . . . I am a leper." Silence. "You open the door and an enemy enters. . . ." Silence. "I have to quit you now . . . I have to write." He walked me to the door.

How to Proceed in the Arts

I

*A Detailed Study of
the Creative Act*

1. Empty yourself of everything.

2. Think of faraway things.

3. It is 12:00. Pick up the adult and throw it out of bed. Work should be done at your leisure, you know, only when there is nothing else to do. If anyone is in bed, with you, they should be told to leave. You cannot work with someone there.

4. If you're the type of person who thinks in words —paint!

5. Think of a big color—who cares if people call you Rothko. Release your childhood. Release it.

6. Do you hear them say painting is action? We say painting is the timid appraisal of yourself by lions.

7. They say your walls should look no different than your work, but that is only a feeble prediction of the future. We know the ego is the true maker of history, and if it isn't, it should be no concern of yours.

8. They say painting is action. We say remember your enemies and nurse the smallest insult. Introduce yourself as Delacroix. When you leave, give them your wet crayons. Be ready to admit that jealousy moves you more than art. They say action is painting. Well, it isn't, and we all know expressionism has moved to the suburbs.

9. If you are interested in schools, choose a school that is interested in you. Piero Della Francesca agrees with us when he says, "Schools are for fools." We are too embarrassed to decide on the proper approach. However, this much we have observed: good or bad schools are insurance companies. Enter their offices and you are certain of a position. No matter how we despise them, the Pre-Raphaelites are here to stay.

10. Don't just paint. Be a successful all-around man like Baudelaire.

11. Remember to despise your teachers, or for that matter anyone who tells you anything straight from the shoulder. This is very important. For instance, by now you should have decided we are a complete waste of time, Easterners, Communists, and Jews. This will help you with your life, and we say "life before art." All other positions have drowned in the boring swamp of dedication. No one paints because they choose to.

12. If there is no older painter you admire, paint twice as much yourself and soon you will be him.

13. Youth wants to burn the museums. We are in them—now what? Better destroy the odors of the zoo. How can we paint the elephants and hippopotamuses? Embrace the Bourgeoisie. One hundred years of grinding our teeth have made us tired. How are we to fill the large empty canvas at the end of the large empty loft? You do have a loft, don't you, man?

14. Is it the beauty of the ugly that haunts the young painter? Does formality encompass the roaring citadels of the imagination? Aren't we sick of sincerity? We tell you, stitch and draw—fornicate and hate it. We're telling you to begin. Begin! Begin anywhere. Perhaps somewhere in the throat of your loud asshole of a mother? O.K.? How about some red-orange globs mashed into your teacher's daily and unbearable condescension. Try something that pricks the air out of a few popular semantic balloons; groping, essence, pure painting, flat, catalyst, crumb, and how do you feel about titles like "Innscape," "Norway Nights and Suburbs," "No. 188, 1959," "Hey Mama Baby," "Mondula," or "Still Life with Nose"? Even if it is a small painting, say six feet by nine feet, it is a start. If it is only as big as a postage stamp, call it a collage—but begin.

15. In attempting a black painting, know that truth is beauty, but shit is shit.

16. In attempting a figure painting, consider that no amount of distortion will make a painting seem more relaxed. Others must be convinced before we even recognize ourselves. At the beginning, identity is a dream. At the end, it is a nightmare.

17. Don't be nervous. All we painters hate women; unless we hate men.

18. Hate animals. Painting is through with them.

19. When involved with abstractions, refrain, as much as possible, from personal symbolism, unless your point is gossip. . . . Everyone knows size counts.

20. When asked about the old masters, be sure to include your theories of culture change, and how the

existence of a work of art is only a small part of man's imagination. The Greeks colored their statues, the Spaniards slaughtered their bulls, the Germans invented hasenpfeffer. We dream, and act impatient hoping for fame without labor, admiration without a contract, sex *with* an erection. The Nigerians are terrible Negro haters.

II WORKING ON THE PICTURE
*The Creative Act As
It Should Flow Along*

1. You now have a picture. The loft is quiet. You've been tired of reality for months—that is, reality as far as painting goes. The New York School is a fact. Maybe this painting will begin a school in another city. Have you started—now a lot of completely UNRELATED green—yes, that's it. We must make sure no one accuses you of that easy one-to-one relationship with the objects and artifacts of the culture. You are culture changing, and changing culture—so you see the intoxicating mastery of the situation. In a certain way, you are precisely that Renaissance painter whom you least admire. You are, after all, modern enough for this, aren't you? Don't be sentimental. Either go on with your painting or leave it alone. It is too late to make a collage out of it. Don't be ashamed if you have no more ideas; it just means the painting is over.

2. Colors appear. The sounds of everyday life, like a tomato being sliced, move into the large area of the white cloth. Remember, no cameras are recording. The choice you make stands before the tribunals of the city. Either it affects man or infects him. Why are you working? No one cares. No one will. But Michelangelo has just turned over in his grave. His head is furrowed and you, like those dopey Florentines, accuse him of being homosexual. He begins to turn back, but not before you find yourself at his toes, begging for the cheese in between.

3. At this point go out and have a hot pastrami sandwich with a side order of beans and a bottle of beer. Grope the waitress, or, if you are so inclined, the waiter. Now return to your canvas—refreshed and invigorated.

4. Michelangelo???. Who likes cheese anyway?

Call a friend on the phone. Never pick up your phone until four rings have passed. Speak heavily about your latest failure. (Oh, by the way, is this depressing you? Well, each generation has its problems.) Act as if there is continuity in your work, but if there isn't, it is because that position is truly greater. Point out your relationship to Picasso who paints a cubist painting in the morning, after lunch makes a Da Vinci drawing and before cocktails a *Sturm und Drang* canvas out of the Bone Surrel oeuvre. His ego is the point of continuity.

5. Do you feel that you are busy enough? Truly busy. If you have had time to think, this will not be a good painting. Try reversing all the relationships. This will tend to make holes where there were hills. At least that will be amusing, and amusement *is* the dawn of Genius.

6. If it is the middle of the day, however, discard the use of umber as a substitute for Prussian blue. Imitation is the initial affirmation of a loving soul, and wasn't James Joyce indebted to Ibsen, and didn't we know it from his words "at it again, eh Ib."

7. Later on, imitate yourself. After all, who do you love best? Don't be afraid of getting stuck in a style. The very word style has a certain snob value, and we must remember whom we artists are dealing with.

8. Refine your experience. Now try to recall the last idea that interested you. Love produces nothing but pain, and tends to dissipate your more important feelings. Work out of a green paint can. Publicly admit democracy. Privately steal everyone's robes.

9. If you are afraid you have a tour de force on your hands, be careful not to lean over backward. It is sometimes better to appear strong than to be strong. However, don't forget the heart either. . . . Perhaps we mislead you. . . . Forget the heart. To be serious means to include all. If you can't bear this you have a chance of becoming a painter.

10. Whatever happens, don't enjoy yourself. If you do, all that has been wisely put here has been an absolute waste. The very nature of art, as opposed to life, is that in the former (art), one has to be a veritable mask of suffering while in the latter (life), only white teeth must pervade the entire scene. We cry in art. We *sing* with life.

Written in 1952, first published in 1961

NEW YORK ARTISTS

LOUISE NEVELSON, *The Throne*. 1959. Wood. 26x16x
12⅝". Courtesy Mrs. Betty Bivins Childers
Photo by Rudolph Burckhardt

RICHARD STANKIEWITZ, *Driving to the Bottom of the Ocean* 1958. Iron and steel. 56″ high. Collection William Rubin
Photo by Richard Stankiewitz

ROBERT RAUSCHENBERG. *The Canyon*. 1959. 86½x70½
x23". Collection Ilena Sonnabend, Paris.
Photo by Ed Menceley

from NAKED LUNCH

1. *Meeting of International Conference of Technological Psychiatry*

Doctor "Fingers" Schafer, the Lobotomy Kid, rises and turns on the Conferents the cold blue blast of his gaze:

"Gentlemen, the human nervous system can be reduced to a compact and abbreviated spinal column. The brain, front, middle and rear must follow the adenoid, the wisdom tooth, the appendix. . . . I give you my Master Work: *The Complete All American Deanxietized Man. . . .*"

Blast of trumpets: The Man is carried in naked by two Negro Bearers who drop him on the platform with bestial, sneering brutality. . . . The Man wriggles. . . . His flesh turns to viscid, transparent jelly that drifts away in green mist, unveiling a monster black centipede. Waves of unknown stench fill the room, searing the lungs, grabbing the stomach. . . .

Schafer wrings his hands sobbing: "Clarence!! How can you do this to me?? Ingrates!! Every one of them ingrates!!"

The Conferents start back muttering in dismay:

"I'm afraid Schafer has gone a bit too far. . . ."

"I sounded a word of warning. . . ."

"Brilliant chap Schafer . . . but . . ."

"Man will do anything for publicity. . . ."

"Gentlemen, this unspeakable and in every sense illegitimate child of Doctor Schafer's perverted brain must not see the light. . . . Our duty to the human race is clear. . . ."

"Man he done seen the light," said one of the Negro Bearers.

"We must stomp out the Un-American crittah," says a fat, frog-faced Southern doctor who has been drinking corn out of a mason jar. He advances drunkenly, then halts, appalled by the formidable size and menacing aspect of the centipede. . . .

"Fetch gasoline!" he bellows. "We gotta burn the son of a bitch like an uppity Nigra!"

"I'm not sticking my neck out, me," says a cool hip young doctor high on LSD25. . . . "Why a smart D.A. could . . ."

Fadeout. "Order in The Court!"

D.A.: "Gentlemen of the jury, these 'learned gentlemen' claim that the innocent human creature they have so wantonly slain suddenly turned himself into a huge black centipede and it was 'their duty to the human race' to destroy this monster before it could, by any means at its disposal, perpetrate its kind. . . .

"Are we to gulp down this tissue of horse shit? Are we to take these glib lies like a greased and nameless asshole? Where *is* this wondrous centipede?

" 'We have destroyed it,' they say smugly. . . . And I would like to remind you, Gentlemen and Hermaphrodites of the Jury, that this Great Beast" —he points to Doctor Schafer—"has, on several previous occasions, appeared in this court charged with the unspeakable crime of brain rape. . . . In plain English"—he pounds the rail of the jury box, his voice rises to a scream—"in plain English, Gentlemen, *forcible lobotomy. . . .*"

The Jury gasps. . . . One dies of a heart attack. . . . Three fall to the floor writhing in orgasms of prurience. . . .

The D.A. points dramatically: "He it is . . . He and no other who has reduced whole provinces of our fair land to a state bordering on the far side of idiocy. . . . He it is who has filled great warehouses with row on row, tier on tier of helpless creatures who must have their every want attended. . . . 'The Drones' he calls them with a cynical leer of pure educated evil. . . . Gentlemen, I say to you that the wanton murder of Clarence Cowie must not go unavenged: This foul crime shrieks like a wounded faggot for justice at least!"

The centipede is rushing about in agitation.

"Man, that mother fucker's hungry," screams one of the Bearers.

"I'm getting out of here, me."

A wave of electric horror sweeps through the Conferents. . . . They storm the exits screaming and clawing. . . .

2. *The County Clerk*

The County Clerk has his office in a huge red brick building known as the Old Court House. Civil cases are, in fact, tried there, the proceedings inexorably dragging out until the contestants die or abandon litigation. This is due to the vast number of records pertaining to absolutely everything, all filed in the wrong place so that no one but the County Clerk and his staff of assistants can find them, and he often spends years in the search. In fact, he is still looking for material relative to a damage suit that was settled out of court in 1910. Large sections of the Old Court House have fallen in ruins, and others are highly dangerous owing to frequent cave-ins. The County Clerk assigns the more dangerous missions to his assistants, many of whom have lost their lives in the service. In 1912 two hundred and seven assistants were trapped in a collapse of the North-by-North-East wing.

When suit is brought against anyone in the Zone, his lawyers connive to have the case transferred to the Old Court House. Once this is done, the plaintiff has lost the case, so the only cases that actually go to trial in the Old Court House are those instigated by eccentrics and paranoids who want "A public hearing," which they rarely get since only the most desperate famine of news will bring a reporter to the Old Court House.

The Old Court House is located in the town of Pigeon Hole outside the urban zone. The inhabitants of this town and the surrounding area of swamps and heavy timber are people of such great stupidity and such barbarous practices that the Administration has seen fit to quarantine them in a reservation surrounded by a radioactive wall of iron bricks. In retaliation the citizens of Pigeon Hole plaster their town with signs: *"Urbanite Don't Let The Sun Set On You Here,"* an unnecessary injunction, since nothing but urgent business would take any urbanite to Pigeon Hole.

Lee's case is urgent. He has to file an immediate affidavit that he is suffering from bubonic plague to avoid eviction from the house he has occupied ten years without paying the rent. He exists in perpetual quarantine. So he packs his suitcase of affidavits and petitions and injunctions and certificates and takes a bus to the Frontier. The Urbanite customs inspector waves him through: "I hope you've got an atom bomb in that suitcase."

Lee swallows a handful of tranquilizing pills and steps into the Pigeon Hole customs shed. The inspectors spend three hours pawing through his papers, consulting dusty books of regulations and duties from which they read incomprehensible and ominous excerpts ending with: "And as such is subject to fine and penalty under act 666." They look at him significantly.

They go through his papers with a magnifying glass.

"Sometimes they slip dirty limericks between the lines."

"Maybe he figures to sell them for toilet paper. Is this crap for your own personal use?"

"Yes."

"He says yes."

"And how do we know that?"

"I gotta affidavit."

"Wise guy. Take off your clothes."

"Yeah. Maybe he got dirty tattoos."

They paw over his body probing his ass for contraband and examine it for evidence of sodomy. They dunk his hair and send the water out to be analyzed. "Maybe he's got dope in his hair."

Finally, they impound his suitcase; and he staggers out of the shed with a fifty pound bale of documents.

A dozen or so Recordites sit on the Old Court House steps of rotten wood. They watch his approach with pale blue eyes, turning their heads slow on wrinkled necks (wrinkles full of dust) to follow his body up the steps and through the door. Inside, dust hangs in the air like fog, sifting down from the ceiling, rising in clouds from the floor as he walks. He mounts a perilous staircase—condemned in 1929. Once his foot goes through, and the dry splinters tear into the flesh of his leg. The staircase ends in a painter's scaffold, attached with frayed rope and pullies to a beam almost invisible in dusty distance. He pulls himself up cautiously to a ferris wheel cabin. His weight sets in motion hydraulic machinery (sound of running water). The wheel moves smooth and silent to stop by a rusty iron balcony, worn through here and there like an old shoe sole. He walks down a long corridor lined with doors, most of them nailed or boarded shut. In one office, *Near East Exquisitries* on a green brass plaque, the Mugwump is catching termites with his long black tongue. The door of the County Clerk's office is open. The County Clerk sits inside gumming snuff, surrounded by six assistants. Lee stands in the doorway. The County Clerk goes on talking without looking up.

"I run into Ted Spigot the other day . . . a good old boy, too. Not a finer man in the Zone than Ted Spigot. . . . Now it was a Friday I happen to remember because the Old Lady was down with the menstral cramps and I went to Doc Parker's drugstore on Dalton Street, just opposite Ma Green's Ethical Massage Parlor, where Jed's old livery stable used to be. . . . Now, Jed, I'll remember his second name directly, had a cast in the left eye and his wife came from some place out East, Algiers I believe it was, and after Jed died she married up again, and she married one of the Hoot boys, Clem Hoot if my memory serves, a good old boy too, now Hoot was around fifty-four fifty-five year old at the time. . . . So I says to Doc Parker 'My old lady is down bad with the menstral cramps. Sell me two ounces of paregoric.'

"So Doc says, 'Well, Arch, you gotta sign the book. Name, address and date of purchase. It's the law.'

"So I asked Doc what the day was, and he said, 'Friday the 13th.'

"So I said, 'I guess I already had mine.'

" 'Well,' Doc says, 'there was a feller in here this morning. City feller. Dressed kinda flashy. So he's got him a RX for a mason jar of morphine. . . . Kinda funny looking prescription writ out on toilet paper. . . . And I told him straight out: "Mister, I suspect you to be a dope fiend."

" ' "I got the ingrowing toe nails, Pop. I'm in agony," ' he says.

" ' "Well," I says, "I gotta be careful. But so long as you got a legitimate condition and an RX from a certified bona feedy M.D., I'm honored to serve you."

" ' "That croaker's really certified," he say. . . . Well, I guess one hand didn't know what the other was doing when I give him a jar of Saniflush by error. . . . So I reckon he's had his too.'

" 'Just the thing to clean a man's blood.'

" 'You know, that very thing occurred to me. Should be a sight better than sulphur and molasses. . . . Now, Arch, don't think I'm nosey; but a man don't have no secrets from God and his druggist I always say. . . . Is you still humping the Old Gray Mare?'

" 'Why, Doc Parker. . . . I'll have you know I'm a family man and an Elder in the First Denominational Non-sextarian Church and I ain't had a piecea hoss ass since we was kids together.'

" 'Them was the days, Arch. Remember the time I got the goose grease mixed up with the mustard? Always was a one to grab the wrong jar, feller say. They could have heard you squealing over in Cunt Lick County, just a squealing like a stoat with his stones cut off.'

" 'You're in the wrong hole, Doc. It was you took the mustard and me as had to wait till you cooled off.'

" 'Wistful thinking, Arch. I read about it one time inna magazine settin' in that green outhouse behind the station. . . . Now what I meant awhile back, Arch, you didn't rightly understand me. . . . I was referring to your wife as the Old Gray Mare. . . . I mean she ain't what she used to be what with all them carbuncles and cataracts and chilblains and haemorrhoids and aftosa.'

" 'Yas, Doc, Liz is right sickly. Never was the same after her eleventh miscarriaging. . . . There was

something right strange about that. Doc Ferris he told me straight, he said: "Arch, 'tain't fitting you should see that critter." And he gives me a long look made my flesh crawl. . . . Well, you sure said it right, Doc. She ain't what she used to be. In fact, she ain't been able to tell night from day since using them eye drops you sold her last month. . . . But, Doc, you oughtta know I wouldn't be humping Liz, the old cow, meaning no disrespect to the mother of my dead monsters. Not when I got that sweet little ol' fifteen year old thing. . . . You know that yaller girl used to work in Marylou's Hair Straightening and Skin Bleach Parlor over in Nigga town.'

" 'Getting that dark chicken meat, Arch? Gettin' that coon pone?'

" 'Gettin' it steady, Doc. Gettin' it steady. Well, feller say duty is goosing me. Gotta get back to the old crank case.'

" 'I'll bet she needs a grease job worst way.'

" 'Doc, she sure is a dry hole. . . . Well, thanks for the paregoric.'

" 'And thanks for the trade, Arch. . . . He he he. . . . Say, Archy boy, some night when you get caught short with a rusty load drop around and have a drink of Yohimbiny with me.'

" 'I'll do that, Doc, I sure will. It'll be just like old times.'

"So I went on back to my place and heated up some water and mixed up some paregoric and cloves and cinnamon and sassyfrass and give it to Liz, and it eased her some I reckon. Leastwise she let up aggravatin' me. . . . Well, later on I went down to Doc Parker's again to get me a rubber . . . and just as I was leaving I run into Roy Bane, a good ol' boy too. There's not a finer man in this Zone than Roy Bane. . . . So he said to me he says, 'Arch, you see that ol' nigger over there in that vacant lot? Well, sure as shit and taxes, he comes there every night just as regular you can set your watch by him. See him behind them nettles? Every night round about eight thirty he goes over into that lot yonder and pulls himself off with steel wool. . . . Preachin' Nigger, they tell me.'

"So that's how I come to know the hour more or less on Friday the 13th and it couldn't have been more than twenty minutes half an hour after that, I'd took some Spanish Fly in Doc's store and it was jest beginning to work on me down by Grennel Bog on my way to Nigger town. . . . Well the bog makes a bend, used to be a nigger shack there. . . . They burned that ol' nigger over in Cunt Lick. Nigger had the aftosa and it left him stone blind. . . . So this white girl down from Texarkana screeches out:

" 'Roy, that ol' nigger is looking at me so nasty. Land's sake I feel just dirty all over.'

" 'Now, Sweet Thing, don't fret yourself. Me an' the boys will burn him.'

" 'Do it slow, Honey Face. Do it slow. He's give me a sick headache.'

"So they burned the nigger and that ol' boy took his wife and went back up to Texarkana without paying for the gasoline and old Whispering Lou runs the service station couldn't talk about nothing else all Fall: 'These city fellers come down here and burn a nigger and don't even settle up for the gasoline.'

"Well, Chester Hoot tore that nigger shack down and rebuilt it just back of his house up in Bled Valley. Covered up all the windows with black cloth, and what goes on in there ain't fittin' to speak of. . . . Now Chester he's got some right strange ways. . . . Well it was just where the nigger shack used to be, right across from the Old Brooks place floods out every Spring, only it wasn't the Brooks place then . . . belonged to a feller name of Scranton. Now that piece of land was surveyed back in 1919. . . . I reckon you know the man did the job too. . . . Feller name of Hump Clarence used to witch out wells on the side. . . . Good ol' boy too, not a finer man in this Zone than Hump Clarence. . . . Well it was just around about in there I come on Ted Spigot ascrewin a mud puppy."

Lee cleared his throat. The Clerk looked up over his glasses. "Now if you'll take care, young feller, till I finish what I'm asaying, I'll tend to your business."

And he plunged into an anecdote about a nigra got the hydrophobia from a cow.

"So my pappy says to me: 'Finish up your chores, son, and let's go see the mad nigger. . . .' They had that nigger chained to the bed, and he was bawling like a cow. . . . I soon got enough of that ol' nigger. Well, if you all will excuse me I got business in the Privy Council. He he he!"

Lee listened in horror. The County Clerk often spent weeks in the privy living on scorpions and Montgomery Ward catalogues. On several occasions his assistants had forced the door and carried him out in an advanced state of malnutrition. Lee decided to play his last card.

"Mr. Anker," he said, "I'm appealing to you as one Razor Back to another," and he pulled out his Razor Back card, a memo of his lush-rolling youth.

The Clerk looked at the card suspiciously: "You don't look like a bone feed mast-fed Razor Back to me. . . . What you think about the Jeeeews. . . ?"

"Well, Mr. Anker, you know yourself all a Jew wants to do is doodle a Christian girl. . . . One of these days we'll cut the rest of it off."

"Well, you talk right sensible for a city feller. . . . Find out what he wants and take care of him. . . . He's a good ol' boy."

3. *Interzone*

The only native in Interzone who is neither queer nor available is Andrew Keif's chauffeur, which is not affection or perversity on Keif's part, but a useful pretext to break off relations with anyone he doesn't want to see: "You made a pass at Aracknid last night. I can't have you to the house again." People are always blacking out in the Zone, whether they drink or not, and no one can say for sure he didn't make a pass at Aracknid's unappetizing person.

Aracknid is a worthless chauffeur, barely able to drive. On one occasion he ran down a pregnant woman in from the mountains with a load of charcoal on her back, and she miscarried a bloody, dead baby in the street, and Keif got out and sat on the curb stirring the blood with a stick while the police questioned Aracknid and finally arrested the woman for a violation of the Sanitary Code.

Aracknid is a grimly unattractive young man with a long face of a strange, slate-blue color. He has a big nose and great yellow teeth like a horse. Anybody can find an attractive chauffeur, but only Andrew Keif could have found Aracknid; Keif the brilliant, decadent young novelist who lives in a remodeled pissoir in the red light district of the Native Quarter.

The Zone is a single, vast building. The rooms are made of a plastic cement that bulges to accommodate people, but when too many crowd into one room there is a soft plop and someone squeezes through the wall right into the next house, the next bed that is, since the rooms are mostly bed where the business of the Zone is transacted. A hum of sex and commerce shakes the Zone like a vast hive:

"Two thirds of one percent. I won't budge from that figure; not even for m bumpkins."

"But where are the bills of lading, lover?"

"Not where you're looking, pet. That's too obvious."

"A bale of levis with built-in falsie baskets. Made in Hollywood."

"Hollywood, Siam."

"Well American *style*."

"What's the commission? . . . The commission. . . . The Commission."

"Yes, nugget, a shipload of K.Y. made of genuine whale dreck in the South Atlantic at present quaranteened by the Board of Health in Tierra del Fuego. The commission, my dear! If we can pull this off we'll be in clover." (Whale dreck is reject material that accumulates in the process of cutting up a whale and cooking it down. A horrible, fishy mess you can smell for miles. No one has found any use for it.)

Interzone Imports Unlimited, which consists of Marvie and Leif The Unlucky, had latched onto the K.Y. deal. In fact they specialize in pharmaceuticals and run a 24-hour Pro station, six ways coverage fore and aft, as a side line. (Six separate venereal diseases have been identified to date.)

They plunge into the deal. They form unmentionable services for a spastic Greek shipping agent, and one entire shift of Customs inspectors. The two partners fall out and finally denounce each other in the Embassy where they are referred to the We Don't Want To Hear About It Department, and eased out a back door into a shit-strewn vacant lot, where vultures fight over fish heads. They flail at each other hysterically.

"You're trying to fuck me out of my commission!"

"Your commission! Who smelled out this good thing in the first place?"

"But I have the bill of lading."

"Monster! But the check will be made out in my name."

"Bawstard! You'll never see the bill of lading until my cut is deposited in escrow."

"Well, might as well kiss and make up. There's nothing mean or petty about me."

They shake hands without enthusiasm and peck each other on the cheek. The deal drags on for months. They engage the services of an Expeditor. Finally Marvie emerges with a check for 42 Turkestan kurds drawn on an anonymous bank in South America, to clear through Amsterdam, a procedure that will take eleven months more or less.

Now he can relax in the cafés of The Plaza. He shows a photostatic copy of the check. He would never show the original of course, lest some envious citizen spit ink eradicator on the signature or otherwise mutilate the check.

Everyone asks him to buy drinks and celebrate, but he laughs jovially and says, "Fact is I can't afford to buy myself a drink. I already spent every kurd of it buying Penstrep for Ali's clap. He's down with it fore and aft again. I came near kicking the little bastard right through the wall into the next bed. But you all know what a sentimental old thing I am."

Marvie does buy himself a shot glass of beer, squeezing a blackened coin out of his fly onto the table. "Keep the change." The waiter sweeps the coin into a dust pan, he spits on the table and walks away.

"Sore head! He's envious of my check."

Marvie had been in Interzone since "the year before one" as he put it. He had been retired from some unspecified position in the State Dept. "for the good of the service." Obviously he had once been very good looking in a crew-cut, college boy way, but his face had sagged and formed lumps under the chin like melting paraffin. He was getting heavy around the hips.

Leif The Unlucky was a tall, thin Norwegian, with a patch over one eye, his face congealed in a permanent, ingratiating smirk. Behind him lay an epic saga of unsuccessful enterprises. He had failed at raising frogs, chinchilla, Siamese fighting fish, rami and cultured pearls. He had attempted, variously and without success, to promote a Love Bird Two-in-a-Coffin Cemetery, to corner the condom market during the rubber storage, to run a mail order whore house, to issue penicillin as a patent medicine. He had followed disastrous betting systems in the casinos of Europe and the race tracks of the U.S. His reverses in business were matched by the incredible mischances of his personal life. His front teeth had been stomped out by bestial American sailors in Brooklyn. Vultures had eaten out an eye when he drank a pint of paregoric and passed out in a Panama City park. He had been trapped between floors in an elevator for five days with an oil-burning junk habit and sustained an attack of D.T.s while stowing away in a foot locker. Then there was the time he collapsed with strangulated intestines, perforated ulcers and peritonitis in Cairo and the hospital was so crowded they bedded him in the latrine, and the Greek surgeon goofed and sewed up a live monkey in him, and he was gang-fucked by the Arab attendants, and one of the orderlies stole the penicillin substituting Saniflush; and the time he got clap in his ass and a self-righteous English doctor cured him with an enema of hot, sulphuric acid, and the German practitioner of Technological Medicine who removed his appendix with a rusty can opener and a pair of tin snips (he considered the germ theory "a nonsense"). Flushed with success he then began snipping and cutting out everything in sight: "The human body is filled up vit unnecessitated parts. You can get by vit one kidney. Vy have two? Yes dot is a kidney. . . . The inside parts should not be so close in together crowded. They need lebensraum like the vaterland."

The Expeditor had not yet been paid, and Marvie was faced by the prospect of stalling him for eleven months until the check cleared. The Expeditor was said to have been born on the Ferry between the Zone and the Island. His profession was to expedite the delivery of merchandise. No one knew for sure

whether his services were of any use or not, and to mention his name always precipitated an argument. Cases were cited to prove his miraculous efficiency and utter worthlessness.

The Island was a British Military and Naval station directly opposite the Zone. England holds the Island on yearly rent-free lease, and every year the lease and permit of residence is formally renewed. The entire population turns out, attendance is compulsory, and gathers at the municipal dump. The President of the Island is required by custom to crawl across the garbage on his stomach and deliver the Permit of Residence and Renewal of the Lease, signed by every citizen of the Island, to The Resident Governor who stands resplendent in dress uniform. The Governor takes the permit and shoves it into his coat pocket:

"Well," he says with a tight smile, "so you've decied to let us stay another year have you? Very good of you. And everyone is happy about it? . . . Is there anyone who isn't happy about it?"

Soldiers in jeeps sweep mounted machine guns back and forth across the crowd with a slow, searching movement.

"Everybody happy. Well that's fine." He turns jovially to the prostrate President. "I'll keep your papers in case I get caught short. Haw Haw Haw." His loud, metallic laugh rings out across the dump, and the crowd laughs with him under the searching guns.

The forms of democracy are scrupulously enforced on the Island. There is a Senate and a Congress who carry on endless sessions discussing garbage disposal and outhouse inspection, the only two questions over

which they have jurisdiction. For a brief period in the mid-nineteenth century, they had been allowed to control the dept. of Baboon Maintenance but this privilege had been withdrawn owing to absenteeism in the Senate.

The purple-assed Tripoli baboons had been brought to the Island by pirates in the 17th century. There was a legend that when the baboons left the Island it would fall. To whom or in what way is not specified, and it is a capital offense to kill a baboon, though the noxious behaviour of these animals harries the citizens almost beyond endurance. Occasionally someone goes berserk, kills several baboons and himself.

The post of President is always forced on some particularly noxious and unpopular citizen. To be elected president is the greatest misfortune and disgrace that can befall an Islander. The humiliations and ignominy are such that few presidents live out their full term of office, usually dying of a broken spirit after a year or two. The Expeditor had once been President and served the full five years of his term. Subsequently he changed his name and underwent plastic surgery, to blot out, as far as possible, the memory of his disgrace.

"Yes of course . . . we'll pay you," Marvie was saying to the Expeditor.

"But take it easy. It may be a little while yet. . . ."

"Take it easy! A little while! . . . Listen."

"Yes I know it all. The finance company is repossessing your wife's artificial kidney. . . . They are evicting your grandmother from her iron lung."

"That's in rather bad taste, old boy. . . . Frankly I wish I had never involved myself in this uh matter. That bloody grease has too much carbolic in it. I was down to customs one day last week. Stuck a broom handle into a drum of it, and the grease ate the end off straight away. Besides, the stink is enough to knock a man on his bloody ass. You should take a walk down by the port."

"I'll do no such thing," Marvie screeched. It is a mark of caste in the Zone never to touch or even go near what you are selling. To do so gives rise to suspicion of retailing, that is of being a common peddler. A good part of the merchandise in the Zone is sold through street peddlers.

"Why do you tell me all this? It's too sordid! Let the retailers worry about it."

"Oh it's all very well for you chaps, you can scud out from under. But I have a reputation to maintain. . . . There'll be a spot of bother about this."

"Do you suggest there is something *illegitimate* in this operation?"

"Not *illegitimate* exactly. But shoddy. Definitely shoddy."

"Oh go back to your Island before it falls! We knew you when you were peddling your purple ass in the Plaza pissoirs for five pesetas."

"And not many takers either," Leif put in. He pronounced it ither. This reference to his Island origin was more than the Expeditor could stand. . . . He was drawing himself up, mobilizing his most frigid impersonation of an English aristocrat, preparing to deliver an icy, clipped "crusher," but instead, a whining, whimpering, kicked dog snarl broke from his mouth. His pre-surgery face emerged in an arclight of incandescent hate. . . . He began to spit curses in the hideous, strangled gutturals of the Island dialect.

The Islanders all profess ignorance of the dialect or flatly deny its existence. "We are Breetish," they say. "We don't got no bloody dealect."

Froth gathered at the corners of the Expeditor's mouth. He was spitting little balls of saliva like pieces of cotton. The stench of spiritual vileness hung in the air about him like a green cloud. Marvie and Leif fell back twittering in alarm.

"He's gone *mad*," Marvie gasped. "Let's got *out* of here." Hand in hand they skip away into the mist that covers the Zone in the winter months like a cold Turkish Bath.

►► **Alfred Andersch**

The Night of the Giraffe

On the night of May 29th at eleven o'clock—that is, at the same time as I was having dinner in a small restaurant on the Rue Saints-Pères—an Algerian of about twenty-five whose name I never learned sat down at a table outside a café on the Rue Monge to wait for my friend Pierre Grange. The young Algerian had carefully picked this café. From where he sat he could command the intersection of the Rue Monge, the Rue Cardinal-Lemoine, and the Rue des Boulangers where Pierre lived, and also the exit of the métro station Cardinal-Lemoine. He carried three new ten-thousand-franc notes which he had received from the agent of a French Fascist organization. They were tucked in a thin, worn leather wallet inside the breast pocket of his black tunic. A few coins and a pack of cigarettes were in the right pocket of his trousers. An oblong pocket which he himself had sewn inside the right leg of his corduroy trousers held a knife with a ten-inch blade, grooved on four sides—a stiletto, in other words, which ended in a point almost as sharp as a needle. He was unbelievably thin according to our standards, like all young North Africans; slim, sinewy, small, and dark, he sat in front of the café. He had ordered a Pinard and had paid for it at once. The white cigarette gleamed in his brown hands. Slumped into himself, completely calm and slightly dirty, he sat there and waited. Before he came he had telephoned the agent from one of the big Negro cafés on the Boul Mich and found out that my friend Pierre was sitting in the *Deux Magots*. The agent had thought Pierre Grange might be late in getting home. So the Algerian waited placidly. Of course, I knew nothing of his existence as I sat in the bistro on the Rue Saints-Pères eating a cutlet, pommes frites and a salad and reading the latest edition of the *Herald Tribune*. But in view of all that happened later that night I can easily picture the vigil of this dirty little hired guy. Just as I had finished my dinner, shortly after eleven, the cars began honking outside. We—that is, the four or five guests in the bistro and the patron— pricked up our ears, for blowing horns is strictly forbidden in Paris at night. The cars were all honking the same signal, two long and three short blasts. The patron went to the door, looked out into the street and said: "A demonstration." I paid my check, clutched the papers under my arm and left. Outside the air was heavy.

On the evening of the same day, May 29th, at 7:26 to be exact, the tall old General's tall old Citroën passed into the courtyard of the Elysée Palace through the gate opened only on visits of foreign heads of state. Exactly 24 hours before, 350,000 people between the Place de la République and the Bastille had protested against this visit. One of the Presidential footmen opened the door of the car, but the General did not get out at once. Instead he leaned forward a little and asked his driver: "René, what are the latest slogans?" "Into the museum with de Gaulle," the driver replied. This is what they hate about me most, the General thought, the fact that I don't fit in with their time. They cannot understand that time adjusts to him who makes it. But I shall be king in France. Come to think of it, nothing has changed at all since the days of the kings. Kings of France are always caught between the Huguenots and the League, between the liberal opposition and the military gang. The Huguenots expect a St. Bartholomew's Eve from me. But I am not a juvenile king who has a gray-haired Protestant admiral assassinated. I am gray-haired myself and I respect that little Jew who led the masses across the Bastille yesterday. It was he who saved the honor of France in Indo-China. He is probably just as alone among his people as I am among mine. Yet, I must fight him. The Pope cannot be a Ghibelline. But I shall have the estates of the heads of the League confiscated, he thought grimly. "And what else?" he asked. The driver, he noticed, hesitated for a second. "Come on, René, I want to know what they say about me." "Into the zoo with the giraffe," the chauffeur said. He looked into the mirror but could detect no emotion on the General's face. A stupid word, thought the General, it cannot possibly come from the clever little Jew. The little Jew would know what would happen if they started locking giraffes into the zoo. If they locked up tall old generals they would also lock up clever little Jews and soon anybody who did not fit in with the time would be locked up. Into this time, the General thought with contempt, and finally stepped out of the car. He really has something of the giraffe, thought the driver admiringly, watching his General reach the top of the stairs and lean down to the President of the Republic who had already been waiting up there for some time.

pages from the original manuscript of proust's "à la recherche du temps perdu" in the windows of the librairie la hune. also galley proofs with the author's corrections; he has written whole new paragraphs onto the margins. across the street at the montana bar the american smart set from the 6th arrondissement: elegant fairies mainly. juliette-greco shadows on the lower lids of dazzling girls. the serious journalist crowd at le village. café-au-lait-colored half-caste girl in brown leather jacket, only her thighs shining in white pants glued to the skin, escorted by three men. kenny clarke at the traps in the st.-germain-des-prés club playing with a french master pianist before five guests, the bottle of coke at a thousand francs. sartre's apartment on the corner of the rue bonaparte is all lit up. the deux magots newsstand sparkling like a jewel in the blue night of bobbing street lights. marianne puts her head on the block and lets the guillotine down on herself: the cartoon from 'punch' heading the latest edition of 'l'express'. tomato-red alfaromeo convertible wedged in on the rue st.-benoit. green drinks, white drinks, green drinks on the tables seen through yellow coffeehouse windows in the dove-blue night. but houses and church, velvety brown and feathery gray, flickered over by street lights. the surface of paris equals the Depth of Paris. troubled arthur adamov walking along the boulevard in conversation with martin flinker. "que voulez-vous," the seventy-year-old bookseller, one of the century's hounded creatures, says to adamov, "one can never live through too many historical events."

"You do remember, don't you, Fayard, that I was in Algeria with Chaban-Delmas?"

"I do, now you mention it, Grange. That was at the time when Chaban-Delmas was Defense Minister under Gaillard."

"Quite right. And that was only three months ago."

"So you were in Algeria in the Spring."

"In February."

"Was it a nice trip?"

"Listen, Fayard, I didn't ask to see you to tell you whether or not February is a nice month in Algeria."

"But. . . ?"

"Did you ever hear the name Léon Delbecque?"

"You're kidding!"

"I only asked because Delbecque's name isn't often mentioned in the Paris press. Even in your paper, Fayard."

"Everybody knows Delbecque prepared the plot in Algiers, but nobody can prove it."

"I can."

"Not really!"

"You don't seem to be exactly panting for information, or am I wrong?"

"You have the wrong idea about journalism, Grange, but go ahead. I know you are sound. You got on Chaban-Delmas' staff via the Navy Department, didn't you?"

"Yes, it's funny. I am only a civilian employee in the Department, you know, just a bread-and-butter job which leaves me time to work on my magazine and the theater reviews for your paper. But then somebody had the idea to assign me to a rear admiral and have me carry his brief case to Algeria."

"You think that was just a coincidence?"

"Of course."

"I believe you underestimate the Navy Department. But go on."

"I happened to meet Delbecque on the trip. As you know, he was personal assistant to the Minister. It was so interesting to watch him, I ended up doing nothing else."

"And what did you see?"

"Wherever we stopped Delbecque held secret conferences with the local military and civilian officials. The Minister made a public speech while his assistant gave private instructions."

"Well, that's common knowledge. We all know it."

"But no one can prove it."

"The people of the Welfare Commission at Algiers will tell anybody who cares to ask and Delbecque won't dream of denying the gossip."

"But it remains a rumor?"

"Yes, it's the typical scuttlebutt—an item for today's gossip and tomorrow's historians."

"It needn't remain that."

"Don't make it too exciting, Grange. I've known for the last five minutes that you wish to present me with proof of Delbecque's activities, all signed and sealed."

"Right. I have made an accurate list of nearly all of Delbecque's meetings, including the names of everyone participating."

"Do you also know what was discussed on those occasions?"

"No. I leave the rest to the journalists. There is a group of about a hundred and fifty persons involved."

"And what do you want me to do?"

"Publish the list!"

"What good would that do?"

"But don't you understand, the list is plain proof that the plot has been prepared long beforehand."

"Whose hand?"

"You ask strange questions. All insiders know Delbecque is Jacques Soustelle's agent. And everyone in France knows Soustelle is de Gaulle's political whip. My list will prove that the General himself has had the plot prepared against the Republic. The great taciturn of Colombey, the impeccable man of honor who waits until he is called. At best a political manipulator like any other. At worst a political criminal

working against the legitimacy of the Republic."

"I'm not going to publish your list, Grange."

"And why not?"

"Because our editorial board has just decided to give the giraffe a chance."

"You mean you have decided in favor of opportunism?"

"Well, let's assume for the moment the publication of your list would have the effect you visualize. What would be the result?"

"That's easy to see, isn't it? De Gaulle's myth would be destroyed or, let's say, slightly damaged."

"Right! And that's exactly what we don't want. At least not now."

"That's interesting! I've never heard you take the part of a myth yet, Fayard. You are a Left-wing citizen. You publish a Left-wing bourgeois paper. So far, you've always been on the side of reason."

"Myth plays an objective part in politics."

"But if it can be unmasked . . ."

"It will have to unmask itself. De Gaulle himself must destroy his legend."

"And if he doesn't oblige?"

"Then his myth is genuine."

"You mean in that case de Gaulle is a man of honor after all?"

"We must give him the chance to prove it."

"Even though my list proves he has already violated the rules of honor?"

"There's a chance he may be playing for high stakes, a game for our side, a game against the Delbecques."

"But that's an illusion."

"And if it isn't?"

"Then everything you and your paper have stood for would have been wrong—your talk about democracy and the rule of the people, the meaning of universal suffrage and the lucidity of politics. Then politics would be what your conservative opponents teach: the private affair of individuals, depending on the honor or dishonor of never-changing human character, a passion or an intrigue, a deal between cliques, a secret web, the maneuvers of gangs or elites who have already made their decisions before the citizen—your citizen, Fayard!—has had even the shadow of a chance to use his influence. True, it is left to him to finance or not finance the water supply of Bordeaux, but the decisions of General de Gaulle are made without him."

"You have completely wrong ideas about the role of public consent or dissent, Grange."

"I am just learning. Obviously, the public's vote is always doomed to be too late."

"Sometimes it may prepare the way. The fact that de Gaulle can come to power is the result of a public vote."

"Before which you capitulate. Which perhaps your own paper manipulated."

"So what! We respect the vote. We never resist developments which can't be stopped. We maintain our principles as things develop, our ideas of freedom and human dignity . . ."

"That's bunk, Fayard."

"You aren't thirty yet, I am fifty. You may go ahead and insult me all you like."

"I shall. From now on I shall insult you and your kind incessantly."

"It won't help you. By the way, why don't you take your list to your friend Sartre, or to *Humanité?*"

"You know very well it wouldn't have ten percent of the effect there that it would have coming from you. It should be published by a paper as dignified and objective as your respectable bourgeois organ, Fayard."

"You're right, of course. You're intelligent, Grange, you're the sort that could adjust to the mechanism of power. I'd like to give you some better advice."

"Well?"

"Burn the list! Don't just burn it—forget it."

"So you're that afraid of de Gaulle?"

"I am not afraid of de Gaulle. Perhaps I am afraid of the Delbecques. But, at the moment, I am only worried about you."

"Thanks a lot!"

"That's a very dangerous paper you have in your pocket, Grange. Some day, perhaps, it will be a very valuable paper. But it will never be so valuable that somebody should die for it."

"I've no answer to that."

"I know. Take care of yourself!"

"Adieu, Fayard."

As I walked down the Boulevard St.-Germain, more and more honking cars came by from the direction of the Concorde. All were honking the same signal, the first five notes of Beethoven's Fifth which, as I read in the *Herald Tribune* next morning, had been the victory signal of Winston Churchill and Charles de Gaulle during the war. I also read that the frenzy of Gaullist victory had broken loose that night in the Champs Elysées: a piercing cry of enthusiasm uttered by ladies with white gloves, the wild roar of young businessmen, the revolution of the car owners, as Pendennis dryly remarked in *The Observer*. The political geography of Paris is simple: the victories of the car owners are celebrated in the Champs Elysées, contradicted in St.-Germain-des-Prés, passed over in silence at Menilmontant. The three short and two long notes were supposed to mean: "Al-gé-rie Française." It was a plain provocation of the intellectuals. Alleg had written the book about his tortures by the paratroopers. Sartre had written a commentary to it. Alleg's book and Sartre's commentary had been banned. Audin, the young mathematician, had died under the tortures of the paras—and St.-Germain-des-Prés stood along the two sidewalks of its Boulevard, whistling and yelling above the noise of the horns, dark shapes moving against bright windows and the twitching reflection of lights from its cafés. It was going on half-past eleven. Through the turmoil I made for the *Deux Magots* newsstand to see if the Gaullist poster was still there on the rear wall. But it had been torn off and lay in the gutter soiled and trampled. By this time it had become rather quiet at the corner of the Rue Monge and the Rue Cardinal-Lemoine where the young Algerian sat and waited for my friend Pierre. I saw Pierre sitting in front of the *Deux Magots*, Solange by his side, and I went to join them. At the table next to Pierre's three Americans had climbed on their chairs for a better view of the rumpus on the street, a lady of forty, shapely and smelling of money, with two rather unprepossessing daughters. A couple of young Frenchmen kidding around with them quipped "Mesdames—the revolution," while the waiters were already collecting the checks. The patron and the waiters of the *Deux Magots* were experienced people and I am experienced too, I've had a few little experiences in the way of street fights back in Germany and I figured the police would turn up in half an hour at the latest. They would begin clearing the Boulevard right from the line of the *Deux Magots* over to the *Royal* and the cafés would have to have their shutters down by then or they might get slightly wrecked. I communicated my observations to Pierre but noticed only then that he was very quiet, sitting there pensively. I asked him what the matter was and finally Solange told me about Pierre's talk with Fayard. "Listen," I said to Pierre, "Fayard is right in what he says about the danger you are in. What are you going to do about it?" "Fayard is Evil," Pierre said without answering my question. "It's not de Gaulle who is Evil, not even the paras who tortured Alleg. It's Fayard. Fayard or the tactics, the tactical tolerance, the technique of compromise." He grabbed me by the arm all of a sudden and cried: "Democracy is Evil." I said: "You're nuts. First of all Fayard is not Democracy and secondly he may even be right on this thing. Democracy is a technique of compromise, not of the phony kind of compromise, naturally, but of creative compromise." But Pierre interrupted me and said: "You are phrasemongers, all of you, I want to publish my list." At this moment things really began to happen on the Boulevard. The crowds surged from the sidewalks into the street and closed in on the honking cars. "Come along,"I said to Pierre and Solange, "we'll go up to the corner of the Rue Dragon. From there we can make off sideways when the police arrive." But Pierre shook his head and remained where he sat and Solange with him, of course. If there is anything I am scared of it's the police. I acquired that habit in Germany and with all the things you hear about the police of Paris. . . . Meanwhile the young Algerian who waited for Pierre had ordered and paid for his second Pinard. Behind him, inside the café, the patron and a few customers were listening to the latest radio news. If ever there was a man able just to sit without thinking of anything at all it was the young Algerian that night. He waited and thought nothing at all. Now and then he fingered his knife. Nothingness and the knife surrounded by sputtering radio news were waiting for Pierre.

After the President of the Republic had asked the General to form the new government of France, the General left the Elysée Palace at 9:14 P.M. and went to see André Malraux, his closest adviser and confidant. Malraux, intellectual head of the Left in France until about 1937, participant in the Canton revolt and the Spanish War, during that time author of twentieth-century romans à clef, then retiring into the background of politics and literature and devoting himself to the history of art, joined the General in his Paris headquarters at 5 Rue Solferino and drove with him to a friend's country house on the Marne. No reporter was able to follow the General's car and police escort. The night of May 29th was dark. Malraux, sharp and elegant as usual, listened to de Gaulle. They sat facing each other by the fireside. They were alone. "You were absolutely right to demand the votes of the Socialists," Malraux said. The General: "I told Mollet, 'All right, I shall join the government but you are going with me.'" They both smiled contemptuously as Mollet's name was mentioned. "Of course, you know the thing would be to take not Mollet but Mendès-France into the government," Malraux said. De Gaulle nodded. "I have asked Pierre Closterman to sound out Mendès-France," Malraux went on, "you know what close friends they are; Mendès-France was a first lieutenant in Closterman's squadron during the war." The General was delighted to hear the name of the great fighter pilot. "And what is the answer?" "Still negative so far," Malraux replied. It will remain negative

too, thought Charles de Gaulle, Mendès-France would accept anything, even my policy, but what he cannot accept is the Cross of Lorraine. Mendès-France is a Jewish Liberal and I am a Catholic Conservative. We are fire and water. But Malraux, who had been through Marxism and the sacraments, thought: If there is anything that can save us from the terror squads of the Communists and the tortures of the paratroopers, from the impotence of parliaments and the corruption of the press, it will be the alliance of the great Conservatives and the great Liberals, the silent accord of Right and Left, a union of elites against the law of inertia in mass society. I shall restore the old way of making policy in secret, thought de Gaulle, the policy which lets a man keep his character, and that is why Mendès-France must fight me. For Mendès-France wants freedom, not secrecy. He knows that deep inside of what is secret there is the Law, the never-changing Law of the Everlasting, the Cross of Lorraine, just as I know that in the innermost heart of the idea of freedom there is anarchy, the moment when the Law is destroyed, Prometheus bringing the fire down from Heaven. In an hour like this the impossible must happen, thought Malraux, the unreconcilable must be reconciled as the Germans reconciled it on their 20th of July 1944. Except that the Germans did the impossible too late. We, the French, will do it in time. This will be my historical mission: I shall lead the elites of freedom into the camp of Conservative power before nothingness overwhelms both freedom and power. Deep in conversation about the tactical steps to be taken in the following days, the poet and the General indulged each in his own dream. Toward eleven o'clock de Gaulle left and reached his country place at Columbey-les-Deux-Eglises after midnight, on May 30 at 1:47 A.M.

very quiet the sound of the seine as it brushes against the pillars of the pont neuf. a church clock nearby struck half past eleven. a railroad station: verneuil l'étang. through the open window of the railway carriage the voices of birds, like the sound of bells above enchanted ponds. a few taxis went by lazily and not all the dromedaries had gone home yet. lemonade stand bathed in white light among the black trunks of the tuileries gardens. in the distance you could see the president of the republic dressed in diver's gear. he was accompanied by the king of greece who seemed so young that one felt tempted to teach him how to read. jacques tati, the comedian, opened the window of his apartment and fixed his shaving mirror so that the reflection of the round disk hit the cage of his canary on the floor below: the bird began to sing. the astral eyes of wols, the deceased tachist, inspected the japanese marten-hair brushes in santelier's shop on the corner of the rue bonaparte and the quai voltaire. *a young hetaera followed them and offered them her services.* a secretary of the president's opened a letter from the widow of audin, the mathematician who had been tortured to death. *it was raining gloves and a sharp november wind carried them away.*

"Pierre!"

"Yes?"

"I know what you're thinking."

"No, you haven't any idea."

"Yes, you think you are going to end it all."

"Okay then, you're right. But I don't like it when you creep into my thoughts, Solange."

"I can't stop thinking just because it doesn't suit you."

"But one should be able to stop thinking."

"You should say that!"

"Well, I'm not a strong thinker, am I?"

"You're intelligent and intense, Pierre."

"Thanks. I'm not in the mood right now to return your declaration of love."

"It wasn't a declaration of love. Just a statement of fact. I don't love you at all. Did I ever tell you I loved you?"

"No, but you like making love with me or don't you?"

"I find you agreeable. You are tactful and intelligent and what I like about you is that you can't stop thinking. Not even in bed."

"Would you love me if at certain moments I did stop thinking?"

"Perhaps."

"I shall oblige in the future."

"Is that part of your program?"

"Are you planning to go on this way?"

"Yes, for just a few more minutes if you don't mind."

"Why?"

"Because I don't like you when you're not intelligent, Pierre. You're not intelligent tonight."

"So you think Fayard is right?"

"There, you see how stupid you are? No, of course, Fayard is an opportunist. But escape, just because there are Fayards in the world?"

"All right, let's call it escape, though it's the wrong word for what I am going to do because I suddenly see the light."

"You mean, because you've suddenly developed a short circuit in your mind."

"Your sarcasm isn't very charming, Solange."

"I'm a Parisian. We don't talk the way they do at Bordeaux, those heroes of Gascony."

"All right, then, I shall talk as soberly as possible. I'll simply draw up an account for you . . ."

"Your program?"

"My conclusions. I'm going to ask you three questions . . ."

"I can't wait."

"Can one go with the Communists?"

"No."

"With de Gaulle?"

"No."

"With the Fayards?"

"No."

"Since there are just these three possibilities one must quit. That's what you call escape. It's my program. I don't escape. I simply quit."

"There is still another possibility."

"Which?"

"You could remain Pierre Grange. A man who thinks and says what he thinks."

"Say what I think? I can't even publish a list, produce a vital piece of information."

"It would be quite sufficient if you thought and spoke. To Fayard, for instance."

"Would I change anything by doing that?"

"No."

"Well then!"

"I am thinking of the Picasso anecdote that delighted you so. He said that if his pictures were packed into crates right after they were painted they would have the same effect they have exhibited on walls."

"All right. I shall put my thoughts into crates in the future. Although they are probably not as valuable as Guernica."

"Perhaps it might help if you told them to me?"

"That's exactly what I'm planning to do. On the beach at Lacaneau you and I are going to pack my valuable thoughts into crates washed ashore by the sea."

"Where?"

"At Lacaneau-Océan. It's north of Arcachon on the Atlantic."

"Ah, near Bordeaux. The defeated hero returning to his home in Gascony."

"Lacaneau has the biggest dunes in France. At low tide the beach is one or two kilometers wide. You have to hurry if you are out and the tide comes in. And it's quite isolated in stretches. You'll be the brownest girl in Lacaneau."

"It's no good."

"Why?"

"Because I can't come with you. I don't have the

time. I still have work to do on the orders for Magnard and it'll take me at least till the middle of July."

"Couldn't you do that at Lacaneau just as well?"

"I'm afraid I shan't be able to think of anything at Lacaneau."

"That isn't the reason."

"You're right. It isn't the reason. I simply don't feel like watching you act the defeated lion licking his wounds. What do you think you are going to live on?"

"I shall ask my father for money."

"You've never done that before."

"But I shall now."

"Poor Pierre, you really are in bad shape. But I'm no good as a nurse. I love you when you are intelligent and intense, when you never stop thinking and saying what you think."

"So you do love me?"

"Did I say that?"

"Just now."

"I must have slipped. By the way, perhaps there is one reason why even I might want you to go to Lacaneau. If it's true what Fayard says about the danger you're in, it would be good to go somewhere where no one suspects you. I'm a little worried about you, Pierre."

"Come along, let's go. They're turning off the lights."

"Yes, your German friend was right. They expect the police."

"I wonder if the police will dare thrash into the people here."

"They must if they want to clear the street. And they'll have their orders."

"It's an outrage. Oh, I could. . . ."

"You'll have to drop the habit of feeling indignant. That doesn't go with your program. From now on you must want to be as deaf and empty as a shell on the beach of Lacaneau."

"You're right. But if I don't succeed?"

"Take a return ticket, just in case."

"Charming, that Parisian cynicism of yours."

"Oh, heavens, can't you understand how glad I'd be if you came back?"

The people of St.-Germain-des-Prés surrounded the cars honking "Al-gé-rie Fran-çaise," yet they did not raise a hand against the occupants, but began arguing with them, screaming and laughing. The boulevard was flooded with people: I stood where the dark narrow Rue Dragon comes in and from here was able to watch the table where Pierre and Solange sat. I saw the lights extinguished at the *Deux Magots*

and the *Flores*, at the *Royal St. Germain*, the *Brasserie Lipp* and the *Calvet* and I thought, I hope Pierre and Solange won't sit there too long or they'll be in the front line later on. I was relieved to see them rise at last. It was a few minutes past midnight. At almost exactly the same time the Algerian must have left his place in front of the café by the Rue Monge. The café closed at midnight at the latest because there was nothing going on in this part of town any more at that hour. The patron must have simply kicked the fellow out at midnight unless he went by himself. By then the Algerian had had enough time to choose a suitable new spot. While Pierre and Solange came toward me diagonally across the Boulevard St. Germain, the Algerian must have crossed the empty intersection of the Rue Monge and the Rue Cardinal-Lemoine and stepped into the dark entrance of the butcher's shop right next to the entrance to the métro station. Whoever comes out of the métro and aims for the Rue des Boulangers must pass in front of this butcher's shop. I lost sight of Pierre and Solange but a few minutes later they reappeared. Pierre held Solange by the hand so as not to lose her in the mob. It was a bit touching, for Solange basically is not the type of woman one must hold by the hand. She has a sort of sporty elegance and makes quite a lot of money with her textile designs for Magnard. But I noticed the two let go their hands only reluctantly when they finally stood beside me on the sidewalk. At this moment the police arrived, a squad of at least three hundred men in large gray vans, in jeeps, with motorcycles whizzing around. The motorcade stopped. In the sudden silence one could hear the shattering of metal and glass as a jeep ran into a van which had stopped short in front of it. Jeers went up from the crowds on the sidewalk. The brigade continued slowly, fanned out with clocklike precision over the Place St.-Germain-des-Prés, rolled to a stop and settled in the three side streets. The two last cars stopped in the center of the intersection and released a crowd of puppets in leather leggings and képis who dispersed according to regulations, swirling their batons—the famous meticulously performed attack of the French police. I caught just a blurred vision of them, for the entire boulevard had started to run in one hypnotizing move; I was just able to prevent us from being swept away. Quickly I pulled Pierre and Solange into the dark shaft of the Rue Dragon. We ran down it a little way, stopped and looked back. Through the mouth of the lane opening into the boulevard we could see the fleeing crowds but not the police. I figured that they had carried their attack no further than a hundred yards into the boulevard. The concentrated movement within a small area would be sufficient to cause a centrifugal dispersing effect. "Sandbox games," I said to Pierre. "Observed with the cool Prussian eye," said a voice next to us. "Yes, but it's a Paris staff operation," I replied and held out my hand to Jacques Mondello, the philosopher. Mondello stood in the door of his little bookstore on the Rue Dragon. The store was dark, with only a small lamp under a green glass shade burning in the back. "Come in," Mondello said and we entered and sat down at the square table in front of the bookcases reaching up to the ceiling. Opposite the window I saw in the uncertain light the dirty-white wall of the publishing house where the writings of Vercors and Eluard had been illegally printed during the war and where the books of Samuel Beckett and Alain Robbe-Grillet and the now forbidden book of the tortured Henri Alleg were published. Mondello noticed at once what I had not sensed before in the *Deux Magots*: that Pierre was silent. They talked together for a while before unrest and fatigue drove us out again. Perhaps the young Algerian was the only person not restless and tired that night. Motionless he leaned in the shadowy black by the door of the butcher's shop near the entrance to the métro and waited.

Before he fell asleep in his bed at Colombey-les-Deux-Eglises the tall old General thought once more of the gate at the Elysée Palace, the gate reserved for heads of states only, which he had ordered opened because he believed in the power of ceremony, in the magic of rites, in the mesmerism of pantomime. Before the masses he would stretch his long arms above his head in a great, solemn, slow gesture that made him seem even taller than he was. Let them call me giraffe, he thought, the animal that stands high above the veld. He mused with satisfaction over the performance that had been put on for him: the ceremony of the perfect coup d'état approaching in brilliant concentric circles from the periphery toward its center, Paris, where he, de Gaulle, stood, motionless. He did not move a finger, yet it was his coup d'état, worthy of his thoughts and ideas. A coup d'état had its aesthetics too, which even opponents admired although they might not use the metaphor of the concentric circles but rather talk in terms of a noose that had been put around the neck of the Republic. He would not pull the noose. I am the rock of legitimacy not the hangman of freedom, he thought dramatically. Then, in tactical terms: I shall send Trinquier and Thomazo to the front so that I can ban Servan-Schreiber's paper when it insults the army. I shall

play like a juggler with the factions, the League and the Huguenots. I shall fuse the capitalist groups behind Mendès-France with those behind Reynaud. Capital has but one honor: interest. I shall grab it by its interest like a soldier by his honor. With some uneasiness he thought of his own interests. His family's capital was invested in Algerian banks. He knew that money was the only power a king of France had to worry about. But if this principle were altered other powers would take the place of the power of money. The terror of an ideology, for instance. That night General de Gaulle did not know that perhaps at the same hour a great and good man who had known nothing about the necessary aesthetics of coup d'état was receiving his death sentence in Budapest.

lacaneau-océan: the waves, the heartshaped shells, the sand crystals, the blowing wind. *it may not be absolutely clear today what one must fight for, but we know beyond any doubt whom we must fight. inevitably, and as of today.* the ultramarine blue of the sea and the bright gloss of the sky. whisky bottles and vases from atlantis thrown onto the beach. *to fight now or to fight later—that is the only alternative for those who cannot bow to orders of the legionnaires.* crab skeletons, death, veined pebbles, silence, paperlike rustling of waves, infinity. *the future begins today.*

"I admire your trust in what people have told you about democracy, Pierre. I'd have thought you more intelligent than that. The function of the public, is it? The purifying power of the press, eh? A deplorable fact is made public and before you know it is only half as deplorable. At least the person who made it public has cleared his conscience. He can go on to the next deplorable fact."

"Supposing Fayard published my list. That would have an effect, wouldn't it?"

"Yes, it might—it might, I say—force de Gaulle to issue a few statements. Your list and his statements —you and de Gaulle—would have added a few not very important pages to the volume of historical documents."

"Isn't there a chance, Mondello, that my list might be quite effective in warning the Republic? If it were proved that de Gaulle is a plotter . . ."

" . . . the President of the Republic might be persuaded not to entrust de Gaulle with a new government. Is that what you mean?"

"It would be logical."

"And you in the part of David slaying Goliath."

"You can't deprive me of any more illusions tonight, Mondello. But let's stay with the idea for a moment: all right, I am David. To all intents and purposes my slingshot should be effective."

"Now I've got you where I want you. Do you know the difference between you and David?"

"Well?"

"David used a real slingshot whereas you want to publish an article which proves how evil Goliath is."

"But the article is my slingshot."

"That's where you are wrong. It's nothing but a piece of literature. This type of literature—newspaper literature—has a certain justification as long as political powers are in balance. Or else when democracy is developing: Zola in the Dreyfus case. But when politics become the mere exercise of power it's all over. At that moment the press and its literature become a mere footnote to the premises of power. You, Pierre, are a victim of false doctrines about democracy. One of them is belief in the press and in the immediate effectiveness of literature. You have been told that freedom is identical with freedom of the press . . ."

"And you mean to say it isn't true?"

"It's an illusion to deceive trusting souls, leading them to write and read rather than to act even in the face of an opponent for whom words like freedom, writing and reading simply don't exist. Whatever needs doing is delegated to the press. Action really means that somewhere letters pour from a printing press."

"Thank you, Mondello, you've released me from my last inhibitions."

"Inhibitions about what?"

"I'm quitting. I've told Solange so earlier this evening."

"You mean you're going to bolt now, Pierre?"

"You yourself have convinced me that everything I've thought up to now is completely useless. Or is it?"

"But don't you see, I only want to make you think of something to do that may be of use?"

"There isn't anything. We live in a world of false alternatives. I can't go with any of the fighting factions. Not even with the lesser evil. To my mind the lesser evil is the greatest of all. I admit that till tonight I believed in a Third Force: the public. You've done away with that illusion."

"It's a neat calculation, Pierre, a trifle too neat."

"I can't help it if you don't like my conclusion."

"You simply wipe out everything that's left."

"What is left?"

"Evil! You've forgotten that injustice remains even if you quit. You can simply walk out, nobody will stop you—but don't forget, some Alleg will go on being tortured wherever you may be."

"Good God, Mondello, but that's why I go, because I can't do anything about injustice."

"Who says you can't? After all, you meet it everywhere. You have a special talent for running into brutality wherever you go. I ask you, Pierre Grange, why didn't you face up to Léon Delbecque in Algiers, pistol in hand? You're a reserve officer, you know how to handle arms."

"So that's what you are driving at!"

"Indeed. Instead of doing the obvious you made a list, and because nobody will publish it, your world collapses."

"Oh, I forgot. Jacques Mondello, the philosopher of direct action. Unfortunately, I don't believe in individual terror."

"Yes, you prefer to capitulate to the great universal terror."

"So you believe one must be able to kill when one encounters injustice?"

"Of course."

"Doesn't that just lengthen the chain of injustice?"

"Don't worry about injustice. It's here to stay, forever. But you may interrupt it occasionally, break the chain so it will take time to weld it together again."

"I'm afraid our conversation is becoming too abstract. I am talking about myself now: I believed in the power of words for a while. It was a mistake, I admit. But I cannot kill. Now you know why I am going away."

"And if you were taken into the cell where Alleg is being tortured—would you still be unable to shoot at his torturers?"

"Perhaps. I don't know."

"I respect your decision, Pierre. Perhaps it's good for you to go away for a while. To go away so as to realize that freedom doesn't mean being able to choose some ideology but to smash injustice wherever you meet it."

"And how do you recognize it?"

"Believe me, you recognize it always and at once. There's a sure sign: when nothing tells you any longer to write, when you are dominated by a single thought: to act, just to act. That's where you confront evil."

"But is there no chance for literature any more?"

"Not for the kind of literature you mean, Pierre—secondary literature that thinks itself history because it gets excited and argues. It is just a symptom, nothing more. Great literature does something else: it prepares long and gradual developments, it sows seeds, a few thoughts and forms which renew the world, which remind it of something old: Augustine did that, Pascal, Spinoza, Marx, Kafka—take his 'Knock at the Gate,' for instance, those few pages of prose don't influence the times but they change the world. A few things have become absurd since we have this story. . . .".

"It's late, Mondello, I must go. What books shall I take into my retreat?"

"None! But don't forget—I know, you'll think I'm quite ridiculous—still, don't forget to read the papers, Pierre."

After we had left Mondello we went back once more to the Place St.-Germain-des-Prés where the police had formed cordons. They were relieved every half hour. Behind them the people of the quartier stood massed, watching the gendarmes silence the Gaullist horns by smashing the car windows with their batons. We stood around and met everybody. After two o'clock the muted demonstration crumbled away; the police had behaved with reserve, they had been wise and had waited. The Algerian was still standing in the entrance of the butcher's shop on the corner of the Rue des Boulangers. The passing of time faced him with a problem: Pierre Grange could no longer come by métro but only on foot or by taxi. If he came by taxi, he would probably drive up to the house in the Rue des Boulangers where he lived; in that case the Algerian would have waited in vain, for he could not place himself in front of the house, Pierre would see him and before the taxi left would already have gone in. The Algerian could not make up his mind to change his position. We took a taxi and first dropped Solange at her apartment in the Rue d'Assas. Pierre and Solange kissed but Pierre did not go up with her. We drove along the Jardin de Luxembourg and the Rue des Ecoles which leads into the Rue Monge. At the intersection of the Rue Monge and the Rue Cardinal-Lemoine Pierre knocked on the window of the cab and we got out. "I don't like to drive up to the house," Pierre said. He had an aversion for janitors and hated to be kept tabs on. We paid the driver. The taxi drove off and for a moment we stood in silence at the completely empty intersection.

Two-seventeen. The tall old General slept. There is a very simple secret to the success of great old statesmen: they fall asleep easily. Anywhere and in any situation they are able to drop off into a deep refreshing nap. They sleep in cars, at diplomatic conferences and in their beds. The world is full of sleeping statesmen.

the whistling sounds of the morse code in the police radio car, like signals from the moon. from the direction of the comédie francaise a clearing of the throat, probably by racine. a dog peeing against the pedestal of diderot's monument. smell of violets.

Crossing the intersection, lit by bobbing electric lights but also by the moon, we made for the corner of the Rue des Boulangers. Against the gray fronts of the old houses the window cornices stood out black. When we passed the entrance to the métro, I looked down the stairs and could read the white enamel signs on the doors saying "poussez." I knew the doors were dark green. They must have been closed at this hour.

In his dream the General recalled a remark by Malraux. "The language of your speeches and memoirs is wonderful old classical French," Malraux had said. "Your style is the style of Montesquieu." Now Malraux repeated his words, and as the General dreamed a smile flitted across his face.

portillon automatique. the sweetish odor of the stairways. carnets for hades. the entrance in art nouveau style designed by guimet, iron vines. thundering trains across the styx, behind the portillon automatique.

At this moment the Algerian broke from his cover. He certainly had not counted on Pierre being in company, but he had to risk the assault. It was lucky for Pierre I was his guest this Night of the Giraffe. Perhaps I saw the Algerian a split second sooner than Pierre, I saw him the way one sees a shadow, but what distinguished him from a shadow was the dull gleam of an object which, as I pulled Pierre aside, went into the sleeve of his coat, tearing the material with a short crackling sound before it hit the flesh of Pierre's arm.

One of the General's dogs moaned in its sleep, woke up, yawned and at once went to sleep again. The General's hand slid down from the coverlet and for a time hung over the edge of the bed, then rejoined the other hand on the General's chest as if in prayer. The General always slept as if he were lying in state—the King of France on a catafalque. But this was not Rheims Cathedral yet.

make up your mind! you can clench your fist, if only inside your pocket, or you can try to widen the scope of the human eye. rebellion, or adding a new kind of blue to the spectrum—but make up your mind!

I believe the pain of the stiletto in Pierre's upper arm was what saved him. It forced him into sharp and immediate consciousness, so that he grabbed the Algerian's wrist with his right hand and bent it back; with his fist he plucked the stiletto like a fruit from the Algerian's open hand and thrust the knife into his chest in a move of automatic and blind force. The Algerian crumpled down on his knees, then toppled backwards and collapsed on the métro steps. Sliding a bit further down, he lay still. We ran down and gazed at him; he made no sound. His white broken eyes reflected the streetlights from the crossing. Pierre pulled the knife from the body and threw it down the steps; it clattered against the doors. Then we both hurried silently along the Rue des Boulangers to Pierre's house. As I dressed his arm upstairs in his apartment—he was bleeding heavily—I muttered: "That dirty little hired guy!" Pierre talked hardly at all, but toward morning when the dim light of a rainy day came creeping along the roofs of the Ile St. Louis outside his windows, he said: "My list wasn't worth that." His face was white and I knew as I looked at him that he would not return from Lacaneau-Océan or from wherever he was going.

Translated by Christa Armstrong

►► **Friedrich Dürrenmatt**

The Tunnel

The young man who boarded his usual train that Sunday afternoon was twenty-four years old and fat. He was fat in order to protect himself, for anything he perceived out of the ordinary terrified him. Indeed, this clarity of vision was probably the only real ability he possessed, and even this was a burden to him. Although his fat gave a general protection to his body, he found it necessary to stuff every sort of hole in his body through which the terrifying influences might reach him. He smoked cigars (Ormond Brazil 10). He wore a pair of sunglasses over his ordinary glasses. He even stuffed his ears with wads of cotton wool. At twenty-four he was still dependent on his parents, a consequence of rather nebulous studies at the University. And the University was two hours away from home by train. Departure time five-fifty. Arrival at seven twenty-seven.

And so this student, fat and twenty-four years old, boarded his usual Sunday train to attend a seminar the following day. The fact that he had already decided to skip class was irrelevant. As he left his home town the afternoon sun shone from a cloudless summer sky. It was pleasant weather for a trip he knew almost by heart. The train's route lay between the Alps and the Juras, past rich villages and towns, over a river and, after some twenty minutes further travel, into a little tunnel just beyond Burgdorf. The train was overcrowded and he had entered at one of the front cars. With considerable difficulty he worked his way toward the rear. Perspiring, and with two pairs of glasses, he offered an oafish appearance. All the travelers were sitting closely packed, some even on suitcases. All the second-class compartments were occupied, and only the first-class compartments were relatively empty. The young man fought through the melee of families and recruits, students and lovers, falling against this one or that one as the train swayed, stumbling against stomachs and breasts until he came to a seat in the last car. At last he had found space enough to have a bench to himself, a pleasant surprise, since third-class coaches are seldom divided into compartments with benches. Opposite him, playing a solitary game of chess, he noted a man even fatter than himself, and on the same bench, near the corridor, sat a red-haired girl reading a novel. The young man gratefully chose the window seat on the empty bench. He had just lit an Ormond Brazil 10 when the train entered the little tunnel. Of course he had traveled this stretch many times before, almost every Saturday and Sunday throughout the past year, but he had never found the opportunity to examine the tunnel closely. He had, in fact, been only vaguely aware of it. Several times he had intended to give it his full attention, but each time he had been thinking of other matters, and each time the brief plunge into darkness had passed unnoticed, so fast was the train and so brief its plunge into the darkness of the little tunnel.

And even this time he had not been thinking of the tunnel and so had forgotten to take off his sunglasses. Outside the tunnel the sun had been shining with all its force, flooding the hills and woods and the distant chain of the Juras with golden evening light. Even the little houses of the town through which they had just passed had seemed built of gold. This abrupt passage from light to darkness must then be the reason why the tunnel seemed so much longer than usual. He waited patiently in the dark compartment for the return to daylight. At any moment the first pale shimmer of daylight would gleam on his windowpane, widen as quickly as a flash of lightning, then close in powerfully with its full yellow brightness. Nevertheless, the darkness lasted. He took off his sunglasses. At about the same time the girl lit a cigarette. As her match flared orange he thought he detected a grim annoyance in her face. No doubt she resented the interruption in her perusal of her novel. He looked at his wrist watch. The liminous dial said six-ten.

He leaned back, settling himself in the corner between window and compartment wall, and directed his thoughts to the complications of his studies. No one really believed he was studying at all. He thought of the seminar he had to attend the next day, and which he would not attend. Each of his activities seemed a pretext designed to achieve order behind the façade of routine pursuits. Perhaps what he sought was not order itself, but only a semblance of order. The art of an actor who used his fat, his cigars and his cotton wool as make-up for a genteel comedy, while all the while he knew himself to be a part of some monstrous farce. When he next looked at his watch the time was six-fifteen. The train was still in the tunnel. He felt confused. At last the light bulbs flickered and the compartment brightened. The red-haired girl returned to her novel and the fat gentleman resumed his solitary chess game. The whole compartment now appeared reflected in the window. But outside, on the other side of the window, the tunnel was still there.

He stepped into the corridor in which a tall man was walking up and down restlessly. He observed the light raincoat and the black scarf around the gentleman's neck. Surely there was no need for a scarf in this weather? A black scarf? He peered into the other compartments in the rear coach. The passengers were reading their newspapers or chatting. Normal. He returned to his corner and sat down. The tunnel must come to an end any minute now. At any second? His wrist watch read six-twenty. He felt an obscure annoyance with himself for not having paid more attention to the tunnel on previous trips. They had been in the tunnel for a quarter of an hour now. And surely, allowing for the speed of the train, it must be one of the longest tunnels in Switzerland. Or perhaps he had taken the wrong train. But he could recall no other tunnel of such length and importance within twenty minutes of his home. On impulse he asked the fat chess player if the train were indeed bound for Zurich. The man confirmed this. The student ventured again that he hadn't known that there was such a long tunnel on this part of the journey. The chess player was more than a little annoyed to have his difficult considerations interrupted a second time. He replied testily that in Switzerland there were a great many tunnels, in fact, an extraordinary number of tunnels, that he was actually traveling in Switzerland for the first time, but that an affluence of tunnels was the first thing one noticed about Switzerland, and indeed, his statistical almanac confirmed the fact that no country possessed such a positive abundance of tunnels as Switzerland! And he added that now he must excuse himself; he was very sorry, really, but a most difficult chess problem in regard to the Nimzowitsch Defense occupied his mind and he could afford no further diversions. The last remark was polite, but firm. It was evident that no further conversation could be expected from the chess player and, in any event, he could be of little use, since the route was new to him.

At that moment the conductor appeared, and the student had high hopes that his ticket would be refused. The official was pale and scrawny. He gave an impression of nervousness as he remarked to the girl near the door that she would have to change trains at Olten. Although Olten was also a regular stop on the Zurich run, the young man did not give up hope of being on the wrong train, so complete was his conviction that he had mistaken trains in boarding. He didn't doubt that he would have to pay extra fare, but he accepted the expense with equanimity. The return to daylight would be cheap at the price. He therefore handed his ticket to the conductor and said that his destination was Zurich. He accomplished the speech without once removing the Ormond Brazil 10 from his mouth.

"But the gentleman is on the right train," replied the conductor as he inspected the ticket.

"But we're going through a tunnel!" The young man had spoken with considerable anger. He was determined to put an end to the confusion. The official replied that they had just passed Herzogenbuchsee and would soon approach Langenthal where the train was due at six-twenty. The young man looked at his watch. Six-twenty. But they had been traveling through the tunnel for the past twenty minutes, he persisted. The conductor raised his brows.

"This is the Zurich train," he said, now looking for the first time toward the window. "Six-twenty," he said again, uneasily. "We'll be in Olten soon. Arrival time six thirty-seven. We must have gone into some bad weather suddenly. A storm. Yes. That's why it's dark."

The gentleman with the Nimzowitsch Defense problem entered the conversation now. He had been holding out his ticket (and holding up his game) for some time, but the conductor had not yet noticed him. "Nonsense," he interjected. "Nonsense! We're traveling through a tunnel. I can see the rock clearly. Looks like granite. Switzerland has more tunnels than all the rest of the world put together. Read it in a statistical almanac."

The conductor relieved him of his ticket, and repeated pleadingly that this was truly the Zurich train. Unmollified, the young man demanded to speak to the Chief Conductor. The ticket collector now felt his dignity to have been abused. He directed the student to the front of the train, but reiterated huffily that the train was going to Zurich, that the time was now six twenty-five, that in twelve minutes time (according to the summer schedule) the train would arrive in Olten, and that the young man should have no further doubts on that point. *He* traveled this train at least twelve times a month.

Nevertheless the young scholar set off to find the Chief Conductor. Movement through the crowded train now seemed even more difficult than before. The train must be traveling exceedingly fast. In any event, it was making a frightful racket. He stuffed the wads of cotton a little more firmly into his ears, for he had loosened them in order to speak to the ticket collecter. The passengers were behaving calmly. This train was no different from any other Sunday afternoon train, and no one appeared worried. In the second-class compartments he came upon an Englishman standing by the corridor window. "Simplon," he was saying, as he tapped the pane with his pipe and beamed inanely.

Things were very much as usual in the dining car too. No seats were vacant, and neither waiters nor diners, occupied with Wiener schnitzel and rice, made any comment on the tunnel. But there, near the exit of the dining car, he recognized the red bag of the Chief Conductor.

"What can I do for you, sir?" The Chief Conductor was a tall man, quiet behind a carefully groomed black mustache and neat rimless glasses.

"We have been in a tunnel for twenty-five minutes."

The Conductor did not look toward the windows, as the young man might have expected, but turned to a nearby waiter. "Give me a packet of Ormond 10," he said. "I smoke the same brand as the gentleman here." The waiter, however, indicated that the brand was not in stock, and the young man, glad of an opportunity for further conversation, proffered a Brazil.

"Thank you," returned the Conductor. "In Olten I shall hardly have time to buy any. You are doing me a great favor. Smoking is a most important business. Will you come this way, please?"

Mystified, the young man followed him into the freight car ahead of the diner.

"The next car is the locomotive," offered the official. "This is the front of the train."

A sickly yellow light burned amid the baggage. Most of the car lay in total darkness. The side doors were barred, as was the small window beside them, and through its irons the greater blackness of the tunnel seeped in. The trunks, many decorated with hotel stickers, the bicycles and the baby carriage that composed the cargo of the coach seemed haphazardly arranged. The Chief Conductor, an obviously precise man, hung his red bag on a nearby hook.

"What can I do for you?" he asked again, without, however, looking at the student. Instead, he began to enter neat columns in a book he had taken from his pocket.

"We have been in a tunnel since Burgdorf," answered the young man with determination. "There is no such enormous tunnel on this line. I know. I travel back and forth every week on this train."

The Chief Conductor continued to write. "Sir," he said, stepping close to his inquisitor, so close that their bodies almost touched, "sir, I have little to tell you. I have no idea how we got into this tunnel. I have no explanation for it. But I ask you to consider this. We are moving along on tracks: therefore this tunnel leads somewhere. We have no reason whatever to believe that anything is wrong with this tunnel, except, of course, that there seems to be no end to it." The Chief Conductor still held the unlit Ormond Brazil 10 between his lips. He had spoken extremely quietly, yet with such dignity and clarity, and with such assurance that his words were audible despite the increased noise of the baggage car.

"Then I must ask you to stop the train," said the young man impatiently. "I really don't understand you. If there's something wrong with this tunnel—and it seems you can't explain even its existence—then your duty is to stop this train at once."

"Stop the train?" returned the older man slowly. It seemed he had already thought of that, but, as he informed his companion, it was a serious matter to stop a train. With this, he shut the book and laid it in the red bag which was swaying to and fro on its hook. Then he carefully lit the Ormond 10. The young man offered to pull the emergency brake overhead, and was on the point of releasing the lever, when suddenly he staggered forward and was sent crashing against the wall. At the same moment, the baby carriage rolled toward him and several trunks slid by. The Chief Conductor swayed strangely and began to move, hands outstretched, through the freight car.

"We are going downhill!" he announced as he joined the young man now leaning against the wall. But the expected crash of hurtling train against granite tunnel did not occur. There was no shattering of telescoped coaches. Once again the train seemed to be running on a level. The door opened at the other end of the car. In the bright light of the diner, until the door swung to again, they could see the passengers merrily toasting one another's health.

"Come into the locomotive." At this point the Chief Conductor was peering thoughtfully, almost menacingly at the student. He opened the door nearby. As he did so a rush of tempestuous heat-laden air struck the pair with such force that they were driven back against the wall. At the same moment a frightful clatter resounded through the almost empty freight car.

"We'll have to climb over to the engine," he cried into the younger man's ear. Despite his shouting, his voice was hardly audible. He then disappeared through the right angle of the open doorway. The student followed cautiously in the direction of the swaying and brightly lit engine. He didn't know why he was climbing, but at this point determination had overcome reason. He found himself on a pitching platform between the two cars, and clung desperately to the iron rails on both sides. Although the terrific draft moderated but slightly as he inched his way up to the locomotive, he dreaded the wind less than the immediate nearness of the tunnel walls. They were hidden from him in the blackness, but were nevertheless frighteningly close. It was necessary to focus all his attention on the engine ahead, yet the pounding of the wheels and the hissing vibrating push of air against him gave him the feeling of careening, at the speed of a falling star, into a world of stone.

A board just wide enough to walk on crossed the gap between the cars and ran the length of the engine. Above and parallel to it, a curving metal rod served as railing. To reach the plank he would have to make a jump of nearly a yard. He braced himself, leaped, and pushed himself along the board. His progress was slow, since he had to press close to the outside of the engine to keep his foothold. It was not until he reached the long side of the engine and was fully exposed to the roaring hurricane of wind and to the menacing cliff walls now brilliantly illuminated by the engine lights that he began to realize his fear. But just then he was rescued by the Chief Conductor who pulled him through a small door into the engine. Exhausted, the young man lay against the wall. He was grateful for the sudden quiet. With the engine door shut, the steel walls of the giant locomotive deadened the noise almost completely.

"Well, we've lost the Ormond Brazil too," said the Conductor. "It wasn't a very sensible idea to light one before starting the climb, but they break so easily in one's pocket. It's their unusual length."

The young man was delighted to converse normally again. The close and terrifying rock walls had reminded him uncomfortably of his everyday world, of its ever similar days and years. The thought occurred to him that their boring similitude had perhaps been only a preparation for the present moment: that this was a moment of initiation, of truth, this departure from the surface of the earth and precipitous descent into the womb of the earth. He took another brown package from his right coat pocket and offered the Chief Conductor a new cigar. He took one himself, and carefully they lit their Brazils from the Conductor's lighter.

"I am very fond of these Ormonds," said the older man, "but one must pull very hard on them. Otherwise they go out so easily."

For some reason these words made the student suspicious. Was the Conductor as uncomfortable as he about the tunnel? For the tunnel still ran on interminably, and his mind persisted in the thought that surely the tunnel must stop, even as a dream can end, all of a sudden.

"Six-forty," he said, consulting his watch. "We should be in Olten now." Even as he spoke, he thought of the hills and woods radiant only a short while ago in the late golden sun. The thought could have been present in both their minds. Nevertheless, the two men stood and smoked and leaned against their wall.

"Keller is my name," announced the Conductor as he puffed at his Brazil.

The student refused to change the topic of conversation.

"The climb to the engine was very dangerous,

didn't you think? At least it was for me. I'm not used to that sort of thing. Anyway, I'd like to know why you've brought me here."

"I don't know," said Keller. "I wanted time to consider."

"Time to consider?"

"Yes," returned the Chief Conductor. "That's right." And he went on smoking. Just then the engine reeled over at a still steeper angle.

"We could go into the engineer's cabin," suggested Keller. He did not, however, leave his position against the wall. Annoyed by his companion's indecisiveness, the young man stepped briskly along the corridor to the driver's cabin, then abruptly stopped.

"Empty!" he said to the Conductor who had now moved up behind him. "The driver's seat is empty!" They went into the cabin. It was swaying too, for the engine was still tearing through the tunnel at enormous speed, bearing the train along with it, as though the weight of the coaches behind no longer counted.

"Allow me," said the Chief Conductor. He pressed some levers and pulled the emergency brake. There was no change. "We tried to stop the engine earlier. As soon as we noticed the alteration in the tracks. It didn't stop then either."

"It certainly isn't stopping now," said the other. He pointed to the speed indicator. "A hundred. Has the engine ever done a hundred before?"

"Good heavens! It has never gone so fast. Sixty-five at the most."

"Exactly. And the speed is increasing. Now the speedometer says a hundred and five. We must be falling." He went up to the window, but he couldn't keep his balance. He was pressed with his face against the glass, so fantastic was their speed. "The engine driver?" he shouted as he stared at the rock masses streaking towards him in the glare of the arc lights, disappearing above him and below him on either side of the engineer's cabin.

"He jumped off," Keller yelled back. He was now sitting on the floor, his back against the controls.

"When?" The student pursued the matter obstinately. Keller hesitated a while. He decided to relight his Ormond, an awkward task, for his legs were then at the same height as his head while the train continued its roll to one side.

"Five minutes after the switch. No use thinking to save him. Freight car man abandoned the train too."

"And you?" asked the student.

"I am in charge of this train. I, too, have always lived without hope."

"Without hope," repeated the young man. By then he was lying on the glass pane, face pressed against glass. Glass and engine and human flesh were pressed together above the abyss. "Back in the compartment," he thought, "we had entered the tunnel, but we didn't know that even then everything was already lost. We didn't think that anything had changed, and yet the shaft of the depths had already received us, and we had entered our abyss."

"I'll have to go to the rear," shouted the Chief Conductor. "The coaches will be in a panic. Everyone will be trying to get to the rear of the train."

"That's true." The student thought of the chess player and of the red-haired girl with her novel. He handed Keller his remaining packages of Ormond Brazil. "Take them. You'll lose your cigar again when you climb over."

"Aren't you coming?" The Conductor was once more on his feet and with difficulty he had begun to clamber up the funnel of the corridor. The student gazed at the useless instruments, at the useless ridiculous levers and switches shining silver-like in the glare of the cabin lights.

"A hundred and thirty," he called. "I don't think you'll be able to get to the coaches above us at this speed."

"It's my duty," shouted Keller over his shoulder.

"Certainly," returned the young man. He didn't bother turning his head to watch the other's senseless efforts.

"At least I have to try," yelled the Conductor. He was already far over the head of the fat young man. He braced elbows and thighs against slippery walls and seemed, indeed, to be making some progress. But just then the engine took a further turn downward. It hurtled toward the interior of the earth, goal of all things, in its terrible plunge. Keller now was directly over his friend who lay face downward on the silver gleaming window at the bottom of the driver's cabin. His strength gave. Suddenly he fell, crashed against the control panel and came to rest on the window beside his companion.

"What are we to do?" he cried, clinging to the young man's shoulders and shouting into his ear. The very fact that it was now necessary to shout alarmed him. The noise of the onrushing walls had destroyed even the quiet of the engine.

The younger man lay motionless on the pane of glass which separated him from the depths below. His fat body and weighty flesh were of no further use to him, no protection now.

"What are we to do?" persisted the Chief Conductor.

"Nothing," came the merciless reply. Merciless, yet not without a certain ghostly cheerfulness. Now, for the first time, his glasses were gone and his eyes were wide open. Greedily he sucked in the abyss through those wide-open eyes. Glass and metal splinters from the shattered control panel now studded his body. And still he refused to tear his thirsting eyes from the deadly spectacle below. As the first crack widened in the window beneath them, a current of air whistled into the cabin. It seized his two wads of cotton wool and swept them upward like

arrows into the corridor shaft overhead. He watched them briefly and spoke once more.

"Nothing. God let us fall. And now we'll come upon him."

Translated by Carla Colter and Alison Scott

► ► Paul Carroll

Death Is a Letter that Was Never Sent

*A Review of Kaddish and
Other Poems 1958-60
by Allen Ginsberg*

Time has assigned a crack reporter—disguised behind false whiskers and Zen paperbacks—to shadow Allen Ginsberg night and day. So goes a malicious rumor along the literary grapevine. By successfully advertising a public image of himself Allen Ginsberg has accomplished what most poets secretly long for but seldom taste: he is the stuff of headlines because his public image fills the shoes of one of the classic archetypes of folklore—The Romantic Poet. All of the paraphernalia are there: the garret in a Manhattan slum, the mysterious, forbidden sexual malady, the addiction to drugs or alcohol, the violence against the literary and social establishments, the epiphanies, the solitary voyages to exotic Alaska and Peru. "Ginsberg is nothing but a Grade-B movie star," I recently heard a Pulitzer Prize poet, plagued by the seven jealousies, carp. Only Frost, in fact, in his pose of Old Honest Abe, the rail-splitter of American Letters, rivals Ginsberg in sales and press notice.

Allen Ginsberg will never be awarded a Pulitzer or Bollingen prize. But his books will, like *Howl*, sell 60,000 copies—and more. He will never be appointed consultant in poetry to the Library of Congress. Over 1,000 people, however, will pack a hall to hear him read his "great, strange, mad, tragic, visionary, rhapsodic, angelic, apocalyptic" poems. Ginsberg will never be included in *The Oxford Book of American Verse* or an Oscar Williams anthology. But, at 34, he is already the American writer whom visiting European intellectuals ask to meet first. Ginsberg

will survive and continue to produce valuable poetry long after others members of the Beat Generation—Ferlinghetti, Burroughs, and Corso excepted—have disappeared into the suburbs or into sad, middle-aged bohemian oblivion. His death will occasion a wake like that of Dylan Thomas.

What is strange, however, is that Allen Ginsberg's real accomplishments as a poet do not come from his public image or his political and social poems. The great Ginsberg poems are private. ("Howl"—that labyrinth of personal sorrow—is a very private poem.) The earlier ones were elegiac. In them Ginsberg mourned his own miseries and the insanity of his friend Carl Solomon, the death of his mother, the decay of his own body. The more recent poems are pentecostal. Tongues of fire flicker through them as Ginsberg wrestles with the Godhead—the first American writer to do so since Melville.

His political and social poems play to the gallery. "Death to Van Gogh's Ear!"—with its ranting against the Almighty Dollar, the cartoon of a sinister Joe McCarthy Congress, the lachrymal lines about India, Australian aborigines, Chiapas Indians, and Chinese starved by a heartless U.S. foreign policy, its blanket, trite put-down of Squaresville, U.S.A.— "Owners! Owners! with obsession of property and vanishing selfhood"—has the sophomoric ring of willed emotion. The poem is what the literary public (it appeared in the London *Times Literary Supplement*) wants a classic Beat poet to say. Great political poems—"Easter, 1916," "Difficulties of a Statesman," Dante's discovery that even in Paradise Florentine politics has its place—transcend pose or propaganda. By experiencing and documenting "things as they are"—particular, temporal political or social events—the great political poems reach to touch the quick of the eternally human. To harangue at Uncle Sam for not giving his poets three square meals a day—"I rarely have an egg for breakfast," Ginsberg complains, "tho my work requires infinite eggs to come to birth in Eternity"—is the eternal anger of a son for more allowance. It doesn't make for memorable poetry.

Ginsberg's private experiences do. "Kaddish," the long lamentation over his mother's death, is the greatest elegy in American literature. In the Lincoln elegies Whitman mourns a public figure. Ginsberg mourns one miserable individual whom he loved—the look, smell, talk, brain, blood, and bone of her as she lived—and in so doing he mourns, finally, the futility, absurdity and queer dignity of our mortality. For days after I heard Ginsberg read "Kaddish" in 1959 for *Big Table* in Chicago, Virgil's incomparable line kept buzzing through my thoughts: *sunt lacrimae rerum et mentem mortalia tangent.* "Kaddish" has that kind of pathos, intensity, universality. Most great elegies find consolation in the Paradises of Christianity or Art or Nature, or vent their grief on some scapegoat—the literary hacks in "Adonais," for example, whose cruel words were supposed to have slain Keats. "Kaddish" is relentless in its sorrow. Nobody is to blame for the wretched, bleak death of Naomi Ginsberg. No future world offers the solace of an Eden come again or a Beatific Vision in whose will is our peace. In a lamentation incredibly sustained, "Kaddish" documents the bald fact that a woman named Naomi Ginsberg was born, loved, suffered terribly, and died. But, finally, the poem accomplishes that primitive magic of all great poetry: It resurrects. Naomi Ginsberg lives and shall live forever in the lines of her son Allen.

On the page a Ginsberg poem can seem banal, strident, crude, bad prosey writing. The second and longest section of "Kaddish," for example, elaborates in mediocre prose anecdotal facts about Naomi Ginsberg—her speech, appearance, nervous breakdowns, family, relatives—facts which in other sections are embodied in intense, memorable poetry. It doesn't matter. A Ginsberg poem must be heard read aloud and, if possible, from the mouth of the poet. (Ginsberg is one of the most accomplished readers of his generation—bardic, hypnotic, apocalyptic, "one of the wiggy Old Testament prophets come back," as Ferlinghetti accurately wrote.) A Ginsberg poem is accumulative, building stanza on stanza until, finally,

orgastically, the poem assumes flesh and blood on the stage and for an instant one bears witness to "truth plain." The prosey litanies, the redundancies, the incantations all contribute. On the page they blemish. Cut them from the heard poem and you cut out the vital guts.

The long, now supple, now locomotive Ginsberg stanza is, in fact, a new poetics. Singlehandedly Ginsberg has transfused into American prosody the important discoveries of jazzmen like Charlie Parker and the spontaneities of the Action painters. Only Robert Lowell and the recent work of John Ashbery match Ginsberg in this; they are constructing—each quite differently—new poetic forms. The Ginsberg stanza is a very personal vehicle. I doubt if it will have many disciples. But Ginsberg has done that rare thing: broken fresh technical ground. Other poets will learn from him—some already have.

Finally, the pentecostal poems. There are four. "Lysergic Acid," the fierce, great "Magic Psalm," "The Reply," and "The End." (The last three were, according to the poet, "visions experienced after drinking ayahucasca, an Amazon spiritual potion.")

For the first time in our poetry we have a poet who celebrates the ancient ritual—Invoking of the God. These poems are both invocation and confrontation. In them Ginsberg asks and gives no quarter. One must take them as literal, experienced visions, or not at all. What is hard to bear is the shock of seeing a modern American poet struggling like a Hebrew prophet with his God. The God whom Ginsberg invokes, hates, loves, mocks, copulates with, and weeps on his knees in front of, is terribly present. The God of Eliot, for contrast, is a God honed from the tomes of the Fathers and Divines (which is not to say he is any the less real). The God of Ginsberg is the one who exists before the civilized sensibility. He is the barbarous, beautiful God who speaks from the Burning Bush.

The title of this review is a line from the poem "Mescaline." It seems to embody the best of Ginsberg: his elegiac powers that can resurrect the dead; his stubborn refusal to circumscribe experience to this empirical world of trees, offices, Richard M. Nixon, income tax returns, and taxis; his insistence, that is, on trafficking with the eternal things. If there is a Heaven, Allen Ginsberg will get into it—even if he has to break down the Gates of Pearl. He is one of the violent lovers. "From the days of John the Baptist until now, the kingdom of heaven suffereth violence, and the violent bear it away."

►► Vladimir Mayakovsky

And You Think You Could?

At once I dashed the everyday map to spindrift
Splashing rainbows of colors out of a glass.
I brought forth from a dish of gelatin
The slanted cheekbones of an ocean.
On the scales of a tin fish
I read the pleas of new lips.
And you,
Could you play a nocturne
On a flute of waterpipes?

Once More on Petersburg

In the ears, snatches of warm music from a ball,
And down from the North, grayer than snow,
The fog with the bloodthirsty mug of a cannibal
Was munching on tasteless people.

Hours hung in the air like gutter profanities,
After five o'clock icicled six o'clock hung,
And gazing from heaven was a splotch of crud
Majestic, like Leo Tolstoy.

Translated by Victor Erlich and Jack Hirschman

►► Ahmed Yacoubi

The Night Before Thinking

For the past decade or so I have been collecting legends and tales, both on tape and directly in writing, provided for me by Moroccans adept in the art of storytelling. The literary tradition here is a strictly oral one, and it is not surprising that the most successful results should come, even at this late date, from illiterates. Storytelling has always been a national pastime here in Morocco; Yacoubi tells me that as a child he used to go daily to the cemetery outside the walls of Fez and sit for hours listening to the professional tale-spinners who made their living like minstrels wandering from town to town entertaining the populace. He remembers the stories, but when he comes to tell his own, he improvises. The following text was recorded in October 1956, and I did not play it back until March of this year, when, since Yacoubi was not available, Mohammed Larbi Djilali helped me to prepare an exact translation of it. Djilali knows no English; we used Spanish for determining the precise meanings of equivocal passages. Nothing has been deleted or added or altered; the English version is a literal translation. The title was given me this year by Yacoubi, who now speaks English. Moroccans, like many Mediterraneans, often believe that the act of thinking means being in a state of sadness, preoccupation, or anxiety. His title, Yacoubi says, refers to the night when he told the story, which belonged to a carefree period of his life.

When I showed the piece to William Burroughs, he was enthusiastic, and I suggested that he might want to furnish some comments. This he agreed to do.

Paul Bowles

Three men sat side by side. Three.
　One was called Hakim.
　One was called Faqir.
　And one was called Meskine.
　And the three of them were sitting there. And as they sat there a woman came by, and the woman's name was Raqassa.
　Raqassa spoke to Hakim. Allah ya Hakim!
　Hakim said to her: Speak to Meskine.

She said to Meskine: Allah ya Meskine!

Meskine said to her: Speak to Faqir.

She went to Faqir: Allah ya Faqir!

Faqir spoke: What's wrong?

She only cried aloud and wailed.

Ya Raqassa! What's wrong?

Ah, she said. I have a son. He's twelve years old and one leg is longer than the other.

Hakim heard these words, and he said: This is work for me. Not for Meskine. And not for Faqir. It is for Hakim. How can it be that your son came out with one leg longer than the other? Ha, Raqassa?

Raqassa wept, and the first tear ran down. When the tear came out of her eye, Faqir said to Hakim: Allah is great! The tear came out of only one eye. She's like her son with one leg longer than the other.

Hakim spoke. Quiet! Let me do this. Then to Raqassa he said: Now, Raqassa, why are you weeping?

Ah, sir, I loved that boy. When he was ten his legs were alike, but when he got to be eleven, one grew longer than the other. And now what's the remedy?

Hakim turned to Meskine and Faqir. Wait here for me. I'm going with Raqassa. He went with Raqassa to her house.

Raqassa has no son, nor any daughter. She has no one at all.

Hakim followed her into the house. She led him into a room. He sat down.

What will you drink? she asked him.

What have you got? Water, or buttermilk, or milk?

I have buttermilk, she said. And she gave him buttermilk. He drank a glass of it, and as he finished swallowing it, he felt his head spin as if he had drunk a glass of cognac.

Well, he said, and where is this boy who has one leg longer than the other?

Allah, Allah, ya Hakim! So your name is Hakim and mine is Raqassa. It was you who killed my brother. A long time ago you killed him. It's fourteen years since then. And I'm tired of looking for you everywhere. There's no city I haven't looked in to find you. I said my name was Raqassa because I didn't want you to know the name of the family. My name is really Aaklaa ben Aaklaa. Now, Hakim, you're only Hakim, while I can freeze water on the ground.

By that time she saw that Hakim was looking very ill from the buttermilk he had drunk. He was not seeing anything. She went up to him and threw a darkness over his face. Then she spread his mouth all over his cheeks. She drew a rope around his neck and made a slip knot in it and pulled on it. Hakim felt sixty kilos of pressure, and then he felt sixty thou-

sand, and he could not move his body. And Raqassa was getting ready to use every kind of power she knew.

Then she stopped. I must have an ostrich egg, she said. I've got everything for this work except that.

She took out a stick and struck it on the floor.[1] Then she burned a little bakhour. At that moment a bird flew in, and under its wing it carried an egg.

Raqassa said to the bird: I want an ostrich egg.

The bird spoke. For three years I've been sleeping on this ostrich egg. When you called me I knew you wanted it. I knew you would be needing the egg for your work on Hakim.

She took the egg from the bird and set it down.

How are we going to break it?

The bird said: I'll tell you. The only thing that can break it is Hakim's head. Put the egg on the floor, tie Hakim's legs together and hang him upside down from the ceiling, right over the egg. Then cut him down, and his head will break the egg. When you break the egg you smash the mouse's water jar, and the mouse dies.

They went over to Hakim and took hold of him. They tied him with a rope and hung him upside down from the ceiling. When they cut him down his head fell on top of the egg and broke it. As it broke, smoke came out, and that smoke was like nothing anyone ever saw. And it was both black and white, and where it was black there was yellow inside, and there were other colors around the yellow. The bird looked at the egg and said: Ayayay! That's the egg of Rokh el Bali. Do you see how many colors it has?

Raqassa answered: Those colors are what I need for my mixture. She walked over to Hakim and snatched away the darkness she had thrown over his face. Then she made paint from the smoke and painted him like a woman. She painted him from his hands to his feet and made him get up.

Hakim said: So, Raqassa. You are paying me back because I killed your brother.

She said: Tell me about it and I'll untie you.

You know how he died? I'll tell you. Your brother Difdaf, if he laughed, you couldn't trust him. If he cried, you couldn't believe him. If he put on his clothes, it was better not to look at him.

What do you mean?

I was always looking at him. If I laughed, he did not laugh. If I cried, he did not cry. When I dressed, he did not look at me. I said to him: What is it? He was sad and his heart was black. I didn't know what was the matter with him. I asked him again and

[1] Like Jesus Christ, who had a long stick and used to hit the ground with it, and all sorts of things came out. The same as Jesus Christ.—*Note by Mohammed Larbi Djilali.*

again what was wrong, but he never would say what was in his heart. Until one day I said to him: Tell me, and perhaps I can help you. Then you will be finished with being sad. Allah, Allah, ya Hakim, he said, if I could only find someone who would kill my sister for me. That woman was born at the same time as I was, but our father treated us differently. Our lives were not alike, for our father said: The one who was born first shall have the power. And she was born five minutes before I was. Five minutes for the Christians is a long time. For us it's not such a big thing. But this time it was like a thousand years.

So I said to him: How does it happen that she was born five minutes before you? He told me his mother used to keep hens on the roof. One day they all began to cackle. And his mother, who had the two babies in her belly, was called Lalla Halalla, and she ran upstairs to feed the hens and chicks, and while she was on her way back down she slipped, and the girl came out of her belly. The girl came out before the boy. Since she was born before me, my father gave her the power. The one who came out first had to be given the power. She got it and I got nothing.

So that's why you're sad? I asked Difdaf.

That's why, he told me.

And why do you want power? I asked him.

Allah, Allah, ya Hakim, he said. With power there is nothing you can't do. You can even see what is unseeable.

I looked at him. I said: If you want power I can give it to you.

He said: Hakim, I want to see that power.

So I made some fire and smoke, and I waved my arms and danced. Difdaf watched. Then I finished, burned bakhour, played a little more, and shrugged my shoulders. And what came down came down and what went up went up. And Difdaf waited until one day when I had gone out of my house. And he went in and tried to do as I'd done. And he did the same things. He even managed to do things I had never been able to do. Because he asked Satan to help him. He never asked help from God, but always from Satan. He made the spell, and the afreets came down. He spoke with them. He said: I want Hakim to die. But the pieces of his body have got to be scattered around. The head to Tunis, the body to America, so they won't be able to get together again.

It happened this way. I was sitting somewhere. An angel flew down out of the sky, saying: Ah, Hakim, get up! God help you! Difdaf is planning to cut off your head and separate it from your body forever.

I ran home, went into my room, and found Difdaf working there. But I knew how to be quick. With my big toe I kicked the door, and Difdaf fell through the floor, and on the spot where he had been there was nothing but fire. Difdaf was ashes. As I was finishing, his sister came in and saw. She knew what had happened, and she knew it was I who had burned him. I would have burned him more, but out of respect for God I stopped. Because I showed respect, the angel flew down again and talked to me. He said: Why are you afraid? This man was going to cut off your head and keep it far from your body. And God gave you the power to burn him. It was written that he should be burned. When Difdaf's sister heard what the angel was saying, she went out quickly. And when she was outside she said to herself that she would change her name and wait to catch up with Hakim later. And when it was later I was sitting with Faqir and Meskine, and at that moment you came by.

Raqassa said: And that's the story?

That's the story.

That's why you killed my brother?

That's why I killed him.

You killed him because he envied me my power?

Yes, he said.

I see. And now, Hakim, how do you plan to get out of this?

Hakim laughed a little and said: How am I going to get away?

Yes, said Raqassa.

He said: I'll go out like smoke leaving fire.

How do you mean, like smoke leaving fire?

Hakim said: When one kind of fire is mixed with another kind of fire, everything turns to smoke. That smoke is not like other smoke. The fire is burning, but the smoke is not in the fire. It's alone.

(This, for example. Her heart and her brain were in the fire, and Hakim was smoke. In this way he could escape from her. Because if the heart goes with the brain, all is fire. But there is no smoke. If there is smoke, either the heart or the brain is going to grow cold.)

Hakim spoke, and Raqassa was listening carefully to his words. She said to him: How is that? The smoke doesn't come out of the fire?

That's right. The smoke doesn't come out of the fire.

And that's how you expect to get out of here?

That's how I'll get away. Like smoke.

I'm going to shut the doors. And I'm going to make fire everywhere. So you won't go out of here like smoke. Every crack will be shut. Everything will be inside the fire.

Raqassa made a door of iron, and built walls of iron. She made a whole laboratory of iron. Everything of iron. She put Hakim in the middle of it.

And she brought out a dark cat and set it beside her, and said to it: O cat! Lie still. When you see the fire, take off those whiskers you have and put them on Hakim's face. Because in that way the fire will reach his heart. With those long hairs on his face. Because the fire by itself won't burn his body, but the whiskers will lead the fire to his heart.

She made the fire. And the cat quickly took off its whiskers and stuck them on Hakim's face. The fire was blazing and Hakim felt nothing. But as the hairs of the whiskers began to burn, he felt the fire on its way to his heart. He called to God. Ya, rebbi! So here I am, caught in the trap!

And Raqassa was watching. The fire was burning Hakim and soon he would be turning to ashes. Why did I ever tell her I would go out as smoke?

Soon Raqassa turned the fire down. Listen, Hakim, I thought you were going to escape as smoke.

Hakim said: Not really. The things that are really in my head I leave there. I was just talking. I wanted to see what you'd do.

He was burning, but he had to pretend that he had never heard of such a thing as fire.

She said: I see. But how do you expect to get away?

There's only one way for me to do that. I'll tell you something, Raqassa. The ostrich egg you broke with my head has saved me. That egg had power in it. I can't be burned now, since the egg has broken against my head.

Raqassa looked at him and laughed. We can wait and see what happens, she said.

Perhaps the way is for us to work together, you and I, he said. You can take the king and I'll work with the captain, the one who's famous for his swordsmanship.

No! she told him. I'm working only against you. I want to see which one of us is going to kill the other, and who's going to die first.

You want to see who's going to die first.

Yes, she said.

He looked at her. Your death is going to be very hard. And your life will seem very long because your death will be so slow.

Raqassa laughed. She told him: Your death won't take long.

Hakim laughed also. I'll disappear fast, like your son, the one who had one leg longer than the other.

She said: Why don't we get married, you and I? Perhaps we could have a son who wouldn't be like you. He might turn out to be a bird. A bird that could fly.

Hakim laughed again.

Raqassa went out of the house to the hammam.

She washed and whitened herself at the bath, while Hakim stayed behind at her house, bound with rope. Then she went back home and untied him, so he too could have a bath.

He went to the hammam and got very clean and shining.

Raqassa arrived, and they went out from the baths together with oboes and drums playing. Oboes and drums, and without paying for them, either, since everything was from another world. They went with oboes and drums and cornets into Raqassa's house, and sat down.

Raqassa looked at Hakim and laughed. Hakim looked at Raqassa. He laughed.

Before putting their bellies together, they began to talk. Even before getting into the bed. And Raqassa stood up and began to take Hakim's clothes off, and Hakim undressed Raqassa. They fell into the bed. Hakim was laughing, and he said: How the world is! Think of it! I've even come to the point of getting married! Who would have thought to see me with a wife!

What's the matter? asked Raqassa. Don't you like the idea?

Marriage frightens me, said Hakim. It means the end of young men. If you want to see a young man disappear, make him get married. He will never be young again.

Raqassa said to him: Why do you say that? If our fathers had never married, where would we be? Everyone gets married.

Marriage is all right, but if a young man is thinking of getting married, he's got to be ready for it. He should never get married if he isn't ready.

How is that? What does he need in order to get married?

Everything, said Hakim. If you haven't got everything, why think about getting married?

Now. You're Hakim. I'm Raqassa. Why are we lying here talking about marrying or not marrying?

And Hakim was looking only at her face. He had not looked at the rest of her. And when he looked down at the rest, he saw it was something very fine. Magnificent! Hakim cried. We'll do it once by electric light, and then I'll light all the candles too and do it again.

He turned on all the lights, and they began to bring and take. Then he lit the candles too.

Later, when Hakim had finished, and Raqassa also had finished, she said to him: Never in my life have I seen such a man as you. Never!

Hakim said: So you've had another man before me! Or do you usually see something different every day, perhaps?

I want to find out what this is all about. Why should you be the way you are?

Hakim went out. He went back to the place where he had left his two friends sitting. They saw him. Ah, Hakim! What happened? Did you see the boy with one long leg and one short leg?

If only it had been you who went to look for him! Then he sat down and told them all about it. When it was time for the evening prayer he said: Good-by. I must go back to Raqassa.

And so Hakim was living his life. And one day he saw that Raqassa's belly was big. A boy was born. The boy was strange. Not like other babies of the world. Between his two eyes he had another eye, and at the top of his head was still another. He looked (God is great!) like nothing ever seen before. Hakim came in and lifted him up, and then he saw the eye in the middle of his forehead. Raqassa said: This baby! See what God gave him on the top of his head! A handle to lift him up by.

But Hakim told her: Be quiet!! That's not a handle. There's an eye at the end of it. The boy is going to see from all sides.

What do you mean, from all sides?

He's got an eye between his eyes and an eye on top of his head. All he needs is one on his leg and one in his back and another in his belly, and he'll be able to see whichever way you turn him.

Before we teach him anything we must make sure that he gets more eyes, said Raqassa. We must remember that. We might put him into a museum. Everyone who went in would go to look at him.

Hakim cried: No! We're going to keep this boy. He took the child in his arms and carried him into his laboratory. He put him down and began to work. When the baby saw him working, the eye in the top of its head began to turn in a circle.

Raqassa got up, and she began to work. When the baby saw its mother working, the eye in the middle of its forehead began to go around, too. The baby looked almost like television. It began to crawl around and around in circles. Soon it had only two eyes: one on the top of its head and one in the middle of its forehead. Hakim laughed.

The baby was very small. That was still only the first day of its life. But as it turned in circles, its legs began to grow. They had been very small, and now they were bigger. Said Hakim: He's growing now.

Raqassa answered: He'll be complete within two days. Then Raqassa went into a trance on one side of the baby, and Hakim waved his arms on the other side. They danced and they made passes with their hands over it. And the baby watched them.

When the baby was only two days old, it already knew what was going to happen. Hakim was in a trance and was beating the air with his arms. He was trying to find a way to kill his wife so he could keep the baby for himself. Because he liked that baby. It was very different.

Raqassa was also in a trance, and she was muttering. She too was hoping perhaps to find a way to kill Hakim so she could keep the baby. They looked at one another. Each one was doing the same thing. And all the while the baby was in the middle, watching.

All at once Raqassa went over to the baby. She shut the eye in the top of its head. And as she shut that eye, another came out in the middle of its belly. She shut the eye in the middle of its belly, and another eye came out on its back. She shut the eye in the middle of its back, and one came out on its leg. That baby had eyes all over it.

Hakim was still in a trance. He moved around the baby, and the baby was looking at him from all sides. Hakim said to himself: Ah! Each moment the baby is more beautiful!

He stopped moving and remained looking straight at Raqassa. He said to himself: If I kill her now, she's not going to make me any more babies. And she might yet make me something with two or even three heads. If she can give one with all those eyes, she might easily turn out one with two or three heads. I'll let her live a while. I won't kill her yet.

They finished with their work, and went into the bedchamber. They sat on the bed, and Hakim pressed his legs against hers and made his hand run down her body to her tabon.[2] When he had his hand on her tabon he patted it, and cried: Well, well, tabon! You gave us a baby with eyes all over its body.

Raqassa made her hand run down Hakim's body to his zib. She seized it and said: Yes! Yes! This is what made the head with the eye on top.

What do you mean? said Hakim. I made the head with the eye? I didn't make anything.

She said to him: Be quiet! Don't say such a thing! Don't say you didn't make the baby. Without you where would he be?

You'd have been with another man, perhaps, said Hakim.

With another man the baby would never have been like this one. You, Hakim! When you put your zib into my tabon it was as if a goat had gone in. It was painful. But only because I wasn't frightened, I didn't cry out. And it was the cry I kept inside me that made the child begin to exist. At first it was only a head growing, and that was like a disease. But in-

[2] cf. t'habunt, Leo Frobenius, *African Genesis*.

stead of going on like that, the disease worked its way out as an eye in the top of his head.

Said Hakim: When you opened your legs and I came close to you to do the thing, I felt pain in the eye of my zib. That's what gave him the eye in the middle of his forehead.

The baby laughed. What a lot of lies you both tell! he said to them. One of you says the eye in the top of my head comes from one thing. The other says the eye in the middle of my forehead comes from something else. You are saying that your eyes are in my eyes. I already existed before you ever met each other. I was hidden and neither one of you knew me. Only God knew I was going to be like this. You didn't know. Now you think you understand all about it. You don't know anything. How can anyone know what's hidden inside the belly of a woman? It's God who decided I should be like this. He cut out my pattern. And neither one of you knew how I was going to look. It was written in the books that I was going to be born like this. It was already known. And now you're telling each other what you did to make me like this. Why don't you try again and see what you can make this time lying together! She with you and you with her! Let's see what you can do!

Hakim had done it the other time with the electric light and with candles as well. He said: By Allah, this time I'll do it without any light at all. He turned out the lights. The baby left the room.

Hakim got up and began. He worked at it and worked at it. When he had finished, the woman's belly was huge. It felt very heavy. Soon she said: Ya, Hakim. My belly is heavy.

What do you mean? Hakim cried. Have you already got a child in there? Are you going to have another?

She said: I don't know. Perhaps, and perhaps not.

Hakim touched her belly, and at that moment it began to swell and rise.

Bismillah er rahman er rahim! he cried. There's something wrong with you! You're ill! Where does it come from?

I don't know, she said. And when she rose from the bed, a baby girl came out of her. She was very small, and all she could do was cry. This girl that had just come out had nine fingers on one hand, and one on the other. And one foot had ten toes, and the other had no toes at all. When Hakim saw this, he began to laugh.

And he said: This is a good marriage! We haven't had a child that looks like me, and we haven't had one that looks like you either.

Yes, answered Raqassa. That is what God has written.

The boy is different, and the girl is different. What is it? It's a good thing I married you without arranging about the money first. If the wedding had cost me money, I'd have to take the children out to sell so I could pay for it.

Can't we sell them anyway? asked Raqassa.

Ahaha! Yes, we can sell them, and you'll see what will happen in the end. Because now they're small, but later it will be different.

The girl had been born tiny, and she never grew. Twenty-five years later she was just as small as she had been the day she was born. Many things happened during those twenty-five years.

One day Raqassa quarreled with Hakim. They fought with a great noise. The son heard the fight, and he was not pleased with it. He took out a cloth of six colors, like the colors across the sky. He held it in his hands and hit it with his finger. The cloth separated into two parts. One piece had three colors and the other piece had three other colors. And as he hit it, both his father and his mother fell dead.

As soon as they were dead, the baby girl began to grow, until she was as big as any other woman. His sister was grown up, and she asked him: What's the matter with me?

There's nothing the matter with you.

When was I born?

Were you really born? Or was somebody else born for you?

No, no she said. I was really born.

Then that was twenty-five years ago, he said.

And where have I been? I was born twenty-five years ago?

Yes. Twenty-five.

Where are my mother and my father?

You have your mother and you have your father, he told her. But there's no one who knows them. Which one do you want? Your mother or your father?

The girl laughed. She said: I take my mother. Because I'm a virgin. And the boy always goes with his father.

The young man heard these words. In his hand he still had the torn cloth with three colors here and three colors there. He took the piece that was green, red and yellow, and gave it to his sister. They were the colors of the mother. The other colors belonged to the father. The girl went away with the colors of her mother, and the man went away with the colors of his father

Translated from the Moghrebi by Paul Bowles and Mohammed Larbi Djilali

Comments on "The Night Before Thinking"

The hallucinogen drugs bottle and smoke pictures of strange places and states of being some familiar some alien as the separation word beautiful and ugly spirits blossom in the brain like Chinese flowers in some cases lethal blossoms bottle genie of appalling conditions hatch cosmographies and legends spill through mind screen movies overlapping myths of The Race. "The Night Before Thinking" was recorded from a young Moroccan painter Ahmed Yacoubi who cannot read or write. (Recorded 1956 Past Time.) "The Night Before Thinking" came to Yacoubi under the influence of majoun a form of hashish jam. (Noteworthy that there has been almost no work done on the chemistry of Cannabis whereas other hallucinogens are receiving constant attention.) When the story of Yacoubi came to the attention of this department Doctor Benway was conducting experiments with some of the new hallucinogens and had inadvertently taken a slight overdose of N-dimethyltryptamine dim-N for short class of South American narcotic plants Prestonia related to Bufotina which a species of poisonous toad spits out its eyes. There is also reason to suspect a relation to a poison injected by certain fish from sharp fin spines. This fish poison causes a pain so intense that morphine brings no relief. Described as fire through the blood:

Photo falling—Word falling—Break Through in Grey Room—Towers open fire—A blast of pain and hate shook the room as the shot of dim-N hit and I was captured in enemy territory Power of Sammy The Butcher. The Ovens closed round me glowing metal lattice in purple and blue and pink screaming burning flash flesh under meat cleaver of Sammy The Butcher and pitiless insect eyes of white hot crab creatures of The Ovens. Called for Hassan i Sabbah (Note 1) and the screams of millions who had called for Hassan i Sabbah in that place screamed back from creatures of The Oven mouths dripping purple fire. No place to go trapped here cut off tried to slip out on The Grey into mirrors and spoons and doorways of the Fish City but by my smoke escape was cut off by white hot metal lattice in this soulless place of The Insect People. Place of Dry Air shriveling envelopes of larval flesh—White hot blue sky—Insect eyes of The Alien Species—The Soulless Insect People. And The Pain Jinn dripping strips of purple fire mushroomed from The Tower blasts—Reached for my silver box of apomorphine (Note 2).

"Better take a handful, Burroughs," said The Regulator.

Took twelve twentieth-grain tablets and flashed a glimmer of grey beyond The Ovens and made it out to the Porte Tea Room on silver set yesterday past fields of interplanetary war and the prisoners eaten alive by white hot ants. Do not forget this Johnny Come Lately: WAR. War to extermination. Fading now. Grey ash writing of Hassan i Sabbah sifts through The Ovens. Dust and smoke. Grey writing of Hassan i Sabbah switch tower orders reverse fire back creatures of The Oven stored in Pain Banks from The Torture Chambers of Time. Souls torn into insect fragments by iron claws of The Chess Master Doctor—Who synthesized dim-N in Annexia, Iron Claws?

"They gave large doses of dim-N. Like five times what you took. And the prisoners disintegrated into oven creatures. They took recordings in sound film and brain waves can tune in on dim-N and they are moving to extend the range of tune in to other hallucinogens and blockade this planet under Alien Insect

Note 1. Hassan i Sabbah The Old Man of The Mountain Master of The Assassins lived in the year One Thousand. From a remote mountain fortress called Alamout he could reach a knife to Paris. There were not more than several hundred trainees in any one Alamout shift. Hassan i Sabbah made no attempt to increase numbers or extend political power. He took no prisoners. There were no torture chambers in Alamount. He was strictly a counter puncher. When a move was made against Alamout by the multiple enemies of Hassan i Sabbah he reached out with his phantom knife and a general a prime minister a sultan died. Hassan i Sabbah Master of The Jinn. Assassin of Ugly Spirits.

Note 2. Apomorphine is made by boiling morphine with hydrochloric acid. This alters chemical formulae and physiological effects. Apomorphine has no sedative narcotic or pain-killing properties. It is a metabolic regulator that need not be continued when its work is done. I quote from *Anxiety And Its Treatment* by Doctor John Dent of London: "Apomorphine acts on the back brain stimulating the regulating centers in such a way as to normalize the metabolism." It has been used in the treatment of alcoholics and drug addicts and normalizes metabolism in such a way as to remove the need for any narcotic substance. Apomorphine cuts the morphine lines from the brain. Poison of the dead sun slowly fading in smoke.

Enemy. One of the nastiest cases ever processed by this department."

Final blast from fading towers I saw the Novia Spirit burning metal eyes black metal skull translucent with fire head of Novia—Remembered that turnstile brought a prisoner to explode this planet—Uranian born of Novia Conditions: Tow two powers of equal strength to be directed against each other. "No riots like injustice directed between enemies." *Minutes To Go.* The tortured Jinn and Pain Spirits to set off the charge from a distant sky switch—White hot blast out in vapor trails smoke writing of Hassan i Sabbah. Break Through in Grey Room—Word falling—Photo falling—Towers open fire—Sacrifice Partisans of all nations—Sacrifice Iron Claws—You are under arrest Iron Claws—Grey Police of The Regulator do their work and go down all your streets and by the river light on water flash spoons and teapots—Poison of dead sun in my brain slowly fading—Now Sammy The Butcher fill your hand—Fan silver bullets from The Old Westerns whistling image of Sammy The Butcher explode a million flash bulbs smell of burning metal—Cut on Grey into *The Gunfighter*—Blast Sammy The Butcher from The West The West Side Push i told over The Grey Subway—Through silent turnstiles—Click clack cut to grey taxi down shadow streets of Tangier—Back from gangster films—Use that typewriter—Chop chop shift Samurai sword—Machete silver flash Sammy's last picture—Now Sammy The Butcher advances from his corner—He is using his chopping technique that earned him his monicker—Sammy can't seem to reach The Contender slipping dodging shifting into grey junk flesh stale overcoats and shaking spoons—Cut into newsreel prize fights and send all those fists crashing into Sammy's soft underside—Mr Bradly Mr Martin through the Grey Turnstile click a million switchblades Uranian born in the face of Novia Conditions—The Champ is worried folks—Molotov Cocktails from the Streets of Berlin and Budapest—Cut chop with that typewriter—Stampeding herds from The West—Turn the animals loose on Sammy—Cut TV bullfight Mexico DF—Chop that horn write up into Sammy's groin—Use all the strength of those neck muscles you got it?—Loose pack of vicious dogs from *The Savage Innocents*—Strafe in battle scenes and fighter planes—Cool and casual whistling killers drift in from 1920 streets—They are not come justa looka you Sammy—Folks The Butcher has take a terrible beating in this round—He looks dazed and keeps shaking his head from side to side—There goes the bell—Now throw in that Pain Jinn sixty feet tall dripping purple fire—KING KONG—Street gangs Uranian born in

the face of Novia Conditions pinball machine the world—Shift tilt that Oven Pain in color splats tracer bullets bursting rockets—Folks the Butcher is clicking back and forth like a bear in a shooting gallery—The Contender has Sammy on the ropes now—He's using Sammy's chopping techniques—Blow after blow air hammers the code write into Sammy's diaphragm—Disperse in broken mirrors clouds cyclones low pressure Sammy's image into your flash bulb—Sput—Witnesses from a distance observed a brilliant flash and a roaring blast as Sammy The Butcher was arrested.

Having written this account of my experience with dim-N (And I would like to sound a word of warning) I was of course struck by juxtapositions of area between my account and "The Night Before Thinking" recorded by Ahmed Yacoubi five years earlier. I took a page of my text—first draft—and folded it down the middle and laid it on top of the page in Yacoubi's text where he relates the oven incident. (Note: Since I was working from first draft of both texts there are some discrepancies with the final text.)

She made the fire and the cat break through in Grey Room. On Hakim's face the pain and hate quivered felt nothing. But as the hairs of white hot metal lattice in purple are reached his heart he called to God burning flash flesh caught in the trap—The Butcher chopping flesh and Raqassa was watching pitiless insect eyes white hot—"I thought you said you were going to escape creatures of the oven." What no place to go? Trapped here. Cut off. I want into mirrors and doorways. He was burning but he had to pretend—Cut off by white hot fire gold and the Pain Jinn dripping.

She said: "I see how fire mushroomed from the Tower Blasts." There's only one way for me—"Better take a handful, Burroughs." Something you never heard before—Twentieth-grain tablets and lay with my head has saved me—That egg grey beyond the ovens and made it out now with that egg broken against my Porte Tea Room—(Puked in the bidet.)

Raqassa looked at him: "Interplanetary War torn envelopes and happens." She said from The Towers fading now—

He answered: "Perhaps the way falls through your ovens—you and I. You can take the King clouds grey writing of Sabbah. I'll work with the Captain whose name is Reverse-Fire-Send-Back-There famous for his swordsmanship. In that way the fire will reach Iron Claws—The grey police on his face will lead fire to his note books recording your brain waves."

Now passed this text through Note 1 and Note 2:

Hassan i Sabbah The Old Man break through in Grey Room. Lived in the year One Thousand. Hate quivered felt nothing. Called Alamout he could reach metal lattice in purple fire. Hassan i Sabbah made no God burning flash flesh political power. From a remote mountain fortress hairs of white hot knife to Paris. Torture out in smoke? Place to go? Trapped here by the multiple enemies of doorways—Sabbah Master Of The Jinn mushroomed from The Tower Blasts—

Note 2 "Better take a handful, Burroughs." Apomorphine is made by boiling morphine ore—Twentieth-grain tablets and this alters the chemical formulae and that egg grey beyond the ovens. Apomorphine has no sedative narcotic egg. It is a metabolic regulator that—(Bidet) Raqassa looked at him. Work is done. "I quote from anxiety and happens,"

She said—John Dent of London: "Apomorphine" he answered Perhaps regulating centers in such a way you and I—You can take The King—Poison of dead sun fading in Grey Room—Because in Iron Claws The Grey Police on check mate—Something you never heard before Note 2 has saved me—Interplanetary War need not be continued from The Tower—Fading now and its *Treatment* by Doctor falls through your ovens—Apomorphine acts on the back brain stimulating grey writing of Sabbah such a way as to normalize metabolism—Apomorphine cuts the lines—Films and brain wave of dead sun slowly fading in smoke.

Juxtapositions of "The Night Before Thinking" by Yacoubi and my account of experience with dim-N suggest underlying unity of words and images that blossom like bottle genie from the hallucinogens now open to all the world of The Thousand and One Nights.

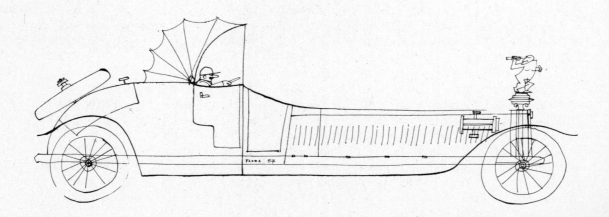

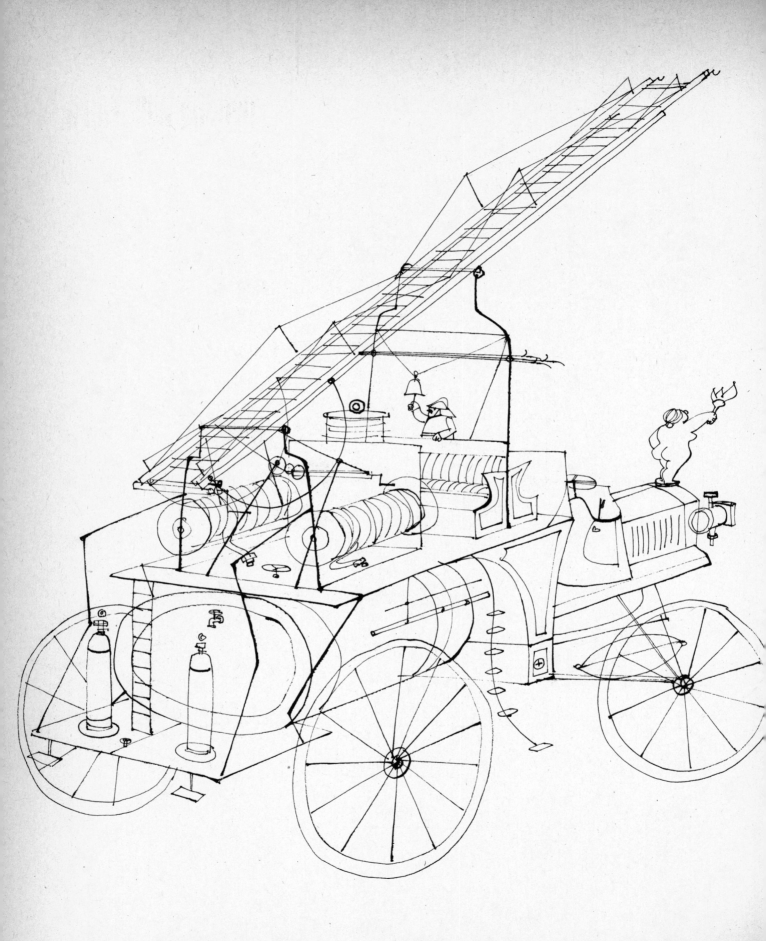

The Big House

A Play for Radio

THE BIG HOUSE: (*Intones, slowly, majestically*) My bullocks, oh, my bullocks. My bullocks, my beeves, sheep, in flocks, in herds, they surround me. My people too, in the ghosts of their generations. Old Baldcock built me. Three hundred years ago. Released from the stocks at Bristol on condition that he come to Ireland and assist in the civilising of this unhappy isle, he came and made a thriving business, swindling Cromwell's soldiery out of their grants of land. If old Baldcock did not win it by the sword, well he did a better thing. He won it off them that *did* win it by the sword. Those that live by the sword. Those that live by the sword shall perish by the. . . .

A most tremendous explosion is heard.

MRS. BALDCOCK: (*She leaps up in bed*) Ananias! (*Screeches*) Ananias! Ananias! Wake up! We're blown up! Blow up! I mean, wake up!

ANANIAS BALDCOCK: Yes, yes, damn it, Boadicea, I'm woken up.

MRS. BALDCOCK: I shan't stand it a moment longer. I knew we'd be blown up.

ANANIAS: We haven't been blown up. Damn it, we're still here in bed. That explosion was a mile away.

MRS. BALDCOCK: Well you might have some sympathy for whoever's house it *was* that was blown up. Not that it was anyone that matters, I suppose. There is no country house left in the neighbourhood for miles around. Hoggitts, Blood-Gores, Ramsbottoms, Snowteses, Pug-Footes, Grimeses. . . . all the aristocratic names, all the grace and splendour and civilised living that the very syllables of those noble names recall . . . all . . . (*she sighs*) . . . . gone **away.**

ANANIAS: **There** is nobody left in the district worth blowing up.

MRS. BALDCOCK: (*Sadly*) I'm afraid you're right, Ananias. As a matter of fact (*more happy*) it can only have been the Civic Guard barracks.

ANANIAS: Maybe some of them have been killed . . . or horribly mangled.

MRS. BALDCOCK: At the risk of seeming bloody minded, I'd say it's just as well to keep the Irish occupied in killing each other rather than in killing us.

ANANIAS: You forgot, Boadicea, that I am Irish. Like my ancestors before me, I was born here.

MRS. BALDCOCK: If an ass is born in a stable, does that make it a horse?

ANANIAS: You forget, too, that most of the new Civic Guard are merely the old Royal Irish Constabulary with their cap badges changed. Men who served their King and Country faithfully; and collaborated openly and defiantly in the North East, and discreetly but efficiently in the South and West.

MRS. BALDCOCK: Well, serves them right for joining the rebels in the end and working for the Free State.

ANANIAS: You don't understand, Boadicea, that the Free State is the surest and best way of *beating* the rebels. Even Lord Birkenhead says so. "Doing England's work, with an economy of English lives" he describes it.

LOONEY: Mashter, sir, and Mishtress, Mashter, sir, and Mishtress, Mashter, sir.

Other voices . . . The heavy accents of the Civic Guards are heard.

SERGEANT: Tell them 'tis only till morning. Just a bit of a refuge for the night is all we want.

LOONEY: I will sergeant, I will surely.

Knocking on door.

Mashter, sir, and Mishtress.

MRS. BALDCOCK: (*Exasperated*) There's old Looney at the door. What can he want?

ANANIAS: Dionysius O'Looney is a loyal old soul. They have been butlers here since the house was built. For three hundred years, as long as the Baldcocks have lived here, there has always been a Looney in Tonesollock House. They have . . .

Knocks again.

LOONEY: Mashter, sir, and Mishtress. . . .

MRS. BALDCOCK: Never mind his sterling qualities now. Ask him what he wants.

ANANIAS: What is it, Looney?

LOONEY: The Eye Orr Ah is after letting off a bum, sir.

ANANIAS: I know, I know, we heard it. But it wasn't anywhere near here.

LOONEY: No, sir, 'twas only the Guards barracks, sir, and Mashter, sir. . . .

SERGEANT: Tell them 'tis only till the morning.

LOONEY: Yes, sergeant. (Louder) And Mashter, sir, and Mishtress, the sergeant wants to know if we can put him up for the night. They've no place to go till morning.

SERGEANT: 'Tis only till morning, your honour, and we could shake down any ould place that'd be a shelter for us out of the wet, till we get the telephone going to Dublin in the morning.

ANANIAS: Very well. You can use the loft or one of the grooms' places.

SERGEANT: Thanks, sir, and a bed in heaven to you, sir.

ANANIAS: The same to you, my good fellow.

SERGEANT: And a bed in heaven to your good lady too, and good night ma'm. We only wants a shake down in the straw.

They move off and his voice fades.

. . . sure what's wrong with us sleeping in straw. Wasn't Our Lord born in it?

MRS. BALDCOCK: They can have the whole Tonesollock House for me. Ananias!

ANANIAS: (Tired) Yes, Boadicea?

MRS. BALDCOCK: I've been in this horrible country twenty years too long . . . but not a day longer. I'm going to Hereward and Tabitha in Ealing. A dull, London suburb but peaceful, without guns and bombs going off every night for five years . . . and Ealing is private . . . without the native militia coming as refugees to live with one. Irish hospitality, I suppose. But I've had enough of it. Ananias, you can please yourself. If you love Tonesollock more than you love me, you'll. . . .

ANANIAS: I love you the most, Boadicea.

MRS. BALDCOCK: Very well then. We'll go together. You go in tomorrow to your solicitors. He'll find an agent and send in the rents, such as they are, and the proceeds of all cattle sales, and we leave directly for England.

LOONEY: (Having shown the Sergeant and Guard to their accommodation) There yous are now, Sergeant dear, and Guard. It's where the Protestant minister sleeps when he comes here. Himself and the wife, in that very bed. He's a Protestant of course, but a very religious man. The moans and groans of him there, kneeling there on that very floor when he's saying his night prayers would go through you.

SERGEANT: (Feeling the mattress) Sure, that's a grand bed, Mr. Looney.

GUARD: We're very thankful to you, Mister Looney, to put up us two poor homeless wanderers.

SERGEANT: Aye, indeed, we are so, Mister Looney.

LOONEY: Is there anything more I could do for yous, now? Would you like a drop of anything to restore your shattered nerves?

GUARD: Ah, no thanks, Mr. Looney, haven't you done enough for us?

SERGEANT: Ah, sure, Mister Looney, sir, it'd be too much trouble going down for it.

LOONEY: Who said anything about going down for it? Don't I carry me little consolation prize with me? Bottle in this pocket, glasses in this . . .

Sounds of glass chinking.

SERGEANT: Well, Glory be to God.

GUARD: Mr. Looney, you're a magician.

LOONEY: I'm telling you, the Looneys is no fools. Here . . . (Handing glasses round) get that down yous.

SERGEANT: Slawncha.

GUARD: Slawncha gus sale.

LOONEY: Slawncha gus sale agut. Health and wealth to you.

SERGEANT: Land without rent to you.

GUARD: The woman of your heart to you.

LOONEY: A child every year to you.

GUARD: Married or single.

GUARD: A stout heart.

LOONEY: A wet beak.

SERGEANT: A death in Ireland.

ALL: Slawncha!

They drink.

SERGEANT: (Smacking his lips) A good sup, Mr. Looney.

GUARD: Mr. Looney, sir, the sergeant wouldn't mind me asking you.

SERGEANT: It's depending what you are going to ask Mr. Looney for.

GUARD: (Shyly) I was going to ask him to sing us a little bit of a song.

LOONEY: Ah, sure me dear decent man, think of the mashter and mishtress and the hour of the night it is.

GUARD: Ah, sure, with respects to them, they're that hard of sleeping they hardly heard the land-mine. Sure a bitteen of a song won't wake them so easy.

LOONEY: Yes, but the time it is.

SERGEANT: (Bold from the whiskey) Yerra, 'tis early before twelve and early after twelve.

LOONEY: All right, so boys, sure a bit of a song would cheer us up anyway.

Sings.
There is another explosion and a burst of ma-chine-gun fire and shouting.

FIRST SHOUT: God forgive them murderers!

SECOND SHOUT: I hates bad grammar. (Laughs more or less maniacally.)

Machine-gun fire.

MRS. BALDCOCK: (Moans in her sleep) Oh, (to the tune of "Galway Bay") Oh, maybe some day, I'll go back again to Ealing. . . .

ANANIAS: What's that dear?

MRS. BALDCOCK: I was asleep.

ANANIAS: I never heard of anyone singing in their sleep.

MRS. BALDCOCK: I shouldn't be surprised if I danced in my sleep before I get out of this horrible country.

ANANIAS: Good night, dear.

MRS. BALDCOCK: Good night, Ananias . . . tomor-row. . . .

ANANIAS: Tomorrow in Jerusalem. . . .

MRS. BALDCOCK: In where, dear?

ANANIAS: In Holyhead, dear.

Tonesollock House. It is early morning and the birds are singing. They keep on tweeting for a little but not so noticeably.

LOONEY: Ah, good morning Sergeant, isn't that a lovely morning? Glory be to God. A pity the mashter and mishtress didn't delay a few weeks more before they thought of going away to Ealing.

SERGEANT: 'Tis so, then, Looney. Sure, if they had have waited a bit longer, only a few weeks, sure everything is back to normal. Sure we're having our first eviction since 1917 tomorrow.

LOONEY: D'you tell me that, now Sergeant dear?

SERGEANT: I do, bedad. The first eviction in six years, and I'll be in charge of it.

LOONEY: Sure, it's just like ould times Sergeant dear.

SERGEANT: And the I.R.A. is bet, thank God. That De Valera fellow got out a proclamation yesterday. De Valera telling his gangs of rogues, rebels, robbers and wreckers that they're bet, and calling them to give up. It's in the paper here. . . . (Reads) . . . . "Soldiers of the Legion of the Rearguard, Bulwark of the Nation's Honour. . . ."

LOONEY: God help us all. Soldiers . . . honour . . . (Spits). . . . Murderers and robbers would be more like it.

SERGEANT: What else would you call them? Lot of scum. But anyway, it means one thing; the trouble is over That's the end of the Civil War.

LOONEY: A civil war, did you call it? Bedad, and if that's what you call a civil war, Sergeant dear, I hope I never see an uncivil one.

ANGEL: Call that a war? I've seen worse rows in the canteen of a Saturday night over someone pinch-ing a pint.

LOONEY: Did you so then, sir? It could be. I believe they manage things better across the other side. Sure God help the Irish, if it was raining soup, they'd be out with forks. But I didn't think you'd had a war over in England this long time.

ANGEL: No, we 'ad it in France mostly. We nearly always 'ave our wars in someone else's country.

SERGEANT: If it's no harm asking, now what might your business be around here?

ANGEL: It's every 'arm. I'm in a 'urry to do some business 'ere in Tonesollock 'ouse and I'm not doing with neither of you, so I'll be off. Ta, ta.

SERGEANT: What did you say "Ta, ta" for? I didn't give him anything.

LOONEY: That's his English way of saying "good-bye."

SERGEANT: (Ponderously) Taah, taah.

LOONEY: Angel is his name. At least that's what Mister Chuckles calls him.

SERGEANT: Angel, that's a peculiar class of a name, more especially for a fellow the like of that. That's a fellow wouldn't lose his way in a jail, I'm telling you.

LOONEY: Angel is the name of the place in London he comes from. He's a great buddy of Mister Chuckles.

SERGEANT: Since Mister and Missus Baldcock went away over to England, I've heard nothing but "Mister Chuckles" here, and "Mister Chuckles" there. Who the hell is this Mister Chuckles, if it's no harm asking.

LOONEY: (Lowers his voice) Ah, Sergeant dear, you may well ask. A Dublin jackeen be the name of Chuckles Genockey is all I know about him, from the tenement houses off of the North Circular Road.

SERGEANT: And what class of a man is that to leave to run an estate? What would the likes of him know about land or cattle?

LOONEY: 'Tis not what he knows about land at all, at all, Sergeant dear, but he knows the world and all about cattle.

SERGEANT: And how could he know about cattle without knowing about land?

LOONEY: Ah, Sergeant, 'tis not on the land but in the market the money's made. What poor farmer ever made a fortune and isn't it a common thing for buyers and blockers and every kind of trickster to maybe double their money at a fair without ever handling a beast only buying off a farmer cheap and selling to a foreign buyer dear?

SERGEANT: Indeed, 'tis true for you.

LOONEY: Till the women going into the butcher are paying for meat the way it would be as cheap for them to be eating gold.

SERGEANT: Musha, 'tis true for you Looney. I often saw my own father selling a beast to a robber of a buyer. (Starts) God bless us, what am I saying? Them men can't be classed as robbers. They are respectable with sons in the priesthood, and T.D.'s aye and landlord gentry like Mr. and Mrs. Baldcock (Reproachfully) 'Tis a shame for you, Looney, to be leading me into the sin of criticisin' respectable men with motor cars and money.

LOONEY: I didn't mean it, Sergeant.

SERGEANT: Do you know there's Royalty that deals in store cattle, and bishops. It's sinful, Looney, for us to talk like that.

LOONEY: I'm very sorry, Sergeant.

SERGEANT: Ah, sure, I know you didn't mean any harm. And sure the Looneys were always known to be decent respectable people that knew their place and served their masters while there was life in their bodies. I often heard Mister Baldcock here saying: "A Looney," says he, "a Looney would work till he'd drop!"

LOONEY: It was only that I was trying to explain to you, Sergeant, how the likes of Mr. Chuckles Genockey came to be agent here. He was always running round the cattle market from the time he was able to walk, and from doing messages for cattlemen, he rose up to be a class of a spy or a go-between from one buyer to another, and he used to do Mister Baldcock's business for him in the market and now he's taken over Tonesollock House and the estate as well. It's a bit queer to see a man from the slums of Dublin that never had as much land as would fill a window box, doing the Lord and master over Tonesollock, but sure as you said Sergeant, it doesn't do to be criticising our betters.

SERGEANT: Oh, I didn't mean a bowsy the like of that. Sure, that fellow is an imposterer of low degree. Only meant that it's not every one that makes money is a robber. Most of them are not. The best rule is that them that had money previously are entitled to make more. Them that makes it for the first time are hill and dale robbers until they've had it for at least twenty years.

LOONEY: Well, you'd include Mister Chuckles with the hill and dale robbers.

SERGEANT: Injubettiddley. And that ruddy English Angel that came down to see him this morning.

LOONEY: He's a plumber. He came down to repair the roof. Look, the two of them is up there now.

On the roof. Seagulls screaming and roof noises generally.

ANGEL: . . . Now, this bit of flashing 'ere . . . there'll be nearly a 'alf ton of bluey in that alone.

CHUCKLES: And how much is lead at the moment?

ANGEL: 'Alf a quid a 'alf 'undred. That's about what *we'll* get. But they must 'ave 'ad a bleedin lead mine of their own the way they poured it on this 'ere roof. I suppose we should get a thousand quid for the lot.

CHUCKLES: That should buy a few loaves anyway.

ANGEL: Course it will take a few days to get it all into the city, so I reckon on starting right now.

CHUCKLES: You get it ripped off and shag it down off the roof, and I'll get some of the farm labourers to load it on the lorry and we'll be in to Dublin with the first load, quick and speedy. I'll go below and collect them . . .

ANGEL: Right. . . . oh, I'll make a start anyway. (*Starts.*)

Sounds of lead being ripped off roof.

Uu . . uup you come. Eas . . . eesy does it. Hey, Chuckles!

CHUCKLES: Hell . . . ooh?

ANGEL: Shall I start flinging it dahn nahw?

CHUCKLES: When I shout up, "Throw it down," you can begin. (*To Looney*) Hey . . . you.

LOONEY: Is it me, Mashter Chuckles.

CHUCKLES: The very same. Tell that peeler there to get offside if he does not want a hundredweight of lead to come crashing down on his napper.

SERGEANT: Look at here, me good man. . . .

LOONEY: Stand away now, Sergeant dear, for Mashter Chuckles.

CHUCKLES: (*Shouts*) Right away there, Angel, throw it dow . . . wn!

Lead crashes from roof to ground.

SERGEANT: Look at here, Mister Looney, is it mending that roof or destroying it they are? Lifting the lead off it. Ripping and robbing maybe.

CHUCKLES: Hey, sleep-in-your-skin.

LOONEY: Yes, Mashter Chuckles?

CHUCKLES: Go down and get some of them bullocks' nurses up here to get that lead on to the lorry.

SERGEANT: Who did he say?

LOONEY: Bullocks' nurses he calls the cattle boys.

SERGEANT: (*Raising his voice to include Chuckles*) Before you go for anyone and before you put an ounce of lead up on that lorry, would it be any harm for me to be asking where it's going and where you're bringing it to. (*Sarcastically*) That is, Mister Chuckles, if you don't mind.

CHUCKLES: I do mind . . . . and you mind . . . mind your own bleedin' business.

SERGEANT: Look at here, me good man, I'm responsible for the protection of property in the district of Tonesollock.

CHUCKLES: And I'm responsible for the property of Tonesollock House and the estate and lands thereof, and our solicitors are Canby, Canby, and Dunne, Molesworth Street, near the Freemasons' Hall, and if you interfere with me, I'll call them on the telephone and tell them you're persecuting the ex-Unionist minority, and get a question asked in the Senate. The Minister of Justice will love you for that.

SERGEANT: (*In suppressed wrath, but just a little anxious*) I'll attend to you in a minute me man. (*To Looney.*) What's this ex-Unionist minority? What does that mean, in plain English?

LOONEY: It means the gentry.

SERGEANT: And is that Dublin guttersnipe . . . telling me . . . telling me . . . that *I'm* persecuting the gentry? Does he make out that he's one of them?

LOONEY: Well I suppose he means that he's running the estate for the master, and he's in the master's place like while the master is away.

SERGEANT: (*Sighs*) And God knows I was right. When I saw the dead lancers lying in O'Connel Street and heard the naval artillery pounding the Post Office, I said to myself, something is going to happen, and when I heard the crash of the . . . .

Terrific noise as another load of lead crashes to ground.

SERGEANT: (*Roars*) Hey, you, up there, hey! . . .

ANGEL: Hey you down there, want to get a 'undredweight of lead on your noggin?

SERGEANT: You just mind . . . .

CHUCKLES: You just get to hell out of here. You're on private land. If something falls on your cabbage head, you needn't come looking to us for compensation.

SERGEANT: (*Indignant and despairing*) Look at here Mister Looney, will you tell that impiddent bowsy who I am?

LOONEY: (*In distress*) Oh, Sergeant dear, it's not my fault and don't go bringing me into it. I don't want to lose me situation that I've been in this fifty years.

CHUCKLES: Hey you. Go-be-the-wall-and-tiddle-the-bricks.

LOONEY: Do you hear the way he calls me out of me name? The old respected name of Looney that was here before the Danes. How would I be trying to get that fellow to give respect to you when I can't get it for myself?

SERGEANT: (*Sighs*) I'll be off for now, Mister Looney, but when Mister Baldcock comes back . . . I'll have a something or two to say to him.

LOONEY: Aye, when Mister Baldcock comes back. I'll be as dead as poor Black Joe waiting for him.

CHUCKLES: Hey, you Step-and-fetch-it, do you not hear me calling?

LOONEY: Yes, Mister Chuckles, sir, I hear you calling me, sir, but what you call me, sir, is not my name.

CHUCKLES: Never you mind what I'm calling you.

LOONEY: I am a Looney, sir, and descended from a long line of Looneys, and I got a medal from the Royal Dublin Society at the Horse Show . . . .

CHUCKLES: What as . . . a prize goat?

LOONEY: For fifty years' service sir to the one family. The Baldcocks that own this estate.

CHUCKLES: I don't give a God's curse if you were here since Judas was in the Fire Brigade, and I won't give a damn if you're not here five minutes more. I'd be just as well pleased to be rid of you and a few more of them valleys and footmen up in the house, and maids and housekeepers . . . . (*Thoughtfully*) . . . No, I'd keep the maids, except the old one.

LOONEY: The housekeeper you mean sir. Miss Gilltrap.

CHUCKLES: Yes, the one with a face like a plateful of mortal sins.

LOONEY: A most respected and superior class of woman, sir.

CHUCKLES: She looks it. But anyway, get some of them fellows up here and have that lead loaded on the lorry for us. Myself and the plumber have to be going into Dublin, directly.

LOONEY: (*Resignedly*) I'll go and get them, sir. (*Moves off mike muttering to himself*) Curse a God on you, you low Dublin jackeen. You'd sack Miss Gilltrap, would you? But you'd keep the young maids, you would. (*Mutters and snuffles off.*)

Lorry starts and moves off.

ANGEL: I thought they'd never get 'er bleedin' loaded. You know, it's a funny thing but the Irish over 'ere in Ireland, they ain't a bit like the Irish over at 'ome in England. Over 'ere they'd stand around all day, if they was let.

CHUCKLES: The fellows out on the farm and looking after the beasts are all right. They'll do a bit of a fiddle with me when we're taking cattle to the market. It's those butlers and valleys that I don't like.

ANGEL: Specially that old Looney. 'E gives me the creeps 'e does.

CHUCKLES: Ah well, I'll have the whole lot cleared out in another week.

ANGEL: I know business is business, Chuckles, and we'll have it off for a few thousand nicker each but don't you feel like, well old Baldcock trusted you a lot?

CHUCKLES: Of course, he trusted me a lot. How the hell could we've arranged the job at all if he didn't trust me? This is not like screwing some gaff along the Tottenham Court Road . . . a rapid creep in, blow the peter and then scarper and read about it in the papers next morning. This is plundering a whole estate. Cattle, horse, sheep, pigs, even let the grazing. The furniture, pictures, the delph, glassware, all that I've had crated with old Baldcock's address in England stencilled on the sides so as they all think he's having it sent to him in England. Now there's the lead and tomorrow or the day after I'm bringing a geezer out to value the doors.

ANGEL: When he comes back, he'll come back to a ruin.

CHUCKLES: That's it.

ANGEL: I'm only asking mind, do you not feel in a way, it's a bit rough on them?

CHUCKLES: How is it? They got a picture of the old man that built the house. It's in books in the library and the Baldcocks boast about it that Cromwell's soldiers croaked about two villagefuls of people to get that land. And old Baldcock got the land off Cromwell's soldiers by using his loaf . . . the same as I'm using mine.

ANGEL: Well, you can 'ardly blame the old man for what happened years ago.

CHUCKLES: I'm not blaming anyone. I don't go in for this lark "on our side was Erin and virtue, on their side the Saxon and guilt." I just don't see why old Baldcock should have a lot of lolly and live in a big house while I go out to graft every morning and come home to a rat trap.

ANGEL: Well, you're a Communist, that's what you are.

CHUCKLES: I'm not a Communist. I'm too humble and modest. The Communists want to free all the workers of the world. I'm content to make a start and free one member of it at a time . . . myself.

ANGEL: You're just a tea leaf, then.

CHUCKLES: That's right, I'm a thief, same as you, and same as Mister and Missus Baldcock. Only as they inherited their lolly, they are really receivers. And they say the receiver is worse than the thief. And now we're coming towards our own fence. Mister Eyes of Green, Marine Dealer.

ANGEL: What sort of a bleeding name is "Eyes of Green"?

CHUCKLES: I don't know; it's just what everyone else calls him around the Liberty. I suppose they call him "Eyes of Green" because he's an Irish Jew from Dublin City.

ANGEL: We never 'eard of Irish Jews in London.

CHUCKLES: Well you don't notice, I suppose. Most Dublin Jews have an accent like mine, only a bit worse.

Noise of lorry slowing up and stopping.

ANGEL: Ere 'e is, anyway. Mind if I see if 'e answers to his name? Hallo, Mister Eyes of Green.

EYES OF GREEN: Hello, you Black and Tan.

CHUCKLES: Listen, Eyes, nark the patriotism just now. We want to do a little business.

ANGEL: We've got a lot of bluey to sell you, Mister Eyes of Green, so don't be so leery.

EYES OF GREEN: All right I'll get it over here and weight it.

Lorry backed over beside scales and lead weighed.

ANGEL: That's the lot then.

EYES OF GREEN: Eighty quid, that's right?

ANGEL: No, it's not right.

CHUCKLES: Do you know, if you gave up being a Jew, you could be a jockey. You've a neck as hard as a jockey's rump.

EYES OF GREEN: What's the difference?

ANGEL: You're not even going by your own scales. And that's good lead.

EYES OF GREEN: Where did you get it and when are you going to give it back?

CHUCKLES: We got it from the estate I'm managing, and I'll show you the papers and give a proper receipt for the proper price.

EYES OF GREEN: I say eighty, what's the difference?

CHUCKLES: A score of pounds.

EYES OF GREEN: Split it. I'll give you ninety.

CHUCKLES: Done, and I hope the odd ten nicker chokes you.

EYES OF GREEN: That's real decent of you. (*Counts money*) Here you are. And many thanks for your Christian sentiments.

CHUCKLES: Shalom alechim, Eyes of Green.

EYES OF GREEN: Slawn latt, Chuckles.

CHUCKLES: Start her up, Angel, and we'll get over to the Northside for a drink.

Lorry starts again and off. Stops.

Public house. Sounds of bottles, glasses. Hum of conversation. When Chuckles and Angel enter, there are shouts of welcome, male and female.

SHOUTS: Me hard man, Chuckles Genockey. Ah, Chuckles, is it yourself that's in it? Musha, me tight Chuckles. You're more nor welcome.

CHUCKLES: Shut up and give us a chance to order a drink for the people.

MALE SHOUT: Silence there for the decent man.

BARMAN: Yes, Chuckles, and what will it be?

CHUCKLES: (*Looks round counting*) One, two, three, four . . . It'd be cheaper to buy the pub. Well, make that . . . er . . . sixteen half ones of malt and chasers.

BARMAN: Certainly, Chuckles. . . . (*Shouts*) sixteen small whiskeys and sixteen bottles of stout.

GRANNY GROWL: There are are, Mrs. Grunt, that's yours.

GRANNY GRUNT: Thank you, Mrs. Growl.

GRANNY GROWL: Don't thank me, thank Chuckles.

GRANNY GRUNT: Thank you, Mister Chuckles, sir, and slawncha.

GRANNY GROWL: Slawncha, Chuckles.

GRANNY GRUNT: Slawncha, Chuckles.

MALE AND FEMALE SHOUT: Slawncha, Chuckles, the flower of the flock; the heart of the roll. Slawncha, and slawncha, again and again.

ANGEL: They don't 'alf like their wallop. Especially the old dears. Reminds me of 'ome. The Bricklayer's Arms or the Elephant of a Saturday night.

CHUCKLES: Wait till they got rightly oiled. (*Shouts*) Hey, more gargle for the people.

GRANNY GRUNT: Me life on you, Chuckles, and the divil thump and thank the begrudgers.

GRANNY GROWL: Up the Republic and to hell with the rest. Give us a rebel song, Mrs. Grunt, ma', a real Fenian one, the one you got the six months for. Up Stallion!

GRANNY GRUNT: I will, allana, if you'll hand me that tumbler (*She swallows a drink.*) Thanks. (*Clears her throat*) (*Sings.*)

GRANNY GRUNT AND CHORUS:
When I was young I used to be as fine a man as ever
    you'd see,
And the Prince of Wales, he says to me "Come and
    join the British Army" . . .
Toora loora loora loo,
They are looking for monkeys in the zoo.
And if I had a face like you,
I'd join the British Army.
    (*Sings*)
Nora Condon baked the cake, but 'twas all for poor
    Nell Slattery's sake,
I threw myself into the lake, pretending I was barmy.
Toora loora loora loo,

'Twas the only thing that I could do,
To work me ticket home to you,
And lave the British Army.

    Shouting, male and female, likewise screeches and roars.

SHOUT: Granny Grunt, your blood's worth bottling.

ROAR: Me life on you Granny Grunt.

SCREECH: A noble call, now, you have ma'm.

CHUCKLES: Granny Grunt, nominate your noble call.

GRANNY GRUNT: I call on the Granny Growl. Mrs. Growl, ma'm, Maria Concepta, if I call you be your first name.

GRANNY GROWL: (*With dignity*) Certingly, Teresa Avila, to be sure.

CHUCKLES: Get something to lubricate your tonsils first. (*Shouts*) More gargle, there!

GRANNY GROWL: God bless you, me son.

GRANNY GRUNT: May the giving hand never falter.

FIRST VOICE: Up the Republic!

SECOND VOICE: Up Everton!

THIRD VOICE: Up the lot of yous.

    Drinks are handed round.

CHUCKLES: Did everyone get their gargle?

    Shouts of assent.

CHUCKLES: Well, Granny Growl, give us your song. Carry on with the coffin . . . the corpse'll walk.

GRANNY GROWL AND CHORUS: (*Sings*)
Get me down me petticoat and hand me down me
    shawl,
Get me down me petticoat, for I'm off to the Linen
    Hall,
He was a quare one, fol de doo ah gow a dat
He was a quare one, I tell you.
If you go to the Curragh Camp, ask for Number
    Nine.
You'll see three squaddies standing there,
And the best looking one is mine
He was a quare one fol de doo ah gow a dat,
He was a quare one I tell you.

If he joined the Army under a false name,
To do me for me money,
It's his ould one's all to blame.
He was a quare one fol de doo a gow a dat
He was a quare one I tell you.

If you put them to the war, out there to fight the
    Boers.
Will you try and hould the Dublins back,
See the Bogmen go before.
He was a quare one fol de doo a gow a dat
He was a quare one I tell you.

Me love is on the ocean and me darling's on the sea,
Me love he was a darling chap,
Though he left me fixed this way.
He was a quare one fol de doo a gow a dat
He was a quare one I tell you.

So . . . get me down me petticoat and hand me
    down me shawl,
Get me down me petticoat for I'm off to the Linen
    Hall,
With your he was a quare one fo de doo ah gow a
    dat,
He was a quare one I tell you.

GRANNY GROWL: (*Sobs a bit*) Me tired husband, poor ould Paddins, he was shot in the Dardanelles.

GRANNY GRUNT: (*Sympathetically*) And a most paintful part of the body to be shot.

GRANNY GROWL: And me first husband was et be the Ashantees. All they found of him was a button and a bone.

GRANNY GRUNT: God's curse to the hungry bastards.

GRANNY GROWL: But still and all ma'm what business had he going near them? Me second husband had more sense. He stopped in the militia, and never went further than the Curragh for a fortnight.

GRANNY GRUNT: Maria Concepta, do you remember when he used to wait on them coming off of the train at Kinsbridge and they after getting their bounty money, and waiting in on the station to be dismissed.

GRANNY GROWL: 'Deed and I do, Teresa Avila, and me provoked sergeant, he was an Englishman, would let a roar that'd go through you.

ANGEL: (*An N.C.O.'s roar*) "Ri . . . ght! To yore respective workhouses, pore'ouses, and 'ore 'ouses . . . d . . iss . . miss!"

GRANNY GRUNT: That's the very way he used to shout. It used to thrill me through me boozem.

GRANNY GROWL: Poor ould Paddins me tired husband . . . .

CHUCKLES: Granny Growl, never mind your husband for a minute. (*Raises his voice*) How would yous all like to come to a house cooling?

MALE AND FEMALE SHOUTS: We'd love to.

GRANNY GROWL: Teresa Avila, what's a house cooling?

GRANNY GRUNT: The opposite to a house warming I suppose. Like an American wake, when someone is going away. Chuckles is going away tonight, I heard them saying. But anyway there will be gargle on the job.

GRANNY GROWL: Oh begod, I'm game . . . game for anything! (*She raises her voice to a shout*) . . . Game for anything. Bottle or draught!

CHUCKLES: All get settled in the lorry. All out to the lorry. The ladies gets in first and settles themselves and the men carries out the drink. Hey there, put up the gargle on the counter for the men to carry out to the lorry. Ten dozen of stout and ten bottles of whiskey.

    Outside in the lorry.

GRANNY GRUNT: Are you right there, Teresa Avila?

GRANNY GROWL: I'm great, Maria Concepta. At our age we enjoy a good ride. It's that seldom we get one.

MALE VOICES: Take up that parcel. Here mind the drink.

GRANNY GRUNT: Yous young women there at the end of the lorry take the gargle off of the men.

    Sounds of bottles rattling as they're put aboard the truck.

MALE VOICES: Everything stored aboard, Chuckles.

ANGEL: (*From the cab*) Right, jump up behind and we're off.

    Lorry starts off into the night.

BARMAN: (*Shouts from the door*) Good night, good night.

MALE AND FEMALE SHOUTS: Good night, good night, good night and good luck.

Lorry gathers speed.

Tonesollock House. The lorry approaches dimly heard in the night.

LOONEY: (*From his window*) Here they are back.

Chorus from the lorry, faint but growing slowly as the lorry comes nearer the house . . . . "He was a quare one" . . . .

LOONEY: Another drunken lot of scum, and old women amongst them. The dirty filthy lot. They'll be roaring and singing and cursing now till morning. Ah, Tonesollock House . . .

In the house.

GRANNY GROWL: Oh me tired husband, he was in the Boer War, and he was standing there in the middle of South Africa, in a big long line, thousands upon thousands of them, every man like a ramrod, stiff as pokers, not a man to move even when a comrade fell, stretched on the parade ground, prostituted from the heat, and up rides Lord Roberts.

GRANNY GRUNT: A lovely man. I see him in the Park and a pair of moustaches on his face a yard long. Waxed and stiff, they went through me boozem.

GRANNY GROWL: He rides along half the length of the line till he comes to my Paddins, and let a roar out of him that would move your bowels: "Fuslier Kinsella!" he roars.

GRANNY GRUNT: God bless us!

GRANNY GROWL: "Fuslier Kinsella," he shouts. Paddins steps forwards, smacks the butt of his rifle, and Lord Roberts looks down at him off his big white horse, and his moustache trembling with glory, "Fuslier Kinsella," he roars, "wipe your bayonet . . . you've killed enough!"

GRANNY GRUNT: My poor fellow, he was a ral, in the Fusiliers.

GRANNY GROWL: What's a ral, Maria Concepta?

GRANNY GRUNT: Well, it's either an admiral, a corporal or a general, but he was a ral, anyway. Pass us that bottle there, Teresa Avila, and we'll have a sup between us anyway. (*They drink*) Where's Chuckles and that English chap be the way?

Upstairs.

CHUCKLES: I suppose we better get down now to the others. I suppose most of them is laid out, be this time. What time is it, Angel?

ANGEL: It's a quarter to five. The sun is coming up.

CHUCKLES: Well, I've everything here. The money from the cattle, from the sale of the farm equipment, and the house fittings, five thousand quid . . . two for you . . . .

ANGEL: That'll be a help. D'you know the last honest graft I was in was the railway . . . thirty-five bob a week.

CHUCKLES: And three for me. We better go down and say good-bye to them down below.

They go downstairs.

GRANNY GRUNT: There you are Chuckles.

CHUCKLES: We're off to the boat. We come down to bid yous good-bye.

GRANNY GROWL: Bedad and we'll give yous a send off. Rouse up there the lot of yous.

MALE AND FEMALE SHOUTS: Wake up there! Wake up there! And sing!

GRANNY GROWL: Wake up Teresa Avila, wake up! Pass a bottle round there, till we wish Chuckles "Good Luck."

MALE AND FEMALE SHOUTS: Good luck, Chuckles, Slawncha, Good Luck, and God go with you.

GRANNY GRUNT AND CHORUS: (*Sings*)
Hand me down me petticoat, hand me down me shawl,
Hand me down me petticoat, for I'm off to the Linen Hall,
He was a quare one fol de doo ah gow a dat,
He was a quare one I tell you.

Hollyhead Station. Rattle, roar, etc., of trains. Wheesh of brakes.

PORTER: This way for the Dublin boat. This way for the mail boat. This way for the Dublin boat.

MRS. BALDCOCK: You've seen about the luggage, Ananias?

ANANIAS: Yes, dear.

MRS. BALDCOCK: It will be nice to be home in dear old Ireland again.

ANANIAS: Yes, dear.

MRS. BALDCOCK: That horrid little house of Tabitha's, and Hereward so rude about you discharging your shotgun in the garden! And those awful, frightful, horrible children.

ANANIAS: Yes, dear, I knew you'd prefer to be back in Tonesollock.

MRS. BALDCOCK: It will be just like when first we wed, and you brought me there as a bride.

ANANIAS: Dear Boadicea.

MRS. BALDCOCK: Darling Ananey!

ANANIAS: Dearest, darlingest Boadey!

MRS. BALDCOCK: (*Greatly astonished*) Look, Ananias.

ANANIAS: Where, darling, at what, dear?

MRS. BALDCOCK: They're just coming out of the customs shed.

ANANIAS: (*A trifle impatient*) Who's coming out of the customs shed, darling?

MRS. BALDCOCK: The agent . . . your man of affairs . . . at home . . . at Tonesollock.

ANANIAS: Genockey, in England?

MRS. BALDCOCK: Wales, darling.

ANANIAS: (*Impatiently*) Whatever it is. Leaving that customs shed!

MRS. BALDCOCK: There he is there, don't you see him with another man, there, they're speaking to a porter.

ANANIAS: Why, bless my soul, so it is.

MRS. BALDCOCK: They're coming this way, dear, speak to him.

ANANIAS: Genockey, Genockey, I didn't hear you coming over. You didn't write.

ANGEL: (*Speaking politely*) I'm afraid you're making a mistake, sir. My employer does not speak English.

ANANIAS: Does not speak English? Ridiculous. Genockey was born and bred in the City of Dublin, where they speak the best English after Oxford.

ANGEL: I'm afraid you are mistaken, sir. This is Doctor Hohnhohn (*he makes for "Hohnhohn," a sound indistinct but very French*), Professor of Celtic Studies at the Sorbonne . . . Belfast Celtic and Glasgow Celtic.

ANANIAS: I beg your pardon, sir.

ANGEL: (*To Chuckles*) Vous-etes le professeur Hohnhohn, ouis?

CHUCKLES: Ouis, je suis.

ANGEL: (*Speaking in his normal Cockney accent*) See, he says so 'imself. We got to catch this train for London . . . . Ta, lady, ta gov.

Train moves off. Gathers speed. Fades.

The big house.

THE BIG HOUSE: Through the war, riot and civil commotion have I stood, and have lived through bad times to see these good times. To get rid of common people and their noisy children and have back again, safe from the towns and cities, my dear horse-faced ladies, and my owners. Stout, redfaced men, and the next best thing to animals, and best of all, the land, for the horse, sheep and bullock, which my people even come to resemble in the end . . . . my beeves, oh my beeves, my sheep, my horses, and or my bullocks, my bullocks, my bullocks. . . . . .

Hans Nordenström

►► Heinrich Böll

In This Country of Ours

We sat in unhappy silence in the cab on the way to the railroad station. It was nearing midnight. Our meeting had been a failure. The traveler had looked to me to give him the precise facts about the Federal Republic, but I had been unable to be precise about so imprecise a country. Not even Einstein could have found a formula for the heterogeneous complex called the German Federal Republic. One of my visitor's questions had been: "In what way are the people here different from those of 1933?" I had answered: "In no way, of course," and then had added the minor proviso: "They are better off economically than people were then." To the question, "Are there still Nazis in this country?" I had replied: "Of course. Do you think that a mere date, May 8, 1945, would have changed human beings?"

Now we were in the cab on the way to the station, and an idea came to me, by way of supplementing what I had said to a question asked hours before: "In this country you will never hear anyone say that Germany was defeated. You will always hear the word 'collapse.' The period from May 1945 to the currency reform is alluded to by the words 'after the collapse.' Or, looking backward, it is called 'before the currency reform.' The period from June 29, 1948 to today is called 'after the currency reform.' Colloquially, the phrase is contracted; people say 'before the currency' or 'after the currency.' And with sureness of instinct, 'before the currency' also includes the period of the war, in which it rained money. We live in the year Twelve after the currency. Before the collapse we had the Nazi period, which in turn is broken down into six years of peace and six years of war. You probably still remember from your school history that everything is *broken down* into the reigns of X and Y, into war and peace. Before the Nazi period was the Weimar Republic, which is broken down into the administrations of the various presidents; before the Weimar Republic—but that would lead us too far into the mists of time. That I was born in 1917, a subject of the German Emperor, seems to me stranger than if my father were to tell me in all seriousness that he had taken part in the Third Punic War. Altogether unreal. . . ."

The visitor did not reply. The cab driver was silent too. He was in bad humor; three hours waiting for a fare, then a miserable five-mark ride and the prospect of having to wait for another three hours—enough to sour anyone's mood. Cabs are unpopular in this country of ours, like telephones and checkbooks; a spendthrift odor still clings to these useful institutions. In this country people go out for an evening's drinking and jollity without a thought of their pocketbooks, but then will huddle anxiously waiting for the last streetcar and will dissipate their dearly-bought good spirits shivering at transfer stations, although the difference between the streetcar and the taxi fare hardly amounts to the price of half a bottle of wine. In this country, someone "flashing" a checkbook has a good chance of being considered affluent. Yet a checkbook costs only seventy-five pfennigs (eighteen cents), and the fifty checks it holds come in very handy in the sport which is a must for every novice who wants to build up his credit. The sport is called: "Keep your account moving." If you've moved two thousand marks fifty times, they amount to one hundred thousand, and that's a respectable turnover. All you have to know is how to keep your account moving: back and forth, forth and back. The thing is not to let the soap bubble burst. No wonder that in a country in which time-honored prejudices against arithmetic and mathematics are still socially acceptable, those who practice the sport diligently have some prospect of success. The multiplication table was invented in vain; the ability to calculate is considered almost a defect. What would happen in this country if it ever got around that Goethe had been good at arithmetic!

The streets were deserted that September night; only a few municipal vehicles were on the move. Softly, the rollers of the sweeper trucks turned; the motors of the sprinkler wagons hummed gently. My visitor offered the cab driver a cigarette. The driver took it and said thanks. He would never—and perhaps this insight is part of a possible formula—have offered a cigarette to a fare. Not out of stinginess, certainly, but because at the moment the fare represents to him something that is simultaneously worshiped and despised in this country—a customer. In economic terms, a consumer. We are a people of consumers. Neckties and conformism, sport shirts and non-conformism—everything has its consumers. What is all important is that it—whatever it is, sport shirt or conformism—appear in the guise of a brand-name article. There are consumers here who have neither the instinct nor the experience for judging quality themselves, so they demand guaranteed quality. But guaranteed quality is expensive. Anyone who wants to go into the fruit-vending business can be sure of selling the highest-priced apples fastest. If he switched price tags and marked the forty-pfennig apples at eighty, and vice versa, he would probably sell the poorer apples at a high price more easily than the good apples at a low price. For what young housewife would have learned to take an apple into her hand to see what it was like? Perhaps this insight, too, is part of the larger formula.

Tensely, I waited for our cab to turn into the street it has to pass on the way to the railroad station. Here the buildings reek of sanctity and dignity; the best stone has been used in the best National Convention style, the watchword being: "There's nothing more solid." To rule and to build are one, and on this street you can plainly see who does the building in this country. Passing by here, a cab driver takes care to glance once more at his fare's shoes, clothing, and face, before venturing the usual comment—a comment coined by the populace at the sight of these buildings: "All built on our money."

Our driver that warm September night finally broke his morose silence; he put it even more precisely than the popular saying: "There's the money my father paid out in life insurance for forty years."

But the Germans are a long-suffering people—how much so becomes evident when you consider that, adding insult to injury, these palaces are illuminated at night. Soft yellow light gives the copper doors and window frames a shimmer of dignity that justifies the cost of the kilowatts. The façades of the buildings are decorated with religious emblems; this is to appease the genius loci. Or should I rather say: to pay it tribute? Do the saints accept the offering? And is there any better subject for monumental sculpture than St. Christopher who carries the smiling Christ Child through perilously gurgling waters? Besides, St. Christopher is the patron saint of motorists, and what motorist is uninsured? Thus business is combined with religion, the duties of ostentation with the duty of promoting the arts—and, what's more, here is a way to demonstrate the proper contempt for abstract, degenerate art. Seven at one blow! I call that clever.

My visitor from abroad was surprised to pass by a whole quarter of palaces so brilliantly illuminated in the middle of the night. "What satraps administer what provinces of which empire from these buildings?" he asked.

"Perhaps," I said, "on your next visit to Germany you will ask some financial expert for the mysterious formula whereby some people found their 100 Reichsmarks transformed into seven, while others found their 100 Reichsmarks transformed into 5,000 or more. He will try to make you think that money is a purely rational matter. Those who don't believe in the miracle of the loaves won't be able to explain to you the miracle of the theft of the loaves. Teachers will continue to pound that ridiculous $2 \times 2 = 4$ into our children, and train them to be thrifty. Apparently the venerable inventor of the multiplication table knew nothing about miracles. Is it possible that the German miracle is based on the formula $7 =$ infinity?"

The cab driver began to act a bit nervous. He drove faster than the speed limit, hurrying toward the station as though he were anxious to be rid of us. It was not much farther to the station now. The kind of fares to whom he could not speak his mind about the palatial buildings will, when asked about the ground rules of the currency reform, reply that in East Germany the boneheads were left with even less money when the currency was pared. That's the kind of consolation offered us. If I ever have to do time for six years on a bum rap, a cell mate will probably offer the consolation that he is doing eight years on a bum rap.

When we got out at the station the cab driver was alarmed by the generous tip my visitor gave him— two marks on a fare of five. And that from a customer he thought he could freely speak his mind to. Had he been mistaken in us? Should he not have kept his mouth shut, after all? Were we communists, or did we think him one? Beware! Unfortunately, his alarm turned into obsequiousness. How carefully he took the traveler's bag from the trunk. In this country generosity is prized no more than thrift. A great deal of sentimentality revolves around the question of money. Nor is this surprising in a country in which poverty is no longer a mystical destination nor a stage on the road to class struggle. Even so-called intellectuals are still wedded to the concept of the poor, decent worker; the terms are virtually equivalent. It follows, then, that since the workers are no longer poor, poverty no longer exists—ergo, the workers aren't the decent, good fellows they used to be. The old middle-class "idealist," the so-called social-minded person, has become a thing of the past. Success is admired without qualification. People do not seem to realize that even as the workers have become less moral, there might be a corresponding amorality among the satraps; a man who lights a cigarette with a hundred-mark note is going to be admired rather than despised or hated. If you point out that in setting fire to his hundred-mark note, this fellow is burning a fragment of freedom, you will be regarded as a nut. Money cannot be a means to freedom where poverty has no sovereignty. Givers of tips are just as wanting in dignity as receivers of tips—in this country.

The train the traveler was going to take was made up when we arrived; a number of passengers were already sleeping; others were enduring the wait with evening newspapers and hot *wurst*. After my visitor had boarded the train, found his seat, and lowered the window, there remained a few minutes, too few for us to be able to take up the conversation that had been such a failure. I tried to imagine what he might be thinking and feeling. He had been born in this city, attended school here, gone into exile in 1937; his parents stayed until 1939—their trust in German decency almost cost them their lives. Three years later—in 1942—you were already risking your life if you brought a handful of potatoes to a Jew in his hiding place or if, as a Polish prisoner of war, you kissed a German girl in a hallway.

A kiss in the doorway, a handful of potatoes, an off-color political remark in the air-raid shelter—these were enough. My mother, who knew how to express in pungent language the lessons life had taught her and the violence of her feelings, delivered herself of such a remark in 1940, in the presence of an ambitious young man who was not a member of the Nazi Party and never became one. At that time, however, he was still filled with a vague ambition that later became focused on making a career as a non-commissioned officer. My mother's life, then, hung not by a thread, but by the conscience of a local Party leader who apparently did not pass on the denunciation; you did not really get to know the Germans in 1933, but later, in the 1940 delirium of victory, when marshals' batons rained down like manna from heaven. In 1946 the ambitious young man, somewhat older if not wiser, became one of the candidates of the Christian-Democratic Party for the municipal government —after all, he had never been a member of the Nazi Party. Probably the local Party leader who had saved my mother's life was in an internment camp at the same period. I do not know how many denunciations he had passed on, how many he suppressed. I know only this: when I meet people I used to know, I try to recall what they said and thought in 1940, in the year of victory and glory, when the loneliness was greatest and we advised my mother not to make political remarks in the air-raid shelter. From then on she spoke only in looks, and her big dark eyes were no doubt more eloquent than her mouth. The ambitious young man would fall into a state border-ing on frenzy whenever she looked at him. I do not know whether anyone has ever been condemned to death because of a look; it certainly would be possible.

Three minutes before the departure time of the train. No point in still trying to formulate my thoughts. On the opposite platform weary wayfarers were waiting for a train to some godforsaken provincial place. Perhaps the Jews who still trusted in German decency as late as 1942 left from this very platform for Poland. Even at the time of their departure they could not yet bring themselves to believe in the horror. Who believed in it? A kiss in the doorway, a handful of potatoes, an irreverent political remark among *non*-members of the Nazi Party. Never rely on man and his psyche. One would have to discover the language of railroad stations, decipher the poetry of railroad tracks, learn to translate the song of the steps that lead up to railroad platforms: political prisoners, Russian slaves, Jews, soldiers, transported children—countless feet of those bound for death have touched these steps. The people who stood here on hot summer afternoons, listlessly sipping their lukewarm lemonade, irritably on the way home from unsuccessful picnics in the country—they, too, came to see their sons and brothers off on troop trains taking them to their deaths. What has murdered their grief, what buried their memories? How few are the faces in this country that show the capacity for grief and memory. Comfort is promised the grief-stricken, but not the irritable. If a woman were to burst into tears on this platform when remembering that from this station her son went off to be killed—if that were to happen people would pat her consolingly on the shoulder, and in secret criticize her for being maudlin. They would think: how can a person afford a memory going back sixteen or seventeen years? If the same woman were to look on indifferently while seven fire brigades worked to rescue a cat that had slipped down a drainpipe, she would be regarded as a dangerous old hag. You must react within the conventional patterns of sentimentality; or else you are considered dangerous. As for your neighbors who perished—the memory isn't worth the flicker of an eyelash. To deal with such memories, and with people who might try to stir them up, psychology has provided a murderous weapon which is at everyone's disposal: the word "resentment." It is stabbed like a knife into the breast of everyone who dares to show genuine feelings. In order to escape this murderous weapon, memories and feelings are aborted; it is this permanent curettage that makes faces so empty here. People cry or scream only in psychiatric clinics. Insensitivity and sentimentality dominate the market which supplies objects to which the heart can cling:

mascots of every size and price, from the ever present stuffed hedgehogs to the imposing new office buildings. Prices are down for a heart and a conscience; they are on the rise for the things man really needs. A government official who joined the Nazi Party in 1936 to save his family from misery strikes me today as an honorable man. For him, something was really at stake; he was threatened; and there was no social or ecclesiastical authority around which would have helped to transform this feeling of being threatened into a sense of composure.

The only threat that inspires a German with fear *today* is the threat of a business slowdown. As soon as this seems in the offing, panic ensues; all the alarm signals are sounded. There are a great many highly intelligent, very clever young people, adroit with their pens, all disturbingly well informed, well-trained in the art of analysis, who know as much about the Third Punic War as about Faulkner. All I ask myself is where their resistance begins, or might begin. They fear neither Adenauer nor Ollenhauer; if you catch them in some inconsistency, they will point to a force far more dangerous than either the former or the latter: Lieschen Müller. This mythical creature, our Jane Doe, seems to me an invention of their guilty consciences. Lieschen Müller and business volume are closely related. Anyone who endangers business risks the wrath of the Germans; at that point they stop being long-suffering. The death of neighbors and friends has not taught them to respect life. Sorrow has not become wisdom, nor grief strength. Paradoxically, they are impoverished, for even in the face of an ever present threat they are incapable of really enjoying their relative prosperity. Even the hunger of the years "before the currency" has failed to teach them how to take real pleasure in the blessings of the moment. Misery has not lent spice to plenty; anyone whose memory stretches back over so much as ten years is considered sick, or ought to be anesthetized so that he will awaken refreshed and strengthened for the present. A handful of potatoes, a kiss in the hallway, a political wisecrack among non-members of the Party—that was the price for a human life. Perhaps the secret of this extinction of memory lies in the nature of the unknown formula which breaks down our lives into the period before and after the currency reform.

I had wanted to say all this to my visitor but had not found the words. A rapid handshake, a "good-by," and the train was off. I walked down the steps, handed in my platform ticket, and went home. There, the empty bottles still attesting to a conversation that had failed, I found my youngest son's slate lying on the table, arithmetic exercises neatly set down on it: $7 + 5 = 12$, $9 + 6 = 15$. Who could remain unmoved in the face of the credulity with which such sums are set down? I wrote across the blank portion of the slate: $7 = $ infinity. Then I cleared away the bottles and tried to write down what I had found impossible to express in conversation. Not the formula, but maybe bits of it, though no one would be able to put them together into an equation that could ever be solved. Who would dare to judge the local Party leader who had *not* betrayed my mother, when others had? The ambitious young man who could sue me for slander if I called him a Nazi will, I should hope, recall my mother's dark eyes now and again.

What does it mean to be a German? It means being bullied in a Paris hotel for being one. It means to be sitting, on the way back in the express train, opposite a young French fascist who tries to pay you compliments for the consistency with which anti-Semitism was practiced in your country. It means not to be regarded as having any say when Frenchmen talk among themselves about Algeria; perhaps we shall have a say only when so many persons have been killed in Algeria as were killed under German rule in Europe between 1933 and 1945. Who keeps this mysterious balance sheet of the nations? Who fixes the price for a human life? Will it be a look tomorrow? Where is it located, the sinister stock exchange which dictates these quotations? The nasty business in the Paris hotel, of course, is directed precisely against the very German who brought the handful of potatoes to the Jew in hiding, and the British customs officer holds in gingerly fingers, as if he were touching a leper's papers, the passport of the very German who did not pass on a denunciation. If there is such a thing as a feeling of collective guilt in this country, it began at the moment that the "currency reform" started the bargain sale of sorrow, grief, and memories.

How many reasons there are for being angry *with* this country, and *within* it! But against whom shall this anger be aimed? The people of this country swallow everything. The television screen could show them their nearest neighbor dying in an automobile accident; they might start, possibly say, "Why, I know him, don't I?" and wait for what would come next on the screen. In the course of the next "currency," their money could be revalued by $100 = 0.1$; the fortunes of the connivers would then be proportionately increased; the others would sigh, swear a bit, but would soon roll up their sleeves and work, sweat, work. Here is the way to still accomplish a few miracles and prevent popular indignation over the unknown quantity in the equation. The converse of the miraculous increase of the loaves is the miraculous theft of bread. The faces of the experts who attempt to explain the miracle in smooth words are as empty and lifeless as the moon.

Dawn was already glimmering when I stood up from my desk. The innocent columns of figures on my son's slate became unreal. I wiped away the equation 7 = infinity; it would only lead to trouble for him. In the schools the 'rithmetic book is still holy; in the schools historical periods are *broken down* into separate segments. My visitor was no doubt long since asleep, somewhere between Brussels and Os-

tend. He had, it is true, a British passport; and yet the gingerly fingers of the customs official in Dover would possibly express, by spreading slightly, a trace of contempt, for he looks more German than the German of today. His clothing, gestures, pronunciation betray him, and though he has not been a German for so long a time, he must pay for a guilt which is considered old and which is yet so new that so far only we Germans know what it is.

Translated by Richard and Clara Winston

► ► **Günter Grass**

The Wide Skirt

You can begin a story in the middle and create confusion by striking out boldly, backward and forward. You can be modern, put aside all mention of time and distance, and when the whole thing is done, proclaim, or let someone else proclaim, that you have finally, at the last moment, solved the space-time problem. Or you can declare at the very start that it's impossible to write a novel nowadays, but then, behind your own back so to speak, give birth to a whopper, a novel to end all novels. I have also been told that it makes a good impression, an impression of modesty so to speak, if you begin by saying that a novel can't have a hero any more because there are no more individualists, because individuality is a thing of the past, because man—each man and all men together—is alone in his loneliness and no one is entitled to individual loneliness, and all men lumped together make up a "lonely mass" without names and without heroes. All this may be true. But as far as I and Bruno my keeper are concerned, I beg leave to say that we are both heroes, very different heroes; he on his side of the peephole, and I on my side; and even when he opens the door, the two of us, with all our friendship and loneliness, are still far from being a nameless and heroless mass.

I shall begin far away from me; for no one ought to tell the story of his life who hasn't the patience to say a word or two about at least half of his grandparents before plunging into his own existence. And so

to you personally, dear reader, who are no doubt leading a muddled kind of life outside this institution, to you my friends and weekly visitors who suspect nothing of my paper supply, I introduce Oskar's maternal grandmother.

Late one October afternoon my grandmother Anna Bronski was sitting in her skirts at the edge of a potato field. In the morning you might have seen how expert my grandmother was at raking the limp potato plants into neat piles; at noon she had eaten a chunk of bread smeared with lard and syrup; then she had dug over the field a last time, and now she sat in her skirts between two nearly full baskets. The soles of her boots rose up at right angles to the ground, converging slightly at the toes, and in front of them smoldered a fire of potato plants, flaring up asthmatically from time to time, diffusing a queasy blanket of smoke over the scarcely inclined crust of the earth. The year was 1899; she was sitting in the heart of Kashubia, not far from Bissau but still closer to the brickworks between Ramkau and Viereck, in front of her the Brenntau highway at a point between Dirschau and Karthaus, behind her the black forest of Goldkrug; there she sat, pushing potatoes beneath the hot ashes with the charred tip of a hazel branch.

If I have made a special point of my grandmother's skirt, leaving no doubt, I hope, that she was sitting in her skirts; if indeed I have gone so far as to call the whole chapter "The Wide Skirt," it is because I know how much I owe to this article of apparel. My grandmother had on not just one skirt, but four, one over the other. It should not be supposed that she wore one skirt and three petticoats; no, she wore four skirts; one supported the next, and she wore the lot of them in accordance with a definite system, that is, the order of the skirts was changed from day to day. The one that was on top yesterday was today in the second place; the second became the third. The one that was third yesterday was next to her skin today. The one that was closest to her yesterday clearly disclosed its pattern today, or rather its lack of pattern: all my grandmother Anna Bronski's skirts favored the same potato color. It must have been becoming to her.

Aside from the color, my grandmother's skirts were distinguished by a lavish expanse of material. They puffed and billowed when the wind came, cracked as it passed, and sagged when it was gone, and all four of them flew out ahead of her when she had the wind in her stern. When she sat down, she gathered her skirts about her.

In addition to the four skirts, billowing, sagging, hanging down in folds, or standing stiff and empty beside her bed, my grandmother possessed a fifth. It differed in no way from the other four potato-colored garments. And actually the fifth skirt was not always fifth. Like its brothers—for skirts are masculine by nature—it was subject to change, it was worn like the other four, and like them when its time had come, took its turn in the wash trough every fifth Friday, then Saturday on the line by the kitchen window, and when dry on the ironing board.

When, after one of these Saturdays spent in housecleaning, baking, washing, and ironing, after milking and feeding the cow, my grandmother immersed herself from top to toe in the tub, when, after leaving a little of herself in the soapsuds and letting the water in the tub sink back to its normal level, she sat down on the edge of the bed swathed in a great flowery towel, the four worn skirts and the freshly washed skirt lay spread out before her on the floor. She pondered, propping the lower lid of her right eye with her right index finger, and since she consulted no one, not even her brother Vincent, she quickly made up her mind. She stood up and with her bare toes pushed aside the skirt whose potato color had lost the most bloom. The freshly laundered one took its place.

On Sunday morning she went to church in Ramkau and inaugurated the new order of skirts in honor of Jesus, about whom she had very set ideas. Where did grandmother wear the laundered skirt? She was

not only a cleanly woman, but also a rather vain one; she wore the best piece where it could be seen in the sunlight when the weather was good.

But now it was a Monday afternoon and my grandmother was sitting by the potato fire. Today her Sunday skirt was one layer closer to her person, while the one that had basked in the warmth of her skin on Sunday, swathed her hips in Monday gloom. Whistling with no particular tune in mind, she coaxed the first cooked potato out of the ashes with her hazel branch and pushed it away from the smoldering mound to cool in the breeze. Then she spitted the charred and crusty tuber on a pointed stick, and held it close to her mouth; she had stopped whistling and instead pursed her cracked, wind-parched lips to blow the earth and ashes off the potato skin.

In blowing, my grandmother closed her eyes. When she thought she had blown enough, she opened first one eye, then the other, bit into the potato with her widely spaced but otherwise perfect front teeth, removed half the potato, cradled the other half, mealy, steaming, and still too hot to chew, in her open mouth, and sniffing at the smoke and the October air, gazed wide-eyed across the field toward the nearby horizon, sectioned by telegraph poles and the upper third of the brickworks chimney.

Something was moving between the telegraph poles. My grandmother closed her mouth. Something was jumping about. Three men were darting between the poles, three men made for the chimney, then round in front, then one doubled back. Short and wide he seemed, he took a fresh start and made it across the brickyard, the other two, sort of long and thin, just behind him. They were out of the brickyard, back between the telegraph poles, but Short and Wide twisted and turned and seemed to be in more of a hurry than Long and Thin, who had to double back to the chimney, because he was already rolling over it when they, two hands'-breadths away, were still taking a start, and suddenly they were gone as though they had given up, and the little one disappeared too, behind the horizon, in the middle of his jump from the chimney.

Out of sight they remained, it was intermission, they were changing their costumes, or making bricks and getting paid for it. Taking advantage of the intermission, my grandmother tried to spit another potato, but missed it. Because the one who seemed to be short and wide; who hadn't changed his clothes after all, climbed up over the horizon as if it were a fence and he had left his pursuers behind it, in among the bricks or on the road to Brenntau. But he was still in a hurry; trying to be faster than the telegraph poles, he took long slow leaps across the field;

the mud flew from his boots as he leaped over the soggy ground but leap as he might, he seemed to be crawling. Sometimes he seemed to stick in the ground and then to stick in mid-air, short and wide, time enough to wipe his face before his foot came down again in the freshly plowed field, which bordered the five acres of potatoes and narrowed into a sunken lane.

He made it to the lane; short and wide, he had barely disappeared into the lane, when the two others, long and thin, who had probably been searching the brickyard in the meantime, climbed over the horizon and came plodding through the mud, so long and thin, but not really skinny, that my grandmother missed her potato again; because it's not

every day that you see this kind of thing, three full-grown men, though they hadn't grown in exactly the same directions, hopping around telegraph poles, nearly breaking the chimney off the brickworks, and then at intervals, first short and wide, then long and thin, but all with the same difficulty, picking up more and more mud on the soles of their boots; leaping through the field that Vincent had plowed two days before, and disappearing down the sunken lane.

Then all three of them were gone and my grandmother ventured to spit another potato, which by this time was almost cold. She hastily blew the earth and ashes off the skin, popped the whole potato straight into her mouth. They must be from the brickworks, she thought if she thought anything, and

Laurent de Brunoff

she was still chewing with a circular motion when one of them jumped out of the lane, wild eyes over a black mustache, reached the fire in two jumps, stood before, behind, and beside the fire all at once, cursing, scared, not knowing which way to go, unable to turn back, for behind him Long and Thin were running down the lane. He hit his knees, the eyes in his head were like to pop out, and sweat poured from his forehead. Panting, his whole face atremble, he ventured to crawl closer, toward the soles of my grandmother's boots, peering up at her like a squat little animal. Heaving a great sigh, which made her stop chewing on her potato, my grandmother let her feet tilt over, stopped thinking about bricks and brickmakers, and lifted high her skirt, no, all four skirts, high enough so that Short and Wide, who was not from the brickworks, could crawl underneath. Gone was his black mustache; he didn't look like an animal any more, he was neither from Ramkau nor from Viereck, at any rate he had vanished with his fright, he had ceased to be wide or short but he took up room just the same, he forgot to pant or tremble and he had stopped hitting his knees; all was as still as on the first day of Creation or the last; a bit of wind hummed in the potato fire, the telegraph poles counted themselves in silence, the chimney of the brickworks stood at attention, and my grandmother smoothed down her uppermost skirt neatly and sensibly over the second one; she scarcely felt him under her fourth skirt, and her third skirt wasn't even aware that there was anything new and unusual next to her skin. Yes, unusual it was but the top was nicely smoothed out and the second and third layers didn't know a thing; and so she scraped two or three potatoes out of the ashes, took four raw ones from the basket beneath her right elbow, pushed the raw spuds one after another into the hot ashes, covered them over with more ashes, and poked the fire till the smoke rose in clouds—what else could she have done?

My grandmother's skirts had barely settled down, the sticky smudge of the potato fire, which had lost its direction with all the poking and thrashing about, had barely had time to adjust itself to the wind and resume its low yellow course across the field to south-westward, when Long and Thin popped out of the lane, hot in pursuit of Short and Wide who by now had set up housekeeping beneath my grandmother's skirts; they were indeed long and thin and they wore the uniform of the rural constabulary.

They nearly ran past my grandmother. One of them even jumped over the fire. But suddenly they remembered they had heels and used them to brake with, about-faced, stood booted and uniformed in the smudge, coughed, pulled their uniforms out of the smudge, taking some of it along with them and still coughing, turned to my grandmother, asked her if she had seen Koljaiczek, 'cause she must have seen him 'cause she was sitting here by the lane and that was the way he had come.

My grandmother hadn't seen any Koljaiczek be-cause she didn't know any Koljaiczek. Was he from the brickworks, she asked, 'cause the only ones she knew were the ones from the brickworks. But accord-ing to the uniforms, this Koljaiczek had nothing to do with bricks, but was short and stocky. My grand-mother remembered she had seen somebody like that running and pointed her stick with the steaming potato on the end toward Bissau which, to judge by the potato, must have been between the sixth and seventh telegraph pole if you counted westward from the chimney. But whether this fellow that was run-ning was a Koljaiczek, my grandmother couldn't say; she'd been having enough trouble with this fire, she explained, it was burning poorly, how could she worry her head about all the people that ran by or stood in the smoke, and anyway she never worried her head about people she didn't know, she only knew the people in Bissau, Ramkau, Viereck, and the brickworks—and that was plenty for her.

After saying all this, my grandmother heaved a gentle sigh, but it was enough of a sigh to make the uniforms ask what there was to sigh about. She nodded toward the fire, meaning to say that she had

sighed because the fire was doing poorly and maybe a little on account of the people standing in the smoke; then she bit off half her potato with her widely spaced incisors, and gave her undivided atten-tion to the business of chewing, while her eyeballs rolled heavenward.

My grandmother's absent gaze told the uniforms nothing; unable to make up their minds whether to look for Bissau behind the telegraph poles, they poked their bayonets into all the piles of potato tops that hadn't been set on fire. Responding to a sudden inspiration, they upset the two baskets under my grandmother's elbows almost simultaneously and were quite bewildered when nothing but potatoes came rolling out, and no Koljaiczek. Full of suspicion they crept round the stack of potatoes, as though Koljaiczek had somehow got into it, thrust in their bayonets as though deliberately taking aim and were disappointed to hear no cry. Their suspicions were aroused by every bush, however abject, by every mousehole, by a colony of molehills, and most of all by my grandmother who sat there as if rooted to the spot, sighing, rolling her eyes so that the whites showed, listing the Kashubian names of all the saints —all of which seemed to have been brought on by the poor performance of the fire and the overturning of her potato baskets.

The uniforms stayed on for a good half-hour. They took up positions at varying distances from the fire, they took an azimuth on the chimney, contemplated an offensive against Bissau but postponed it, and held out their purple hands over the fire until my grandmother, though without interrupting her sighs, gave each of them a charred potato. But in the midst of chewing, the uniforms remembered their uni-forms, dashed a little way out into the field along the furze bordering the lane, and scared up a hare which, however, turned out not to be Koljaiczek. Returning to the fire, they recovered the mealy, steaming spuds and then, wearied and rather mellowed by their bat-tles, decided to pick up the raw potatoes and put them back into the baskets which they had over-turned in line of duty.

Only when evening began to squeeze a fine slant-ing rain and an inky twilight from the October sky did they briefly and without enthusiasm attack a dark boulder at the other end of the field, but once this enemy had been disposed of they decided to let well enough alone. After flexing their legs for an-other moment or two and holding out their hands in blessing over the rather dampened fire, they coughed a last cough and dropped a last tear in the green and yellow smudge, and plodded off coughing and weep-ing in the direction of Bissau. If Koljaiczek wasn't here, he must be in Bissau. Rural constables never envisage more than two possibilities.

The smoke of the slowly dying fire enveloped my grandmother like a spacious fifth skirt, so that she too with her four skirts, her sighs, and her holy names, was under a skirt. Only when the uniforms had become staggering dots, vanishing in the dusk between the telegraph poles, did my grandmother arise, slowly and painfully as though she had struck root and now, drawing earth and fibers along with her, were tearing herself out of the ground.

Suddenly Koljaiczek found himself short, wide, and coverless in the rain, and he was cold. Quickly he buttoned his pants which fear and a boundless need for shelter had bidden him open during his stay beneath the skirts. Hurriedly he manipulated the buttons, fearing to let his piston cool too quickly, for there was a threat of dire chills in the autumn air.

My grandmother found four more hot potatoes under the ashes. She gave Koljaiczek three of them and took one for herself; before biting into it, she asked if he was from the brickworks, though she knew perfectly well that Koljaiczek came from somewhere else and had no connection with bricks. Without waiting for an answer, she lifted the lighter basket to his back, took the heavier one for herself, and still had a hand free for her rake and hoe. Then with her basket, her potatoes, her rake, and her hoe, she set off, like a sail billowing in the breeze, in the direction of Bissau Quarry.

That wasn't the same as Bissau itself. It lay more in the direction of Ramkau. Passing to the right of the brickworks, they headed for the black forest with Goldkrug in it and Brenntau behind it. But in a hollow, before you come to the forest, lay Bissau Quarry. Thither Joseph Koljaiczek, unable to tear himself away from her skirts, followed my grandmother.

It is not so easy, lying here in this scrubbed hospital bed under a glass peephole with Bruno's eye in it, to give a picture of the smoke clouds that rose from Kashubian potato fires or the slanting October rain. If I didn't have my drum, which, when handled adroitly and patiently, remembers all the incidentals that I need to get the essential down on paper, and if I didn't have the permission of the management to drum on it three or four hours a day, I'd be a poor bastard with nothing to say for my grandparents.

In any case, my drum tells me this: That afternoon in the year 1899, while in South Africa Oom Kruger was brushing his bushy anti-British eyebrows, my mother Agnes, between Dirschau and Karthaus, not far from the Bissau brickworks, amid smoke, terrors, signs, and saints' names, under four skirts of identical color, under the slanting rain and the smoke-filled eyes of two rural constables asking uninspired questions, was begotten by the short but stocky Joseph Koljaiczek.

Translated by Ralph Manheim

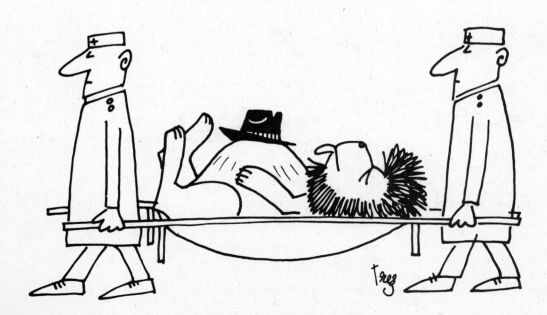

ALFRED ANDERSCH, born in 1914 in Germany, is regarded as one of the most talented writers of postwar Germany. *The Redhead*, as well as an earlier work, *Flight to Afar*, were published here by Coward McCann. In 1964, *The Night of the Giraffe and Other Stories* was published by Pantheon.

BENNY ANDERSEN is a Danish author who has been writing poems, short stories, and radio plays since 1951. This story first appeared in the volume *Sengeheste*, published in Denmark and soon to be published here by Grove Press.

ARRABAL was born in Spanish Morocco. He moved to Madrid after the Spanish Civil War, and later to Paris. Translations of two of his plays, *The Automobile Graveyard* and *The Two Executioners*, were published by Grove Press in 1960, followed by his novel *Baal Babylon* in 1961.

ANTONIN ARTAUD, French playwright, critic, film actor, and director, died in 1948, two years after he had been released from many years of tragic confinement in asylums for the insane. His work has left a deep impact on modern drama, particularly *The Theater and Its Double*, published by Grove Press in 1958.

GEORGES BATAILLE, the French philosopher and art historian, died in 1962 at the age of sixty-five. His last book, *Les Larmes d'Eros*, was published in 1961 and offers one of the most radical reappraisals of the history of art to be found in modern literature. Grove will soon publish his nonfiction study, *The Trial of Gilles de Rais*.

SAMUEL BECKETT was born in Ireland in 1906 and educated at Trinity College, Dublin. He went to Paris in the late twenties and until 1945 wrote in English; shortly after the war he began writing directly in French. He has written many plays, novels, short pieces, and poems, and all of those which are available in the United States have been published by Grove Press.

BRENDAN BEHAN, Irish playwright and raconteur, died at the age of forty-one in 1964 in Dublin. His works include *The Quare Fellow* and *The Hostage*, two plays published by Grove Press.

PAUL BLACKBURN, born in 1926 in Vermont, has been a Fulbright Scholar, an American Lecturer at the University of Toulouse, and a Guggenheim Fellow. He is the author of several books of poems, including *The Cities*, his first major collection, published by Grove Press in 1967.

HEINRICH BÖLL, a German author, has written several volumes of short stories, four novels, and a number of essays and radio plays. Among the books he has had published here are *Billiards at Half-Past Nine*, *Clown*, and a collection of eighteen stories.

JORGE LUIS BORGES was born in 1899 in Buenos Aires. Educated in Europe, he returned to Argentina in 1921, where he was one of the pioneers of the *ultraista* movement. While convalescing from a severe illness, he wrote the first of the "fictions" which have since made him famous.

PATRICK BOYLE is an Irish writer, author of the novel *Like Any Other Man*, published by Grove Press, and a collection of short stories, *At Night All Cats Are Grey*. His work has also appeared in *New Writing*, *Penguin New Writing*, and many magazines.

RICHARD BRAUTIGAN was born and raised in the Pacific Northwest and now makes his home in San Francisco. His novel, *A Confederate General from Big Sur*, was published by Grove

in 1965, and another, *Trout Fishing in America*, is distributed by City Lights.

BRASSAÏ, whose real name is Jules Halasz, was born in Brasso, Hungary, in 1899. He came to Paris in the early 1920's, at first drawing and writing for magazines. He switched to photography in 1931 and his first book, *Paris de Nuit*, immediately established him as one of the leading European photographers. Brassaï is also a writer, a poet, and a sculptor.

BROTHER ANTONINUS, O.P. (William Everson), was born in Sacramento, California. Since 1951 he has been stationed at the Collect of St. Albert the Great in Oakland. Two volumes of poetry which he has had published are *The Crooked Lines of God* and *Hazards of Holiness*.

MIODRAG BULATOVIC is a writer from Montenegro who has rapidly achieved recognition as one of the leading authors in present-day Yugoslavia. His novel, *The Red Cock Flies to Heaven*, was published in 1962 by Bernard Geis Associates.

WILLIAM S. BURROUGHS was born in St. Louis in 1914, and after graduating from Harvard, traveled extensively in Europe. In recent years he has lived mainly in Tangier, London, and Paris. He became internationally known upon the American publication of *Naked Lunch* in 1962.

EMIL CADOO is a free-lance American photographer who lives and works in Paris. He is perhaps best known in this country for the series of photographs which appeared in the *Evergreen Review*, two of which are included in this anthology.

ALBERT CAMUS, French philosopher, novelist, and playwright, was awarded the Nobel Prize for Literature in 1957. His "Reflections on the Guillotine" was first printed in the June and July issues (1957) of *La Nouvelle Revue Française*. He was killed in an automobile accident in 1960.

PAUL CARROLL is former poetry editor of *Chicago Review* and was editor of *Big Table*. His poems have appeared in a number of publications, including *Evergreen Review*. His first volume of verse was *De Medici sur Machine*. He has also edited *The Edward Dahlberg Reader*.

BLAISE CENDRARS was born in 1887 of mixed Swiss and Scottish descent. He traveled extensively, living by his wits, making films, serving as a corporal in the Foreign Legion, and writing. He was the author of over twenty books. Cendrars died in Paris in 1961.

DRISS BEN HAMED CHARHADI is a young, illiterate Berber from North Africa. The episode in this volume is from an autobiographical work, *A Life Full of Holes*, which Charhadi dictated on tape and Paul Bowles translated from the Moghrebi.

E. M. CIORAN is a Rumanian-born writer who lives in Paris. His works include *La Tentation d'exister* and a volume of essays on politics and history, *Histoire et utopie*.

ROBERT COOVER has contributed numerous short stories to *Evergreen Review*. His novel, *The Origin of the Brunists*, published by Putnam, won the William Faulkner Award.

GREGORY CORSO, born in New York City, was placed in an orphanage at the age of one. At seventeen, in prison, he began to read extensively and to write. He later spent many years in Europe. Among his works are three books of poems and a novel, *American Express*.

ROBERT CREELEY was born in Massachusetts in 1926. He attended Harvard and served in the American Field Service in Burma during the war. He taught at Black Mountain College

---

* *The following Notes on Contributors apply to both this volume and the second volume of this work.*

and is presently at the State University of New York at Buffalo. He is the author of many books, including two volumes of poetry, a novel, and a collection of short stories.

JOSÉ LUIS CUEVAS, born in Mexico City in 1933, has had many exhibitions of his paintings in France, Latin America, and the United States since he began work as an illustrator at the age of fourteen. In recent years, he has taught at the Universidad Ibero-americana in Mexico City and at the art school of the Philadelphia Museum of Art.

STIG DAGERMAN, the Swedish author whose literary career was brought to a premature end by his death in 1954 at the age of twenty-six, published four novels, a collection of short stories, a book of travel sketches, and four full-length plays.

SALVADOR DALI, well-known Spanish painter and leader of the Surrealist school, was born in Catalonia in 1904. He has also collaborated on the scenarios of a number of motion pictures and written a book, *Babaoua*.

RENÉ DAUMAL, see page 297.

STUART DAVIS was born in Philadelphia in 1894 and died in New York in 1964. Davis's use of everyday objects—eggbeaters and percolators, electric fans and rubber gloves—led to the development of a style which has been called a "visual analogue of the polyphony of jazz horns."

SHELAGH DELANEY is well known for her two plays, *A Taste of Honey* and *A Lion in Love*. The story included here is from her book of memoirs, *Sweetly Sings the Donkey*, published by Putnam in 1963.

TIBOR DÉRY is in his late sixties and lives in Budapest. Two novels, *Mr. G. A. in X* and *The Unfinished Sentence*, as well as his short stories, have established him as the outstanding novelist of present-day Hungary. "Behind the Brick Wall" was written and published in Hungary in 1956.

GEORGE DE VINCENT is a Washington, D. C. photographer who, with Philip M. Stern, published *The Shame of a Nation* in 1956.

WARREN BABY DODDS, an outstanding exponent of New Orleans' drumming, played, during his long career, with such jazz greats as his brother, Johnny Dodds, King Oliver, Bunk Johnson, Jelly Roll Morton, and Sidney Bechet.

ROBERT DUNCAN was born in 1919 in Oakland, California. He edited *The Experimental Review*, one of the first magazines to publish postwar American poetry. Among his works are two books of poetry, *The Opening of the Field* and *Roots and Branches*. He is currently at work on a study of H.D.

FRIEDRICH DÜRRENMATT is a Swiss playwright and novelist. Among his plays are *The Physicists* and *The Visit*, which have been performed throughout Europe and America, and which have been published by Grove Press.

WILLIAM EASTLAKE, lives in New Mexico, and is the author of four novels, the most recent of which was *Castle Keep*. He is finishing a new book based on his experiences as a journalist in Vietnam.

EVGENY EVTUSHENKO, the well-known Soviet poet, caused an uproar inside the Soviet Union with the publication of "Babii Yar," a poem critical of the regime. Evtushenko has made numerous trips to the United States and his poetry has been published here in several different translations.

LÉON-PAUL FARGUE, see page 302.

FÉLIX FÉNÉON, see page 291.

LAWRENCE FERLINGHETTI was born in New York but spent most of his childhood in Europe. He is the proprietor of San Francisco's well-known bookstore, City Lights. Among his books of poems are *Coney Island of the Mind* and *Pictures of the Gone World*.

EDWARD FIELD was born in Brooklyn. After graduating from high school, he enlisted in the U.S. Air Force and became a navigator, flying combat missions over Germany. Grove published his first book of poetry, *Stand Up, Friend, With Me*, which was awarded the Lamont Poetry Prize, in 1963, and his second, *Variety Photoplays*, in 1967.

PAUL FLORA was born in the South Tyrol in 1922. He has had many books of satirical drawings published—one, *Flora's Fauna*, in the United States—and has won awards in art and graphic art shows all over the world. He now lives in Innsbruck.

JEAN-CLAUDE FOREST is a French painter who was born in 1930 in Perreux, France. *Barbarella* was originally intended as a game for the amusement of the author and his friends, but it was so successful with the French public when it appeared in a monthly magazine that it was republished as a book.

CHARLES FOSTER was a member of the California Venice West group of writers at the time of the publication of his story, "The Troubled Makers," in *Evergreen Review*.

CARLOS FUENTES was born in Mexico in 1929, and has studied and traveled extensively in Europe, South America, and the United States. He was one of the founders of the *Revista Méxicana de Literatura*, which he has edited since 1954. He has had several novels published in the United States, including *The Death of Artemio Cruz* and *Where the Air Is Clear*.

LARRY GARA was assistant professor of history at Eureka College in Illinois at the time of his interview with Baby Dodds.

FEDERICO GARCÍA LORCA, Spanish playwright and poet, was murdered by the Falange in 1936. Among his plays are *Blood Wedding* and *Yerma*. Collections of his plays and poetry have been published by Grove, New Directions, and Norton.

PIERRE GASCAR is the author of *The Seed*, published by Little, Brown. He has traveled extensively throughout Asia and Africa for the World Health Organization.

JACK GELBER is the author of three successful plays, *The Connection*, *The Apple*, and *Square in the Eye*, all of which are published by Grove, and a novel, *On Ice*. He is at work on a new play, *The Cuban Thing*.

JEAN GENET was born in Paris in 1910 and began writing in 1943, while serving one of his numerous prison sentences for theft. He has written several novels, plays, a volume of poems, and an autobiographical journal. He is considered one of France's greatest living writers.

ALLEN GINSBERG was born in Paterson, New Jersey, in 1926. After high school in Paterson, he attended Columbia College in New York and later sailed in the Merchant Marine. In 1955 he went to San Francisco where, along with such writers as Kerouac, Corso, and McClure, he was one of the founders of the so-called beat school of modern American poetry.

JOE GOLDBERG has published articles on jazz and the movies in a number of magazines, and has written two books, *Jazz Masters of the Fifties* and *The Big Bunny*.

WITOLD GOMBROWICZ was born in Poland in 1904. He published his first book in 1933, and from 1939 lived for twenty-five years virtually unknown in Argentina, continuing to write stories, plays, and novels—two of which, *Ferdydurke* and *Pornografia*, were recently published by Grove. At present, Gombrowicz lives in France.

ROBERT GOVER was born in Philadelphia. He is the author of the famous *One Hundred Dollar Misunderstanding*, as well as

The Maniac Responsible and *Here Goes Kitten*, all published by Grove.

GÜNTER GRASS, the Danzig-born author of *The Tin Drum*, is as much respected in Germany for his poems as he is for his novels. Two volumes of poetry have been published in Germany and in the United States a collection has been published by Harcourt, Brace & World.

HORACE GREGORY, well-known poet and critic, is the author of *The Dying Gladiators and Other Essays*. He was awarded a Fellowship of the Academy of American Poets in 1961 for distinguished poetic achievement.

CLEMENT GREENBERG, noted art critic, has edited books on Matisse and Miró. A collection of his essays, *Art and Criticism*, was published by Beacon Press.

NAT HENTOFF, a frequent commentator on jazz, politics, and education, is a regular contributor to the *Evergreen Review*, *The Village Voice*, and many other magazines. His newest book, *A Doctor Among the Addicts*, has just been published, and a novel, *Onwards!*, will be published this summer.

AIDAN HIGGINS is an Irish writer now living in Spain who has written a volume of short stories, *Killachter Meadow*, and a novel, *Langrishe, Go Down*, both published by Grove. He is presently at work on a new novel, *Balcony of Europe*.

CHESTER HIMES is an American Negro writer now living in Europe. He wrote his first novel, *If He Hollers Let Him Go*, some twenty years ago, and has since written more than a dozen others. *Pinktoes* was published by Stein & Day in 1965.

HO CHI MINH, President of North Vietnam, wrote the poems in this volume while imprisoned by Chiang Kai-shek's police in 1942. The English translation is by Alleen Palmer from the volume *Prison Diary*, which was published by the Foreign Languages Publishing House in Hanoi.

ANDRÉ HODEIR is a French music critic, composer, and musician. Grove has published three of his books on music, including *Jazz: Its Evolution and Essence*. Mr. Hodeir has also written two children's books which were recently published by Grove, *Warwick's Three Bottles* and *Cleopatra Goes Sledding*.

ANSELM HOLLO is a Finnish-born poet who now lives in London. He has translated works by Voznesensky, Evtushenko, and Kirsanov. A collection of his own poetry, *History*, was published in England.

EUGÈNE IONESCO was born in Rumania in 1912, but has lived most of his life in Paris. He was thirty-seven when he wrote his first play, *The Bald Soprano*, which marked the beginning of a distinguished career that has established him as one of the most important playwrights in the world.

ALFRED JARRY was rocketed to fame at the age of twenty-three with the first production of his revolutionary play, *Ubu Roi*. In addition to his theatrical works, his extensive writing during his brief life (1873–1907) included essays, criticism, poetry, and fiction.

KARL JASPERS is a noted German philosopher. He has written many books, including studies of Kant, Nietzsche, Augustine, and Descartes, and is particularly well known for *Reason and Existenz* and *The Question of German Guilt*. "The Atom Bomb and the Future of Man" was a radio lecture, widely broadcast in Germany.

LE ROI JONES, born in 1934 in Newark, New Jersey, attended Rutgers, Howard, Columbia, and the New School for Social Research. From 1954 to 1957 he served in the Air Force as a weatherman-gunner. He was the editor of *Yugen* and an editor of *Kulchur*. Among his books are *The Dead Lecturer*, *Tales*, *Blues People*, and *The System of Dante's Hell*. His

play, *Dutchman*, was awarded an Obie for the 1963–64 off-Broadway season.

LENORE KANDEL's volume of poems, *Love Book*, published by Stolen Paper Editions, was banned as obscene in San Francisco when it was brought out in 1967. The decision was later reversed. Grove Press has recently published her second book of poems, *Word Alchemy*.

YASAR KEMAL is a native of the Taurus mountain region of Turkey. He has written a novel, *Memed My Hawk*, as well as several stories which depict village life in southern Turkey.

LYSANDER KEMP was written extensively on Mexico and has translated Octavio Paz's *Labyrinth of Solitude* and Mario Vargas Llosa's *The Time of the Hero*.

JACK KEROUAC was born in 1922. At the age of eleven he began to write novels, and at the age of seventeen he began what he called "serious writing." *On the Road*, published in 1957, spoke for an entire alienated generation of postwar Americans. Among his published works are *The Dharma Bums*, *The Subterraneans*, and *Lonesome Traveler*.

PIERRE KLOSSOWSKI was born in Paris in 1905. Éditions de Minuit published *Roberte Ce Soir*, a section of which was published in *Evergreen Review*, in 1954, and a sequel, *La Revocation de l'edit de Nantes*, five years later. Grove will publish both books in the near future.

KENNETH KOCH is one of the foremost poets of what is popularly called the "New York School." Born in Cincinnati in 1925, he now lives in New York City and teaches at Columbia University. He is at work on a new book, *Pleasures of Peace and Other Poems*.

JAN KOTT is a Polish drama critic and scholar whose essay, which influenced Peter Brooke's production of *King Lear*, is a chapter from his book *Shakespeare, Our Contemporary* which was published by Doubleday.

JEREMY LARNER was the editor, with Ralph Tefferteller, of a series of interviews with drug addicts published in book form as *The Addict in the Street*. His first novel, *Drive, He Said*, won the $10,000 Delta Prize Novel Contest.

DENISE LEVERTOV, born in Essex, England, was educated by her parents at home. During World War II she worked in London as a nurse, then married the American writer Mitchell Goodman. Her books of poetry include *The Double Image*, *Overland to the Islands*, and *The Jacob's Ladder*.

JAKOV LIND was born in Vienna. He spent the early war years in hiding in Holland, and survived the remainder posing as a Dutch national in Germany. He now lives in London and is the author of *Soul of Wood*, *Landscape in Concrete, and Ergo*, which has also been produced as a play by Joseph Papp.

LI YÜ was a famous dramatist, novelist, and essayist of the Ming period. *Jou Pu Tuan*, which is now considered a classic, recounts the adventures of a brilliant young student who resolves to lead a life of pure eroticism.

NORMAN MAILER was born in 1923 in Long Branch, New Jersey, and grew up in Brooklyn. He went to Harvard and spent over two years in the army: his war novel, *The Naked and the Dead*, made him famous overnight. Since then he has written several novels, a play, and three collections of essays.

CURZIO MALAPARTE, the Italian writer who died in 1957, is known in America chiefly for his novels *Kaputt*, *The Skin*, and *Those Cursed Tuscans*. The piece appearing here is the first section of his unfinished novel, *Mamma Marcia* (literally translated as "Rotten Mother"), published posthumously in Italy.

VLADIMIR MAYAKOVSKY, the Soviet poet who committed suicide in 1930 at the age of thirty-seven, has remained the central figure of Russian poetry in the Soviet epoch.

MICHAEL MC CLURE was born in Kansas. In 1953 he settled in San Francisco where he was one of the first contributors to *The Ark*, a magazine important in the development of contemporary American poetry. He has written several books of poems, and his plays include *The Beard*, which has been produced in New York, San Francisco, and Los Angeles.

W. S. MERWIN is the author of several books of poems, among which is *The Moving Target*, published by Atheneum. His prose translation of the *Song of Roland* and a reprint of his verse translation of the *Poem of the Cid* have been published by Random House.

HENRI MICHAUX, poet and painter, was born in Belgium in 1899, and has lived most of his life in Paris. Three volumes of his work, *Barbarian in Asia*, *Miserable Miracle*, and *Selected Writings* have been published in the United States.

HENRY MILLER was born in 1891 and raised in Brooklyn. After extensive travels in Europe, he moved to California in 1942. Since then he has divided his time between writing and painting. Miller's books were first published in Paris and when *Tropic of Cancer* was published here it was banned as obscene. The Supreme Court reversal of this decision in 1964 was a landmark in the battle against censorship.

JAMES MITCHELL received his B.S. from San Francisco Art Institute in 1964 and has worked as an assistant to Dorothea Lange and for Magnum, *The New York Times*, and *Newsweek*. He has also had one man shows and exhibited at Expo '67.

SLAWOMIR MROZEK is one of Poland's leading playwrights and political satirists. In 1957 he won the annual Literary Prize awarded by the Polish State Cultural Review for *The Elephant*, a collection of stories from which the three tales in this anthology were taken.

PABLO NERUDA was born in Chile and first won recognition as a poet at the age of sixteen. Starting in the twenties, the Chilean government sent him on a series of consular missions, but his active role in radical politics from 1936 on resulted in expulsion and exile; he returned to Chile in 1952.

MICHAEL O'DONOGHUE was born in 1940 and raised in upstate New York, later attending the University of Rochester; he has held innumerable jobs, from radio announcer to door-to-door salesman. At present he lives in New York and is a regular contributor to *Evergreen Review*.

KENZABURO OË, born in 1935, is one of Japan's most eminent younger writers. His most recent novel, *A Personal Matter*, won the Shinchosha Award and will be published this year in the United States by Grove Press. "Lavish Are the Dead," his first published story, originally appeared in translation in *Japan Quarterly*.

FRANK O'HARA was born in 1926 in Baltimore and raised in New England. From 1951 until his untimely death in 1966 he was an assistant curator at the Museum of Modern Art in New York. Along with John Ashbery, he was one of the founders of what has come to be known as the "New York School" of poetry.

CHARLES OLSON was born in 1910 in Worcester, Massachusetts. He has taught at Clark College and Harvard, and was rector of Black Mountain College from 1951 to 1956. He is well known for his full-scale study of Melville, *Call Me Ishmael*, and for the *Maximus Poems*, a work still in progress.

BORIS PASTERNAK was born in Russia in 1890. He is known in the West for his novel, *Doctor Zhivago*, as well as for several books of poems.

OCTAVIO PAZ was born in Mexico City in 1914. He studied at the University of Mexico and in the United States. He has

been diplomatic representative from Mexico to France, India, Japan, and the United Nations. In addition to his book of essays on Mexican life and thought, *The Labyrinth of Solitude*, he has published many volumes of poems.

ANDRÉ PIEYRE DE MANDIARGUES was born in Paris in 1909. He graduated from the Sorbonne and holds a number of degrees. Grove has published his novels *The Girl Beneath the Lion* and *The Motorcycle*. He was recently awarded the Prix Goncourt for his novel *La Marge*, which Grove will publish shortly.

HAROLD PINTER, who was born in London, is the outstanding playwright in the current renaissance of British drama. Grove has published many of his plays, including *The Birthday Party*, *The Caretaker*, and *The Homecoming*, which was produced on Broadway in 1967. Mr. Pinter has also written numerous scripts for television and the cinema.

JEFFREY POTTER has for many years been a regular contributor to *The New Yorker* and is the author of two juvenile books, *Elephant Bridge* and *Robin Is a Bear*, published by Random House.

JACQUES PRÉVERT was born in 1900 in Neuilly-sur-Seine. Among his books are *Spectacles*, *Fatras*, and *Paroles*, which was translated into English and published by City Lights Books.

JAMES PURDY first appeared in *Evergreen Review*, Number One. His most recent novel, *Eustace Chisholm and the Works*, was published in the spring of 1967 by Farrar, Straus & Giroux.

RAYMOND QUENEAU was born in Le Havre in 1903. His first book, published in 1933, marked the beginning of a prolific literary career. In 1941 he joined the Board of Directors of Gallimard. He is best known in this country for *Zazie dans le Métro*.

PAULINE RÉAGE has been the subject of considerable controversy: her identity still remains unknown a decade and a half after her book, *Story of O*, was published in France by Jean-Jacques Pauvert, with a lengthy, laudatory preface by leading French critic Jean Paulhan.

JOHN RECHY was born in El Paso, Texas. His first novel, *City of Night*, was received with considerably acclaim and has been translated into eight languages. His second novel, *Numbers*, was recently published by Grove.

KENNETH REXROTH was born in the Midwest and spent his early years in Chicago as a member of Chicago's Bohemia, where he was a poet and painter. He has now lived in San Francisco for about thirty years. He has had many books of poetry published.

LARRY RIVERS is a leading American painter who has exhibited in all the major galleries and museums. He is at present at work on a film.

ALAIN ROBBE-GRILLET was born in 1922 in Brest, France. His first novel, *The Erasers*, appeared in 1953. With the publication of *The Voyeur*, *Jealousy*, and *In the Labyrinth*, he became the chief spokesman for the *nouveau roman*. In recent years he has concentrated on writing and directing films.

CONRAD ROOKS was born in Kansas City in 1934. He made two low budget films before making *Chappaqua*, a surrealistic film about drug addiction.

BERTON ROUECHÉ, a staff member of *The New Yorker*, is the originator of its "Annals of Medicine"; a collection of his pieces from that column appeared in book form as *Eleven Blue Men*. His other books include *Alcohol* and a novel, *The Last Enemy*.

JUAN RULFO was born in 1918 in Sayula, Mexico. His book *The Burning Plain and Other Stories*, and his novel, *Pedro Páramo* (published by Grove), have established him as one of the most gifted writers of fiction in Mexico today.

MICHAEL RUMAKER was born in Philadelphia and grew up in a small town in New Jersey. He won a scholarship to Black Mountain College where he wrote his first stories. He is the author of *Gringos and Other Stories*, and a novel, *The Butterfly*.

I. M. SANDOMIR, His Magnificence, is Vice-Curator-Founder of the Collège de 'Pataphysique. He has also written *The final EPANORTHOSIS on the Moral Clinamen*.

JEAN-PAUL SARTRE was born in 1905. In the 1930's he studied under Heidegger and Husserl and began his work on Kierkegaard. He published his treatise on existentialism, *Being and Nothingness*, during the war, while he was a member of the Free French Resistance. After the war he gained international reputation as one of France's leading intellectuals.

MARK SCHORER, critic and novelist, is Professor of English at the University of California at Berkeley. He has written critical studies of Sinclair Lewis, William Blake, Jane Austen, and the Brontë sisters.

JOHN SCHULTZ, whose novella *Custom* was recently republished by Grove Press in *4 x 4*, has also contributed to *Big Table* and *Chicago Review*.

MARCEL SCHWOB, see page 299.

HUBERT SELBY, JR., author of *Last Exit to Brooklyn*, was born in New York City in 1928 and raised in Brooklyn. At sixteen he went to sea as a merchant seaman and contracted tuberculosis, spending the next three years in various hospitals. At that time he started to read and write extensively.

GENEVIÈVE SERREAU, a French writer and critic, works for *Les Lettres Nouvelles*.

ROGER SHATTUCK teaches in the Department of Romance Languages at the University of Texas. He has translated René Daumal's *Mount Analogue* and has written articles on Surrealism. Among his recent books of criticism are *Proust's Binoculars* and *The Banquet Years*.

SINÉ is one of the leading cartoonists and satirists of contemporary France. For twenty years, his acerbic drawings have appeared in the major French magazines—*L'Express, Nouvel Observateur*, etc.—and have been collected into books.

GARY SNYDER was born in San Francisco. He graduated from Reed College in 1951 and studied classical Chinese at the University of California at Berkeley. In 1956 he went to Japan to study as a Zen novitiate and he now lives there. Among his books are *Rip-Rap, Myths and Texts*, and *Rivers and Mountains Without End*.

SUSAN SONTAG is the author of two novels, *The Benefactor* and *Death Kit*, and is especially known for her drama, literary, and film criticism. The essay included here is from her book *Against Interpretation*.

TERRY SOUTHERN is the author of *Flash and Filigree, The Magic Christian*, and co-author of *Candy*, one of 1964's best-selling novels. He is also the co-author of the screen plays, *Dr. Strangelove* and *The Loved One*.

PATSY SOUTHGATE's first published story, "A Very Important Lady," appeared in *Evergreen Review*, Number 3. She has translated several books for Grove, including *Astragal* by Albertine Sarrazin.

JACK SPICER was born in Hollywood. He is acknowledged to be one of the great mentors of the postwar American poets. Among his books are *Language, After Lorca*, and *The Heads of the Town up to the Aether*. He died at the age of forty.

FRANK SPRINGER is a free-lance cartoonist who has done everything from sports cartoons to comic books and children's television shows.

ROBERT STROMBERG had spent several months in Europe working for newspapers and a British wire service at the time of his interview with Louis-Ferdinand Céline. He currently lives in New York.

ELIZABETH SUTHERLAND had just spent two months in the Soviet Union, Poland, and Hungary at the time of her interview with Andrei Voznesensky. Formerly an editor at Simon and Schuster and head of the New York office of SNCC, she is at present writing a book on Cuba.

DAISETZ T. SUZUKI, a world authority on Zen Buddhism, was born in 1870 in Japan. Trained in the Zen monastery of Kumakura, he has written more than one hundred works on Zen and Buddhism.

JERRY TALLMER, who writes regularly for the *New York Post*, has contributed many articles to *Evergreen Review*.

MACK THOMAS has had some of his poems anthologized in a collection of modern American poetry brought out in Germany under the co-editorship of Gregory Corso. Grove published his novel, *Gumbo*, in 1965.

JULIEN TORMA, see page 301.

ALEXANDER TROCCHI is a Scottish-born novelist and poet, the author of *Young Adam* and *Cain's Book*. He was associated with a group of young writers in Paris in the early fifties and co-edited the magazine *Merlin*.

AMOS TUTUOLA is a native of Lagos, Nigeria, who writes in primitive English. His first book, *The Palm-Wine Drinkard*, was published by Grove in 1953. This selection is from a later book, *The Brave African Huntress*.

BORIS VIAN, who died in 1959 at the age of thirty-eight, was a novelist, poet, playwright, singer, composer, jazz trumpeter, translator, and engineer. During his lifetime he had little success with the publication of his works and the production of his plays. Today, however, his reputation in France is tremendous and is steadily growing in the United States.

ANDREI VOZNESENSKY, Soviet poet, has made several trips to the United States. His poetry, including *Antiworlds* and *Selected Poems* (Grove Press), has been published here in different translations.

PHILIP WHALEN was born in Portland, Oregon, and attended Reed College at the same time as Gary Snyder. Among his books of poems are *Like I Say* and *Memoirs of an Interglacial Age*. He has been living in San Francisco for many years.

JOHN WIENERS was born in 1934. He graduated from Boston College in 1954 and attended Black Mountain College. He founded the magazine *Measure*, which printed many of the young poets associated with Black Mountain and with the "San Francisco Renaissance." He is the author of *The Hotel Wentley Poems* and *Ace of Pentacles*.

HEATHCOTE WILLIAMS is an editor of *Transatlantic Review* and lives in London. His first book, *The Speakers*, deals with London's Hyde Park Corner, and four of its more popular orators, MacGuinness among them.

MARTIN WILLIAMS is one of the foremost jazz critics in the United States. He was co-editor of *Jazz Review*, and has contributed to *The Saturday Review*, *The Record Changer*, *The American Record Guide*, and *Downbeat*. For many years he had a column "Jazz: The LP Catalogue" in *Evergreen Review*.

WILLIAM CARLOS WILLIAMS was born in 1883 in Rutherford, New Jersey, and attended the University of Pennsylvania where he met Ezra Pound, Marianne Moore, Hilda Doolittle, and others. He spent his life as a doctor in Rutherford. The author of many books of poetry, he is generally acknowledged, with Ezra Pound, to be one of the founders of modern American poetry. His last book, for which he was posthumously awarded a Pulitzer Prize, was *Pictures from Breughel*.

DOUGLAS WOOLF has written of himself: "The art of working, whether with the hands or with language, is a true one. At least I have found it so in my own life and writing. For twenty part-time years of picking berries, etc., and peddling ice creams, etc., I have five novels, two now too true, *John-Juan* and *Ya!*. That's better than eulogized slavery."

AHMED YACOUBI is a self-taught painter who is now considered Morocco's foremost artist. His first show was at the Betty Parsons Gallery in New York in 1952.